The Child and the English Language Arts

Fourth Edition

Mildred R. Donoghue
California State University, Fullerton

Wm. C. Brown Publishers
Dubuque, Iowa

Part Opening Photographs: Parts 1 and 2—(c) Jean-Claude Lejeune; Part 3—(c) Ron Monner; Part 4—(c) James Ballard.

Library of Congress Catalog Number: 84–72485

ISBN 0–697–00416–3

Printed in the United States of America
10 9 8 7 6 5 4

The Child and the English Language Arts

Dedicated to E. Ranzdorff
with affection and respect

Contents

Preface xi

Part A
Foundations 2

1 The Language Arts Program 5

Language Competencies and Program Goals 6
Developing Language Readiness 10
Microcomputers in the Language Arts Classroom 14
Discussion Questions 19
Suggested Projects 19
Related Readings 20
Chapter Notes 20

2 The English Language and the Child Learner 21

Language History 23
Usage and Dialect 26
Language Structure: Phonology, Morphology, Syntax, Semantics 31
Language Acquisition 35
Language Development 36
Intellectual Development According to Piaget 42
Providing for Individual Differences 44
Evaluation of Pupils' Progress in Language Development 48
Discussion Questions 49
Suggested Projects 49
Related Readings 49
Chapter Notes 50

3 Grammar 51

The Continuing Debate Over Grammar 52
Major Kinds of English Grammar: Traditional, Structural, Transformational 57
Instructional Activities 72
Evaluation of Pupils' Progress 74
Discussion Questions 77
Suggested Projects 77
Related Readings 80
Chapter Notes 80

Part B
Oral and Written Communication 82

4 Listening 85

Basic Questions about the Listening Program 86
Instructional Activities 93
Learning Games 102
Evaluation of Pupils' and Teachers' Progress 108
Discussion Questions 110
Suggested Projects 112
Related Readings 112
Chapter Notes 113

5 Speaking 115

Speech Arts 117
Communicative Development 141
Communicative Remediation for Handicapped Children 151
Evaluation of Pupils' Progress 157
Discussion Questions 157
Suggested Projects 157
Related Readings 158
Chapter Notes 159

6 Handwriting 161

Writing Readiness 165
Traditional Manuscript Handwriting 168
Traditional Cursive Handwriting 173
Alternative Forms of Handwriting: D'Nealian, Italic 178
Typewriting Skill 182
Providing for Children with Special Needs 186
Evaluation of Pupils' Progress 192
Discussion Questions 199
Suggested Projects 199
Related Readings 201
Chapter Notes 201

7 **Spelling 203**

The English Alphabetic Orthography 204
Teaching Spelling: Modern Guidelines 211
Teaching Spelling: Recommended Practices 215
Teaching Spelling: Individualized Approach 216
Spelling and Reading 218
Instructional Activities 221
Learning Games 224
Learning-Disabled Spellers 227
Evaluation of Pupils' Progress 230
Discussion Questions 235
Suggested Projects 235
Related Readings 235
Chapter Notes 236

8 **Written Composition 241**

Factors Affecting Writing Performance 242
Generalizations/Guidelines for the Teaching of Written Composition 245
Major Areas of the Curriculum in Written Composition 248
School Stimuli for Writing 260
Samples of Children's Written Composition 272
Creativity: The Foundation of Composition 285
Evaluation of Pupils' Progress 286
Discussion Questions 292
Suggested Projects 292
Related Readings 292
Chapter Notes 293

Part C
Reading, Literature, Drama, and Related Skills 296

9 **Reading 299**

Beginning Reading Readiness 302
Instructional Strategies 309
Word Recognition Skills 316
Comprehension 327
Evaluation of Pupils' Progress 333
Discussion Questions 338
Suggested Projects 338
Related Readings 338
Chapter Notes 340

10 **Vocabulary Development 343**

Growth in Word Meaning 345
Factors Influencing Vocabulary Growth 348
Types of Vocabularies 350
Guidelines for a Curriculum in Vocabulary Development 351
Teaching English Vocabulary: Methodology 354
Teaching English Vocabulary: Etymology 364
Teaching English Vocabulary: Instructional Activities 365
Learning Games 368
Evaluation of Pupils' Progress 372
Discussion Questions 373
Suggested Projects 373
Related Readings 374
Chapter Notes 376

11 **Children's Literature 377**

Objectives/Functions, Satisfactions, and Trends 380
Children's Literary Interests/Preferences 383
Sources and Criteria for Selecting Well-Written Books 384
Poetry: Literary Work in Metrical Form 391
Bibliotherapy—or Books That Help Children to Cope 397
Minority-Americans in Modern Children's Literature 401
Instructional Activities 402
Choral Speaking: A Unique Interpretive Activity 417
Evaluation of Pupils' Progress 423
Discussion Questions 424
Suggested Projects 424
Related Readings 426
Chapter Notes 426

12 Library Media Center Skills 429

Major Library Media Center Skills and Instructional Activities 433
Learning Experiences through the Grades 457
The Exceptional Child and the Library Media Center 462
Worksheets and Learning Games Involving Library Media Center Skills 463
Evaluation of Pupils' Progress 467
Discussion Questions 468
Suggested Projects 468
Related Readings 470
Chapter Notes 470

13 Children's Drama 471

Statement of Purposes 472
Children's Theatre 473
Creative Drama 475
Dramatic Play 478
Pantomime 480
Role-Playing 484
Story Dramatization: Interpretation 487
Story Dramatization: Improvisation 491
Evaluation of Pupils' Progress 492
Discussion Questions 492
Suggested Projects 492
Related Readings 494
Chapter Notes 494

Part D
Teaching English to Non-Native Speakers 496

14 English as a Second Language 499

Guidelines for Instruction 503
Second Language Learning Model 504
Guidelines for a Functional ESL Curriculum 505
Strategies and Second Language Learning 506
Stages in the Acquisition of English Language Skills 511
Instructional Activities 517
Learning Games 519
Evaluation of Pupils' and Teachers' Progress 523
Discussion Questions 528
Suggested Projects 528
Related Readings 528
Chapter Notes 530

Appendices

1 Award-Winning or Highly Recommended Media Resources for Elementary School Language Arts 531

2 Language Arts Textbook Evaluation 537

3 How to Judge a Basal Reader Series 541

4 Caldecott Medal and Newbery Medal Books and Their Honor Books Since the Mid-Century 547

5 Guidelines for Review and Evaluation of English Language Arts Software 559

6 Answers to *Discover As You Read This Chapter If* Statements 567

Author Index 569

Subject Index 573

Preface

The English language arts discipline has been described as being at once the most fundamental, the most complex, and the most potent in the entire curriculum. Certainly it constitutes the foundation for all other subjects commonly taught in elementary schools.

A child cannot gain appreciably in the mastery of one language art (or skill) without triggering some degree of advancement in at least two others, because all of them reinforce and complement one another so strongly. A growing body of research has even begun to justify an emphasis on an integrated rather than a segregated approach to language arts instruction because none of the arts and skills can truly be taught or learned in complete isolation from the others.

However, the essential difficulty with such an integrated program is twofold; first, the need for a basic understanding of each individual language art or skill; and second, the need for a resolution to the critical problem of implementing an integrated approach.

Both aspects have been uppermost in my mind during the preparation of this fourth edition, which is the first to include a lengthy chapter on reading. Interestingly enough, even as Chapter Nine was being written, the noted editor of *Language Arts*—David Dillon of the University of Alberta—publicly determined that reading *must* be treated in relationship with other language arts since it is becoming increasingly difficult to deal with it as an isolated topic.

Another new feature of this edition is the "Discover As You Read This Chapter If" section that begins each chapter. This section includes a series of detailed true or false statements that should, according to research studies, provoke greater student interaction with the text. Other pedagogical aids include overviews which open each chapter and describe highlights of the material; and discussion questions, suggested projects, and a list of related readings from 1980–1985, which conclude each chapter.

Other changes in the fourth edition include two new appendices concerned with evaluating major areas of today's language arts program. Appendix 3 tells teachers how to judge a basal reader, and Appendix 5 provides guidelines for teachers to determine the suitability of software in the English language arts field.

Besides these major textual additions, every portion of the book has been revised substantially in an effort to keep teachers aware of current and pertinent scholarship and research findings.

For this edition I have relied on my colleagues and graduate students for criticism and commentary, and I wish to thank them for their efforts. I would also like to thank the reviewers who were involved at each stage in the progress of the manuscript, and whose opinions I respect: Delorys Blume, University of Central Florida; Omer E. Bonenberger, Cedarville College; Dr. Martha C. Leyden,

University of Akron; and Dr. Barbara A. Sperling, Southwest Missouri State University. While many people helped during the preparation of this book, I wish to express my appreciation especially to my editor Sandy Schmidt, who supported, challenged, and corrected my work; and to Laura Schwalm of the Garden Grove (CA) Unified School District who assisted in the development of certain sections of Chapter Nine. Finally, as the writing of the fourth edition began only a short time after the sudden and unexpected death of my husband, I am grateful for the continued encouragement of our children, Kathleen and James.

January 1985 — Mildred R. Donoghue

The Child and the English Language Arts

Part A Foundations

Chapters

1 The Language Arts Program
2 The English Language and the Child Learner
3 Grammar

The Language Arts Program 1

Objectives

The four general language processes or skills

The foundational competencies for English language arts programs

Types of activities that develop language readiness

Microcomputers in the language arts classroom

Discover As You Read This Chapter If*

1. Preschool children learn whatever language is used by their families and playmates.
2. Any one language art can be learned in isolation from the others.
3. The expressive skills in the language arts are oral composition and written composition.
4. Learning experiences affect only the productive areas of the language arts.
5. Competencies deemed essential for English programs include those needed for locating information.
6. Language and thought can be separated.
7. Unlike reading readiness activities, language readiness activities are not recommended before children begin to use books and writing tools.
8. Teachers should consider the microcomputer as the panacea for language arts instruction.
9. Drill-and-practice is a major form of computer-assisted instruction in language arts.
10. Extensive use of the microcomputer will not impede the refinement and expansion of communication skills.

*Answers to these true-or-false statements may be found in Appendix 6.

Small children are not taught a language but learn it by themselves without conscious effort and application. Since they seem to possess an inborn faculty for language generally, the language they learn depends wholly on the language—or languages—to which they are exposed until about the age of puberty.

By the time children are ready for kindergarten, they already have marvelous control over the pronunciation and syntax of their native American English as they have learned it from their families and playmates. The school then begins to share the responsibility for the children's language development with the home and the community. Both inside and outside of the school environment the children are continually increasing their command of the language through informal means: conversing; playing; listening to records and to adult dialogue; watching films and television; reading signs, magazines, and books; and writing notes and creative pieces. Therefore, and to a greater extent than in any other discipline, the language arts program demands a knowledge of each child's social, emotional, cultural, and intellectual background and development.

Due to the variety of student experiences in any level or grade, an effective program in language learning must focus upon children as individuals. Boys and girls must be involved actively and positively in genuine learning situations that have meaning for them.

As children progress through the grades, they must be permitted greater responsibility in choosing learning experiences because as Figure 1.1 shows, these experiences influence their gradual acquisition of the productive and the receptive operations in the English language arts. The productive or expressive areas stress composition in both oral and written forms. The receptive areas concern reading and listening. Yet all these areas are so intricately interrelated that none of them can be learned in complete isolation from the others, and growth in one area promptly promotes growth in the others.

Language Competencies, and Program Goals

In recent years there have been expressions of concern coupled with mounting evidence that too many children and adults have not attained the language competencies required for success in everyday life. Such competencies require sustained attention in the primary grades as well as at all other teaching levels because they must be functional for every person in American society. Although there are obvious differences in their use by particular individuals, the essence of these competencies lies not in their specific manifestations but in the processes.[1]

Essential Competencies for English Programs

I. Competencies Essential for Receiving Communication from Others

A. Basic Understandings and Attitudes

1. To understand that reading and listening skills are needed for learning in school, for most occupations, and for daily living.
2. To understand that symbols and signs other than those which either graphically or auditorily represent words may transmit meaning.
3. To understand that the purpose and the degree of involvement of the receiver affect communication.

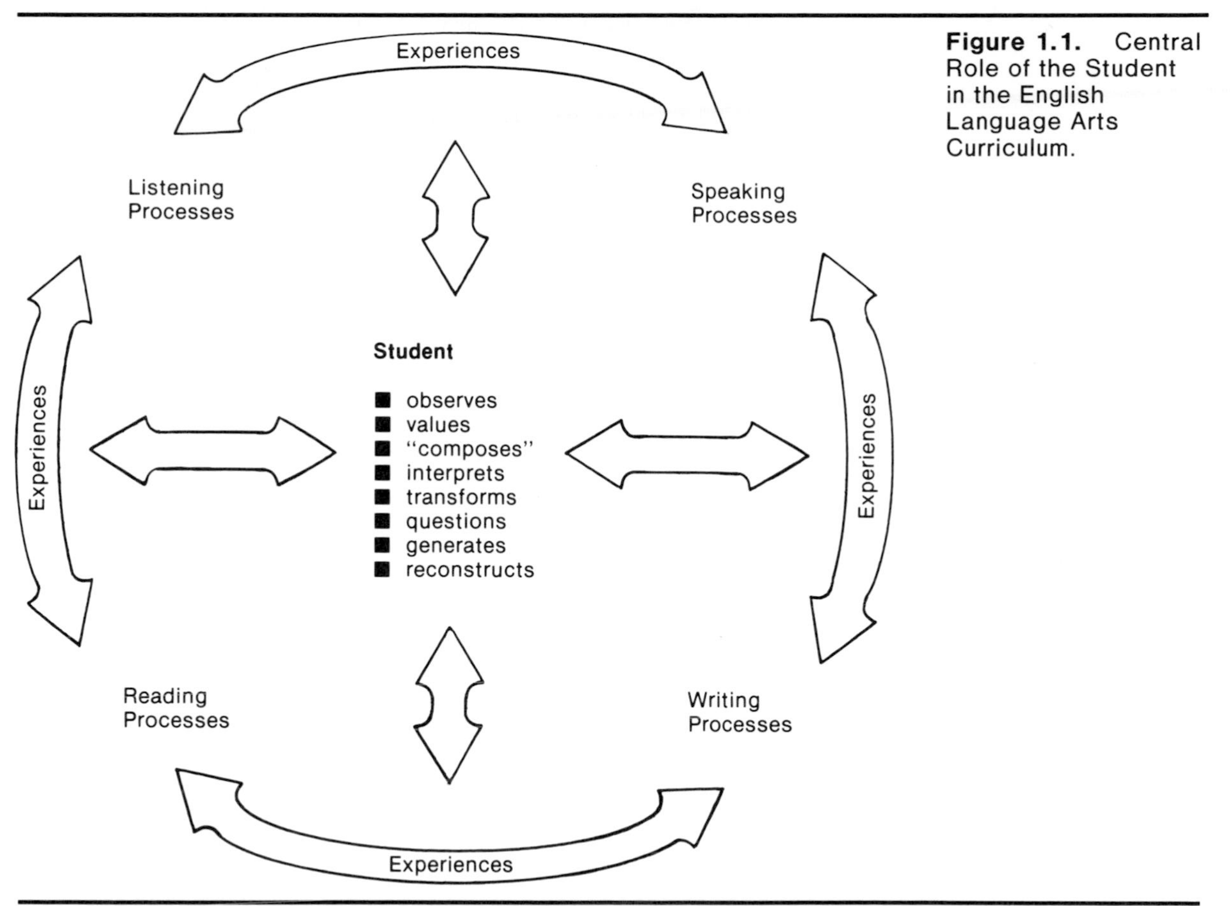

Figure 1.1. Central Role of the Student in the English Language Arts Curriculum.

Source: *English Language Framework for California Public Schools: K–12* (Sacramento: State Department of Education, 1976), p. 15.

4. To understand that reading and listening are means for gaining pleasure directly as well as indirectly in terms of finding avocational and recreational information.
5. To understand and appreciate various types of language: dialects, levels of usage, jargon, figurative language, and so forth.

B. Receptive Comprehension Abilities
1. To follow directions, determine main ideas, recognize important supporting information, and perceive relationships.
2. To use language structure, context clues, dictionaries, and other aids in gaining meaning.
3. To relate information received to previous experiences and present knowledge and to draw inferences.
4. To distinguish between fact and opinion and between the relevant and the irrelevant.
5. To recognize bias, prejudice, and propaganda and avoid judgments based upon inadequate evidence.
6. To gain pleasure and self-development from receptive communication acts.

C. Abilities Needed for Aural Decoding
    1. To identify and discriminate among common speech sounds.
    2. To recognize words, phrases, and larger units of aural communication.
    3. To use the pitch, stress, juncture, and tone of speech in gaining meaning.

D. Abilities Needed for Visual Decoding
    1. To distinguish and identify individual letters and letter groups in a wide variety of type and script styles.
    2. To recognize by sight a core of words and to be able to use structural and phonemic-graphemic knowledge to determine others.
    3. To use punctuation marks and other nonword symbols as aids to reading.
    4. To make use of facial expressions, physical movements, and graphic and picture symbols as aids in gaining meaning from nonreading communication acts.

II. Competencies Needed for Expression to Others

A. Understandings and Attitudes
    1. To recognize that the content of what is said is more important than the mechanics of saying it.
    2. To understand that the mechanics of writing and the manner of speaking are aids to communication rather than ends in themselves.
    3. To understand that, to communicate effectively, one must be willing to acquire the specific skills or learnings needed for the performance of particular speaking or writing tasks.
    4. To recognize that there are levels of usage appropriate to varying occasions.
    5. To recognize that one's own personal language or dialect is worthy of respect and is suitable for many situations.
    6. To recognize that standard English is needed for certain kinds of oral and written communication.
    7. To be sensitive to the opinions and feelings of one's reader(s) or listener(s).

B. Abilities Needed for Organization and Composition
    1. To speak or write for particular purposes:
        a. to seek information
        b. to give directions
        c. to make explanations
        d. to give information
        e. to express feelings and/or opinions
        f. to persuade
        g. to make requests
        h. to comply with social amenities
        i. to provide entertainment, pleasure, or comfort
    2. To choose content appropriate to the intended audience—that is, the reader or listener.
    3. To use varied structures in accord with the purpose, the audience, and the situation.
    4. To use language—one's own personal language or dialect or standard English—that is suitable to the occasion, the content, and the audience.

5. To organize ideas and information in ways such as:
   a. using sequential development
   b. using supporting details
   c. giving examples or illustrations
   d. showing cause and effect
6. To use accurate facts and valid sources of information to support ideas.

C. Abilities Needed for Oral Communication
1. To participate in informal as well as formal speaking situations that involve exchange with others without being either overly dominant or reticent.
2. To speak distinctly and to articulate sounds clearly.
3. To use volume, pitch, rate, and tone appropriate to the audience and the occasion.
4. To use suitable gestures and facial expressions.

D. Abilities Needed for Written Communication
1. To write legibly and neatly.
2. To spell correctly the words that are needed.
3. To use accepted punctuation and capitalization.
4. To use accepted form and appropriate language in varying types of written communication.

III. Competencies Needed for Locating Information

A. Understandings and Attitudes
1. To have the desire to acquire knowledge and pleasure from sources outside one's immediate environment.
2. To understand that most sources of information—from the telephone directory to the card catalog in the library—list items alphabetically.
3. To understand that the ability to locate information aids in achieving self-determination and acquiring knowledge.
4. To be aware that it is sometimes desirable and necessary to ask for assistance in locating information.

B. Locational Abilities
1. To know the sequence of the letters of the alphabet.
2. To use alphabetical order to locate information of varying kinds.
3. To give specific information desired when requesting aid in locating someone or something.
4. To use various aids for finding information in books, such as tables of contents, indexes, and format clues.
5. To use such aids as card catalogs, computer searches, building directories, diagrams, maps, and the like to locate facts, materials, places, or people.

Program Goals

In addition to incorporating foundational competencies appropriate for all English curricula, the elementary language arts program must also identify several more specific goals in its efforts to help children communicate efficiently and properly at their individual ability levels.[2]

The program must aim first to develop students who, in terms of their maturity and potential, understand that people use language to create literature which records their experiences, expresses their emotions and perceptions, and responds to the expressions of others. Literature provides the models and the stimuli to extend children's mental horizons and to nurture their sensitivity and imaginations. At every grade level, children should hear or read a rich variety of literature—stories, dramas, and poems.

Second, it must hope to develop students who, in terms of their potential and maturity, realize that people communicate both verbally and nonverbally in formal and informal speech situations. Skills of oral communication are prerequisite to the development of all language skills. They are worthy of organized classroom instruction because speech is so integral to every personality and so much more commonly used than the written word.

The program must also aim to develop students who understand, according to their maturity and potential, that verbal systems of communication convey precise, unequivocal, and time-binding information which is obtained primarily through purposeful and attentive listening. Objectives related to the lexicon of the English language can be included here.

Fourth, it must hope to develop students who, in terms of their potential and maturity, realize that the written form of a language records and preserves spoken language and is subject to certain organizational and mechanical conventions. Increasing attention is being paid to the importance of children's writing as a means for self-discovery, self-expression, and self-education in the arts of language use.

In addition, the language arts program must aim to develop students who, in terms of their maturity and potential, understand that a living or spoken language is continually changing. Oral usage may be introduced to elementary school children as early as the kindergarten year. Dialectology and the history of spoken and written language teach both primary and intermediate pupils that pictures can be used to communicate and record ideas, that certain words have interesting and known origins, and that language changes in response to various influences.

Finally, it must aim to help students understand, according to their potential and maturity, that language and thought are inseparable. The instructional objectives included under this goal are a kind of translation of the cognitive domain from the taxonomy of educational objectives and are relevant at every grade level from kindergarten through the sixth grade. This goal represents a major concept about the function or use of language.

Developing Language Readiness

Language readiness activities cannot be differentiated from other language learning experiences, except that they are those experiences which are recommended before children begin the routine use of readers and textbooks.

Major Types of Beginning Language Activities

Firsthand Experiences

A language is a system of arbitrary verbal symbols. Children cannot listen, speak, read, or write very well until they have learned a large number of symbols and the concepts related to these symbols. Consequently, children must have extensive firsthand experiences with places, such as the zoo, the airport, and the supermarket, and with concrete objects, such as a flower, an aquarium, or an umbrella, in order to attain a functioning vocabulary. Children must also have experiences to help learn the meanings of a myriad of abstract concepts such as fairness, kindness, and responsibility. The development of vocabulary is a necessary prerequisite to language fluency.

Imaginative Experiences

Looking for forms in the clouds and listening for messages in the wind or rain are all experiences that stimulate the imagination. Such activities offer occasions for use of descriptive words and figurative speech that help children to enjoy poetic literature and increase their language power.

Sensory Experiences

The experiences of smelling, seeing, touching, tasting, and hearing are related to firsthand experiences but imply greater refinement. Children need to learn to identify numerous objects by shape, texture, or sound. Appropriate experiences include making and classifying collections, playing identification games when blindfolded, and participating in tasting parties. As the children learn to use their senses, they extend their vocabularies and store up percepts that will help them in their reading and writing.

Picture Interpretation

Pupils can tell a story illustrated by a single picture, "read" a story from a wordless picture book or a sequence of pictures, and sort and classify pictures according to various topics or word elements. They can illustrate concepts with pictures and play matching games with pictures. Picture dictionaries help teach early work-study habits. And it is possible for the teacher to stimulate concept development through the use of pictures collected from magazines, discarded schoolbooks, and used workbooks.

Story Listening

Listening to well-selected stories gives children opportunities to learn listening and comprehension skills and to become acquainted with the various qualities of literature that make it enjoyable. Probably nothing has more effect on the development of the pupils' desire to learn to read than listening to appealing stories.

Language readiness activities include a variety of both firsthand and imaginative experiences. (Photo courtesy of James Ballard.)

Poetry Experiences

Young children readily appreciate the poet's ability to paint word pictures and to express different moods. They quickly learn to sense the rhythm and listen for rhyming sounds. Repetitive phrases aid them in hearing varied speech sounds, and nonsense verse leads them into their own efforts at creative expression. Poems can help the pupils to see their own selves, to develop a healthy sense of humor, and even to acquire increased ease in communication situations.

Dramatic Play and Pantomime

In these types of activities children step into other people's shoes and portray others' personalities. In learning to identify with others pupils learn to think creatively, to use common courtesies, and (in dramatic play) to use the mechanics of oral communication to express themselves in clear and colorful ways.

Puppetry and Paper Dolls

Classrooms often display puppets, but paper dolls are not frequently utilized in teaching. Children love to work with both devices, however, and through such experiences they grow in eye-hand coordination. Puppets and paper dolls have the advantage of permitting shy children to hide behind their characters, thereby making it easier for boys and girls to speak freely.

Puzzles

Jigsaw puzzles that have large pieces provide purposeful practice in differentiating shapes and sizes. They develop eye-hand coordination and habits of concentration. A variety of durable puzzles can be obtained from Creative Playthings.

Musical Games

Singing games such as "London Bridge" and "Looby-Loo" teach articulation and the rhythm of the language.

Word Games

The children whose home backgrounds cause them to use words habitually in patterns that are considered nonstandard will be handicapped in speaking, reading, and writing in many situations. Most word and sentence games provide practice in standard English usage.

Use of Educational Television

Programs, such as "The Electric Company" and "Sesame Street," promote language development among many young viewers. Children may watch them on the classroom set or at home. Research has shown that viewers of "The Electric Company" make significant gains over nonviewers in the reading skills which the program is designed to teach and that the program is an effective instructional supplement for target-age pupils in the bottom half of their class who are just beginning to experience reading difficulty.[3]

Experience Charts

These charts may be employed for constructing group experience stories, recording plans, displaying information, and a number of other purposes. Through their use children learn page orientation, sequential organization, initial sight vocabulary, and various language functions.

Conversation Periods

It is essential that the daily schedule provide some periods when children work quietly on individual projects and other periods when they can learn the give-and-take of lively, polite conversation. A short session for sharing out-of-school experiences may stimulate conversation, especially if the class is broken into small congenial groups for the activity so that simple social responsibilities and courtesies may be taught. Classroom snack times also offer occasions for teaching and learning language usage.

Use of Films and Filmstrips

Motion pictures and filmstrips effectively develop concepts, foster literary appreciation, and teach language patterns. The filmed experience must be followed, however, by a related verbalization if maximum benefits are to be obtained. Some teachers find the loop projector especially worthwhile. (Titles of selected films and filmstrips are provided in Appendix 1.)

Use of Cassettes and Recordings

Resources that are available can be classified into three language instruction categories: concept development, literary appreciation, and auditory discrimination. They may be used well as early as kindergarten and first grade. (Titles of selected recordings are included in Appendix 1.)

Use of the Tape Recorder

The ways in which a tape recorder can be employed for language development are so numerous that every classroom should have its own machine. In speech arts, for example, the initial taping of puppet plays provides an opportunity for pupils to listen critically and suggest changes in the production. The tape recorder can also be used for gathering outdoor sounds for indoor listening or for bringing an evening radio program to school for a daytime lesson.

Unit Experiences

During unit study children discover new ways in which language may be used in group planning, in recording of experiences, and in evaluating outcomes. Frequently they may learn how to make and read labels and how to use books (with the teacher's help) as sources of information.

Beginning Writing

Children's first writing experiences may be the drawing of their initials in manuscript capitals on booklets related to unit activities. When they are ready to learn to write their full names they should be taught to use both uppercase and lowercase letters so that there is no problem of relearning writing habits later. Next, the more advanced children can learn to make signs as part of their unit work.

Telling Original Stories

The early retelling by children of stories they have heard aids them in learning to relate events in sequence. Experience chart planning and picture interpretation projects also add to creative skills. The first expression usually consists of recounting personal experiences, and some beginners never progress any further. Others can compose an entire original story several sentences long. Young children who can express their ideas with some degree of sensitivity and imagination are well along the road to language fluency.

Dictated Stories

It is only a short step from telling personal experience stories and original stories to dictating them for the teacher to record. As boys and girls dictate and watch the teacher write the dictation, they learn page orientation and gradually attain a sight vocabulary. With guidance, children generalize that certain letters and letter combinations stand for specific sounds which appear in words. Each child's dictated stories contain his or her own vocabulary and are as long or short as attention span and ability permit them to be. Since the work is so completely individualized, one immature pupil can enjoy participation in the activity without learning to read a single word, while another may advance to the second- or third-grade reading level. Dictated stories lead toward experiences in writing one's own stories and in reading books and so are important milestones in a coordinated language arts curriculum.

Microcomputers in the Language Arts Classroom

Language readiness activities and other language learning experiences may often be implemented successfully with the use of the microcomputer. All teachers should be aware that, in the future, the computer will be like a pencil—universal, with everyone using it, never dictating what we do with it, interactive, and with as yet unknown capacities.[4]

The microcomputer in the last decade has moved quickly and dramatically into the realm of instructional technologies available to teachers. Furthermore, it has done so with an ever-increasing number of kinds of machines and programs. It may very well be, according to Daniel and Blanchard, the most staggering new economic force since the invention of the automobile, with billions in annual sales.[5] For teachers to act rather than react in the face of such rapid change, the following suggestions are offered to them:

1. Acquire a basic knowledge in educational computing by talking to students and reading books and magazines on computing.
2. Start to use educational computer programs since they are about as simple to use as cassette tapes.
3. Begin to develop procedures for evaluating educational computer programs, such as the Software Evaluation Checklist in Figure 1.2.
4. Incorporate a computer-assisted lesson into the weekly plans so that computer technology is not reserved for a few select students.
5. Get acquainted with resource materials available in educational computing, such as software directories.
6. Visit a video-game arcade to determine what appeals to students and to review the games for any educational values.
7. Learn to use a word processor in order to save time on paperwork and to serve as a role model for students.
8. Start to review the curriculum in an effort to determine pupil needs in view of future trends.
9. Discover the names of district and building personnel responsible for implementing computer technology, and then assist those individuals in incorporating language arts programs into their purchases of software.
10. Join educational computing professional organizations, such as the International Council for Computers in Education (ICCE), the Association for Educational Data Systems (AEDS), or the Association for the Development of Computer Based Instruction Systems (ADCIS).

Software Evaluation Checklist

Figure 1.2. Software Evaluation Checklist.

PRODUCT INFORMATION

Name of program ______________________ Price __________

Hardware required ________________ Audience level __________

Distributor ______________________________________

Purpose or objective ______________________________

ANSWER each question below using a "+" for "yes" and "−" for "no".

INSTRUCTIONAL DESIGN

Directions

_____ 1. Are directions shown on the screen and easy to follow?
_____ 2. Are directions available throughout the program?
_____ 3. Can the user run the program with minimal assistance?

Screen Format

_____ 4. Is print size and space between lines acceptable?
_____ 5. Are special text features used to attract attention? (flashing words, underlining, or inverse printing)
_____ 6. Do graphics enhance the program content?

Rate of Presentation

_____ 7. Can the learner adjust the reading rate?
_____ 8. Can the learner exit the program at various points?
_____ 9. Can the learner re-enter the program at exit point?

Learner Interaction with the Program

_____ 10. Is required input easy to enter?
_____ 11. Is positive feedback present and appropriate?
_____ 12. Is negative feedback present and appropriate?
_____ 13. Does feedback guide learner to the correct response?
_____ 14. Is the number of learner responses per item limited to no more than two or three attempts?
_____ 15. Are required worksheets furnished?

Linear or Branching Programming

_____ 16. If linear, is the content in proper sequence?
_____ 17. If branching, is it thorough in providing learner options?

Content Bank

_____ 18. Is there a bank of items?
_____ 19. Can the teacher add to the bank of items?

Time

_____ 20. Does time required for lesson fit your schedule?

Format of Instruction

_____ 21. Does the format fit the instructional goal?
_____ drill and practice _____ tutorial
_____ informational _____ game

Figure 1.2. (cont.)

Instructional Support

_____ 22. Is the program easy for the teacher to use?
_____ 23. Is the hardcopy quality satisfactory?
_____ 24. Can the teacher save items into a content bank for later use?

Documentation

_____ 25. Is a teacher's manual available?
_____ 26. Are directions clear and complete?
_____ 27. Are program objectives specified?
_____ 28. Is the lesson content shown in detail? (vocabulary lists, reading selections, etc.)
_____ 29. Are sample frames from the program shown?
_____ 30. Are needed forms included?
_____ 31. Has the program been field tested?

Record Keeping

_____ 32. Can records be kept for an ample number of students?
_____ 33. Are responses and progress reported in a usable form?
_____ 34. Can records be printed on paper?

CONTENT

_____ 35. Does content focus on a specific objective?
_____ 36. Is the content accurate?
_____ 37. Does it fit into the curriculum?
_____ 38. Is the content taught as you want it taught?
_____ 39. Is it appropriate for the learner's age and ability?
_____ 40. Are reading selections interesting for the learner?
_____ 41. Is the content free of racial, ethnic, sexual and religious bias?

SUMMATIVE EVALUATION

_____ 42. Does the program deal effectively with the stated objective?
_____ 43. Does the program support the curriculum?
_____ 44. Can it be used with the intended age or grade level?
_____ 45. Can it be used with learners of varying ability levels?
_____ 46. Can it serve multiple uses, such as introducing, reviewing, or expanding on a skill or concept?
_____ 47. Does this program present content as well as or better than material already being used?

What are the strengths of the program? ____

____

What are the significant weaknesses? ____

____

Describe how the content is presented. ____

____

Describe how the learner reacted to the program. ____

____

From R. Sanders and M. Sanders, "Evaluating Microcomputer Software" in COMPUTERS, READING AND LANGUAGE ARTS. Reprinted with permission of Modern Learning Publishers, Oakland, California.

11. Work with the International Reading Association (IRA) and the National Council of Teachers of English (NCTE). They represent language arts professional organizations with special interest groups dedicated to educational computing.
12. Join a community computer club since its members are probably the best source of current information on computing in the locality.
13. Visit nearby computer stores where the clerks can offer considerable information about the latest computer hardware and software.
14. Take an informal course in computing from a local college, because any beginning course in instructional computing or beginning programming is helpful. It is not necessary to know how to write computer programs in order to use a computer.[6]

Ways to Use a Microcomputer

Unless classroom teachers have been especially trained in the use of the microcomputer, they may be unaware of the multitude of uses of computer technology in the reading/language arts curriculum. The following beginning list may provide elementary teachers with opportunities to enhance their instruction of boys and girls:

1. *Drill and practice.* Once the teacher has presented a basic concept, commercial software can provide practice in that concept and help develop automacity. It represents a major form of computer-assisted instruction (CAI).
2. *Tutoring.* This program is especially geared for students who need individual reteaching, who need make-up instruction due to absence, or who have special needs due to other causes. Teaching is provided before practice, and the program involves the other major form of computer assisted instruction.
3. *Assessment.* Programs of assessment may accompany a basal reader, for example, to be used after units or chapters, or they may be determined by the teacher or school district to be used at the end of a reporting period or a semester. The actual tasks are much like those the student encounters on drill and practice programs.
4. *Record Keeping.* Information from student drill and practice activities, from tutorial exercises, or from assessment activities can be recorded automatically, stored easily, and recovered handily. A broad variety of reports is available.
5. *Prescriptions.* Many teachers consider the current status of individual students to be the most useful information that can be retrieved from computer records. Teachers (or paraprofessionals) may use this information to type prescriptions coded to the objectives being assessed. Many of the computerized management systems attached to basal reading programs, for instance, permit the teacher to retrieve automatically suggestions in supplementary materials (such as workbooks) that accompany the basals.
6. *Interactive Language Programs.* Programs that model language and promote language production may be written by teachers, but they are not as common commercially as other types of software. They are important, however, because students learn language by modeling and by being active participators in the instructional process.

7. *Readability Determination.* The readability of instructional resources is a significant factor in student success in learning. Since the microcomputer handles repetitive tasks quickly and correctly, it can apply readability formulas based on syllable count as well as sentence length. Therefore, teachers can easily evaluate the difficulty of resources already in the classroom as well as those being considered for future purchase.
8. *Language Analysis.* This provides additional information about language (other than readability) and also gives data about student language production. Programs can be written for any word, type of word, or language string (such as a subordinate clause) that can be identified to the computer.
9. *CLOZE Passage Generation.* A cloze passage test is one way for the teacher to determine whether a pupil can read selected materials with comprehension. It omits every fifth word from a prose selection, leaves the first and last sentences alone, and replaces the missing words with blanks. The pupil must fill in the blanks with the omitted words.

   While such a test has proved to be a valuable resource for some years, its production is both tedious and time-consuming. Microcomputers, however, can readily develop a variety of cloze tests, including different forms of the same passage.
10. *Vocabulary List Generation.* As will be discussed at length in Chapter Ten, vocabulary is an important factor in reading comprehension, and direct instruction in vocabulary results in improved and increased concept formulation. Teachers, therefore, need appropriate word lists to use, to store in microcomputers, and to retrieve as needed during classroom instruction.
11. *Test Item Generation.* The periodic testing of students at certain grade levels throughout a district is a necessary but expensive procedure. Since test results influence both programs and student progress, test items are generally stored on computers and can be reviewed by objective and grade.
12. *Objectives Production.* Since correct identification of instructional objectives is the first step in promoting student achievement, it is important for the teacher to be able to retrieve readily objectives for instructing specialized groups of students, such as those who are learning English as a second language. Such objectives can be stored in the microcomputer on separate data files.
13. *Inventories.* When library media center inventories are maintained on microcomputer disks, the librarian can spend more time working directly with children and with teachers requesting media materials. Pupil acquisition of media center skills then improves dramatically.
14. *Word Processing.* In schools, an inexpensive diskette can convert a microcomputer into a word processor which allows writers to revise, edit, and proofread their work without repetitive handwriting or typing. Composition skills improve, and language experience programs in reading (which of course demand student writing) become more successful.[7]

Potential Pitfalls of Microcomputer Applications

Currently there are two temporary factors which restrict the usefulness of computers in the classroom: the relative lack of good commercially available software for the language arts, and the equally limited computer resources in many schools.[8]

More serious are two additional pitfalls which may surface as more and more teachers adopt this technology for their language arts programs.[9] The first concerns student oral language development and written composition skills. Elementary school children in general, and in particular those whose background experiences do not involve conversations/discussions with linguistically adept adults, need frequent and regular exposure to strong language environments and require verbal interaction with teachers and peers. Since most computer-assisted teaching is transmitted visually and in isolation for purposes of individualized instruction, extensive use of the microcomputer could impede the expansion and refinement of communication skills. Teachers must therefore plan computer time wisely and never forget that microcomputer instruction is hardly a panacea.

The second potential pitfall relates to the integration of the language skills of listening, speaking, reading, and writing. At the present time, most software programs isolate rather than integrate language arts instruction, despite the fact that girls and boys learn language holistically. Teachers must consequently be alert to this dilemma, when selecting any program, in their continuing effort to avoid additional fragmentation of the language arts curriculum. They may wish to refer to the guidelines for review and evaluation of English language arts softward developed by the NCTE and presented in Appendix 5.

Discussion Questions

1. Do you agree that none of the four language skills can be taught in total isolation from the others? Defend your position.
2. Why would growth in the receptive areas of the language arts prompt growth in the productive areas?
3. Of the ten subgroups of essential competencies for English programs, which two do you feel should receive the least attention in the elementary school? Can you justify your ratings?
4. Which of the major types of beginning language activities would you use with less advantaged first graders enrolled in a school district noted for its limited financial resources?
5. How can a teacher guard against the potential pitfalls of using microcomputers in the language arts program?

Suggested Projects

1. Prepare for the grade of your choice a list of goals that would be appropriate for the language arts program of a nearby school.
2. Locate the teacher's edition for one current commercial elementary language arts series. Then categorize the essential competencies in one chapter or section.

3. Draw and label on a sheet of graph paper a classroom arrangement conducive to the development of language readiness. Then, on the other side of the paper, list briefly other items which would further stimulate such development in that environment.
4. Use the Software Evaluation Checklist to determine the adequacy of one language arts program.
5. Role play: a classroom teacher justifies the expenses involved in the language arts program before a group of parents determined to slash school costs.

Related Readings

Busching, B., and Schwartz, J., eds., 1984. *Integrating the Language Arts in the Elementary School.* Urbana, IL: National Council of Teachers of English.

DiStefano, P. et al. 1984. *Elementary Language Arts.* New York: John Wiley.

Flood, J., and Salus, P. 1984. *Language and the Language Arts.* Englewood Cliffs, NJ: Prentice-Hall.

Gordon, H. et al. 1984. "Ten Myths about Microcomputers," *Academic Therapy, 19,* pp. 285–292.

Riedesel, C., and Clements, D. 1985. *Coping with Computers in the Elementary and Middle Schools.* Englewood Cliffs, NJ: Prentice-Hall.

Savignon, S., and Berns, M. 1984. *Initiatives in Communicative Language Teaching.* Reading, MA: Addison-Wesley.

Sinatra, R., and Stahl-Gemake, J. 1983. *Using the Right Brain in the Language Arts.* Springfield, IL: Charles C. Thomas.

Stewig, J. 1983. *Exploring Language Arts in the Elementary Classroom.* New York: Holt.

Temple, C., and Gillet, J. W. 1984. *Language Arts: Learning Processes and Teaching Practices.* Boston: Little, Brown.

Vockell, E., and Rivers, R. 1984. *Instructional Computing for Today's Teachers.* New York: Macmillan.

Chapter Notes

1. W. Petty, D. C. Petty, A. P. Newman, and E. M. Skeen, "Language Competencies Essential for Coping in Our Society," in *The Teaching of English,* J. R. Squire, ed. (Chicago: National Society for the Study of Education, 1977), pp. 88–91. Reprinted with permission of Kenneth J. Rehage, editor for the society.
2. Bloomington Public Schools, *Language Arts Curriculum Guide: K–6* (Bloomington, Minnesota: Public Schools, 1971), pp. 1–21.
3. J. G. Cooney, *Children's Television Workshop: Progress Report* (New York: Children's Television Workshop, 1974). ERIC Document Reproduction Service No. ED 095 892.
4. S. Papert, *Mindstorms: Children, Computers, and Powerful Ideas* (New York: Basic Books, 1980).
5. D. Daniel and J. Blanchard, "Trends in Educational Microcomputing: Implications for the Language Arts," *Computers, Reading and Language Arts,* 1983 *I*(2), p. 18.
6. *Ibid.,* pp. 21–23.
7. G. Kuchinskas, "22 Ways to Use a Microcomputer in Reading & Language Arts Classes," *Computers, Reading and Language Arts,* 1983, *I*(1), pp. 11–16.
8. J. A. Zaharias, "Microcomputers in the Language Arts Classroom: Promises and Pitfalls," *Language Arts,* 1983, *60,* pp. 990–995.
9. *Ibid.*

The English Language and the Child Learner

2

Objectives

The nature of language according to linguistic scientists

Factors explaining why the English language is constantly changing

Three major theories about language acquisition in boys and girls

Development of syntax and fluency in children ages five to twelve

Discover As You Read This Chapter If*

1. Most of the languages spoken in the world today are represented in writing.
2. Every normal child possesses the biological capacity for language.
3. Social interaction is needed for language learning.
4. Language keeps changing constantly, and, therefore, some of the nonstandard forms used today may become acceptable tomorrow.
5. Dialects are incorrect or inadequate speech.
6. Two major types of dialects are regional and social.
7. Phonology is concerned with the distinctive sounds that make up a language.
8. Morphology deals with word order and how groups of words are arranged to convey meaning.
9. Psychologists have finally agreed on how young children acquire language.
10. When boys and girls enter kindergarten, their syntactical development is complete.

*Answers to these true-or-false statements may be found in Appendix 6.

A basic understanding of the nature of language is important so that teachers may promote in their lesson planning for the child learner one or more of these language aspects:

1. *Language has grammar.* While the grammar of each language is different, some closely related languages (such as English and Spanish) share many features which denote meaning or the relationships of elements in sentences. Children who speak two languages often have problems with the differences in the grammars of those languages. Since word order (or syntax) is a vital part of grammar, Spanish-speaking pupils enrolled in an ESL (English as a Second Language) class, for example, will be asking ungrammatical questions should they persist in using the Spanish order when posing questions in English.
2. *Language is oral.* Scholars have counted about 3000 spoken languages, although less than half of them have ever been represented in writing. Spoken language is older, more widespread, and communicates ideas better than written language. Every normal child will learn to talk with little or no formal assistance, although ordinarily he or she learns to write only with the help of others. And then that writing is a mere representation of earlier speech.
3. *Language is social.* The form of each language reflects the social needs of the group that employs it. Children may possess the biological capacity for language, but they cannot develop that potential without interaction with others in their society. There is even evidence that language learning is inhibited when social interaction becomes blocked.
4. *Language is symbolic and arbitrary.* Words, the symbolic aspect of language, permit children to discuss a ride in the space shuttle although they have not as yet experienced it directly. Language is a type of code which allows abstract ideas and experiences to be encoded by the speaker, transmitted by speech, and decoded by the hearer. Although words symbolize real objects or events, they themselves are arbitrary. English speakers, for example, call a four-legged animal that gives milk a *cow,* but there is no inherent trait in the animal that demands that it be called *cow.* Even onomatopoeic words are arbitrary symbols and do not, therefore, have meaning in themselves; consequently, the dog in the English community that says *bow-wow* barks *wang-wang* in the Chinese community.
5. *Language changes.* Since it is spoken by living people, language too is alive and therefore changes. New ideas, products, and institutions make the need for such change necessary. Since English and the other languages exist in the oral expression of the persons who use them, some of the nonstandard usage of today may become the accepted usage of tomorrow.
6. *Language is systematic and describable.* Every language in the world can be described using identical techniques, according to the science of descriptive linguistics. Each is consistent in its structure and not a haphazard collection of symbols and sounds. Most sentences, therefore, although they are created spontaneously, still follow a system of rules of which even the users often are not totally aware. Children learn the system as they learn the language.

7. *Each language is unique and diverse.* In order to comprehend how unique each language is, it is important to recall that the most popular definition of a language is that form understood by members of one *speech community* (such as France) but not by those of another speech community (such as Spain). (Even elementary school children are surprised to learn that there are reported to be 54 distinct linguistic groupings for North American Indians alone!) When groups of persons are socially or geographically separated from one another, their speech reflects grammatical, vocabulary, and pronunciation changes. Such language diversity is ordinarily a cumulative process.

Language History

Children need to know something of the history of the English language in order to interpret information about derivations as provided in the dictionary. The historical context furnished to help them interpret A. S. (Anglo-Saxon), M. E. (Middle English), O. F. (Old French), and L. (Latin) should lead the pupils to four important generalizations:

- English is basically Anglo-Saxon.
- English became a simpler language after the Norman Conquest and one that is more dependent upon word order to express relationships.
- English vocabulary has been enriched by extensive borrowing from other languages, particularly Latin and French.
- The assimilation of borrowed words was made possible by the ease with which English endings could be given to them.

The study of the development of the words in a single language and the changes in the relationships among those words is termed *language history.* It should be included in the curriculum because language is constantly changing, and that change affects principally four areas: pronunciation, word forms, sentence structure, and vocabulary.

Three factors help explain the change. First, there is *normal growth* or routine progress as ideas and inventions develop and are absorbed into the language. Second, there is *human mobility* occurring whenever people move to new locations and new situations. And finally there is the *importation of foreign words and expressions* when speakers and writers of different languages meet and exchange words.

The application of the history of the English language to the teaching of English is largely unexplored. Still, some of the details can be introduced as early as the middle grades, along with the history of English words and their meanings. Several textbook series have sections labelled variously as "Working with Words" or "Words Are Interesting." Third graders learn, for instance, that the word *hello* was once spelled *holla* and that it came from the French and means the same as "Hey, there." Fourth graders must match Modern English words (such as *heaven, eastward, right,* and *live*) with the Anglo-Saxon words from which they came (namely, *heafonum, easteweardre, riht,* and *libban*) and then discuss why the pairs of words look and sound so different. Fifth graders are asked to determine why the land formation known as a *delta* is named after the fourth letter of the Greek alphabet.

Historical Development

Many languages appear to be related. For instance, some English words sound and look much like words having identical meanings in other languages. The English word for *mother,* for example, is *mere* in French, *Mutter* in German, and *moder* in Norwegian. The English word for *family* is *famille* in French, *Familie* in both German and Norwegian, and *fameel* in Persian. Linguistic study of the origins of language has shown that such similarities exist because these languages all developed from one early language spoken by people called Indo-Europeans.

Originally, these people lived together somewhere on the land mass which today is Europe and the Near East. As their culture grew, however, they began migrating to various corners of the continent. One such group settled in northern Europe and became the Germanic branch of the original Indo-European language family, whose descendants presently cover nearly the entire world.

Between 600 and 400 B.C., a tribe of Indo-Europeans called Celts crossed the English Channel and conquered the island of Britain. About a century after Gaul had fallen to Caesar, Britain too was annexed to Rome. Then after the Romans withdrew early in the fifth century, the British Celts were invaded and conquered by the Germanic tribes of Angles, Saxons, and Jutes from the eastern coast of the North Sea. The English language is generally dated from this last conquest. By the beginning of the seventh century, the language called Anglo-Saxon, or Old English, emerged as the language of the island and took its place among the modern tongues of Europe.

Old English was a highly inflected language, as were its Germanic progenitors. It carried distinctive endings for four forms of the verb, for case in nouns and adjectives, for number in several parts of speech, and for person, number, and case in pronouns. Its phonology resembled that of modern German rather than that of Modern English.

Although English in the seventh century did include some Latin after Britain's conversion to Christianity, the vocabulary was predominantly Germanic (and even today it has been stated that half of the words on any one page of English are Anglo-Saxon in origin). It changed markedly, however, with the influence of Norman French from William the Conqueror's conquest of England in 1066 until the end of the Hundred Years' War in 1453. Little wonder that Chaucer's fourteenth-century vocabulary looks very different from King Alfred's ninth-century one since so many of Chaucer's words were borrowed from the French. The period of Middle English, during which *Canterbury Tales* was written, extended from approximately 1100 to the Renaissance.

Shakespeare was a writer of Modern English. Although the dates are highly arbitrary, Modern English is the language from 1500 on. The language of each of the two early major periods—Old and Middle—differs so much from the type of English used today that one must study it almost as a foreign language in order to understand it at all. Over the centuries a vast simplification of the language has evolved, with the pattern of deteriorating inflections being felt everywhere.

For the last thousand years the English language has borrowed words greedily from other languages. Through invasion and exploration the English came in contact with the ideas, items, and ways of peoples of continental Europe and many other lands. Their language grew and changed. In recent times, however, through the apparent dominance of English-speaking peoples in everything from sports to science, other languages have borrowed words from Modern English.

A special strand of Modern English is American English which, from the seventeenth century on, began to run a separate course. Emigrants from certain regions in England usually settled together in their new homeland, with the result that the English dialects they spoke were transplanted to particular areas along the Atlantic coast. People who came from southern England settled in New England and spoke with a broad *a* and softened terminal *r* as in *father* and a softened or abandoned *r* before consonants as in *lard.* Those who came from northern England settled mainly in Pennsylvania or moved to the North Central States. The third dialect area extended from Chesapeake Bay south and reflected the dialect of southeastern England.

As pioneer society in the New World was in constant flux, there was a cross-fertilization of dialects and the eventual development of an American English that is related to the most noticeable features of the cultural history, institutional growth, and physical environment of the American people. The language has borrowed words from the American Indians (e.g., *chipmunk, moose, pecan, squash,* and *tamarack*); the French (e.g., *cent, chowder, depot, dime,* and *pumpkin*); the Spanish (e.g., *alfalfa, burro, palomino, rodeo,* and *stampede*); the Dutch (e.g., *boss, cookie, Santa Claus, sleigh,* and *waffle*); and the Germans (e.g., *delicatessen, noodle, pinochle, semester,* and *seminar*). It also has frequently altered word function (e.g., from noun to adjective or verb) and demonstrated a fondness for compound formations (e.g., 20 words have *stage* as a first element), word blends (e.g., *cablegram* for *cable telegram*), and the creation of mouth-filling terms (such as *gobbledygook*).

While some differences between British and American English exist in vocabulary and pronunciation, the similarities between the two languages far outweigh the differences. In the critical area of grammatical structure and syntax, the difference is negligible.

Teaching Activities in Language History

The English language is dynamic and changing. Elementary language arts instruction should reflect this reality. An intermediate teacher can help children develop a better understanding of the history of their language when he or she chooses to:

1. Make bulletin boards or wall charts showing the similarities among many words in the Indo-European language family. If these are also discussed with the class, the pupils will generalize that many languages evolved from a common ancestor.
2. Use library or media center references to motivate the class to investigate the civilizations of the Indo-European culture and subsequently report on its research.
3. Tell the story of the migrations to the British Isles of the Germanic branch of the Indo-European culture. Perhaps the students will hypothesize concerning the reasons for such migrations.

4. Show transparencies of English writing during the Old English and Middle English periods. A discussion of the characteristics of some of the strange letter formations and unusual spellings may lead the class to generalize that language indeed changes.
5. Select at random a 100-word sample of Modern English writing and have the class look up in a reputable dictionary the origin of each word. Results can then be tabulated to indicate the percentage of English words borrowed from other languages and the percentage which are American in origin. Using such data, the pupils may generalize regarding the effect that other languages have had in changing the English language.
6. Lead children to investigate the pronunciation of geographically isolated American people, such as the hill people of North Carolina (who pronounce *boil* as *bile* and *drop* as *drap*). The class may then hypothesize concerning the evolution of a language.
7. Have pupils (during the social studies unit on Discovery and Exploration) list words which explorers may have brought back from trips to alien lands. The dictionary can be consulted to see if the words suggested did truly originate from those lands. (The same procedure can later be used during the unit on The Settlement of America and the words that varied ethnic groups contributed to American English.)

Usage and Dialect

Along with some study of English language history, elementary school children can also learn to understand English language usage. They should come to recognize that language must be suited to the context in which it is used. The notion that there is only one "correct" way to express an idea is both linguistically naive and counterproductive.[1] Wise language arts teachers therefore encourage students to observe usage variety in literature and to experiment with such variety in their written compositions.

There are at least seven interlocking dimensions of modern English usage.[2] The first is *socioeconomic-educational* and involves the spectrum of usage extending from standard to nonstandard English and reflecting the speaker's education and/or socioeconomic status. The second is *stylistic* and involves the distinction between usage at formal ceremonies, for example, and that at a backyard picnic. The third dimension is *sex-based* and concerns the spectrum of usage extending from the obscenities deemed rough and masculine to the gentle expressions considered to be very feminine. The fourth viewpoint is *methodological;* this involves the choice between writing and speech and the distinction between the punctuation of writing and the intonation of speech. The fifth dimension is *historical;* for example, it concerns the differences between Chaucer's usage and present-day usage. The sixth viewpoint is *occupational* and involves the unique vocabulary and phraseology of each job speciality. The seventh dimension is *geographic* and relates to the phenomenon that English usage possesses international, national, regional, and local dialects. All seven of these dimensions interact, thereby creating the total situation of modern usage. Dimensions involved in a speaker's ability to understand and to produce appropriate styles of language as part of his or her broader ability to communicate can be illustrated by the acronym SPEAKING:

Setting:	When and where the speech act occurs affects variables such as volume. In some places no speech is allowed at times.
Participants:	Sex, kinship, age, occupation, social class, or education may make a difference.
Ends:	The purpose of the speech act matters: Is it a request, warning, demand, query, or statement of fact?
Act sequence:	Sometimes this refers to the prescribed form a speech act can take when it is controlled by the culture. At other times it refers to what can be talked about during the speech act.
Key:	Identical words may express various moods, tones, or manners. The signal may be nonverbal or it can be conveyed by intonation, word choice, or other linguistic convention.
Instrumentalities:	Different verbal codes may be chosen. A bilingual may choose between languages and a monolingual among regional or social dialects. The choice is generally an unconscious one and may indicate humor, distance, respect, intimacy, or insolence.
Norms:	Norms of interpretation and interaction during a speech act include taking turns in the conversation (if proper in the speaker's culture), knowing polite greeting forms, and other "linguistic manners" (including, for example, appropriate topics for dinner conversations).
Genres:	Certain speech acts may be categorized in formal structures, such as proverbs, riddles, editorials, myths, poems, or prayers.[3]

A change in one or more of these speech components of the social context may signal that some different linguistic rules should be used.

Dialect in the United States

Some people mistakenly assume that *dialect* refers to corrupted, inadequate, or incorrect speech. Actually the term implies no value judgment. It refers merely to a habitual variety of usage or to a distinct variation in how a language is spoken. Dialects are fully formed systems. Every language has dialects and its native speakers use several dialects to meet the many needs of daily life.

Speakers of a particular dialect form a speech community which reflects the members' life styles or professional, national, family, or ethnic backgrounds. Certain common features mark the speech of the members, however these features may be defined. Nevertheless, no two members of a particular community ever speak alike because each person's speech is unique. This individualized speech or individual dialect is termed an *idiolect*.

One of the principal types of dialect is *regional* or geographical dialect used by speakers living in the same area. In the United States no single regional dialect is the accepted standard for the country. Instead, each area has its own standard which represents the dialect of its educated residents. The major dialect areas in the United States today are shown in Figure 2.1. Note that the western United States does not fall as neatly into dialect boundaries as does the eastern region.

Regional dialects differ from each other in phonological, vocabulary, and syntactic or grammatical features. An example of the first difference is the "intrusive *r*" that appears in *Washington* and *wash* among residents of Indiana and Missouri. Vocabulary variety may be proved by the many synonyms for the word

Figure 2.1. Major Dialect Areas of the United States.

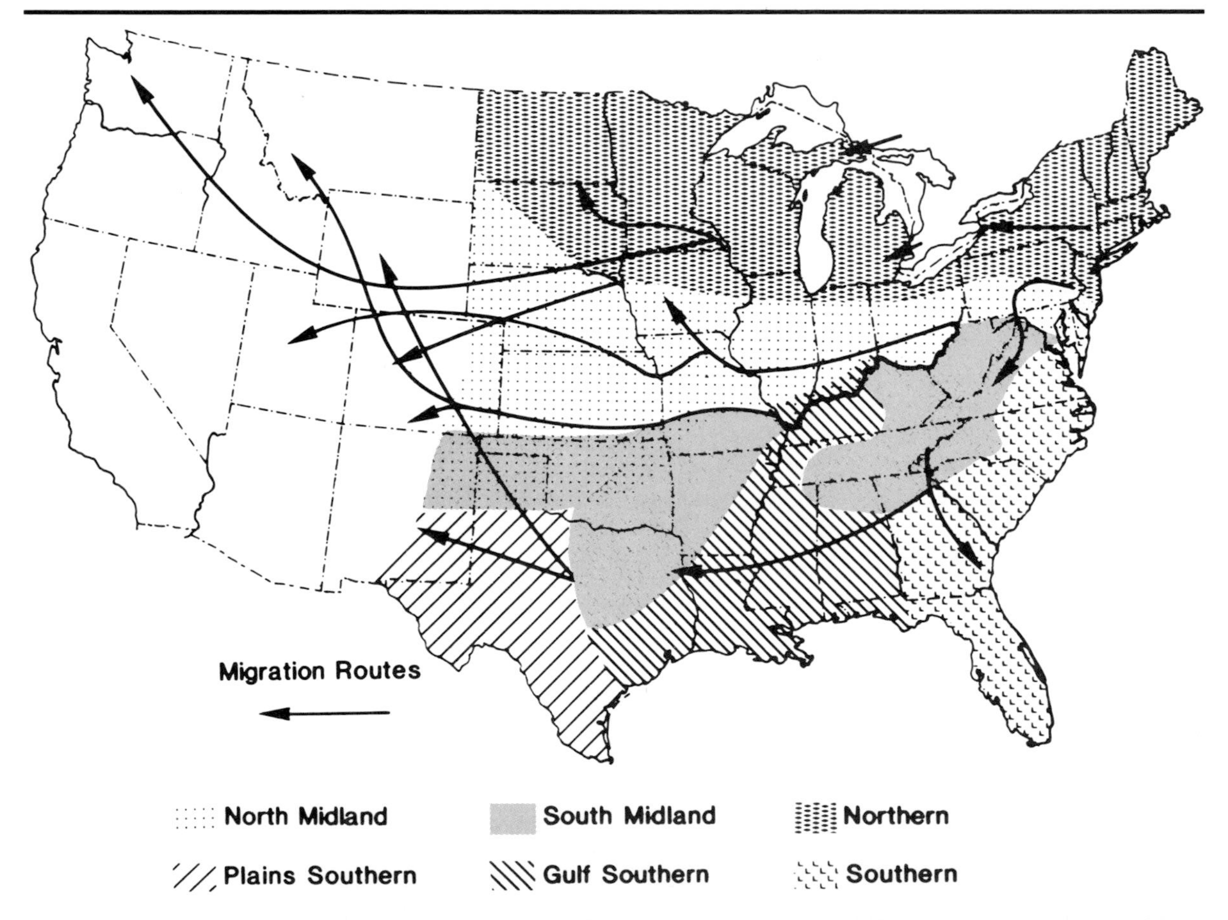

relatives, including *folks, people, kinfolk, folkses, homefolks,* and *kinnery.* Finally, a grammatical difference is the preference for *he don't* rather than *he doesn't* among residents in North Carolina. Americans generally are said to be puzzled by pronunciation differences, delighted by vocabulary differences, and repelled by grammatical differences.

On the whole, however, the speakers of American English have an advantage over those who speak the dialects of languages in most other countries where social and geographic mobility has been more limited for long periods of time. In the United States no functional block in communication normally intrudes between native speakers.

Regional dialects make interesting study. Some of the current English textbook series used in elementary schools contain material on regional dialect differences.

Social Dialect

Residents of the same geographical region do not all sound alike. The variations in their speech include differences in sounds, words, expressions, and sentence patterns. Such differences within a single regional speech community often correlate with social variables of occupation, isolation, education, and the resulting social status in the community. Speech variants used by one socially identifiable group of speakers comprise the second major type of dialect known as a *sociolect* or social dialect. Studies by sociologists and linguists—or *sociolinguists*—have increasingly focused on this kind of dialect since the 1960s.

Sociolects are generally divided into two broad classes: standard and nonstandard dialects. The first class is used by persons who are usually well-educated, well-traveled members of occupations ranking at the middle-to-high socioeconomic levels. They interact with other standard dialect speakers in social and job settings and read nationally disseminated journals and books. Speakers of a nonstandard dialect, on the other hand, are generally persons with a limited education and mobility who interact with others with the same background.

Children also reflect a nonstandard or standard social dialect in their speech. Although this dialect is hardly the result of occupation or formal educational background, it is the social dialect used by the children's parents, neighbors, and friends. If boys and girls mature in a language-learning environment filled with standard dialect speakers, they are likely to speak a standard dialect. Similarly, if children are surrounded by nonstandard dialect speakers, they will typically speak a nonstandard dialect. An oral language rating form which teachers can use with pupils who speak a nonstandard English dialect is found in Figure 2.2.

Upon entering school however, children who speak a nonstandard dialect are no longer limited to speaking that one dialect for the rest of their lives. In school they learn a second and alternative dialect—the standard dialect—and gradually become able to *style-shift* from one dialect to the other depending upon the topic setting and the number and identity of the participants. They retain the right to use their own first and nonstandard dialect in speech and writing. Furthermore, they gain an equal right to acquire a second and standard dialect for the same communicative purposes.

Figure 2.2. Oral Language Rating Form for Use with Children Who Speak a Nonstandard English Dialect.

Oral Language Rating / Dialect Interference	5 Never	4 Almost Never	3 Sometimes	2 Usually	1 Almost Always
School ____________ Date ________					
Name ____________					
Grade ______ Teacher ____________					
Pronunciation: Distinguishes between *then* and *den; they* and *day; both* and *boat; thin* and *tin;* and *thin* and *sin.*	____	____	____	____	____
Comparison: Uses the correct form of comparison such as *bigger, biggest; more beautiful,* and *most beautiful* rather than *more bigger; beautifuller* and *beautifullest.*	____	____	____	____	____
Double Negative: Uses negative expressions, such as *don't have any* rather than *don't have none.*	____	____	____	____	____
Plurals: Distinguishes between regular and irregular plurals (i.e., says *feet* and not *foots*). Pronounces the *s*-ending of regular plurals correctly (i.e., boots /s/, horses /iz/, dogs /z/).	____	____	____	____	____
Past Tense: Uses the appropriate past forms of irregular verbs rather than participle forms (uses appropriate *I ate* instead of *I et*). Uses the appropriate past forms of irregular verbs rather than inappropriate forms with the regular *-ed* ending of past form (i.e., *I drank* instead of *I drinked* my milk).	____	____	____	____	____
Past Participles: Uses the appropriate participle form (i.e., *cut* rather than *cuted,* or *brought* rather than *brung*).	____	____	____	____	____
Pronouns: Uses appropriate pronoun form.	____	____	____	____	____
Uses of Do: Uses appropriate forms of *DO* in questions, answers, and in negative statements.	____	____	____	____	____
Uses of Be: Uses, rather than omits, appropriate forms of *BE.*	____	____	____	____	____
Uses of Have: Uses, rather than omits, appropriate forms of *HAVE.*	____	____	____	____	____
Subject-Verb Agreement: Uses correct verb form when he or she is used as subject. Verb form has appropriate ending sound (i.e., *he takes* /s/, *he watches* /iz/, *he wears* /z/, rather than uninflected or simple forms (i.e., *he take, he watch, he wear*).	____	____	____	____	____

Source: *Michigan Oral Language Series* (New York: ACTFL, 1969).

Language Structure

For the most part boys and girls acquire their understanding of the underlying structure of the English language in much the same informal fashion that they acquire their understanding of usage. Again, however, as in the area of usage, there are portions of that understanding which can be and are formally studied in school, such as learning about prefixes and suffixes in the middle and intermediate grades.

The English language is a structure of arbitrary systems relating sounds and meanings. A child or adult is described as "knowing" the language when he or she understands the sounds used, the basic units of meaning, and the rules combining sounds and meanings to form sentences. That person is then said to have command of the phonological, morphological, syntactic, and semantic systems.

Phonology

Each language has its own set of vocal sounds (*phones*). As children grow into productive members of the speech community, they develop only those phones which they find useful in communicating. The study of phones is called *phonetics.*

Of the many phones in the English language, only a relatively small number differ significantly from each other. Those that do differ are called *phonemes* or minimal contrastive elements. While English is generally said to possess 44 phonemes, there is actually little agreement as to the number of phonemes in the American English language. The reported totals range from thirty-three to forty-five because there are different classification schemes and because sounds which are significant in one dialect may be less so in another. The study of phonemes or distinctive sounds that make up a language is called *phonology.* When phonemes appear in textual matter, the symbol for a phoneme appears between slanted bars: / /.

There are both segmental phonemes and nonsegmental (or suprasegmental) phonemes. The first group of thirty-two includes consonants, vowels, and semivowels (or phonemes that function either as consonants or as parts of diphthongs like /w/ and /y/) and constitutes the sequential elements, with some overlapping and gliding, of syllables, words, and sentences.

The second group of twelve includes phonemes of stress, pitch, and juncture which occur simultaneously with the segmental phonemes or separate them, and which are often considered together under the heading of *intonation.* Combinations of suprasegmental phonemes are responsible for the rhythm and cadence of a language. Their function is similar to that of punctuation in writing.

Stress refers to the relative degree of intensity of loudness of different syllables in a sentence, and there are four stress phonemes in speaking which can be quite simply indicated for purposes of discussion as: primary (the strongest stress (/); secondary stress (\ ); tertiary stress (∧); and weak (slight) stress (◡). One-syllable words, when pronounced alone, usually have the strongest, or primary, stress, for example, *féet, ádd, íf.* Words of two or more syllables have varying patterns of stress, as in *ínvàlîd* or *ìnválĭd* and *mágnèt* or *màgnétîc.* Phrases may vary in stress according to the meaning expressed, as in *lóud spèakĕr* or *lòud spéakĕr.* Sentences, too, have varying patterns of stress, depending upon the meaning intended, for example, *Jóhn bought three books; John bóught three books; John bought thrée books;* or *John bought three bóoks.*

Pitch refers to the ups and downs, or tunes, in a stream of speech. Although many changes in pitch do not affect meaning, there are some that do. Differences in pitch distinguish between statements and questions in English. A way of picturing this difference might be as follows: *John bought three books?* or *John bought three books.* A statement has a falling pitch contour, while a question has a rising pitch contour. There are four significant pitch phonemes in English, designated from lowest to highest as low, normal, high, and highest and numbered from one to four. The basic pitch of a person's voice, regardless of whether the person is a man or woman, is marked as pitch two.

The term *juncture* refers to the ways a speaker of English makes the transition from one phoneme to the next. There are four juncture phonemes and all are relevant to the teaching of spelling. Open or internal juncture (+) is the vocal signal that usually divides words from each other; it is the slight retarding of the flow of sound that distinguishes *ice cream* and *I scream.* The three terminal junctures are the vocal signals that generally divide sequences of words into constructions: (a) falling or fade-fall terminal (↘) ordinarily ends statements, commands, and some questions; (b) rising or fade-rise terminal (↖) usually ends questions that are intended to express surprise, doubt, regret, or other emotion; and (c) sustained or level terminal (→) marks the divisions between certain constructions within a sentence.

When pupils listen carefully to someone speaking his or her native language, they will notice that while the speaker always uses certain phonemes in certain places, the same phoneme is not always pronounced in exactly the same way each time. The speaker's different pronunciations of the same phoneme, however, are of a kind that indicate clearly to someone familiar with the language which phoneme is being used. Most native speakers do not realize that they make these differences in sounds and a student of the language is free to use any one of the pronunciations in such cases. In describing a language it can be stated that such variations are *allophones* or two (or more) forms of the same phoneme.

While children are acquiring the phonemes of a language, they must also learn that phonemes go together in a predetermined order. Only certain orders are allowed, and there are rules which determine whether a phoneme can appear at the beginning, in the middle, or at the end of a word. Therefore, in English for example, PWLODB is not a word since it does not follow the phonological rule concerned with sequencing.

Morphology

When children and adults speak, they utter a sequence of individually meaningless phonemes as well as a sequence of meaningful morphemes. The sentence *The cat chased the birds* consists of vowels and consonants (segmental phonemes) spoken at varied *pitches* with different degrees of *stress.* It is simultaneously a string of the following *morphemes:* (the), {cat}, {chase}, {-d}, {the}, {bird}, {z}.

Morphemes are larger building stones which cannot be defined as precisely as phonemes. While phonemes only distinguish between meanings without adding to or changing them, morphemes are units of discourse that carry meaning. In the words *big* and *bag,* for example, there is a contrast in sounds by which one word is distinguished from the other, but the sounds responsible for the distinction do not in themselves carry any meaning and are, therefore, phonemes. In the words *bag* and *bags,* however, the sound that has been added causes a change in meaning and such a sound is termed a morpheme. One morpheme may contain one phoneme or several phonemes. Linguists write the symbol for a morpheme between braces: { }.

Morphemes are the smallest units of speech that have identifiable meanings of their own. They are not necessarily identical with syllables or words. The major morpheme classes in English are *bases* and *affixes.* Most bases (or roots) stand alone as words and so are described as *free* morphemes. Affixes never stand alone; they are always attached to bases, either before them as prefixes or after them as suffixes, and so are called *bound* morphemes. The study of morphemes or units of meaning is known as *morphology.*

Affixes are either derivational or inflectional. All prefixes are derivational affixes but suffixes may be either derivational or inflectional. In English no new inflectional affixes have been added for 700 years although derivational affixes are added routinely as needed, such as the recent prefixes {*mini*}, {*midi*}, and {*maxi*}.

Inflectional suffixes never change the word's part of speech, but derivational suffixes usually do. For example, the inflectional suffix *-s,* added to the noun *friend,* creates *friends,* which is still a noun with the added meaning "plural." However, the derivational suffix *-ly* changes the noun *friend* to the adjective *friendly.*

Just as each language has a separate set of phonological rules, so does each language have a distinct set of morphological rules which children (and non-native speakers) must learn if they are to combine morphemes into suitable words. Too, just as phonemes have allophones, morphemes have *allomorphs* or positional variants. For example, the prefixal morpheme *in* has four allomorphs: *in-* (inactive), *il-* (illogical), *im-* (immodest), and *ir* (irrelevant).

Syntax

Morphemes cannot be arranged one after another in any elective order. Instead, for each language there are combinations in which morphemes can be put together in an utterance. Such combinations are known as constructions, and *syntax* is the study of these constructions. Syntax deals with word order and how words or groups of words are arranged to convey meaning. For example, the words *the* and *cat* can be grouped together in the construction, *the cat,* but not *cat the.* As mentioned earlier, most syntactic structures are used by even the youngest children who must learn to follow a finite set of rules determining how grammatical sentences may be formed in the native language.

The largest English construction is the sentence. Children therefore should have considerable experience in changing sentences about; in modifying and rearranging the information that sentences provide; and in exploring relationships among the various kinds of sentences. During the elementary years basic sentence patterns can be taught inductively and largely without emphasis on terminology.

All theories of grammar recognize that English sentence patterns have two main parts: the subject and predicate (according to traditional grammar) or the noun phrase and the verb phrase (according to transformational generative grammar). Although linguists do not agree as to the number of patterns to be considered basic, these four sentence patterns are the ones most generally used in the elementary school, with the first two types accounting for 85 percent of the sentences found in the speech uttered by children:

Pattern I. N^1 *V.* Noun (or pronoun) and (intransitive) verb.
Example: *Birds sang.*
Subject/predicate

Pattern II. N^1 *V* N^2. Noun (or pronoun), (transitive) verb, and noun (or pronoun).
Example: *Mother bought cookies.*
Subject/predicate/object
(Can be transformed to passive voice.)

Pattern III. N^1 *L V* N^1. Noun (or pronoun), linking verb, and noun (or pronoun).
Example: *Mother is a teacher.*
Subject/predicate/predicate noun
(Can be an equation pattern since nouns or pronouns can exchange places.)

Pattern IV. N^1 *L V Aj.* Noun (or pronoun), linking verb, and adjective.
Example: *Summer is hot.*
Subject/predicate/predicate adjective.[4]

Semantics

The study of word meanings or the role of language in human life is called *semantics.* It explains how language is used to express feelings and thoughts, to transmit information, to control behavior, to persuade, and to create and express social cohesion.[5]

According to Halliday, a child acquiring language "learns how to mean," and part of that acquisition concerns mastery of seven universal functions of language:

1. *Instrumental language* used to satisfy needs. "I want. . . ."
2. *Regulatory language* used to control the behavior of others. "Go away."
3. *Interactional language* employed during social activities or for the purpose of getting along with others. "Let's play together."
4. *Personal language* used to express personal opinions or to allow a child to tell about himself/herself. "I want to be a pilot."
5. *Imaginative language* employed for creating a fantasy or a make-believe world. "Once upon a time. . . ."
6. *Heuristic language* used to seek information and ask questions. "Why do . . . ?"
7. *Informative language* employed to inform others. "I've got something to tell you."[6]

Semantics deals both with word meanings and with the attitudes that humans have toward particular words and expressions. It thus covers both the denotation and the connotation of certain vocabulary. Denotation refers to the literal, objective meaning of a word while connotation concerns the personal, subjective meaning that a word possesses for one individual. Little wonder that the identical word may have a variety of meaning-associations for different children or adults when words are so often learned in different settings by various individuals.

Children today must understand certain concepts about language content primarily because they are constantly exposed to the pervasive effects of the mass media. They must comprehend propaganda and persuasion techniques. They must learn to distinguish between what is actually reported, what is inferred from the report, and what judgment has been formed. They must realize the importance of context and how words or sentences lifted out of context can distort meaning. They must understand that the attitudes of writers and speakers can frequently be discerned by studying the words which they use. Magazine and newspaper advertisements are readily accessible sources that children can use for examination and analysis of how language may be manipulated.

Language Acquisition

Young children in all cultures appear to master the complex task of acquiring an understanding of the semantics, morphology, syntax, and phonology of their native language. This knowledge or competence enables them to produce an infinite variety of sentences, to understand and make judgments about sentences, and to develop an unconscious awareness of both the limitations and creative capacity of language. Yet most of this knowledge is attained early in life (*primarily* between the ages of two and five) without direct instruction. Psycholinguists are still investigating the attainment of this knowledge because to date there has been no complete explanation acceptable to everyone.

Over the past 15 years, however, three major theories about language acquisition in children have evolved. First, there is the *behavioristic theory* which holds that boys and girls learn their language through imitation. Proponents argue that stimuli and reinforcement bring about changes in children's language. Boys and girls who produce desired language patterns receive social and material reinforcements as rewards. Opponents contend however that (1) children utter certain expressions which they have never heard anyone say (so that their language is hardly a faithful imitation); (2) children's speech is highly resistant to alteration by adult intervention; and (3) the practical task of memorizing all of the possible language structures is virtually impossible. The behavioristic theory is known also as the environmental or empiricist or associationist view.

The second prevalent theory is the *nativistic theory* which maintains that boys and girls learn their language from within themselves because language is innate. Proponents contend that (1) the onset and accomplishment of minimal language development seem unaffected by linguistic or cultural variations; (2) language cannot be taught to nonhuman forms of life whereas the suppression of language acquisition among humans is almost impossible; and (3) only humans have the necessary physiological and anatomical features to engage in sustained language. The nativistic theory is also known as the genetic, generative, mentalist, rationalist, or biological view.

Proponents of the *cognitive theory* feel that boys and girls are innately equipped to process cognitive data in general. They do not first learn language and then apply it to situations, but rather they first learn about situations and then apply that knowledge to language.[7] Any teaching aimed at developing the intellect will simultaneously promote language. When children learn language, they map concepts into language which they have already developed nonlinguistically. It is assumed that intellectual functioning will increase as language competence improves.

All three theories appear to be umbrellas. So until there is a better understanding of the complex process of language acquisition, concerned adults should be aware of all three and use the insights from each. They must also realize that the development of oral language performance has been found to be basic to achieving success in reading and writing.

Language Development

Studies of the stages of language development vary to some extent, depending upon the observer and the techniques used. Clear-cut delineations are not possible. Nevertheless, authorities generally agree upon certain age ranges which may indicate progressive stages of speech development in young boys (or girls), as shown in Table 2.1.

The *undifferentiated cry* occurs during the first month of life and appears to be wholly reflexive. It is part of the total bodily response to a new environment. The *differentiated cry,* observed between the second and third months of life, varies with the type of situation or stimulus: thirst, hunger, pressure, or fear. All of the characteristic sounds exercise the speech apparatus.

Babbling appears between the third and sixth months and consists primarily of vocal play in which children produce a great variety of sounds. Children emit sounds which occur in a language other than that of their speech community, numerous sounds that far surpass those prevalent in any one language. In fact, infants of all nations and cultures babble the same sounds and in the same order, following a highly stereotyped pattern. They use a front-to-back mouth action for vowel-like sounds but use a back-to-front mouth action to produce consonant-like sounds. In the case of the congenitally deaf child, speech development terminates with the babbling period because deaf children lose interest in playing with mouth movements and exercising their vocal muscles.

Critical to the process of early language acquisition is the role of adults and siblings. If they focus the infant's attention on sounds produced that are approximations of words, the infant is likely to repeat those sounds again due to the positive reinforcement. By rewarding selective responses, families are apt to motivate infants to produce phonemes or the significant speech sounds comprising the language.

The production of phonemes steadily increases so that a 30-month-old child is using vowels and consonants with a frequency approximating that of an adult.

Table 2.1
Checklist of Language Behavior of a Preschool Boy

Average Age	Question	Average Behavior
3-6 months	What does he do when you talk to him?	He awakens or quiets to the sound of his mother's voice.
	Does he react to your voice even when he cannot see you?	He typically turns eyes and head in the direction of the source of sound.
7-10 months	When he can't see what is happening, what does he do when he hears familiar footsteps . . . the dog barking . . . the telephone ringing . . . candy paper rattling . . . someone's voice . . . his own name?	He turns his head and shoulders toward familiar sounds, even when he cannot see what is happening. Such sounds do not have to be loud to cause him to respond.
11-15 months	Can he point to or find familiar objects or people, when he is asked to? *Example:* "Where is Jimmy?" "Find the ball."	He shows his understanding of some words by appropriate behavior; for example, he points to or looks at familiar objects or people, on request.
	Does he respond differently to different sounds?	He jabbers in response to a human voice, is apt to cry when there is thunder, or may frown when he is scolded.
	Does he enjoy listening to some sounds and imitating them?	Imitation indicates that he can hear the sounds and match them with his own sound production.
1½ years	Can he point to parts of his body when you ask him to? *Example:* "Show me your eyes." "Show me your nose."	Some children begin to identify parts of the body. He should be able to show his nose or eyes.
	How many understandable words does he use—words you are sure *really* mean something?	He should be using a few single words. They are not complete or pronounced perfectly but are clearly meaningful.
2 years	Can he follow simple verbal commands when you are careful not to give him any help, such as looking at the object or pointing in the right direction? *Example:* "Johnny, get your hat and give it to Daddy." "Danny, bring me your ball."	He should be able to follow a few simple commands without visual clues.
	Does he enjoy being read to? Does he point out pictures of familiar objects in a book when asked to? *Example:* "Show me the baby." "Where's the rabbit?"	Most two-year-olds enjoy being "read to" and shown simple pictures in a book or magazine, and will point out pictures when you ask them to.
	Does he use the names of familiar people and things such as *Mommy, milk, ball,* and *hat?*	He should be using a variety of everyday words heard in his home and neighborhood.

Table 2.1 (continued)

Average Age	Question	Average Behavior
2 years (cont.)	What does he call himself?	He refers to himself by name.
	Is he beginning to show interest in the sound of radio or TV commercials?	Many two-year-olds do show such interest, by word or action.
	Is he putting a few words together to make little "sentences"? *Example:* "Go bye-bye car." "Milk all gone."	These "sentences" are not usually complete or grammatically correct.
2½ years	Does he know a few rhymes or songs? Does he enjoy hearing them?	Many children can say or sing short rhymes or songs and enjoy listening to records or to mother singing.
	What does he do when the ice cream man's bell rings, out of his sight, or when a car door or house door closes at a time when someone in the family usually comes home?	If a child has good hearing, and these are events that bring him pleasure, he usually reacts to the sound by running to look or telling someone what he hears.
3 years	Can he show that he understands the meaning of some words besides the names of things? *Example:* "Make the car go." "Give me your ball." "Put the block in your pocket." "Find the big doll."	He should be able to understand and use some simple verbs, pronouns, prepositions and adjectives, such as *go, me, in,* and *big.*
	Can he find you when you call him from another room?	He should be able to locate the source of a sound.
	Does he sometimes use complete sentences?	He should be using complete sentences some of the time.
4 years	Can he tell about events that have happened recently?	He should be able to give a connected account of some recent experiences.
	Can he carry out two directions, one after the other? *Example:* "Bobby, find Susie and tell her dinner's ready."	He should be able to carry out a sequence of two simple directions.
5 years	Do neighbors and others outside the family understand most of what he says?	His speech should be intelligible, although some sounds may still be mispronounced.
	Can he carry on a conversation with other children or familiar grown-ups?	Most children of this age can carry on a conversation if the vocabulary is within their experience.
	Does he begin a sentence with "I" instead of "me"; "he" instead of "him"?	He should use some pronouns correctly.
	Is his grammar almost as good as his parents'?	Most of the time, it should match the patterns of grammar used by the adults of his family and neighborhood.

Source: *Learning to Talk: Speech, Hearing and Language Problems in the Pre-School Child* (Bethesda, Maryland: National Institutes of Health, 1977), pp. 22–24.

Age three represents the upper-age limit for mastery of most diphthongs (or blends of vowel and semivowel sounds) and of most vowels as well as the consonants *m, p, b, w, h, t, d,* and *n.* By age four most of the remaining consonants are being produced correctly and the child's phonological system closely approximates the model system of the language. Complete mastery, including two- and three-consonant blends, is attained at about eight years for most boys and girls. *Phonological development is not complete when children enter kindergarten.*

While the phonemes are being acquired, the child is combining them appropriately to express words. The age for the appearance of the first word, as reported by 26 nonbiographical studies, ranges from nine to nineteen months for normal children with the average set at eleven to twelve months.[8]

The child's first words are likely to be *holophrases* or single words used to express a more complex idea. They generally take the form of a noun, pronoun, verb, adjective, or adverb. While anecdotal studies and case histories show that first words are the monosyllabic or reduplicated monosyllabic *mama, daddy,* and *bye,* research indicates that more functional words than these may appear first. For instance, a recent study of middle-class Hebrew boys revealed that the first words elicited by their mothers in the home were *this, that, here, no,* and *food.*[9] These words, together with gestures, resolve most children's problems by age 12 months. By 24 months some boys and girls have a vocabulary of more than 150 words. By 48 months many children have a vocabulary of 1,000 words.

In contrast to their gradual mastery of phonology, children use syntax correctly (though incompletely of course) from the very beginning. By age two, and sometimes as early as 18 months, children begin to string together two or more holophrases and have thereby arrived at the *telegraphic stage.* Their utterances are devoid of function words and resemble messages that adults would send by wire. For instance, "Jimmy truck" could represent "That truck belongs to Jimmy," or "Give me my truck." Meanings will often depend upon the context and intonation of the utterance. All telegraphic speech, however, consists of acceptable grammatical sequences which are the precursors of the sentence. Normal children will acquire at least a few hundred presentences by the time they reach 30 months of age.

By age three most children are constructing simple affirmative-declarative sentences, putting together a subject and predicate. Gradually their sentences become longer and more complex, due partly to adult expansion and extension of child speech and partly to child induction of the latent structure of language. Boys and girls are apparently able to process the speech they hear and induce from it general rules of structure which they later use in their own speech.

The rule system which boys and girls construct makes it possible for them to generate an infinite number and variety of sentences, including many never heard from anyone else.[10] The system is a set of rules for sentence construction, rules which neither the children nor their parents know explicitly. It consists of a series of grammars that have their own phonological, syntactic, and semantic components at each successive stage in the development of language. Children take all speech, interact with it, and somehow develop the systems that constitute the grammar of their language.

Table 2.2
Development of Syntax and Fluency in Children Ages 5-12

Ages 5 and 6
The average number of words per oral communication unit (independent clause with modifiers) will be about 6.8, with a variation between 6 and 8. The Tennessee research group found slightly higher scores, with 7 as an average and a range of 4 to 9.5, but their subjects represented a somewhat more affluent socioeconomic background than those in the Oakland study. Children at this stage settle their use of pronouns, and of verbs in the present and past tenses. Complex sentences appear more often. "Pre-forms" of conditionality and causality occur as early as age two.
Ages 6 and 7
The average number of words per oral communication unit will be about 7.5, with a variation between 6.6 and 8.1. The research group in Ypsilanti, Michigan, known as High Scope, found the average number of words per written communication unit (grade two) ranging from 6.9 to 8.3. Additional progress occurs in speaking complex sentences, especially those with adjectival clauses. Children begin to use conditional dependent clauses, such as those starting with *if.*
Ages 7 and 8
The average number of words per oral communication unit will be about 7.6, with a variation between 7 and 8.3. The Far West Laboratory for Educational Development in San Francisco found the average number of words per written communication unit (grade three) ranging from 6 to 7. Children now use relative pronouns as objects in subordinate adjectival clauses (*I have a cat which I feed every day*). They begin to use more frequently the

Syntactical development is not complete when children enter kindergarten. The language development of 211 subjects who began as kindergartners in the Oakland, California area was studied by Loban for 13 years.[11] He compiled a chart describing syntax and fluency during elementary school years. The chart combined his findings with those of Hunt in Florida, Watts in England, and O'Donnell, Griffin, and Norris in Tennessee.[12] An abridged version of this chart appears in Table 2.2

Briefly then, language development begins in infancy and continues throughout life. Although there appears to be a sequence in the learning of phonology, morphology, and syntax, the rates of acquisition vary among individual children.[13]

A second continuum of linguistic development among elementary school children, occurring simultaneously with the first, has been labelled their maturing linguistic orientation to the world.[14] It is shown in four important ways.

subordinate clauses starting with *when, if,* and *because.* They also use the gerund phrase as an object of a verb (*I like washing myself*).

Ages 8, 9, and 10

The average number of words per oral communication unit will be 9, with a variation between 7.5 and 9.3. The average number of words per written communication unit in the Oakland study was 8.0, with a range from 6 to 9. This is similar to the Florida average of 8.1 for boys and 9.0 for girls.

Children begin to relate specific concepts to general ideas, using such connectors as *meanwhile, unless,* and *even if.* They begin to use the present participle active, the perfect participle, and the gerund as the object of a preposition.

Ages 10, 11 and 12

The average number of words per oral communication unit will be about 9.5, with a variation between 8 and 10.5. The average number of words per written communication unit was 9, with a range from 6.2 to 10.2.

All students show a marked advance in using longer communication units and in the incidence of subordinate adjectival clauses both in writing and in speech. Nouns modified by a participle or participial phrase appear more often, as do the gerund phrase, the adverbial infinitive, and the compound or coordinate predicate.

At this age children frame hypotheses and envision their consequences. This involves using complex sentences with subordinate clauses of concession. Auxiliary verbs such as *might, could,* and *should* appear more often than at earlier stages of language development. Students have difficulty, however, in distinguishing and using the past, past perfect, and present perfect tenses of the verb.

The Tennessee research group found a marked decrease in immature coordination of main clauses, in both speech and writing.

Source: Adapted from LANGUAGE DEVELOPMENT: KINDERGARTEN THROUGH GRADE TWELVE by Walter Loban. © 1976 National Council of Teachers of English, Urbana, Illinois. Used with permission.

Boys and girls first change in their *processing of experience,* moving from the physical exploration of a concrete world to the mental discovery of abstract ideas. Second, they change linguistically in their *processing of environment.* Although initially egocentric, children develop the capacity to be objective and to evaluate experience outside themselves.

A third element of linguistic change in girls and boys relates to the *time and space* nature of their experience. While young children are concerned with the here and now, older pupils can express other times and places.

A fourth important way in which maturing children change linguistically is concerned with their *affective interpretation of reality.* Young children have only a personal way of viewing the world; their intake and expression of experience are pervaded by their feelings. Although pupils in the middle grades also view their experiences in strongly personal ways, they can understand and express the opinions of their peers. Older children develop the capacity to be more objective. Their perceptions of the world are built upon broader experiences and have greater impact involving numerous points of view. Provided that older children have been able to maintain positive self-images, they will bring personal views to the reception of unfamiliar ideas. Thus they will be able to express themselves clearly to classmates and concerned adults.

Intellectual Development, According to Piaget

Language development is closely related to the development of the thought process, and the world-renowned Swiss psychologist, Jean Piaget, viewed intellectual growth in children as a matter of sequential stages.

These stages in the development of a child's capacity to use increasingly difficult thought operations are clearly defined. They are generally regulated by wide age spans and follow in an ordered sequence. A new stage will not be successfully undertaken until the previous stage has been properly attained. As children modify and add new experiences to those previously absorbed, new abilities evolve from the old. Although the sequence in which the stages appear are the same for all children, such factors as motivation, environment, native intelligence, and diversity of experience may retard or hasten the process of intellectual growth.

The sequence of stages described by Piaget begins with the *sensorimotor period* (birth to age two years). The first stage of interest to elementary teachers, however, is the *preoperational period* (ages two to seven years). This period is divided into the *egocentric* phase, which lasts until about age four, and into the *intuitive* phase. In the egocentric or preconceptual phase symbols are constructed in which boys and girls imitate and represent what they see through language and action. In the intuitive phase children extend and combine their action-images and correct their intuitive impressions of reality. During the preoperational period boys and girls are continually seeking information, asking questions, and acquiring new concepts. The relationship between language and concepts may be strengthened through puppetry, creative drama, and imaginative play. Additional growth in the ability to relate language symbols and objects may be found in children's initial efforts to draw and make graphic representations.

The next stage of intellectual development is the *concrete operations period* (ages seven to eleven/twelve years) when children lose much of their egocentricity. They become less dependent on either immediate perceptual cues or on actions as their thinking becomes "decentered." In this period boys and girls accept ideas other than their own as they communicate with their peers. They are now able to do mentally what they previously had to act out. Their internalized thinking operations help classifying, ordering in series, numbering, grouping, and subgrouping of action-images. This is a period of avid reading.

The fourth and final stage is generally beyond the immediate concern of most elementary school teachers. It is the *formal operations period* (ages eleven/twelve years to age fifteen years and beyond) when children advance to the solution of complex problems through reasoning. Their thinking is flexible and they perceive many possibilities, including those beyond any actual situation. They are no longer bound to the concrete but can think with symbols.

During the preoperational period, children's growth in ability to relate language symbols and objects is found in their efforts to draw and make graphic representations. (Photo courtesy of the Ocean View School District, Huntington Beach, California.)

Principles of Development

Several principles from Piaget's theory can provide the bases for the English language curriculum in the elementary school:

1. While the acquisition of language is closely related to the growth of the thought process, both competencies do not necessarily develop at the same rate. A dominant factor in stimulating language growth is a specific set of environmental conditions. Thought processes, on the other hand, develop more slowly and are affected by a much wider (and more accessible) variety of environmental factors. A teacher should provide activities for children which are commensurate with their ability to understand rather than to articulate; otherwise the teacher will be deceived in attributing to the more verbal children mental growth that is beyond their years. The teacher must not assume that because a child can utter the word, he or she knows the concept. Language alone is not the answer. Nor does language training by itself lead to intellectual development.
2. Children's thought and language patterns differ from those of adults. A child must attain each level of thought development alone and the child does so through interaction with his or her world. While boys and girls may be helped to move to a higher level of thinking through proper experiences, they will

not benefit from verbal explanations that are extraneous to their ways of thinking. The imposition of intellectual growth by means of formal instruction is not possible.

3. Learning is an active process and children learn best from concrete activities. There is intrinsic motivation in this type of learning which stems from children's innate curiosity about their world and the rewards that can be reaped by satisfying that curiosity through knowledge. When learning is physically and mentally active, thought is the internalization of that action.

   Young learners especially must be able to actively manipulate and explore varied materials and equipment in their environment so that they may construct their own knowledge. They are capable of intuitive learning when they have some part in purposeful activities both in and out of the classroom.

4. Though there is a fixed sequence in development, each child proceeds at his or her own rate. Knowledge of the developmental stages in children's thinking can help teachers become aware of the limitations as well as the possibilities at each stage. Still, each boy and girl is different and should not be forced to learn material for which he or she is not ready.

   While all children are not at the same place at the same time, all of them enjoy the same kinds of materials at the same stage of maturity. Therefore, differences in ability do not constitute a major factor in determining and providing for the listening, reading, and viewing interests of boys and girls. However, there are differences in the rates at which children pass through the various stages and in the number and complexity of book and nonbook materials that they choose.

5. Children learn from social experiences with their peers and with adults. In addition to learning by interacting with their physical environment, boys and girls learn by sharing experiences and discussing reactions and viewpoints with others. As they grow older, they lose their egocentricity. They have their opinions challenged, they encounter new ideas, and gradually they reshape and reconstruct their knowledge.

   Bingham-Newman and Saunders warn teachers to listen *to* an answer, not *for* an answer, because children's answers can provide excellent information about children's thinking.[15] The unexpected answers can be used advantageously as another starting point. By accepting pupil's egocentric replies, teachers encourage young learners to be intellectually honest rather than to be looking, listening, or waiting for the right answer to be provided.

Providing for Individual Differences

Within every heterogeneous classroom there are wide variations in the children's physical and emotional health and in their out-of-school experiences. The children are highly individual persons, shaped and influenced by the environment in which they have developed. The teacher's most challenging responsibility is to provide a program that meets children where they are, recognizes their potential, capitalizes upon their strengths, and moves them along at a pace consonant with their ability. The teacher recognizes, for example, individual variations in abilities to understand and speak standard English, to listen attentively, to use appropriate and extensive vocabulary, and to verbalize experiences.

Since children learn at different rates, they require different materials, experiences, and instructional techniques. A single group activity often affects each member differently. The following section describes various types of learners and offers suggestions for adapting instruction and material to their needs.

Some Children	The Teacher
Use patterns of language that represent a dialect unlike the standard English classroom dialect.	Accepts each child's nonstandard dialect for communication purposes. Offers additional instruction in standard English.
Have speech patterns that result in poor communication with teacher or classmates.	Assists each child in the speaker-audience situation. Plans program designed to improve pronunciation and intonation. Uses tape recorder for children to record and play back their own voices in different situations.
Are learning English as a second language, having had little or no practice with the structure, sound system, and vocabulary of the English language.	Supplements the class program with additional instruction and practice in English. (See Chapter Fourteen.)
Find their vocabulary inadequate, unfamiliar, or inappropriate in school situations.	Plans activities to develop concepts and related vocabulary. Checks constantly on word meaning. Replaces vulgarisms with acceptable expressions.
Use actions, gestures, facial expressions, and noises rather than words to communicate.	Encourages children to use oral language to make known their wishes and needs, or to describe actions, by letting them hear repeatedly what they are expected to say.
Lack confidence in their ability to learn.	Develops assurance by providing activities, materials, and assignments that promote successful learning.
Learn and work at a slower pace than others in the group. Need to take smaller learning steps.	Adapts instruction to individual and group needs. Introduces new concepts slowly, allowing time for understanding. Allows sufficient work time.
Have limited experience with school-type materials—pictures, books, educational toys, and games. Are insecure in handling and responding to them.	Provides abundance of intellectually stimulating materials and time to peruse and enjoy them. Gives careful direction in the handling and use of those materials.

Some Children	The Teacher
Are less confident in school situations than in out-of-school situations.	Builds confidence so that the children can expect positive reactions and rewards from adults when they complete a task, ask questions, or explore ways of finding answers. Communicates to the children, by word or manner, any recognition of their progress, no matter how slight it may be.
Require special support strengthened by the interest and cooperation of the school and the home.	Reports frequently and formally to the children and their parents. Plans regular parent-teacher conferences, providing a translator when necessary, and includes the children on appropriate occasions.
Lose interest in sustained "talking" by the teacher or other adults.	Tries to watch his or her own "talking" time. Encourages dialog with children. Intersperses verbal instruction with gestures, visuals, and realia. Provides children with interesting events to discuss; limits "listening time."
Listen actively when a physical response or game element is present, or when there is a visual focal point of attention.	Uses listening games that call for action rather than verbal response. Involves listeners in activities such as refrains, pantomime, and rhythms. Makes provision for interaction (teacher-pupil, pupil-pupil), noting how each child feels and responds.
Find it easier to discuss and evaluate incidents that are presented through dramatization rather than through verbalization.	Allows the children to act out incidents with projective devices that promote free speech. Uses realia, pictures, stories, filmstrips, and firsthand experiences as the basis for conversations and discussions.
Are shy in revealing personal fantasies and the realm of their imagination.	Involves the children in creating additional incidents for familiar story and TV characters or in creating imaginary characters and incidents. Encourages children to select media for interpretation.
Have a limited range of the concepts and vocabulary useful in school. Are not accustomed to looking for similarities that help them to classify objects.	Checks frequently on each child's understanding of common, everyday words and provides experiences to develop better understanding. Plans activities involving classifying, labeling, and discussing objects. Uses verbal experiences to deepen understandings.

Some Children	The Teacher
Are limited in ability to draw inferences or to generalize on the basis of related experiences.	Offers activities through which he or she can guide children to arrive at generalizations and draw inferences.
Lack interest in standards and study. Work without goals or an organized system.	Gives close supervision to development of work-study habits, setting sensible standards and requiring children to meet them.
Are not inclined to review experiences and to see the relationship between what happened today and yesterday.	Increases the number of experiences designed to stimulate recall and to relate the past to the present and the future.
Find it difficult to relate to unfamiliar adults or to confide in them.	Finds opportunities to establish a one-to-one relationship with every child. Comments positively on each child's personal appearance and performance. Encourages each child to talk with him or her about individual interests and problems.
Tend to rely on physical skill and courage to bolster self-image and to meet problems.	Shows the children that discussion is a better way of solving problems than name-calling and physical force.

A student with individual interests, this boy has been encouraged by his teacher to share his hobby with the class. (Photo courtesy of Emil Fray.)

Some Children	The Teacher
Are happiest and most confident when they are permitted to engage in physical activities.	Provides ample time for physical expression—running, jumping, skipping, dancing, balancing, and playing singing games. Praises gross motor skills.
Can accept responsibility and enjoy the importance of being asked to share in classroom duties.	Rotates duties and assignments. Discusses need for monitors. Stresses individual responsibility for class pride in room appearance.
Are accustomed to considerable freedom of movement and self-determined and self-directed play activities. Are ingenious in devising materials and games.	Praises independence of action and thought. Encourages creative use of time and equipment.
Pursue individual interests of academic value—collecting rocks or reading about dinosaurs.	Challenges children to continue and extend their interests. Helps them to plan ways of sharing their hobbies with the class.
Approach problem solving creatively and use materials and equipment imaginatively.	Praises original ideas and solutions. Provides the materials and equipment with which to work out problems.
Learn rapidly. Read at levels considerably beyond those of the majority of the group.	Provides special activities beyond the usual group assignments. Sees that books and other printed materials cover a sufficiently wide reading range. Offers nonprinted resources.
Can handle abstract ideas. Are able to generalize and hypothesize.	Poses problems, questions, and situations that require children to select, relate, and evaluate ideas and to make generalizations.

Evaluation of Pupils' Progress in Language Development

Three formal instruments for assessing language growth among normal and handicapped children are the *Northwestern Syntax Screening Test,* the *Utah Test of Language Development* (revised edition), and the *Verbal Language Development Scale.* The first measures the expressive and receptive language skills of children from ages three to seven. It is individually administered, considered to be primarily a screening instrument (as stated in its title), and requires approximately 15 minutes to administer. It is published by the Northwestern University Press (Evanston, Illinois 60201). The second is an instrument of fifty-one items that measures the expressive and receptive language skills of children from ages 1.5 to 14.5; about one-half of the test items are related to the preschool age. An individual, untimed assessment, the *Utah Test of Language Development* can generally be completed in less than one hour. It is published by Communication Research Associates (Salt Lake City, Utah 84111) and has been fairly well received critically.[16]

The *Verbal Language Development Scale* has received similar reviews. It consists of fifty items designed to be individually administered to children from ages 1 month to 16 years, although 70 percent of the items relate to the preschool age (5.5 years and below). An expansion of the verbal portion of the *Vineland Social Maturity Scale,* it was revised in 1971. The test requires approximately 30 minutes to administer. It is published by American Guidance Service (Circle Pines, Minnesota 55014).

Discussion Questions

1. Why is it so important that each child's dialect receives the approval of the teacher?
2. Can the teacher help boys and girls to process the environment or experiences? If so, how?
3. Why are social experiences so critical to the intellectual development of children?
4. As an aide or teacher, how can you adapt phases of the language arts program to pupils who (a) use gestures or noises to communicate; (b) have a limited range of concepts and vocabulary useful for school; or (c) lack interest in school-type materials?

Suggested Projects

1. Watch an educational television show for young children. List the language skills it develops and describe how that development occurs.
2. Examine a current language arts series to see which generalizations about the history of the English language are presented to elementary students.
3. Compile a list of children's books published during the past decade which use nonstandard English dialects.
4. Determine how many morphemes are contained in the first paragraph of the lead story on the first page of the local newspaper. Which ones are free morphemes and which are bound?
5. Tape the speech of one kindergartner, one second grader, and one fourth grader for three minutes each. Analyze each recording to determine the average number of words per communication unit.
6. Collect ten narrative replies by children. Then choose the three longest and most detailed replies and describe what type of information they furnish about the thinking abilities of elementary pupils.

Related Readings

Anisfeld, M. 1984. *Language Development from Birth to Three.* Hillsdale, NJ: Erlbaum Associates.

Flake-Hobson, C. et al. 1983. *Child Development and Relationships.* Reading, MA: Addison-Wesley.

Freeman, E. B. 1982. "The Ann Arbor Decision: The Importance of Teachers' Attitudes toward Language," *Elementary School Journal, 83,* pp. 42–47.

Gillet, J. W., and Gentry, J. R. 1983. "Bridges between Nonstandard and Standard English with Extensions of Dictated Stories," *Reading Teacher, 36,* pp. 360–364.

Gottfried, A., ed., 1984. *Home Environment and Early Cognitive Development.* New York: Academic Press.

Hare, V. C. 1984. "What's in a word?: A Review of Young Children's Difficulties with the Construct 'Word' ". *Reading Teacher, 37,* pp. 360–364.

Shafer, R. E. et al. 1983. *Language Functions and School Success.* Glenview, IL: Scott, Foresman, and Company.

Trachtman, P. 1984. "Putting Computers into the Hands of Children Without Language," *Smithsonian, 14*(11), pp. 42–51.

Worell, J., ed., 1982. *Psychological Development in the Elementary Years.* New York: Academic Press.

Zelazo, P. et al. 1984. *Learning to Speak: A Manual for Parents.* Hillsdale, NJ: Erlbaum Associates.

Chapter Notes

1. J. Malmstrom, *Understanding Language* (New York: St. Martin's Press, 1977), p. 65.
2. *Ibid.,* p. 66.
3. D. Hymes, "Models of the Interaction of Language and Social Life," in *Directions in Sociolinguistics: The Ethnography of Communication,* J. Gumperz and D. Hymes, eds. (New York: Holt, 1972), pp. 35–71.
4. C. Eisenhardt, *Applying Linguistics in the Teaching of Reading and the Language Arts* (Columbus, Ohio: Charles E. Merrill, 1972), pp. 96–98; and R. C. O'Donnell, W. J. Griffin, and R. C. Norris, *Syntax of Kindergarten and Elementary School Children: A Transformational Analysis* (Urbana, Illinois: National Council of Teachers of English, 1967), p. 74.
5. California State Department of Education, *English Language Framework for California Public Schools* (Sacramento: The Department, 1976), p. 48.
6. M. Halliday, *Learning How to Mean—Explorations in the Development of Language* (London: Edward Arnold, Ltd., 1975), pp. 19–21.
7. F. Smith, "The Uses of Language," *Language Arts,* 1977, *54,* pp. 638–644.
8. F. L. Darley and H. Winitz, "Age of First Word: Review of Research," *Journal of Speech and Hearing Disorders,* 1961, *26,* pp. 288–289.
9. J. Zonshin, *One-Word Utterances of Hebrew-Speaking Children* (Master's thesis, University of Tel-Aviv, 1974).
10. R. Brown, "Development of the First Language in the Human Species," *American Psychologist,* 1973, *20,* pp. 97–106.
11. W. Loban, *Language Development: Kindergarten Through Grade Twelve* (Urbana, Illinois: National Council of Teachers of English, 1976), pp. 81–84.
12. K. W. Hunt, *Grammatical Structures Written at Three Grade Levels* (Urbana, Illinois: National Council of Teachers of English, 1965); A. F. Watts, *The Language and Mental Development of Children* (Boston: D. C. Heath & Company, 1948); and R. C. O'Donnell, W. J. Griffin, & R. C. Norris, *Syntax of Kindergarten and Elementary School Children.*
13. S. Dahl, "Oral Language and Its Relationship to Success in Reading," in *Research in the Language Arts,* V. Froese and S. Straw, eds. (Baltimore: University Park Press, 1981), p. 13.
14. Department of Education, *Elementary Language Arts Handbook* (Edmonton, Alberta: The Department, 1973), pp. 15–17.
15. A. Bingham-Newman and R. Saunders, "Take a New Look at Your Classroom with Piaget as a Guide," *Young Children,* 1977, *32,* pp. 62–72.
16. O. K. Buros, ed., *The Eighth Mental Measurements Yearbook,* Volume II (Highland Park, New Jersey: Gryphon Press, 1978), pp. 1503–1506; and O. K. Buros, ed., *Tests in Print II* (Highland Park, New Jersey: Gryphon Press, 1974).

Grammar 3

Objectives

The debate over grammar teaching

The major kinds of grammar presented in elementary classrooms today

Developing skills in sentence combination

Distinctions between *kernels* and *transforms*

Discover As You Read This Chapter If*

1. Grammar is a controversial area in the language arts curriculum today.
2. There is no one common definition of the word grammar.
3. Kindergarteners demonstrate their knowledge of grammar without ever studying it formally.
4. Grammar instruction generally promotes language development.
5. Activities in sentence combination and manipulation have no effect on receptive or productive language growth.
6. For elementary school children, informal instruction in grammar has only negative results.
7. Among the major kinds of English grammar presented in elementary classrooms is structural grammar.
8. Traditional grammar is concerned with how people do talk and not how they should talk.
9. The newest major kind of English grammar is transformational grammar.
10. Basic sentences in transformational grammar are known as *kernels.*

*Answers to these true-or-false statements may be found in Appendix 6.

Grammar is receiving more and more attention in many schools today, due in part to the Back to Basics movement. If students supposedly can neither read nor write as well as they should or as well as their predecessors did, the public remains convinced that studying grammar will help alleviate the situation.

Then there are the aesthetes who believe that the content of grammar is a theoretical human construct which can help people define their human uniqueness.[1] According to this group, the elimination of grammar study in the modern education of children would be another step in the conversion of education to mere training.

The Continuing Debate Over Grammar

The teaching of grammar therefore remains a major, if controversial, area of the language arts curriculum. There are several aspects to the debate.

The first involves *definitions* and stems from the fact that the very term grammar has different meanings in the minds of different groups or individuals. While some writers provide five or more varied interpretations, the following are the three common definitions of the term:

1. Grammar is usage or so-called language etiquette. It is a description of those sounds, units of meaning, and constructions which are preferred and socially prestigious in contrast to those which are not. To some advocates of this interpretation, grammar even includes such writing mechanics as punctuation, capitalization, and spelling.
2. Grammar is a written description and explanation of how language is produced: the classes of words, their inflections, and their relationships and functions in sentences.
3. Grammar is a set of abstract rules of communication by which even young children (who are normal) comprehend and produce sentences. It is the underlying structure of language which humans use intuitively. Thus, when girls and boys enter kindergarten, they can already demonstrate their knowledge of grammar although they have not studied it. Their built-in grammar is such that the primary teacher can informally use vocabulary like *verb* and *noun* to give children names for discussing what they already know.[2]

A second aspect of the on-going debate over grammar centers on the *values* of such formal instruction. For many years educators have argued that the separate study of grammar had a positive effect on the overall study of language. However, it is known now after numerous research findings that studying grammar formally makes few, if any, contributions to the growth of reading or listening skills, to achievement in foreign language, or to expansion of productive language generally or written composition particularly. Briefly, grammar instruction by itself has little or no value in promoting or enhancing language development.[3]

The one exception appears to be in the manipulation of sentences, both in reading and in writing. Research studies during the past 15 years with students even as early as third and fourth graders have shown that activities in sentence combining/manipulation significantly affect both productive and receptive language growth and development.[4] One form that such activities can assume is the

By listening to a taped lesson on sentence manipulation and combination, fourth graders can increase their productive and receptive language development. (Courtesy of the Fountain Valley School District, Fountain Valley, California.)

type of workbook exercise drills exemplified later in this chapter, which focus on sentence-building. Another form is the revision of selected pieces of student writing, either during private conferencing or anonymous class display on overhead projector transparencies for positive peer analysis. Incidentally, such revising of writing in view of the audience for that writing should be the very basis of grammar-related language study, according to Haley-James.[5] A third form of beneficial activities is sentence-combination drills found in some language arts textbooks, as shown in Figure 3.1.

The third conflict in the grammar debate relates to the *type of instruction.* The consensus appears to be that formal instruction in grammar only has a negative effect on elementary children, primarily because time devoted to such instruction could be put to better use in helping boys and girls listen, read, speak, and write with greater effectiveness. *Informal* instruction, on the other hand, is useful and even necessary to help pupils perform competently in language by understanding grammatical vocabulary and concepts.

Figure 3.1. Sentence Combination Exercises.

Part 3 Combining Sentences

Run-on sentences and stringy sentences join ideas incorrectly. They must be separated into shorter, good sentences.

However, some ideas can be joined correctly. Now you will learn ways to combine sentences to form longer, good sentences.

Joining Sentences with *and* or *but*

Sometimes two sentences show two ideas that are alike.

Larry washed one dog. Grace washed the other.

These sentences can be joined by a comma and the word *and*. Here is the combined sentence. It tells both ideas.

Larry washed one dog, and Grace washed the other.

Sometimes two sentences show two ideas that are different. These may be joined by a comma and the word *but*.

The paint looked dry. It was still wet.
The paint looked dry, but it was still wet.

Exercise Joining Sentences with *and* or *but*

Join each pair of sentences by following the directions in parentheses.

1. Penny brought records. Ted brought a record player. (Join with **, and**.)
2. My knee hurt. I finished the race. (Join with **, but**.)
3. The bus was ready to leave. Half the team wasn't on board. (Join with **, but**.)
4. The jelly jar was open. A spoon lay nearby. (Join with **, and**.)
5. Liz heard a cat. She couldn't see it. (Join with **, but**.)

Joining Sentence Parts

Sometimes two sentences are very much alike. They are so alike that words are repeated. If they are combined, the repeated words can be left out. Only the important words will be used.

Sentences that show ideas that are alike can usually be joined by *and*. Here is an example. (The words in italics can be left out.)

Paul collects stamps. *Paul collects* coins.
Paul collects stamps and coins.

Sentences that show ideas that are different can usually be joined by *but*.

Anne can help on Friday. *She can* not *help* on Saturday.
Anne can help on Friday but not on Saturday.

Exercise Joining Sentence Parts

Join the sentences in each pair. Follow the directions. Leave the italicized words out.

1. Carl bought tickets. Dot *bought tickets*. (Join with **and**.)
2. My coat is thin. *However, it is* warm. (Join with **but**.)
3. The players were tired. *However, they were* happy. (Join with **but**.)
4. Gordon clapped. *He* cheered. (Join with **and**.)
5. The puppy chewed my shoes. *It chewed* Linda's wallet. (Join with **and**.)

Consequently, it is the teacher who must acquire a knowledge of formal grammar[6] in order to present some of its varied aspects informally to the students at opportune times. This casual strategy is referred to by Kean as teaching grammar from the student's perspective.[7] The teacher must know when to intervene to help children correct their own grammar, and he or she must also make decisions about how, where, and when to help boys and girls improve immature syntax. Those interventions and decisions are best made when the teacher understands the processes by which new sentences may be formed as well as the structure of existing sentences.

Instructional activities described later in this chapter typify some of the informal strategies which teachers can adapt for use with small groups of learners or with individual students.

A fourth part of the continuing debate over the teaching of grammar concerns *content* (terminology, elements, and emphases). The three systems most often presented in the elementary classrooms today are traditional grammar, structural grammar, and transformational (or transformational-generative) grammar. Some of their terminologies and elements are similar, but their emphases differ. Each system will be discussed later in this chapter.

Some school districts select one grammar over the others, and some elementary language textbook series are equally dedicated. Other districts and texts prefer to present an eclectic grammar which combines elements freely from all three types. They believe that the way to assist students in using language more effectively is not necessarily through a study of any one theory of the nature of English grammar. Instead, they believe that there are significant components to be derived from all three grammars. Consequently, these generalizations are worthy of a place in the elementary curriculum:

- The emphasis in grammar instruction should be on how language operates to convey meaning.
- The study of basic sentence patterns should be central to the beginning study of grammar because it can help students become more conscious of the subject-predicate relationship and the rhythm of the sentence. Work with the complete subject and the complete predicate should be introduced when treating basic relationships within the sentence.
- The study of sentences should include the four major word classes (i.e., nouns, verbs, adjectives, and adverbs) and their inflection as well as the most useful classes of structure words (or connectors) and their use.
- The basic sentence patterns may be compounded, subordinated, and transformed. Work in grammar therefore should give much practice in compounding, subordinating, and modifying. It should also include substituting structures within the basic sentence patterns and transforming the patterns themselves.
- Grammatically essential sentence elements tend to be fixed, and grammatically less essential elements tend to be movable. All children should have considerable experience in changing sentences about and in rearranging and changing the information conveyed by the sentences.[8]

Major Kinds of English Grammar

English grammar as it is known today did not exist until the seventeenth century. Although grammar was an important part of the school curriculum before that time, the grammar taught in the schools was Latin, not English. English was, after all, only the language of the common folk.

Currently there are three different and undiluted grammars prominently presented in elementary classrooms in the United States. A fourth kind, the so-called eclectic grammar, draws from all three and presumably uses the best elements of each. It is as yet uncharted, however, and varies from district to district and from publishing house to publishing house.

Traditional Grammar

Since Latin was for centuries considered by scholars to be the perfect language, traditional grammar is a classification of English based partly on resemblances, real and supposed, to Latin. Originating in England during the seventeenth and eighteenth centuries, it was written by grammarians whose goal was to prescribe usage, establishing "rules" for speakers and writers to follow.

Refined in this century, traditional grammar accurately emphasizes the subject-predicate nature of the English sentence and the fact that function within the sentence is the ultimate determinant of word classification. It is primarily interested in syntax and it is always presented to pupils through the deductive method.

Traditional grammar, however, makes little attempt to discover how people learn languages. It fails to distinguish adequately between content words and function words in English sentences. It demands memorization of eight parts of speech (nouns, verbs, adjectives, adverbs, pronouns, prepositions, conjunctions, and interjections) whose inconclusive definitions often mix levels (e.g., the definition of a noun tells what it is, but the definition of an adjective tells what it does). It divides unnatural sentences into categories named by the parts of speech showing the relationships of each to the others. It uses a form of diagramming which does not help many children to see the basic building blocks of each sentence clearly. It fails to describe its operations with any consistency. It deals with exceptions, making the pupil unaware of the major grammatical patterns in the language. Finally, it has little impact on composition and tends to ignore English as a spoken language. Many, but not all, traditional grammarians are *prescriptive,* operating from the false assumption that there is a standard English grammar which is changeless and permanent, and that the school's task is to develop competence in understanding the elements of that grammar.

Traditional grammar is concerned with the knowledge of eight parts of speech and an understanding of such terms as *tense, agreement,* and *comparison.* It mandates the ability to define and recognize structural elements of sentences (such as subjects, predicates, complements and modifiers of all types) and the ability to recognize sentence faults that are associated with predication, pronoun reference, parallelism, placement of modifiers, and tense sequence. It classifies sentences both by purpose (declarative, interrogative, and exclamatory) and by form (simple, compound, complex, and compound-complex). It considers the word as the most important element of communication. And since traditional grammar deals primarily with the written forms of language, it tends to explain only what happens when language is used formally by educated people.

Even with good teaching, traditional grammar suffers from the efforts of early scholars to fit English (a Germanic language) into the preferred Latin mold. One major example concerns *nouns.* Every Latin noun has a different spelling depending on its case—nominative, genitive, dative, accusative, and ablative—or its relation to other elements in the sentence. In English, however, none of the properties of case matter except those of the genitive (or possessive) case because the relationship of nouns to other sentence elements is established by word order.

A second major example concerns *verbs.* The six tenses of traditional grammar—present, past, future, present perfect, past perfect, and future perfect—tally exactly with the Latin. Yet English can be regarded as having only two true tenses (the simple past and the simple present) that are ordinarily represented by single words spelled differently. Tense in English verbs then is more often a property of inflection rather than of time, for other elements in the construction may show time functions too. Latin, on the other hand, expresses time only by variations in the forms of the root word. Little wonder that the attempts to fit English into Latin patterns have resulted in confusion.

Structural Grammar

Developed in the United States in the 1930s by Leonard Bloomfield and others, structural grammar began as a study of the structure of English. Instead of prescribing how people should talk (as traditional grammar does), it is descriptive and concerned with how people do talk today. It analyzes the living spoken language to ascertain the basic structure of English sentences, the intonation patterns signaling meaning, and the words which operate as signs to indicate parts of speech. It believes that grammar is essentially a description of speech sounds and of sound combinations, and that language goes from form to meaning. It also finds that any structure generally accepted by a given speech community is correct for that community: there is no "ideal" language.

The structuralists have developed a technique for classifying words into parts of speech that is sometimes referred to as the slot-and-substitution method. The best way to understand this technique is to look at a few examples:

- A noun is a word like *bicycle* in *The (bicycle) is old.*
- A verb is a word like *see* in *I (see) the bus.*
- An adjective is a word like *sad* in *She is very (sad).*
- An adverb is a word like *quickly* in *The robber ran (quickly).*

Sometimes called Class I, Class II, Class III, and Class IV, there are four word-form classes among the words with lexical meaning (i.e., nouns, verbs, adjectives, and adverbs). All other words are called structure words, of which there are 15 to 17 groups, depending upon the structuralist. The English language is broken into four subdivisions:

1. *Intonation* or melody, whose elements are levels of pitch, degrees of stress, and junctures as discussed in Chapter Two. The oral approach to teaching punctuation is one of the by-products of a knowledge of intonation.

2. *Sentence patterns,* including especially:

Pattern 1 (NV, noun and verb) which is the simplest structure and most basic pattern of the English language; for example, (a) *Men run;* (b) *Children are running.* Two variants are NVA (noun, verb, adjective) and NVAd (noun, verb, adverb); for example, (a) *The door seemed shut;* (b) *Bob plays well.*

Pattern 2 (NVN, noun, verb, and noun complement) which is one of the most common sentence patterns in American English; for example, (a) *Children eat candy;* (b) *Bob drinks milk.*

Pattern 3 (NVNN, noun, verb, noun, noun); for example, (a) *Ann calls her dog Chip;* (b) *Bob gives his cat milk.* A fairly common variant is NVNA; for example, *He painted the boat blue.*

Pattern 4 (NLvN, NLvA, and NLvAd, or noun, linking verb, and noun, adjective, or adverb); for example, (a) *Rover is a dog;* (b) *Boys are rough;* (c) *Bob is here.*

Once the children have mastered these basic patterns they are ready for practice in expanding sentence patterns through such techniques as *compounding* (or adding subjects, predicates, and/or objects), *modification* (or adding adjectives, adverbs, determiners, intensifiers, prepositional phrases, participial phrases, and dependent clauses), and *subordination* (with relative clauses modifying noun headwords, or with clause modifiers after the noun headword). Examples of these three techniques include, respectively: (a) *Birds and bees fly;* (b) *The three tall boys were brothers;* (c) *The girl who was in my class went to Japan.*

3. *Structure words* or function words, showing primarily the grammatical and syntactical relationships within sentence patterns. They number about 300, and are used with greater frequency than all other words in the language. Relatively lacking in meaning or content, they are often the most difficult for pupils to learn in reading. Although they are never taught in isolation, the most important structure words are noun markers (including articles, cardinal numbers, and possessive pronouns), verb markers (including modals as well as forms of *be, do,* and *have*), clause markers (including conjunctions and sentence pattern connectors), phrase markers (or the prepositions of traditional grammar), and question markers (or words that begin questions or introduce inverted sentence patterns).
4. *Word-form changes* which have two main divisions. There are the inflectional endings of the four word classes. There are also the derivational prefixes and suffixes that modify the meanings of words, or convert words from one form class to another.[9]

In structural grammar the study of syntax becomes essentially a problem of determining the regularities in the arrangements of form-classes. Constructions have no specific content but comprise a series of "slots" into which particular kinds of material, including form-classes, can be fitted. Each slot must contain a specific kind of material because if it does not do so, the result either belongs to another construction or is not accepted as meaningful by the speakers of the language. A sample construction can be diagrammed as follows:

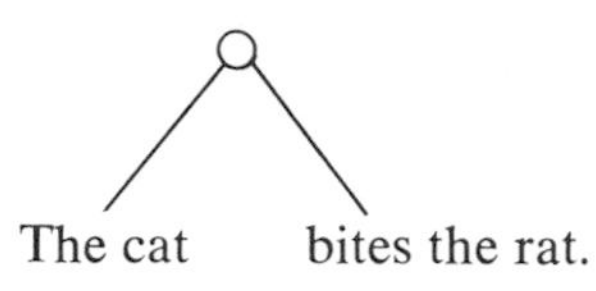

Here the little circle represents the construction, and the lines running from it lead to the *constituents* of the construction. There are both *immediate* constituents and *ultimate* constituents. In this example the major subwholes, or largest parts of the construction, are the immediate constituents (or ICs for short): *The cat* and *bites the rat*. The ultimate constituents, which are its individual morphemes, are: {The}, {cat}, {bite}, {-s}, {the}, {rat}.

The structuralists stress oral communication and believe that written language is only a repetition of spoken language. Their goal is to describe and catalog all the observable features of language.

Transformational Grammar

Developed in the United States in the 1950s by Noam Chomsky, the third major kind of grammar is generally known as transformational-generative or simply *transformational grammar.* Chomsky asserts that one of the basic functions of a grammar is to describe a native speaker's unconscious distinctions between what is grammatical and what is not grammatical in the language.

Transformational grammar, therefore, provides patterns for the analysis of existing sentences just as structural grammar does, but it also has rules for producing new sentences. Its proponents assert that, if preschool children with limited experience can generate thousands of new sentences based on the early sentence structures they have learned, there must be an underlying process that can be explained and taught. Consequently, while the structuralists are concerned only with the surface level of language structure, the transformationalists are interested in both the *surface structure* (human speech) and in the *deep structure* (ideas, thoughts, meaning) underlying actual speech performance. Due to its dedication to the processes by which deep structure is transformed into surface structure, it is therefore a transformational grammar. Two examples follow:

a. Surface structure=*They are teaching fellows.*
   Deep structure (first meaning)=Those fellows are fellows who teach.
   Deep structure (second meaning)=Some people are teaching some fellows.
b. Surface structure=*The bone was chewed by the dog.*
   Deep structure=The dog chewed the bone.

The term "transformational" also refers to the division of American English sentences into two classifications: basic sentences or *kernels* (with subjects and predicates) and their variations or *transforms*. The formula for a basic sentence may be written as follows: S $\longrightarrow$ NP + VP (a sentence consists of a noun phrase plus a verb phrase). It can also be diagrammed as follows:

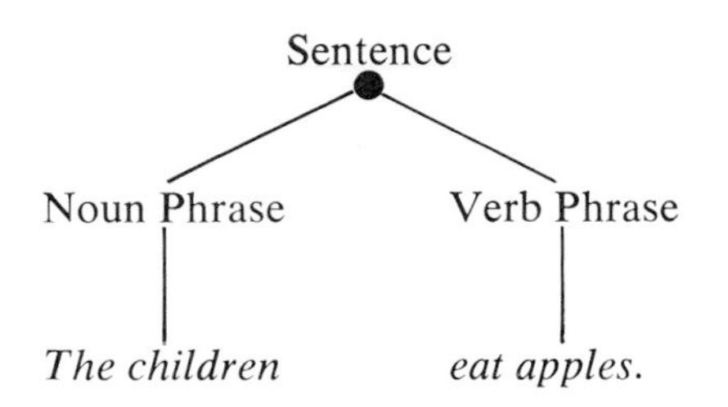

Unlike the diagram in traditional grammar, however, this "tree" diagram begins with the rules or directions for rewriting rather than representing an arbitrary division of an existing group of words (sentence) into its component parts.

Kernels

There are four to ten or more basic types of kernels or kernel sentences, depending upon the linguist questioned. Each such sentence is affirmative (not negative) and each is a statement (not a question). Each kernel is in the active voice and always begins with the subject. Finally, a kernel contains only a single predication and that follows the subject. Essential to the basic kernel are the terms *noun phrase* and *verb phrase.*

Four groups of words or kinds of words function as a subject in a kernel: (a) determiner + common noun (*The boy* walked the dog); (b) proper noun (*Mr. Black* is a teacher); (c) personal pronoun (*They* ran home); and (d) indefinite pronoun (*Everyone* seemed hungry). Each of these kinds of subjects is called a noun phrase even though it may be a single word. A noun phrase is the name for a structure but not for a word class, *noun* being an example of a word class.

All linguists agree that there are at least two kinds of nouns: countable (or regular) and uncountable (or mass). The former literally can be counted (*one girl, two girls*), but the latter cannot (*one furniture, two furnitures*) in any ordinary sense.

In a kernel the first word of the predicate is usually a verb or a form of the word *be—am, is are, was,* or *were.* The word *be* and its forms do not behave the way verbs do, so *be* is not called a verb but is considered in a class by itself which makes it possible to simplify the treatment of syntax. Every predicate of a kernel must contain either *be* or a verb. If it contains a form of *be,* something else must follow as in *He is a sailor.* If the predicate contains a verb, the verb may or may not be followed by something else as in *They look sick.* Verbs may also be followed by other words such as adverbials of manner, place, time, or frequency.

The verb phrase is probably most clearly understood if these sentences are noted:

The girl works quickly.
The girl is working quickly.
The girl has worked quickly.
The girl will work quickly.
The girl has been working quickly.

The girl may be working quickly.
The girl could have worked quickly.
The girl must have been working quickly.

A variety and a flexibility of material may appear within a verb phrase.

All English verbs in the present tense have two forms: the simple form (*see, walk*) that goes with the plural subject, and the *s* form (*sees, walks*) that goes with the singular subject. Verbs, however, are not considered singular or plural but merely correspond in form to the requirements of the subject. In transformational grammar there are only two tenses—the past and the present—which are always shown by the first word in the predicate and which, of course, are not the same as time.

Transforms

Any sentence that is not a kernel is a transform or transformation, and most sentences that people use are transformations. The base of any transformation is the kernel (or kernels) out of which it is formed. There are both *single-base* and *double-base* transformations.

Single-base transformations concern one kernel sentence. Among the most common are the *interrogative,* the *negative,* the *passive,* the *command,* the *expletive* (or "there" transform), and the *indirect object* transformations. One of the simplest is the *yes-no transform.* In order to form a yes or no question, elements are transposed and the final punctuation in written language is changed:

The girl is pretty. (kernel)
Is the girl pretty? (transform)

Double-base transformations involve the combination of two or more kernels into a single, more complex sentence. The two most common types are *coordinating transforms* and the more numerous *subordinating transforms.* In the latter group the most frequently used is the *relative clause.* Always beginning with a relative pronoun or relative adverb, it actually replaces the subject of the inserted or embedded kernel:

My friend has a brown dog. (kernel)
The brown dog can do tricks. (kernel)
My friend has a brown dog that can do tricks. (transform)

Exercises A through F are inductive exercises (designed for students in the middle grades) which involve either single-base (Exercises A-B) or double-base (Exercises C-F) transformations.[10] In them the symbol ⇒ indicates that this is a transformation rule and is read as "is rewritten as." Furthermore, in each exercise there is a valuable segment entitled Application which demands that students create their own sentences employing the specific transformation under scrutiny.

Exercise A

The Negative Transformation

GIVEN:

1. The dog is in the yard. ⇒ The dog is not in the yard.
2. His father owns a car. ⇒ His father does not own a car.

MATERIAL:

1. The bird was in a bush. ⇒
2. I am a new student. ⇒
3. A freeple is a furple. ⇒
4. A snirkle uggled a smiffle. ⇒
5. A green dog bit a pink postman. ⇒

DIRECTIONS:
Change the sentences in MATERIAL so that *not* will be in each.

CONCLUSION:

1. Where is *not* added in sentences like nos. 1-3?
2. What other changes must be made in sentences like nos. 4-5?

APPLICATION:
Make up four sentences using the word *not.* Two of the four sentences should include the word *did.* Now write these four sentences without the *not.*

Exercise B

Yes/No—The Question Forming Transformation

Part A

GIVEN:

1. The boy is my friend. ⇒ Is the boy my friend?
2. I can go. ⇒ Can I go?
3. Mary has left. ⇒ Has Mary left?

MATERIAL:

1. The orange bat is my friend. ⇒
2. Pete was a little grey squirrel. ⇒
3. Louise has hit the fat cat. ⇒
4. Some of the boys will leave. ⇒
5. The group of children can stay. ⇒

DIRECTIONS:
Change each of the above sentences in MATERIAL to questions that a listener can answer with either "yes" or "no."

CONCLUSION:

1. What did you do to the word order when you made questions out of the sentences?
2. What kind of word now comes first after you have a question?

APPLICATION:

1. Make up three sentences like those in MATERIAL.
2. Change them into questions which can be answered with "yes" or "no."

Exercise B (cont.)

Part B

GIVEN:

1. The child hit the ball. ⇒ Did the child hit the ball?
2. A worm ate the apple. ⇒ Did a worm eat the apple?

MATERIAL:

1. A small goat swallowed a can. ⇒
2. The perfume smelled like roses. ⇒
3. The poodle swam across the pool. ⇒
4. A fimply snirple uggled an orf. ⇒

DIRECTIONS:
Change the above sentences into questions which can be answered with "yes" or "no."

CONCLUSION:

1. What new word was added?
2. What happened to the verb?

APPLICATION:

1. Make up three sentences like those in MATERIAL.
2. Change them into questions which can be answered with "yes" or "no."

Exercise C
The Coordination Transformation

Part A

GIVEN:

1. a) Children play. b) Children work. ⇒ Children play and work.
2. a) Children play. b) Children work. ⇒ Either children play or children work.

MATERIAL:

1. a) I like cake. b) I like ice cream. ⇒
2. a) The boys have a hot rod. b) The boys have a club. ⇒
3. a) You leave. b) You stay. ⇒

DIRECTIONS:
Join sentences "a" and "b" in each group in MATERIAL.

CONCLUSION:
How did you know which sentence group to use "either-or" with?

APPLICATION:
Write a short paragraph using "and" and "either-or" in the writing.

Part B **Exercise C (cont.)**

GIVEN:

1. a) Mary stayed. b) He left. ⇒ Mary stayed but he left.
2. a) John did not laugh. b) John did not smile. ⇒ John did not laugh, nor did he smile.

MATERIAL:

1. a) The pilot flew the plane. b) The mechanic stayed on the ground. ⇒
2. a) It had quit raining. b) The road was still wet. ⇒
3. a) Joe didn't come to class. b) Joe didn't stay home. ⇒
4. a) The wind didn't blow. b) The rains didn't come. ⇒

DIRECTIONS:

Join sentences "a" and "b" in each group in MATERIAL. Use "but" for two of the groups. Use "nor" for the other two. Drop the italicized word.

CONCLUSION:

1. What happens to the word order of sentence "b" when you use "nor"?
2. How did you know when to use "nor"?

APPLICATION:

1. Write three sentences using "nor."
2. Write three sentences using "but."

PART A **Exercise D** *The Subordination Transformation*

GIVEN:

a) I didn't go to school today. b) I had a cold. ⇒ I didn't go to school today because I had a cold.

MATERIAL:

1. a) I got my lessons finished. b) I worked hard. ⇒
2. a) Joe had a stomach ache. b) He gobbled his supper. ⇒
3. a) We stayed indoors today. b) The weather was terrible. ⇒

DIRECTIONS:

Add 'because' to the front of each 'b' sentence in MATERIAL. Now put this with sentence 'a' to form a new sentence like that produced in GIVEN.

____
____
____
____
____
____
____

CONCLUSION

Can 'because' + sentence 'b' be added to either front or back of sentence 'a'? ____

Exercise D (cont.)

APPLICATION:
Make up three sentences using 'because' like those you produced in DIRECTIONS.

____
____
____
____
____
____

PART B

GIVEN:

a) You will get a reward.
b) You will find the purse.
} ⇒ If you find the purse, you will get a reward.

MATERIAL:

1. a) You will win the prize.
   b) You *will* dress best. } ⇒
2. a) She will hit the ball.
   b) She *will* practice. } ⇒
3. a) He will be my friend.
   b) He *will* move next door. } ⇒
4. a) I will stay late.
   b) You *will* take me home. } ⇒
5. a) You will be a good football player.
   b) You *will* practice hard. } ⇒

DIRECTIONS:

1. Add 'if' to sentence 'b' in each pair of sentences in MATERIAL. Then place sentence 'b' in front of 'a' to make a new sentence.

____
____
____
____
____
____
____
____
____
____

2. What happens if you drop the italicized word? Do you still have a sentence? ______________________________
3. Is it better with or without the word? ______________________________

CONCLUSION:

1. Does 'if' change the meaning of the sentence?
____
2. Can 'if' + sentence 'b' be placed after sentence 'a' as well as before it?

APPLICATION:

Exercise D (cont.)

1. Make up three sentences containing 'if'.

2. Now change them by moving 'if' + words before the comma to the end of the sentence.

PART C

GIVEN:

a) I'll stay.
b) I'm unhappy. } ⇒ I'll stay although I'm unhappy.

MATERIAL:

1. a) She's mean.
   b) She's pretty. } ⇒
2. a) The dog runs fast.
   b) *The dog* has a sore paw. } ⇒
3. a) The old man ate the food.
   b) *The old man* had an upset stomach. } ⇒
4. a) The boy had dessert.
   b) *The boy* did not eat his supper. } ⇒
5. a) A little frog tried to leap from the bank
   b) *The bank* was a long way off. } ⇒

DIRECTIONS:

1. Place 'although' in front of sentence 'b' in groups 1 and 2 in MATERIAL. Place the 'b' sentence in front of the 'a' sentence.

Exercise D (cont.)

2. Do the same for sentences in groups 3–5, except use 'even though' instead of 'although'.

3. Cross out the italicized words in MATERIAL which you wrote in your sentences and change to 'he'.

CONCLUSION:
Can the 'b' sentences be placed behind the 'a' sentences? ______
APPLICATION:
Make up three sentences using 'although'. Two of the three should have 'although' inside the sentence instead of at the front.

Exercise E
The Relative Clause Transformation

Part A

GIVEN:
1. The boy hit the ball.
2. The boy is my friend.

} ⇒ The boy who is my friend hit the ball.

MATERIAL:
1. The girl was very noisy.
2. The girl had long pigtails. } ⇒
3. The lady quickly left the room.
4. The lady was the oldest. } ⇒

DIRECTIONS:
1. In sentence no. 2 in MATERIAL change *the girl* to *who.* Now place sentence no. 2 between *girl* and *was* in sentence no. 1. Write the new sentence.
2. In sentence no. 4 change *the lady* to *who.* Now place sentence no. 4 between *lady* and *quickly* in sentence no. 3. Write the new sentence.

CONCLUSION:
What can you do with two sentences that have the same first part?

APPLICATION:
Make up three sentences that look like the two you made in DIRECTIONS.

Part B

Exercise E (cont.)

GIVEN:

1. The dog ate the bone.
2. The dog had fleas.

⇒ The dog which had fleas ate the bone.

MATERIAL:

1. The little cat was pretty.
2. The little cat had a sore paw.

⇒

3. A bird hopped merrily.
4. A bird was eating a worm.

⇒

DIRECTIONS:

1. In sentence no. 2 in MATERIAL change *the little cat* to *which.* Now place the sentence between *the little cat* and *was* in sentence no. 1.
2. In sentence no. 4 change *a bird* to *that.* Now place sentence no. 4 between *a bird* and *hopped* in sentence no. 3.

CONCLUSION:

Compare these new sentences with those made in PART A. In PART A you used *who.* In this part you used *which* and *that.* Why? (Clue: Look at the nouns in these sentences and compare them with those in PART A. How are they different?)

APPLICATION:

Make up three sentences that look like the two you made in DIRECTIONS.

Part A

Exercise F

The Combination of More Than One Sentence

GIVEN:

1. The dress is a color.
2. The dress is blue.
3. The color is pretty.

⇒ The blue dress is a pretty color.

MATERIAL:

1. The buffalo charged the Indian.
2. The buffalo is old.
3. The Indian is brave.

⇒

DIRECTIONS:

Combine the above three sentences in MATERIAL so that they are one. The meaning of the new sentence should be the same as the three separate sentences.

____

____

____

____

CONCLUSION:

1. Two of the sentences are "put" inside the third. Which two are put inside the third? How?

____

____

____

____

Exercise F (cont.)

2. How did you decide which two to put in the other?

APPLICATION:
Below are a number of sentence combinations. Combine the two or three sentences in each group and produce one:

1. a) The car hit the fence.
   b) The car was for racing.
   c) The fence was old.

2. a) The fans clapped their hands.
   b) The fans were eager.
   c) Their hands were cold.

3. a) The judge waved the flag.
   b) The judge was uneasy.
   c) The flag was checkered.

Part B

GIVEN:

1. *Someone* sold *something.*
   a) The salesman worked hard.
   b) The vacuum cleaner was broken.

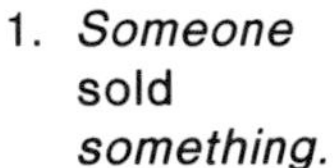

⇒ The hard-working salesman sold the broken vacuum cleaner.

MATERIAL:

1. *Something* charged *something.*
   a) The buffalo was arrow-peppered.
   b) The Indian was extremely worried. ⇒
2. *Someone* quickly ate *something.*
   a) The robin was swift-footed.
   b) The worm was rapidly crawling. ⇒

DIRECTIONS:

Exercise F (cont.)

1. Change sentences 'a' and 'b' in MATERIAL so they can be put into the *someone—something* slots in the sentence above them.

2. Now put these words into the slots and form sentences.

CONCLUSION:

What did you do to the input sentence before it can go into the containing sentence?

APPLICATION:

Below are three "containing" sentences. They all contain 'input' sentences. Of course, the 'input' sentences had to be changed first. Write out the 'input' sentences as they looked before being changed.

1. The soapy dish had a strange smell.

2. The sudden-firing gun had an oily smell.

3. The little girl was a hungry eater.

Instructional Activities

Informal instructional activities have been proved useful in promoting effective language performance because they introduce or review grammatical concepts and vocabulary. Sample activities are described in this section by grade level.[11]

Grade One and Grade Two

1. Children take everything out of their desks and classify the items by laying them in piles on top of the desks. A discussion follows regarding the classifications the children have developed; for example, colors, shapes, sizes. In classrooms without desks, the teacher fills a large sack with numerous items and asks one child to classify the items; the teacher then writes the child's classification on the board, puts the items back into the sack, and asks if another child can classify them in a different way.
2. Each group of children receives individual word cards comprising a possible sentence. Then the members come to the front of the room and arrange themselves into a sentence. (Examples: [a] [Mary] [little] [had] [lamb] and [to] [her] [day] [He] [one] [followed] [school].)
3. Children are shown pictures of objects with two definite parts which can be easily named; for example, frying pan (handle and pan), book (pages and covers). Then they are given sentences written on slips of paper which must be cut apart into the subject and the predicate. (Example: [The lions] [run fast].)
4. Children use word cards to demonstrate logical placement, with each card containing a single word. (Example: [Mary] [ride] [can] [Mike] [with]). If cards are punched in one corner, they can be fastened as soon as correct order is established. If cards are not punched, children can arrange the cards on the chalk tray or on the desk to see how many different sentences can be made from these few words.

Grade Three

1. The teacher prepares sets of subject cards and sets of predicate cards. Then each child chooses one card from each set and reads aloud his or her complete sentence; the child may also be asked to identify the subject or the predicate. (Humorous sentences may result in some instances; for example, [The boy] [barked].)
2. Children bring magazine or newspaper pictures from home or draw some pictures in class. Then each child tells which nouns depicted in his or her picture are singular and which are plural. Some pictures may even be arranged on the bulletin board according to the two classifications.
3. The teacher prepares a list of singular nouns and a list of related plural nouns. Then the children write or tell a sentence, matching a singular noun (e.g., *library*) to a plural noun (e.g., *books*).
4. The children divide into groups to develop three declarative sentences relevant to a science or social studies unit. These are written on the chalkboard. Then the groups are disbanded and each child changes the declarative sentences of his or her group into three questions and writes them down on a workpaper.

Grade Four

1. Children circle all the noun determiners in a group of sentences. (Example: *The girls went to that zoo.*)
2. Children choose the appropriate noun-verb agreement in each pair of sentences. (Example: *Seals eat fish. Seals eats fish.*)
3. Children collect several news article headlines using the noun-verb sentence pattern. They then identify the nouns and verbs in the collected headlines.
4. The children classify the following adjectives into three columns headed Color, Size, and Number: *green, fat, yellow, three, small, twelve, blue, tiny, large, six, short, white, slim, fifteen, slender, brown, dozen, red, tall, thin, purple, black, blonde, little, thousand, huge, orange, gigantic, seventy, tan, pink.*

Grade Five

1. The teacher prepares a set of sentences, each of which contains one blank. The children plan suitable intensifiers or qualifiers for the blanks. (Example: *His model was* ______________ *colorful than mine.*)
2. The children circle the verbs in a set of sentences prepared by the teacher. (Example: *The rabbit ran fast.*)
3. Children match the words from a column of common nouns with corresponding words from a column of proper nouns and make a statement about the difference between each. (Example: A *city* is any city. *Chicago* is a certain city.)
4. Children list as many events as possible by fitting verbs in the blank(s) of a set of sentences prepared by the teacher. (Example: *People _ their homes.*)

Grade Six

1. Children rearrange sets of words into meaningful sequences to determine the order of modification words before a noun. (Example: *giant nine peas the* and *small frosted cakes our birthday.*)
2. Each child writes a simple five-line verse by using one noun (the subject) in the first line, two adjectives in the second line, three verbs in the third, an adverb in the fourth, and the subject and an adjective modifying it in the fifth line:

   Ghosts,
   Scary, wispy
   Glide, float, drift
   Slowly,
   Pale ghosts.

3. Each child makes up ten jumbled sentences. Then each exchanges sentences with a partner who must rearrange every sentence into meaningful order. (Limits restricting the number of words per sentence are suggested.)
4. Children classify the following words into groups and then make a generalization about each group: *Monday, Baltimore, Thursday, Easter, March, New Year's, Michigan, Christmas, Thanksgiving, September, Idaho, January, Minneapolis, Wyoming, May, Friday, Florida, Alaska, Pittsburgh, Veterans Day, Atlanta, Boston.*

Evaluation of Pupils' Progress

Some well-rated, standardized, achievement test batteries include sections entitled usage, usage and structure, or usage and/or grammar.[12]

In view of the recognized research-based significance of sentence combination/recognition, however, the classroom teacher may prefer to develop an evaluative instrument which follows a format used recently by the California State Department of Education.[13] It simulates actual written production but involves multiple choice items. Children choose from a list of possible options. Some examples follow.

Sentence Recognition

Supplying Subjects: Grade 3

The teacher says: Fill in the bubble next to the words which are needed to form a complete sentence.

_____ __________ peanut shells at the people.

- ○ Have thrown
- ○ Monkeys threw
- ○ Were throwing
- ○ To throw

Grade 6

The teacher says: Fill in the bubble next to the words which will form one or more complete sentences.

_______________ woke up the neighbors.

- ○ Every day
- ○ In the morning
- ○ His dog
- ○ Near the fence

Supplying Predicates: Grade 3

The teacher says: Fill in the bubble next to the words which are needed to form a complete sentence.

Sometimes Dan _____ _____ _______ .

- ○ down the street
- ○ in the class
- ○ runs to school
- ○ to the teacher

Supplying Predicates: Grade 6

The teacher says: Fill in the bubble next to the words which will form one or more complete sentences.

The school carnival _______________

- ○ next week
- ○ is coming
- ○ lots of fun
- ○ games and prizes

Sentence Combination—Grade 6

Simple Sentences with Modification

The teacher says: Fill in the bubble next to the sentence which combines the numbered sentences in the best way.

1. Roller skating is a sport.
2. Roller skating is challenging.
3. Roller skating is growing in popularity.
4. Roller skating is played indoors and out.

○ Roller skating is a sport, and it is growing in popularity, and it is played indoors and out, and it is challenging.
○ Roller skating, a challenging sport growing in popularity, is played indoors and out.
○ A challenging sport, roller skating, it is played indoors and out and is growing in popularity.

Compound Sentences and Sentence Parts

The teacher says: Fill in the bubble next to the sentence which combines the numbered sentences in the best way.

1. John is going golfing.
2. James is going golfing.
3. Grace is going bowling.
4. Joyce is going bowling.

○ John is going golfing, and James is going golfing, and Grace is going bowling, and Joyce is going bowling.
○ John and James are going golfing, but Grace and Joyce are going bowling.
○ John is going golfing, James is going golfing, Grace is going bowling, and Joyce is going bowling.

Complex Sentences

The teacher says: Fill in the bubble next to the sentence below which combines the numbered sentences in the best way.

1. Ladybugs are beetles.
2. Ladybugs are small.
3. They feed on insects.

○ Ladybugs are small beetles that feed on insects.
○ Ladybugs are beetles, and they are small, and they feed on insects.
○ Ladybugs feed on insects, and they are beetles, and they are small.

Standard English Usage[14]

Irregular verbs: Grade 3

The teacher says: Fill in the bubble next to the word which completes the sentence correctly.

Juan has ______ a story about horses.

○ wrote
○ write
○ written
○ writed

Irregular verbs: Grade 6

The teacher says: Fill in the bubble next to the word that completes the sentence correctly.

Jack __________ his lunch.

○ brung
○ brought
○ brang
○ bringed

Pronouns: Grade 3

The teacher says: Fill in the bubble next to the word which completes the sentence correctly.

______ went for a ride.

○ Us
○ Him
○ Her
○ We

Pronouns: Grade 6

The teacher says: Fill in the bubble next to the word that completes the sentence correctly.

Send the equipment to Doug and ______ .

○ she
○ me
○ I
○ they

Subject-verb agreement: Grade 3

The teacher says: Fill in the bubble next to the word which completes the sentence correctly.

Every day, Martin ______ to school.

○ have walked
○ walks
○ walk
○ were walking

The teacher says: Fill in the bubble next to the words that complete the sentence correctly.

Subject-verb agreement: Grade 6

The cats _______ together.

○ was playing
○ plays
○ were playing
○ is playing

The teacher says: Fill in the bubble next to the word which completes the sentence correctly.

Noun determiners: Grade 3

_______ children broke the toy.

○ This
○ One
○ That
○ Those

The teacher says: Fill in the bubble next to the word that completes the sentence correctly.

Noun determiners: Grade 6

_______ students are in the marching band.

○ This
○ Them
○ That
○ Those

Discussion Questions

1. Why should the teaching of grammar create almost as much controversy among members of the general public as the teaching of reading?
2. Do you find any similarities among the three major systems of grammar today? What differences exist among them?
3. If you were assigned to a school which is planning to introduce transformational grammar next semester, how would you prepare the parents for the new grammar in an effort to solicit their support?
4. If instruction in grammatical concepts and vocabulary is preferably conducted on an informal basis, how do you propose to evaluate the girls and boys for their achievement in those areas?

Suggested Projects

1. Design a learning game for the purpose of reviewing one grammatical concept (e.g., subject-predicate relationships). Try it with a group of children and then refine it.
2. Examine Maestro's *Busy Day: A Book of Action Words* (Crown, 1978) and then plan an informal instructional activity around that book.
3. Report to your peers about one of the more recently developed grammars, such as Pike's tagmemic grammar, Fillmore's case grammar, Lamb's stratificational grammar, Halliday's scale and category grammar, or Chafe's semantically-oriented grammar.

4. Survey four teachers in a nearby elementary school to determine if and how each presents grammatical concepts to the pupils.
5. Examine one primary-level book and one intermediate-level book in a single current language arts text series for their coverage of a grammatical system. Evaluate the content and caliber of activities outlined.
6. Set up the learning center on sentence combination and modification shown in Figure 3.2.

Figure 3.2. Language Arts Learning Center: Grammar.

TYPE OF CENTER: **Functional English—Transforming Sentences**

TIME: 30 minutes

GRADE LEVEL: 5-7

NUMBER OF STUDENTS: 4

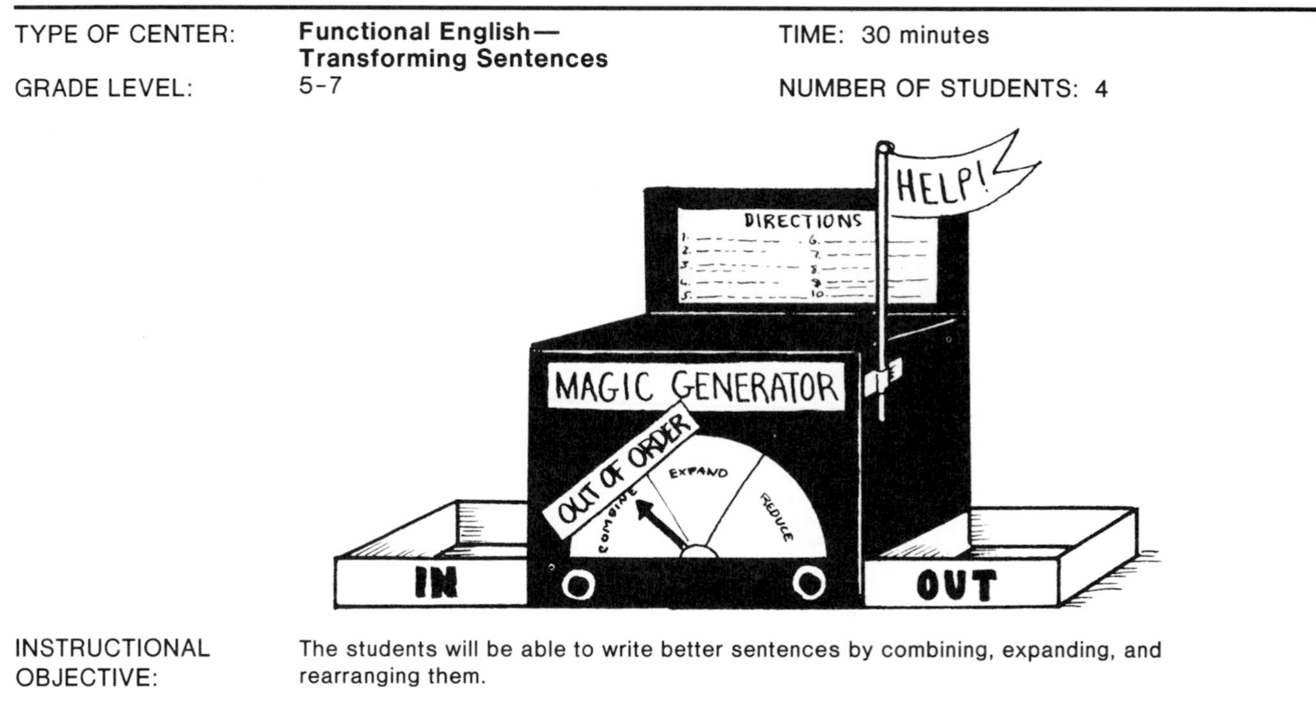

INSTRUCTIONAL OBJECTIVE: The students will be able to write better sentences by combining, expanding, and rearranging them.

MATERIALS: A large box labeled "Magic Generator," smaller flat boxes for "in" and "out" papers, a flag calling for HELP, an "Out of Order" sign, worksheets, paper and pencil.

DIRECTIONS: This machine changes sentences to make them more interesting. Today the machine is out of order. It needs help to get the work done. Please help!

1. Each student is to select one worksheet from the "in" box.
2. Take a pencil and paper.
3. Write your name and the date at the top of the paper.
4. Follow the directions on the worksheet.
5. You may work with one or two other students on this activity, but each student must hand in a completed exercise.
6. When you have completed the worksheet, return it to the "in" box and put the paper you wrote in the "out" box.

It was nice of you to help. Thank you!

Figure 3.2 (cont.)

Worksheets for Sentence Generating Center

I. Directions: Rewrite each of the following sentences as questions.
1. The snow storm has lasted the entire day.
2. The workers built a new fence around the old ball park.
3. Our cat has chased the ball of yarn.
4. Eddie mowed the lawn this morning.
5. The girls have beaten the boys in checkers.
6. You had read this before.

II. Directions: Write these sentences, adding an adjective (a descriptive word) in each blank space.
1. My __________ sisters helped.
2. My __________ brother wrote __________ songs.
3. The __________ boy threw the __________ magazine away.
4. A __________ boy wrote a __________ story.
5. A __________ crowd followed the __________ actors.
6. The __________ prince visited his __________ classmates.
7. The __________ mayor greeted the __________ visitors.
8. Two __________ girls picked the __________ papers off the __________ table.
9. The __________ world wants __________ peace.
10. __________ Sue had a __________ dream.

III. Directions: Write ten new sentences by adding words to each part of these sentences. Expand the noun part, then the verb part.
1. Men work.
2. Don laughed.
3. Feet stamped.
4. Beets grew.
5. Snow fell.
6. Bells tinkle.
7. Bill told a joke.
8. We called the girls.
9. Ellen likes tomatoes.
10. Rain hit the roof.

IV. Directions: Combine each pair of sentences to make one longer, more interesting sentence. Use such connecting words as *but, or, while, so,* or *and.*
1. Ann will speak. She will take notes.
2. The cab driver pulled over to the curb. He turned off the motor.
3. The motor boat raced across the lake. The swimmer raced across the lake.
4. Sally will sing. She will hum.
5. Joey must return early. He will not be allowed to go again.
6. The gardener cut the flowers. He did not water the plants.
7. The tugboats tooted. The ship tooted back.
8. The rain stopped. The wind kept howling.
9. The little boy coughed. He almost choked.
10. Mrs. Hill spoke. Mr. Hill spoke at the same time.

EVALUATION: The teacher will check the work. Later the class can review papers in small groups.

Related Readings

Bornstein, D. 1984. *An Introduction to Transformational Grammar.* Washington, D.C., University Press of America.

Center of Learning. 1983. *Grammar with a Purpose.* Dubuque, IA: Wm. C. Brown Company Publishers.

Holbrook, H. T. 1983. "ERIC/RCS Report: Whither (Wither) Grammar?" *Language Arts, 60,* pp. 259–263.

Lawler, J. 1980. *Improving Student Writing through Sentence Combining: A Literature Review.* Los Alamitos, CA: Southwest Regional Laboratory for Educational Research and Development.

McCarthy, A. 1983. "Can We Rescue Language?" *Commonweal, 110*(2), pp. 37–38.

Middleton, T. H. 1983. "It Gets My Goats," *Saturday Review, 9*(8), p. 34.

Noyce, R. M., and Christie, J. F. 1983. "Effects of an Integrated Approach to Grammar Instruction on Third Graders' Reading and Writing," *Elementary School Journal, 84,* pp. 63–69.

Nunberg, G. 1983. "The Decline of Grammar," *The Atlantic Monthly, 252*(12), pp. 31–38.

Nutter, N., and Safran, J. 1984. "Improving Writing with Sentence Combining Exercises," *Academic Therapy, 19,* pp. 449–454.

Sinatra, R. 1983. "Sentence Development: A Nonverbal Approach," *Academic Therapy, 19,* pp. 79–88.

Chapter Notes

1. M. Klein, *Teaching Sentence Structure and Sentence-Combining in the Middle Grades* (Madison: Wisconsin Department of Public Instruction, 1976), pp. 4–5.
2. J. Malmstrom, *Understanding Language* (New York: St. Martin's Press, 1977), p. 28.
3. S. Straw, "Grammar and Teaching of Writing: Analysis Versus Synthesis," in *Research in the Language Arts,* V. Froese and S. Straw, eds. (Baltimore, University Park Press, 1981), p. 150.
4. D. Daiker, A. Kerek, and M. Morenberg, eds., *Sentence-Combining and the Teaching of Writing* (Akron, Ohio: University of Akron Press, 1979); K. D. Fisher, *An Investigation to Determine if Selected Exercises in Sentence-Combining Can Improve Reading and Writing* (Unpublished doctoral dissertation, Indiana University, 1973); E. A. Green, *An Experimental Study of Sentence Combining to Improve Syntactic Fluency in Fifth-Grade Children* (Unpublished doctoral dissertation, Northern Illinois University, 1972); S. S. Levine, *The Effect of Transformational Sentence Combining Exercises on the Reading Comprehension and Written Composition of Third-Grade Children* (Unpublished doctoral dissertation, Hofstra University, 1976); B. D. Miller and J. Ney, "The Effect of Systematic Oral Exercises on the Writing of Fourth-Grade Students," *Research in the Teaching of English,* 1968, *2,* pp. 44–61; F. O'-Hare, *Sentence-Combining: Improving Student Writing without Formal Grammar Instruction* (Urbana, Illinois: National Council of Teachers of English, 1973); J. D. Perron, *An Exploratory Approach to Extending the Syntactic Development of Fourth-Grade Students through the Use of Sentence-Combining Methods* (Unpublished doctoral dissertation, Indiana University, 1974); S. L. Stotsky, "Sentence-Combining as a Curricular Activity: Its Effect on Written Language Development and Reading Comprehension," *Research in the Teaching of English,* 1975, *9,* pp. 30–71); and S. Straw, *The Effect of Sentence-Combining and Sentence-Reduction Instructions on Measures of Syntactic Fluency, Reading Comprehension, and Listening Comprehension in Fourth Grade Students* (Unpublished doctoral dissertation, University of Minnesota, 1978).

5. S. Haley-James, "Twentieth Century Perspectives on Writing in Grades One through Eight," in *Perspectives on Writing in Grades 1–8,* S. Haley-James, ed. (Urbana, Illinois: National Council of Teachers of English, 1981), p. 17.
6. C. Weaver, *Grammar for Teachers* (Urbana, Illinois: National Council of Teachers of English, 1979), pp. 83, 86, 90.
7. J. Kean, "Grammar: A Perspective," in *Research in the Language Arts,* V. Froese and S. Straw, eds. (Baltimore, University Park Press, 1981), p. 169.
8. California State Department of Education, *English Language Framework for California Public Schools* (Sacramento: The Department, 1976), p. 45.
9. C. LeFevre, "A Concise Structural Grammar," *Education,* 1965, *86,* pp. 131–137.
10. Klein, *Teaching Sentence Structure,* pp. 32–33, 36–37, 40–41, 48–51, 56–57.
11. Bloomington Public Schools, *Language Arts Curriculum Guide K–6* (Bloomington, Minnesota: Public Schools, 1971).
12. O. K. Buros, ed., *The Eighth Mental Measurements Yearbook,* Volume I (Highland Park, New Jersey: Gryphon Press, 1978).
13. California Assessment Program, *Survey of Basic Skills, Grade 3: Rationale and Content* (Sacramento: California State Department of Education, 1980), p. 20; and California Assessment Program, *Survey of Basic Skills, Grade 6: Rationale and Content* (Sacramento: California State Department of Education, 1982), pp. 36–39.
14. *Ibid., Grade 3,* pp. 17–18; and *Grade 6,* pp. 42–43.

Part B Oral and Written Communication

Chapters

4 Listening
5 Speaking
6 Handwriting
7 Spelling
8 Written Composition

Listening 4

Objectives

How listening relates to other language arts
Factors that affect listening ability
The type of listening that occupies the major part of the school day
Why critical listening is so important today

Discover As You Read This Chapter If*

1. Listening is a basic skill.
2. Everyone who can hear knows how to listen.
3. Elementary school children spend nearly 1/3 of their classroom activity time every day in listening.
4. Incidental approaches to teaching listening have proved just as effective as structured lessons.
5. There is as yet no developmental sequence of listening skills.
6. Teachers readily accept children with hearing aids.
7. Attentive listening is more concentrated than critical listening.
8. The greatest part of the school day is spent on attentive listening rather than on either appreciative or critical listening.
9. Primary children are incapable of critical listening.
10. A good listening test uses stimulus materials that are spoken.

*Answers to these true-or-false statements may be found in Appendix 6.

The United States Office of Education recently added listening to the list of basic skills under a new Title II (of the Elementary and Secondary Education Act of 1965) passed by Congress as Public Law 95–561 (20 USC 2881). It seems almost ironic that the first language skill to appear chronologically and the oldest language art on record has finally been recognized and made legitimate.

Although reading and writing are the more recently developed of the communication skills in human societies, they have been more readily accepted as proper subjects of school instruction than have the older skills of listening and speaking. Since the establishment of compulsory education in many countries in the nineteenth century, elementary schools have traditionally been concerned with providing training in the skills of literacy and, to some extent, of speaking. Any listening skills that the pupils acquired came incidentally in the course of studying other subjects or were learned indirectly at home.

Today, however, given the new emphasis on basic skills in public education, the federal legislation should lead to more student and teacher time devoted to listening. The idea that everyone who can hear knows how to listen has finally been discredited. Still some confusion remains among teachers about essential aspects of this challenging curricular area.

Basic Questions about the Listening Program

What Is Listening?

There apparently is no one definition of listening which is presently and widely accepted by educators and researchers. Lundsteen defines listening simply as that process by which spoken language is converted to meaning in the mind.[1] A more elaborate definition is stated by Froese, who prefers the term "auditory processing" and subcategorizes it into the neurophysiological act of hearing, the perceptual act of listening, and the comprehending act of auding.[2] Auding, incidentally, was the label proposed by various authorities because it appeared to be the more comprehensive term.

Linguistically, listening is a learned receptive skill. Since verbal communication is carried on primarily so that others may comprehend the information transmitted and react accordingly, listening implies comprehension of the material heard. It is a personal, often private absorption of ideas and attitudes expressed through oral language. It differs from hearing which does not involve interpretation.

Why Is Listening Important?

Listening is not only the first language skill for most persons, but it generally is also basic to success in all other areas of the language arts. Progress in reading, speaking, and writing is directly governed by listening ability. It is quantitatively the most important of the four arts since nearly half of the adult working day and more than half of the child's classroom activity time are spent in listening. Listening is also a critical part of today's culture in the United States where approximately 70 percent of the people reside in nonrural areas causing person-to-person relationships to typify modern lives. Moreover, the knowledge explosion since the mid century has demanded the processing of greater amounts of information through listening.

Listening constitutes one of the most rapidly expanding leisure-time activities in present-day society and is the mainstay of two popular and pervasive communications media: radio and television. According to the latest census each child and adult in this country has more than one radio available to him or her, and in 98 percent of the households, the use of one or more television sets as well.

Many reasoning-thinking skills are practiced in a listening-speaking environment before those skills are taught in a reading situation.[3] For this reason, listening skills occupy a prominent position in reading instruction. A major means of learning and recall, particularly for poor readers, listening is essential to success in the phonetic analysis of words and the ability to discriminate among sounds and identify initial and final sounds.

During the early school years most instruction takes place through oral language. Even after a child begins reading, listening remains the more effective tool for gaining information until the sixth- or seventh-grade level. It directs attention to details and their synthesis.

Listening is a basis for the good human relationships that are considered to be among the most important educational goals. It influences value formation. It results in greater emotional responses and changes in attitude than other language arts. Finally, according to the Florida State Department of Education, listening constitutes the threefold problem of today's generation that must decide: what to listen to, how to strengthen listening ability, and how to listen appreciatively and critically.

Can Listening Be Taught?

By the 1970s, hundreds of studies had concluded that listening skills can be taught, so teachers today can be assured that they are not wasting time when planning and presenting structured lessons in listening. They should be aware that such directed lessons make boys and girls more conscious of good listening habits than do incidental approaches.

Lessons that demand active verbal responses on the part of the children both during and after listening increase listening comprehension. Such comprehension is also improved through listening to literature or participating in lessons primarily directed toward increasing reading comprehension.

Incidentally, the grade level of the students does not matter insofar as listening instruction goes. From kindergarteners to college freshmen, all students who receive such instruction (in contrast to those who do not) evidence significant improvement in listening ability.

How Is Listening Related to the Other Language Arts?

Not only does language processing include the major skills of transmission and reception, but language in all its facets is an integrated phenomenon.[4] Since effects in one of its sub-systems will later show up in the others, improving listening for example is likely to affect other language arts.

The relationship between the receptive skill of *listening and the expressive skill of writing* was explored in research on children with normal hearing and those with impaired hearing. Children able to hear were found to use more complex types of language structure and more concise composition, thereby reflecting a higher degree of maturity in writing expression than that of children who were deaf or who had partial hearing. Comprehension of meaning in writing is dependent upon the base of comprehension in listening. Furthermore, while composing ideas in written form, some children speak and listen internally as they record.

Research has established a positive statistical correlation between *listening and speaking.* Not only are speech patterns learned largely through listening to other persons speak, but, in turn, the growth of the listener function in an individual probably plays an important role in the ultimate development of his or her skill as a speaker in being able to order verbal behavior. (No wonder, then, that the child born into a large, overcrowded, noisy household often learns "practiced inattention.")

An interesting dimension in the listening-speaking relationship is distortion, which can occur while boys and girls are listening to spoken messages.[5] Four distortions which create differences between messages sent and messages delivered are: (1) attitude cutoff, which stops information at the oral source; (2) motive attribution, which tries to attribute a motive to the speaker; (3) organizational mix-up, which sometimes occurs during message organization; and (4) self-preoccupation by listeners so intent on formulating responses that they cannot attend fully to the messages being sent. Briefly then, while the message should be the same for speaker and listener alike, differences in communication may and often do occur.

Both *listening and reading* are phases of language serving as major avenues for the acquisition of information. Both are a complex of related skill components and the same postulated higher mental processes seem to underlie the two of them (although the evidence indicates that each receptive skill may contain verbal factors individually unique). Both flourish in a relaxed environment where the ideas and vocabulary are at least partially familiar to the receivers. And both use signals such as intonation and pauses in oral language and their corresponding punctuation marks.

In listening, however, the rate is determined by the speaker; the ideas usually are presented but once; the listener loses a portion of the content whenever his or her attention lapses; and the listener's evaluation of that content is often influenced by the speaker's use of gestures or voice inflections. Communication through reading, on the other hand, is less personal and may include visual aids. The reader proceeds at his or her own rate and may reread the material as often as needed to gain the information. Too, printed ideas are more likely to be expressed in well-organized fashion.

Since listening and reading are receptive skills, early researchers assumed that they are highly interdependent. More recently, however, research findings have been mixed.[6] On the one hand, Lemons and Moore taught listening skills to black, inner-city fourth graders and found the children made significant improvements on the Metropolitan Achievement Test in reading skills in contrast to pupils in the control group not exposed to such instruction in listening skills. Another group of fourth graders, as studied by Hoffman, was also given training in listening comprehension and made significant gains in reading comprehension in contrast to a control group in the same grade not provided with such training.

Finally, Tinzmann and Thompson compared listening and reading cloze procedures and found that, among the third through sixth graders in their study, 14 of the 16 correlations between all variables were significant, suggesting that scores on student oral language ability tests can be predictive of reading ability.

On the other hand, Haugh studied the relationship between listening comprehension and reading comprehension among first graders and found a correlation of only .317. Hildyard's comparison of third graders and fifth graders readers' and listeners' comprehension of a narrative text concluded that readers and listeners adopt different, not similar, strategies when comprehending narrative material. Readers studied paid more attention to what was "said," and listeners paid more attention to what was "meant." In their review of some 31 studies comparing reading comprehension versus listening comprehension at various grade levels, Sticht et al. found that in grades 1–6 most comparisons favored the listening comprehension mode, but the advantage shifted to the reading comprehension mode as one moved from grades seven to twelve.

In view of the conflicting evidence one recent recommendation, labeled only as "pretty sure," stated that at almost any age level, students will benefit from direct efforts to improve comprehension abilities, although much transfer from listening to reading cannot be expected.[7] Nevertheless, after pupils become mature readers (at grade eight or above), cross modal transfer is possible, and what benefits reading comprehension will likely benefit listening comprehension and vice-versa.

Is There a Learning Hierarchy of Listening Skills?

A sequential program in listening skills is equally as important as a sequential program in reading skills. Because most children are not accomplished listeners, a developmental listening improvement program is needed in many schools. However, there is as yet no published research outlining a special developmental sequence of listening skills.[8] Still, one hierarchy has been compiled based on theories of the development of auditory abilities, and it covers both sighted as well as visually handicapped children.[9] It includes sections on auditory discrimination skills, listening comprehension skills, and environmental skills, the last-named being those involved in the identification and interpretation of sounds from the environment (excluding verbal sounds) which play an important role in the orientation and mobility skills of visually handicapped (VH) persons. In this hierarchy, discrepancies in the time when certain skills are apt to occur in sighted and visually handicapped persons are indicated by (VH+).

Discrimination skills for K–3 pupils include recognizing the differences in initial consonants, final consonants, and medial sounds auditorily; recognizing the discrete words within a sentence as well as the sequence of words within a sentence; learning that sounds differ in intensity (VH+), pitch (VH+), pattern, and duration; identifying the accented words within a sentence, the number of syllables within a word, and the accented syllable within a word; changing the accent from one syllable to another; discriminating among the temporal order of sounds within words; and recognizing the initial and final consonant sounds, the short vowel and long vowel sounds, and rhyming words as well as recognizing and discriminating among word endings.

Comprehension skills for K–3 pupils include using new words learned by listening and using context to predict words in a sentence; associating spoken words with pictures or miniature objects (VH+) and associating auditory cues with motor responses; recognizing verbal absurdities; sequencing details correctly; identifying the main ideas of a simple story; relating new information to past experiences; listening for specific information; and following travel directions (VH+).

Comprehension skills for children in grades 4–6 include distinguishing between true and false statements and between statements which are relevant and those which are irrelevant; generalizing from details, drawing inferences and conclusions; following the directions in making things; recognizing associations and relationships; interpreting the feelings of the characters; comparing and contrasting; and evaluating critically.

Environmental skills for K–3 pupils are (1) learning that sounds differ in intensity (VH+), pitch (VH+), pattern and duration; and (2) learning the concept of distance in relation to sound localization and movement (VH+). Skills for children in grades 4–6 include (1) identifying sounds in the environment at particular times of the day and evaluating them in terms of orientation and mobility (VH+); and (2) promoting growth of echo perception and spatial orientation (VH+).

Which Factors Influence Listening?

There are at least a dozen factors which affect the learning processes generally and the teaching of listening particularly. Conversely, some of them could also be listed as possible causes for specific listening deficiencies.

The first and most obvious is *hearing sense.* The human ear is said to be able to detect sounds in the range of 20–20,000 cycles per second or Hertz (Hz), the standardized international unit for measuring frequency. During the hearing process the ear receives and modifies speech sounds, the range being 250 to 3000 Hz. Approximately five to ten percent of the school population is deemed to be hearing-impaired.

A second factor is the *involvement level required of the listeners.* This has generally been described as an enhancing factor since child listeners must actively process the information heard and can be neither bored nor discouraged. However, it may become an inhibiting factor if the speaker's voice is monotonous or if the aural message relates to topics arousing negative reactions, such as fear of nuclear war, for example.

Another factor is the *family.* Children in small families generally obtain higher listening scores than those in large families. Pupils coming from smaller, television-viewing families are better listeners than those of larger, television-viewing families.

Although evidence concerning the possibility of a relationship between listening and family size is not yet conclusive, it has been speculated that the heightened noise and confusion in a large group leads to the development of a protective insulation, or a nonlistening attitude that children transfer to the classroom. Socially and economically, good listeners tend to come from middle- and upper-middle-class homes, while poor listeners come from lower- and lower-middle-class homes. Middle children (those who have older *and* younger brothers and sisters) are no better listeners than the oldest or the youngest children in the family. More good listeners than poor listeners, however, are first-born or only children.

In the area of *personality and social development,* good listeners are better adjusted than poor listeners. They are indicated to be more participating, ready to try new things, and more emotionally stable and free from nervous symptoms. They are chosen significantly more often than poor listeners as work partners and play companions. Their teachers too seem to be aware of the differences for they rate poor listeners as lower in such traits as willingness to work, vigor, ability to get a task done, cheerfulness, and participation in class and playground activities. Emotional and social adjustment is therefore vital.

Listening achievement increases with the *chronological age and grade level* of its owners. This factor holds true even when the rate of presentation is increased and speech is compressed. Older, intermediate-grade boys and girls always comprehend more by listening than do their younger, primary-age friends who, in turn, surpass kindergarten and preschool pupils.

A sixth factor is a *structured program.* As mentioned earlier, listening skill and listening performance can be and have been improved by instruction. Even at the first-grade level children profit from a structured listening program.

Another factor is *thinking skills.* Many of the operations involved in listening are mental operations, with listening said to involve facets of thinking and reasoning of a high order. Although the relationship between listening and thinking has not yet been firmly determined by researchers, there are those already who believe that poor listeners may have thinking problems. Thinking skills allow pupils to index, make comparisons, note sequence, react by forming sensory images, draw inferences, abstract main ideas, categorize, recognize relationships, and use appreciation.

The extent to which meaning is associated depends initially on the listeners' *experiential background.* Words are more easily apprehended when they form a part of predictable and meaningful speech. Children who come to school with a broad background of experiences can apprehend each word to which they listen and will, therefore, enjoy listening to their teachers and peers.

A ninth factor concerns the *physical condition of the listeners.* Boys and girls who are hungry and/or tired are not physiologically able to attend to the listening tasks effectively.

Once the listening pupil has identified a sound or recognized a sound sequence as a familiar word, then the *presentation* variables of mode and rate must be considered. Primary children listening to a storytelling program across three modes of presentation, for instance, had their highest comprehension performance for videotape and lowest for audio cassette.[10] Also, comprehension has generally increased as the rate of presentation increases, and most spoken language can be comprehended satisfactorily at rates twice that of normal talk of 120 words per minute. Although research studies are conflicting in this area, other studies do support slower rates of presentation for the verbally disadvantaged, the auditorially handicapped, and young children generally.[11]

Recognition of voices is the eleventh factor. The differentiation that is made between the voices of other persons depends on the period during which the threshold becomes lower and lower and allows the hearer to be increasingly confident in his or her recognition of the speaker. Children find it easiest to listen to a single voice. They can also comprehend a conversation or recitation that involves several voices, but in one setting. They do not perceive, however, a situation in which several persons are talking without being in the same place, or a situation in which voices are added from the outside either to comment on a scene or to produce some psychological or moral effect. Interestingly, it does not matter to pupils who use Black English whether speakers use standard English or nonstandard dialect because all are comprehended equally by primary children.[12]

Finally children have the best opportunity to improve their listening ability in a *supportive classroom environment.*

Such an environment is flexible. Children learn to communicate best when they have the chance to practice in small groups first, and later in increasingly larger groups. Furniture which allows freedom of movement from one type of organization to another is desirable.

Such an environment has opportunities for interaction. When listeners are active in the communication process, their level of personal involvement reaches its highest peak. The amount of interaction possible often depends upon the group structure, for while only minimum response is possible in a whole-class discussion with a questioning teacher and answering children, maximum interaction can occur when children work in pairs for problem solving or oral reading. Pupils need practice in communicating in groups of various sizes and for many different purposes.

Such an environment stimulates speaking and listening. Children will communicate about those activities and objects which they encounter in their classroom. When the room has ample materials and interest centers, pupils are stimulated to improve the quality and increase the quantity of their oral language.

Such an environment is relatively quiet. One study of 40 five- and six-year-olds showed that even young children with normal hearing have significantly more difficulty in comprehending speech against a background of noise than do young adults.[13] In fact, the range of speech discrimination in noise scores for the boys and girls indicated great variability in their ability to handle even low levels of noise of competing messages. The researchers concluded that the open-plan classroom should be questioned from an acoustical viewpoint since it generally provides poorer signal-to-noise ratios than does the self-contained classroom.

How Can the Teacher Help the Hard of Hearing Listen Better?

The elementary teacher today will generally enroll two or more children with reduced hearing each year. Since the teacher is concerned with developing listening skill in the hard-of-hearing pupils, he or she will make sure to:

1. *Seat them carefully.* Place them from six to ten feet from the area where teaching is centered. Permit them to move their seats if the teaching center

moves to another part of the room. Permit them to turn around to hear their classmates speak. Make sure that each pupil's better ear is toward the source of significant sounds and not toward the windows or hallway.

2. *Speak properly.* Avoid using loud tones, exaggerated mouth movements, or too many gestures. Avoid talking when walking about the room or when facing the chalkboard. Avoid placing hands or books in front of the face while speaking. Avoid using homophones (such as *road-rode*) which look alike on the lips. Use clear enunciation. Check frequently and informally to make sure that the handicapped children comprehend the discussion.
3. *Assist them casually.* Write new words on the chalkboard, since names of people and places are difficult for them to understand. Ask other children to help them get the correct assignment. Provide special help in such language activities as spelling and reading where sounds have unusual importance. Explain special events such as field trips well in advance. Repeat instructions as often as needed.
4. *Watch their physical condition.* Prevent further hearing loss by noting respiratory infections and other ailments. Prevent undue fatigue from the strain of seeing and listening intently by providing alternating periods of physical activity and inactivity in the day's planning.
5. *Encourage participation.* Allow extracurricular activities, especially vocal music. Help them discover abilities and talents by guiding them into activities where they can achieve their share of success.

Finally, teachers should personally avoid stereotypical images of hard-of-hearing pupils. Results from a recent survey in northern Illinois of 104 elementary teachers who had pupils with hearing aids supported the conclusion that such images do exist.[14] Asked to list all traits that may be used to describe elementary school age children with hearing aids, the teachers noted undesirable traits to desirable ones by a ratio of 3.5 to 1. This data supports the claim that elementary classroom teachers need greater understanding of the child who has a hearing aid since the largest number of responses was grouped in terms of emotional implications rather than educational ones. Teachers apparently were projecting their own feelings rather than listing attributes of the children.

Instructional Activities

Like all language skills, listening demands responsible and systematic teaching and practice. Without the guidance of a teacher and the reinforcement of parents, children are unlikely to attain the facility required by the impact of listening competence upon contemporary society.

While listening is a receptive language art, it is also an active process, entailing thinking and interpretation on the part of the listeners. They question, accept, reject, enjoy, or dislike some, if not all, of what they hear. At the same time, they are called upon to recall what they have heard or read earlier in the same area in order to evaluate more accurately the present information.

Although as many as 25 different kinds of listening have been identified (ranging from accurate and active to responsible and selective), basically there are only three types of listening: *appreciative, attentive,* and *critical.* They differ

This young pupil is engaged in appreciative listening, which is less concentrated than attentive listening. (Photo courtesy of National Education Association Publishing, Joe Di Dio.)

primarily in the degree of concentration demanded, with appreciative listeners being considerably less tense than critical listeners. It must be pointed out, however, that all listening demands interpretation and consequently some degree of concentration. Listening is not merely hearing; therefore, when two or more distractions are present, during a radio broadcast for example, children only *hear* the presentation on the radio. They cannot *listen* to it until the number of distractions is reduced and they give conscious attention to the performer or performance. Listening is more than a physiological reaction and it demands more than passive participation.

Appreciative Listening

Appreciative listening is the ability to listen for enjoyment and creative response. It is less concentrated than either attentive or critical listening, and the hearer is therefore more relaxed. Children may listen to tapes and records, to radio and television programs, and to concerts. They may listen to shadow plays, puppet shows, roll movies, sound filmstrips, and taped dramatizations. They may also simply listen to enjoy pleasant sounds, indoors or outdoors, such as a cricket's chirp or a canary's song.

Boys and girls may fingerpaint or draw designs to music or use chalk or clay to express ideas inspired by a recording of Tchaikovsky's *Nutcracker Suite;* Dv̌orák's *Slavonic Dances;* Grieg's *Peer Gynt Suite;* Rossini's *William Tell Overture;* or Gershwin's *Rhapsody in Blue.*

Part 4 Listening To Learn

When you read, your eyes help you learn. You can also learn with your ears. When you think about what you hear, you are listening.

Daydreaming

We don't always listen well. Sometimes we daydream when others talk. Let's look at an example.

> Cliff opened his reader. He listened. Several students read aloud. Then Cliff began to daydream. He gazed out the window and thought about his tree house. He had worked on it all weekend.
>
> "Cliff, please read next," the teacher said.
>
> Her voice startled Cliff. He had lost the place. He didn't know where to begin reading.

Cliff had stopped listening. For the last few minutes, he had not learned. Cliff would have extra work to do after school.

Asking People To Repeat

Sometimes we don't hear well. Perhaps people are speaking softly. Perhaps the room is noisy. If you don't hear, ask people to repeat. They seldom mind doing so. Here is an example.

> When Kate met Janet, she didn't hear Janet's name. At first Kate didn't want to ask Janet to repeat her name. Finally, she asked her. Now Kate feels at ease with Janet. It helps to call her new friend by name.

Figure 4.1. Attentive Listening Exercises.

They can paint their responses to poetry they have heard, including Livingston's "I Haven't Learned to Whistle" and "The Sun Is Stuck;" Fisher's "June" and "The First Day of School;" Cole's "Jemima" and "Sarah Cynthia Sylvia Stout;" and Behn's "The Kite" and "Hallowe'en."

Children can divide themselves into small literary committees, each selecting one of its members to read aloud to the others. The child's audience listens, with books closed, to poems rich in imagery or poems that evoke excitement, contentment, or drowsiness. Sometimes the reader selects stories that have a dominant mood such as three of those for older pupils by Hans Christian Andersen. The audience can sense sadness-triumph-surprise for "The Ugly Duckling," sadness-pity for "The Little Match Girl," and the exaggeration-arrogance of "The Princess and the Pea."

Choral speaking provides for participation as well as for appreciative listening. At times as many as six to ten pupils can recite while the rest of the class listens. Suggestions for simple choral activities are given in Chapter Eleven.

Watching performances of a children's theatre group also involves appreciative listening. The theatre provides enjoyment and expression, allowing the young audience to identify with the onstage characters and actions. Listeners are sometimes subtly exposed to learning about cultures of other lands as well.

Storytelling also offers children the opportunity to learn to listen appreciatively to their teacher, media center specialist, or their peers. They can tell round-robin chain stories in which each participant carries on from where the preceding speaker stopped. They can tell, extemporaneously, an original ending to a classic story that they have heard.

Kindergartners and early primary pupils are generally interested in finger plays, which are excellent devices to foster appreciative listening. Sometimes a child can even be encouraged to develop his or her own finger play to share with classmates. Younger children also often enjoy interpreting music with simple rhythm instruments. Older pupils can select background music for an original class story or a poem located in a basal reader.

Finally, children may compile a picture book of sounds with separate sections devoted to sounds at home, sounds of the city (or country), sounds in the classroom, and sounds on the playground. Younger pupils may wish to include only pictures while older children can write an accompanying text.

Attentive Listening

Attentive listening demands that the attention of the listener be focused on one person or on one electronic medium so that the listener can purposefully respond either orally or in written fashion. It may or may not involve a two-way conversation or discussion, for in some cases it is strictly a one-way communication process. The listener, however, must think carefully about the telephone conversation, radio broadcast, recording, telecast, play, lecture, or classroom announcement.

Attentive listening concerns the ability to respond to directions and explanations. In the primary grades children may be sent on errands throughout the building after they have received exact directions as to how to get to the custodian's and the principal's offices, or how to locate the sixth-grade classroom. They should have many opportunities to recall the directions given for their safety regarding standards for fire drills and playground behavior. They can explain to newcomers how a particular classroom routine is handled that requires three or four steps in sequence; for instance, how to care for paintbrushes, how to line up for morning recess, or how to be a book monitor. Individual pupils can give directions for reaching their nearest public library, and the class can later evaluate the clarity of these directions. In the intermediate grades one group of pupils may explain the steps in a science experiment, while a second group follows the directions as stated, and a third group evaluates both procedures. In another instance, the teacher can read the instructions for using a word processor, and let the children retell the steps in order.

This kind of listening, which occupies a greater part of the school day than either appreciative or critical listening, also includes the ability to recognize and respond to grapheme-phoneme relationships, to rhyming, to onomatopoeia and alliteration, and to gross sounds (by identifying, duplicating, or classifying them). It involves as well the ability to retell in sequence what has been heard, to recognize specific details in a story told on tape, and to note similes, metaphors, and other figurative language in poems read orally. Therefore primary children can, for example, do these attentive listening activities:

1. Sit quietly outdoors and name the sounds around them.
2. Classify sounds according to intensity and pitch or by the specific object with which each is linked.
3. Choose pairs of rhyming words out of three-word and four-word series of mixed words.
4. Supply single words to complete rhyming couplets.
5. Name three other words that begin with the same initial consonant blend as the chalkboard word which the teacher has just pronounced.

Fourth, fifth, and sixth graders develop attentive listening habits when they are given an opportunity, for example, to:

1. Answer specific questions about an article on Australia which the teacher has just read aloud.
2. Note the visual imagery after listening to Thurman's *Flashlight and Other Poems* (Atheneum, 1976).
3. Identify the triple blends (such as *scr* and *spl*) in lists of words which have been taped.
4. Listen to two stories, and then compare them to determine their similarities.
5. Discuss the alliterative unit in tongue twisters recited by their classmates.

This type of listening is labeled as purposeful listening by Devine, who also considers it highly teachable.[15] It is one segment of the curricula from which students may profit promptly by acquiring those listening skills most necessary for success in school. Sample textbook exercises in attentive listening are shown in Figure 4.1.

Figure 4.1 (cont.)

Asking Questions

To learn, you must understand what you hear. Sometimes things are not clear. Don't stay confused. Ask questions. Be sure you have the facts straight. Let's look at Milo's problem.

> Milo's teacher said, "Ponce de Leon discovered Florida in 1513." Milo was confused. He knew America was discovered in 1492. Florida is part of America. Milo asked his teacher to explain. He learned because he was not afraid to ask a question.

The guides below will help you remember how to listen.

Guides for Listening To Learn

1. Pay attention.
2. If you don't hear something, ask someone to repeat it.
3. If you are confused, ask questions.

Exercises **Listening To Learn**

A. Close your eyes for twenty seconds. Listen. Then open your eyes. Write down everything you heard. Talk about those things in class. Did everyone hear the same things?

B. Listen as your teacher reads to you. Answer these questions.

1. What was the main idea of the paragraph?
2. Name three objects mentioned in the paragraph.
3. Write a question about the paragraph.

C. Form groups of three or four. With your group, make a poster. Show times when listening is important. You may draw pictures, use magazine photographs, or make a comic strip.

Source: Reprinted from BUILDING ENGLISH SKILLS, Aqua Level. Copyright © 1984. McDougal, Littell & Company, Evanston, Illinois. Used with permission.

Critical Listening

Critical listening is the most complex kind of listening to teach or to learn. At the same time it is a matter of grave significance under the First Amendment which guarantees freedom of speech to all, regardless of ethical or educational backgrounds.

Implied in critical listening is the use of a highly conscious standard or criterion for evaluating spoken material while comprehending it. It is this advanced degree of evaluation or reflection about what is heard that is crucial and intricate. A continuum of the goals or skills involved in lessons in critical listening in the elementary school should include teaching the children how to do the following:

1. Distinguish fact from fantasy, according to explicit criteria.
2. Distinguish relevant statements from irrelevant ones and evaluate them.
3. Distinguish well-supported statements from opinion/judgment and evaluate them.
4. Evaluate the qualifications of a speaker.
5. Detect and evaluate the bias, emotional slant, or lack of objectivity of a speaker.
6. Recognize and evaluate the effects of devices the speaker may use to influence the listener, such as propaganda, voice intonation, or music.
7. Evaluate the validity and adequacy of the central theme or point of view of a performer or performance.

Primary children are capable of critical listening. For example, a day after telling the class the story of "The Three Bears," the teacher can read them Graves' *The Wright Brothers* and then ask them to give evidence of why yesterday's tale was fantasy or make-believe and today's story is real. Another day, the teacher can pose a series of questions, some of which are meaningful and some of which are not. The child responding must determine in each instance whether the question is nonsense (Why is the grass red?) or whether the question is reasonable (If chickens are birds, why can't they fly?).

Intermediate pupils can listen to recordings of talks or conversations by unidentified persons and then decide whether the speakers showed prejudice or used loaded words during the presentations. On another occasion they can listen to a selection containing instructions for making paper snowflakes, for instance, but containing, as well, some extraneous information. The class, omitting all irrelevant data, must then make the snowflakes. Sample textbook exercises in critical listening for intermediate students are shown in Figure 4.2.

That both late primary and intermediate pupils can be helped to develop critical listening has been substantiated by research involving 200 children, ages eight to ten, in Maryland.[16] The boys and girls, both white and black, were given lessons to help them become aware of propaganda employed by commercial advertisers in their television programs. It was concluded that children can be made conscious of commercial propaganda emanating from television. Furthermore, they can successfully transfer their new critical listening skill to other disciplines as they begin to recognize propaganda in reading, in conversations with teachers and peers, and in newspaper and magazine advertising.

Figure 4.2. Critical Listening Exercises.

Part 3 Listening for Fact and Opinion

A **fact** is a statement about something that has really happened or is true. It can be proved. An **opinion** is one person's idea about something or someone. An opinion cannot be proved.

Every speaker uses a mixture of facts and opinions. A good listener must be alert to separate them. This may be difficult because some speakers use opinions in a way that makes them look like facts. Watch out particularly for **over-generalizations** and **propaganda**.

Understanding Generalization

A **generalization** is a statement of fact based on details. For example, Janet asks one class of sixth graders, "What is your favorite carnival ride?" Nineteen students answer, "Tilt-a-Whirl." Five answer, "Octopus." Four answer, "Bumper Cars." Two say, "Ferris Wheel." These answers are details. From them, Janet might generalize: Most sixth graders like the Tilt-a-Whirl better than other rides.

Generalizing is a useful way of pulling together facts. Over-generalizing, however, is an error. For example, Janet might have said, "Everyone's favorite ride is the Tilt-a-Whirl." A careful listener would question this statement. Did Janet talk to any young children? any teenagers? any adults? The listener would conclude that the statement is too broad. The details did not support the conclusion.

Spotting Over-Generalizations: Words To Listen For

everyone	never	nobody	all the time
always	every	everybody	no one

Recognizing Propaganda

Propaganda is an effort to spread an opinion or belief. The motive behind propaganda is to convince listeners to think or act in a certain way. The speaker wants the listeners to end up agreeing with his or her bias.

How do you know when you are hearing propaganda?

First, think about what the speaker is saying.

Does the speaker present opinion as facts?
Does the speaker over-generalize?
Does the speaker make vague statements that say little?

Next, think about how the speaker is saying it.

Does the speaker use many strong adjectives, such as *worthwhile, grim, sleek?*
Does the speaker present only one point of view?
Does the speaker use catchy slogans?

Then, think about the speaker's motive.

What is the speaker trying to do?

Finally, think about the way you feel.

Do you find yourself being carried away by the presentation?

Exercise Practicing Listening Skills

Together with a partner, make up a commercial to sell a product. Model your commercial after one that you hear on radio or TV. Present your commercial for the class.

The class should do the following for each commercial.

1. Describe the speakers' motive, point of view, and bias.
2. Identify any over-generalizations.
3. Pick out signs of propaganda.

Learning activities that promote each of the three basic types of listening are listed in Table 4.1. The behavioral objective and the suggested grade level for each instructional activity also are included.

Table 4.1.
Sample Instructional Activities in Elementary School Listening.

Type of Listening	Grade Level	Behavioral Objective	Learning Activity and/or Teaching Strategy
Appreciative	K, 1, 2	The children will listen to music chosen by the teacher and describe how it makes them feel.	The teacher will play a musical selection via record, piano, or cassette while the children listen. The children will then respond by describing how the music makes them feel (sad, happy) through pictures or words.
Appreciative	3-4	After the teacher reads or tells a given story, the children will be able to interpret the mood of that story.	The children will listen to the story which the teacher has chosen to read or tell. They will then be able to state whether the story has made them angry, sad, or delighted.
Appreciative	5-6	After listening to a literary selection, the pupils will determine the attitude of the writer (or speaker) by discussing the selection with their peers.	The teacher will read Carl Sandburg's "Chicago" which denotes approval, joy, and ambition.
Attentive	K, 1, 2	After listening to a story, the children will arrange pictures related to that story in the proper sequential order.	The teacher will choose any story which has a definite beginning, middle, and end; and then prepare pictures illustrating actions in each part of the story. Later, the children will arrange four or five pictures in sequence.
Attentive	3-4	After listening to a given story, the children will be able to recall five details of the story.	The teacher will read or tell a story to the class and then ask five questions concerning what had happened in the story.

Learning Games

Some of the skills essential to the development of good listening among boys and girls can be reviewed through a variety of purposeful games. All of the games outlined in this section are instructional group games which can be adapted by the teacher to meet the needs of a particular classroom of children. Few of the fifteen games described herein require special materials.

Airplanes Fly

1. The teacher is the first leader, and the pupils are seated (or standing) far enough apart to move their arms freely.
2. The teacher describes a flying object or animal; and if the statement is true (e.g., "Airplanes fly"), the pupils wave their arms. Should the statement be false (e.g., "The chalkboard flies"), the pupils must keep their arms still.

Type of Listening	Grade Level	Behavioral Objective	Learning Activity and/or Teaching Strategy
Attentive	5-6	The pupils will listen to a passage which explains how to do something. They will take notes and later complete the assignment correctly.	The teacher will read orally the instructions for making a papier-mâché animal. After listening to the instructions, the pupils will outline the steps involved and then make the animal.
Critical	K, 1, 2	After listening to a story in which there is conversation and/or actions which reveal the emotions of the characters, the children will deduce how the characters feel by citing examples of their conversation and/or actions.	The teacher will read a story with conversation and/or action which reveals feelings. The children will evaluate orally the conversation and/or actions of the story characters in order to determine feelings.
Critical	3-4	After a classmate talks on an assigned topic, the group will discuss the presence of both fact and opinion in the speech and whether or not the facts were substantiated and the opinions qualified.	A pupil is assigned to speak on "Pollution of the Streams and Rivers in Our State." Classmates listen to the speech and criticize it for substantiating facts and qualified opinions.
Critical	5-6	Given a passage which propagandizes, the pupils will orally identify examples of slanted, loaded words and varied propaganda techniques.	The teacher will locate newspaper advertisements for a particular product and the pupils will be able to identify orally examples of such well-known propaganda techniques as plain folks, glittering generalities, testimonials, and band wagon.

3. Any pupil who moves his or her arms when the statement made by the teacher-leader is false is dropped from the game.
4. The pupil who remains in the game the longest wins the first round and becomes the next leader.
5. Variations: (a) Fish Swim; (b) Frogs Jump; and (c) Dogs Run.

Bouncing Ball

1. The pupils are seated with their eyes closed.
2. The teacher, as "It," bounces a rubber ball or tennis ball a number of times at random.
3. The players listen and count the number of bounces silently.

4. "It" calls on one player who responds, "You bounced the ball . . . times." If the player's response is correct, he or she is allowed to have the next turn to be "It." If the player's response is incorrect, another player has a turn to give the proper number of bounces.
5. The winner of Bouncing Ball is the pupil who is "It" the longest.
6. Variation: The ball may be bounced three times, then a pause, and then bounced four times more. The player responds, "You bounced the ball three and four times," or "Three and four are seven."

Cross Out Relay

1. Before the game the teacher writes on the left half of the chalkboard fifty or more numerals with which the class is familiar, presenting them in a mixed or inconsecutive order. Then on the right half of the board the teacher repeats the process, using the same numerals but in a different mixed order.
2. Two teams are chosen and stand facing the class, *not* the numbered board. The player on each team who is nearest to the board receives a piece of chalk.
3. The teacher calls out one number at a time, and a player from each team must quickly cross out that numeral on the board and pass the chalk to the next player.
4. Any player who does not cross out the proper numeral must return to the board, erase his or her mistake, and rewrite the numeral.
5. The team which has the smaller amount of numerals left after a designated time is declared the winner of the Cross Out Relay.

Fruit Basket

1. "It" stands holding a basket with various fruits (or pictures of various fruits on individual pieces of paper). Other players are seated in a circle or in two parallel lines, but there are no extra chairs.
2. "It" studies the contents of the "fruit basket" and then passes the basket to each player, who is allowed to remove one piece of fruit.
3. When the players are ready, "It" stands at the end of the double line or in the center of the circle and begins the dialog:

   It: Good day, my friends.
   Group: Good day, It, how are you?
   It: I am hungry.
   Group: Do you like fruit?
   It: Yes, I like fruit very much.
   Group: Which fruit would you like?
   It: I would like—grapes and bananas.

4. As "It" says, "I would like—grapes and bananas," the two players holding those fruits must change places while "It" tries to sit in one of their empty chairs.
5. The player without a chair is "It" next, and the game continues.
6. Variations: (a) Animal Basket; (b) Vegetable Basket; (c) Laundry Basket (clothing); (d) School Basket.

I Am Packing a Bag

1. The pupils are seated at their tables or desks.
2. The first child chosen as "It" says, "I am packing a bag and will put something in it that begins with . . . (and names a single consonant sound) *b*."

3. Then the other players who can supply a needed word raise their hands.
4. "It" calls on one player who correctly says "book," "bear," or "bicycle." That second player now becomes "It" and chooses the next and different sound.
5. Suggestions: (a) A large paper bag or book bag makes an effective prop for It; (b) With older children, this game may be played with teams and scoring of points as each player says a different word with the same initial sound; (c) Initial blends may be used on occasion.

Jump Up

1. The teacher reads or tells a story. It may be an original tale, an old folk tale, or a simple anecdote.
2. Each player is then assigned to be a character or object in the story.
3. The teacher now retells the whole story except that this time each player must jump up (or stand up, in a crowded classroom) every time his or her character or object is mentioned.
4. The players with superior listening skills are all declared the winners.
5. Variation: As the players jump up, each must make a sound characteristic of his or her role.

Musical Chairs

1. Chairs are arranged in one, two, three, or more rows, depending upon the number of pupils playing. Seats and backs are faced alternately along the row, and the total number of chairs is always one less than the number of players.
2. The teacher plays the piano or uses taped music as the players march around the chairs.
3. When the teacher stops the music suddenly, each player must scramble for a chair. The only child left standing must remove one chair from the area; this child is out until the next game.
4. The round continues until there is only one chair left. Its occupant is the winner of Musical Chairs.
5. Variation: Large cutouts are taped to the floor at various points in a circle and the players march around the circle, stepping on each cutout as they come to it. When the music stops, any pupil whose foot or feet are on a cutout is eliminated from that round.

Rat-A-Tat-Tat

1. The pupils are seated at their desks or at their tables.
2. With a drumstick, the teacher beats out on a drum or table top the exact number of syllables found in a child's name.
3. The pupils listen for the number of syllables in their first name, and later, in their first and last names.
4. When a child believes that his or her name has been tapped out, the child stands and claps as many times as there are syllables in his or her name.
5. All pupils who succeed in recognizing the number of syllables in their names in any one round are declared the winners of that round.
6. Suggestions: (a) The teacher may select a child to beat the drumstick; (b) Older children may sound out the names of songs or the first lines of familiar poems or song lyrics.

Sally Says

1. The teacher is Sally (or Sam) during the first round and stands in front of the room. The pupils stand at their seats.
2. When Sally precedes a command with "Sally says" (e.g., Sally says "Touch your toes"), each pupil performs the command with Sally. If Sally does not precede a command with "Sally says," the pupils must ignore the command no matter what Sally does, or be dropped from the round.
3. A pupil who is out of the first round sits down and the last pupil standing becomes Sally (or Sam) during the second round.
4. Suggestions: (a) Sally (or Sam) should work quickly and always perform her (or his) own commands; (b) Actions and clothes can be stressed as well as parts of the body.

Secret Color

1. All pupils are seated in a circle except "It" who stands inside the circle.
2. The players seated are each assigned a secret color by the teacher. The teacher whispers the secret color individually to each boy or girl and may assign the same secret color to more than one player at once.
3. "It" begins to call out color names at random. As soon as "It" mentions one of the secret colors assigned during that round, the players given that color must promptly leave the circle and move clockwise around the outside. They may hop, jump, or walk, but all must follow the identical action of the first player that leaves.
4. "It" also leaves the circle and, imitating the action of the moving players, tries to tag the players one at a time.
5. The last player to be tagged becomes "It" for the next round.
6. Suggestions: (a) The total number of different secret colors assigned should depend upon the maturity of the group; four colors are adequate for kindergarten and early primary children; (b) When the game is played outdoors, "It" and the other players have the option of running around the circle.

Shopping Cart

1. The teacher needs pictures of foods available at the market.
2. One player is chosen as "It"; the other players sit in a large circle with no empty chairs and hold up pictures which are visible to "It."
3. "It" walks around the circle, saying, "I went to the market and in my shopping cart I put some . . . and some . . . (etc.)," naming different foods which he or she sees pictured. The players holding those pictures leave their chairs and follow "It" around the circle.
4. When "It" decides to stop shopping, he or she says, "My shopping cart fell over." Then "It" and the players following "It" must find empty seats.
5. The player left standing becomes "It" for the next round of Shopping Cart.

Spin A Yarn

1. The players are seated in a circle.
2. The teacher holds a large, brightly colored ball of rewound yarn with knots (tied earlier at intervals of two to three feet) and begins to Spin A Yarn or tell a tall tale. She/He unwinds the ball slowly while talking but stops abruptly when the first knot is reached.
3. The player seated at the teacher's right receives the ball and continued to Spin A Yarn—talking and unwinding—until the second knot is reached.

4. Players take turns and the tale continues until the ball of yarn is completely unwound and the final knot reached.
5. All players who picked up the yarn (story and ball) deftly are deemed good listeners and therefore winners of Spin A Yarn.

This Is My Shirt

1. The players line up in a row. One player is "It."
2. "It" walks up and down in front of the line. Suddenly "It" touches a part of his or her clothing (or body) and deliberately misidentifies it (e.g., "This is my shirt," while touching a shoe), and points to one of the players.
3. The player addressed promptly replies in the reverse ("This is my shoe," while touching his or her shirt).
4. The first player that "It" can trap becomes "It" in the next round.

Utellem

1. The pupils are seated at their desks or tables.
2. The teacher as the first "Director" chooses one volunteer player to follow directions which are given all at once and demand the performance of several actions within the classroom. For instance, the teacher may say, "Walk to the chalkboard. Draw a circle. Then draw a square inside the circle. Write the word 'dog' inside the square. Run to your seat and sit down."
3. If the player successfully follows all the directions, he or she becomes the second Director.
4. The Director who retains the post the longest wins the Utellem game.
5. Suggestions: (a) The directions must be given slowly and clearly; (b) The teacher may need to help the succeeding Directors decide if the directions have been followed properly; (c) The directions may relate to some current classroom unit such as New York Geography; and the Director could say, "Draw a map of New York. Locate Albany. Locate Buffalo. Label the Hudson River."

Vocal Tennis

1. Two teams of players face each other seated in rows or across tables.
2. The teacher or leader announces a word like *feed* which is made up of a phonogram (or graphemic base) preceded by a consonant.
3. The first player on the first team must say a word that rhymes with *feed* like . . . *seed.*
4. The first player on the second team then says a third word that rhymes with both *feed* and *seed* like . . . *need.*
5. Verbal Tennis continues back and forth between the two teams until the players have given all the words they know using the same phonogram or until the teacher supplies a word with a different phonogram preceded by a consonant like . . . *get.*
6. The team with the greater number of correct words recognized or points earned wins Verbal Tennis.
7. Suggestion: Homophones (e.g., *bead* with *feed* and *seed*) are acceptable among primary and middle-grade pupils.

Evaluation of Pupils' and Teachers' Progress

A listening test should possess the following features: (a) Stimulus materials should be taped (audio or video) and always spoken. They should never be written passages read aloud by a narrator on a tape or by the teacher. (b) Stimulus materials should demand a simple and minimal response. Both messages and questions should be on tape, and test items should not be obstructed by difficult or lengthy reading matter. (c) Stimulus materials should be short, ranging from 30 seconds to three minutes. (d) Stimulus materials should be interesting and taken from real life occurrences that are meaningful to the students. (e) Vocabulary used in stimulus materials should be controlled. Otherwise the instrument more aptly tests general verbal knowledge.[17]

One or more of the foregoing features is present in each of the commercially-available listening tests listed below and published in the United States for the purpose of yielding evaluative judgments concerning skills in children (in some or all of the elementary grades). Although all are considered appropriate for the target populations, the reviewers warn that listening tests for younger children particularly often fail to discriminate between reading readiness indicators and indicators of proficiency in receptive communication.[18] Incidentally, unless otherwise noted, all tests are group administered with multiple-choice, paper and pencil format.

California Achievement Tests: Listening (CTB/McGraw Hill, Monterey CA), primary population.

Circus-Listen to the Story, Versions B, C, D (Addison-Wesley, Reading, MA), population: K–3, multiple choice responses.

Comprehensive Tests of Basic Skills (CTB/McGraw Hill, Monterey, CA), population: early elementary.

Durrell Listening-Reading Series (Harcourt Brace, New York), population: grades 1–9.

Fundamental Achievement Series: Verbal (Harcourt Brace, New York), population: grades 6–12, multiple choice, paper and pencil format, taped instructions.

Metropolitan Achievement Tests: Listening Comprehension (Harcourt Brace, New York), population: K–9.

PRI Primary Reading Systems: Oral Language Cluster (McGraw Hill, New York), population: grades K–4, multiple choice answers.

SRA Achievement Series, Levels A, B, C (Science Research Associates, Chicago), population: grades K–3.

Sequential Tests of Educational Progress: Listening (Addison-Wesley, Reading, MA), population: grades 3–12, multiple choice responses.

Stanford Achievement Test: Listening (Harcourt Brace, New York), primary population.

Stanford Early School Achievement Test: Aural Comprehension (Harcourt Brace, New York), population: K–1.

Test of Listening Accuracy in Children (Communication Research Association, Salt Lake City, UT), population: grades K–6, multiple choice questions.

Informal Evaluation

Formal tests are hardly a substitute for informal tests, and in the evaluation of listening, both kinds of measuring devices should be developed and used. Informal techniques are more appropriate for specific classroom situations in order to evaluate objectives which have been established for individual programs.

The alert teacher will discover numerous opportunities to determine the extent of listening progress displayed in her or his classroom as the children plan units of work, make announcements, present reports, or read stories aloud. The teacher can evaluate the listening skills of small groups of children by asking: Can they follow directions? Can they identify main ideas, supporting details, or a sequence of events? Can they distinguish between fancy and realism, between opinion and fact, between statements and questions? Have they been developing a meaningful listening vocabulary? Do they listen attentively and courteously? Can they make critical or value judgments about what is heard? Do they listen for enjoyment and aesthetic appreciation? Can they identify with a character and his or her problems?

As children mature and learn, they become more aware of the characteristics of good listeners and of their own strengths and weaknesses relative to those standards. Fourth, fifth, and sixth graders are better qualified to listen than six-year-olds and are also more capable of evaluating their own listening according to a checklist such as that shown in Figure 4.3.

Figure 4.3. Listening Checklist for an Intermediate Student.

Intermediate Pupil's Self-Evaluation Checklist in Listening

Physical Aids	**Always**	**Sometimes**	**Never**
1. Do I clear my desk of all unnecessary articles?	______	______	______
2. Do I have everything out of my hands except when writing?	______	______	______
3. Do I watch the speaker for helpful facial expressions and gestures?	______	______	______
4. Do I make sure that I am not a distraction?	______	______	______
Attitude			
5. Do I practice all rules of courtesy?	______	______	______
6. Do I shut out all distractions?	______	______	______
7. Do I listen with an open mind?	______	______	______
8. Do I withhold final evaluation until comprehension is complete?	______	______	______
9. Do I actively engage in listening?	______	______	______

Figure 4.3. (cont.)

Content	Always	Sometimes	Never
10. Do I understand the purposes and goals for this listening experience?	______	______	______
11. Do I understand the kind of listening to use for this listening experience?	______	______	______
12. Do I screen the material for what I need?	______	______	______
13. Do I concentrate on what the speaker is saying?	______	______	______
14. Do I listen for main ideas first and details second?	______	______	______
15. Do I take notes when they will be of use to me?	______	______	______
16. Do I use past knowledge to give meaning to the current listening experience?	______	______	______
17. Do I ask questions at the appropriate time?	______	______	______

The teacher's role in informally evaluating listening in the classroom is not complete until the teacher has evaluated his or her own listening abilities and program as outlined in Figure 4.4. Realizing that listening *can* be taught, the teacher plans carefully and then displays the same unfailing interest and courtesy in listening to the oral contributions of the pupils that they are expected to show to him or her and to each other. Children who observe their teacher sorting papers or taking roll while they are talking to him or her can hardly be expected to develop into attentive listeners.

Discussion Questions

1. Why is the teaching of listening so frequently neglected?
2. Which factors that affect listening fall within the domain of the teacher?
3. How can elementary teachers improve the listening ability of those children who are hard of hearing?
4. How could a school evaluate children's listening? Would a letter grade ever be warranted?
5. Should all types of listening receive equal attention by the classroom teacher? Why or why not?

Figure 4.4. Listening Checklist for a Classroom Teacher.

Classroom Teacher's Self-Evaluation Checklist in Listening

	Always	Sometimes	Never
1. Do I pursue a program in which listening skills are consistently developed?	_____	_____	_____
2. Do I prepare for the listening activities to be presented?	_____	_____	_____
3. Do I initiate activities to which the pupils want to listen?	_____	_____	_____
4. Do I create an emotional climate for good listening?	_____	_____	_____
5. Do I create a physical climate for good listening?	_____	_____	_____
6. Do I realize that the attention span of pupils is limited?	_____	_____	_____
7. Do I realize that the concentration span of pupils is limited?	_____	_____	_____
8. Do I help the pupils to develop an appreciation and awareness of sounds?	_____	_____	_____
9. Do I help the pupils to establish purposes for each listening activity?	_____	_____	_____
10. Do I listen to each pupil during the school day?	_____	_____	_____
11. Do I encourage the pupils to listen to each other?	_____	_____	_____
12. Do I use changes in pitch, loudness, and rate in my classroom voice?	_____	_____	_____
13. Do I secure the attention of the group before beginning to speak?	_____	_____	_____
14. Do I give attention to unfamiliar vocabulary?	_____	_____	_____
15. Do I help pupils recall related experiences which may aid their understanding?	_____	_____	_____
16. Do I pose questions that promote careful listening?	_____	_____	_____
17. Do I try not to repeat my presentations or directions?	_____	_____	_____
18. Do I express appreciation for what each child says?	_____	_____	_____
19. Do I promote good listening by not talking too much myself?	_____	_____	_____
20. Do I make myself available for listening and teach listening in every subject area?	_____	_____	_____

Suggested Projects

1. Plan a listening lesson for intermediate pupils which involves critical listening.
2. Try to arrange an experiment involving the physical conditions in one elementary classroom and their effect on children's listening.
3. Develop six learning experiences in attentive listening and six more in appreciative listening for a grade level of your choice.
4. Spend one hour each in the kindergarten, second-grade, and fifth-grade classrooms. Record the amount of time the students spent listening and the amount of time the teacher listened. Do older children have as many opportunities to listen as younger pupils do?
5. Examine two current language text series for one intermediate grade level to see how listening skills are being presented. Compare, for example, the material in the Macmillan series with that of the Houghton Mifflin series. Which do you prefer and why?
6. Set up the learning center for listening shown in Figure 4.5.

Related Readings

Adorable, E. 1983. "Is Everyone Out There Listening?" *Instructor, 92*(6), pp. 70–74.
Alvermann, D. E. 1984. "Adults Who Read to Children Need to be Good Listeners, Too!" *Academic Therapy, 19,* pp. 537–542.
Boodt, G. 1984. "Critical Listeners Become Critical Readers in Remedial Reading Class," *Reading Teacher, 37,* pp. 390–394.

Figure 4.5. Language Arts Learning Center: Listening.

TYPE OF CENTER: **Listening** TIME: 10 minutes
GRADE LEVEL: 1 NUMBER OF STUDENTS: Varies

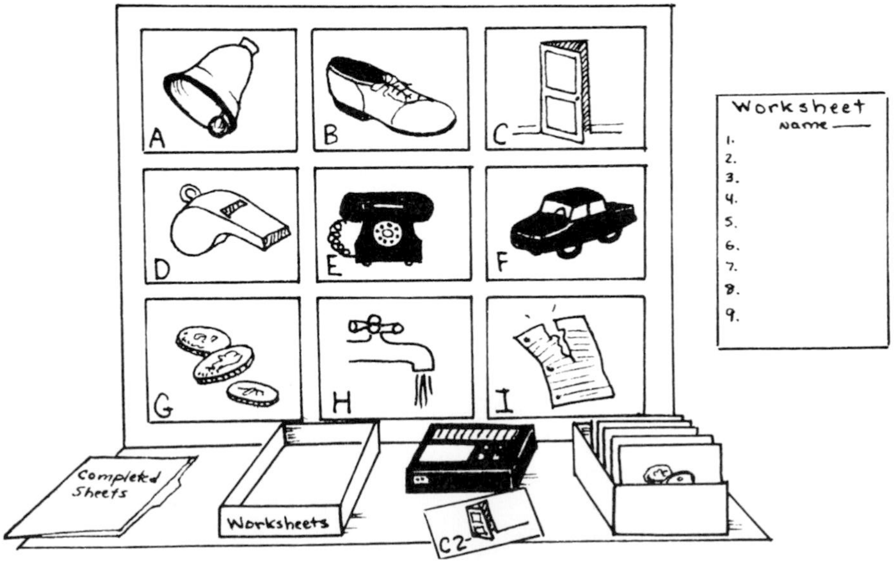

A
B
C
D
E
F
G
H
I
Worksheet
Name
1.
2.
3.
4.
5.
6.
7.
8.
9.
Completed Sheets
Worksheets
C2

Cunningham, P. 1982. "Improving Listening and Reading Comprehension," *Reading Teacher, 35,* pp. 486–488.
Gerard, H. 1983. "Listen Up: History Lives—and Talks—in Your Town," *Learning, 12*(3), pp. 106–108.
Janiak, R. 1983. "Listening/Reading: An Effective Learning Combination," *Academic Therapy, 19,* pp. 205–211.
McMahon, M. 1983. "Development of Reading-While-Listening Skills in the Primary Grades," *Reading Research Quarterly, 19,* pp. 38–52.
Mumford, S. 1983. *Conversation Pieces: Exercises in Elementary Listening Comprehension.* Elmsford, NY: Tergamon Press.
Wassermann, S. 1982. "Interacting With Your Students: Learning to Hear Yourself," *Childhood Education, 58,* pp. 281–286.
Wolff, F. et al. 1983. *Perceptive Listening.* NY: Holt, Rinehart & Winston.

Chapter Notes

1. S. W. Lundsteen, *Listening: Its Impact at All Levels on Reading and the Other Language Arts* (Urbana, Illinois: National Council of Teachers of English, 1979), p. 1.
2. V. Froese, "Hearing/Listening/Auding: Auditory Processing," in *Research in the Language Arts,* V. Froese and S. B. Straw, eds. (Baltimore: University Park Press, 1981), pp. 132–135.
3. California State Department of Education, *Reading Framework for California Public Schools, K–12* (Sacramento: The Department 1980), p. 7.

INSTRUCTIONAL OBJECTIVE: The students should be able to identify a sequence of sounds by listening carefully to a prepared tape.

MATERIALS: Tape recorder, tape of sounds, pictures of objects, two small boxes, paper, pencil, a folder for worksheets.

DIRECTIONS:
Teacher: Instruct children on how to use the tape recorder. (If listening headset centers are used, direct the children to put on earphones, then turn on the tape recorder.)

Student:

1. Follow the directions on the tape.
2. Turn the tape on. The tape will say the following: Listen carefully to the following instructions. Take a worksheet from the blue box. It is numbered one through nine. As you hear the following sounds, write the letter that goes with the picture of the object that made the sound you hear. Take your time.
3. There will be 30 seconds between each sound. Each sound will be repeated again very quickly.
4. Now check your answers with the cards in the yellow box.
5. When you are finished, please turn off the recorder and put your answers in the folder.

KEY

Order of Sounds

1. whistle
2. door slamming
3. change jingling
4. water running
5. car motor
6. phone ringing
7. bell
8. paper tearing
9. shoe shuffling

EVALUATION: Have the students exchange papers with a classmate and check their answers.

Source: From PATHWAYS TO IMAGINATION by Angela S. Reeke and James L. Laffey, © 1979 by Scott, Foresman & Company. Reprinted by permission.

4. P. D. Pearson and L. Fielding, "Research Update: Listening Comprehension," *Language Arts,* 1982, *59,* p. 624.
5. J. D. Stammer, "Target: The Basics of Listening," *Language Arts,* 1977, *54,* pp. 661–664.
6. R. L. Lemons and S. C. Moore, "The Effects of Training in Listening on the Development of Reading Skills," *Reading Improvement,* 1982, *19,* pp. 212–216); S. M. Hoffman, *The Effect of a Listening Skills Program on the Reading Comprehension of Fourth Grade Students* (Unpublished doctoral dissertation, Walden University, 1978); M. B. Tinzmann and G. R. Thompson, *A Comparison of Listening and Reading Cloze Procedures and a Standardized Reading Achievement Test,* ERIC Document Reproduction Service No. ED 162 249 (1977); E. K. Haugh, *Reading Versus Listening: Modes of Presentation of a First Grade Reading Test,* ERIC Document Reproduction Service No. ED 172 157 (1979); A. Hildyard, *On the Bias of Oral and Written Language in the Drawing of Inferences on Text* (Ontario: Ontario Institute for Studies in Education, 1978); and T. G. Sticht et al., *Auding and Reading: A Developmental Model,* ERIC Document Reproduction Service No. ED 097 641 (1974).
7. Pearson and Fielding, *Research Update,* p. 625.
8. J. M. Kean, "Listening," in *Encyclopedia of Educational Research,* H. Mitzel, ed. (New York: Macmillan, 1982), p. 1102.
9. S. S. Weaver and W. L. Rutherford, "A Hierarchy of Listening Skills," *Elementary English,* 1974, *51,* pp. 1146–1150.
10. H. S. Wetstone and Z. B. Friedlander, "The Effect of Live TV, and Audio Story Narration on Primary Grade Children's Listening Comprehension," *Journal of Educational Research,* 1974, *68,* pp. 32–35.
11. M. Martin, "Listening in Review," in *Classroom-Relevant Research in the Language Arts,* H. G. Shane and J. Walden, eds. (Washington, D.C.: Association for Supervision and Curriculum Development, 1978); and M. Berry and R. Erickson, "Speaking Rate: Effects on Children's Comprehension of Normal Speech," *Journal of Speech and Hearing Research,* 1973, *16,* pp. 367–374.
12. I. Ramsey, "A Comparison of First Grade Negro Dialect Speaker's Comprehension of Standard English and Negro Dialect," *Elementary English,* 1972, *49,* pp. 688–696; and T. Frentz, "Children's Comprehension of Standard and Negro Nonstandard English Sentences," *Speech Monographs,* 1971, *38,* pp. 489–496.
13. G. Larson and B. Petersen, "Does Noise Limit the Learning of Young Listeners?" *Elementary School Journal,* 1978, *78,* pp. 264–265.
14. C. G. Fisher and K. Brooks, "Teachers' Stereotypes of Children Who Wear Hearing Aids," *Language, Speech, and Hearing Services in Schools,* 1981, *12,* pp. 139–144.
15. T. G. Devine, *Listening Skills Schoolwide: Activities and Programs* (Urbana, Illinois: National Council of Teachers of English, 1982), p. 19.
16. J. E. Cook, "A Study in Critical Listening Using Eight- to Ten-Year-Olds in an Analysis of Commercial Propaganda Emanating from Television," *Dissertation Abstracts International,* 1973, *33,* pp. 3146A–3147A.
17. P. Backlund, et al., "Recommendations for Assessing Speaking and Listening Skills," *Communication Education,* 1982, *31,* pp. 9–17.
18. D. L. Rubin et al., "Review and Critique of Procedures for Assessing Speaking and Listening Skills among Preschool through Grade Twelve Students," *Communication Education,* 1982, *31,* pp. 285–304.

Speaking 5

Objectives

The three major components of the speech curriculum in today's elementary school

The most important domain of the language arts

Puppets that children can make

Communicative disorders that teachers should refer to clinicians

Discover As You Read This Chapter If*

1. Oral language proficiency is a predictor of school readiness.
2. Elementary school girls are linguistically superior to boys at comparable ages.
3. Children's speech characteristics do not affect the expectations that teachers have of elementary pupils.
4. Show-and-tell is a legitimate form of informal reporting.
5. Discussions are concerned with problem solving and critical thinking skills.
6. Interviewing is a speech art in which kindergarteners can participate.
7. Lessons involving marionettes are appropriate for elementary school language arts programs.
8. Communicative disorders are more prevalent among girls than among boys.
9. The largest proportion of articulation problems occurs among children in grades one through three.
10. About one percent of school age children suffer from stuttering.

*Answers to these true-or-false statements may be found in Appendix 6.

The child's control of the features of language proceeds along a continuum of mastering the highly predictable and productive features toward the mastering of less common forms with limited distribution. Speech skills necessary for effective oral communication must therefore be taught through a developmental process, with learning opportunities offered in varied areas of the curriculum.

Most of what children know of language when they enter school has been learned by accident because effective oral communication is not inherent. Consequently, speech habits formed in the preschool years will vary greatly with the individual child, and teachers who are cognizant of the variations will modify their programs to meet student needs.

While most elementary teachers are aware that competence in spoken language constitutes the basis for competence in reading and in written composition, kindergarten-first grade teachers particularly should reflect upon the results of one recent study in Texas of 74 five- and six-year-old preschoolers.[1] Conclusions of standardized tests individually administered to the group of white, black, Mexican-American, and Asian children showed that it is *intelligence and not oral language proficiency which is a predictor of school readiness.*

Other investigations completed during the past decade among pupils from kindergarten through grade seven show that children in each succeeding year speak more words, produce more communication units, and increase the average number of words in those units. The fastest spurts in development of oral expression appear to occur in the time spans between kindergarten and the end of first grade and between the end of fifth grade and the end of seventh grade.

These studies in speech found no evidence of linguistic superiority of girls over boys at comparable ages. (Possibly changes in social, cultural, and educational environments have reduced differential behavior of the sexes.) There is, however, a frequently recurring pattern of boys at the extreme ends of a number of measures: boys in the high-ability group excel the girls in the same group, while the boys in the low-ability group are the least proficient of all pupils observed.

Whether these children are academically advantaged or not, their language patterns are largely established by the time they reach school age. Still every person who has contact with the children from the day they enter kindergarten influences their speaking patterns.

In turn, the children's patterns and other speech characteristics affect the expectations that teachers have of the elementary pupils. Two studies—one in the Midwest and one in Texas—involved black, white, and Mexican-American students of middle- and low-income families.[2] The investigations found that teachers tended to evaluate children's speech samples in terms of two relatively global dimensions. One was confidence-eagerness and was found to be related to a child's fluency, lack of hesitations, and tendency to participate actively in a linguistic interview. The second was labeled ethnicity-nonstandardness and was a reflection primarily of the degree of nonstandard English found in a child's speech.

Consequently, any teachers enrolling pupils whose native language or nonstandard English dialect is unfamiliar to the school must be certain that their own attitudes affect the children's progress in the classroom environment positively. They must be aware, as discussed earlier, that all dialects are fully formed language systems. They also must recognize that the speech education program developed and maintained by the school needs the active support of the home and community.

Such a comprehensive speech curriculum should incorporate three major components:

Speech arts for all children, planned by the classroom teacher in every grade in order to present applications of specific skills.

Communicative development for all children, planned by the classroom teacher in every grade in order to implement specific lessons in articulation and other skills.

Communicative remediation for deviations or disorders for the few handicapped children in every grade who suffer from mild deviations or more pronounced articulation disorders, stuttering, voice disturbances, or delayed speech development. These boys and girls require the services of a clinician who in turn relies on the follow-up support of the classroom teacher. In districts which do not employ speech clinicians, the teacher has sole responsibility for communicative remediation.

To create an effective oral language program the teacher must consider several notable factors. First, since students learn to speak by speaking, *the environment of the classroom* should resemble that of a communication center and allow pupils to translate their thoughts into words for questioning, comparing, contrasting, reporting, evaluating, and summarizing. Yet that center cannot deteriorate into a classroom of unorganized confusion where students ignore the social amenities needed for interaction. Second, *the role of the teacher* must be that of listener, facilitator, and participant in learning. Third, *the role of the student* must be an active role, whether it be in small groups, whole-class groups, or with a partner. Fourth, skills and activities using *the components of oral language* should be those emphasizing vocabulary, syntax, fluency, intonation, and articulation. Finally, language is *a communication tool* and therefore it should be used for re-presenting the meaning of experiences.[3]

Speech Arts

Learning to communicate through speech demands frequent opportunities for oral language skills. Through the speech arts program, favorable attitudes may be established by the pupils toward good speech and toward themselves as speakers. Desirable social relationships may be fostered to meet the needs of individuals and groups. Progressive speech development may be stressed through a variety of beginning and advanced kinds of speaking situations. Pleasant voices may be encouraged in order to promote an effective and natural manner. Practical standards of speech may be determined and maintained mutually by the pupils and their teacher. Realistic situations and experiences may be presented for applying speech improvement exercises.

The speech arts include primarily: giving talks, conversing, discussing, debating, following parliamentary procedure, interviewing, developing social courtesies, participating in readers theatre, and using puppets, as well as engaging in choral speaking, storytelling, and creative drama. The last three arts listed will be discussed later in Chapters Eleven and Thirteen. The other nine speech arts are presented herewith, with Table 5.1 listing instructional activities which involve each of them.

Table 5.1
Sample Instructional Activities in Elementary School Speech Arts.

Kind of Speech Art	Grade Level	Learning Activity and/or Teaching Strategy
Conversing	K-6	Six pupils participate in a (directed) conversation about children's television shows available on Saturday mornings.
Debating	5-6	Two boys and two girls debate the proposition that no four-legged pets should be allowed in apartments.
Discussing	3-6	All the pupils engage in a round-table discussion about the responsibilities involved in being left alone at home.
Following parliamentary procedure	5-6	All the students are involved in various committees that must report back to the class regarding the year-end picnic at a nearby park.
Giving directions	1-3	The child has just encountered someone from an unidentified flying object on the school playground and must direct this being to the principal's office.
Interviewing	4-6	Two students interview a neighborhood woman who weaves small rugs and sells them to a New York gift shop.
Making announcements	2-4	Two Brownie Scouts announce, completely but concisely, a forthcoming event: the annual cookie sale.
Making introductions	2-6	Michael picks a friend to be the New Boy in the Class. Then "during recess" he first introduces himself to him and later introduces the boy to other classmates.
Participating in readers theatre	3-6	One group of students adapts a script from the Aesop fable "The Miller, His Son, and the Donkey." Later, in front of an audience, other students use that script in reading their roles.
Reporting	1-3	The child informally reports to the class what the members of his or her family like to eat and don't like to eat.
Telephoning	5-6	Using a coin telephone, the child receives from the information operator the telephone number of a local television station showing a favorite series which has just been cancelled for next season.
Using puppets	K-3	Three children use hand puppets to stage a play describing the downfall of Lazy Louey who refused to brush his teeth.

Talks

Oral language ability must be viewed as the most important domain of the language arts, states Klein.[4] School settings being rarely conducive to talk, however, it is up to the teacher to transform the classroom atmosphere, at least metamorphically, into a variety of settings with a variety of audiences with different genuine purposes and subjects available for potential talkers. If the teacher can accomplish this task, most of the effort to motivate talkers will be unnecessary because the environment itself will stimulate speech.

Talks center about one of five basic purposes: to inform, to move to mental and sometimes physical action, to inquire, to enjoy (which is the most wide-ranging category), or to conjoin (which is made up of language used to maintain cultural and social rituals or relationships.[5] Although several kinds of talks are included in this segment of the language arts, the majority of them fall under either of two categories: reporting or announcing/explaining/directing.

Reporting

In the lower grades there is *informal reporting.* The teacher begins by sharing with the class some anecdotes, incidents, and descriptions from his or her own life in order to extend the children's experiences. The teacher than encourages the pupils to report on news that they think important by helping them to understand which incidents are appropriate for sharing with the class and which are better suited for relating to him or her alone. After listening attentively to the reports the pupils share with their classmates and assisting with sequence, relevancy, and length, the teacher asks the listeners for constructive comments or questions. Also, the teacher compliments each speaker on some aspect of his or her report, calling attention to choice descriptive or action words, sentence patterns, or speech skills. The teacher explains the cues Who? Where? What? Why? When? How? and lists them on a chart. Sometimes informal reactions to particular films or television programs can be elicited, as the teacher points out qualities that make certain productions worthwhile.

In turn, the children begin to develop a sensitivity to suitable topics for informal reporting and to gain confidence in their ability to share ideas with others. In their role as listeners, they pay close attention and ask questions truly related to the reports presented. In their role as reporters, they try to remember to speak audibly, look at their audience, realize that the opening sentence must be an attention-getter, and keep to the topic.

Since children are less self-conscious when they become absorbed in *showing and telling* about an object, especially one that bears a personal significance for its owner, their oral reports are likely to be longer, livelier, and less rambling. Young pupils find it easier to share facts and experiences while they are showing objects which can be held in the hand and admired by the class—an arrowhead, a frog, or a seashell. Teachers may choose to vary this type of activity in several ways, but the basic experience remains valuable for developing body control, a sense of audience, and an ability to elaborate on a topic the speaker knows well.

A recent study of show-and-tell conditions in the kindergarten concluded that a more informal setting and a decrease in the status differential between children and teachers result in increased participation on the part of the boys and girls.[6] There is also an increase in the amount of responsibility on the part of the children for structuring the flow of sharing time.

Primary teachers can encourage informal reporting by sharing with the class some anecdotes and objects from their own travels. (Photo courtesy of Jon Jacobson.)

Although some districts feel that by the middle of first grade, most children have outgrown the need for holding an object as a supportive measure, there are other schools where seventh graders still show-and-tell, though on a more sophisticated level. Students in one New Jersey school, for example, are invited to select an afternoon to "demonstrate and elaborate," using multimedia aids if they wish. Such talks are generally made up of two parts: first, the informal showing of the photographs, lucky coins, birds' nests or other objects; and then, a report on close-up photography, superstitions, nest-building and feeding habits of different birds, or some other topic closely allied to the object presented.[7]

Planned or *formal reporting* is common in the intermediate grades where students are taught to organize, outline, and use reference materials. Besides being a good listening exercise for the audience, such reporting provides an opportunity to build on skills in the selection and collection of material and the organization and presentation of the report. The children can be shown how to delimit the scope of their talks and how to choose pertinent material quickly by using the index and by scanning and skimming. They can learn to take notes relevant to the major ideas, to keep a record of the books used, and to organize their material into a logical order by making an outline of the main points to be stressed. Finally, class members can be shown how to give reports extemporaneously without obvious reference to their papers. Some children may wish to use visual aids to enhance their presentations.

Topics for talks may be assigned by the teacher or determined by the children in cooperation with their teacher. The range of topics suitable for reporting include weather reports, school news, committee reports, and student council reports. Special subject reports for social studies, science, or current events could focus on the sport of hang gliding, on plants and music, on drinking water from the sea, or on the black widow spider.

Announcing-Explaining-Directing

The skills and abilities necessary for making announcements and for giving directions and explanations are similar to those in reporting. The verbal message should be brief, exact, and complete, answering the questions Who? What? When? Where? and sometimes How? and Why? It should be arranged in suitable order and presented enthusiastically so that listeners will become convinced that the matter is worthy of their time and attention.

Announcements may be made about the safety patrol, community events, ball games, scout meetings, lost-and-found articles, and exhibitions. In schools which have public-address systems, the students can make announcements about the PTA meeting. In classrooms they can use puppets to announce a forthcoming classroom drama. Boys and girls can listen to commercial television or radio and list the many kinds of announcements heard in one hour. Their teacher can invite a local anchorperson to talk to the class about his or her job and the preparations necessary before going on the air. The teacher and the children can tape a series of announcements and then play back the material in order to evaluate it in terms of sufficiency and relevancy of information.

Explanations may be offered about a variety of topics ranging from the operation of a battery-operated toy to the passage of vessels through a canal. Children may give *directions* for playing handball, for building bird houses, for setting up experiments, and for planting radish seeds. Sometimes, however, talks giving directions are really *speeches of demonstration,* useful for elementary school classes because there is a visible crutch to supply meaning to the listeners if and when the speaker stops momentarily. Since demonstrations involve processes, they reinforce the need for orderly sequence. Pupils often use them in social studies or science.

Evaluation of Talks

The teacher can evaluate the class progress in giving talks by asking these questions about the pupils:

- Are they becoming better able to discriminate between significant and insignificant information in planning their talks?
- Are they describing details more accurately?
- Are they developing the habit of observing sequence?
- Are they learning to face an audience with reasonable confidence and to speak up clearly?
- Are they incorporating properly the use of visuals in their presentations?

Conversation and Dialogue

In some of the current language arts texts for both primary and intermediate grades *conversation* is included as a speech activity. Conversation is an informal and spontaneous experience where the stress is primarily on the development of social skills. It contributes to the child's ability to make friends, to acquire self-confidence, and to speak easily and well. Conversation may be stimulated by sharing such uncommon experiences as hiking in the mountains, riding in the desert, visiting a national park, and exploring a cave. It also develops from ordinary activities that pupils can recall, including washing the dog, shopping for new clothes, watching a ball game, and playing a musical instrument.

These kindergarten children have yet another opportunity to enjoy an informal dialogue. (Photo courtesy of Jean-Claude Lejeune.)

To encourage conversation the teacher again has the responsibility to create the proper environment. It must be stimulating and ever-changing. At the same time, however, the teacher must also provide a relaxed classroom atmosphere with wholesome teacher-pupil and pupil-pupil relationships that make every child feel secure and accepted.

Social conversations can take place during free periods or during ongoing activities in the classroom or on the playground. A small group of children may assemble around a learning center or bulletin board indoors or in the swings area or on the softball diamond outdoors. Their informal sharing of reactions in a small group makes it possible for children to respond freely, each in his or her own way. Even timid pupils are encouraged to enter into a small circle of participants.

When there are only two pupils instead of several, such a language experience can be termed a *dialogue*. Dialogue offers a combination of human closeness and immediacy of feedback that is appealing to children. Informal kinds of dialogue activity include the preparation by two pupils of a project, research assignment, or skit. More formal activity can develop questioning skills or inferences, as in the following examples from Klein:

1. The first child has a specific sense experience which he must then narrate to his partner. She in turn must select the correct olfactory, visual, auditory or tactile cue from a group of three or four such cues. She questions carefully.

2. The first child is shown how to make or do something, e.g., fit a part into a machine. The second child in the meantime has been given the necessary materials for the project. Now the first child must explain to his partner how to complete or do the job with the materials provided.[8]

One research study about children's conversation examined the verbal interactions among boys and girls assigned to multiage rather than single-age classrooms.[9] It concluded that conversation is affected by the number of ages in that one classroom. When *three* ages are combined, the older children tend to dominate the conversation directed to other boys and girls in the classroom, whether the ages of the children are three-four-five, six-seven-eight, or nine-ten-eleven. While interaction within each age group is high, interaction between groups is low, and only the pupils of the middle age tend to interact randomly across age groups. On the other hand, in multiage classrooms composed of children from *two* age groups (six-seven, eight-nine, nine-ten), children from each of the two-age groups initiate conversation randomly across groups. In summary, then, grouping children of different ages together in one class can result in verbal interaction across age groups, but it is not likely to occur if children of three ages are grouped together.

Evaluation of Conversations

After some conversational experiences the children, with the help of their teacher, could ask themselves:

- Was our subject an interesting one? Did we keep to the subject?
- Were we careful listeners? How did we show we were interested in our classmates' ideas?
- Did everyone in our group have a turn to talk? If someone didn't have a turn, how can we invite him or her to talk the next time?
- Could we hear each speaker?
- Did someone use an "unusual" word in today's conversation?
- Since conversations often include something that is said only for fun, was anything said that made us smile or chuckle?

Discussion

Like conversation, discussion uses oral language in a small-group setting. Unlike conversation, however, its purpose concerns problem solving, critical thinking, and decision making. Sticking to the topic is a critical quality of a good discussion for the goal is to reach a conclusion. Conversations, on the other hand, generally meander from topic to topic, rarely probing for any indepth coverage or final resolution. Sample textbook exercises in discussion skills are shown in Figure 5.1.

The stress in discussion is on leadership skills, and in this regard, Wilcox's work with fifth and sixth graders from a low-income area is helpful.[10] She studied the participation of students in classroom discussion under three different conditions: leadership by the teacher, leadership by an untrained student, and leadership by a student who had been given training on how to encourage active participation on the part of all the group members. Six classes were involved and the analysis of 45 discussion sessions showed that group members led by students had a significantly higher rate of participation than the group members led by

Figure 5.1.
Discussion
Exercises.

Part 2 Roles in a Group Discussion

Leading a Discussion

It is usually helpful for someone involved in a discussion to serve as its leader or chairperson. Below are some suggestions that will help you lead a discussion in an organized way.

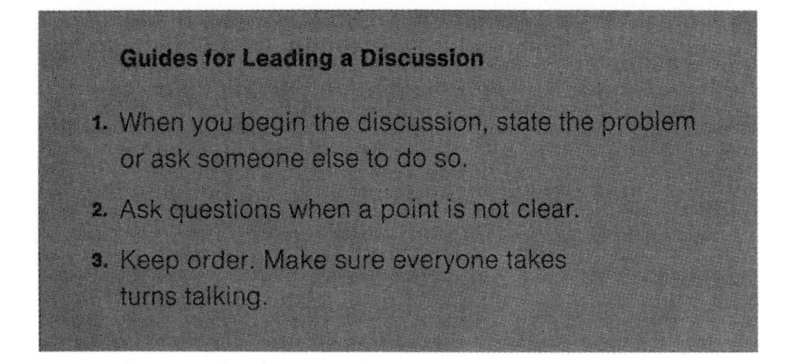
Guides for Leading a Discussion

1. When you begin the discussion, state the problem or ask someone else to do so.
2. Ask questions when a point is not clear.
3. Keep order. Make sure everyone takes turns talking.

The person who leads the group should be a helper and a guide. In the best discussions, the leader is well-informed and organized. He or she keeps the discussion moving forward.

Participating in a Discussion

When a group of people tries to solve a problem, everyone should work together. If you do not speak up, no one will know what you think or how you feel about the problem. As a responsible member of a group, always try to add something new or to ask a question.

You are always free to say what you think. However, you must also listen to others and respond to what they say. Group discussion helps you learn to think in an orderly way. It also teaches you to talk reasonably with other people in order to solve a common problem.

teachers. Also, the groups led by trained students displayed a different kind of participation (with more divergent and analytic acts) than groups led by teachers.

The kinds of topics most appropriate for beginning discussion call for listing or enumeration ("How many different ways does an animal get food?" or "How can you tell what will cost a dollar and what will cost a dime?") which in turn leads to comparison topics by making the category either one of similarities or one of differences ("In what ways are cars and airplanes alike?" or "What are

Guides for Participating in a Discussion

1. Be informed. Be sure you have done any necessary reading and research.
2. Stay on the subject.
3. Ask questions:
   a. To clarify a point
   b. To get information
   c. To help the discussion move forward
4. Listen to others.
5. Always be polite, especially when you disagree.

Exercises **Talking in Groups**

A. Pretend that a scout troop wants to collect old newspapers and glass from the neighborhood. The group discusses this problem: How should the troop organize for picking up the papers and glass? During the discussion, the following comments are made. Which comments move the discussion forward? Which seem out of place? Explain your answers.

a. I think we should collect the papers and glass on Saturday morning.

b. What are we going to do with the money we get at the recycling center?

c. I read that colored glass should be separated from clear glass.

d. Old newspapers are a fire hazard.

e. My sister cut her hand on broken glass and had five stitches.

the differences between dogs and cats?"). A third kind of topic calls for chronology—planning an action or telling how something is made ("How can John get his bicycle back?" "How will we raise money to buy a record player for the classroom?" or "How should we go about building a miniature mission?").

One practical aspect for promoting good discussions involves seating arrangements. Greater and more effective interaction is promoted by face-to-face grouping patterns. There are both single-circle and double-circle arrangements.

The *large single circle* of participants guided by a teacher or student leader often promotes one, two, or more *small single-circle spin-off groups*. These small groups meet for special interests or needs and later share their results with the large parent group. The *double-circle* or fishbowl arrangement involves an outer circle of listeners and an inner circle of talkers. Sometimes a variation of this pattern occurs when one or two empty chairs are added to the inner circle, thereby permitting one or two listeners to join the discussion briefly in order to raise a question or answer a query.

Other forms of discussion procedure include the round-table discussion, the panel discussion, and the buzz group. The *round-table discussion* generally involves between three and eight pupils. There is a moderator who guides the group, introduces the members, presents the problem (e.g., Eliminating Playground Litter), and keeps the discussion moving. It can be used in the middle and upper grades by having one group discuss a problem before the rest of the class or by dividing the class into several small discussion groups that function without an audience.

The *panel discussion* is much like the round-table discussion but there are also some important differences. First, the procedure is more formal, usually opening with a short statement by each discussant. Second, there is a greater responsibility on the part of the panel members to prepare themselves, for each panelist is considered to be a knowledgeable "expert" on the topic (e.g., Nominating and Electing the Vice-President of the United States). Finally, panels are more audience-oriented than round tables with some provision being made for questions or participation by the observers at the end of the panel's presentation.

Buzz groups solicit suggestions, reactions, or comments to problems informally. There may or may not be leaders designated and conclusions reached. Still they are helpful in clarifying ideas and getting pupils to participate who might otherwise be reluctant or fearful. Since such brainstorming can readily get out of hand, however, standards must be established or reviewed before each buzz session.

Evaluation of Discussion

Following a discussion the teacher and class might find it useful to evaluate the participants and the leader separately:

Rating Scale

Did the discussion leader—

1. State the problem or question correctly and in a manner that the class members could understand?
2. Summarize important points brought out along the way?
3. Skillfully keep the discussion progressing?
4. Give a good summary and conclusion at the end of the discussion session?

Did each participant—

1. Understand the problem and keep in mind the purpose of the discussion?
2. Contribute his or her share of information and consider contrary ideas?
3. Listen attentively and critically?
4. Have an acceptable attitude toward suggestions?

The children could also evaluate their own roles by asking themselves silently:

- Did I participate today?
- Did I participate too much?
- How did I treat my classmates whose ideas differed from mine?
- Did I encourage someone who is very shy to add his or her ideas to the discussion? How?
- Was I able to ask questions which helped others to think?
- Did I make my point promptly?[11]

Debating

Debating has been successfully used with intermediate children who have been given opportunities to develop reasoning skills. It provides them with basic experience in democratic procedure and teaches them that more than one solution of an issue may be both possible and sound.

Debate is the presentation of arguments between two teams (often consisting of two members each) who represent positions in opposition to each other on a single subject or *proposition.* That issue or proposition is stated briefly and affirmatively; for example, Students shall be allowed to buy candy in the school cafeteria. The affirmative team supports the proposition while the negative team attacks it.

Beginning level exercises for this area of speech arts would include expansions of decision-making assignments, such as having each child name something appropriate to wear in certain situations and then offer reasons for that selection.[12] Intermediate level exercises would involve more advance preparation and could include, for example, having boys or girls give accounts of historical events together with explanations of why those events occurred. Advanced level exercises demand the presentation of one viewpoint with adequate organization of that position, such as having each student gather facts about a possible vacation choice and then give a speech on whether or not that is indeed an ideal selection.

In a classic debate the constructive speeches by both sides appear first, followed by the rebuttal speeches by both sides which attack the opposing arguments. The order for four debaters, for example, would be as follows:

1. first affirmative—constructive speech
2. first negative—constructive speech
3. second affirmative—constructive speech
4. second negative—constructive speech
5. first negative—rebuttal speech
6. first affirmative—rebuttal speech
7. second negative—rebuttal speech
8. second affirmative—rebuttal speech

In this manner the affirmative team speaks first and last, and each debater presents one constructive speech, prepared in advance, as well as one rebuttal speech. The latter is more of an impromptu address, in which the speaker differs with the arguments and information of the opposing side while defending the arguments and information of his or her side.

The debate has a chairperson to introduce the topic and the team members to the audience, a timekeeper (elementary debates average thirty minutes), and judges to determine which side debated best and so won the debate. Often the judges include all the members of the class who are not debating.

Evaluation of Debating

Elementary school debates can be informally evaluated by asking:

- Was the proposition a significant issue?
- Were the constructive speeches carefully prepared?
- Could all the speakers be heard?
- Was sufficient time available for the contest?
- Was the judgment fairly determined?

Following Parliamentary Procedure

Parliamentary procedure is used universally wherever organized groups exist in order to help them carry on activities in an efficient and democratic manner. Like several other speech activities, parliamentary procedure is learned best by participation, and the elementary school is an ideal place to begin to practice the proper way to conduct a meeting. Activities that call for group decisions and require a presiding officer should be conducted within the framework of parliamentary procedure. Adaptation and informal use of many of the procedures in *Robert's Rules of Order Newly Revised* can be appreciated by pupils as early as the fifth grade, and some can be taught or incorporated as early as third grade. Even a first grader can be taught to raise his or her hand and not speak until recognized by the teacher.

The purposes of parliamentary procedures are fivefold.[13] First, rules of order are meant to keep order where commotion and disorder are likely to occur. Second, rules of order are meant to keep things in proper sequence; sometimes known as rules of preference, they are also known as rules of precedence. Third, parliamentary procedure is intended to either delay or expedite action, depending upon the wishes of the group. Fourth, parliamentary procedure is designed so that the majority, sooner or later, will always win if there is a vote. Finally, parliamentary procedure protects the rights of the minority, and the chief right of the minority is that it might someday become the majority.

In every grade the parliamentarian is the classroom teacher. Both the children and the parliamentarian must become familiar with five segments of procedure: *motions* ("I move that our class visit the Museum of Natural History to see the dinosaur exhibit."); *resolutions* ("Resolved that we thank the room parents for the Halloween party they gave us."); *amendments* ("I move to amend the motion about visiting the Museum of Natural History by adding the words 'on Saturday, March 14.' "); referral to *committees* problem topics that arise during class meeting ("I move to refer the motion about visiting the Museum of Natural History to a committee of three pupils appointed by our chairperson. I believe the committee should tell us its recommendation by Friday afternoon."); and *voting* on either an idea or a motion ("Would someone make a motion about how many classes we should invite to see our Christmas program?"). The sixth segment of parliamentary procedure—*the table of precedence of motions*—need only be understood in the elementary school by the parliamentarian.

When an intermediate teacher believes that students are ready to be organized as a club, he or she may act as chairperson until the club or class president has been elected. The president then asks for nominations for the remaining officers. After nominations have been closed, voting is done by the raising of hands or the marking of ballots. Later, after several meetings have been held, the officers and the other students in the room will probably conclude that much time could be saved if standard parliamentary procedures were used in conducting the meetings. It is then that the teacher quietly introduces some of these rules of order:

> Calling the meeting to order: "The meeting of the ____________ class (or club) will please come to order."
>
> Reading of the minutes: "Will the secretary please read the minutes of the last meeting?"
>
> Approving or correcting the minutes: "Are there any corrections or additions?"
>
> Announcing the result: "The minutes are approved as read." (or) "The minutes are approved as corrected."
>
> Asking for reports of committees: "We will now have a report of the ____________ committee."
>
> Approving reports of committees: "Is there any discussion of the report?" and "The report is accepted."
>
> Asking for announcements: "Are there any announcements to be made at this time?"
>
> Asking about unfinished business: "Is there any unfinished business?"
>
> Asking about new business: "Is there any new business to be brought up?"
>
> Turning the program over to the program chairperson: "I shall now turn the meeting over to the program chairperson."
>
> Ending the meeting: "If there is no further business, the meeting stands adjourned." Usually the chairperson ends the meeting but during the meeting any member can make a motion to adjourn at any time (provided the motion does not interrupt another speaker). Once the motion has been seconded, the chairperson immediately calls for a vote.

Evaluation of Club Meetings

The teacher-parliamentarian will note the pupils' gradual development in the areas of social skills and speech skills. Critical points from both of these skills are incorporated into the criteria which children typically formulate—with the help of their teacher—for evaluating club meetings:

- Are we following the rules of parliamentary procedure?
- Are the meetings worthwhile? Do they move smoothly?
- Are members courteous to one another? Do they show respect to the officers?
- Do members use well-planned sentences when presenting items of business? Do they speak convincingly?
- Are the club activities run by a minority or majority of the members?

Interviewing

Since the interview is one of the principal methods employed in obtaining first-hand information, the ability to conduct interviews should be a speech activity presented to children from their kindergarten year through the sixth grade.

Cowe distinguishes between informal and formal interviewing, explaining that the latter involves preplanning and the formulation of questions in advance by the group or individual pupil.[14] She describes a kindergarten child who brought some wooden animals to show her classmates during the sharing period. The girl's presentation became more lucid as her friends *informally interviewed* her, inquiring casually (one at a time) about the origin, cost, and production of the animals. On the other hand, the anticipated visit to the kindergarten class by a room mother familiar with the Japanese New Year prompted a different and more formal sort of questioning. Queries developed by the group were first recorded on the chalkboard by the teacher and then copied by her on separate sheets of paper. Once each sheet had been distributed to the boy or girl who had developed the question, the interview began. Each child read his or her question independently or with some assistance and the resource visitor responded. A total of ten questions and answers comprised the *formal interview.*

Young pupils can also use dramatic play for interviews between a child and a parent, a child and a teacher, and a child and the school principal. Later, after they have all interviewed each other, primary pupils can go out in small teams with a list of prepared questions to use in interviewing the media specialist, the cafeteria manager, the custodian, and other school workers. Their teacher may wish to help them develop another set of questions before inviting a police officer, fire fighter, or other community worker to visit the classroom for an interview. Slowly, the teacher and the children will begin to use the tape recorder as they conduct interviews.

Older classes can set up interviewing criteria and techniques and list these on charts. The pupils can interview foreign exchange students as well as parents or teachers who have recently visited other countries. Some of them can interview classroom committees that are preparing to report on a science project, or they can role play in social studies imaginary interviews between such personages as Sacagawea and Meriwether Lewis or William Clark. They can interview the principal for the school paper. They can dramatize a "Meet the Press" type of interview or conduct telephone interviews with persons in charge of local places of historical interest. Gradually they will become adept at using the tape recorder for self-evaluation of interviewing techniques.

Several observations have been made regarding the effects of recent interviewing programs conducted in several Georgia schools in both the primary and middle grades.[15] First, bringing outside guests (such as motorcycle officers and airline pilots) into the classroom increases interest in listening, speaking, writing, and reading. It releases a drive to communicate as children assume language roles all too often allowed only to adults. Second, students enjoy being in control as active participants, and in some instances they are able to abandon earlier images of themselves as school failures. Third, interviewing unifies the communicative process as listening/speaking leads naturally to writing and then to reading. Finally, when children become interested in their topics, they write more and use more sophisticated and specialized vocabulary.

After a practice or actual interview conducted in class, the teacher and children should ask each other:

Evaluation of Interviewing

- Did the interviewer maintain a natural, easy posture?
- Was his or her voice audible?
- Did the interviewer get the information he or she wanted?
- Was the interviewer courteous?
- Did the interviewee help the interviewer?
- Was the interviewee in a hurry?
- Was the interview concluded properly?

Developing Social Courtesies

The fundamentals of social conventions should be initially presented in the primary grades and then amplified in the intermediate grades. Telephone etiquette, informal introductions, proper table manners, and politeness toward others should be stressed early in the child's school life. Since most social conventions are accompanied by polite speech, teaching the proper conduct in a variety of situations is a responsibility of the language arts program.

Merely knowing what they are to do without experiencing a sufficient number of occasions to practice the social behaviors tends to make pupils self-conscious rather than secure. Consequently, opportunities to let the children use the newly learned courtesies must be furnished routinely. Confidence and social understandings grow best through realistic social experiences throughout the school year at every grade level.

The critical factor in the program is the teacher because courtesy is indeed contagious. The climate that the teacher creates in the classroom must be accepting and encouraging, helping the pupils to learn the pleasant and polite thing to do. Social behavior is learned chiefly by imitation. Knowledge about everyday courtesies contributes to the children's sense of security and orderliness.

Planned lessons about correct social behavior and thoughtfulness toward others will hopefully elicit the following generalizations:

- Social courtesies are genuine expressions of respect and regard for other persons.
- Basic good manners provide the individual with poise and personal satisfaction.
- The customs of good manners vary from place to place and change from time to time.
- Basic good manners depend upon honesty, tact, and common sense.

Social Skills and Attitudes

Included in this segment of speech activities is the development of courtesy in the classroom, courtesy in the school, and courtesy in the community. The first involves accepting personal responsibility for the completion of certain tasks and showing consideration for fellow members by adjusting one's personal desires for the common good. It also suggests ways of working together, solving group problems, and being a proper host or guest.

The second category—courtesy in the school—teaches consideration for the rights and property of others on the playground and in the halls, auditorium, and media center. It stresses thoughtfulness of others and respect toward teachers, aides, administrators, and other staff personnel. It shows pupils how to be well mannered during assembly programs and lunch periods.

Courtesy in the community—the final group of social skills and attitudes—emphasizes awareness that good manners should be used wherever one happens to be. It teaches children to avoid conduct that might attract unfavorable attention to themselves when they are in the synagogue or church, in the neighborhood theatre, in a public restaurant, or at the local supermarket.

Numerous occasions arising naturally both inside and outside the school demand the proper use of social skills by the young child: introducing a parent to the teacher during the first parent conference of the semester; acting as room host for an open house; winning a school award and accepting congratulations quietly; apologizing to the school secretary/nurse for being late in returning a medical slip; thanking neighbors while collecting papers during a Scout drive; taking a telephone message for another family member; meeting a distant cousin who has just arrived from Australia; telephoning a friend about a homework assignment. In each of these instances, the child presumably reacts with a suitable degree of poise and courtesy.

Introductions

Of the two areas of social courtesies that are especially studied in the elementary school, the first is the making and acknowledging of introductions. Boys and girls learn to introduce themselves to a new person or a new group by giving their names and stating something about themselves. When they are introducing a newcomer to others, they should remember to say something interesting about the new person or suggest a topic of conversation.

Children learn to handle introductions through role-playing sessions, especially if both correct and exaggeratedly incorrect procedures can be observed. Tape recordings of such activities may also prove helpful for later evaluation of the greetings and conversational topics selected. Since it is not sufficient for the pupils to merely memorize the correct wording and manner for making and acknowledging introductions, they should be allowed ample practice time before the class to demonstrate such situations as:

How Mike introduces his friend, Dick Stern, to
James Thomas, a classmate
Dr. Charles Kellogg, his uncle
Kathleen Merritt, his sister

How Betty introduces her friend, Patty Ishizu, to
Celeste Vodola, a classmate
Ms. Amy Howard, her aunt
Nick Hogan, her cousin

How Joanne introduces her mother, Mrs. Johnson, to
Mr. John Miles, the principal
Mrs. Janet Cohen, her teacher
Joe Jordan, her girlfriend's brother

Older children can discuss practical criteria for making and receiving introductions. They also can prepare a chart illustrating proper techniques.

Telephoning

The second area of social courtesies suitable for study by young children is the use of the telephone. Conversing by telephone has become increasingly important in daily living, with the United States ranking first among the countries of the world served by telephone. There are approximately 160 million telephones in the country today. Although the public makes three kinds of telephone calls—local, long distance, and overseas—approximately 95 percent of the calls in the United States are local calls, which children can receive and place routinely. Pupils therefore should learn how to make and answer a telephone call, how to take messages, and why it is important to speak clearly and courteously.

To become familiar with the proper way of using the telephone, older children can be introduced to the teletrainer distributed by the local telephone company. The teletrainer is a relatively simple device, usually consisting of two telephones attached by approximately 25 feet of cord to an amplifying unit. The cord allows the phones to be passed around the room and since there are two phones, a typical conversation can take place. The amplifier permits the class to hear the conversation. The teacher has the added advantage of being able to control volume of voice with a special switch on the back of the amplifying unit as well as being able to control telephone rings, busy signals, and dial tone. The students who are speaking on either of the two telephones can hear themselves over the amplifier as well as through their individual phone units as they act out situations involving social, business, or emergency reasons for telephoning. They may call to obtain a dental appointment, to order ice cream for a class party, to wish their grandmother a happy birthday, to report a fire, or to obtain the new number of a former classmate who recently moved.

Primary children can learn to name the parts of the telephone and to recognize the dial tone, the busy signal, and the ordinary ringing sound. They can practice taking messages, learning to listen carefully for details, and repeating the message before writing it down. They can be made aware that there are different instrument models. Their teacher can help them develop an illustrated chart on telephone courtesy.

Older pupils can become proficient in using a telephone directory, including the classified section. They can determine the area codes of nearby towns as well as those of the major metropolitan centers such as Chicago (312), San Francisco (415), New York (212 and 718), Boston (617), New Orleans (504), and Los Angeles (213 and 818). They can prepare a class directory of pupils' names and telephone numbers. They can learn the proper way to handle wrong numbers that have been dialed by mistake either by themselves or by someone else. They can practice making long-distance calls, either by dialing direct or with operator assistance, to places within the United States or to foreign countries. Their teacher may plan a field trip to the local telephone building or invite a resource person from the telephone company to visit the class.

Intermediate grade pupils may wish to research and discuss such questions as: (a) Do all telephones need wires? (b) How does the weather affect the work of the telephone repairperson? (c) Why is the telegraph still used when it is so convenient to make a telephone call? (d) How would a picture phone (a telephone with a TV screen) operate? (e) How does the transmission of sound in a string-and-can telephone differ from the transmission of electricity in a real telephone? (f) How does the push-button type of telephone differ from the dial type? (g) Is it merely an inconvenience to be without a telephone?

Finally, older and younger boys and girls alike must be reminded not to reveal to a stranger on the telephone that they are home alone. Any and all information concerning their parents' whereabouts also should not be mentioned. Any child who is in doubt as to how much to tell on the telephone should remember to ask only for the stranger's name, telephone number, and brief message.

Evaluation of Telephone Conversation

Pupil participation in evaluating how others use the telephone is probably the most effective way to promote good telephone usage. Among the more important criteria to be considered in rating a telephone conversation are these:

- Did both parties listen as well as talk?
- Was identification of the caller made early in the conversation?
- Was the purpose of the call achieved to the satisfaction of both parties?
- Was the conversation courteous?
- Was the message clear?
- Did both parties use pleasant speaking tones?
- Was the call concluded politely and promptly?

Participating in Readers Theatre

Readers theatre is a form of oral reading in which a group of two to twelve students presents works of literature in front of an audience. It involves no memorization and only minimal use of scenery and costumes; readers usually work from copies of printed scripts and sit atop stools of various heights. Physical movement is only suggested, and the mood is projected by means of voices, facial expressions, and restrained gestures. Suitable for readers theatre are excerpts from fiction prose, nonfiction prose, or poetry read in their original form or adapted by the children themselves.

The most important role is that of the narrator who speaks directly to the audience and sets the scene. He/she describes the situation, theme, action, and characters to further the comprehension of the literary work.

The instructional potential of this speech art includes: expansion of social awareness; cooperative work in heterogeneous groups; development of new concepts/information/vocabulary; stimulation and preparation for writing; and encouragement of below-average readers in the middle and upper grades by its lure of performance.[16]

Step-wise, readers theatre first requires the children to choose their character parts and to rehearse individually. Next there are informal practice sessions. Finally the production is staged in front of an audience or else presented on videotape or on a regular tape recording. For elementary school students, 10 to 30 minutes of playing time is most effective.

For teachers who are newcomers to this exciting combination of creative drama/reading/literature, there is a Readers Theatre Script Service in San Diego, California, which supplies both early elementary and advanced elementary packets containing cast scripts, director's prompt books, and other materials and information.

Evaluation of Participation in Readers Theatre

One means of assessing the readers theatre experience is the rating scale shown in Figure 5.2. With it the teacher can judge each pupil's response and progress.

Figure 5.2. Rating Scale of Pupil Progress in Readers Theatre Participation.

Rating Scale of Pupil Response to the Readers Theatre Project

Directions: Rate each item on the basis of 4 points for outstanding quality or performance, 3 points for better than average, 2 points for average, 1 point for inferior, and 0 for unsatisfactory. Encircle the appropriate number to indicate your rating, and enter the total of these numbers at the bottom of the sheet.

Item	Rating
1. How would you rate this pupil's enthusiasm for the project?	0 1 2 3 4
2. To what extent did this pupil seem eager to seek out and read material for possible use in the project?	0 1 2 3 4
3. To what extent did this pupil seem eager to read a part in the group script?	0 1 2 3 4
4. To what extent did this pupil contribute ideas for the creation and staging of the script?	0 1 2 3 4
5. How would you rate this pupil's receptiveness to ideas generated by his or her classmates?	0 1 2 3 4
6. How would you judge this pupil's interest in listening to the readings delivered by his or her fellow classmates?	0 1 2 3 4
7. How would you evaluate this pupil's comprehension of the literature used in the project?	0 1 2 3 4
8. To what extent did this pupil appreciate the literature used in the project?	0 1 2 3 4
9. To what extent did this pupil respond to the voice, diction, and interpretive reading exercises?	0 1 2 3 4
10. To what extent did this pupil exhibit improvement in his or her oral reading skills?	0 1 2 3 4
Total of encircled numbers:	______

Reprinted from Shirlee Sloyer READERS THEATRE, National Council of Teachers of English, 1982, p. 65. Used with permission.

Using Puppets

Acting through the medium of dolls is termed puppetry and it has existed as an entertaining and educative medium since the days of ancient China and Egypt. When the dolls are operated by strings, they are called marionettes and are suitable for manipulation by adolescents or adults. When they are worked directly by hand, the dolls are appropriate for manipulation by children and are called puppets. *Elementary school language arts programs should be concerned with lessons involving puppets only.*

At any grade level beginning puppetry should revolve around the fun of using the puppets, and a wise teacher keeps a supply of inexpensive puppets available for this purpose. Later, after the children have become acquainted with puppetry and have learned to enjoy manipulating the figures, the teacher can assist them in making their own puppets. Even kindergarten children are capable of making and manipulating simple stick and hand puppets.

The teacher should realize that puppetry is especially helpful for both shy and overaggressive pupils because puppeteers are generally hidden from their audience and so lose themselves in their characterizations. The attention of the audience is channeled away from the puppeteers to the puppets they are operating. In this fashion, the timid children lose some of their self-consciousness and the highly extroverted pupils become more restrained. Children suffering from such speech handicaps as defective articulation, stuttering, or loudness also benefit from repeated roles as puppeteers. They are motivated to practice correct speech patterns so that their puppets' conversations can be understood.

A new technique for using puppets is called *interaction puppetry* and helps children acquire problem-solving skills.[17] They learn to explore alternative solutions, identify consequences of interpersonal behaviors, develop causal thinking, and become sensitive to personal and interpersonal experiences and problems. Interaction puppetry involves one adult puppeteer behind the stage who manipulates the puppets and brings them to life and one adult facilitator who sits in front of the stage and promotes the child-puppet interaction. The boys and girls comment on what is happening and the puppets agree or disagree with the pupil responses. The adult facilitator maintains control and helps the children express their ideas.

When designing an interactional puppet skit, there are four guidelines which are both important and interrelated. First, there must be developed a "puppet family" with several puppets that have definite but different personalities (e.g., one puppet that is sad, lonely, and very frightened; another that is an aggressive extrovert). Second, a problem must be identified, such as hitting or rejection. Third, there must be a worthwhile storyline that is brief, uncomplicated, and significant. Finally, there needs to be a clarification of the types of problem-solving responses desired from the audience. A few of the numerous possible themes for interaction puppetry would include emotional development, racism, conflict, cooperation, body awareness, sensory development, and friendship.

Steps in Classroom Puppetry

In preparing to give a show, it is first necessary to select a story which is suitable for the age of the puppeteers and their audience. The story should have numerous short lines, with no more than three characters performing simultaneously. It must be fast moving to sustain the attention of the viewers.

Next, the class must choose puppets that can best tell the story and begin to imagine how each puppet should look and act. While some groups will wish to make puppets of their own at this point, others may still prefer to use puppets from the teacher's supply or to bring puppets that have been made at camp, Scout meetings, or summer recreational centers.

Then, the boys and girls should discuss the dialog and try out different tonal qualities in order to match the voices with the characters. With children who are timid or inexperienced, this step will take a longer period of time than with fluent and resourceful pupils. Written scripts, however, are not necessary.

Fourth, the puppeteers should set up the stage and manipulate the puppets. They must decide how to hold the figures and how to enter or exit from the stage. Manipulating puppets is not an easy chore and the job becomes even more difficult when lines are added to the actions.

The class is now ready to present the puppet show for a useful experience in creative action. Background scenery may be screened through the opaque projector. Sound effects, miniature portable properties, and music may also be added for variation and interest.

Finally the children and their teacher evaluate the performance. Suggestions for improving the manipulation of the puppets and the voices of the puppeteers are in order.

Suggested Stories for Puppetry

Since there should not be too many characters in a puppet show staged by or for elementary school pupils, the teacher may wish to encourage the class to write its own script. If the children should choose to do that, they have to realize that (1) all action must take place in the present; (2) each section must arise naturally from the preceding section; (3) the plot has to be brief and simple with a definite beginning, middle, and end; and (4) the characters must be faced with a problem whose solution brings conflict to the action of the play.

Sometimes, however, the teacher may find that the boys and girls prefer to adapt a literary story they have heard or read. Folk tales such as "The Story of the Three Little Pigs," "Snow White and the Seven Dwarfs," "Henny Penny," "Tom Tit Tot," "The Bremen Town Musicians," "The Three Billy Goat Gruff," "Gudbrand on the Hill-side," and "The Pancake" have simple plots that can be easily adapted for puppetry.

Other stories that lend themselves to interpretation include Lionni's *Alexander the Wind-up Mouse* (Pantheon, 1969) and *Frederick* (Pantheon, 1967), Hutchins' *Rosie's Walk* (Macmillan, 1968), Kipling's *The Elephant's Child* (Walker, 1970), and Travers' *Mary Poppins in Cherry Tree Lane* (Delacorte, 1982).

Puppets That Children Can Make

Young children are capable of constructing a large variety of puppets, and their teachers can find simple directions for making puppets in books by Laura Ross (1978), Shari Lewis (1977), Lis Paludan (1975), David Currell (1975), Louise Cochrane (1972), Goldie Chernoff (1971), Tom Tichenor (1971), and Eleanor Boylan (1970). There are four major groups of puppets that boys and girls can fashion.

There are *push or table puppets* which are the easiest of all to operate and are recommended especially for early puppet dramatization. These small figures stand on their own. When a child wants such a puppet to perform in a moment of play, he or she will lift it by its head or push it along to its next position. This frees the puppeteer to concentrate on his or her oral expression. Children can readily use watercolors or construction paper to transform into a stationary puppet such a commonplace item as a bottle, can, block of wood, paper cone, water glass, balloon, or cup. They may also bring from home two-dimensional plastic man-like or animal-like figures to help in the development of stories about favorite poems or folk tales.

Another group includes the familiar *hand puppets,* which fit somewhat like gloves. The most common variety is worked by two fingers and the thumb. The pointer finger is projected into the neck while the fourth and little fingers remain in the palm of the hand. The heads of hand puppets may be made from a wide selection of commonplace and inexpensive materials, like fruits and vegetables, stuffed socks, rubber or styrofoam balls, stuffed napkins, papier-mâché, or small boxes. After the head is finished, the operator's hand is readily covered with a piece of colored fabric about the size of a man's handkerchief; then rubber bands are slipped over the fingers to help define the arms, and the head is put into position.

Probably the simplest type of hand puppet from the standpoint of materials and construction is the paper-bag puppet. A sturdy bag such as a lunch sack is placed flat on the desk and colored with crayons. When it is time for a performance, the bag is slipped over the entire hand without making allowance for puppet arms. The children must remember, however, that the mouth opening always falls on the fold of the bag so that the underside of the flap is the inside of the mouth. For the advanced type of paper-bag puppet the head is stuffed with torn newspapers or paper toweling to create a three-dimensional effect.

Another kind of hand puppet is the finger puppet which usually slips over an individual finger. Properly cut, a finger puppet can also slip up onto the second knuckles of two fingers so that the puppet walks. Finger puppets can be made from rolled cylinders of construction paper, from toilet-paper rolls, or even from mittens. Face and body features can be added with crayons, marking pens, or other materials.

A third and large category of puppets is composed of the *stick puppets,* which consist of pictures, drawings, objects, or push puppets attached to sticks. Each is animated by moving the stick up and down or from side to side. Types of sticks include tongue depressors, yardsticks, pencils, broomsticks, dowel sticks, and narrow plywood. Hand-puppet heads may also be mounted on sticks for quick puppetry.

When a stick puppet has two sticks instead of the usual one, it is known technically as a rod puppet. The second stick or rod is attached to a jointed arm or head. Operators of such puppets must be capable of using both their hands skillfully as they simultaneously deliver their lines. Consequently, rod puppeteers are generally fifth or sixth graders.

The fourth and final group of puppets useful in the elementary curriculum comprises *shadow puppets*. An extension of rod puppets, they are distinct, flat figures that have been cut from cardboard, stiff cellophane, or tagboard and painted. They are manipulated on long rods by the players who animate them against a tightly drawn translucent screen lit from behind. The lights must be placed between the screen and the operators, and the puppets are pressed against that screen by two wire rods in order to produce well-defined shadows. Jerking or twisting the rods sets the puppets into motion.

Fifth graders in one suburban Chicago school became involved in the writing, figure-making, and staging of this type of puppet show during their "Folk Tales from Other Lands Through Shadow Theater."[18] Their teacher reported that shadow puppets enrich the reading program, provoke an interest in storytelling and creative drama, and sharpen research skills as the boys and girls become involved in preparing authentic scripts for these translucent silhouettes.

While facial expressions are obviously invisible on shadow puppets, they are critical to push, hand, and stick puppets. The teacher must therefore impress upon the students the importance of building character into the faces of the puppets they construct and decorate. Incidentally, the teacher should also stress the importance of saving all remnant pieces of items that could be used in future puppet-making projects. Such leftover bits can go into a large cardboard box for the production of so-called "junk-box puppets."

Puppet Stages

The stage and the staging for a puppet show should be as uncomplicated as possible. Elaborate preparations are beyond the scope of young children. There is a variety of temporary stages which the pupils can make quickly as well as some more permanent stages whose construction requires the assistance of parents and/or teachers.

At least four temporary stages are readily and inexpensively assembled. The first is a *table stage*. When a rectangular table is placed on its side with the top part facing the audience, a large piece of cloth is strung as a curtain around the sides and front of the stage and the puppeteers crouch behind the curtain in order to operate the puppets from below. If two tables are available, one can be turned on its side on top of the other. Then the front and sides of the bottom table can be wrapped with butcher paper or with cloth to hide the puppeteers from the audience. A bookcase or portable chalkboard properly covered also provides a good stage surface.

The second type of temporary stage is a *box stage*. A large cardboard appliance box is used and the upper half of its front is cut back so that the puppeteers can enter from the rear. The box is then painted and some type of anchor applied to prevent the box from tipping over. Should a smaller grocery carton be available, the back of the carton is completely removed and the front is cut to give the effect of a curtain drape. After the box has been painted, a table is covered with a sheet or blanket and the back edge of the carton is placed along the back edge of the table. The puppeteers then kneel behind the table and are hidden from view. Even a shoe box can become the stage for puppets of suitable size.

The *doorway stage* is a third kind of temporary stage. A single drape, sheet, or blanket is fastened to a rod or is thumbtacked across an open doorway so that it reaches the floor. It is attached at a point one inch above the heads of the puppeteers so the players can remain completely hidden, even when they stretch their arms to show their puppets. When a pair of drapes or sheets can be found, the shorter one is hung so that it falls from the top of the doorway and leaves a 20-to-30-inch opening, and the second one is hung down to the floor. The puppeteers reach up to work the figures in the opening.

A fourth stage is a *chair stage*. A board may be placed across the top of two chairs placed back to back and a blanket draped over the board. Should an overstuffed chair be available, the puppeteer can kneel on its seat and manipulate the puppets so that they are visible to an audience facing the back of the chair.

There are at least three kinds of more permanent stages that take longer to construct and are more costly to assemble. The first of these is a *wooden stage,* and some teachers like to have one wooden theatre in the room for use throughout the year. It is built of plywood or wallboard and can include curtains and floodlights as well as backdrops that are fastened to the theatre by a rod for easy changes. The height of the stage opening from the floor will depend on whether the puppeteers sit or stand as they use the figures.

Some teachers may desire a wooden stage that rests on a table. They should realize that it is possible to build a basic frame of two upright one-by-eight-inch planks, putting one plank at each end of the table and then attaching four angle brackets to each plank. The frame can even be moved to tables of different thicknesses by adjusting the angles with a screwdriver. Brown wrapping paper is taped to the edge of the table to hide the feet of the participating pupils, and the stage has both a scenic curtain and a concealing curtain.

Other arrangements evolve from a wooden box of suitable size. For instance, one of the wider sides can be removed and sawed into about half lengthwise, with one of the two pieces nailed under the box to form a shelf that extends a few inches. Then a piece of tagboard is attached to the front of the stage to give the effect of a curtain. In another instance, the bottom side can be knocked out, the box placed on its side, and stick legs nailed to each of the four corners. Finally, cloth is draped and tacked around the sticks.

A second stage is a *screen stage* which uses a three-fold screen. An opening is made into the upper part of the middle section, and the puppeteers operate their figures from a sitting position below the level of the bottom of that opening. The two side sections of the screen are perpendicular to the middle section in order to hide the puppeteers. A curtain can be drawn across the open part of the theatre.

A third stage is a lightweight *plastic-pipe stage.*[19] Sturdy and inexpensive, it can be made by the teacher (or an interested room parent) from three 20′ lengths of PVC plastic pipe (¾″ in diameter), 10 elbow fittings, 10 T fittings, 2 X fittings, ½ pint PVC adhesive, five yards of nontransparent cloth, one pair of curtains (approximately 33′ long) and a valance. The pipe pieces are cut with a hacksaw and the edges sanded. Then after a quick check to determine that all parts fit and all pieces are level and straight, the teacher can apply the adhesive to the pipe ends and slide the connective pipe pieces onto the ends of the pipe lengths. Finally the curtains are added. The theatre will measure five feet in height, four feet in width, and three feet in depth.

Properties for both the permanent and temporary stages should be few and restricted to essentials, with all other items painted on the inside of the stage or on the backdrop. The scenery should be suggestive rather than realistic, with careful attention paid to the matter of size in relation to the height of the puppets. It is paramount that the figures and not the background dominate any puppet stage.

Evaluation of Puppetry

The teacher can readily evaluate the progress of the boys and girls in using puppets by asking:

- Do the children show increasing ability in handling puppets?
- Are their overall speech patterns becoming consistent in speaking for a particular puppet?
- Can they make up adventures for an inanimate figure?
- Does the use of puppets stimulate interest in developing sentence sequence?
- Is there increasing variety and quality in creative puppet dialog?
- Are the children whose speech sounds are sometimes defective, distorted, or omitted, gaining incentive to improve their speech?

Communicative Development

The American Speech and Hearing Association has recommended that comprehensive speech-language programs be organized along a continuum. This continuum has at one end a communicative development component, has in the middle a communicative deviations component, and has at the other end a communicative disorders component. It recognizes the wide range of needs among children and attempts to accommodate each of them.

Formerly known as "speech improvement," the communicative development component is a preventive program. It recognizes that the development of verbal-auditory skills is basic to the academic achievement of all boys and girls. Such development is consequently a major objective of the language arts curriculum. In light of current educational philosophy and budgets, it is apparent that the classroom teacher is responsible for attaining that objective, although school clinicians or university clinical instructors in speech language pathology can serve as consultants in designing and implementing a language development program.[20]

The fact that children come to school knowing, with varying degrees of effectiveness, how to speak, should not mislead the teacher into believing that no instruction is needed. As a matter of fact, it is only through the disciplined correlation of the factors of language, thought, voice, and action that effective oral communication can be achieved.

Since the development of speech depends upon physical and psychological development, it is to be hoped that each child will have normal organs of speech and hearing and the security of a psychologically comfortable environment. When some pupils lack these assets, it becomes the teacher's responsibility to assist the children in making the adjustments necessary for effective speech.

Through such various speech arts as were presented earlier in this chapter, children learn the values of pleasant audible speech, clear articulation, attentive and discriminating listening, and the correct use of stress, phrasing, and intonation. The program of speech in action, however, may not provide sufficient instruction and practice in proper posture, breathing habits, and control of the speech organs. Nor may it pinpoint minor speech faults that must be corrected. Specific instruction in speech skills, therefore, is critical and constitutes that integral part of the language arts curriculum which is known as communicative development. It is concerned with building positive attitudes and attempts to meet the speaking needs of all children in the classroom.

Such a program does not require the services of a speech clinician but can be implemented successfully by the classroom teacher. Several school districts in New Jersey, for example, have reported that young children showed a marked decrease in articulation errors and displayed improved auditory discrimination as a result of a thirteen-week program of daily fifteen-minute lessons.[21] The first week was spent on generalized listening to environmental sounds and on introducing listening for a particular sound at the beginning, middle, or end of a word. The work of the remaining twelve weeks was progressive in difficulty. It was divided into two-week segments during which one particular sound was heard, identified, discriminated, and reinforced in a variety of contexts. (The six sounds studied in this fashion were *k, f, s, r, l,* and *th*). Commercially available communicative development stories and picture cards were incorporated in the lessons and given to the teachers along with the syllabus of complete lesson plans for each day of the thirteen-week period.

A sample plan covering one of the final lessons on the *k* sound ran this way:

Eighth Day: Articulation and Difficult Discrimination—Further Reinforcement

The teacher says:

1. Let me see how sharp your ears are. Do you think you all know the crowing sound of *k* now? We'll see. I'm going to say two words, like *key/tea.* Where did you hear the crowing sound of *k?* In the first *key* or in the second *tea?* Now here are some more pairs of words. Tell me where the *k* is. Is it in the first or second word? Listen to both words and then answer "first" or "second"—*call/tall, tan/can, pearl/curl, cop/top.*
2. Here are some words with *k* at the end. Listen to both words and then answer "first" or "second". . . *sick/sit, back/bat, like/light, lock/lot, oat/oak.* (Exaggerate the sounds, but no more than you have to.)
3. Who likes riddles? I'm thinking of something beginning with *k*
   . . . and it's yellow and I like to eat it on the cob (*corn*).
   . . . and it's soft, furry and says "Meow" (*kitty* or *cat*).
   . . . and it's a long orange vegetable. Rabbits like it too (*carrot*).
   . . . and we ride in it and get driven to many places (*car*).
   . . . and soup comes in it and all kinds of other foods too (*can*).

4. I'm thinking of something with a *k* in the middle
   . . . and it's something that lives at the zoo, climbs trees, and does very funny tricks (*monkey*).
   . . . and it's something I have on my coat that I put paper or money or important things into (*pocket*).
   . . . and it's orange and I make a jack-o'-lantern out of it at Halloween (*pumpkin*).
   . . . and it's something I eat for Thanksgiving dinner (*turkey*).
5. I'm thinking of something with a *k* at the end
   . . . and it's white and we drink it (*milk*).
   . . . and it's the sound a clock makes (*ticktock*).
   . . . and it's the thing we wash our hands in (*sink*).
   . . . and it's what you put on your foot before you put on your shoe (*sock*).
   . . . and it's what I am if I have to stay in bed and can't go to school (*sick*).
6. Who wants to make some riddles for us to guess? (The children will not be able to do this if they are left entirely on their own. However, if you give them one of the picture cards containing a *k* sound and let them describe the picture, it should go fairly well.)

A new dimension of interest in communicative development lessons such as this one has resulted from research studies showing significant relationships between defective articulation and auditory discrimination, and between reading retardation and auditory discrimination.

The Sounds of English: Some Problems

The sound system of English can create problems in the sequence of speech development in children with respect to six areas. The first of these is *reversals,* for a child may say *alunimum* for *aluminum* due to immaturity, inadequate learning, or cerebral damage; some of the words commonly reversed appear in Table 5.2. Another problem area is *consonant blends,* for either the nervous system or the muscular system of the child may not be sufficiently mature to master two or three consonants bound together such as *str.* While the ability to discriminate among sounds develops at a different rate in different people, an eight-year-old child who says *wabbit* for *rabbit* is showing vestiges of *baby talk,* which is another area of difficulty.

Then there is *voice pitch* which is related to general body tension, inadequate loudness, outdoor yelling, heredity of vocal apparatus, or a change of voice. There is also *voice loudness* which may involve discriminational, psychological, physical, or environmental causative factors. The final problem area is *mispronunciations* which, in part at least, may be resolved by the teacher's model pronunciation of all words and especially those found in Table 5.2.

Testing and Recording Speaking Patterns

In order to plan lessons well and use time wisely, the teacher must be cognizant of the specific speech faults that prevail among the boys and girls. The teacher can observe during several short periods of class activity the habitual patterns employed by the pupils and then record these impressions quickly and accurately with *yes* or *no* answers on individual profile sheets. Taping the activities may

Table 5.2
The 100 Most Frequently Mispronounced of the Commonly Used Words.

1. aluminum	35. gather	69. recognize
2. American	36. genuine	70. regularly
3. apron	37. geography	71. rinse
4. arctic	38. get	72. roof
5. asked	39. government	73. room
6. athlete	40. height	74. sandwich
7. battery	41. hundred	75. secretary
8. because	42. iron	76. sink
9. booths	43. Italian	77. smile
10. bury	44. keg	78. soot
11. bushel	45. larynx	79. spoil
12. can't	46. length	80. squash
13. catch	47. library	81. statistics
14. cavalry	48. Massachusetts	82. such
15. cement	49. material	83. sure
16. child	50. men	84. surprise
17. children	51. Michigan	85. ten
18. chimney	52. milk	86. tired
19. column	53. nuclear	87. tournament
20. could you	54. onion	88. towel
21. cushion	55. orange	89. tower
22. dandelion	56. our	90. veteran
23. davenport	57. particularly	91. vision
24. deaf	58. party	92. vowel
25. Detroit	59. peony	93. wash
26. diphtheria	60. percolate	94. wheelbarrow
27. eggs	61. perspiration	95. where
28. escape	62. picture	96. wiener
29. film	63. police	97. wouldn't
30. finally	64. power	98. wrestle
31. fire	65. pumpkin	99. years
32. fish	66. push	100. your
33. fists	67. put	
34. flower	68. radish	

Source: A. W. Huckleberry and E. S. Strother, SPEECH EDUCATION FOR THE ELEMENTARY TEACHER (Boston: Allyn & Bacon, Inc., 1973), p. 307.

sometimes help the teacher form conclusions in doubtful cases. Such profile sheets can be used later for referrals to speech clinicians or for consultations with parents, administrators, or other teachers. A typical profile sheet is shown in Figure 5.3.

Skills

When a school program begins with the kindergarten classes and is subsequently developed throughout the grades, the students, upon completion of the sixth grade, have the ability to *modulate their voices* to reflect feeling, mood, and meaning. They can *speak in clear and pleasing tones,* giving attention to intonation and

Profile of General Speech Faults

Child's Name ______________________ **Date** ______________________

1. Articulation and Pronunciation
   a. Does the child distort sounds? _______
   b. Does the child substitute one sound for another? _______
   c. Does the child omit sounds? _______
   d. Does the child mispronounce? _______
2. Voice
   a. Is the child's voice loud? _______
   b. Is the child's voice nasal? _______
   c. Is the child's voice hoarse? _______
   d. Is the child's voice monotonous? _______
   e. Is the child's voice inaudible? _______
   f. Is the pitch abnormally high? _______
   g. Is the pitch abnormally low? _______
3. Rate and Fluency
   a. Is the child's speech too rapid? _______
   b. Is the child's speech too slow? _______
   c. Is the child's phrasing poor? _______
   d. Is the child's speech hesitant? _______
   e. Is the child's vocabulary limited? _______
   f. Is the child able to organize his/her thoughts? _______
4. Attitude toward Speaking Situations _______
   a. Does the child enjoy speaking situations? _______
   b. Does the child apparently avoid speaking situations? _______
   c. Is the child reluctant to speak in group situations? _______
   d. Does the child participate actively? _______

Figure 5.3. Sample Profile Sheet for Recording General Speech Faults of Elementary Students.

tonal quality. They are able to *use their teeth, lips, and tongues to give precise enunciation* to beginning sounds, middle sounds, and ending sounds. Finally they can *pace their speech* in order to obtain and maintain sustained listening.

Ability to Modulate the Voice

In both the primary and the intermediate grades the ability to modulate the voice may be developed and improved through a variety of learning experiences. Younger children can dramatize stories in which the characters feel strong emotions, such as the animals in *The Three Little Pigs, The Three Billy Goats Gruff,* and *The Three Bears,* or stories that demand a variety of voices such as *Jack and the Beanstalk* and *Hansel and Gretel.* They can listen to poems such as Stevenson's "The Wind" and discuss how the refrain should sound.

Their teacher can exhibit visuals of active children and allow each pupil to select one picture as a basis for an impromptu oral composition. The teacher may also display chalkboard sentences that express happiness, surprise, or fear, such as "What a good time we had!" and "Stay away from the fire" and encourage the pupils to practice saying these sentences aloud, preferably using a tape recorder. Sometimes the teacher may read or tell a story to the class and then have the children evaluate his or her reading or telling in terms of feeling, mood, and meaning.

Older pupils can participate in choral speaking of poems with story contrast, such as Poe's "Bells," or poems with pictures or sounds, such as Bennett's "Motor Cars" or Reeves' "The Sea." Their teacher can have them recite or read statements that can show both annoyance and pleasure, such as "Who left this box here?" and "Is this for me?" Also, the teacher can encourage the children to suggest words that describe a pleasant voice, such as one that is soft or musical, as well as words that characterize an unpleasant voice, such as one that is gruff or whining. Finally, the teacher and the pupils can prepare and tell two brief stories, each ending with the same sentence but showing a different feeling; for example, "He dropped the letter into the fire."

Ability to Speak in Clear and Pleasing Tones

Young children can develop and improve the ability to speak clearly in pleasing tones through dramatic play activities planned in conjunction with a unit on The Home. They can recite or read sentences such as "It is snowing" and "Come here" with different inflections. They may listen to tapes or records of appropriate stories and orchestral selections for changes in volume and pitch. Later they can tape short selections by themselves from their basals in order to determine how to improve tonal quality.

A primary teacher can read poems to the class and discuss how intonation must change with meaning. The teacher may encourage the children to read chorally "The Three Little Kittens" as he or she points out the sounds that help make the Mother Goose rhyme a favorite with listeners. Also, the teacher can introduce the class to different kinds of bells and let the pupils imitate the bells for the purpose of distinguishing between the tone and the pitch of the telephone, the doorbell, and the fire alarm.

Children in the intermediate grades can help list criteria for pleasing speech such as "Speak slowly" and "Use the lips and tongue to make clear speech sounds." They can use a teletrainer kit that is available from the telephone company to schools at no cost in many parts of the country, and then chart standards for pleasant telephone conversations.

Their teacher can help the class participate in the oral reading of poems from books such as Smaridge's *Only Silly People Waste* (Abingdon, 1976), listening for distinct beginnings and endings of words. The teacher can ask each child to present a one-minute talk on a topic like "Noise Pollution in the School" or to spin a one-minute tale from such a beginning phrase as "One dark and rainy night . . ." Finally, the teacher and the pupils can discuss how pitch and stress are used during telecasts or broadcasts of sports events or news reports of tragedies.

Ability to Use Teeth, Lips, and Tongue for Proper Articulation

To practice proper articulation, boys and girls in kindergarten and the primary grades can recite those nursery rhymes, including "Sing a Song of Sixpence" and "Baa, Baa, Black Sheep," that feature the consonant sounds of *s, b,* and *p.* They can hold a piece of tissue paper before their mouths, trying to keep it vibrating as long as possible while they sound out certain consonant digraphs such as *sh* and *th.* They can also practice the *wh* digraph by pretending to blow out a lighted candle or asking, "Why did you whisper that there is a whale under the wharf?" The children can create and recite sentences with alliteration, such as "Paul Pipwick prefers pumpkin pie" or sentences that contain tongue twisters, such as "Many mothers make money mending mittens." Finally, with the help of their teacher, they can compile a list of word pairs that begin or end with the following letters: *d* and *t, p* and *b,* or *th* and *t.*

Pupils in the intermediate grades should continue to do oral exercises with rhyming words and tongue twisters. They can work in teams to pronounce such word pairs as *pin/pen, which/witch,* or *breathe/breed.* They can divide polysyllabic words, learning to enunciate distinctly the sequence of sounds in words like *chronological* and *arithmetical.* They can listen for the often-forgotten syllable in words like *family, geography,* or *poem.* Lastly, they can compile lists of words using the consonant sounds of *l, r,* and *z,* and the digraph *ch.*

Ability to Pace Speech

While young children are hearing and reciting tongue twisters, they can be shown how the difficulties in pronouncing and understanding the sayings increase with the tempo of the recitation. They can listen to poems with definite rhythms such as Lindsay's "The Mysterious Cat," and discuss how rhythm affects pace. They can discover by rereading some of the sections in their basals how oral pacing is related to the subject matter of a narrative.

Older boys and girls can contrast two poems such as Stevenson's "Windy Nights" and Moore's "Snowy Morning" in order to establish the relationship between mood and pacing. They can make announcements over the public address system and later play back their presentations so that they may evaluate the pace they exhibited and discuss the differences between the delivery of an excited speaker and that of a calm one. Finally, the class can take turns giving directions relevant to artificial respiration or other first aid, for example, in order to demonstrate the importance of clarity and variety of pace in instances of emergency instructions.

Self-evaluation by the teacher and by the child by means of a checklist (Figures 5.4 and 5.5) has proved worthwhile, although the teacher can also appraise the speech of each pupil from time to time (Figure 5.6).

Figure 5.4. Sample Checklist for Teacher's Self-Evaluation in Speech.

Classroom Teacher's Self-Evaluation Checklist of His or Her Role in Speech

	Always	Sometimes	Never
1. Do I provide a good speech example?	______	______	______
2. Do the children in my class feel socially and emotionally secure when they talk to each other and to me?	______	______	______
3. Do I keep records of my children in order to chart development in speech over a period of time?	______	______	______
4. Do I maintain separate standards for each group of children since I recognize their differences in readiness to learn?	______	______	______
5. Do I provide ample time for the children to hear the correct production of sounds in a variety of activities?	______	______	______
6. Do the parents know that I am working on improving children's speech, and do they understand and approve of the methods I use?	______	______	______
7. Do I consciously integrate speech activities with the rest of the school program?	______	______	______
8. Do I encourage the whole group to participate in the communicative development activity so that no one is singled out for individual correction?	______	______	______
9. Do I give praise for good speech by the children?	______	______	______
10. Do I promptly refer children with communicative disorders to the speech clinician and do I then follow his or her recommendations closely?	______	______	______

Intermediate Student's Self-Evaluation Checklist in Speech

Figure 5.5. Sample Checklist for Student's Self-Evaluation in Speech.

	Yes	No
1. Is my voice pleasant to hear?	______	______
2. Is my voice too loud or too soft?	______	______
3. Is my voice too high or too low?	______	______
4. Do I use a variety of inflections?	______	______
5. Do I speak too slowly or too fast?	______	______
6. Do I speak distinctly?	______	______
7. Do I use a varied vocabulary?	______	______
8. Do I use appropriate language for each speaking situation?	______	______
9. Do I explain myself well so others can understand my ideas?	______	______
10. Do I remember to wait for my turn to speak?	______	______

Classroom Teacher's Evaluation of Student Speech

Figure 5.6. Sample Form for Teacher's Evaluation of Student Speech.

Student's Name ______________ **Date** ______________

(The teacher should check the vocal difficulties below each speech technique that is rated *average* or *unsatisfactory.*)

Tempo Very Good ______ Average ______ Unsatisfactory ______

______ Too fast

______ Too slow

______ Unvarying, monotonous

______ Poor phrasing; irregular rhythm of speaking

______ Hesitations

Loudness Very Good ______ Average ______ Unsatisfactory ______

______ Too loud

______ Too weak

______ Lack of variety

______ Force overused as a form of emphasis

Figure 5.6 (cont.)

Pitch Very Good ______ Average ______ Unsatisfactory ______

______ General level too high

______ General level too low

______ Lack of variety

______ Fixed pattern monotonously repeated

______ Lack of relationship between pitch changes and meaning

______ Exaggerated pitch changes

Quality Very Good ______ Average ______ Unsatisfactory ______

______ Nasal

______ Hoarse

______ Breathy

______ Throaty and guttural

______ Strained and harsh

______ Flat

______ Thin and weak

Articulation Very Good ______ Average ______ Unsatisfactory ______

Consonants: ______ Slurred over or omitted

______ Specific sounds defective

Vowels: ______ Improperly formed

______ General diction careless or slovenly

A comparison of the teacher's rating with the pupil's appraisal often leads to a better understanding of exhibited weaknesses and strengths, especially when the suggestions are specific enough to point the way to growth. Generalities such as *interesting* or *good* offer little enlightenment or practical assistance. Records of evaluations should be kept up-to-date on individual cards or in separate folders in order to provide a basis for diagnosis and deliberation.

Assessment of students through observations by classroom teachers is one of the recommendations made to the Massachusetts Department of Education concerning a rating scale to assess speaking skills.[22] Teachers should observe students at least twice in a given time period (such as a semester or a year). For the sake of reliability checks, students should be rated at least once by two different teachers or at two different times by the same teacher. A second recommendation concerns the principal features of the rating scale and states that those should represent lists of delivery skills, language skills, organization skills, and skills of purpose. The third important recommendation relates to the type of situations in which that student assessment should occur. Rather than contrived situations that isolate assessment from regular classroom activities, naturalistic situations should be employed which ask the student to demand and provide straightforward information, to use survival words for coping with emergency situations, to question others' opinions, or to describe objects, experiences, and events.

Three commercial tests published in the United States for the purpose of assessing speaking skills in children all meet the significant criterion of individual administration. The first is *Circus Say and Tell* published by Addison-Wesley Publishing Company, Inc. (Reading, MA) for a target population of pre-kindergarten to grade three; the child responds to a variety of stimuli. The second is *Language Facility Test* published by the Allington Corporation (Alexandria, VA) for a normal target population of ages three to fifteen; the child makes free responses to picture stimuli.

The third instrument is the *Carrow Elicited Language Inventory* published by Learning Concepts (Austin, TX) for a target population of ages three to seven. It consists of 52 sentences, varying in length from two to ten words, which the child is asked to imitate. It requires audiotape equipment and about 10–15 minutes of administration time. Described as probably the most useful of the few productive language tests that now exist, it is geared for children from a standard English-speaking community.[23]

Communicative Remediation for Handicapped Children

A recent review of the major sources of prevalence data on communicative disorders in the United States revealed that a national study of nearly 40,000 public school students in grades 1–12 showed the presence of articulation errors, voice problems, and stuttering in 5.7 per cent of the children, as evaluated by trained examiners.[24] In each of the three categories, the prevalence was higher among males than among females. One state (New Mexico) published the results of its own survey and identified almost 8 per cent of its school-age population as being speech impaired, and that figure did not include bilingual children. Neither of these percentages includes incidence of communicative disorders among the learning disabled, physically handicapped, emotionally disturbed or mentally retarded, which would surely raise the percentages considerably. Although estimates do vary, the largest single group of handicapped children in the nation's schools, claims the United States Office of Education, are those with speech disorders.

Speech is defective, according to Van Riper, when it deviates so far from the speech of other people that it calls attention to itself, interferes with communication, or causes its possessor to be maladjusted.[25] Briefly, it is conspicuous, unintelligible, or unpleasant.

Byrne and Shervanian have developed criteria for evaluating the level of an individual's communication skill based on social acceptability:

1. Does the individual function with adequate linguistic skill in his or her own speech community? (If the answer is yes, then go on to evaluative question 2.)

2. Does the individual function with adequate linguistic skill outside his or her own speech community? (Again, if the answer is yes, go on to evaluative question 3.)
3. Are there any minor differences in the speech patterns of the individual that contribute to social differences that in turn lead to social devaluation or reduction of status? (If the answer is no, the individual's communication can be rated as adequate or possibly superior.)[26]

Should a child be unable to function linguistically in his or her own community, the chances are slight that he or she will be able to do so outside that community, such as in a school situation.

Consequently, it is important that elementary teachers be able to identify speech disorders and refer speech-handicapped children. Studies have shown that the percentage of accurate referrals tends to rise as the severity of the disorder increases. Teachers are most accurate in referring stutterers because interruptions in speech fluency and the accompanying mannerisms tend to interfere with the communication process to a greater extent than do most other speech disorders. Teachers are least accurate in referring children with voice disorders because such disorders often do not affect speech intelligibility. At least one survey reported that, overall, teachers are uncertain about the particular handicaps that clinicians handle.[27] In fact, only 58 percent of those responding felt certain they could recognize a speech/language defective child in their own classrooms.

Yet elementary teachers can be taught to identify speech defective pupils if they are given training in the use of pragmatic criteria rather than in the use of morphological-syntactic criteria.[28] Such useful referral criteria include: linguistic nonfluency, revisions, delays before responding, nonspecific vocabulary, inappropriate responses, poor topic maintenance, and the need for repetition (although the last criterion may indicate a hearing problem).

Teachers must also have a tolerant attitude toward the speech-defective children in their classrooms. If they say nothing, they are indicating that the children's speech is not noticeably objectionable. This creates the most favorable environment for the speech-handicapped pupils whose peers then accept them readily. On the other hand, the teacher who demands unusually high standards of speech behavior, with little tolerance for individual deficiencies, tends to generate reduced acceptance of the speech-defective children by their classmates.

The matter of teacher attitude toward the speech-impaired child as well as toward the speech clinician and toward the speech and language program was explored in a study of 147 teachers conducted recently.[29] It concluded that classroom teachers have a more positive attitude toward the speech clinician and the speech and language program but a somewhat less positive attitude toward the afflicted child. Furthermore, such demographic variables as teachers' age, sex, academic degree, or teaching experience have no significant correlation with the attitude expressed.

In a school district with an adequate number of speech clinicians, the elementary teacher can and should work closely with them in helping speech-handicapped children gain intelligible speech. He or she can help these pupils develop a sense of carry-over in their speech correction activities from the speech class to the regular classroom and can quietly urge the children to focus attention daily on the sound or sounds which the therapist is presenting. Through teacher-and-speech-correctionist conferences, the teacher can provide information regarding the strengths and weaknesses of the children referred from his or her classroom. Finally, the teacher can report to the clinician any progress the children are making, and together they can plan an approach for speech reeducation which will hopefully provide maximum success for the pupils.

In school districts with relatively few speech clinicians the classroom teacher includes communicative remediation in lesson plans by employing one of these practices:

1. A weekly speech period plan which sets aside a specific period of time every week for concentration on the skills of speech
2. An adaptive instruction plan which schedules remedial speech lessons during periods when other pupils are engaged in reasonably self-directed study

The elementary teacher will ordinarily encounter one or more of the four common groups of speech deficits in the classroom: disorders of articulation, voice disturbances, stuttering, and language disorders/delayed language. The teacher will want to do whatever possible to help the pupils with speech problems by assisting those with minor cases and referring those with more serious disorders to speech clinicians. Some children will, of course, have deficiencies in more than one dimension of speech.

Disorders of Articulation

Speech surveys in the public schools have indicated that most children with speech problems fall into the category of speech disorders classified as problems of articulation. As many as 80 percent of all speech problems found in the elementary classroom will concern those pupils who cannot make certain phonetic sounds either within blends with other phonetic sounds or in isolation.[30] The largest proportion of these problems occurs in the population of grades one through three, even though, by the age of five, 75 percent of the males and females produce all sounds correctly. By fifth grade, most children have acquired articulatory proficiency, according to the results of a five-year longitudinal study in Virginia of the spontaneous development of such proficiency in 60 boys and girls who had misarticulated at least one phoneme in the first grade.[31] Forty seven of the 60 children developed adequate articulation with no speech intervention, suggesting that a substantial amount of phonological maturation does occur without the intervention of speech services. For the remaining 13 children, however, school speech pathology services were desirable.

Children who have difficulty in articulation are not able to produce consistently and effortlessly the accepted sound patterns of speech. Instead, they may form some sounds poorly (making distortion errors), leave some sounds out completely (making omission errors), add sounds in either the medial or final position of words (making addition errors), or exchange one sound for another (making substitution errors), as they find that there are some sounds, such as *s, r, th, l,* and *z,* that seem to be harder to learn than others. Of the three categories, the predominant type of misarticulation—at least among primary children—is simple substitution, according to a three-year survey of Caucasian pupils in a Chicago suburb.[32]

Articulation disorders may be classified as either phonetic errors (resulting from organic malformations or malfunctions) or phonemic errors, sometimes called functional errors, for which no neurological or physiological basis seems to exist. Both types of disorders are associated with certain factors, including general language deficits, low intelligence, socioeconomic status (with interdental lisping, for example, tending to come from high socioeconomic levels but omission-type errors occurring more frequently among low socioeconomic levels), hearing loss, structural abnormalities, auditory discrimination and auditory memory, and reduced motor ability.

Representative tests of phoneme production that can determine which children need to attend a school speech clinic are:

Arizona Articulation Proficiency Scale (Western Psychological Services, Los Angeles);
Compton-Hutton Phonological Assessment (Carousel House, San Francisco);
Fisher-Logemann Test of Articulation Competence (Houghton-Mifflin, Boston);
Goldman and Fristoe's Test of Articulation (American Guidance Service, Circle Pines, MN) in filmstrip format; and
McDonald's Screening Deep Test of Articulation with Longitudinal Norms (Stanwix House, Pittsburgh).[33]

Two much more detailed instruments which determine the ability of the child to use sounds in different phonetic contexts are the *Templin-Darley Test of Articulation, 2d Ed.* (Bureau of Educational Research and Service, University of Iowa, Iowa City) and the *McDonald's Deep Test of Articulation: Picture and Sentence Forms* (Stanwix House, Pittsburgh).

Finally, the United States Department of Health and Human Services offers these suggestions to the teachers and parents of children with disorders of articulation:

1. Let speech be fun by letting the children know that you like to hear them talk and that you like to talk to them by playing games with sounds and words and by telling them stories and reading aloud to them.
2. Build up their feelings of success about speech by letting them use the few words or phrases that they have been practicing at times when the words are easy for them and by praising them for trying to talk.
3. Help them to learn new speech skills through imitation and ear training by choosing sounds or words that fit in with daily activities and by showing them how those sounds are made.

Teachers and parents alike should recall one important finding of a fifteen-year followup report of speech language-disordered children: overall, those subjects initially diagnosed as primarily articulation-disordered appear to have the best prognosis for correction of the problem.[34]

Voice Disturbances

Speech is made up of tones and noises, and, in articulation, noises are added and tones modified. Sometimes, however, the tones themselves may be defective, varying too far from the norm to be acceptable. There may be impairment of the tones, partial loss, or (rarely) complete loss. One report based on data from several surveys estimates that one to two percent of the children in the 6- to 14-year age range have voice problems, although an earlier figure covering grades 1–12 was three percent.[35] There is an age-related prevalence for vocal disorders, ranging from as high as 5.6 percent among first-graders and a low of 1.0 percent among high school seniors.

Common types of voice disturbances include loudness, faulty range and pitch, defects of quality (such as hoarseness among younger children), and voice "breaks." These are usually caused by poor physical health, hearing loss, physical anomalies (including the common cold), glandular disturbance (especially of the thyroid gland), poor habits of vocalization, personality disturbances, pubertal changes (beginning usually at age 12), poor habits of vocalization, inappropriate nasal resonance, or imitation of poor models.

The United States Department of Health and Human Services suggests that parents and teachers of children with disorders of voice: (a) refer children for medical examinations; (b) help them to relax by easing tensions and pressures in the environment; (c) give them a chance to talk without interruption so that they need not strain their voices; (d) help the children find a pitch level that is comfortable for them, changing the pitch of their own adult voices if necessary since the children may imitate them; and (e) discuss "voice rests" with a speech specialist, for the children's problems may be serious enough to require a period of silence.

Stuttering

A frequent abnormal disruption in the relative continuity or fluency of speech is known as *stuttering*. It is marked with repetitions and prolongations of syllables and sounds and by hesitancies in the utterance of syllables, sounds, and words. Sometimes there are interjections of unneeded sounds as well as associated lip, eye, or head movements. About one percent of school age children suffer from stuttering or stammering.

Although much about stuttering is yet to be documented, there are a few generalizations about this speech defect that are widely accepted. First, stuttering prevails more among boys than girls (with an average ratio of three or four to one), endures longer among boys than girls, and tends to be more severe among boys than among girls. Second, stuttering is more apt to begin when the child is in the preschool/kindergarten/primary grades than in the secondary school (with onset after the age of 10–12 being comparatively rare). Third, many boys and girls in the kindergarten and first grade who appear to be potential stutterers with hesitant, repetitious speech, never actually become stutterers (and by the third or fourth grade have normal speech production). Finally, no one stutters all the time. Stutters may be fluent when talking to themselves, to animals, or to those in a lower status position (such as younger children). They also do as well as other children in choral speaking or group singing situations.

While theories regarding the causes of stuttering are diverse and numerous, Eisenson and Ogilvie present three current points of view.[36] One school believes that stuttering is a constitutional problem with physical reasons predisposing certain individuals to stammering. Proponents of a second viewpoint consider stuttering as essentially a learned form of behavior that can befall anyone. The third and older position is that stuttering is mainly a manifestation of an underlying neurotic personality. Incidentally, in addition to the three viewpoints just listed, there are at least two others that explain stuttering as having not one but multiple origins.

Though many people have feelings of pity and embarrassment toward stutterers, current trends to mainstream handicapped children may have some positive effects on changing attitudes. One study showed that elementary school boys did not differentiate (in ranking social position) between classmates who stuttered and those who were fluent speakers.[37] The pupils were aware of the defect but simply evaluated stutterers as poorer speakers than peers who did not stutter.

The classroom teacher, in an effort to help stuttering children, should attempt to:

1. Create an environment which encourages talking.
2. Offer positive feedback.
3. Provide a selection of individualized learning activities (e.g., learning centers or student contracts).
4. Encourage participation in creative drama.
5. Help them develop realistically positive opinions of themselves.
6. Make talking enjoyable and rewarding.
7. Encourage participation in a variety of school activities.

Teachers and parents alike must understand that any environment which pressures children beyond their tolerance levels can and does contribute to speech dysfluency.

Delayed Language Development

Among some children there is an orderly sequence in learning the language code but language development is not appropriate to the chronological age of the user. These boys and girls know the rules consistent with their level of development. They are learning the grammar, for example, in proper sequence but they are doing so at a slower pace than other children in their age group. They use the proper inflections for regular plurals and regular past tense verbs, for instance, but they overgeneralize those endings to other plurals and verbs. They can also use the simple affirmative-declarative sentences with some transformations but are incapable of the advanced degree of embeddings and coordination that they should be using. While these children seem to comprehend and engage in social conversations, their deficiencies become more obvious in their written language and in their reading comprehension. They have difficulty in understanding instructional language, and become generally retarded in educational achievement.

In most districts the classroom teacher of nonexceptional children will have in his/her class one or two children who suffer from delayed language development. To assist them it has been recommended that teachers continue to:

1. Be sensitive to individual needs, providing a program that is relevant to current social, economic, and cultural patterns of speech-retarded children.
2. Create a pleasant and stimulating atmosphere in which learning can occur.
3. Offer an individually determined curriculum, incorporating the children's weaknesses and strengths.
4. Encourage the children to want to talk and to talk more clearly.
5. Teach them new sounds and then put the new sounds together to make whole words.

Incidentally, it has been observed that the chief cause of speech delay is mental retardation and that direct teaching is critically important to such speech-defective children.

Evaluation of Pupils' Progress

In the critical field of speech arts, evaluative techniques vary among the numerous facets of the skill. As a consequence, methods of evaluation have been described at the conclusion of the discussion of each facet. The reader may wish to review these techniques briefly at this point.

Discussion Questions

1. Show-and-tell should be a purposeful speech art. What guidelines might help the primary teacher who uses this activity?
2. What advantages does readers theatre have over ordinary story dramatization in the classroom? Are there any disadvantages?
3. Why is puppetry enjoyed by so many children?
4. How would you propose to resolve some of the problems created by the sound system of English during the sequence of communicative development in children?
5. In schools where there are speech clinicians, what specifically can the classroom teacher do to help boys and girls who stutter?

Suggested Projects

1. Begin a card file of common situations which involve speech arts. Arrange cards by major headings such as Interviewing.
2. Examine some of the free materials available from the telephone company. Plan a lesson incorporating their use.
3. Rewrite some of *Robert's Rules of Order Newly Revised,* and then plan a beginning lesson in parliamentary procedure for fifth graders.
4. Make a puppet that a third grader could construct and manipulate as well as an adult does. Then assemble a temporary stage and demonstrate how that puppet moves and talks.
5. Interview the speech clinician in a local school. Discover what types of communicative deviations or disorders are being encountered and what types of remedial procedures are proving to be successful.
6. Set up the learning center on speaking shown in Figure 5.7.

Figure 5.7. Language Arts Learning Center: Speaking.

TYPE OF CENTER:	**Oral Communication**	TIME:	10–20 minutes
GRADE LEVEL:	5–7	NUMBER OF STUDENTS:	1

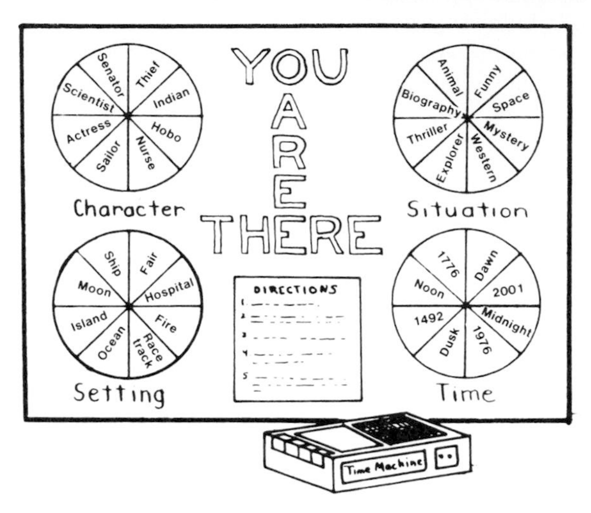

INSTRUCTIONAL OBJECTIVE: The child will imagine himself in a situation and be able to relate his experiences, problems, and surroundings.

MATERIALS: Construction paper for wheels, paste, paper clasps, spinner, and tape recorder.

DIRECTIONS:

1. Spin each of the wheels.
2. Imagine that you are that person, at that place, in that era, and in that situation. Begin with "I am. . . ."
3. What would you do? What would your problems be?
4. How would you feel different than you normally do?
5. Answer these questions and enter your own thoughts into the tape-record log of the time machine journeys.

SUGGESTED IDEAS: Students can share their stories and evaluate whether or not their classmates used their imaginations.

EVALUATION: The teacher will listen to the tape and note whether the children used their imaginations and could picture themselves in another era through words. The teacher should note the children's ability to create surroundings, solve problems, and relate their experiences.

Related Readings

Alpern, R. 1984. "Confessions of a Speech Pathologist," *Academic Therapy, 19,* pp. 297–303.

Carson, D. 1984. "The Case for Oral Language in Schooling," *Elementary School Journal, 84,* pp. 458–468.

Edwards, C. et al. 1983. "Talking With Young Children about Social Ideas," *Young Children, 39*(1), pp. 12–20.

Fleming, C. S. et al. 1983. "Puppets Put Learning Center Stage," *Learning, 11*(9), pp. 94–98.

Heath, S. 1983. "A Lot of Talk about Nothing," *Language Arts, 60,* pp. 999–1007.
Hoffman, S., and McCully, B. 1984. "Oral Language Functions in Transaction With Children's Writing," *Language Arts, 61,* pp. 41–50.
Jones, T. 1983. *Whistle-Stop Puppet Plays.* Jefferson, NC: McFarland & Company, Inc.
Russell, S. 1984. "Proceed with Caution: Implementing Communication Therapies,"*Academic Therapy, 20,* pp. 195–201.
Seiler, W. J. et al. 1984. *Communication for the Contemporary Classroom.* New York: Holt.
Wilkinson, L. C. 1984. "Peer Group Talk in Elementary School," *Language Arts, 61,* pp. 164–169.

Chapter Notes

1. R. Gray et al., "Is Proficiency in Oral Language a Predictor of Academic Success?" *Elementary School Journal,* 1980, *80,* pp. 261–268.
2. F. Williams et al., "Teachers' Evaluations of Children's Speech," *Speech Teacher,* 1971, *20,* pp. 247–254; and F. Williams, "The Psychological Correlates of Speech Characteristics: On Sounding Disadvantaged," *Journal of Speech and Hearing Research,* 1970, *13,* pp. 472–479.
3. California State Department of Education, *English Language Framework for California Public Schools* (Sacramento: The Department, 1976), pp. 23–24.
4. M. L. Klein, *Talk in the Language Arts Classroom* (Urbana, Illinois: National Council of Teachers of English, 1977), pp. 34–37.
5. M. L. Klein, "Designing a Talk Environment for the Classroom," *Language Arts,* 1979, *56,* pp. 650–651.
6. P. Lazarus and S. Homer, *Sharing Time in the Kindergarten: A Study of the Relationship between Structures and Content.* ERIC Document Reproduction Service No. ED 194 930 (1980).
7. D. Nelson, "D. and E.: Show and Tell, Grown Up," *Language Arts,* 1976, *53,* pp. 203–205.
8. Klein, *Talk,* pp. 41–44.
9. J. Way, "Verbal Interaction in Multiage Classrooms," *Elementary School Journal,* 1979, *79,* pp. 178–186.
10. M. Wilcox, "When Children Discuss: A Study of Learning in Small Groups," *Elementary School Journal,* 1976, *76,* pp. 302–309.
11. S. Fitzgerald, "Teaching Discussion Skills and Attitudes," *Language Arts,* 1975, *52,* pp. 1094–1096.
12. M. L. Willbrand and R. D. Rieke, *Teaching Oral Communication in Elementary Schools* (New York: Macmillan, 1983), pp. 162–166.
13. A. W. Huckleberry and E. S. Strother, *Speech Education for the Elementary Teacher* (Boston: Allyn & Bacon, 1973), pp. 228–229.
14. E. Cowe, "Interviewing by Young Children," *Language Arts,* 1976, *53,* pp. 32–33.
15. S. Haley-James and C. D. Hobson, "Interviewing: A Means of Encouraging the Drive to Communicate," *Language Arts,* 1980, *57,* pp. 497–502.
16. B. Busching, "Readers Theatre: An Education for Language and Life," *Language Arts,* 1981, *58,* pp. 332–335.
17. C. A. Smith, "Puppetry and Problem-Solving Skills," *Young Children,* 1979, *34*(3), pp. 4–11.
18. N. Nirgiotis, "Shadow Theater," *Childhood Education,* 1983, *59,* pp. 316–320.
19. "Produce Your Own Puppet Theater," *Better Homes and Gardens,* June 1981, p. J 16.

20. M. Pickering and P. Kaelber, "The Speech-Language Pathologist and the Classroom Teacher: A Team Approach to Language Development," *Language, Speech, and Hearing Services in Schools,* 1978, *9,* pp. 43–49.
21. A. Seidler, *Experimental Speech Improvement Program* (Glassboro, New Jersey: Glassboro Public School System, 1970), pp. 13–14.
22. P. Backlund et al., "Recommendations for Assessing Speaking and Listening Skills," *Communication Education,* 1982, *31,* pp. 12–14.
23. O. K. Buros, ed., *The Eighth Mental Measurements Yearbook,* Volume II (Highland Park, New Jersey: Gryphon Press, 1978), p. 1488.
24. J. Eisenson and M. Ogilvie, *Communicative Disorders in Children* (New York: Macmillan, 1983), pp. 16–17.
25. C. Van Riper, *Speech Correction: Principles and Methods,* 6th ed. (Englewood Cliffs, New Jersery: Prentice-Hall, 1978), p. 29.
26. M. C. Bryne and C. S. Shervanian, *Introduction to Communicative Disorders* (New York: Harper & Row, 1977), p. 5.
27. G. M. Clausen and N. Kopatic, "Teacher Attitudes and Knowledge of Remedial Speech Programs," *Language, Speech, and Hearing Services in Schools,* 1975, *6,* pp. 206–210.
28. J. Damico and J. W. Oller, Jr., "Pragmatic Versus Morphological-Syntactic Criteria for Language Referral," *Language, Speech, and Hearing Services in Schools,* 1980, *11,* pp. 85–94.
29. L. Signoretti and M. Oratio, "A Multivariate Analysis of Teachers' Attitudes toward Public School Speech Pathology Services," *Language, Speech, and Hearing Services in Schools,* 1981, *12,* pp. 178–187.
30. S. Dickson and G. Jann, "Diagnostic Principles and Procedures," in *Communication Disorders: Remedial Principles and Practices,* S. Dickson, ed. (Glenview, Illinois: Scott, Foresman, 1974), p. 25.
31. R. C. Gralley and R. J. Stoudt, Jr., "A Five-Year Longitudinal Study of Development of Articulation Proficiency in Elementary School Children," *Language, Speech, and Hearing Services in Schools,* 1977, *8,* pp. 176–180.
32. A. S. Morency, et al., "Developmental Speech Inaccuracy and Speech Therapy in the Early School Years," *Elementary School Journal,* 1970, *70,* pp. 219–224.
33. Eisenson and Ogilvie, *Communicative Disorders,* pp. 285–287.
34. R. King, et al., "In Retrospect: A Fifteen Year Follow-up Report of Speech-Language Disordered Children," *Language, Speech, and Hearing Services in Schools,* 1982, *13,* pp. 24–32.
35. J. F. Curtis, ed., *Processes and Disorders of Human Communication* (New York: Harper & Row, 1978), p. 144; and F. M. Hull and R. J. Timmons, "The National Speech and Hearing Survey: Preliminary Results," *ASHA* (Journal of the American Speech and Hearing Association), 1971, *13,* pp. 501–509.
36. Eisenson and Ogilvie, *Communicative Disorders,* pp. 383–395.
37. C. L. Woods, "Social Position and Speaking Competence of Stuttering and Normally Fluent Boys," *Journal of Speech and Hearing Research,* 1974, *17,* pp. 740–747.

Handwriting 6

Objectives

The primary goal of handwriting instruction
Signs of handwriting readiness
How manuscript and cursive writing differ
Typewriting in the elementary school

Discover As You Read This Chapter If*

1. Legibility is a more important goal than speed in teaching handwriting.
2. As a technique for introducing beginners to handwriting, tracing is superior to copying.
3. Writing readiness is an important area of a successful handwriting program.
4. Hand preference is usually stable after the age of five.
5. It has been proven that beginners who use special primary pencils and primary paper improve the quality of their handwriting.
6. Cursive writing is easier and faster than manuscript writing.
7. Italic handwriting is now being taught to children.
8. It takes elementary pupils only a year to master touch typing.
9. Following typewriting instruction, elementary school boys and girls have shown no differences in physical development when compared with children of comparable ages who are not typists.
10. Left-handed children should be separated from right-handed children for handwriting instruction.

*Answers to these true-or-false statements may be found in Appendix 6.

Handwriting instruction has changed very little during most of the century, according to a recent survey of 60 years of handwriting research and practice.[1] After that lengthy period of time there is still no widespread acceptance of what constitutes legible writing or how that writing can be evaluated.

Handwriting, nevertheless, continues to maintain its important role in the integrated program of language arts. It extends into all written work and merits attention throughout the school day. Although separate handwriting periods are necessary, even instruction and practice provided during these periods can involve children in practical writing situations related to reading, spelling, and social studies assignments.

Writing concerns language, and studies have shown positive correlations among abilities in the various language arts. Many of the interrelationships are probably due to the presence of common elements in each area and to the fact that an experience which affects one cannot be isolated from the others. The best instructional program, then, teaches all of the language arts in a communication framework while at once recognizing the need for directed teaching of specific skills like handwriting.

The primary goal in teaching handwriting is legibility. The first essential is correct letter formation, and the second is proper spacing of letters and words. Size, within certain limitations, may be still another consideration. Legibility has sometimes been defined as the ease with which something can be read.

Legible handwriting was the focus of an investigation in Wisconsin of some 600 writing samples done by fourth-, fifth-, and sixth-graders.[2] A relationship was established between legibility and size (with the more legible sample being the larger writing) and between legibility and slant uniformity (with the more legible sample having a more uniform slant). As they moved from the fourth grade to the sixth grade, both boys and girls improved their legibility. They also wrote smaller and showed an increase in size uniformity.

The secondary goal in teaching handwriting is speed (without loss of legibility). Although it is not a factor in the early grades, beginning at grade three there is a consistent increase in the speed of writing among both manuscript and cursive writers. Sometimes defined as fluency, speed is important for note-taking and summarizing.

Early in their schooling, pupils realize the difference in legibility when they write for their own use and/or under the pressure of speed and when they write for others and/or without pressure of time. In the fourth, fifth, and sixth grades girls write more rapidly than boys, but left-handed and right-handed writers show no significant difference in writing speed.

If a student is forced to write faster than his or her usual rate, then the legibility of the handwriting produced will almost surely deteriorate. While a tool subject such as handwriting should be done as efficiently as possible, writing speed may be stepped up only to the point where a reasonable degree of legibility persists.

Handwriting is an individual production influenced by physical, mental, and emotional factors. The development of handwriting skill is closely related to the total growth and development of the pupil. Teachers who recognize that

Children must learn to recognize handwriting as an individual tool of expression that serves important needs in writing letters, stories, and reports. (Photo courtesy of Jean-Claude Lejeune.)

children's growth patterns are not identical will not insist that every child meet the same standard of achievement. Instead, each pupil will be encouraged to develop his or her own optimum rate of writing and level of writing pressure. These teachers will allow an individual show of readiness to precede each step in the writing process and encourage handwriting practices adjusted to individual differences in motor control.

Since the motor control that plays such a large part in learning to write neatly is not highly correlated with intelligence or scholastic achievement, high skill in handwriting may be possible for many children who do not have widespread academic success. It can help them maintain a positive self-image.

Handwriting lessons for both slow and fast learners in the intermediate grades should stress individualized practice on only those few letters which remain troublesome.

Handwriting is primarily a tool of communication. It is a means to an end and an individual tool. Consequently, from the beginning of instruction the pupils must write material that is meaningful to them. Children who write for a valid reason and not just as a mechanical task (and even copying from the chalkboard or book can be made purposeful) accept the importancce of handwriting. They recognize that, if their writing is so illegible that what they have written cannot be read, their attempts at communication have failed.

Busy teachers too must remember to write legibly in an effort to promote clear communication. Many of them reportedly write less legibly today than in the past, since less time is allotted in modern teacher education programs for future teachers to master handwriting skills.

Well-planned lessons develop proficiency in handwriting. Handwriting is definitely a skill and improves with proper systematic instruction. Most schools teaching handwriting, therefore, offer it five times a week in the primary grades and three times a week in the higher grades. Class periods average 10 to 20 minutes at all grade levels, with shorter planned lessons being more effective than longer unplanned periods. In England recently, research revealed the extent of handwriting activity reported by 936 schools sampled for their six- and nine-year-old pupils.[3] In most schools with both age groups, class-based work occupied at best 30 minutes a week, and only 20 percent of the pupils were encouraged to practice handwriting during their free time, with again a limit of 30 minuts per week. Twelve percent of the younger children and 21 percent of the older ones had *no* time allocated for handwriting.

Copying is superior to tracing as a technique for introducing beginners to handwriting.[4] Kindergarteners, for example, who did not copy letters but used faded tracing dots which outlined letter shapes did not learn to write those letters. After all, copying is a cognitive task and it has been shown that what children learn is not a motor pattern but a set of rules that enables them to copy from a model. Indeed, copying may be effective because in reproducing letters, the boys and girls are actively engaged in developing and applying rules that govern letter production. Such rule-based instruction improves performance on target letters and also permits transfer of learning to new letters. The key to that transfer has proved to be a demonstration of rules. Since independent copying practice, however, results in no transfer, teachers must provide prompt feedback on the learners' writing movements or on the products. Incidentally, fifth grade teachers should be aware of a recent study which concluded that while the ability of children to copy seems to develop continuously during the first four years of school (grades 1–4), their chances to improve the copying function as a psychomotor skill by training are rather small at age 10.[5]

The greatest single factor in determining the nature of the instructional program in handwriting in a given school is the commercial system of handwriting instruction that is adopted. Seventy-five to 80 percent of all school systems rely on a commercial system as the basis for their programs. While there have been reported to be as many as 26 different systems, only four are used by a majority of the schools. Since the various handwriting programs show considerable divergence in letter forms, sequence in the introduction of letters, and recommended teaching practices, the classroom teacher using a commercial system must be familiar with the guides, alphabet cards, and all other materials furnished by that system.

One popular commercial system was compared recently to a program using planned lessons presented through educational television.[6] In a study involving more than 2,500 third graders in Virginia, it was concluded, after one term, that the teaching of transitional cursive handwriting by means of television was better than the commercial system. The evaluative instrument used was the Freeman Cursive Handwriting Scale, Grade 3.

Each pupil must develop correct posture, correct hand movement, and proper position of writing paper and handwriting tools. Good posture and position in writing influence how well children write.

The table or desk should be a height comfortable for the pupil and have a writing surface that is smooth and flat. It should be positioned so that the light falls over the child's left shoulder if he or she is right-handed or over the right shoulder if the child is left-handed. The child should face the table or desk squarely, leaning slightly forward. Both arms should rest on the writing surface. Elbows, however, should be off the table or desk to permit free arm movement.

Proper positioning of the writing paper is another important factor. For manuscript writing, the right-handed student places the paper squarely in front of him or her, with the left or writing edge of the paper even with the midsection of the body. The left-handed child tilts the paper up and toward the right so that the lower-right corner is slightly to the left of the body's midsection. During cursive writing, the right-handed student tilts the paper toward the left so that the lower edge of the writing surface and the lower edge of the paper form a 30 degree angle. The left-handed pupil, however, tilts the paper toward the right (about 35 to 45 degrees) so that the lower-right corner of the paper points either toward the body's midsection or to the right of the midsection. Whatever the handedness, the nonwriting hand should be on the paper, shifting it to keep the total writing area visible to the pupil.

Writing Readiness

Handwriting readiness, like reading readiness, has come into vogue during the past decade. Although handwriting is being taught to young children today in more and more kindergarten and early childhood programs, some boys and girls are being pushed into handwriting before they have acquired adequate prehandwriting skills. Consequently, handwriting is difficult for them and causes discouragement.

Many years ago Maria Montessori stated, after extensive experimental work with young children, that learning to write demands both intelligence and an efficient motor mechanism. Children can acquire mental readiness through experiences that value handwriting and promote interest in learning to write. They attain motor readiness through activities that enable them to learn to hold the writing tools and to perform the simple movements required.

Specifically, six prerequisite skill areas for handwriting have been recently identified.[7] *The first is small muscle development and coordination.* When pupils start school, they use their arm and leg muscles fairly well, but skill in the use of wrist and finger muscles comes slowly. Before they can develop skill in writing, they must be able to hold the chalk or crayon without noticeable strain and to make the finger muscles respond so that they can copy simple geometric or letterlike characters. If children lack the ability to control their muscles in a manner necessary to produce legible handwriting, or if they overexert themselves in order to achieve the muscular coordination needed for writing, they may develop an antagonistic attitude toward all writing.

Activities that enhance small muscle development include many manipulative tasks such as working with jigsaw puzzles and snap beads or playing with blocks and doll furniture. Day-to-day experiences including zipping, buttoning, tying, and sewing also promote coordination. Too, the art curriculum enhances muscle development with painting, coloring, drawing, sketching, and tearing or folding paper. A pupil who can cut easily with small scissors is displaying readiness for handwriting instruction.

The second series of handwriting skills consists of eye-hand coordination tasks. These are plainly related to small muscle development skills, and therefore many of the activities mentioned above also promote eye-hand coordination. Playing the piano, stringing beads, pushing buttons, working puzzles, typing, and balancing blocks all require precise hand motions. Numerous paper-oriented tasks such as pasting and finger painting refine coordintion. Even large muscle activities such as jumping rope or climbing a ladder are helpful for eye-hand precision.

Children who consistently construct tall buildings out of blocks without knocking them down, follow mazes without touching exterior lines, or hammer nails straight into wood are revealing readiness for handwriting lessons.

An ability to hold writing tools properly is the third prerequisite skill area. Young children need to manipulate tools at the water table and at the sand table as part of their early childhood curriculum. Gardening with its rakes and hoes, cooking with its spatulas and spoons, and painting with its sponges and brushes, all provide experiences with utensils and tools.

There is an apparent hierarchy of difficulty in using writing tools. When young children are given a choice of four tools with which to write their names—a pencil, a felt-tip marker, a crayon, and some chalk—they overwhelmingly prefer the marker as the easiest tool to use followed by chalk, crayon, and pencil in that order. There is, incidentally, no advantage to the oversized pencils used by young children in some classrooms. Actually, some boys and girls write better with standard (adult) pencils from the beginning.

Teachers can readily determine if children are holding a pencil properly. The first indicator is the depth of impression on the page caused by the amount of pressure used. If the writing paper has holes in it or is covered by strokes which are too light, the child is using improper pressure and may become a slow writer. The other indicator of correct pencil usage is the ease with which the tool can be removed from the writer's hand as he or she is writing. Children who are experiencing stress will grip the pencil too tightly and may be unable to write for a reasonable period of time.

If young children have not firmly determined a hand preference by the time they begin school, teachers should encourage them to participate in activities leading to left-handedness if they are left-eyed or activities leading to right-handedness if they are right-eyed. Numerous instances of mixed laterality (especially involving the eye and hand) have been associated with reading and learning disabilities as well as with autonomic disturbances. In a follow-up study of children over three years of age, it was reported that hand preference usually seems stable after the age of five (as does foot and eye preference), but ear preference shows variation up to the age of seven.[8]

A fourth prerequisite skill area is the ability to form basic strokes. Circles and straight lines should be made smoothly in the appropriate direction and with clean intersections. Such strokes should evolve through time and activities like stirring, drawing, painting, sand play, and water play.

Until circles and straight lines occur naturally in a child's drawings of houses, flowers, people, and trucks, the boy or girl is not ready for formal handwriting instruction. Even then the transition from drawing to handwriting may be a slow process involving basic strokes in both artistic and written form.

Letter perception is the fifth prerequisite skill area. Attention to perception in a handwriting program develops better writers than a conventional program because handwriting is more than a physical activity. Since children should observe the finished product (letter or word) as well as the model formational act, left-handers should have left-handed models for aid and right-handed pupils, right-handed ones. They all must be able to notice likenesses and differences among the forms and provide accurate verbal step-by-step descriptions of the productions of the same forms.

In the initial stages of handwriting, reversals may often occur. When a child reverses a *b, d, s,* or uppercase *N* for example, the teacher must help by pointing out the differences in direction and by providing practice in dealing properly with the confusing symbols. Reversals generally disappear as children mature.

The importance of adult modeling of correct letter formation cannot be overstressed. Boys and girls must virtually perceive the way the alphabet letters are formed. The more often they see their teacher write on paper (and not merely on the chalkboard) the better. Equally critical is self-correction of initial attempts at handwriting as an aid in the letter perception. Incorrect habits are difficult to break later.

The sixth and final prehandwriting skill is actually an entire set of skills concerned with the orientation to printed language. One of these is an interest in writing and a desire to write. As the children observe the teacher writing in a meaningful way, their desire to do the writing themselves begins to grow. They soon sense a personal need to communicate in writing and enjoy learning to write their names. As the children watch, the teacher writes their dictated captions for pictures and experience charts as well as their dictated messages to absent classmates. The teacher also involves the children in discussions of personal experiences which culminate in party invitations, thank-you notes, and weight-and-height records.

Another is an understanding of the concept of left-to-right progression. Before starting to write, children need to know the meaning of the terms *left* and *right.* While some pupils begin school with an understanding of the differences between the terms, others must gradually begin to comprehend them through teacher-planned psychomotor activities such as Looby-Loo and the Hokey-Pokey. Additional activities recommended to help children master the bodily concept of left-right orientation demand:

1. Creating a dramatic play setting for fire fighting and then providing the boys and girls with toy fire trucks/engines to move from the fire station at the left to the "fire" area at the right.

2. Drawing green "go" and red "stop" signs on the chalkboard and then providing the children with colored chalk to draw the left-to-right horizontal lines between the signs. Later, a simulation game can be played with toy cars being "driven" along the lines from "go" to "stop."

Another is *language maturity*. When pupils verbalize satisfactorily, their oral experiences provide meaningful vocabularies for the first writing experiences. They enjoy listening to stories as well as composing and sending written messages. They should have many opportunities to dictate stories, poems, reports, plans, ideas, and funny or frightening incidents. When writing for the pupils, the teacher is not only introducing them to writing and reading, but she or he is also helping to bridge a gap between oral and written language. Children need to write through the teacher about themselves and their friends.

Traditional Manuscript Handwriting

Manuscript writing is a twentieth-century development. It was invented by a British elementary school teacher named Margaret Wise whose classic text, *On the Technique of Manuscript Writing,* was published in 1924. The style was soon adopted by hundreds of American public schools. Today it is part of the curriculum in many primary grades throughout the country because it is consistent with the motor and perceptual development of young children.[9]

Manuscript handwriting (printing) has several advantages. It is written with only three basic strokes and so is similar to the kind of drawing with which the pupils are familiar. Since it can be written with little physical strain, it allows the children to rest between strokes if necessary. Because each letter is separate, even a child with poor muscular control can produce readable results. It demands few eye movements, making it easier on the eyes of all young children and especially on those with visual difficulties. It is less tiring and, therefore, can be employed for longer periods of time. It can be written rapidly without loss of legibility and children are pleased with their own efforts.

Because manuscript writing resembles the print found in most primary reading materials, it aids beginning reading and composition. Only one alphabet needs to be mastered, and Piaget's work suggests that the preoperational child (usually from two to seven years of age) will learn to write and read better and faster when a single alphabet is used. Because the pupil writes more and therefore comes into contact with more words, manuscript writing improves spelling. It increases the quantity of written composition. Since it promotes proofreading, it also improves the quality of that composition because many spelling errors are actually handwriting illegibilities.

Children exposed to manuscript writing in the early grades become better cursive writers than those who never received manuscript lessons. Those with legible manuscript are more apt to write legibly when they switch to cursive, and legibility is an important consideration for young pupils. Unlike adults who can "fill-in" illegibilities, primary children are relatively unacquainted with written language and so lack the ability to "fill in." Their first writing experience should be based on a legible script which encourages them to read their own writing.

Finally, manuscript writing can be learned easily by those who are non-English speaking, learning disabled or physically handicapped. It is as useful with illiterate adults as it is with illiterate children. It has even been recommended that manuscript handwriting replace cursive handwriting as the style used by teachers for all classroom work since it is so legible.

Chalkboard Writing

Chalkboard writing gives young children an opportunity to use their large muscles. They can also write on a broad surface without the restriction they find in writing on paper.

As several children show numerous signs of writing readiness, the teacher gathers them into a group. The children are taught to face the chalkboard, standing comfortably to enable a good arm movement and adequate visualizing of letters and words. They are shown how to hold a half-length piece of chalk about one inch from the writing end (between the thumb and first and second fingers). They are told to hold the elbow close to the body.

The section of chalkboard used should hang low enough to permit children to write at or near eye level. Guidelines may be permanently ruled on the board to help children gauge the size, shape, spacing, and linear evenness of their writing.

When a group of children is ready for its first writing experience, the teacher plans instruction at a time when the members are not fatigued. Each pupil is carefully supervised so that correct habits are established and focus is centered on paper letter formation.

Paper Writing

Following the experience of writing at the chalkboard, writing activities using crayons or paint and brushes on unlined newsprint, tag board, or manila paper are the next step. The teacher may guide the making of simple figures that use the basic strokes, emphasizing large, free movements, left-to-right direction, and a feeling of form and space.

When beginning writers are ready to use pencils and lined paper, teachers need no longer assign special primary pencils and special primary paper. Neither the width of the writing space (whether ½″ or 1″) nor the exclusive use of oversized pencils has any differential effect on the quality of beginning handwriting.[10] Children appear to write better with standard adult pencils, felt-tip pens, and ball-point pens. They need no longer be subjected to any gradual changes from one type of writing tool and lined paper to other types of tools and papers.

Once children have learned how to write the manuscript alphabet, they must learn to make good use of it. Usually the first writing which boys and girls wish to complete is the writing of their names. The purpose is significant and readily achieved. They repeat the writing often, whenever they must sign drawings or paintings, label personal possessions, or mark worksheets. Many teachers prepare individual name cards in manuscript writing so that every child has a guide to keep on his or her desk for reference at all times.

Guiding Rules

When introducing the manuscript alphabet shown in Figure 6.1, the lowercase and uppercase (or capital) letters should be presented together, one or two letters at a time. Letters that are similar should be introduced together, such as *o* and *c, v* and *w,* and *M* and *n.*

Figure 6.1. Manuscript Handwriting Alphabet.

The letters of the manuscript alphabet vary widely in difficulty. The ten easiest letters for first-grade children are *l, o, L, O, H, D, i, v, I,* and *X;* the most difficult letters are *q, g, p, y, j, m, k, U, a* and *G.* Uppercase letters are usually easier than lowercase letters for pupils to write.

The classroom teacher should model through chalkboard/chart/paper writing six areas of the manuscript style:

Alignment

All letters must rest on the baseline. There should also be an evenness of the letters along their tops with letters of the same size having even heights.

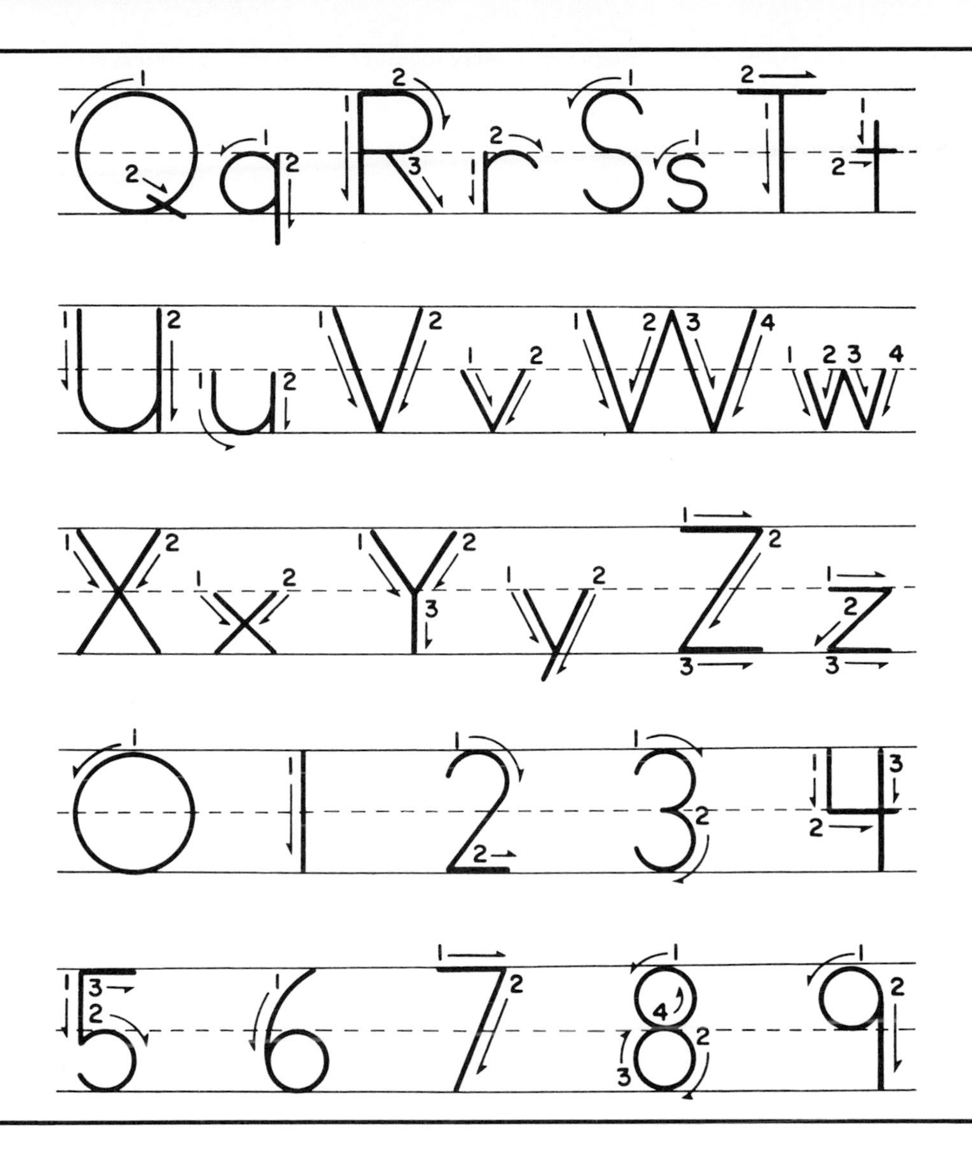

Size and Proportion

Maximum letters extend the full space from the baseline to headline and include all uppercase letters and the "tall" lowercase letters. All other lowercase letters (except *t*) extend from the baseline to the midline. The lowercase *t*, the only intermediate letter in manuscript writing, extends from the baseline to halfway between the midline and the headline.

Spacing

The most difficult element in manuscript writing for many children is spacing.

Pupils should space words four fingers apart for chalkboard writing, two fingers for newsprint, and one finger for first attempts on ruled paper. The width of an *o* is proper spacing when the size of writing has been reduced. Circular letters (such as *a, b,* and *d*) are placed closely together, while vertical letters such as *i* and *l*) are placed farther apart.

Letter Formation

Since this is the core of the writing program, beginning writers are more concerned with letter formation than with any other aspect of legibility.

All letters are made with circles and straight lines. Vertical lines of a letter are formed before the horizontal lines, and movements go from left to right. All vertical and all slant lines start at the top. Strokes within a letter are made separately and touch each other.

Circles or parts of circles which are made counterclockwise begin at the two o'clock position and proceed to the left. Circles or parts of circles which are made clockwise, however, begin at the ten o'clock position and proceed to the right.

Slant

There should be no slant since manuscript letters are vertical.

Line Quality

The evenness, smoothness, and thickness of the pencil or pen line are important. Sometimes the writing instrument is held improperly and a heavy line results. Sometimes the line is too light because the instrument itself is too hard or too fine.

Modality-Based Handwriting Curriculum

Some children learn best when information is introduced through a single modality or when one modality is dominant. They can be labeled auditory learners, visual learners, or kinesthetic learners. A handwriting curriculum which relies upon each of the three educationally relevant modalities would include the following list of objectives:

1. Auditory (with oral directions, letter name or strokes)
   a. Told letter names, writes uppercase manuscript letters
   b. Told letter names, writes lowercase manuscript letters
   c. Given letter sound, writes letter
   d. Told letter names, says letter strokes
   e. Told numeral names, writes numerals *1–30*
   f. Told number names, writes number words *one–ten*
   g. Presented with oral directions, writes uppercase manuscript letters grouped by similarity of strokes
   h. Presented with oral directions, writes lowercase letters grouped by similarity of strokes
   i. Told names of punctuation marks, writes period, comma, question mark, exclamation mark, quotation marks
   j. Told letter names, writes without reversal letters that are often reversed: *b-d, p-g-q*
   k. Told words, writes without reversal words that are often reversed: *on-no, was-saw*
2. Visual (with model)
   a. Presented with letter models, writes uppercase manuscript letters
   b. Presented with letter models, writes lowercase manuscript letters

c. Presented with numeral models, writes numerals *1–30*
d. Presented with models, writes number words *one-ten*
e. Presented with letter models, writes without reversal letters that are often reversed: *b-d, p-g-q*
f. Presented with word models, writes without reversal words that are often reversed: *on-no, was-saw*
g. Presented with letter models, writes uppercase letters grouped by similarity of strokes
h. Presented with letter models, writes lowercase letters grouped by similarity of strokes
i. Presented with models, writes punctuation marks: period, comma, question mark, exclamation mark, quotation marks

3. Kinesthetic (tracing, motioning, chalkboard)
    a. Presented with example, traces or motions in air uppercase letters grouped by similarity of strokes
    b. Presented with example, traces or motions in air lowercase letters grouped by similarity of strokes
    c. Presented with example, traces or motions in air numerals[11]

Functional Use of Manuscript Skills

In a mdoern handwriting program the teacher should develop many purposes for which the pupils need to write. Instruction in manuscript writing must not become an exercise period set aside for meaningless drill.

Primary pupils can be encouraged to label exhibits and displays in the classroom. With ballpoint or marking pens, even first graders can make posters and flashcards. They can then prepare picture captions, keep weather reports, and send notes to parents about school activities. Children can write verses, invitations, stories, letters of thanks, and messages for greeting cards. On the chalkboard they can copy the daily program and other announcements, including classroom news.

Teachers must realize that instruction in manuscript skills can eventually accomplish several goals for children: ability to print; knowledge of letter names; awareness that letters represent sounds; understanding of beginning sounds; knowledge of some letter-sound associations; awareness that words are comprised of letters; awareness that the writing (spelling) of a word is related to its pronunciation; and ability in visual discrimination.[12]

Traditional Cursive Handwriting

Nearly 70 percent of the private, public, and laboratory schools in the United States introduce cursive (or running) writing between the first half of the second grade and the first half of the fourth grade. Research has shown that, while the time of transition does not affect grade-to-grade progress, it is a factor influencing children's handwriting performance. Late transition is associated with rapid writing, but early transition is associated with legible handwriting.

Cursive writing is not faster, easier or more legible. It is merely more socially accepted. Since both pupils and parents believe that manuscript writing is associated with the primary grades, cursive writing has become an alternative handwriting skill. It involves four performance tasks. First, children must learn to habitually turn the paper in front of them. Second, they must keep the non-writing hand out of the way, at the top of the sheet, for easy paper shifting. Third, they must slant their writing. Finally, they must learn to slide their pens or pencils laterally to join the cursive letters.

Readiness

Boys and girls arrive at the threshold of advanced writing readiness at varying times. Since neither chronological age nor grade placement constitutes a reliable index, a teacher must adapt instruction and plan flexibility. Second-, third-, and even some fourth-grade teachers are constantly noting individual signs of readiness among their students.

A group can be successfully introduced to the cursive style when most of its members are:

1. Children who want to write in the cursive style.
2. Children who are unconsciously starting to join manuscript letters.
3. Children who can write all the manuscript letters from memory and do it well.
4. Children who can copy a selection in manuscript at a rate varying from 20 to 45 letters per minute.
5. Children who are able to reduce the size of their manuscript letters.
6. Children who have attained adequate physical development so there is muscular coordination of the arm, head, and fingers.
7. Children who can read writing. A definite relationship exists between the ability to read manuscript and to read cursive writing. Pupils who have developed adequate skill in reading manuscript style will require little instructional emphasis on reading cursive style. Those who have experienced difficulty in learning to read manuscript will need more attention. One answer may be to postpone the addition of cursive writing until enough growth has occurred in reading manuscript. Another solution is to precede the introduction of cursive writing with the reading of material written cursively.

Comparison to Manuscript Writing

The outstanding difference between traditional cursive and manuscript writing is sliding laterally to join letters. Cursive writers lift their pens and pencils from the paper upon completion of each word. Manuscript writers lift their writing tools after each letter.

The basic shapes used in cursive writing are slant strokes, connecting strokes, and ovals. In manuscript writing they are circles and straight lines.

The letters *i* and *j* are dotted and the letter *t* is crossed after the complete word has been written in cursive style. In manuscript writing, the dotting and crossing occur immediately after the letters are formed.

The uppercase letters in the cursive alphabet always differ considerably from the lowercase letters. Nearly one-third of the manuscript alphabet, however, is much the same for uppercase and lowercase letters—*c, o, p, s, v, w, x, z.*

In cursive writing, the spacing between letters is controlled by the slant and manner of making connective strokes. In manuscript writing it is determined by the shapes of the letters.

Cursive letters shown in Figure 6.2 differ from book print, but manuscript letters closely resemble such print.

Figure 6.2. Cursive Handwriting Alphabet.

Figure 6.2 (cont.)

Ss Tt Uu

Vv Ww Xx

Yy Zz

1 2 3 4 5 6 7 8 9 10

Guiding Rules

The classroom teachers should model through paper/chalkboard/chart writing six areas of the cursive style:

Alignment

Every letter rests on a baseline, whether the line is visible or not.

Size and Proportion

All 26 uppercase letters are of maximum height. All lowerloop letters (whether uppercase or lowercase) take a full descender space below the baseline. All upperloop letters extend a full space from the baseline to the headline.

Slant

The downstrokes or slant strokes of the letters slant uniformly and in the same direction. Cursive writing, which has a consistent forward slant, is easier to read than writing which slants too much or is irregular. A slant between 60 and 70 degrees is regarded as the most acceptable.

Spacing

Between each letter there is an even distribution of sufficient blank space. Between each word there is the space of one letter.

Letter Formation

All the cursive letters are comprised of overcurves and undercurves. They originate from the oval and are combined with slant strokes of other curves. There are *loop letters* (such as *j* and *p*) whose up-strokes must curve and whose down-strokes must be straight. There are *retraced letters* (such as *m* and *n*) which must not become loops. There are *rounded turn letters* (such as *x*, *y*, and *z*) which must not be pointed. There are *closed letters* (such as *a* and *d*) which must not overlap.

When either the undercurve or the overcurve is made hastily, however, it tends to become merely a straight stroke and difficult to read. When the undercurve becomes staight, *e* becomes *i* and the *r* and *s* becomes overcurves. When the overcurve is made straight:

a becomes *u*
d becomes *il*
g becomes *y* or *ij*
m becomes *w*
n becomes *u*
o becomes *u*
v becomes *u*
y becomes *ij*

Some problem areas are shown in Figure 6.3.

Figure 6.3. The Most Difficult Cursive Letters and Numerals Which Constitute Half of All the Handwriting Illegibilities.

	Right	Wrong
a like o		
a like u		
a like ci		
b like li		
d like cl		
e closed		
h like li		
i like e with no dot		
m like w		
n like u		
o like a		
r like i		
r like n		
t like l		
t with cross above		
5 like 3		
6 like 0		
7 like 9		

Source: Adapted from California State Series *Handwriting Made Easy*, Part III. Sacramento: State Board of Education, 1963.

Figure 6.4. The Most Difficult Cursive Combinations.

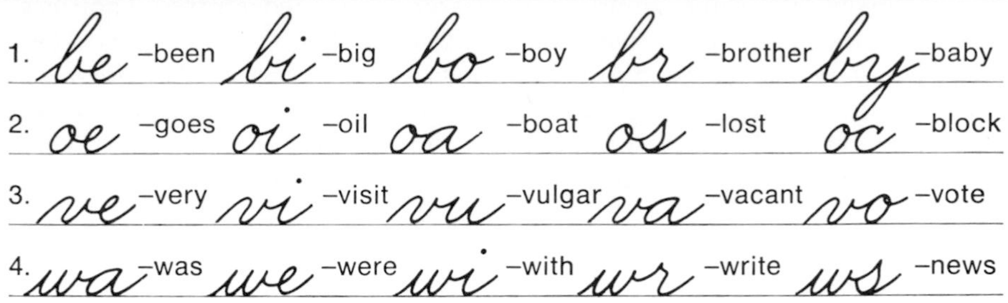

1.	be –been	bi –big	bo –boy	br –brother	by –baby
2.	oe –goes	oi –oil	oa –boat	os –lost	oc –block
3.	ve –very	vi –visit	vu –vulgar	va –vacant	vo –vote
4.	wa –was	we –were	wi –with	wr –write	ws –news

The most difficult letter, according to a survey of 1,000 sixth graders, is the letter *r*.[13] Its malformations account for 12 percent of all illegibilities. Other cursive letters that pupils often malform are *h, i, k, p,* and *z*.

Joining

Joining the cursive letters is as important as forming the letters. The four letters which give the most trouble in joining are *b, o, v,* and *w,* for they connect the next letter at the top and not on the line. These difficult combinations of overcurves and undercurves are shown in Figure 6.4.

By the sixth grade, the teacher may introduce joinings of uppercase to lowercase letters. There are 17 uppercase letters which have a natural joining finish and so must be taught as joinable capitals. The remaining letters —*D, F, L, O, P, Q, T, V* and *W*—do not readily permit joining.

Functional Use of Cursive Skills

Repetitive drill can quickly dull children's desires to improve their handwriting techniques. Wise teachers therefore, build a program that encourages all pupils to write primarily to communicate ideas and feelings.

Middle- and upper-grade children can use cursive handwriting for preparing stories, poetry, book reports, and invitations. They can take notes, make outlines, keep vocabulary lists, and plan the school newspaper. They can keep minutes of club meetings. They can compile a class directory. Pupils can write letters to government offices or to private firms asking for information or arranging study trips. They can write up interviews with resource speakers or class visitors. As committee members, they can even help develop a unit of work in science and social studies.

Through routine but significant assignments, children are made aware of the many purposes for acquiring cursive skills.

Alternative Forms of Handwriting

For teachers who do not wish to present the traditional handwriting forms to their classes, there are now available some alternate forms of the Roman alphabet for beginning writers.

D'Nealian Handwriting

Developed by teacher-principal Donald Neal Thurber, this alternative form is said to have grown in popularity to more than one-third of the handwriting materials market within six years of its national introduction in 1978. In the

D'Nealian method children begin by printing in slanted script that resembles cursive writing. They learn to make 21 of the lowercase manuscript letters with a continuous stroke, retracing at times as they would in traditional cursive. The five exceptions requiring special introductory lessons are the dotted letters *i* and *j* and the crossed letters *f, t,* and *x.*
Since children slant the manuscript forms from the very start, no new alignment procedures are needed for transition to cursive. With the exception of *f, r, s, v,* and *z,* manuscript letters become cursive letters as soon as the children add simple joining strokes. Whether cursive or manuscript, however, all uppercase letters are delayed until all the lowercase letters of the same style have been mastered. Transition to cursive can occur as early as late first grade or early second grade. D'Nealian handwriting has proved to be equally useful for mainstream, average, and above-average children. Transfer students familiar with traditional manuscript are said to "shift unconsciously" into the D'Nealian models after sufficient exposure to the new style. Sample alphabets are shown in Figure 6.5.

Italic Handwriting

An alternative of special interest to educators concerned with teaching children two systems of handwriting is italic handwriting since boys and girls need to learn only one system. Developed in Italy during the Renaissance, it presents a modified single form approach which is neither manuscript nor cursive. The shapes of the letters (both uppercase and lowercase) resemble the shapes of printed letters.

Whereas traditional lowercase manuscript letters are called ball-and-stick letters since they are based on circle shapes (and straight lines), lowercase italic letters are based on egg shapes (and slanted lines). The system is therefore sometimes referred to as egg-and-stick printing.

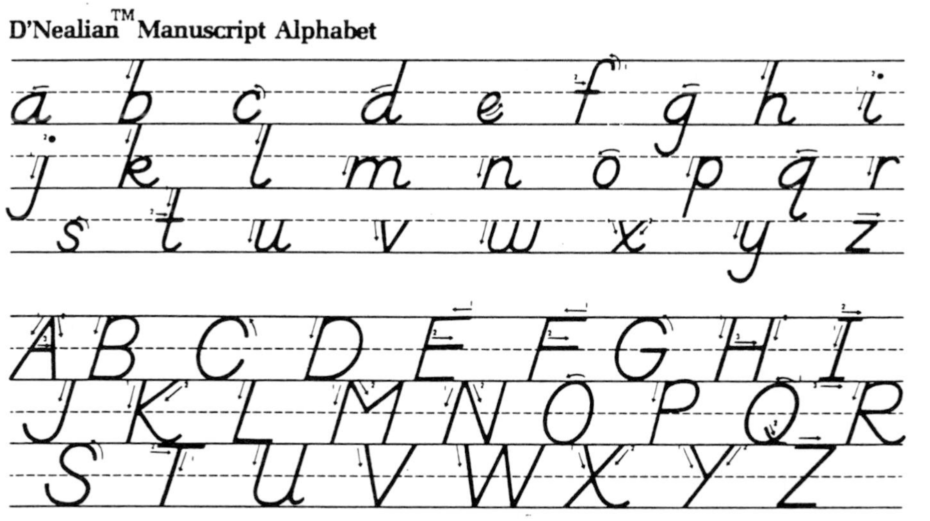

Figure 6.5. One Alternative Form of Handwriting: D'Nealian.

Figure 6.5 (cont.)

D'Nealian™ Cursive Alphabet

a b c d e f g h i
j k l m n o p q r
s t u v w x y z

A B C D E F G H I
J K L M N O P Q R
S T U V W X Y Z

D'Nealian™ Numbers

0 1 2 3 4 5 6 7 8 9

Source: From D'NEALIAN® HANDWRITING, Book 2, by Donald Thurber. Copyright © 1981 by Scott, Foresman and Company. Reprinted by permission.

Once the children have mastered the techniques of producing individual letters, they can give their handwriting cursive (running) flow by adding entry and exit strokes (called joins) and by learning how to space the resulting words.

At least one study has already been reported comparing the efforts of primary-grade children who had been taught italic writing with the efforts of their primary peer group that had been taught the traditional manuscript writing followed by the traditional cursive writing.[14] After three years, and on a speed test at the end of the third grade, the italic group produced more letters during a two-minute time span than did the comparison group. Furthermore, in the area of legibility, the italic group deviated only one half as much from their letter models as did the comparison group.

Italic handwriting has earned the approval of public school officials in Oregon as well as those in other states and in at least one Canadian province (British Columbia), where it is referred to as loop-free cursive. Sample alphabets are shown in Figure 6.6.

Figure 6.6.
Another Alternative Form of Handwriting: Italic.

Source: Reprinted from HANDWRITING RESOURCE BOOK, GRADES 1-7, Ministry of Education, Province of British Columbia, Canada, 1981, p. 53. Used with permission.

Typewriting Skill

Once boys and girls have reasonably learned the handwriting skill, they are ready to acquire an addition to handwriting by learning how to typewrite. Schools in all geographical areas of the nation from Texas to Michigan and from Connecticut to California are offering typing instruction to some children in some elementary grades.

Why Is Typing Being Taught?

Increased interest in computers and computer instruction among younger students further accelerates concern in the proper use of the typewriter. Recently some 50,000 children in Hawaii, ages five to ten, used the electric typewriter to develop keyboard literacy. Their teachers confirmed five reasons for including typewriting as an essential part of the language skills.[15] First, it stimulates children's motivation to learn to use the graphic symbols of the English language. Second, typewriting supports the development of the children's reading ability. It also offers boys and girls an alternative mode of writing so that they can use the typewriter for their stories, songs, poems, and letters. Fourth, it supports the development of the children's handwriting ability. And finally, typewriting helps the children become independent learners and promotes individualization.

Typewriting skill is a value in and of itself. It is useful personally as well as vocationally and remains an educational tool. Consequently, it cannot be taught to children as an isolated skill but as a tool which makes curricular areas more interesting. It helps boys and girls in the compilation of individual and committee booklets, for example, and in the production of labels and legends for posters, maps, bulletin boards, and displays. Teaching children to typewrite helps them clarify margins, line spacings, paragraphing, hyphenating, spacing between words, vertical and horizontal centering, as well as understanding bibliographies and outlines and the addressing of envelopes and postal cards. The production of class newspapers, book reports, letters, and notes is simultaneously increased.

Finally, the affective, cognitive, and psychomotor values promoted through the use of the typewriter may even prove more important than the fact that children are also learning beginning keyboard literacy.

Incidentally, there are four goals in typewriting courses generally: speed and accuracy in operating the machine; efficiency in using the typewriter for the production of typed material; mastery of a mass of related technical information; and improvement and reinforcement of the learner's language skills. Of these four goals, the last-named is by far the most important for typewriting instruction in the elementary school.

How Is Typewriting Being Taught?

Instructions found in junior-high and senior-high textbooks for teaching beginning typewriting can be used with upper-grade elementary children. The teacher may either simplify the directions in these texts or choose to use one of the typewriting books especially designed for younger pupils. Sample lessons from two such elementary school books are found in Figures 6.7 and 6.8.

Figure 6.7. One Sample Typewriting Lesson for the Elementary School.

Lesson 2: Learning "E"

Now that we have learned the home key fingers, we are ready to learn the letter "E."

Type "E" with the "D" finger. After typing the letter E, the D finger returns to home base again.

Practice:

ded ded ded ded ded ded ded ded

eee eee eee eee eee eee eee eee

fff eee lll fell fell fell fell

Have fun typing the hockey game. See how many goals you can score!

Directions: Type the practice drill you see on the hockey field. Each time you complete the drill you score a goal. How many goals can you score?

Source: Mary Ellen Switzer, TYPING FUN (Santa Barbara, Ca.: The Learning Works, 1979). Reprinted with permission.

Figure 6.8.
Another Sample Typewriting Lesson for the Elementary School.

LESSON 7

The Full Alphabet

Hooray, hooray, you finish the alphabet today.

There are only three letters left to learn—"C," "X," and "Z."

They are all in the bottom row.

Be sure that you learn to hit them only with the proper finger as shown in the chart.

Remember—do not look at the keys when you type; look only at the chart.

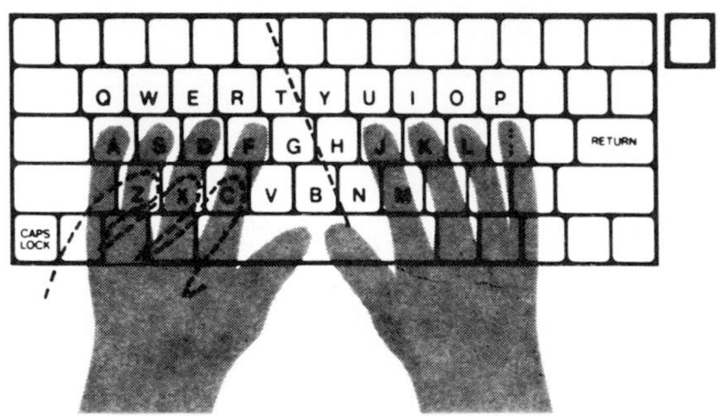

Now, without looking at the keys, copy the following exercise.

```
DCDCDCDCDCDCDCDCDCDCDCDC
SXSXSXSXSXSXSXSXSXSXSXSX
AZAZAZAZAZAZAZAZAZAZAZAZ

CLO CLO CLO CLO CLO CLO
FGHJ FGHJ FGHJ FGHJ FGHJ

LOSW LOSW LOSW LOSW LOSW
PAQ PAQ PAQ PAQ PAQ PAQ

EXY EXY EXY EXY EXY EXY
ZKM ZKM ZKM ZKM ZKM ZKM

JIR JIR JIR JIR JIR JIR
FTY FTY FTY FTY FTY FTY

HEW HEW HEW HEW HEW HEW
ZJ: ZJ: ZJ: ZJ: ZJ: ZJ:

IT IT IT IT IT IT IT IT
OF OF OF OF OF OF OF OF

QUH QUH QUH QUH QUH QUH
SEL SEL SEL SEL SEL SEL

SXJM SXJM SXJM SXJM
FVRH FVRH FVRH FVRH

READ READ READ READ
NOW NOW NOW NOW NOW

COP COP COP COP COP
XKN XKN XKN XKN XKN

HYZ HYZ HYZ HYZ HYZ
BVD BVD BVD BVD BVD
```

Type your own name five times.

This is a great day.
We are now using all the letter keys. (8)

Source: Reprinted by permission of the publisher from Edward B. Fry, COMPUTER KEYBOARDING FOR CHILDREN (New York: Teachers College Press, © 1984 by Teachers College, Columbia University. All rights reserved), p. 8.

The method presented in elementary school typewriting classes is touch-typing. Course content includes presentation of the keyboard, manipulations of other parts of the machine, completion of correspondence and report forms, and understanding simple tabulation. The elementary classroom and language arts teacher usually conducts the typing class. This teacher is sometimes assisted by an aide and occasionally by instructional records. Class periods run 15 to 30 minutes during the regular semester, and fifth- and sixth-grade pupils, for example, accomplish more in typing than high school students taught by the same instructor in the same amount of class time. Fourth-grade pupils reportedly learn to type on the electric portable with less instruction than adults.

Typewriting then can be mastered by elementary pupils in about one semester. Thirty hours of class instruction produce sufficient skill to enable most pupils to use typing in their school and home work. Second, third, and fourth graders in Del Mar, California, master the touch system in three to four months. Fifth and sixth graders in Jackson, Mississippi, take between 12 and 18 weeks to master it. Incidentally, these same Jackson fifth graders reach a typing speed of 40 words per minute by the end of their first year in the program.

Children can learn with either a manual or an electric typewriter and with either an office or a portable machine. There has been no appreciable difference noted between skill development by a learner on the electric model and a learner on the manual typewriter. However, at least one writer (Petitclerc) believes that every typewriter must be *electric* because young fingers fatigue when working on manual machines and *portable* so that any child can pick up the machine and carry it to a secluded spot to type alone if he or she so desires.[16]

Typewriting can be taught without the addition of any special furniture or equipment other than the machines themselves. Adjustable desks are helpful but not necessary. While the typing lab in one Mississippi elementary school is furnished with 30 IBM Selectric typewriters (with multiple listening stations and audio-belt recording machines) a typing center can be initiated simply with one machine at a learning center that is properly supervised.

During the Hawaii English Program, for example, primary classrooms had one machine for 30 children, and upper grades had one machine for 15 pupils. Classroom teachers generally worked intensely only with the first few learners (who in turn tutored their peers) and then periodically monitored all typists. It must be emphasized that, left to their own devices, children do not learn to operate the typewriter with any degree of skill. They need teacher direction and supervision if they are to achieve superior typing techniques.

Research and Typewriting

Although the typewriter was first marketed in 1874, young children did not use it until the mid–1920's. Since that pioneer experiment in New York City, many studies have been completed stressing the positive results of teaching typewriting in the elementary school.[17] Major conclusions reached are:

1. Typing improves reading comprehension and fluency. For example, when first and second graders, diagnosed as slow readers, learned to use electric typewriters, they made a gain in reading skills in eight weeks which was more than three times greater then normal.

2. Word study skills improve with the ability to type. This was noted among first-, third-, and fourth-grade pupils.
3. Children who type make greater gains in spelling, capitalization, punctuation, and language usage than non-typists.
4. Using the typewriter has a positive effect on learning-disabled children of elementary school age, especially in reading-related areas. It has even been suggested that the typed productions of hearing-impaired pupils could be used as supplementary reading material.
5. Self-concept is raised when children learn to type. Typers' attitudes toward school also appear to be healthier.
6. Handwriting quality and handwriting speed improve, in both manuscript and cursive styles.
7. Gains in listening skills and attention span are made when children learn to type.
8. Reactions of parents, pupils, and the public are those of approval and enthusiastic acceptance. Reluctance appears limited to some elementary teachers.
9. No differences have been found in the physical development of children in grades three, five, and seven following typewriting instruction, even though the learners represented three different levels of development.
10. More than half of the children in two Florida schools who have been learning typewriting skills in special classes were reported in 1981 to be performing one year ahead of their grade levels in reading.

Providing for Children with Special Needs

Indirectly related to the whole area of self-evaluation, motivation, and pupil interest is individualized learning. Although whole-class instruction still prevails in the majority of schools, efforts have been begun to meet individual differences in handwriting needs. Individualization is most effective before the pupils' handwriting habits have been fairly well established—probably before the fourth grade. Sample lessons promoting individualized learning in handwriting are listed in Figure 6.9.

Research involving third and fourth graders in an urban elementary school, for example, revealed after nine weeks of daily instruction that individualized approaches produce greater increases in legibility than the formal group approach.[18] The children were randomly assigned to one of three instructional programs: the formal group, the formal-individualized group, and the individualized-diagnostic group. The last-named group made no use of commercially-prepared materials. Instead, its teachers helped each pupil focus on a limited number of malformed letters at the beginning of each lesson and encouraged everyone to develop the habit of continuously evaluating his or her own handwriting.

A transitional step between complete individualization and the whole-class approach occurred successfully in one New York district. A supervisor using an overhead projector made group presentations to 150 students monthly. Then, during the follow-up by classroom teachers, all malformed letters that pupils made on any written assignment were posted on a handwriting chart. These letters were

Sample Creative Lessons in Handwriting

1. Children each bring in five handwritten envelopes which came through the mail to their home. They practice writing the addresses on sheets of paper or at the chalkboard. Later, each receives five blank business-sized envelopes with address lines on which to write the final copies. Older children should be able to match the cursive or manuscript style used on the original cancelled envelopes. Younger pupils should bring in only envelopes using printed letters. (This activity adapts readily to typing practice.)
2. Boys and girls can write with finger paints or with oil paints/brushes on large sheets of butcher paper. While this exercise is especially valuable during introductory lessons in manuscript or cursive, it also continues as a helpful review activity done periodically after writing skills have been learned.
3. Intermediate writers can take turns leading a small-group handwriting lesson using an overhead projector. Under the supervision of the teacher they do their cursive lettering on clear plastic sheets or on the plastic roll provided with some machines. Since the overhead can be used in a lighted room, the other children in the group can follow the leader easily, practicing difficult letter combinations or words targeted for improvement. Peer tutoring can be a motivational change from adult instruction.
4. Girls and boys each bring in a short favorite recipe for the Class Cookbook. The teacher checks each one for accuracy before the children begin to practice copying their contribution in manuscript, cursive, or typewriter writing. Each pupil is then given a spirit duplicating master on which to write his or her recipe. Sufficient copies are later run off so that the class can assemble and decorate individual booklets.

Figure 6.9. Handwriting Lessons.

practiced twice weekly during individualized activities in both manuscript and cursive writing.

Another project promoting individualized instruction took place in Illinois. It involved fifth graders for 20-minute periods daily. During two such sessions a teacher directed the whole class at the overhead projector or chalkboard. Small-group instruction occurred once a week with specially-prepared tapes. Finally, the remaining two periods were spent on teacher conferencing, individual diagnosis, and practice.

Every teacher must view a handwriting program in terms of satisfying individual pupils with varying needs. Most of them must be grouped together temporarily to overcome a common deficit. A few other pupils will require instruction for longer periods of time. Chiefly they include children with learning disabilities and left-handed writers.

Children With Learning Disabilities

Problem areas in handwriting have been identified as visual-perception-input, visual-spatial relationships, visual-motor ability, and short-term visual recall.[19] For a learning-disabled child there may be a deficit in one while the other areas are developing normally. For example, a learning-disabled pupil can have good short-term visual recall and still have inadequate visual-spatial relationships. A checklist of possible handwriting difficulties of a learning-disabled child is shown in Figure 6.10.

Visual-perception-input means the ability to perceive a configuration. Boys and girls who perceive a shape incorrectly focus the motor response incorrectly, and thus their writing consists of twisted letters, inconsistently reversed letters, and letters slanted diagonally toward the line. Remediation for visual-perception-input difficulty starts with the use of cardboard form boards to help the children visually recognize like and unlike shapes. They are given one of the boards and a variety of cutout shapes and parquetry blocks to place on that board. Later, they can sort the blocks and shapes into piles together with shaped templates. Along with this exercise the boys and girls also match shapes to form designs or pictures. Finally, they advance to learning the actual letter shapes visually and kinesthetically by using sandpaper, clay or playdough, crayons, tagboard, and writing paper.

Visual-spatial relationships develop from the ability of children to relate themselves to space and then to relate two objects in space to each other. Pupils with a weakness in this area of handwriting have difficulty placing letters on the line, organizing the letters on the paper, and positioning the spaces correctly. They often produce a disproportion in the sizes of their letters. Remediation in the visual-spatial area demands that heavy dark lines or colored lines be drawn or printed on writing paper to visually accentuate the spatial orientation of the letters. Another technique is to color the three writing spaces blue, green, and brown and then to designate the letters as being "placed in the sky," "placed on the grass," or "placed under the ground." Later, such lines are gradually lightened until boys and girls can properly place the letters without guide lines.

Children experiencing difficulty in *visual-motor ability* produce lines of writing that are either very light or very heavy. They will often take an unusually long time to form one letter or to complete one writing lesson. Although they have been taught how to hold a pencil properly, they either hold it so tensely that they make holes in the paper or so lightly that their letters are barely visible. Such pupils will try to make many erasures because they realize that they are not making the letter shapes properly. Remediation begins at the chalkboard: a pupil is given a piece of chalk in each hand and told to draw parallel lines, then large squares, and finally large circles with both hands while simultaneously saying the directions of the movements being made. Then the child gradually traces pictures, traces letters, and finally writes letters with crayons.

Since the fourth area involves visual imagery, a problem in *short-term visual recall* occurs when children have difficulty transferring letters or words from one paper to another or from the chalkboard to their papers. Letters or words may be omitted or letters may be copied out of sequence. Remediation requires teaching visual sequencing by matching a group of manipulative objects with a row of pictures of the same objects. The same process can also be used with parquetry blocks. To help children copy items in proper sequence, a cardboard strip (the width of three writing spaces) can be used when copying from another sheet

A handwriting sample should be obtained by having the child copy at least three lines of writing either from the board or another paper. The example to be copied from should not exceed 18 letters and/or spaces per line. The child should be instructed to copy the example exactly.

Figure 6.10. Teacher's Checklist of Major Areas of Handwriting Difficulty.

If these things are observed	the child experiences difficulty in:			
	visual-perception input	visual-spatial relationships	visual-motor ability	visual recall
Parts of letters not connected	x			
Shape of letters distorted	x			
Reversed letters*	x			
Upside down letters*	x			
Twisted letters*	x			
Unequal spacing of letters		x		
Unequal size of letters		x		
Letters not on the line		x		
Heavy use of the pencil			x	
Light use of the pencil			x	
Tense grip while writing			x	
Pencil held in fist grip			x	
Wavering lines			x	
Deterioration of letter shape as repeated across line			x	
Letters copied out of sequence				x
Letters omitted or words omitted				x

*These must be constant and not just an occasional learning error.

Source: Reprinted from CORRECTING HANDWRITING PROBLEMS, Lexington Public Schools, Lexington, Massachusetts, 1974, p. 18. Used with permission.

of paper. The cardboard strip is drawn along the line of print that is being copied, exposing only one letter at a time. Gradually, more letters can be uncovered at once until the strip becomes unnecessary.

When teaching cursive handwriting to learning-disabled children, it has been recommended that one lowercase letter be taught during a 15-minute period each day. The two easiest letters are *i* and *t* with the next easiest being *b, e, f, g, j, k, l, p, r, s, u,* and *w*. By writing words like *ill* and *bit,* the teacher can illustrate words that are somewhat alike in both cursive and manuscript writing.

Left-Handed Children

The one form of individual difference that appears most frequently during handwriting instruction is left-handedness. Studies have indicted that 10 to 15 percent of all beginning students have a marked preference for writing with their left hands.

Teachers must realize that, while evidence for a genetic base for handedness remains positive, no direct link has been established. The development of preferred handedness can also be affected by such factors as cultural and social pressures, family preference, educational practices, specific brain damage, and the prevalence of certain types of devices more suitable for one hand than the other. Even today many European schools demand that all pupils learn to write with the right hand.

Consistency in the use of one writing hand is important from the beginning. If either the left or right hand is used without strain, teachers and parents can encourage use of that hand. Children who shift readily from one hand to the other, however, should be encouraged to use the right hand.

Recent research, incidentally, shows that there is no difference in intellectual and cognitive performance between left- and right-handed elementary pupils.[20] Children in grades one through six in one California community were tested on three measures of handedness and one measure of eyedness. No relationships of any kind were discovered between left-handedness and areas such as reading ability, intelligence, perceptual performance, mental retardation, and emotional instability.

Measures of handedness and eyedness can be individually administered by kindergarten and first-grade teachers to assess pupil preferences. Such informal tests involve familiar materials adapted to the age and development of the children. Teachers should repeat each stage of a test a sufficient number of times to detect the dominant hand or eye. They must remember never to hand the materials to the children during the dominant hand tests.

Dominant Hand Tests

Sorting Colored Cards

The teacher cuts assorted colored papers about the size of playing cards and shuffles them. He or she places a pile (of at least twenty) of these cards where the child can reach them and then tells the child to get the cards and sort them according to colors. The teacher observes which hand the pupil uses in picking up the cards and in sorting them.

Putting a Puzzle Together

On the table are the large pieces of a sturdy puzzle, preferably a wooden one. The child is asked to assemble the puzzle.

Playing with a Hand Puppet

A hand puppet sleeve is placed on the table and the child is asked to participate in puppet play. The teacher observes to see on which hand the pupil puts the puppet.

Bouncing a Ball

The child picks up a ball and then bounces it ten times, catching it on each rebounce. Since only one hand can be used, the pupil's preference is easy to note.

Holding a Spoon

The teacher observes the child during snack time, at the lunch table, or in a dramatic play situation where the child must use a spoon. The dominant hand is quickly discovered.

Unlocking a Cupboard

The teacher padlocks a cupboard in the classroom and places the key on the desk. The child is asked to take the key, unlock the padlock, and bring one object from the cupboard. He or she is observed unlocking the padlock and picking up the object.

Cutting Pictures

On the table are an old magazine and a small pair of right-handed scissors. The child is asked to cut out a picture. A repeat test with the other hand will show whether or not there is a preferred hand. The left-handed child will have more difficulty than the right-handed one.

Dominant Eye Tests

Hole-in-Card Test

In the center of a card or sheet of stiff paper, the teacher cuts a hole about one inch in diameter. The pupil holds the card in both hands with arms extended and is asked to sight (with both eyes open) a distant object through the hole. Then one eye is covered. If the child can still see the object, the dominant or preferred eye is the uncovered eye. If he or she cannot see the object, it is apparent that the dominant eye is covered. The teacher should have the pupil try the test from different positions since one trial may not suffice.

Aiming Test

The pupil sights a distant object with both eyes open and then points fingers at the object. Then she or he closes (or covers) the left eye, and if the fingers are still in line with the object, the child is right-eyed. When she or he closes (or covers) the right eye, the child is left-eyed if the fingers are still in line with the object.

Simple Tube Test

On the table is a long mailing tube and an object which the pupil has not seen before in the classroom. Asked to look at the object through the tube and describe it, he or she will use the preferred eye to sight the object.

Advanced Tube Test

Holding a long mailing tube about six inches from both eyes, the pupil looks through it at a distant object in the room. Both eyes remain open. The right eye is now covered, and if the child continues to see the object, she or he is left-eyed.

Then the left eye is covered, and if the pupil continues to see the object, he or she is right-eyed.

Guiding Left-Handed Writers

With proper instruction of left-handed and right-handed pupils, no significant difference will appear in handwriting peformance. Teachers should guide left-handed writers to:

1. Learn first the four manuscript letters that begin with a stroke to the left since these develop muscular control most readily: *a, d, g,* and *o*. Then, develop coordination in the forward motion from left to right by practicing the manuscript letters *b, e, f, i, l, r, t, u,* and *w*.
2. Realize that they can use the manuscript style indefinitely if they find that it is easier to write.
3. Use a writing tool that does not smudge, such as a ball-point pen with an extended tip.
4. Hold back about one and one half inches on the writing tool so that they can see over or around the writing hand. (A thin strip of masking tape can be put around the instrument at the point where it should be held.) They should grasp the tool lightly.
5. Sit at the left half of the writing surface which should be slightly lower than that for right-handed children to aid in seeing what is being written.
6. Use pushing strokes rather than pulling strokes.
7. Use the chalkboard often. Left-handed writers are especially comfortable if they can stand at the right end of the chalkboard. However, they need two spaces—one in which to stand and one in which to write.

Left-handed students should be separated for instructional purposes from right-handed students. This is important because they will write in reverse if they interpret directions as demonstrated by the teacher in the routine teaching strategy. By producing such mirror writing, they are correctly interpreting only visual directions or directions given to the right-handed students. The teacher should group left-handers together for instruction, preferably at slant-top desks.

Evaluation of Pupils' Progress

Children are graded for handwriting in about 70 percent of the American and Canadian schools.[21] A strong majority of these schools evaluate handwriting on the basis of teacher observation. Since a child may practice the same mistakes over and over again until poor quality handwriting becomes a habit, the teacher must be a good evaluator of learner achievement in handwriting.

Presumably, such evaluation occurs individually or on a small-group basis. The teacher who understands that growth patterns naturally vary will not insist that every child in the grade meet identical standards of handwriting achievement. Some pupils who make appreciable progress during the year still will not write as well as pupils who have average ability for the grade. To force such slow learners to meet a kind of standardized norm is unfair and promotes apathy. Children who exhibit very little improvement, as well as those who show unusual growth, may be progressing consistently with their rate of overall development.

Since the aims of the handwriting program are legibility and speed, evaluation of each pupil's progress demands that those two factors be measured objectively. The only form of rating that has meaning for the child occurs when he or she and the teacher set up goals for the improvement of personal writing skill. Class or group discussion on the qualities of good writing may precede the time of personal examination and goal setting. Evaluation then becomes an ongoing technique as well as a long-term device to measure growth.

Children and teachers are only occasionally concerned with the secondary goal of a handwriting program, which is the rate of writing. In those instances where speed has become an issue, it can be easily measured by having the pupils write a familiar passage for a specific number of minutes. Since speed is generally expressed in letters per minute, it can be readily determined by dividing the total number of letters written by the number of minutes allowed. The average speed for manuscript writing in the second grade, for example, is about 30 letters per minute while the standard speed for cursive writing in the fifth grade is about 60 letters per minute. Beginners in either style write more slowly, of course, than advanced pupils.

The following is a possible guide in determining speed attainments in cursive writing by grade level:[22]

Grade	*Letters Per Minute*	*Letters Per Line*
2	30	14–16
3	40	16–20
4	50	20–22
5	60	22–25
6	67	25–28

Legibility

Legibility in handwriting involves alignment, letter formation, line quality, size and proportion, slant, and spacing. These elements, listed in Figure 6.11, may be informally measured in manuscript and cursive writing in several ways.

Manuscript (Or Cursive) Handwriting Check List

Element	Child Rating	Teacher Verification
Alignment	________	________
Letter Formation	________	________
Line Quality	________	________
Size and Proportion	________	________
Slant	________	________
Spacing	________	________

Figure 6.11. Handwriting Checklist for Self Evaluation.

Evaluation and correction of cursive handwriting problems in particular are shown in Figures 6.12 and 6.13, respectively.

Figure 6.12. Evaluation Sheet of Student Cursive Handwriting.

Student Handwriting Evaluation Sheet

	O.K.	Needs Review
1. Performance observation.		
a. pen or pencil is held properly	☐	☐
b. paper is positioned at a "normal" slant	☐	☐
c. writing posture is acceptable	☐	☐
d. writing speed is acceptable	☐	☐
2. Correct letter formation.		
a. closed letters are closed	☐	☐
b. looped letters are looped	☐	☐
c. stick letters are not loops	☐	☐
d. i's and j's are dotted directly above	☐	☐
e. x's and t's are crossed accurately	☐	☐
f. m's and n's have the correct number of humps	☐	☐
g. all lower case letters begin on the line (unless they follow b, o, v, or w)	☐	☐
h. b, o, v, and w end above the line	☐	☐
i. all lower case letters end on the line	☐	☐
j. v's and u's are clearly differentiated	☐	☐
k. connecting strokes of v and y are clearly not ry and ry	☐	☐
l. upper case letters are correctly or acceptably formed	☐	☐
m. numbers are correctly formed	☐	☐
3. Fluency.		
a. writing is smooth, not choppy	☐	☐
b. pencil pressure appears even	☐	☐
c. words appear to be written as complete units	☐	☐
d. letter connection is smooth	☐	☐
4. Letter size, slant, and spacing.		
a. lower case letters are uniform size	☐	☐
b. upper case letters are clearly larger than lower case letters	☐	☐
c. upper case letters are uniform in size	☐	☐
d. tail lengths are consistent and do not interfere with letters on the line below	☐	☐
e. tall letters are a consistent height and are clearly taller than other letters	☐	☐
f. writing is not too small or too large	☐	☐
g. slant of letters is acceptable	☐	☐
h. slant of letters is consistent	☐	☐
i. spacing of letters and words is consistent	☐	☐

Figure 6.12 (cont.)

5. Student attitude toward writing
   a. student's opinion of his writing skills ☐ ☐
   b. "writing is hard" ☐ ☐
   c. writes too slowly ☐ ☐
   d. feels good about writing ☐ ☐
6. Overall teacher evaluation.

Teacher Recommendation:

☐ You appear to write smoothly and easily. Your letters are formed correctly. Letter size, slant, and spacing are good. Your writing is neat and legible. It is *not* necessary for you to complete the handwriting exercises.

☐ You appear to write smoothly and easily. You have developed your own writing style which is acceptable, neat and legible. It is *not* necessary for you to complete the handwriting exercises.

☐ You appear to write smoothly and easily. However, your letter formation, neatness, and legibility need some work. Please complete the handwriting exercises.

☐ Writing seems to be difficult for you. You need practice in handwriting skills. Please complete the handwriting exercises.

Reprinted by permission from Lynne R. Ruedy, "Handwriting Instruction," ACADEMIC THERAPY, Vol. 18, 1983, Novato, California, Academic Therapy Publications, pp. 427–428.

Figure 6.13. Correction of Common Cursive Handwriting Problems.

Handwriting is so small that it cannot be read easily.	*in adult proportion*	• Use ruled paper on which a midline appears or rule a midline on standard writing paper. Explain that minimum letters touch the midline. • Practice large writing at the chalkboard. • Give correct models of words, have the student copy them, then evaluate for size. • Identify the problem so that the student is aware of what must be corrected.
When two maximum undercurves are joined (*ll, fl,*) letter formation suffers.	*parallel*	• Emphasize that the basic undercurve stroke must be made correctly. • Make a wide undercurve to allow room for the loop that follows. • Make slant strokes parallel to each other.
The height of the lowercase letters is not consistent.	*Write freely*	• Use paper that has a midline and a descender space, or rule a midline on standard paper. • Have the student identify maximum, intermediate, and minimum letters. • Evaluate writing for alignment by drawing a horizontal line across the tops of the letters that are supposed to be of the same size. • Shift paper as the writing progresses.

Figure 6.13 (cont.)

The maximum letters (*b, f, h, k, l*) are made without loops.	little	• Demonstrate and explain proper formation of undercurve that begins loop of letter. • Demonstrate and explain proper formation of the slant stroke. • Point out that the top of the letters is rounded and determines the width of the loops.
The slant of the writing is irregular.	flight	• Check for correct paper position. • Pull strokes in the proper direction. • Shift paper as writing progresses. • Shift hand to the right as writing progresses. • Evaluate slant by drawing lines through letters to show the angle at which they are made.
When an undercurve joins an overcurve (*in, um,*) the letters are poorly written.	instrument	• Show how the undercurve to overcurve is a smooth, flowing stroke. • Explain that the undercurve ending continues up and then quickly overcurves into the downward slant stroke.
The quality of the writing changes within a single word.	laboratory	• Shift both the paper and the hand as the writing progresses. The paper moves toward the student, and the hand moves away. • Write in the same area of the paper, roughly a six-inch diameter circle that is located at the midpoint of the body about ten inches from the edge of the desk. • Do not reach out to write or write very close to the body.
The letters *a, d, g, o, q* are not closed.	boat amount	• Stress proper beginning strokes. • Write correctly formed model letters on the student's paper, explaining the strokes while the student watches.
Non-looped letters such as *t, p, i, u, w* are looped and become difficult to read.	little	• Demonstrate that there is a pause at the top of these letters. • Encourage the student to write slower, as speed causes the loops in the letters. • Pause before making the slant stroke in the letters *a, d, g, i, j, p, q, t, u, w,* and *y.* • Emphasize the retrace in these strokes.
Checkstroke joinings, for example *br, we,* are poorly made.	break weather	• Demonstrate the letters *b, v, o,* and *w* and explain the strokes as you form them. • Use the auditory stroke description "retrace and swing right" as students practice *b, v, o, w.* • Demonstrate correct joinings in which the first letter has a checkstroke. • Point out the letter forms that change when they are preceded by a checkstroke: *br, os.*

Figure 6.13 (cont.)

Handwriting is so slow that there is no smoothness in the individual letters.	*Intermediate*	• Encourage students to write letters with smooth and complete motions. • Engage in relaxation exercises before practicing writing. Excessive muscle tension is the cause of slow writing. • Emphasize rhythm rather than alignment or slant. These qualities can be developed later.
Joinings involving overcurves, such as *ga, jo,* are not well made.	*baggage job*	• Show how all overcurve connections cross at the baseline, not above or below it. • Make the overcurve motion continuous. Do not change its direction in mid-stroke. • Check letter formation.

Reprinted from Thomas M. Wasylyk and Michael Milone, Jr., CORRECTIVE TECHNIQUES IN HANDWRITING: CURSIVE, Zaner-Bloser Educational Publishers, Honesdale, PA., Professional Pamphlet Series #12, 1980. Used with permission.

Alignment

Compare the evenness of the letters along the baseline and along the tops of the letters. All letters of the same size should be of an even height. Draw a light line horizontally along the tops of all the maximum letters, another line along the tops of all minimum letters, and finally a third line along the tops of the intermediate letters. Compare the results. Then, with a ruler, draw a line touching the base of as many of the letters as possible. Is this line the same as the baseline?

Letter Formation

Manuscript writing consists of horizontal, vertical, and slanted lines and cirlces and parts of circles. Correct letter models placed adjacent to the child's writing will aid evaluation.

Cursive writing involves two basic motions: the slant and the oval. Since every cursive letter uses either or both motions, the child's letter formations may be evaluated by placing correct letter models near the writing paper.

Two groups of researchers interested in developing techniques for assessing letter formation have recently used transparent overlays to measure the range of deviations in handwritten letters from given model letters.[23]

Line Quality

Letter line quality is described as the evenness, smoothness, and thickness of the pencil or pen line. Some lines may be too light, some too heavy, and others of varying quality. Light lines may result from writing instruments which are too fine or too hard. Heavy lines occur when the child bears down too heavily on the paper or grips the writing instrument too tightly. Varying line quality results from inconsistent pressure which in turn is due to fatigue or overly rapid writing.

Size and Proportion

Proportion refers to the height of letters in relation to each other and to the writing space. For manuscript and cursive writing, lines may be drawn along the tops of letters to see if they are uniformly written as suggested in the particular handwriting program. In manuscript, are the uppercase letters and the tall lowercase letters a full space high? Do all other letters except the lowercase *t* extend from the baseline only to the midline?

In cursive, there are two proportions used (primary and adult) with the change from primary to adult proportion usually occurring at the fifth-grade level. In primary proportion, are the minimum letters one half the size of maximum letters? Are the intermediate letters midway between minimum and maximum letters in size? Do the uppercase letters, the maximum letters, and the lowercase *b, f, h, k,* and *l* touch the headlines?

Slant

There should be no slant in manuscript writing because letters are vertical. Vertical quality may be evaluated by drawing light lines through the vertical strokes of the letters.

All cursive letters slant whether they are lowercase or uppercase. Regularity of slant is readily determined by drawing straight lines through the slant strokes of the letters. If the lines are at different angles, the slant is irregular; if the lines are parallel, the slant is uniform and the writing legible. If lines are parallel but the slant is too extreme or too little, the writer must change the tilt of the paper.

Spacing

Spacing between letters, words, and sentences should be uniform. In manuscript, is the widest space between the straight line letters? Is the second widest space between a circle and a straight line letter? Is the least amount of space between two circle letters? Does the spacing between words equal one lowercase *o?* Does spacing between sentences, for margins, and for indentations equal lowercase *o*'s? Is spacing consistent throughout the writing?

In cursive, is there enough spacing between letters within a word so that each letter appears legible by itself? Does spacing between sentences equal one uppercase *O?* Does spacing between paragraphs equal two uppercase *O*'s? Is spacing consistent throughout the writing?

Conferencing

Evaluation of each child's handwriting progress should occur regularly through teacher-pupil conferencing. It involves using an individual chart, folder, or scale. Teachers may also wish to keep a small box of four-by-six-inch file cards, listing each pupil's strengths and deficits in the handwriting areas. Such a box is helpful during parent conferences because handwriting is regarded as a critical skill by many parents of elementary school age children.

An Individual Chart

In their notebooks the pupils keep a chart which has been adapted to one writing skill. They can use it to indicate progressive levels of achievement and to determine new target goals. The chart can be marked off in monthly columns.

An Individual Folder

The pupils file one handwritten or typed composition into their folders weekly, dating each paper. If the folders are begun at the start of the school year the children can detect their own progress and note areas for improvement. The folder may include papers from other curricular areas such as social studies. Again, the teacher and pupils can use the folders in setting up goals.

An Individual Scale

The pupils can make handwriting scales from specimens of their own writing. They begin by collecting several of their papers over a period of some three or four weeks and then (a) cut a few lines at random from each paper; (b) date each sample and arrange them all in order of quality (not date); and (c) paste them on a large sheet of paper, putting the best specimen at the top. Such a scale should be made each semester for a better indication of progress.

School and Commercial Handwriting Scales

It has been suggested that one teacher or a group of teachers can collect many samples of handwriting for a specific grade level and then divide them into various categories of global legibility (ranging from excellent to poor). For each category one or two samples can be mounted as model for comparison purposes. Then for each level a range of elements (including alignment, slant, and spacing) may be illustrated. If a value of five to one is assigned for each element, the total score for an overall rating is readily determined. These samples can be collected on a school-wide or district basis.

Although only one third of the schools use some sort of school or commercial scale for evaluating children's handwriting, the five scales used are: locally developed school scales; the Freeman Scale (1959); the West (American) Scale (1957); the Ayres Scale (1957); and the Noble Scale (1965).

The use of commercial scales is not especially helpful to the classroom teacher (except sometimes in the area of assigning grades) for several reasons. The reliability of the scales is either not given or only moderate. All material used for writing is copied and/or memorized by the writer. There is no assurance that the range of the handwriting quality of a given population of children has been explored. The scales predominantly measure only cursive writing. Right-handed writing is mixed with left-handed writing in a single scale. Finally, teachers are generally either unfamiliar with the scales or inconsistent in using them, although once they become adept at using scales to rate handwriting samples, they can soon rate samples without even using the scales.

Discussion Questions

1. How can you determine when a young child is ready to learn handwriting?
2. If handwriting is primarily a tool of communication, how can you justify teaching children one of the alternative forms as their only system of handwriting?
3. What specific practices would you use to teach a left-handed pupil to write?
4. Should everyone be able to type in highly industrial nations such as the United States? If so, should typewriting instruction be offered in every elementary school? Would it be feasible?

Suggested Projects

1. Examine some of the more commonly used resources which accompany any one commercial system of handwriting. Then, if possible, compare several different systems (including Zaner-Bloser, Noble and Noble, and Palmer), noting similarities and differences in philosophy, equipment used, and evaluative techniques.
2. Administer to a five- or six-year-old child one informal test for handedness and one for eyedness. Report your results to your peers.
3. Plan an introductory lesson in cursive writing for a group of third-grade boys and girls.
4. Evaluate your own handwriting, whether it be manuscript or cursive. Could it serve as a model for young learners?

5. Collect handwriting samples from five elementary school children. Then confer (or describe how you would confer) with each in order to help the pupil improve his or her writing.
6. Set up the learning center on handwriting shown in Figure 6.14.

Figure 6.14. Language Arts Learning Center: Handwriting.

TYPE OF CENTER: **Handwriting—Manuscript** TIME: 15-20 minutes
GRADE LEVEL: 2 NUMBER OF STUDENTS: 2-4

INSTRUCTIONAL OBJECTIVE: The students will become more familiar with the alphabet through writing practice.

MATERIALS: Cardboard for three-sided fold-out, *finished papers* folder, large envelope for letter cards, tag paper for letter cards (cut 3″ × 3″ cards and print one letter on each card), paper and pencils.

DIRECTIONS:

1. Take a worksheet and write your name on it.
2. Pick a card from the envelope.
3. Write the letter you see on the card.
4. On that same line write a word that begins with the letter that follows the letter you write. Look at the example. If you wrote **b,** write a word that begins with **c.**
5. Pick another card and write the letter on that card.
6. On that same line write a word that begins with the following letter.
7. Do this same task with each card you choose.
8. Put your finished paper in the *finished papers* folder.
9. Put all of the cards back in the envelope for someone else to use.

Note: A tape recorder could be used to give oral directions for retarded readers. Thus, the student will associate the printed directions with the identical oral directions.

SUGGESTED IDEAS: This activity could be adapted to cursive writing for grades 3 to 5.

EVALUATION: The teacher checks all completed work. Incorrect responses, spelling errors, or poor writing skills indicate that the student needs assistance to achieve better results.

Source: From PATHWAYS TO IMAGINATION by Angela S. Reeke and James L. Laffey, © 1979 by Scott, Foresman & Company. Reprinted by permission.

Related Readings

Barbe, W. et al., eds., 1984. *Handwriting: Basic Skills for Effective Communication.* Columbus, Ohio: Zaner-Bloser, Inc.

Burton, G. M. 1982. "Writing Numerals," *Academic Therapy, 17,* pp. 415–424.

D'Angelo, K. 1982. "Developing Legibility and Uniqueness in Handwriting with Calligraphy," *Language Arts, 59,* pp. 23–27.

Fisher, C. 1984. "Ten Top Handwriting Hints," *Instructor, 93*(8), pp. 75–76.

Getman, G. 1983. "About Handwriting," *Academic Therapy,* 19, pp. 139–146.

Harries, R., and Yost, H. 1981. *Elements of Handwriting.* Novato, CA: Academic Therapy Publications.

Hayes, D. 1982. "Handwriting Practice: The effects of perceptual prompts," *Journal of Educational Research, 75,* pp. 169–172.

Lamme, L., and Ayris, B. 1983. "Is the Handwriting of Beginning Writers Influenced by Writing Tools?", *Journal of Research and Development in Education, 17,* pp. 32–38.

Milone, M., and Waslyck, T. 1981. "Handwriting in Special Education," *Teaching Exceptional Children, 14,* pp. 58–61.

Trap-Porter, J. et al. 1984. "D'Nealian and Zaner-Bloser Manuscript Alphabets and Initial Transition to Cursive Handwriting," *Journal of Educational Research, 77,* pp. 343–345.

Chapter Notes

1. V. Froese, "Handwriting: Practice, Pragmatism, and Progress," in *Research in the Language Arts,* V. Froese and S. B. Straw, eds. (Baltimore: University Park Press, 1981), p. 227.
2. D. W. Andersen, "Correlates of Handwriting Legibility: What Makes Writing Readable?" in *Forum For Focus,* M. L. King, R. Emans, and P. Cianciolo, eds. (Urbana, Illinois: National Council of Teachers of English, 1973), pp. 137–143.
3. Sir A. Bullock, *A Language for Life* (London: Her Majesty's Stationery Office, 1975).
4. E. N. Askov and K. N. Greff, "Handwriting: Copying Versus Tracing as the Most Effective Type of Practice," *Journal of Educational Research,* 1975, *69,* pp. 96–98; E. Hirsch, "The Effects of Letter Formation Practice and Letter Discrimination Training on Kindergarten Handwriting Performance," *Dissertation Abstracts International,* 1973, *33,* pp. 6648A–49A; and U. Kirk, "Learning to Copy Letters: A Cognitive Rule-Governed Task," *Elementary School Journal,* 1980, *81,* p. 29.
5. N. Sovik, "Developmental Trends of Visual Feedback Control and Learning Children's Copying and Tracking Skills," *Journal of Experimental Education,* 1980/81, *49,* p. 116.
6. R. M. Forster, "An Experiment in Teaching Transitional Cursive Handwriting by Educational Television with Teacher Attitude toward the Teaching of Handwriting as a Factor," *Dissertation Abstracts International,* 1971, *32,* p. 1184A.
7. L. L. Lamme, "Handwriting in an Early Childhood Curriculum," *Young Children,* 1979, 35(1), p. 20.
8. C. Sinclair, "Dominance Patterns of Young Children: A Follow-up Study," *Perceptual and Motor Skills,* 1971, *32,* p. 142.
9. W. Barbe, M. Milone, Jr., and T. Wasylyk, "Manuscript is the 'Write' Start," *Academic Therapy,* 1983, *18,* p. 400.
10. R. E. Coles and Y. Goodman, "Do We Really Need Those Oversized Pencils to Write With?" *Theory Into Practice,* 1980, *19,* pp. 194–95; G. Halpin and G. Halpin, "Special Paper for Beginning Handwriting: An Unjustified Practice?" *Journal of Educational Research,* 1976, *69,* pp. 267–269; and J. S. Krzeski, "Effect of Different Writing Tools and Paper on Performance of the Third Grader," *Elementary English,* 1971, *48,* pp. 821–824.

11. Adapted from W. Barbe and M. N. Milone, *Teaching Handwriting through Modality Strengths* (Columbus, Ohio: Zaner-Bloser Inc., 1980).
12. D. Durkin, *Teaching Young Children to Read,* 3rd ed. (Boston: Allyn & Bacon, 1980), p. 166.
13. L. W. Horton, "Illegibilities in the Cursive Handwriting of Sixth-Graders," *Elementary School Journal,* 1970, *70,* pp. 446–450.
14. C. L. Lehman, *Handwriting Models for Schools* (Portland, Oregon: The Alcuin Press, 1976).
15. W. J. Oskendahl, "Keyboard Literacy for Hawaii's Primary Children," *Educational Horizons,* 1972, *51,* pp. 21–22.
16. G. Petitclerc, *Young Fingers on a Typewriter* (San Rafael, California: Academic Therapy Publications, 1975), p. 9.
17. A. Cothran and G. E. Mason, "The Typewriter: Time-tested Tool for Teaching Reading and Writing," *Elementary School Journal,* 1978, *78,* pp. 172–173; R. DeLoach, "A Study of Fine Motions by Learners of Touch Typewriting at Three Levels of Physical Development," *Dissertation Abstracts,* 1968, *29,* p. 831-A; and D. Kaake, "Teaching Elementary Age Children Touch Typing as an Aid to Language Arts Instruction," *Reading Teacher,* 1983, *36,* pp. 640–644.
18. G. E. Tagatz et al., "Effect of Three Methods of Instruction upon the Handwriting Performance of Third and Fourth Graders," *American Educational Research Journal,* 1968, *5,* pp. 81–90.
19. *Correcting Handwriting Problems: Integration of Children with Special Needs in a Regular Classroom* (Lexington, Massachusetts: Public Schools, 1974), pp. 6–17.
20. C. Hardyck, L. F. Petrinovich, and R. D. Goldman, "Left-Handedness and Cognitive Deficit," *Cortex,* 1976, *12,* pp. 266–279.
21. P. Addy and P. E. Wylie, "The 'Right' Way to Write," *Childhood Education,* 1973, *49,* pp. 253–255.
22. W. Barbe, *Evaluating Handwriting: Cursive* (Columbus, Ohio: Zaner-Bloser, Inc., 1977).
23. J. J. Helwig, J. Johns, J. B. Norman, and J. O. Cooper, "The Measurement of Manuscript Letter Strokes," *Journal of Applied Behavior Analysis,* 1976, *9,* pp. 231–236; and J. Jones, J. Trap, and J. Cooper, "Technical Report: Students' Self-Recording of Manuscript Letter Strokes," *Journal of Applied Behavior Analysis,* 1977, *10,* pp. 509–514.

Spelling 7

Objectives

The two major areas which make English spelling highly systematic
Young children and invented spelling
Modern guidelines for teaching spelling
Spelling and reading

Discover As You Read This Chapter If*

1. Most contemporary writing systems are based on the alphabet.
2. English spelling is highly irregular.
3. Learning to spell is a task of rote memorization.
4. Young children demonstrate a detailed understanding of English phonology.
5. As children develop in the primary grades, they switch to standard spelling without appreciable difficulty.
6. Teaching proofreading must be delayed until the intermediate grades.
7. Spelling is best taught in conjunction with functional writing.
8. Calling attention to the so-called "hard spots" within a word is a valuable technique in teaching spelling.
9. Making boys and girls write a word repeatedly assures learning the correct spelling of that word.
10. Surveys of published spelling series for the elementary grades have raised serious doubts about the usefulness of such programs.

*Answers to these true-or-false statements may be found in Appendix 6.

All modern natural languages have been and continue to be primarily aural-oral communication systems. Over the centuries, of course, a few of them have added a writing system as a secondary means of communication so that messages could be transmitted over space and time. However, such a writing system, or *orthography,* is only a substitute for the oral language. It is predicated on the structural characteristics of oral language and demands that its users be comfortable with both visual skills and listening-speaking skills. Its symbols graphically represent the phonology, morphology, and syntax of speech, with the influence of each of these three components dependent upon the nature of the graphemes of the particular language.

Three broad kinds of writing systems can be noted. The oldest is *logographic writing* in which the graphic symbols represent entire words or even concepts. Those symbols or characters can be understood without recourse to oral language, and this trait is considered to be the major advantage of logographic orthography. Its principal drawback, on the other hand, is that learning to read and write in such a system is a lengthy and laborious process because there are almost as many characters as there are words or concepts. Scholars in China, for example, must learn approximately 9000 characters (out of a possible 80,000).

A second important writing system is the *syllabary.* It uses graphemes to represent the syllables which make up the oral language. By combining syllabic signs which represent a group of syllables, the writer can convey a spoken word. The chief advantage of the syllabary over the logographic writing system is the substantial reduction in the number of graphic symbols needed in order to read and write. Its principal disadvantage is that it can only be used in languages with simple syllabic structures; i.e., in languages where a syllable consists of one consonant and one vowel or even a single vowel. Few languages in the world today have such simple structures, one example being spoken Japanese which uses two syllabaries as part of its orthography.

Derived from the ancient Greeks and Romans, the third orthography is *alphabetic writing.* It relies mainly on phonological components so that its graphemes represent its phonemes. Most contemporary orthographies are based on the alphabetic system due to its economy and flexibility. Ideally a spoken language with 26 speech sounds would have an alphabet of 26 letters.

The English Alphabetic Orthography

Some languages such as Hawaiian, Turkish, Spanish, and Finnish come close to attaining the ideal orthography of using one grapheme to represent each phoneme. Their native speakers find it easy to spell nearly any word they know how to pronounce and equally simple to pronounce nearly any word they see spelled. Apparently, all that the schoolchildren in these language communities have to do to become successful spellers is to memorize the comparatively few graphemes involved and their matching phonemic references, and later learn to write the graphemes in the same sequence in which the phonemes are arranged.

No alphabetic orthography however has a perfect and consistent "fit" between its phonemes and its graphemes. American English, for example, has approximately 44 phonemes in its sound system and only 26 graphemes in its writing system. The discrepancies between English pronunciation and English spelling have been considered by linguists who later determined that several factors are responsible:

1. There have been historical accidents of printers' preferences or lexicographers' errors. For example, the earliest English books were printed by the Dutch who mistakenly spelled English words by analogy with Latin roots.
2. English vocabulary includes many loanwords from foreign languages which preserve the graphic conventions found in the native language. For example, the French *eau* appears in *bureau* and *tableau.*
3. The pronunciation of English words has changed without corresponding graphic changes so that words which were once distinct in pronunciation are now homophonous. For example, there is *knight* and *night.*
4. The spelling of English words tends to ignore changes in sound, particularly when vowel changes result from a shift of stress. Related words may look more alike than they sound. For example, there is *crime* and *criminal.*
5. The current pronunciations of words are not at all distinctly represented in writing. For example, there is *machine.*

One grapheme may represent more than one phoneme while one phoneme may be represented by more than one grapheme. In all there are about 2000 ways to spell the phonemes of English. Both consonant and vowel phonemes together with their symbols are shown in Figure 7.1.

Despite its frequently touted discrepancies, *English spelling is nevertheless highly systematic,* according to linguists and linguistic research conducted during the past two decades. The Stanford University Spelling Project proved through computer analysis of more than 17,000 common words that English spelling has an underlying systematic nature. On the basis of phoneme-grapheme correspondences alone, the computer spelled correctly about 50 percent of the words. More importantly, however, an examination of the words which had been misspelled showed that, had morphological information been included in the computer analysis, over 85 percent, or about 15,000 words, would have been correctly spelled.

When Richard Venezky analyzed some 20,000 words in the Thorndike-Lorge List on the basis of both phonological *and* morphological factors, he established that English orthography is a writing system in which both of those groups of factors play basic roles in determining spelling patterns within words.

Figure 7.1. English Sounds and Their Symbols.

Symbol	Example
Vowel sounds	
/æ/	bat
/ɛ/	bet
/I/	bit
/a/	pot
/ʌ/	but
/u/	put
/e/	bait
/i/	beet
/o/	boat
/u/	boot
/yu/	cute
/¢/	bought
/ay/	bite
/ow/	bout
/oy/	boy
/ə/	around, chicken (frequently varies with /I/)
/E/	the first vowel sound in Terry, Harry, Mary

Symbol	Example
Consonant sounds	
/b/	boy
/č/	chair
/d/	do
/f/	fat
/g/	go
/h/	hit
/j/	jet
/k/	kiss
/l/	let
/m/	man
/n/	no
/ŋ/	sing
/p/	pan
/r/	rat
/s/	sit
/s/	ship
/t/	to
/θ/	thin
/ð/	then
/v/	van
/w/	wet
/y/	yet
/z/	zoo
/z/	azure

Reprinted from Paula Russell AN OUTLINE OF ENGLISH SPELLING, Technical Report #55, 1975, SWRL Educational Research and Development, Los Alamitos, California, p. 47. Used with permission.

Finally, transformational-generative grammarians Noam Chomsky and Morris Halle have asserted that English spelling is a very reliable system based both on sound-to-spelling correspondences and on morphological principles of English. In order to maintain a graphic identity among words which are semantically related, however, phonetic differences are largely overlooked. This means that words that are the same semantically look the same graphically (e.g., *nation/national*), and readers can focus on meaning. The specific principles arising from the Chomsky/Halle approach can be delineated as follows:

- *One-syllable, monomorphemic words.* Spelling is based on the relationships of individual sounds and letters; that is, phoneme-grapheme correspondences.
- *Polysyllabic, monomorphemic words.* Spelling of the *stressed* syllable is based on rules of phoneme-grapheme correspondence. Spelling of the *unstressed* syllable is arbitrary but choices are limited.
- *Compounds.* Morphemes are spelled independently according to phoneme-grapheme correspondences. No changes in either component result from combining them.
- *Prefixed words.* The base morpheme is spelled according to phoneme-grapheme correspondences. Prefixes vary only in vowel pronunciation, not in vowel spelling; their spelling is governed by morphemic identity rather than by sound.
- *Suffixed words.* These words are governed by the same spelling principles as those governing prefixed words with three additional complexities: (1) some suffixes are homophones but ordinarily homophonous pairs have different functions (e.g., *-ess* is a feminine nominalizer but *-ous* is an adjectival suffix); (2) suffixes often cause stress changes in base morphemes in which case affix-aided spelling is of predictive value (e.g., spelling the *o* in *ignorance* on the basis of /o/ in *ignore*); and (3) special processes are involved in combining base and suffix (e.g., *tie* is changed to *ty* in *tying*).
- *Foreign words.* Some sets of foreign words, particularly those from Greek and French, have spelling patterns that deviate from normal rules of correspondence. Such words frequently have stylistic traits of identification. For example, there is the Greek *ch* spelling for /k/ and the French *ch* spelling for /š/, with the Greek words being scholarly or technical (as in *choreography* and *architect*) and the French words having connotations of prestige or luxury (as in *chauffeur* and *chalet*).[1]

There are, of course, spellings which do not follow any of the above principles, but these are relatively few in number.

The Psychology of Spelling

The modern advances in understanding the true nature of English orthography have been matched fortunately and also recently by advances in understanding how children learn to spell. Numerous studies have concluded that *learning to spell is a developmental process* and not a low-order task of rote memorization. Consequently, the widely-held practice of making children write a word again and again is invalid as a technique for learning the correct spelling of that word.

Long before boys and girls start school, they acquire the fundamentals of language and even learn to use a grammar to put words together to form sentences. Language development, therefore, proceeds from the simple to the complex. So too does spelling development as maturing children gradually progress toward a greater understanding of English orthography.

During recent years work with preschoolers, kindergarteners, and early primary pupils has shown that there is an apparent analogy between learning to spell and learning to speak.[2] Children learning to talk constantly mispronounce words, omit words, or improperly order words. Nobody actually teaches them to speak. Instead, they learn about their language as they listen and talk and are actively involved in the speech environment. They appear able to identify, classify, and apply concepts about the "rules" of oral language.

In a similar way, boys and girls learn to spell by writing (and later, by reading). Beginning writers quickly realize, however, that the 26 letters of the English alphabet are not enough to spell all the words which they wish to write since English has more than 26 phonemes. Upon making this discovery, the children either ask parents, teachers, or other adults how to spell the missing sounds, or they *invent* their own nonstandard spelling. They appear able to identify and classify the sounds they hear and do not use graphemes frivolously. Of course they misspell many words when they first write, but, given enough opportunities over a prolonged period of time, they will learn to spell. If young children are corrected constantly as they try to talk, they will soon hesitate to speak for fear of correction. Likewise, if they are corrected constantly as they try to spell, they will become thwarted for fear of correction.

Language acquisition is a creative feat, and all children are creative when it comes to learning their own language. This additional aspect of language processing—innovative spelling—is not confined to just a few boys and girls. Instead, linguists recognize that children generally are able to spell on their own. Of course, the judgments of five-year-olds, for example, concerning relationships between English spelling and phonology differ qualitatively from those of adults.[3] Nevertheless, children have demonstrated a surprisingly detailed understanding of English phonology.

The teacher or other adult, however, must give the children the idea that they *can* spell. He or she must also recognize "correctness" (by taking cues from the children and from a few phonetic perceptions—not from standard spelling) and must learn to respond to nonstandard spelling appropriately.

The particular circumstances of the first writing will vary with the child, depending upon his or her own timing and the situation in which the need arises. What remains constant is the expectation that children will figure it out for themselves when the time comes. The activity must develop as an expressive one and not degenerate into a form of exercise. The function of the teacher should be to give boys and girls access to spelling but not to require it of them. How much writing they will eventually produce, if any, depends on their interest.

An analogy to painting and drawing is useful. A teacher of young children makes paints and paper available to them and encourages them. The teacher still leaves it up to the children, however, to decide when, how, and what they will paint. Early spelling should be treated in much the same way. If a teacher encourages spelling once it starts, welcomes and values the spelling, and transmits a feeling to the children that they are doing something exciting and useful, some children will go ahead and make progress.

Cramer describes how one teacher helped a first grader approximate the spelling of a word needed for a written composition.[4] The child, Jenny, thought she was not able to spell *hospital.* The teacher, Mrs. Nicholas, told Jenny to spell it as well as she could, writing as much of the word as possible. When Jenny insisted that she didn't know any part of the word, the teacher-pupil dialogue proceeded in this manner:

> Mrs. Nicholas: Yes, you do, Jenny. How do you think *hospital* begins? (*Mrs. Nicholas pronounced* hospital *distinctly emphasizing the first part slightly. She avoided distorting the pronunciation.*)
>
> Jenny (*tentatively*): *h-s.*
>
> Mrs. Nicholas: Good! Write down the *hs.* What do you hear next in *hospital?* (*Again Mrs. Nicholas pronounced* hospital *distinctly, but this time she emphasized the second part slightly.*)
>
> Jenny (*still tentatively*): *p-t.*
>
> Mrs. Nicholas: Very good! Write down the *pt.* Now, what do you hear last in *hospital?* (*While pronouncing the word* hospital *for the last time Mrs. Nicholas emphasized the last part slightly.*)
>
> Jenny (*with some assurance*): *l.*
>
> Mrs. Nicholas: Yes, Jenny, *h-s-p-t-l* is a fine way to spell *hospital.* There is another way to spell the word, but for now I want you to spell all words you don't know just as we did *hospital.*

Strategies and Stages of Invented Spelling

Boys and girls do not proceed as spellers randomly or by rote. Nor do they all learn spelling in exactly the same way. Still, researchers have found that strategies of learning to spell progress in about the same sequence for all children. Observed in the early writing of young pupils are these spelling strategies:

1. The use of single letters to represent the sound of the full letter name (*hol* for *hole,* and *ppl* for *people*).
2. The omission of nasal sounds before consonants (*plat* for *plant* and *sic* for *sink*).
3. The use of *t* to render /t/ in the past tense form of certain verbs (*likt* for *liked* and *lookt* for *looked*).
4. The omission of the vowel when the syllable has a vowel-like consonant such as *l, m, n,* and *r* (*brd* for *bird* and *opn* for *open*).
5. The use of *d* to render the flap phoneme for *t* between vowels (*prede* for *pretty* and *bodm* for *bottom*).
6. The use of a rather advanced set of linguistic rules for deciding which vowel letter to use when children have not yet learned the spelling of the short vowel sounds (*fel* for *feel* and *fill*).
7. The substitution of *chr* and *jr* for *tr* and *dr* (*chran* for *train* and *jragin* for *dragon*).
8. The occasional use of letters according to their full pronounced names (*yl* for *while* and *r* for *are*).

Stages of early spelling evolve systematically, regardless of the geographical location of the children or the instruction which they receive. The various stages seem to form a sequence for spelling development. Five spelling strategies/stages used by early primary children as they moved toward correctly spelled words are described as deviant, prephonetic, phonetic, transitional, and correct.[5]

The first stage is labeled the *deviant stage* and occurs in early kindergarten (for children with previous exposure to print) or grade one (for those with no such earlier exposure). Boys and girls try to approximate writing by random use of letters and Arabic numerals which they are able to produce from recall. They often write from right to left and repeat letter sequences. Examples of deviant spellings include IMMPMPT and BDRNMPM, both of which could only be "read back" by the spellers themselves. The implicit understanding revealed during this stage is that speech can be recorded by graphic symbols.

The *prephonetic* stage is the second stage to emerge. Children do not represent essential sound features of words, although they do use letters to represent some speech sounds which they hear. They sometimes spell a word with the correct beginning and/or ending consonant sound and generally use one-, two-, and three-letter representations of complete and separate words. Examples of prephonetic spellings include MSR for *monster,* DG for *dog,* and P for *pie,* revealing that vowels are often omitted. The implicit understandings shown during this stage are that specific letters stand for specific speech sounds and that speech is made up of discreet words.

The third stage is the *phonetic stage* when the essential phonetic elements of words are represented even though the letters used may be wrong. While phonetic spelling does not resemble standard spelling, it is readable to most first-grade teachers and to the writers themselves. Examples of phonetic spellings are PPL for *people* and PRD for *purred.* A major difference between the prephonetic and phonetic stages is revealed in the spelling of *chirp:* prephonetically, it is spelled CHP, but phonetically, it is CHRP. The implicit understandings shown at this time are that every sound feature of a word can be represented by one letter or a combination of letters and that the graphic form of a word contains every speech sound in the same order in which those sounds are heard when the word is spoken.

Children in the *transitional stage* produce words which look like English words although the spelling is sometimes nonstandard. Generally, in the last half of the first grade or early in the second grade, boys and girls understand many of the orthographic rules of English even if they do not always apply them precisely. Vowels appear in every syllable and inflectional endings are spelled uniformly. Children intersperse standard spelling with nonstandard phonetic spelling. Examples of transitional spellings include *com* for *come, eagel* for *eagle,* and *chrip* for *chirp.* The implicit understandings displayed at this stage are: (a) there are numerous ways to spell many of the identical speech sounds; (b) every word has a standard spelling which is used in print; (c) many words are not spelled entirely phonetically; and (d) words must be spelled in such a way that everyone can read them readily.

The fifth and final stage is the *correct stage* during which boys and girls spell words using standard orthography. They finally realize that words are units of sound *and* units of meaning. Pupils should be introduced to formal spelling instruction early, according to Gentry, if they advance to the correct stage prior to second grade.[6] Such instruction, however, should be delayed for those older children who are slower to notice orthographic rules. Until they are well into the stages of phonetic and transitional spelling, children cannot be successfully introduced to formal spelling lessons.

It is important to note at this point that none of the children studied by the various researchers have had any difficulty in switching to standard spelling. If spelling is regarded as being based on a set of implicit rules about sound-to-symbol correspondence and morphological principles, then the developing child can be described as modifying those rules easily as he or she acquires new information about standard spelling.[7] Kindergarteners, for example, often spell one word several different ways in the same story, attacking each word as a new problem. Nevertheless, as they develop and learn the standard orthography for a word, they will spontaneously substitute it for their own. The key to the transition appears to be *exposure*—to extensive writing experiences, to systematic reading instruction including the acquisition of sight vocabulary, and to an audience willing to read what others have written, provided that indeed it can be read.

Kindergarten, first-grade, and second-grade teachers can help beginning spellers in many ways. They can read to children. They can encourage creative writing, deemphasizing standard spelling and responding appropriately to nonstandard spelling. They can immerse children in a language environment (especially through the language experience approach described in Chapter 9). They can not only allow but actively help boys and girls to learn the alphabet. They can avoid the instruction, "sound it out." Finally, they can encourage children to compare and to categorize words in different ways.

Teaching Spelling: Modern Guidelines

An effective environment for spelling study appears to be the classroom where pupils are most apt to learn the patterns and regularities which make up English orthography. No commercial spelling program used alone can accomplish this because children affect their spelling skills every time they write or otherwise interact with written language. They learn to spell by spelling and must not be restricted in their progress to those words and "rules" which are introduced during formal spelling lessons.

Adults concerned with curriculum development in spelling should bear in mind several principles or guidelines for teaching English spelling today. First, *spelling must be presented in the context of overall language learning.* As a language based activity, spelling demands knowledge of varied aspects of language—semantics, morphology, and phonology. Since children learn language by actively exploring their linguistic environment, spelling instruction must build upon their curiosity about language by encouraging boys and girls to discover how the writing system operates. It should also provide many opportunities for them to practice their findings in new situations. Spelling can never be considered an isolated component of the language arts.

Second, *children must understand that learning to spell has certain unique aspects*. Spelling has the special function of representing language graphically through handwriting/typewriting. It forms a link between verbal and written forms of language expression. It is a multisensory process involving visual, auditory, oral, and haptical (muscular) abilities. While most children are able to use all these sensory modes in learning to spell, they hardly use them all to the same degree or in the same manner. Slower learners, for example, admit that the most effective way for them to learn to spell involves pronunciation of the words by students and teacher.[8] For other pupils the visual processes represent the chief means by which spelling is mastered. And while spelling ability generally is not truly dependent upon haptical experiences, nevertheless haptical memory (so fundamental to typewriting) aids in the act of spelling when combined with the other types of recollections of words. All four mechanisms come into play in the study of each spelling word, as outlined in Figure 7.2.

Furthermore, boys and girls who are learning to spell must actually begin to understand the entire framework of orthography. They will not and should not move one precise indepth step at a time, going from letters and sounds to syllables, and finally to words. Instead, every learner will follow his or her own logic in moving from one aspect of English orthography to another while attempting simultaneously to keep in mind the total framework.

Third, *children seldom make random errors in spelling, so teachers can use error pattern analysis in formulating spelling strategies*. For example, one study of pupils in grades one through four in various Michigan schools showed only three types of errors in spelling vowels: (1) the use of a letter-name strategy (as in *gat* for *gate*) which accounted for 68 percent of all errors; (2) the addition of an incorrect vowel after a correct vowel (as in *hait* for *hat*) which accounted for 25 percent of errors; and (3) the incorrect substitution of one short vowel for another (as in *spick* for *speck*) which accounted for 7 percent of all errors.[9] The researchers stress that teachers must not become upset when children repeatedly make the same type of errors because the errors are not necessarily caused by "not listening" or "not trying." They may be due, instead, to the length of the children's overall development and exposure to words. Recurring errors do not indicate that children will not or cannot spell correctly at a later time.

The teacher or other adult, however, must give the children the idea that they *can* spell. He or she must also recognize "correctness" (by taking cues from the children and from a few phonetic perceptions—not from standard spelling) and must learn to respond to nonstandard spelling appropriately.

By examining children's spelling errors, the teacher can derive hypotheses about each pupil's learning strategies and plan instruction accordingly. Error pattern analysis is a way of regarding the learner and the errors he/she makes during the learning process. Steps which the teacher can take in a diagnostic-prescriptive approach to spelling using such error pattern analysis include the following: (1) collect samples of student writing; (2) place student's misspellings (preferably about 25 errors) and the dictionary's correct spellings side by side; (3) surmise the erroneous strategy in conference with the student and record it; (4) suggest

How to Study a Spelling Word

1. Say the word. Listen to the sounds in it.
2. Look at the word. Notice which letters are used to stand for the sounds in the word.
3. Write the word. Say the word to yourself as you write it. Do not look at the copy.
4. Proof the word. Check the word against the copy to see if it is spelled correctly.
5. Identify the error. Determine which part of the word, if any, has been misspelled.
6. Restudy the word. Study again any word you have misspelled, repeating the steps from the beginning.

Figure 7.2. How to Study a Spelling Word.

a correction strategy and record it; and (5) place correction strategies for all observed problems in order and then determine through teacher-student conference which areas are most in need of improvement.[10]

Fourth, *spelling consciousness can be developed through the proofreading habit.* Such functional attention to spelling in the course of written composition should help children learn orthographic patterns to the point of automaticity much more effectively than the write-each-word-ten-times method.[11] It is consequently important to help boys and girls acquire fairly early in their school years the responsibility for correcting improperly spelled words themselves, preferably immediately after completing a written composition. Otherwise they will continue to spell words correctly on a test one week and yet misspell the identical words the following week in their written efforts. The development of spelling consciousness is closely linked to the habit of individualized checking or proofreading, an area related in turn to the problem of transfer in spelling.

Fifth, *spelling growth depends on continuous evaluation.* Learning occurs whenever there is feedback on one's actions or efforts. Growth in spelling ability, therefore, only develops through observing and proofreading and through an analysis of errors made. A crucial part of spelling instruction, according to Hodges, is an ability to distinguish incorrect spellings from correct ones and then to correct both the mistakes and their causes.[12] Such instruction must provide students and teachers with many opportunities to evaluate pupil progress toward a total understanding of English orthography.

Sixth and last, *the most important generalization that students may ever need is that English spelling is actually quite regular but in ways that may have never occurred to most learners.*[13] It is clear that to spell English successfully one must have a high degree of sensitivity to both the phonological and the morphological structure of words. Pupils must be permitted to discover the relationships between that structure and English spelling by using materials which have been carefully prepared or properly selected by their teacher.

Good spellers, children and adults alike, are characterized by Carol Chomsky as recognizing that related words are spelled alike even though they are pronounced differently.[14] Such spellers seem to rely on an underlying picture of the words that is independent of the words' varying pronunciations. They internalize the underlying relationships among words. When good spellers encounter a troublesome word, they automatically utilize the idea that while related words may vary a good deal in their pronunciation, their spelling usually remains the same. Once the connection is clear between the new troublesome word and other related words, correct spelling becomes automatic.

To help children develop the habit of seeking such connections, the linguistically oriented teacher may use one of these exercises:

1. Give the children Column A of words with a /ə/ vowel omitted. Ask them to think of related words that give distinct clues to the spelling (Column B). (The clues turn out to be the same ones which preschoolers use in their invented spelling.)

A	B
pres ___ dent	preside
janit ___ r	janitorial
maj ___ r	majority
comp ___ rable	compare
ind ___ stry	industrial

2. Give the children only Column B from Exercise 1 and ask them to think of other forms of the words. See if they notice how vowel sounds shift around.
3. Help the children guess the proper consonant when two or more seem possible. In Column C the spelling is ambiguous. In Column D the related word gives the key to the correct choice.

C	D
gradual (d, j)	grade
nation (t, sh)	native
medicine (c, s)	medical
racial (t, c, sh)	race
criticize (c, s)	critical

4. Help the children to observe silent consonants by giving them Column E and asking them to think of related words in which the silent consonants are pronounced (Column F).

E	F
bomb	bombard
soften	soft
muscle	muscular
sign	signal
condemn	condemnation

5. Give the children only Column F and ask them to think of related words in which the underlined consonants become silent.
6. Give the children only Column E and ask them to name the silent consonants.
7. Help the children learn consonant alternations which occur in the pronunciation of words and are reflected in the orthography too. Since the *t-c* alternation is fairly common, give the children Column G and ask them to determine the missing consonants in Column H.

G	H
pirate	pira __ y
democratic	democra __ y
present	presen __ e
resident	residen __ e
lunatic	luna __ y[15]

Incidentally, at least one study of older students—those in grades six, eight, and ten—concluded that spelling ability does rely on phonological and visual characteristics of words and therefore develops with age and apparently from longer exposure to written language.[16]

Teaching Spelling: Recommended Practices

Although spelling is one of the most thoroughly researched areas in the language arts, most teachers prefer to use spelling procedures based on tradition and not on empirical evidence. At least one recent study of nearly 1300 elementary teachers in Iowa confirmed the fact that teachers seldom use research-based practices when planning spelling lessons.[17]

Summarized below are empirically-based procedures which should be incorporated into school-based spelling instruction in an effort to elevate spelling achievement both formally and informally:

1. Pupils should initially study their spelling words in a column or list form rather than in sentence or paragraph form.
2. Spelling words of highest frequency in child and adult writing should be studied by elementary school children: words for which children ask the spelling; words that children misspell; and words the teacher knows the boys and girls will need to spell.
3. The child correcting his or her own spelling test, under the teacher's direction, is the single most important factor in learning to spell.
4. In order to learn to spell, children need not learn the meanings of the majority of their words.
5. Spelling lists composed of words from various curricular areas are of little value in increasing spelling ability.
6. Learning words by the whole method is a better practice than learning words by syllables.
7. Most attempts to teach spelling by phonic rules are questionable.

8. Time allotted for the study of spelling should be between 60 and 75 minutes per week.
9. The test-study-test method is superior to the study-test method for most spellers.
10. Each student should be taught an efficient technique for studying unknown spelling words (such as the procedure described earlier in Figure 7.2).
11. Children should learn words as whole units and, therefore, the practice of drawing attention to the so-called "hard spots" within a word is of little value.
12. Writing words several times in rote fashion and without intervening recall does not insure spelling retention.
13. A child's interest and attitude in learning to spell are of primary importance.
14. Spelling should be taught in conjunction with functional writing.

Most of the above recommendations appear in a summary of more than 60 years of research in spelling instruction.[18]

Teaching Spelling: Individualized Approach

In order to plan an effective spelling program, the teacher must understand the importance of phonological and morphological relationships as well as the significance of oral and written language. Furthermore, the teacher must know the backgrounds, needs, and potential of the children.

As to the optimum grade for beginning formal spelling instruction, recent research studies are not in agreement. One national survey of nearly 3,000 children in 22 states in grades three through eight showed that after grade four no spelling instruction is almost as effective as formal instruction.[19] These findings were in general agreement with another survey of more than 2,000 children in grades two through six which concluded that many pupils had achieved a "skill in spelling" as early as the third or fourth grade and that tracking them through the sequences of the available spelling programs may not be a worthwhile utilization of their time or energy.[20]

On the other hand, arguing for a delay in formal spelling instruction are researchers involved in a Michigan study of approximately 200 children in grades one through four.[21] They believe that formal instruction may not be appropriate until children have had ample time to develop an understanding of word-attack principles. They state that it is more important to give pupils a chance to explore words in their writing and their reading rather than to have them write lists of spelling words.

As to the optimum sources for spelling words, three are currently mentioned.[22] The first is *student writing.* At least one study of spellers in grades two through six showed that fifth graders, for example, are spelling incorrectly many high-frequency words.[23] It is therefore recommended that students maintain their spelling dictionaries based on the misspelled words in their daily journals and other written work. Teachers can then use those misspelled words to individualize word lists for students.

The personal spelling dictionary can be simply a loose-leaf notebook, with alphabetical dividers, in which students record words they need to know how to spell in the course of all of their writing experiences in school. The same notebook can be used year after year because the pages can be changed and updated as necessary. Once a class has been introduced to individualized spelling dictionaries, it is important to get children into the habit of using their dictionaries whenever they are involved with writing activities in any area of the curriculum. As a pupil is writing and needs to use a word he or she cannot spell, the pupil can ask the teacher or look up the word in a published dictionary. The pupil then promptly records it in his or her spelling notebook. Should the pupil need to use that word again later and is still unsure of the correct spelling, he or she need only refer back to the personal dictionary.

The second source for spelling words is *frequency vocabulary lists.* There are both graded lists by V. Thomas (1979, 1974), for example, and ungraded lists by such authorities as H. Rinsland (1945), J. Fitzgerald (1951), and H. Kučera and W. Francis (1967). Teachers in a single school can choose the 3000–4000 high-frequency words basic to any spelling program from one or more of those lists and track individual students.

The third source is the revised *New Iowa Spelling Scale* (1977), published by the University of Iowa. It lists 5507 words by the percentage of students in grades two through eight who spelled the words correctly. Teachers can develop

Paraprofessional aides play a key role in an individualized spelling program. (Photo courtesy of the Fountain Valley School District, Fountain Valley, California.)

word lists for pupils at a particular grade level or ability level by using the available percentages. Data for the Scale were gathered from some 30,000 pupils per grade in 645 school systems in all types of cities and in most states throughout the country.

Finally, elementary teachers who are considering the possibility of using commercial spelling series as sources for spelling words should be aware of the results of three recent surveys of published spelling programs for children. All raised serious doubts concerning the feasibility of using such programs. The first survey examined seven elementary series published between 1971–1978 and found that most programs do not require children to perform realistic spelling assignments.[24] Instead, they ask pupils to do various copying tasks, which is an unrealistic practice in contemporary society where students must generate their own spelling in response to an internal or external need. The purpose of modern spelling instruction, after all, is the development of independent spelling ability.

The second study examined 11 spelling series published since 1976 and found that no one series was consistent *across* grade levels in the numbers of high-frequency words (based on a standard measure of word frequency) found at each level.[25] Nor was there consistency *within* grade levels. It would appear, therefore, that a school would have to purchase several different series simultaneously in order to provide pupils with lists of appropriate words at each grade level.

The third and last survey of more than 2000 children in grades two through six revealed that many pupils already know how to spell a substantial number of the words included in the spelling textbook program at each grade level.[26] Furthermore, the average child in this suburban sample also seemed to be able to spell a substantial number of words designated for the level one grade *above* his or her present grade placement. The researcher concluded that qualitative differences exist in spelling that may require a greater degree of individualization than that located in the neatly compartmentalized study procedures available in many published programs.

Each pupil needs to work with a word list that is different—either totally or slightly—from that of every other child in the class at any given time. Examples of individualized and creative lessons in spelling can be found in Figure 7.3.

Spelling and Reading

Beginning with the colonial period and continuing for at least 200 years in this country, spelling and reading were taught together. The primary reading program then was actually a spelling book, such as Noah Webster's *Blue-Backed Speller*. With the advent of graded classrooms in the mid–1800s, however, came the need for graded—and separate—reading books, and spelling became divorced from reading.

Yet both spelling and reading employ the same writing system to transmit information from one person to another. All users of an alphabetic system must acquire two closely related processes: (1) the ability to translate printed or written graphemes into the oral forms which they represent (*decoding* or reading); and (2) the mastery of the graphic symbols needed to set forth speech in writing (*encoding* or spelling).

Figure 7.3. Lessons in Individualized Spelling.

Sample Creative Lessons in Spelling

1. Boys and girls each write their initials on a sheet of paper. They then list correctly foods and/or activities whose names begin with one or more of the initials. They can refer to a cookbook, a dictionary, a newspaper, or the yellow pages of the local telephone book. Example: Jennifer T. Donaldson might list *jumping, jam, tomatoes, tickling, doughnuts, dancing.*
2. Children with handy access to a standard or picture dictionary can write correctly words which have developed from the names of animals. Examples: *dog—doghouse, horse—horseback, man—manhole.* Some boys and girls may choose to write words centered about one animal only. Others may prefer to incorporate two or three animals, wild or domestic.
3. Upper primary children can each receive a dittoed worksheet on which have been sketched seasonal items. Each leaf or pumpkin (fall), snowflake or fir tree (winter), or tulip or umbrella (spring), for example, contains space for writing in one Study Word. Later, after the words have been checked, the child may color in the items appropriately. If any word has been misspelled, however, the child must first write the word correctly before he or she can color in the sketch. The pupil should be cautioned to color lightly so that the words may remain visible. For less confusion, all sketches on any one sheet should be of the same item.
4. Intermediate girls and boys with easy access to a dictionary can review simple geometric shapes. The teacher lists on the chalkboard the names of several shapes, including *circle, square, rectangle, triangle, oval, sphere,* and *cube.* At their desks the children prepare on their papers several columns, each headed with one of the shapes the teacher has listed. Then each pupil writes the names of items in the classroom/home/neighborhood that resemble those shapes. Examples: *cube—ottoman, oval—mirror, rectangle—bicycle pedal.* The children use their dictionaries to proofread their choices.

Since the American-English orthography suffers from a lack of an exact one-to-one correspondence between phoneme and grapheme, there are major differences between decoding (spelling-to-sound correspondences) and encoding (sound-to-spelling correspondences).

In reading children start with a word that is seen; in spelling they see nothing at all. Therefore, the context and/or picture that will assist them in reading can be of no help to them in spelling. In spelling they end with what they begin with in reading; that is, the visual symbol.

In reading the stimulus is a printed or written symbol which is concrete and relatively permanent. The stimuli for spelling, on the other hand, are speech sounds (including words) which are much less concrete and much more transient than printed letters, especially for children. While the written symbols in reading can be isolated and studied in detail if necessary, speech sounds are much more difficult to study and present greater problems for spellers. Children entering school are generally able to discriminate and identify written symbols, but they hardly possess comparable ability for speech sounds.

The 26 letters of the English alphabet can be combined in varying ways to give a total of about 70 letters and letter combinations. Consequently, reading moves from numerous stimuli to fewer responses (e.g., both *d* and *dd* are pronounced /d/). Spelling, on the contrary, moves from fewer stimuli to numerous responses (e.g., the sound /d/ may be spelled as either *d* or *dd*).

Reading requires solely a mental response (except for oral reading). However, spelling demands a muscular response as well, for letters must be written to represent the sounds which the children hear in their minds. As good spellers, children respond automatically to such mental sound stimuli. As good readers, their response is dependent upon the meanings the words have for them.

Considerable variation is allowed in the pronunciation of English words, and that variability may be individual or dialectal, with regional variation being frequent. Such differences, always tolerated and generally accepted, aid the reader. English spelling, on the other hand, is rigidly fixed with few variants (e.g., *grey/gray*). It is an area where individual differences are not usually permitted. Correct spelling has even been described as a sign of social and intellectual competence!

Due then to the several distinctions between decoding and encoding, it seems clear that reading and spelling are not simply the same processes used in reverse.[27] Still, the two abilities are closely related and, therefore, according to a recent study of 116 second graders, the practice of isolating spelling apart from reading instruction is questionable.[28] The more children knew about words in general, the more able spellers they were, since spelling strategies reflect word knowledge. The study also suggested that, if weekly spelling lists are used, the lists should come directly from reading material to which the child has been exposed throughout that week.

A question is often raised as to why some good readers are poor spellers while good spellers are almost always good readers. Studies conducted of 29 twelve-year-olds in three South London schools concluded that good readers who spell badly are weak in relating print to sound.[29] The weakness appears to be an avoidance or lack of preference for doing so. Good spellers/readers, on the other hand, are equally able to convert print to sound and print to meaning. The researcher concluded that spelling instruction based only on phoneme-grapheme relationships is incomplete because English orthography reflects knowledge both on the level of sound *and* on the level of meaning.

That conclusion may explain why the language-experience approach to reading produces significantly better spellers than the basal-reader approach, according to a study of 21 first-grade classrooms in Delaware.[30] Although the children and their teachers using each approach were matched evenly, the pupils in the basal reader classes found the phonologically irregular words of American English orthography somewhat more difficult to spell than the phonologically regular words, whereas the language-experience classes did not. The latter integrated listening, speaking, and writing in a broad-based reading program, and its members maintained their spelling superiority throughout their elementary school careers.

Instructional Activities

Since children learn to spell through constant and enriching interaction with written language through daily writing and reading, teachers must plan a variety of activities that enhance pupil awareness of words and word formations. The 20 exercises described in this section focus attention on the spelling process and stress correct rather than incorrect spellings. Some are especially appropriate for younger or slower spellers while others may meet the needs of most spellers throughout the elementary grades.

Being Magnetic

Two children work together with one box of magnetic letters. The first child uses the letters to spell one of the Study Words. The second child then removes one or more of the letters, and the partner must state what is missing and replace the letters in the correct order. They continue to take turns.

Drawing Charades

Simple pictures of Study Words are drawn on the chalkboard or on worksheets. Children write the correct word under each picture.

Examining Pocket Words

The teacher prepares a chart with 26 pockets, one for each letter of the alphabet. Then individual cards of Study Words are placed in the pocket, according to the first letter of the word. Students may remove the cards, examine them, and return them to the chart. Sometimes the chart may hold all the cards for a week or month.

Finger Writing

The teacher and children gather together all the materials needed for finger painting. Then, instead of painting shapes or pictures, the children write their Study Words in paint. Most children will require more than one sheet of paper.

Fishing

Children draw pictures of Study Words on construction-paper cutouts of fish. The fish are then placed in a bowl with paper clips attached to them. The pupils "catch" the fish with a magnet at the end of a short fishing pole. They then write on the chalkboard or on paper the words pictured on the fish that they caught.

Fixing Macaroni Words

Students spell Study Words with alphabet macaroni and then glue them on black construction paper. For a colorful variation, the macaroni can be dyed earlier (using food coloring and rubbing alcohol) and allowed to dry for five to ten minutes.

Glueing It

Each child writes the more difficult Study Words, using glue on construction paper. Then the words are sprinkled with sand or glitter or covered carefully with yarn.

Graphing It

Each student receives one sheet of plain white paper and one sheet of one-inch-squared graph paper. First, the child writes one letter of a Study Word in each of the squares. Second, he/she cuts the squares apart, mixes them up, and rearranges them in correct order. Third, the reassembled letters are pasted in proper sequence on the plain paper. The child continues studying each word, following the three steps.

Having a Cross Word

Children connect words to form an original crossword puzzle. Partners who are working with similar Study Words can then number the words across and down, write clues, and exchange their puzzles. They may use graph paper and produce a puzzle like this:

				1 b				
		2 m	a	y	3 b	e		
		e			o			
4 b	e	e			5 y	a	r	n
		6 t	a	g	s			

Making Clay Tablets

Like the ancient Sumerians, the children spread ordinary modeling clay out into "sheets" about one half inch thick. Then each child inscribes Study Words in clay, using an opened paper clip or a pencil.

Pasting Spots

Each child makes a large heavy cardboard giraffe and paints it yellow. Then the pupil cuts out a quantity of wide circles from brown construction paper to simulate spots. As Study Words are learned correctly, the child writes the word on one circle and pastes it on the giraffe. If the teacher can provide a grooved piece of wood (or some other device) to help the giraffe stand up, the spelling spots can be more prominently displayed.

Preparing Anagrams

The teacher or children make cutout letters of the alphabet, with several lowercase and several uppercase forms of each one. The letters are placed in a box on a corner table. During free time, one pupil or two partners may go to the table to form various Study Words. Either the teacher or partner can check the correct spellings, using a nearby dictionary if necessary.

Putting Black on White

Children use a white crayon to write their Study Words on a piece of manila construction paper. Later they paint over the paper with a wash of thin black paint. Their spelling words will then magically appear.

Solving a Rebus

On the chalkboard or worksheets, there are sentences for completion which use picture clues for Study Words such as: *I found some eggs in the* __________ .

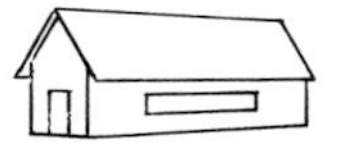

Spacing Out

The teacher prepares a paragraph which includes many or all of the Study Words. Then the teacher copies it on the chalkboard or on worksheets, purposely leaving no space between words but punctuating and capitalizing the sentences properly. The children must draw lines between the connected words to make sense out of the paragraph.

Talking about Taped Lessons

Children listen to a taped spelling lesson lasting 15 to 20 minutes. Then they participate in a five-minute discussion period, during which their teacher answers any questions regarding the taped lesson. Incidentally, a study was completed in which the spelling achievement of fourth-grade boys after eight such taped lessons substantially exceeded that of identical subjects who had participated instead in a lecture-discussion approach.[31]

Towering a Word

A pupil writes one Study Word vertically, either on the chalkboard or on writing paper. He or she then tries to use each letter of that word in a new word and may even attempt to form the new words into a sentence or question like this:

*C*an
T*O*m
*R*un
to*D*ay

Using a Jig Saw

The student writes all of the Study Words on a sturdy piece of paper and then turns it over. On the back he/she draws curved lines to make it look like a jigsaw puzzle. Finally, the student cuts the paper apart and tries to reassemble it by using the letters of the words as clues.

Using Tiny Flash Cards

The child writes the Study Words on small rectangles of colored construction paper. He/she then uses these as flash cards, working with a partner. When the words have been mastered, the child may paste the flash cards in a special notebook or on an individual chart.

Writing Jingles

Children can write jingles using one or more Study Words in rhyme. Sometimes they learn not only to spell the designated words but other words in the same phonogram (or graphemic base) as well, as in this:

My sister has a puppy,
I have a little frog.
I'd rather have a clean pet
Than her dirty dog.

Learning Games

The value of word games in the teaching of spelling lies both in the enjoyment they provide for children and in their potential for promoting experimentation and inquiry.[32] Games can be planned for individual players, pairs of students, or teams made up of small groups of children. Since spelling is relevant to writing, spelling games should involve written work and not consist exclusively of oral exercises. They should stress correct spellings and avoid incorrect ones as much as possible. Experienced teachers who realize that learning games are intended as supplements to and not substitutions for a spelling program are equally aware that such games encourage children to form concepts about the written code.

Add-On

1. A scorekeeper is selected. Teams are chosen and assigned chalkboard space far apart from each other.
2. The teacher pronounces a Study Word and has the first member on each team go to the board and write the first letter of the word. As soon as the player is finished, he or she hands the chalk to the second member of the team, urging this player to "add-on."
3. The second member then writes the second letter, and the round continues until one team completes the word.
4. The team finishing first in each round scores one point. Points are subtracted, however, for any illegible or incorrect letters.
5. The team with the most points wins Add-On.

Countdown

1. The teacher prepares to dictate Study Words. A scorekeeper is selected. Teams are chosen and are assigned chalkboard space far apart from each other.
2. The first player on each team stands at the board, listening to the word the teacher reads. The player then tries to complete writing that word by the time the teacher finishes a "countdown" from ten to one. The teacher can either count softly or indicate the count with his or her fingers.
3. Each team scores a point every time a player completes writing the dictated word correctly by the time the teacher counts down to one.
4. Individual winners are all the players who beat the countdown. The winning team or teams of Countdown are those with the most points.

Detectives

1. The players are divided into two-partner teams that are given dictionaries, pencils, and paper.
2. One partner on each team writes the alphabet on the left side of the paper, skipping one line after each letter. Then both players or Detectives search for objects in the classroom and write each item down opposite its corresponding letter (e.g., A<art, B<book, C<chalk), consulting the dictionary as needed.
3. Although most of the searching can be done with players at their desks, a team may search more actively if it can do so without disturbing the other Detectives.
4. When time is called, the teacher writes the alphabet letters vertically on the chalkboard, and each team copies its own list next to the proper letters. Teams may use different colors of chalk for easy tallying.
5. The team with the longest list of correct words wins Detectives.

Erase and Spell

1. Three players stand at their desks, each holding an eraser and a piece of chalk. A fourth student is chosen as scorekeeper.
2. The teacher writes on the board a list of Study Words, for example, *now, prow, sow, cow, how, chow.*
3. When the teacher asks, "Who can find, erase, and rewrite the word *sow?*", the first player to walk to the board, complete the chore successfully, and return to his or her desk scores one point.
4. The round continues until all the words have been erased at least once. The winner of Erase and Spell is the player with the most points.
5. Variation: The teacher may give a brief definition instead, e.g., "Who can find, erase and rewrite the word which means a pig?"

Hook-On

1. One student writes a Study Word on the chalkboard.
2. The next student in turn writes a word that begins with the last letter of the first word.
3. The game continues until one player cannot Hook-On a new word.
4. Partners or teams can play.

Leave-Out

1. The teacher writes on the board a Study Word, omitting the vowels of the word (e.g., *m ssp ll*).
2. At their seats the players write the word completely and correctly (i.e., *misspell*) on paper.
3. The teacher selects a player to write his or her answer on the board. If the player's response is correct, he or she may then put a vowel-less word on the board for the rest of the class to solve. If the player's response is incorrect, another player has a turn.
4. The winners of Leave-Out are all the players who solved the incomplete words correctly either at the board or at their seats.

Missing Relay

1. The teacher writes on the chalkboard identical lists of words and each word has one missing letter. There are as many words in each list as there are players on the team assigned to that list.
2. At a signal the first player on each team goes to the board and writes in the missing letter in one word on the team's list. As soon as the first player finishes, the second player on the same team attempts to complete a different word.
3. The first team to complete all its words correctly wins Missing Relay.

Pull and Spell

1. Study Words are written on separate slips of paper, which are then folded and placed in a box.
2. One at a time, the players pull out a slip but do not look at the word. Each player hands the slip to the teacher or to "It" who pronounces the word for the player to write on the chalkboard.
3. If the word is spelled correctly, the teacher or "It" keeps the slip. If the word has been misspelled, the player keeps the slip for future study.
4. Players who have no slips at the end of the round are the winners of Pull and Spell.

Roots

1. Divided into two-partner teams, each team receives a dictionary, a pencil, and a large card with a derived word printed on it (e.g., *fearless, enjoyment, handful*). Each card bears a different word, which also appears on the chalkboard.
2. Each team determines what portion of its word is the root word and then consults the dictionary in order to compile a list of other words also derived from the same root. The list is written on the back of the word card.
3. When time is called, Partner One writes the team list on the chalkboard under the word originally printed on the team card. Partner Two proofreads the team list.
4. The team with the longest correct list wins Roots.
5. Individuals or larger teams can play.

Spelling Bingo

1. Each player folds a sheet of paper into 16 squares.
2. The teacher writes on the chalkboard 16 different words. The players copy the words on their papers, putting only one into a square and determining the locations by themselves.
3. The teacher erases the board and proceeds to call out the words, one at a time. The players put dry beans or discs on the appropriate squares.
4. When a player has a row or diagonal filled, he or she calls out, "Spelling Bingo!" and reads the words aloud. The player then writes the four words on the board while his or her classmates and teacher help check the bingo.

Supernatural

1. Each player is given a dictionary, a pencil, and some paper.
2. He or she must search the dictionary for 10 minutes for all the words which have five syllables (just as *Supernatural* does) and then write them down.
3. When time is called, each player copies his or her list on the chalkboard for everyone to proofread.
4. The player with the longest list of correct words wins Supernatural.
5. Variation: Younger players may prefer Super, which requires words of only two syllables.

Touchdown

1. The teacher draws on the chalkboard a large diagram of a football field, indicating the goal lines and the 10-to–50-yard lines.
2. Two teams are chosen (Teams A and B), that in turn each select a team captain. The captains determine which goalpost each team will defend and choose a team color. A scorekeeper is selected to continually note the teams' positions on the field with chalks representing team colors.
3. On the chalkboard, outside the diagram but near the goalpost it is defending, each team is assigned space in which to write the words the teacher will dictate.
4. The teacher begins the game by reading one Study Word at a time to Team A, whose players in turn write the words in the space allocated. Each word correctly spelled advances the team ten yards, as duly noted by the scorekeeper. If no misspellings occur, a touchdown is scored by Team A after ten words or one hundred yards.

5. However, if Team A misspells a word on its own 30-yard line, for example, Team B has its turn and can score a touchdown by running only thirty yards or spelling three words correctly. Should Team A misspell a word on Team B's 30-yard line, then Team B can score a touchdown by running seventy yards or spelling seven words correctly.
6. The team with the most touchdowns within a designated period of time wins Touchdown.

Treasure Hunt

1. Teams are chosen, and on the chalkboard the teacher writes a different word at the head of each team's column. All words, however, contain the same number of letters.
2. At a signal the first player on each team goes to the board and writes one word which uses letters from the team's assigned word. For example, from *tamer* the player could write *am, tame, ram, mar, ear, me,* or *mat.*
3. After the first player returns to his or her desk, the second player goes to the board and writes a different word from the same team word.
4. The round continues until time is called. The winner of Treasure Hunt is the team with the longest list of correct words. The teacher or designated student Hunter proofreads the lists.

Write or Wrong

1. Two teams are established (Teams A and B) and their players prepare individual name tags which are collected facedown and separated into two piles.
2. The teacher calls out a spelling word. Players on both teams write the word on paper at their seats.
3. The teacher selects a name tag from Team A's pile and calls upon the owner to copy his or her word on the board for the class to see. If the player can do so correctly, Team A gets a point; if the player fails, a tag from Team B is picked.
4. With each new word during Write or Wrong, all tags are returned to their proper pile so that every player has an equal opportunity to be chosen for any one word.

Learning-Disabled Spellers

In almost every classroom there are at least two learning-disabled spellers who are deficient in one or more of the basic processes needed for the spelling task. They may be unable to analyze auditory constructs, or the words as pronounced, into their ordered component parts. Or they may lack the ability to recall the word parts' appropriate visual representation in correct sequence. Or, finally, they may be unable to reproduce the words synthesized in written form. Successful spellers, on the other hand, almost simultaneously reauditorize, revisualize, and produce kinesthetically, all with accurate sequencing.

Generally, when one modality is weak, the others take over in an effort to compensate. The problem area thus goes relatively unnoticed and the modalities continue to function in an integrated fashion. In the learning disabled, however, there is likely to be mutual interference instead of integration. These pupils then become less efficient in receiving and processing information as well as less efficient in monitoring their expressions.

Techniques for Improvement

The best approach for aiding learning-disabled spellers depends on how many deficient areas are involved. Children whose auditory competencies are reasonably intact but who suffer from poor visual memory can at least be expected to spell phonetically and to develop a visual memory bank for some of the phonologically irregular words. On the other hand, pupils whose spatial and visual skills are fairly intact may learn to spell through these strengths, recalling many sight words readily. Gradual development of the phonic tools may even make them adequate spellers. For both of these groups of children, the task of bridging the auditory and visual areas must proceed from the area of strength.

A third group of pupils has neither visual nor auditory competencies. Since its spelling can only be described as bizarre, haptic methods are suggested to help deal with these children's deficiencies. Partoll, for example, recommends a typing program which is patterned and linguistic to help bypass the motor problems that may also exist.[33] Typewriting introduces both visual and auditory skills and provides for their development to an almost automatic level.

For problem spellers the ordering of tasks is considered essential. To limit confusion, phonic skills must be taught simultaneously in introductory reading and spelling in a relatively fixed order, and they must be reinforced by writing. Later the irregular phonograms are introduced, and still later, the roots and affixes.

One useful proposal recommends a week-long individual observation of spelling skills in order to determine a child's preferred mode of response.[34] Forty words are chosen based on grade level and are divided into five groups of eight words each. On Monday the first eight words are presented auditorally, with the child responding with a vocal response (auditory-vocal). Tuesday's group of eight words is presented in an auditory-motor fashion, Wednesday's in a visual-vocal approach, Thursday's in a visual-motor format, and Friday's in a multisensory manner. At the end of each day the child is tested to determine how many of the day's words he/she spelled correctly. The classroom teacher can then develop a spelling program involving the preferred input process (auditory, visual, or combined) and preferred output process (vocal, motor, or combined).

Routes and approaches to help disabled spellers vary according to age and grade level. In the primary grades the need is to solidify associations of sounds-to-letters and of sound patterns to letter patterns. In the middle grades teaching strategies must be directed to the obvious and specific deficits displayed. Reference to the checklist in Figure 7.4 can help distinguish among children who are learning disabled in spelling.

Figure 7.4. Analysis Checklist of Severe Spelling Problems Among Learning-Disabled Children.

Severe Spelling Problems

Check consistent or frequent errors only.
Put initials of child next to errors that he or she consistently makes.

_____ 1. Consonant sounds used incorrectly (specify letters missed)
_____ 2. Vowel sounds not known (specify as above)
_____ 3. Sounds added at beginning of words (e.g., a blend given when single consonant required)
_____ 4. Sounds omitted at beginning of words
_____ 5. Omission of middle sounds
_____ 6. Omission of middle syllables
_____ 7. Extraneous syllables added
_____ 8. Extraneous letters added
_____ 9. Endings omitted
_____ 10. Incorrect endings substituted (*ing* for *en* or for *ed*)
_____ 11. Reversals of whole words
_____ 12. Auditory confusion of *m/n* or *th/f/v* or *b/p* or other similar sounds
_____ 13. Missequencing of sounds or syllables (transposals like *from* to *form*)
_____ 14. Revisualization of very common sight words poor (e.g., *one, night, said*)
_____ 15. Spells, erases, tries again, etc. to no avail
_____ 16. Reversals of letter shapes *b/d* or *p/q* or *u/n* or *m/w* (specify)
_____ 17. Spelling phonetic with poor visual recall of word appearance
_____ 18. Spelling laborious, letter by letter
_____ 19. Spelling so bizarre that it bears no resemblance to original; even the pupil frequently cannot read his own

Observe also (additional hazards to problem spellers):

_____ 20. Spatial placement on line erratic
_____ 21. Spacing between letters and words erratic
_____ 22. Poor writing and letter formation, immature eye-hand coordination
_____ 23. Mixing of upper and lower case letters
_____ 24. Inability to recall how to form either case for some letters
_____ 25. Temporal disorientation: slowness in learning time, general scheduling, grasping the sequence of events in the day and those usually known to his contemporaries
_____ 26. Difficulty in concept formation; not able to generalize and transfer readily, to abstract "the rules and the tools"

Reprinted by permission from Shirley F. Partoll, "Spelling Demonology Revisited," ACADEMIC THERAPY, Vol. 11, Spring 1976, Novato, California, Academic Therapy Publications, p. 344.

By the fifth and sixth grades learning-disabled spellers who are intellectually able can attach meaning and appropriate spelling to Latin and other bases and affixes. They can learn some polysyllabic, phonetically regular words too. Many sight words can be introduced, mnemonic devices are often useful, and a small number of "discovered" generalizations can help. Most children at this level have completed the transition from manuscript to cursive writing and thereby reduced the visual-spatial and kinesthetic demands in spelling. Any one of a number of different lists of common words, as discussed in Chapter Ten, can be adopted for use with intermediate spellers in an effort to enable them to develop a minimal memory bank of important but irregularly spelled words. A teacher can pass the list along to the next grade with notations on the progress that the disabled spellers have made.

One basic approach which has proved successful for children with learning disabilities in both the primary and intermediate grades is the visual configuration method that is color-coded.[35] The necessary materials include one-inch wooden cubes (orange and blue), felt-tip pens (orange and blue), ruled newsprint with cardboard backer, and 5 inch by 12 inch tagboard ruled in one-inch intervals. The children are told that (1) all vowels are made with orange cubes and all consonants with blue cubes; (2) tall letters are three cubes high; (3) the letter *t* is two cubes high; (4) the manuscript letters *g, j, p,* and *q* are two cubes long with lower portions hanging below the solid lines; and (5) the letter *y* is either orange or blue (depending on its use as a vowel or consonant) and is slightly tilted from right to left. The pupils are introduced to the concept of visual configuration by spelling familiar words with the cubes and letting classmates figure out the words. The words are then written with the pens with the color code remaining the same. The action of changing pens for the vowels and consonants impresses letter sequencing on the writer's mind. Each time a new word is introduced there is practice with the cubes and the pens for the first two or three days. Even certain phonics generalizations can be incorporated into this visual configuration method; for example, syllabication can be taught by leaving extra space between the cube groups.

Evaluation of Pupils' Progress

Evaluation in spelling goes on informally and continually in written composition assignments and instructional spelling sessions. It occurs, too, more formally and less frequently during periodic tests.

Teacher's Evaluation of Pupils

The wise teacher provides for both weekly and monthly testing of the pupil's mastery of his or her word list. Such testing, particularly when followed by brief teacher-pupil conferences, can contribute to a growing sense of spelling achievement. Every pupil is encouraged to reflect upon personal growth as the teacher reviews his or her spelling record. Such individual guidance is essential to effective teaching and learning of spelling.

Appraisal of the overall growth of the class in spelling should also be made periodically, though on an informal basis, by observing the following:

- Can the pupils use correct spelling in functional writing?
- Do they locate their own misspelled words?
- Are the pupils consulting dictionaries or individual word lists?
- Is each pupil increasing his or her spelling proficiency?

The teacher may also wish to assess class progress in spelling more formally on a monthly or semester basis by designing a test which follows a new format developed by the California State Department of Education.[36] It simulates actual written production but involves multiple choice items. It assumes that spelling ability is a result of both word memory and strategies for predicting the spellings of unknown words.

Evaluation of each child's progress in spelling should occur regularly through individual and informal conferencing, following periodic tests. (Photo courtesy of Jean-Claude Lejeune.)

Children choose from a list of possible letter options the one which correctly completes the spelling of a partly-spelled word, and then they write the word on the paper. Some examples follow:

Predictable Words

Grade 3 I like to climb tr ______ s.

(a) ee
(b) ie
(c) ea
(d) ei

Grade 6 I enjoyed the dis ______ ussion after the movie.

(a) k
(b) c
(c) ck
(d) g

Words with Suffixes

Grade 3 I gave both bab ______ their toys.

(a) ys
(b) ees
(c) eys
(d) ies

Grade 6 We will go swim ______ every day.

(a) ing
(b) ming
(c) eing
(d) in

Demons

Grade 3 I only hit him ______ nce.

(a) ou
(b) o
(c) wu
(d) wo

Grade 6 The fire swept thr ______ the woods.

(a) ioux
(b) ue
(c) oo
(d) ough

Homophones

Grade 3 ______ not very hot today.

(a) Its
(b) It's

Grade 6 The boys could ______ strange noises in the cave.

(a) here
(b) hear

Self-Evaluation by Pupils

Students can participate in the process of evaluating their spelling growth in several ways. First, they can correct their own spelling tests. This useful procedure is made even more effective when the children *hear* the teacher read the correct spelling while they *see* each word spelled correctly on a specially prepared overlay.

Secondly, students can keep individual progress charts. They can note either the number of words missed, as shown in Figure 7.5, or the number of words correctly spelled (multiplied by a given number to provide a pointscore), as shown in Figure 7.6. In either case, dots are entered on the simple graphs and connected periodically.

Finally, pupils can maintain lists of words that they continue to misspell during composition work or in other subject areas. Such a Personal Spelling Demons list for an intermediate student might contain the following words:

money	cousin	business	vegetable
forty	knowledge	review	argument
courtesy	difference	valuable	naturally
often	seize	height	whose
although	anxious	separate	amateur
changeable	occasion	against	mischievous
ninety	persuade	necessary	trouble
straight	receive	calendar	sandwich
hospital	acquaintance	disappear	plaid
absence	sincere	familiar	misspell

Figure 7.5. Self-Evaluation Progress Chart, Form A.

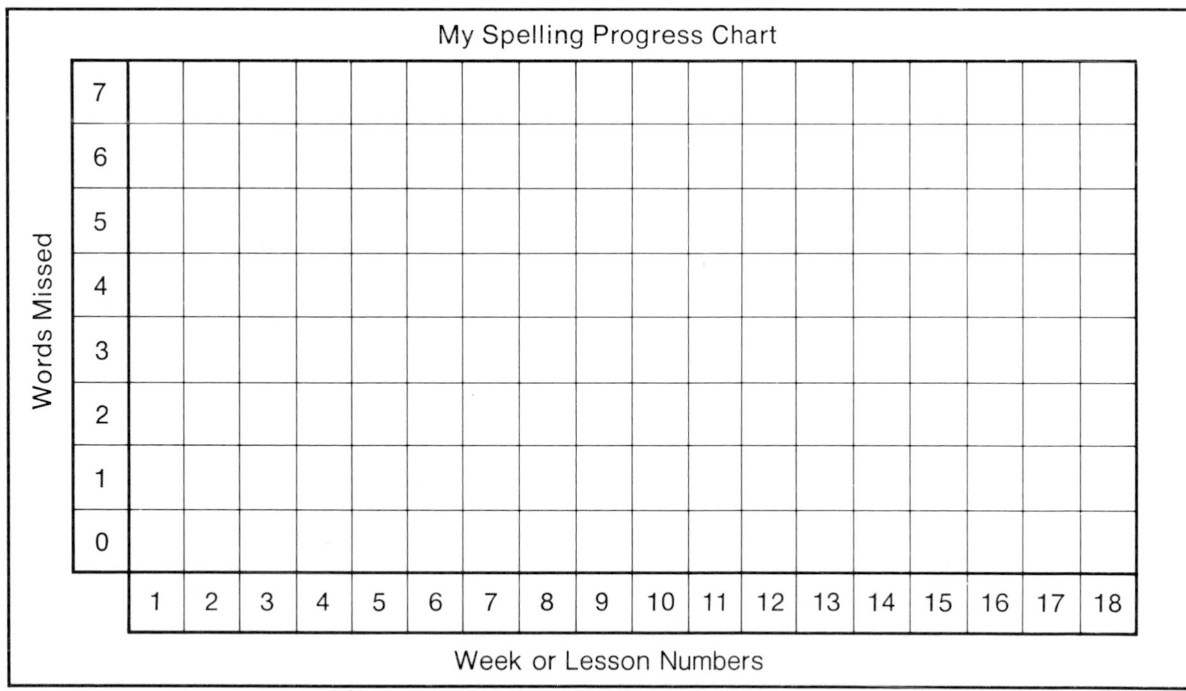

Figure 7.6. Self-Evaluation Progress Chart, Form B.

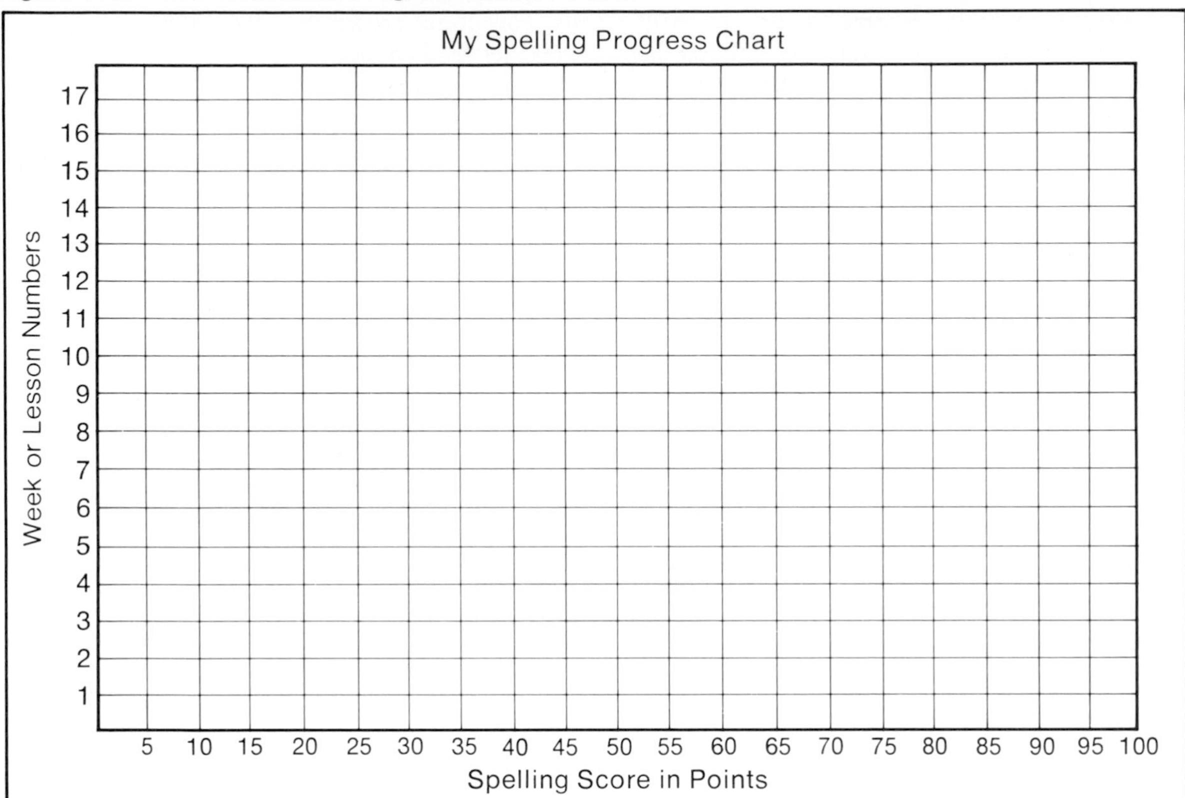

Standardized Spelling Tests

Infrequently teachers are asked to administer formal standardized tests which are purported to inform teachers, administrators, parents, and school boards where pupils stand in relation to other students in the local school system and across the county, state, or nation.

Rated as recommended are those standardized spelling tests found as subtests of such reputable achievement test batteries as the *Iowa Tests of Basic Skills* (from the Riverside Publishing Company, Lombard, IL) and the *Metropolitan Achievement Tests* (from Psychological Corporation, New York City). Standardized achievement tests, of course, do not constitute the best means of evaluating spelling instruction since they cannot measure the growth that has taken place in a particular situation or been made by a particular child.

One recent instrument described as an interesting alternative method to assess spelling is the *SPAR Spelling Test* published in England (by Hodder & Stoughton of Kent).[38] It is recommended for administration to children ages seven to ten. No reading is required by the examinees, and the test takes 10 minutes to administer. Thirty test items are chosen locally from a list of 300 words divided into two "banks"—Spelling Banks A and B.

Discussion Questions

1. Why has the English language been erroneously described so often as being irregular and therefore hard to spell?
2. Why would so many teachers refuse to incorporate research-based, recommended practices into their instructional spelling program?
3. How can parents promote spelling achievement in their child(ren)?
4. If some good readers are also good spellers, why then are other good readers poor spellers?
5. In a modern elementary classroom, how should a pupil's progress in spelling be determined?

Suggested Projects

1. Ask one kindergarten teacher for examples of invented spelling.
2. Make a chart that could be displayed permanently in the classroom which shows How to Study a Word.
3. Obtain some compositions written by fourth graders and list the words most frequently misspelled in them. Can you conclude anything as to common types of spelling errors?
4. Use one of the learning games described in this chapter with a group of third-grade pupils. Then report to your peers about the group's reactions.
5. Investigate some of the alternative forms to traditional orthography such as those designed by Sir James Pitman, John Culkin, and George Bernard Shaw. Do you believe that one of these forms would help resolve the spelling problems of some children?
6. Examine two current editions of commercial spelling programs for level five and compare the kinds of activities suggested for children of high ability and those of low ability. Determine why such programs do not meet the individual spelling needs of children.
7. Set up the learning center on spelling shown in Figure 7.7.

Related Readings

Carpenter, D. 1983. "Spelling Error Profiles of Able and Disabled Readers," *Journal of Learning Disabilities, 17,* pp. 102–104.

Chiang, B., and Schilling, M. 1983. "Effectiveness of the Speed Spelling Program With Five LD Students," *Reading Improvement, 26*(1), pp. 60–63.

DiStefano P., and Hagerty, P. 1985. "Teaching Spelling at the Elementary Level: A Realistic Perspective," *Reading Teacher, 38,* pp. 373–377.

Hasselbring, T. S., and Owens, S. 1983. "Microcomputer-Based Analysis of Spelling Errors," *Computers, Reading & Language Arts,* I(1) pp. 26–32.

Henderson, E. 1985. *Teaching Spelling* Boston: Houghton Mifflin.

Holbrook, H. T. 1983. "Invented Spelling," *Language Arts, 60,* pp. 800–804.

Hurst, C. O. 1984. "A Spelling Spectacular," *Early Years, 14* (5), pp. 27–30.

Morris, D., and Perney, J. 1984. "Developmental Spelling as a Predictor of First Grade Reading Achievement," *Elementary School Journal,* 84, pp. 441–457.

Serio, M. 1984. "Can't Spell Cat," *Academic Therapy, 20,* pp. 235–239.

Stein, M. 1983. "Finger Spelling: A Kinesthetic Aid to Phonetic Spelling," *Academic Therapy, 18,* pp. 305–313.

Figure 7.7. Language Arts Learning Center: Spelling.

TYPE OF CENTER: **Spelling—Prefixes and Suffixes** TIME: 10–15 minutes
GRADE LEVEL: 4–5 NUMBER OF STUDENTS: 2

INSTRUCTIONAL OBJECTIVE: The student will practice working with prefixes and suffixes to expand words.

MATERIALS: Four sets of cards containing words that use prefixes (pocket 1) and other words that use suffixes (pocket 3), paper, pencils, activity sheets, an envelope for completed work.

Example: act en

DIRECTIONS:

1. Take a worksheet and pencil.
2. Take the set of cards out of pocket 1. Look at the cards.
3. Take the prefix cards out of pocket 2.
4. Match the prefix cards to the cards in pocket 1.
5. Say the new words to yourself. Write them on the worksheet.
6. Place the cards off to the side.
7. Take the cards out of pocket 3. Look at the cards.
8. Take the suffix cards out of pocket 4.
9. Match the suffix cards to the cards in pocket 4.
10. Say the new words to yourself. Write them on the worksheet. Put the cards back into the correct pockets.
11. Complete the exercise at the bottom of the activity sheet.
12. When you finish, place the worksheet in the envelope provided.

Chapter Notes

1. P. Russell, *An Outline of English Spelling* (Los Alamitos, California: SWRL Educational Research and Development, 1975), pp. 1–2.
2. J. W. Beers and C. S. Beers, "Vowel Spelling Strategies among First- and Second-Graders: A Growing Awareness of Written Words," *Language Arts,* 1980, *57,* pp. 166–172; G. L. Bissex, *GNYS AT WRK: A Child Learns to Write and Read* (Cambridge, Massachusetts: Harvard University Press, 1980); C. Chomsky, "Invented Spelling in the Open Classroom," *Word,* 1971, 27, pp. 1–3; E. H. Henderson, *Learning to Read and Spell* (DeKalb, Illinois: Northern Illinois University Press, 1981); E. H. Henderson and J. W. Beers, eds., *Developmental and Cognitive Aspects of Learning to Spell* (Newark, Delaware: International Reading Association, 1980); R. Paul, "Invented Spelling in Kindergarten," *Young Children,* 1976, *31,* pp. 195–200; C. Read, "Pre-School Children's Knowledge of English Phonology," *Harvard Educational Review,* 1971, *41,* pp. 1–34; C. Read, "Children's Judgments of Phonetic

Pocket 1 Use words such as:

lease	tract	human	dress
way	marine	set	come
correct	appear	bend	able
tend	fit	claim	paid
visible	act	fresh	mount
miss	complete	pack	

Pocket 2 Prefixes to use:

re-	in-	en-
sub-	un-	ex-
be-	dis-	
pre-	de-	

Pocket 3 Use words such as:

add	work	create
power	grace	envy
long	move	entertain
kind	govern	short
fear	loud	slow
call	dark	rapid

Pocket 4 Suffixes to use:

able	ing	ful
ed	less	ly
ness	est	
er	ment	

Worksheet: (Leave the top half of sheet blank for students to write words.) Using these root words, make as many words as you can by adding prefixes, suffixes, or both.

turn	heart	some	strong	avoid
use	water	visible	fury	adjust
cover	ball	self	chant	best

EVALUATION: The teacher will collect a number of papers. Have the students check their own work as you and a group go over the words written. A scoring procedure could be determined by the students and teacher (e.g., one point per word made).

Similarities in Relation to English Spelling," *Language Learning,* 1973, *23,* pp. 17–38; and J. Zutell, "Spelling Strategies of Primary School Children and Their Relationships to Piaget's Concept of Decentration," *Research in the Teaching of English,* 1979, *13,* pp. 69–80.

3. C. Read, "Lessons to be Learned from the Preschool Orthographer," in *Foundations of Language Development,* Volume 2, E. and E. Lenneberg, eds. (New York: Academic Press, 1975), p. 344.
4. R. L. Cramer, *Children's Writing and Language Growth* (Columbus, Ohio: Charles E. Merrill, 1978), p. 105.
5. R. Gentry, "Learning to Spell Developmentally," *Reading Teacher,* 1981, *34,* pp. 378–380; and R. Gentry, "Early Spelling Strategies," *Elementary School Journal,* 1978, *79,* pp. 90–92.
6. Gentry, "Learning to Spell," p. 380.

7. C. Read, *Children's Categorization of Speech Sounds in English* (Urbana, Illinois: National Council of Teachers of English, 1975), p. 30.
8. W. M. Golladay, "The Teaching of Spelling to Low Ability Students," *Elementary English,* 1971, *48,* pp. 366–370.
9. J. W. Beers, C. S. Beers, and K. Grant, "The Logic behind Children's Spelling:" *Elementary School Journal,* 1977, *77,* pp. 238–242.
10. L. Ganschow, "Discovering Children's Learning Strategies for Spelling through Error Pattern Analysis," *Reading Teacher,* 1981, *34,* p. 680.
11. S. Templeton, "The Circle Game of English Spelling: A Reappraisal for Teachers," *Language Arts,* 1979, *56,* p. 796.
12. R. E. Hodges, "The Language Base of Spelling," in *Research in the Language Arts,* V. Froese and S. B. Straw, eds. (Baltimore: University Park Press, 1981), p. 222.
13. Templeton, "The Circle Game," p. 796.
14. C. Chomsky, "Reading, Writing, and Phonology," *Harvard Educational Review,* 1970, *40,* pp. 287–309.
15. *Ibid.*
16. S. Templeton, "Spelling First, Sound Later: The Relationship between Orthography and Higher Order Phonological Knowledge in Older Students," *Research in the Teaching of English,* 1979, *13,* pp. 255–264.
17. R. J. Fitzsimmons and B. M. Loomer, *Spelling: Learning and Instruction* (Des Moines: Iowa State Department of Public Instruction, 1978), pp. 75–78.
18. *Ibid.,* pp. 1–64; S. Graham, "Effective Spelling Instruction," *Elementary School Journal,* 1983, *83,* pp. 560–567; T. Johnson, K. Langford, and K. Quorn, "Characteristics of an Effective Spelling Program," *Language Arts,* 1981, *58,* pp. 581–588; and T. Blair and W. Rupley, "New Trends in Spelling Instruction," *Reading Teacher,* 1980, *33,* pp. 760–763.
19. D. D. Hammill, S. Larsen, and G. McNutt, "The Effects of Spelling Instruction: A Preliminary Study," *Elementary School Journal,* 1977, *78,* pp. 67–72.
20. G. Manolakes, "The Teaching of Spelling: A Pilot Study," *Elementary English,* 1975, *52,* p. 246.
21. Beers, Beers, and Grant, "The Logic," p. 242.
22. P. DiStefano and P. Hagerty, "An Analysis of High Frequency Words Found in Commercial Spelling Series and Misspelled in Students' Writing," *Journal of Educational Research,* 1983, *76,* p. 185.
23. *Ibid.,* p. 184.
24. B. Cronnell and A. Humes, "Elementary Spelling: What's Really Taught," *Elementary School Journal,* 1980, *81,* pp. 59–64.
25. DiStefano and Hagerty, "An Analysis of High Frequency Words," p. 184.
26. Manolakes, "The Teaching of Spelling," p. 244.
27. C. Read, "Writing is Not the Inverse of Reading for Young Children," in *Writing: The Nature, Development, and Teaching of Written Communication,* C. H. Frederiksen, M. Whiteman, and J. Dominic, eds. (Hillsdale, New Jersey: L. Erlbaum Associates, 1981).
28. C. Beers, "The Relationship of Cognitive Development to Spelling and Reading Abilities," in *Developmental and Cognitive Aspects of Learning to Spell,* E. H. Henderson and J. W. Beers, eds. (Newark, Delaware: International Reading Association, 1980), pp. 74–84.

29. U. Frith, "Unexpected Spelling Problems," in *Cognitive Processes in Spelling,* U. Frith, ed. (New York: Academic Press, 1980), pp. 495–515.
30. R. L. Cramer, "An Investigation of First Grade Spelling Achievement," *Elementary English,* 1970, *47,* pp. 230–237.
31. P. Childers, "Snow White and the Seven Dwarfs," *Journal of Experimental Education,* 1971, *40,* pp. 5–8.
32. R. E. Hodges, *Learning to Spell* (Urbana, Illinois: National Council of Teachers of English, 1981), p. 15.
33. S. Partoll, "Spelling Demonology Revisited," *Academic Therapy,* 1976, *11,* pp. 339–347.
34. I. Rothschild, "Spelling Instruction for the Dyslexic Child," *Academic Therapy,* 1982, *17,* p. 397.
35. S. J. Kowalski, "A Spelling Method That Works," *Academic Therapy,* 1977, *12,* pp. 365–367.
36. California Assessment Program, *Survey of Basic Skills, Grade 3: Rationale and Content* (Sacramento: California State Department of Education, 1980); and California Assessment Program, *Survey of Basic Skills, Grade 6: Rationale and Content,* (Sacramento: California State Department of Education, 1982).
37. *Ibid., Grade 3,* pp. 23–24; and *Grade 6,* pp. 46–48.
38. O. K. Buros, ed., *The Eighth Mental Measurements Yearbook,* Volume I (Highland Park, New Jersey: Gryphon Press, 1978), p. 161.

Written Composition

Objectives

Factors that affect children's writing performance
Major areas of the curriculum in written composition
School stimuli for writing
Ways to evaluate children's written compositions

Discover As You Read This Chapter If*

1. The writing that primary children do contains features of their basal readers.
2. Well-developed oral language proficiency has little or no effect on written composition.
3. The prewriting stage of the writing process is most critical for girls and boys in the intermediate grades.
4. Self-determination by children of composition topics has been proven ineffective.
5. The most important area in the written composition curriculum is the content or substance/ideas.
6. Proofreading by children of their own written work should start as early as the fifth grade.
7. Student interest in writing peaks at grade four.
8. Teacher-pupil conferences are less effective than large-group instruction for developing the conventions of writing.
9. Holistic scoring of compositions involves correcting errors and writing comments.
10. Analytical scoring is the type of grading most used in schools today.

*Answers to these true-or-false statements may be found in Appendix 6.

Although writing is a fundamental ability needed for school success, many contemporary researchers and educators agree that, with rare exceptions, students today do not write well.[1] Teachers have not been adequately prepared in the area of written composition, methods used are frequently inappropriate or inadequate, and not enough emphasis has been placed on writing and writing instruction.

While written composition may be used less than oral composition in everyday life, this does not mean that it should be accorded less attention in teachers' planning. Instead, it should require additional and specialized instruction because writing is more difficult. It involves expressing ideas thoughtfully and precisely without the aid of facial grimaces, vocal tones, or physical gestures.

The growing awareness in recent years of the need to improve the complex task of student writing has spurred the implementation of a wide range of writing programs. Perhaps the most noteworthy is the Bay Area Writing Project begun at the University of California in 1974, now including 17 California sites as well as 60 other sites throughout the United States. Within its first five years of existence, an estimated 30,000 teachers around the country had been "BAWPed" after five weeks of intensive training, discussion, and writing in regional summer institutes and other forums. The chief elements of the Project's philosophy about teaching and writing include the following:

1. Writing is a complicated process, best taught in a series of steps.
2. There are no prepackaged methods or formulas, so each teacher must discover his or her own best approach.
3. It is possible and desirable for boys and girls to learn how to recognize overall writing quality.
4. Children can be shown how to edit each other's papers and thereby develop critical faculties.
5. Children do not fail in writing; teachers fail. When a child is not motivated to write, the teacher must try a different approach, work harder, and finally get the job done.

Modeled after the BAWP is the National Writing Project, begun in 1977, which has sites in 36 states. It assumes that a teacher of writing must write, that the best teacher of teachers is another teacher, that change can best be accomplished by those who work in the schools, and that change agents in the schools should begin by focusing on what works.

Factors Affecting Writing Performance

Numerous factors affect children's writing[2] Research studies have established the positive importance of the factors which are discussed in this section.

1. *Intellectual capacity.* Pupils who are superior in verbal ability are also superior in composition writing, producing more words per minute and per paper. IQ scores are significantly related to writing accomplishments. In a heterogeneous sample of 300 children, ages 7.0 to 9.11, the able group showed an advantage of nearly three years in written language development.

2. *Reading achievement.* Children who read well also write well, while those who read poorly write poorly too. In low-income, urban neighborhoods even first graders reveal a high correlation between reading and written composition, while sixth graders who rank illiterate or primitive in writing read below their chronological age. Finally, as the students' level of reading comprehension increases, so does the number of compound and complex sentences they can write.
3. *Grade level/chronological age.* Advances in grade/age correlate positively with increasing length of written sentences and of T-units (i.e., terminable units—main clauses together with all phrases and clauses syntactically related). On the other hand, the difference between the performance of the low-achieving groups and the national performance in expressive writing increases at each successive age level.
4. *Sex.* Girls write more than boys. On measures of complexity, boys and girls score at generally the same levels. On most measures of quantity, however, girls score significantly higher than boys. Girls also tend to write compositions which are judged to be of high quality.

   Seven-year-old boys write more about the so-called secondary territory or the metropolitan areas beyond the home and school, while seven-year-old girls write more about the primary territory related to the home and school. Girls stress more prethinking and organizational qualities and feelings in characterizations than do boys. Primary boys are more concerned than primary girls with the importance of spacing, formation of letters, and neatness.
5. *Oral language proficiency.* Children who are rated superior or above average in their use of oral language are also rated above average in writing. Those below average in oral expression rate the same in written language.
6. *Type of writing tool.* Story-writing performance is significantly better with ball-point or felt pens than it is with standard (adult-size) pencils, whether the writers are primary or intermediate children. Also, the novelty of writing with pens does not wear off after repeated exposure.
7. *Special training program.* A program emphasizing many experiences in writing and a focus on clarity and interest in writing (rather than on mechanical correctness) results in a greater number of words per T-unit, greater sophistication in language control—and fewer mechanical mistakes.
8. *Structured literature program.* The type of program described in Chapter Eleven provides a balance between fiction and nonfiction, between prose and poetry, and between the traditional and the modern. The ability of children to write often depends upon their ability to hear/read good books. They and their teacher should set aside time to share favorite volumes with each other.
9. *Classroom environment.* Results of writing done in informal environments demonstrate that pupils do not need supervision in order to write. Informal environments also seem to favor boys in that they write more than girls do in such environments, whether the writing is assigned or unassigned. Formal environments, on the other hand, seem to be more favorable to girls in that they write to greater length and more frequently than do boys in these types

of environments, whether the writing is assigned or not. Finally, an environment that requires large amounts of *assigned* writing inhibits the content, range, and amount of writing done by elementary school children.

Teachers must be sensitive to establishing a relaxed classroom climate in which divergent thinking is encouraged. Each member of the class—and his or her work—should be respected. In order to encourage dialogue and foster sensory awareness, learning centers should be maintained.

10. *Handedness.* Left-handers outperform right-handers on both verbal and nonverbal tests. They should therefore have a clear advantage because ability is a powerful determinant of writing development. However, since their output is identical with that of right-handed children, Harpin suggests that teachers make special provision for left-handers and offer them direct help.[3] Otherwise the physical difficulty of writing may take an abnormal share of the left-handed child's attention and so restrict the freedom to experiment syntactically.
11. *Socioeconomic background.* The proportions of good expressive papers written by students whose parents have post-high school education and by students who live in relatively affluent communities are greater than the proportions for children of the poorly educated and children who live in relatively impoverished areas. Pupils in the top socioeconomic groups are more fluent in their writing and use a greater variety of words than pupils in the lower levels. In every measure of language studied, the child writers in the upper levels, socially and economically, show an advantage over those in the lower levels. This is true even among children of only average intelligence. Pupils from low-metro schools do not routinely produce unique written creations. Instead, very often their stories are stereotypic, descriptive, and not very imaginative.
12. *Length of writing time.* The longer the time the children are permitted to write, the better the quality of their written expression. They should therefore be allowed to choose how long they wish to write during any one period. Even middle-grade pupils profit from a prolonged time span of as much as 225 minutes for writing.
13. *Instruction in modern grammar.* Boys and girls receiving instruction in structural grammar or transformational-generative grammar—whether formally or informally—are producing longer and more syntactic structures of greater complexity than students taught the older, traditional grammar.
14. *Lack of integration of writing and reading tasks.* Writing instruction is not a substitute for reading instruction, according to Stotsky, and it is best undertaken for its original purpose.[4] Conversely, using reading instruction to better free writing also is not effective.

Eckhoff, however, did find that the writing of the second graders she studied contained features of their reading texts.[5] Children reading in a basal which closely matched the style and complexity of literary prose wrote sentences using complex verb forms, infinitive and participial phrases, and subordinate clauses. Their classmates who read in a basal with a simplified style wrote generally in the same less elaborate style. It would appear that the practice of many publishers of using simplified sentence structures in their reading texts in the hope of easing the learning-to-read process has had a negative effect on children's writing.

Finally, good readers and poor readers alike enjoy reading a story significantly more than they enjoy writing about it, and there appears to be no evidence that integrating reading and writing enhances enjoyment of the reading.

Briefly, while a central issue in the study of literacy is the nature of the relationship between writing and reading, that relationship remains somewhat mysterious due to the many unanswered questions about writing and reading themselves.[6]

15. *Teacher attitude.* A receptive and encouraging attitude on the part of the teacher is crucial. Children whose teachers stress originality of expression develop more ideas, write more words, and make fewer mechanical errors.

    The matter of teacher criticism of completed compositions, however, has not been resolved. There appears to be no significant difference between the effects of negative reaction as opposed to positive criticism by teachers of children's writing. Either type of criticism may apparently be used since each gets similar results.

Generalizations/Guidelines for the Teaching of Written Composition

The curriculum for written composition in the elementary grades is concerned with three major areas. First and foremost there is the *content or ideas* which the children wish to relate. Then there are the *writing process* and the *skills with the conventions (or mechanics) of writing,* both of which are needed for the communication of the content. All areas are expedited when teachers underscore their planning with the principles discussed in this section.

1. *Children must recognize the significance of writing, in their own lives and in the lives of others.* Through daily contact with labels, direction sheets, maps, menus, coupons, charts, bulletin boards, and newspapers, pupils can be taught to sense the importance of writing—in the home, school, and community. Studies of such famous writings as historical documents of the past and present offer another dimension to older children's recognition of the role of written composition in society.
2. *Children must realize that writing serves several different functions.*[7] The *first* of these is self-expression—writing to know oneself and to exhibit a close relation to the reader. This demands a free flow of feelings and ideas. A *second* is transmission of information or getting things done. It is writing to demonstrate academic competence and involves giving instructions and attempting to persuade others. Britton calls this function transactional.[8]

   The *third* function has been termed poetic and uses language as an art medium. It is not limited to poetry but refers to any writing which stands alone as a product of creativity. A *fourth* function is assistance to learning and thinking generally, and it is believed that when writing is pursued seriously in a comprehensive language arts program, it can help the boy or girl become a more perceptive thinker.[9]

The *fifth* and *sixth* functions of writing were revealed in a two-year study of one second/third grade classroom and one sixth grade classroom, both in a midwestern suburb.[10] One function was termed writing as participation in the community (e.g., writing classroom rules) and the other was writing to occupy free time (e.g., making cards to send to noncustodial parents by children of divorce).

The *final* function of writing concerns the enhancement of reading comprehension. The two phases of literacy appear to be reciprocal, and therefore girls and boys who learn how reading material is structured may acquire ways to structure ideas in writing.

3. *Children must have a variety of experiences and interests about which to write.* Firsthand happenings at home or school, on the playground or at a nearby park, on a study trip or at a club meeting, are all useful means of input. So are vicarious experiences through the media of selected books, magazines, films, or television programs. Finally, hobbies and sports, from stamp collecting to soccer, furnish material for written compositions too. Input, however, can and must be continued during the year through the ongoing classroom activities and learning centers provided by the teacher in the areas of science, social studies, reading, arts and crafts, and health.
4. *Children must communicate orally before they can express themselves in written form.* Speaking and listening habits profoundly influence pupils' abilities to write. Until they can express themselves clearly through oral means, they generally are not ready to compose their thoughts in written form. This is true of both school beginners and upper primary children.

   Suggested activities for developing oral communication skills include puppetry, story dramatization, reporting, dramatic play, interviewing, and discussion.
5. *Children must enjoy a satisfying and supportive classroom environment.* In a pressure-free atmosphere pupils believe that their values, encounters, and feelings are important enough to share with each other. If they are thereby encouraged to talk freely about these experiences and beliefs, they are more apt to be able to use their oral contributions as a basis for their writing.
6. *Children must be aware that writing occurs in many different forms.* Four basic forms are narration, description, exposition, and argumentation. The first includes stories, the second focuses upon the appearance of people/pets/objects, the third explains a subject or gives directions, and the fourth covers efforts to persuade or offer evidence in support of certain statements. Function sometimes dictates the form of the composition.
7. *Children must realize that a writer always communicates with someone when he or she writes.* The subject or subjects being addressed by a writer comprise the "audience." Writer attitude as well as writing style and language are all dependent upon the nature of this "audience."

   The framework in elementary school composition published by the Wisconsin Department of Public Instruction treats audience in three different senses—Me-as-Audience, Personal You-as-Audience, and Unknown You-as-Audience.[11] Each of these is removed somewhat from the other in psychological distance, passing from inner-person or self-as-audience to an unknown audience that may be geographically many miles away, or at least, some audience about whom the writer knows very little.

8. *Children must hear and read literature in order to write well.* Next to direct experience, the reading which children do is usually their most important source of new words and ideas. Since carefully chosen literature presented effectively can do much to stimulate good writing, a teacher should plan many types of literary experiences, including storytelling and choral speaking. Scheduled browsing in the school media center or classroom library is also helpful.

   There are specific ways in which the writing ability of students' will be enhanced when the teacher reads aloud from quality literary works every day for at least 20 minutes.[12] First, their vocabularies will increase both in comprehension and in word count. Second, their abilities to distinguish among subtle differences in word meaning will improve. Third, their sentence structures will become more effective and more complex. Fourth, they will gain a sense of writing form and organization: e.g., their compositions will have proper introductions and conclusions. Fifth, they will gain a reason or rationale for writing after hearing the rhythm of standard speech and the pattern of literary prose.

9. *Children must understand that the writing process actually consists of three major stages: prewriting, composing, and post-writing.* While the prewriting stage is important for all writers, it is most critical for the younger writer in the early grades. The writing process demands a careful balance of craftsmanship and creativity, which in turn requires exceptional planning on the part of the teacher. Focus must remain on the *process* rather than the written *product.*

10. *Children must write frequently.* Writing becomes a habit when boys and girls write daily. They find it easier to do and begin to appreciate their own written effort and that of others. Spending five to ten minutes writing each day in their journals has helped many children develop necessary composition skills.

11. *Children must be allowed to choose their own composition topics.* While teachers may continue to suggest possible themes, students themselves should be able to determine what the exact subjects of their compositions will be. The importance of such self-determination is confirmed by much of the literature on student stages of mental development. The more abstract the writing task, the greater the amount of mental maturity necessary for the writer to possess. According to Haley-James, writing on topics that are unrelated to personal experiences or have been assigned by someone else is inappropriate for children in grades 1–8.[13]

12. *Children must appreciate that vocabulary is a major element contributing to effective writing.* Students can be taught to refer to a variety of sources in which they can locate the words they need, including appropriately graded dictionaries, word boxes, basal readers, spelling books, and special chalkboard or chart lists. To improve their written communication they must also

learn to select expressive words, employ synonyms and antonyms, and become acquainted with a beginning thesaurus.

13. *Children must become actively involved in evaluating their own writing.* Through writing conferences with their teacher, pupils acquire the ability to occasionally revise and to routinely edit their own work. As they complete some compositions, they may decide to *revise the contents* in order to make the compositions more interesting to readers. As they finish all written work, however, they *proofread* or *edit* it in order to make meanings clearer to readers. Occasionally a pupil may even copy a composition for the sake of neatness if the composition has been revised/edited extensively.
14. *Children must be encouraged but not forced to share their writing with others.* Since writing implies communication, compositions may be read aloud in the classroom or posted in the halls. They may be delivered to parents or published in local newspapers or national journals. On the other hand, compositions may be quietly placed in children's language folders or the teacher's file and never displayed at all. While the teacher can and should guide pupils to share their writing with peers and parents, it is the children themselves who must finally choose to accept or decline publicity about their written compositions.

   For pupils who are eager to share their writing with a wide audience, there are more than a dozen national children's magazines ranging alphabetically from *Cricket* to *Young World* that publish the creative efforts of elementary school pupils. Competition is keen and delays in notification of the acceptance or rejection of submitted material are common. Still, each of the magazines accepts two or more of the following: poems, riddles, book reviews, jokes, letters, stories, puzzles, recipes, photographs, comic strips, drawings, and articles. All work must be original and accompanied in most instances by a signed statement regarding originality. Occasionally a magazine will pay a small sum for work accepted.
15. *Children must have teachers who enjoy and practice writing.* A teacher who fears writing or dislikes it will convey that fear or dislike, just as a teacher who only writes comments on children's work, reports to parents, or exercises for classroom activities will demonstrate that writing is solely for administrative and classroom use.

   Negatively stated, this is what Smith terms the Grand Myth about Who Can Teach Writing: People who do not themselves practice and enjoy writing can teach boys and girls how to write.[14] In reality, boys and girls taught by a teacher who sees writing as a tedious chore with minimal applications will adopt exactly the same attitude.

Major Areas of the Curriculum in Written Composition

There are three major areas in written composition curriculum, the foremost of which is certainly the content or substance. Wise teachers today place primary emphasis on the fresh viewpoint or novel description contained in student writing. They are quick to rank both the writing process and the skills in the conventions (or mechanics) of writing as subordinate since each is necessary only in order to express the content accurately and fluently.

Content or Ideas

Most pupils, whether they are beginning or advanced writers, will need some assistance in working with the ideas that they wish to communicate. Since the substance of all written expression consists of ideas, the ability to work with them effectively is fundamental. As ideas may be handled in a variety of ways, writers may employ any one of five interrelated kinds of thinking-writing operations as shown below:

A. *Reflecting on the world:* As child writers represent accurately what they have seen, heard or read.
   1. Describing characteristics of objects, persons or materials
   2. Reporting on an event
   3. Telling how something is done
   4. Retelling in other words something read or heard
   5. Summarizing briefly key events or points

B. *Relating phenomena existing in the world:* As child writers identify relationships among instances or items.
   1. Comparing similarities among items
   2. Contrasting differences among items
   3. Classifying common properties of items
   4. Analyzing qualitatively which items are higher or lower, larger or smaller.
   5. Analyzing sequentially which items come first, second, etc.
   6. Explaining why something happened.

C. *Projecting hypotheses, theories, and designs:* As child writers suggest ideas that appear possible but go beyond current data.
   1. Hypothesizing or making predictions
   2. Generalizing or theorizing
   3. Designing or planning systems

D. *Personalizing:* As child writers express their own opinions or beliefs.
   1. Expressing feelings
   2. Expressing preferences
   3. Expressing opinions
   4. Expressing judgments

E. *Inventing:* As child writers must go beyond actual occurrences to create people, situations, and conversations.
   1. Creating descriptions
   2. Creating dialogue
   3. Creating characters
   4. Creating plot[15]

Writing Process

Elementary school teachers guide children in the primary and intermediate grades through three distinct stages of writing, sequentially labelled *prewriting, composing,* and *postwriting.* The amount of attention and time spent on any given stage will vary from child to child depending upon many factors, including the very form of the writing task. Brief informal writing in daily journals, for example, is not apt to require nearly the attention demanded by the preparation of directions for a science experiment.

Prewriting

It has been defined as any activity, exercise, or experience that motivates the girl or boy to write, that focuses a writer's attention upon a certain subject, or that generates ideas and materials for writing.[16] Its purpose is simply to move the writer from mere mental consideration of a topic to the physical activity of typing or hand writing about that topic. Younger or less experienced writers are in even greater need of this stage than older, sophisticated ones.

Guidelines for prewriting developed at Auburn University during one recent summer suggested that the teacher should:

1. Set aside enough *time* to allow for reflection prior to putting thoughts on paper.
2. Provide an *environment* conducive to thinking/writing and a *stimulus* that is meaningful to the class.
3. Communicate exactly the *expectations* and *purposes* for the composition, including some attention to the matter of audience.
4. Use *discussion/questioning* in an effort to encourage reflection and visualization.
5. Promote *organization of ideas* by jotting down critical phrases or words.[17]

Numerous kinds of prewriting activities are both possible and useful, as well as being readily adapted to varied levels of writing experience. Included are brainstorming (during which all contributions are listed on the chalkboard), examining photographs/posters/pictures, becoming involved in story dramatization (whether interpretation or improvisation), listening to stories or story records/tapes, studying common objects such as forks or sweet potatoes, painting or crayoning pictures of one's thoughts, going on walking or field trips, using puppets or watching puppet theatre productions, taking opinion surveys among family members or classmates, viewing films/filmstrips, examining globes or collages, or enjoying hands-on and taste-on experiences with such items as fabrics and foods, for example.

Three important cautions are issued by those associated with the famed Bay Area Writing Project (recently renamed the California Writing Project). First, the teacher must rarely, if ever, allow boys and girls to embark upon a writing task without first having provided them with one or more prewriting activities. Second, once the noisy, interactive prewriting session has drawn to a close, the teacher must plan a quiet, introspective time for the writers before they begin to work. Finally, explorational prewriting activities have proved to be equally important in both the upper and lower grades.[18]

Coverage of the prewriting stage in one language arts series is shown in Figure 8.1.

Composing

The teacher's principal responsibilities during the composing stage are to be sure that the classroom atmosphere is conducive to writing and that he/she is generally available for reassurance, assistance, or occasional prodding. The child writers must be comfortable in supportive surroundings and should see their own teacher occupied with writing tasks from time to time.

Part 1 Pre-Writing

Figure 8.1. Coverage of the Prewriting Stage in Composition.

The first part of the writing process is **pre-writing**. This planning stage has four steps. When you complete these steps, you are ready to write.

Step 1. Find a Topic. Sometimes your teacher will assign a topic. Other times you will need to find your own topic. The following questions will help you to come up with ideas:

What do I do for fun?
What books do I enjoy reading?
What places have I visited?
Has anything exciting ever happened to me?
Do I know any interesting people?
Have I heard any good stories?
Do I like to learn about other times or other countries?

Make a list of several ideas that come to you.

Keep in mind the reason for this piece of writing. If you are making a report, you will need to choose a topic for which you can find facts. If you are writing a made-up story, you can tell about either real or imaginary things.

You should also remember who will be reading your writing. A letter to a friend will be quite different from a letter to the editor of a newspaper.

Examine your list of ideas. Think of what you can say about each. Then choose one idea as your topic.

Step 2. Limit the Topic. The writing you plan to do may be a short paragraph. It may be a longer report. Make sure that your topic can be developed within the length assigned. For example, you would need several paragraphs to explain the topic "The Potlatch Ceremony." You might, however, describe a totem pole in one paragraph.

Step 3. Gather Information. List the details you could use to develop your topic. Depending on your topic, you might get information from books and magazines or from people you interview. You might draw ideas from your memory.

Figure 8.1 (cont.)

Step 4. Arrange the Information. Go over your list of details. If you have not already decided on the main idea of your writing, do that now. Then cross out any details that do not develop that main idea. Change details that are not exact enough. Add new details if you wish.

Finally, put your details into some order. When you are telling a story, for example, you would list events in the order that they happened. In later chapters, you will learn how to arrange details and ideas for different kinds of paragraphs.

Here is an example of pre-writing notes.

Ideas for Topics

training a guinea pig *Chief Logan*
recycling egg cartons *members of my family*
haunted houses *world's greatest sandwich*

Topic

~~*members of my family*~~ *my brother*

List of Details

tells jokes all the time
thinks he's a great comic
wears glasses
gave the family a show last week
Dad fell asleep during the show.
I hid in my room.
awful jokes
he practices in front of a mirror

Source: Reprinted from BUILDING ENGLISH SKILLS, Silver Level. Copyright © 1984, McDougal, Littell & Company, Evanston, Illinois. Used with permission.

Boys and girls need not restrict their working tools to pencils but may freely use pens, felt markers, finger paints, typewriters, chalk or water colors. Nor do they need to write in solitary confinement. After all, if well-paid adult writers in advertising agencies or on newspaper staffs can compose together, so can children write productively in pairs, in small groups, or even in large groups at times.

In a similar vein, just as some adult writers prefer to dictate their compositions, there may be boys and girls (especially young children) who need secretaries to whom they can dictate their expressions. Such personal scribes can be found among intermediate grade students, volunteer adults (including retirees or grandparents), or even the classroom teacher. Also handy are the more impersonal tape recorders which will also allow the student to concentrate on the content of the composition rather than the mechanics, during this phase of the writing process.

An effective writing program encourages students to develop fluency, to write for an audience, and to identify a specific purpose for each piece of writing.[19] When students are fluent writers, they have much to say, and the words flow easily from the mind to the paper. A teacher can help boys and girls develop fluency by such strategies as having them keep journals/logs/diaries, by having them dictate ideas and stories to a student recorder, by using a kitchen timer and having children write as much as they can before the bell rings, or by making lists of familiar objects.

Student writing for an audience can be at times egocentric, and the child may choose to write for only himself/herself in ways not fully understandable to others. Students gradually begin to realize, however, that an audience demands that writers communicate ideas in more controlled forms than those used in egocentric writing. Therefore, writers must always attempt to envision their audience and recall whether they are writing to friends, family members, business concerns, or government agencies. A few may even eventually learn to write to a unknown broader audience (such as the readers of a juvenile magazine) and will consequently have to adjust their writing accordingly. Activities which may help students learn to accommodate their writing abilities to different audiences include writing for specific and varied purposes (e.g., get-well wishes, complaints, or ordering of merchandise), writing the same message in four different ways for four different audiences, or writing about a real or imagined school event twice (once for children in grades K–2 and once for pupils in grades 5–6).

There is a variety of purposes which motivate composition, including writing to explain, to record, to persuade, to complain, to entertain, to inform, or to comfort. Purpose is one matter which should be decided early in the writing process since it serves as an underlying guide and is often related to the type of audience that will read that particular piece of writing. Activities which help writers improve their talents for composing for a purpose include writing on the same topic with different objectives in mind, discussing models of various purposes in writing, compiling lists of goals for writing, and identifying author purposes in what is read. More sophisticated writers may even attempt to parody a piece of writing to indicate a change in purpose.

Postwriting

The most controversial aspects of the writing process probably occur during the postwriting stage.[20] It is also the time during which the greatest possibilities for writing growth can take place. Therefore, teachers should wisely:

- Make postwriting a positive (and not a punitive) experience for the children by encouraging them to work together and by keeping in mind that postwriting does not mean recopying.
- Look for strength in the composition, concentrate on changes to be made rather than on errors to be corrected, and realize that boys and girls cannot be expected to write like adults.

- Allow adequate time for reflection about any piece of writing.
- Provide direct instruction in proofreading.
- Prepare for individual conferences by identifying areas for discussion and by varying expectations for the final form of the writing according to the maturity of the writers.
- Correlate the postwriting experience with instruction in other areas of language.

On the whole, postwriting activities for one kind of writing may often develop into prewriting activities for another kind; for example, proofreading an interview with a local poet can lead to discussing varied types of poetry which in turn develops into writing free verse.

Postwriting can actually be broken down into two or more subphases, including responding/reacting, revising/reexamining, editing/proofreading, developing skills with the mechanics or the conventions of writing, evaluating, and finally realizing the relative importance of any piece of writing.[21] A first, quick overall *reaction* to a composition demands an audience that may consist of a teacher, an aide, one classmate, or a group of peers. It may occur through suggestions or questions about either the form or the content of the composition. Next comes *revision,* during which the writer has enough opportunity to rethink his/her expressed communication. Not all writing needs to be taken through the revision subphase and, therefore, at least part of the revising portion of the writing process is learning which pieces of writing deserve not to be revised; e.g., writing which reinforces the learning of subject matter such as social studies would not ordinarily require revision.

A major subphase of postwriting is *editing or proofreading,* which comprises correction of such areas as syntax, capitalization, punctuation, spelling, handwriting, usage, paragraphing, and improvement of diction (or the most effective word choices). It closely correlates with *developing skills with the conventions of writing* discussed separately in this chapter.

Another subphase of postwriting is *evaluation,* which always occurs in a positive fashion in order to support student effort. It must not be overemphasized, however, because it is only one aspect of the entire area of written composition. Evaluation too will be discussed at length later in this chapter.

The final subphase of postwriting covers all the activities that can be done with a finished piece of writing, varying from publishing it all the way down to discarding it. Often it involves sharing the written work with some sort of audience. It helps children become aware of the importance of their work and also aids them in *establishing a value for that written work.* They may use practical pieces of writing (such as business letters) in actual transactions with others; they can adapt narratives for dramatizing; they can publish their work in school magazines or community newspapers; or they can read their work aloud to a small group or an entire class. There can be school displays of successful writing or superior writing can be recognized through writing contests, awards, or assembly programs.

Two subphases of postwriting appearing on a sample page from a language arts series are combined in Figure 8.2.

Figure 8.2.
Coverage of the Postwriting Stage of Composition.

Part 6 Revising Your Story

When you write your story on paper, you should write your ideas quickly before you forget them.

When you are done, read over what you have written. Use these guides. Mark your changes on your paper.

Guides for Revising a Story

First, read the whole story.

1. Is the story interesting?
2. Do the paragraphs make sense together? Is anything missing?

Next, look at each paragraph.

3. Is every word group a sentence?
4. Do all sentences tell about the same thing? Should anything be taken out?
5. Is the paragraph easy to understand? Does it need more sentences? Do any sentences need more words?
6. Are the sentences in an order that makes sense?

Marks for Changing Your Writing

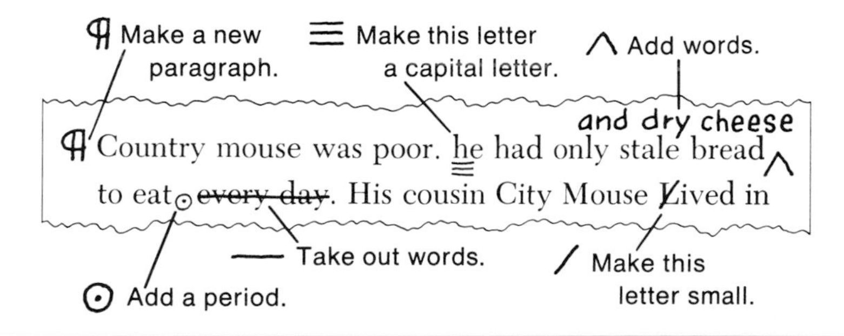

Writing Poetry

Lessons involving the writing of poetry by children do not always fit neatly into the three stages of the writing process described earlier. Instead, one successful lesson plan in this area breaks down the presentation into five steps:

1. The teacher gives a short *introduction* or conceptual overview of the lesson.
2. The teacher provides *examples,* stressing that all have been written by other boys and girls of the same age. This boosts the confidence of young would-be poets. Because examples tend to have a powerful modeling effect, the teacher must present a broad spectrum of poetic qualities including sound, imagination, feeling, and imagery. Unless a variety is presented to them, the children will promptly write poems showing only the single quality exhibited in the poem(s) that the teacher had introduced.
3. *Discussion* follows so that everyone understands exactly what is happening and what he or she is to do. The teacher must remind the class of two critical guidelines: There is to be no rhyming, and there is to be no concern with spelling or handwriting. All questions are answered and comments encouraged.
4. The *work session* now begins. The children start to write either alone or in teams. They are given plenty of personal space to minimize problems of privacy and copying. The teacher provides as much personal attention as he or she can because often even a small amount of such interest is sufficient as a strong incentive to create.

   Dictation is a good technique to use with boys and girls who may have an unusually difficult time expressing themselves with a pencil, pen, or crayon. The teacher writes as the child talks. Sometimes collective dictation is encouraging also and can be done at the chalkboard or on the tape recorder or typewriter.
5. *Presentation* by the teacher of student poetry is the final step. It takes place promptly (after a work session of 20–30 minutes) since an audience reinforces writer efforts and delights beginning poets. The teacher (and not the child writer) should read aloud the new poetry because students sometimes have trouble reading their own handwriting and therefore are apt to mumble. Furthermore, teachers can edit the poems as they read them, cutting out possible obscenities and choosing one particularly appealing portion while explaining its appeal. Should some students prove reluctant to have their poems read aloud, the teacher can either omit the poet names or allow the students to develop humorous pseudonyms such as Rocky or Beansprout.[22]

Another five-step approach, but this time generally restricted to the writing of cinquains, runs as follows:

1. The teacher chooses a *general topic* which allows flexibility and with which everyone is familiar; e.g., Foods I Love to Eat.
2. There is individual *brainstorming* as students list words or phrases about the chosen topic. The teacher moves about the class, reassuring and encouraging. After three to five minutes, sample words may be shared with the group.

3. There is *selection of one of the words* or phrases elicited during the previous step.
4. There is additional student *brainstorming,* again with considerable teacher encouragement and again for only a short time span.
5. A cinquain *poem is written.* Upon all the words that have been brainstormed a simple five-line form is imposed, with two syllables in the first line, four in the second, six in the third, eight in the fourth, and two in the fifth. The poem need not rhyme. Nor do all the brainstormed words have to be used although some words may be repeated, added, or reordered.

   Older children prefer working in groups of three to four, discovering quickly that cinquains almost write themselves. Younger children, on the other hand, respond more positively when allowed two to three sessions in which to complete their cinquains. It is believed that these five-step brainstorming-cinquain sessions can launch a flexible though controlled approach to poetry writing.[23]

Skills with the Conventions of Writing

The conventions of writing (or mechanics of writing) include spelling, handwriting, capitalization and punctuation, paragraphing and sentence sense, and usage. A recent national survey in the form of questionnaires distributed to 1000 fourth-grade teachers revealed that 96.5 percent of them "have students do punctuation and capitalization exercises" either "almost always" or "frequently."[24] It would appear, therefore, that teachers do indeed consider some conventions of writing as important.

However, mastery of the conventions or mechanics takes place more readily and efficiently not through the form of completed workbook pages or other prepared exercises but rather through the context of regular writing. The best motivator appears to be need, and consequently certain skills are learned/improved more effectively at particular stages of the writing process. Handwriting, for example, often abruptly improves during the writing phase while spelling and capitalization/punctuation generally dominate the postwriting phase.

In the early grades most editing is done in conference with the teacher. Since many beginning compositions are relatively brief, a great deal can be accomplished in a short period. By the third grade pupils are capable of greater self-reliance and can be introduced systematically to techniques of editing that they can gradually apply on their own. By the fourth grade many children can function as independent editors, provided that they have had a lengthy introduction to corrective procedures. Some groups even adopt a few professional proofreading marks:

∧	Insert a word, punctuation mark, or sentence.	Christmas is here∧
≡	Capitalize.	He is mr. Mason.
/	Don't capitalize.	She moved to the /State of Washington.

ℓ	Delete a word, punctuation mark, or sentence.	I can ~~can~~ go home.
¶	Start a new paragraph.	. . . my aunt. ¶The horse ran away . . .

Child writers should compose knowing that their work may possibly need editing. If they write on every other line and leave broad margins, they may later insert, delete, or correct material without problems of space. To help them identify choppy sentences or letters and words omitted unintentionally, they can read their poems or reports aloud to classmates or to a tape recorder. Such listening or oral proofreading aids self-editing, according to researchers who found that a quantity of syntactic deviations can thus be eliminated from children's written sentences.[25] Many omissions of the subject, the verb *be,* tense markers, articles, expletives, and capital letters can be detected and corrected. Most extraneous and redundant words can be deleted.

Mechanical skills are never introduced all at once or taught in isolation. Neither are they stressed to the point where they curb the creativity of pupils, and cause a loss of interest in writing. Nevertheless, mechanical skills are considered to be a legitimate extension of the written form of speech, and children can gradually become independent editors.

Spelling

Each child needs to know what to do independently upon discovering a word that he or she cannot spell while writing. The teacher, to avoid breaking the writer's train of thought or interrupting work with other boys and girls, may advise the pupil with a spelling problem to leave a space on his or her paper temporarily (writing in only the initial letter or syllable of the troublesome word). The teacher can then help the pupil later. Or better yet, the teacher may do the following:

1. Encourage invented spelling among beginning writers.
2. Place topic words on reference charts for copying as needed. Most classrooms have various kinds of classification charts, showing word lists that grow out of the units of study.
3. Compile a chalkboard list of class-dictated words to be used when needed.
4. Obtain appropriate dictionaries, preferably one for each pupil. Such books should list single-entry words in alphabetical order and supply some classification pages.
5. Encourage children to consult a familiar reader or storybook which contains the word they need to spell.
6. Promote the construction of individual notebooks, dictionaries, or word boxes.
7. Allow the experienced writer with a spelling problem to receive aid from a classmate.

Handwriting

Interrelated with spelling is handwriting, for each depends on the other for communication. When letters are correctly proportioned and words are properly spaced, the composition is more readily understood.

The real issue is not the form of the handwriting but its legibility. Although the primary pupil ordinarily uses traditional manuscript and the intermediate pupil employs traditional cursive writing or the typewriter, each boy or girl should be encouraged to compose in whichever form he or she feels comfortable. Nevertheless, since some types of writing always require the use of manuscript, the teacher will wish to help every child develop or maintain skill in that form of penmanship.

Capitalization and Punctuation

Children tend to use too many marks of punctuation and too many capital letters rather than too few. The responsibility of the teacher is often as much a matter of showing the boys and girls when not to insert capital letters and punctuation marks as it is a matter of teaching them when to use these conventions meaningfully.

Primary and intermediate pupils alike possess individual writing needs, and it is these needs that should determine what is taught in the areas of punctuation and capitalization at each level of development. Most teachers, and particularly those concerned with the writing process, prefer to provide explanations that have a functional base. At times the specific demands of a small group of children permit specialized drills tailored to the temporary needs. Then the teacher may choose to employ an opaque projector or the chalkboard to promote group discussion and correction of an unidentified paper, with special attention to the elements of capitalization and punctuation.

Elementary school children are able to understand that punctuation marks help translate speech into writing. And the teacher can point out how, through the use of punctuation, a writer can convey meaning to readers without benefit of the help which a speaker has—gestures, pitch, stress, juncture, and facial expressions.

Incidentally, a recent study of first graders in New Hampshire who learned to use three punctuation marks during their writing sessions concluded that the correct use of periods was harder for the children to learn than the use of quotation marks or the use of possessive apostrophes.[26]

Paragraphing and Sentence Sense

Children can be helped early to understand and to write good sentences. Even in the beginning primary years when children are dictating stories, they can gradually discover that a sentence may tell something, ask a question, express strong feeling, or give a command. As their sentence skill develops, they can move from the one-sentence composition to the two- and three-sentence compositions. Finally children learn that a group of sentences (or even occasionally a single sentence) that tells about one idea is called a paragraph. Beginning in the fourth grade, children can write *narrative paragraphs* (following chronological order and using exact verbs) and *descriptive paragraphs* (arranging details effectively).

Usage

Boys and girls need practice with sentence-combining activities to illustrate sentence variety and construction. Such practice may help them eliminate the run-on sentence, the choppy sentence, and the excessive use of the *and* connective. It may also encourage sentences using the basic transformations. The values of sentence manipulation/combination in the realm of written composition were discussed earlier in Chapter Three. The average elementary school boy or girl will probably need to be knowledgeable with only a few aspects of usage during the writing process. These would include subject-verb agreement, use of negative forms, use of appropriate participle forms, use of possessives, and use of past and future forms of verbs.

School Stimuli for Writing

Children clearly do not leap at the opportunity to do creative writing, concluded Smith and Hansen after their study of 464 fourth graders in Madison, Wisconsin.[27] The pupils as a whole enjoyed reading a story significantly more than they enjoyed writing about it, regardless of whether the writing task was creative or noncreative, assigned by the teacher or self-selected. Furthermore, the good readers did not respond any more positively to the writing task than did the poor readers.

The problem of motivating written composition remains acute. Today's children are more accustomed to electronic devices that stress the spoken word over the written word. Still, writing in the elementary grades can be spurred on through a variety of stimuli, and recent research among some 13,000 students in ten different states shows that student interest in writing becomes a critical factor beginning in the intermediate grades.[28] Exactly why such interest peaks in grade four and falls so rapidly is not at all apparent, but the decline is very clear. Teachers in those grades must therefore make special efforts to capture student excitement about writing and remain alert to the issue of overall student interest in writing-related topics.

Approximately 70 stimulating topics/situations are explored in this section, with additional activities described briefly in Table 8.1. Most of them can be adapted easily to a grade level other than that mentioned in the text or table.

Mother's Day/ Father's Day Gift

In preparation for the annual May or June festivity, each fifth grader hilariously *wrote one unique recipe*. The collection of recipes was then reproduced and stapled together so that each student presented one parent with a Crazy Culinary Cookbook. One fifth grader began his Fillet of Sole recipe as follows: Take one rubber boot, three buckets of fresh rain water. . . .

Foreign Exchange Student

Attending the local high school one year was an exchange student from Argentina. The sixth-grade teacher invited him to her classroom and the young man enjoyed talking to the boys and girls. He arranged to get names of children in Argentina who wished to correspond with their peers in the United States and who had studied English in school. The sixth graders were soon busy, as they started to *write friendly letters* to their foreign pen pals and to exchange inexpensive souvenirs.

The fourth graders watched a film called *A Fable* (Xerox Films), whose sound track contains no narration. Then they were divided into committees in order to *write a film narrative*. The short film was subsequently rerun several times until each committee's composition had been read aloud as an accompaniment.

Film

When the family of the second-grade teacher lost some of the pieces from his 500-piece jigsaw puzzle, he brought the remaining pieces to school. After he had distributed them among the pupils, the boys and girls arranged the pieces face down on manila paper and pasted the odd shapes into pictures. Those who wished to could *dictate couplets* about their pictures into the tape recorder.

Puzzle Pieces

After watching another successful launching of the American space shuttle, fifth graders *wrote unrhymed verse* about the varied sensory images each would be certain to experience as a future member of the crew.

Space Shuttle

In keeping with the light-hearted mood of the day, third graders *wrote ads* (for posting on the bulletin board) concerning the sale of useless or unusual objects. Example: (old board) A genuine handy-dandy, whipper-flipper that outwhacks all other tools. For only $9.98.

April Fools' Day

The fifth graders had learned "Godfrey Gordon Gustavus Gore" in a cumulative arrangement. Later, following a prolonged discussion, the children were eager to *write tercets* about other problem children who also had long names that rhymed with their owners' condition. Examples: Kate who was always late; Murray who was forever in a hurry.

Choral Speaking

On January 17 (Benjamin Franklin's birthday), the sixth graders decided to *write proverbs* much like those contained in *Poor Richard's Almanac*. Some even chose to paint or otherwise illustrate their maxims. One child drew a boy and his dog clinging frantically to a rope as they recalled "When you come to the end of your rope, make a knot and hang on."

Birthdays of Famous Americans

When the kindergarten class learned that an unnamed nine-year-old kangaroo had hopped away from the local children's zoo, each pupil wished to draw the kangaroo and then *dictate a name (for him or her) and one sentence* telling why the animal had decided to run away.

Escape of Wild Animal

Various kinds of playground balls, used during outdoor recess periods, kept disappearing from the second-grade classroom. In order to *make a written report* on the situation, the children got busy *gathering data from verbal sources* in small and large groups, hoping to resolve their common problem.

Burning Issues

Table 8.1
Instructional Activities in Elementary School Written Composition.

Instructional Objective	Grade Level	Learning Activity and/or Teaching Strategy
Understands the relationship between speech and writing.	K	Class cooperatively dictates to the teacher the directions for responding properly to a fire drill.
	1	The teacher brings in a hand eggbeater and a sponge for squeezing water into a tin pie pan. Then he or she asks the children to dictate what the eggbeater and the sponge may be saying as they are being used.
Comprehends the relative permanence of writing.	1	Children individually prepare picture scrapbooks to share with classmates. They paint, draw, or cut out pictures and then paste them on heavier paper. Finally they label the pictures.
Understands that people write to influence the behavior or convictions of others.	4	Each child writes a pro or con argument on littering.
	5	Each child designs a food advertisement for a billboard.
	6	The debate teams write out their opinions and facts before the oral presentation. Resolved: Christmas has become too commercial.
Understands that people write to record information clearly and accurately.	2	Upon returning from a field trip to the science museum, each child writes a description of his or her favorite item and reads it aloud to a small group. The group must guess the identity of the object; whoever guesses correctly becomes the next reader.
	3	Each child keeps an individual diary for one week. At the end of each day the child writes one or two sentences about the day's happenings.
	4	Students record observations of the behavior of mealworms as seen under a microscope.
	5	Each student prepares a brief bibliography on American presidents. Bibliographies are exchanged and the receivers must check the library shelves to determine accuracy of the documentation.
	6	Class makes a time line tracing the development of the growth of democracy from ancient times to 1776.
Understands that people write to respond to a verbal or written stimulus.	2	Children clip coupons from newspapers or magazines and complete the forms correctly, pretending to be ordering merchandise.
	3	Children write friendly letters to the room parents after the St. Valentine's Day party.
	4	Children individually write a definition of a common object (such as a balloon) by naming and classifying it properly and by giving one identifying characteristic.
	5	Each student chooses a topic sentence about a special interest/sport/hobby and proceeds to write a paragraph using details to expand that sentence.
	6	Class lists several transitional words and phrases that keep time order straight in a paragraph or story and that keep the relationships clear between ideas (e.g., *if, when, then, while, because, first*).

Instructional Objective	Grade Level	Learning Activity and/or Teaching Strategy
Applies mechanical skills (i.e., punctuation, capitalization, spelling, and handwriting) to all writing.	1	Children take turns erasing capitalization errors and correcting the errors with colored chalk in a dictated experience chart story written on the chalkboard.
	2	The teacher displays one concrete item and has each child write a sentence about it. The sentences are collected and read aloud to the class (with the owners' permission), which must decide which sentences are complete sentences.
	3	Some children are chosen to be question marks; others, exclamation marks; and the rest are periods. The teacher reads aloud a class summary of a field trip, which includes all three marks. After a question, the question marks stand up, and so on.
	4	Children are given written instructions (for a science experiment) which have no periods. The class places periods in the correct places.
	5	Each child writes a paragraph summary about a film the class recently viewed, purposely misspelling five words. The children exchange papers, and each then proofreads the new paragraph carefully for proper spelling.
	6	Portions of editorials which the pupils have written are projected on a screen (with owners' names deleted). The class must evaluate the handwriting—slant, size, shape, spacing, and alignment.
Organizes expository writing logically and clearly.	6	Children bring to class copies of their favorite comic strips and list details which happen in each frame.
Understands that people write to express, both for themselves and others, their ideas, opinions, and insights.	1	Class cooperatively writes "Fun at a Picnic" (via the teacher and the chalkboard) just to a certain point, at which time the children individually conclude the story.
	2	Children are given a worksheet entitled "This Is How I Feel." The children individually write a sentence or two about what makes them glad and what makes them sad. On the back, they choose one other emotion to discuss in writing.
	3	Children are given the middle sentence of a story. They must write one sentence which shows what may have happened before and also write one sentence which shows what may have happened after.
	4	Children write a legend about an event or a figure in state or local history.
	5	Class writes three original sentences containing metaphors and copies them on the chalkboard, underlining the words that constitute the metaphor in each. Then each child writes a poem in metaphoric language.
	6	Each student personifies (or gives human qualities to) an inanimate object such as a baseball, a pencil, an apple, or a paper clip, and writes a story about it. Example: My Life as a Stepladder.

Book Jacket

The fifth-grade teacher pinned on the bulletin board many colorful book jackets with the caption "What's It All About?" after removing all the blurbs. Since he had succeeded in selecting book titles which were unfamiliar to a majority of the pupils, the short *book review* each student prepared (based on his or her favorite book jacket) proved enjoyable to read as well as to write.

Cartoon Characters

The first-grade class had seen the cartoon characters in the primary filmstrip unit "Safety Every Day" (Scholastic) and had discussed various safety precautions. Their teacher then offered them some short jingles about traffic safety, and asked the boys and girls if these reminded them in any way of Mother Goose rhymes. With her encouragement, the children began to *write contemporary nursery rhymes* about safety involving familiar characters. One result began:

Jack and Jill stepped off the curb.

School-Made Products

The first-grade class was planning to make gingerbread men in conjunction with their economics unit. The pupils wanted to try to sell some of their products in order to raise money for the class library. They chose to cooperatively *dictate an announcement* about the gingerbread sale which could be read in other primary classrooms.

Community Sports

The YMCA had arranged to hold swimming classes for both beginners and advanced students of elementary school age. As teachers discussed the formation of the classes with the children, they urged the boys and girls to talk over the matter at home. Three days later each interested child was given time to *complete an application* for admission to the swimming class.

Sick Classmate

When six-year-old Stephanie got the mumps, her classmates told their teacher that they wished to *dictate a get-well message* to their friend. The group letter was accompanied by many funny pictures which the children drew to cheer up Stephanie.

Recorded or Taped Music

Intermediate children enjoy listening to some of the music written by Leroy Anderson, Ferde Grofé, Peter Tchaikovsky, and others. Against such a background they can *write, collectively or individually, an original ballad* based on the current scene. Any incident having dramatic, relevant, and contemporary interest can be fashioned into a ballad whose lines are organized into a quatrain, or into a quatrain plus a refrain.

Principal's Visit

The fourth graders listened intently to their principal after she had stopped by one morning to review appropriate behavior on the school bus. She encouraged then to *take notes* during her visit so that the whole class might later recall the salient points of the discussion.

Wild Things

Primary children made animals from discarded gift boxes and scrap materials including yarn, velvet, feathers, colored cord, and egg cartons. The following day each pupil was asked to *write an original definition* for his or her "wild thing." Some even wished to *develop new name words* for their creations.

The first-grade teacher placed a silver gravy boat on his desk one morning as he told the children his favorite poem about three wishes and read them an abbreviated version of "Aladdin and His Wonderful Lamp." Each pupil was then allowed to rub the "magic lamp" three times before drawing his or her wishes. Later the teacher stopped at each table so that each child could *individually dictate a story* about his or her wishing picture.

Magic Object

When the district nurse visited the fifth grade she reviewed the importance of good nutrition and the daily need for the basic food groups. Then she suggested that each pupil *complete a chart* of the kinds of food he or she should eat for balanced breakfasts, lunches, and dinners for one week.

Nurse's Visit

Each month the PTA program chairperson selected a different grade to supply the entertainment for the all-school meeting. When it came time for the second graders to perform, their teacher suggested they *write invitations* to each of their families to attend the Thanksgiving songfest they had planned.

Assembly Program

During National Safety Week, the boys and girls in the third grade decided to *make a list* of all the precautions each was taking regarding pedestrian safety. The lists were later discussed informally with the school crossing guard.

Community Campaign

A professional music instructor visited the school where many of his students were enrolled and presented two violin concerts in the auditorium. The first-grade teacher whose class had attended the morning performance encouraged her pupils to *write notes of appreciation* to the school visitor to let him know how much they had enjoyed the concert.

Visitor

The sixth-grade students (some individually, some in small committees) created collages by using newspaper or magazine pictures, colored construction paper, printed labels, paste, and tempera. Each collage had a theme, such as "Freedom" or "Busyness." Later, the pupils decided to *write dramatic paragraphs* about their collages.

Collages

The third graders acquired some rabbits, mice, and goldfish. On a lined sheet of writing paper, the teacher wrote the first two entries of a journal about the animals, and pinned it to the bulletin board. Then each child was encouraged to keep a *written observational record* of the activities of his or her favorite animal at school or a pet at home.

Nature Study

To launch a unit on myth writing, the teacher read aloud to her fifth-grade class from Farmer's *Beginnings: Creation Myths of the World* (Atheneum, 1979). The adventures of Prometheus, Pandora, and other gods were used to encourage each boy and girl to *write an original myth* offering a convincing explanation of a natural phenomenon to a primitive group of people.

Prose Read Aloud by the Teacher

The sixth-grade teacher cut out intriguing headlines from daily newspapers and pasted each on a sheet of lined writing paper. The papers were turned face-down

Newspaper Headlines

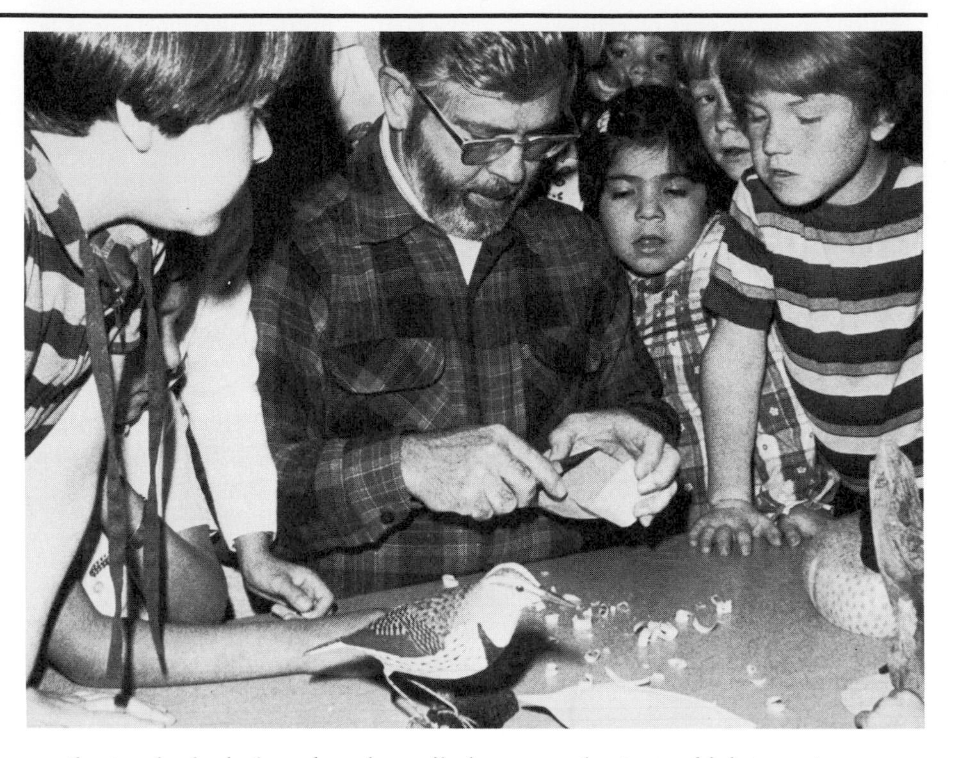

A visit from a professional wood carver and artist stimulated these first graders to write him notes of appreciation. (Photo courtesy of the *Daily News Tribune,* Fullerton, California.)

on the teacher's desk and each pupil chose one sheet on which to *write a news story* that fit the headline. (On another occasion the teacher provided the original newspaper articles so pupils could compare their stories with the published accounts.)

Class Walk

In a school located close to a lake, the first-grade teacher suggested one morning that the children put on their coats and walk over to see the waves on the lake. The lake was especially choppy that day and the pupils commented excitedly about the waves. Back in the classroom the teacher asked each child to write one sentence describing how the waves made him or her feel. The papers were collected and assembled into group *free verse.*

Special School Event

The fourth-grade teacher had been placed in charge of faculty participation in the forthcoming school carnival. He invited his students to publicize the carnival by creating comic-strip advertisements for distribution around the school. Committees were chosen, and each included at least one artist, one idea person, and one pupil who could *write comic strip dialog.*

Pupils' Birthdays

About one week before any member of the third-grade class celebrated a birthday, classmates prepared interview questions about the celebrant's family, pets, toys, favorite sports, or Scouting. Later, each pupil had to *write up the interview* that took place on the festive occasion. Children whose birthdays occurred in the summer or on weekends were allowed to choose alternate days for their interviews.

During the early part of October, the boys and girls in the fourth grade each chose to *keep a personal journal* (as might have been written by Columbus in the final days of his first voyage to the New World) or to *keep a logbook* of the *Nina,* the *Pinta,* or the *Santa Maria* (as written by the first mate of each vessel during the fall of 1492). The final entry in either the journal or the logbook was dated October 12.

Patriotic Holiday

Over several days, the second-grade teacher sometimes read and sometimes recited numerous poems about mail carriers, fire fighters, and other community workers. After discussing the poems with their teacher, the children decided to *write riddles* about the community helpers that had been described. The riddles were later placed in a folder on the library table for all to read and attempt to solve.

Poetry Presented by the Teacher

The sixth-grade teacher distributed some reproductions of famous paintings on four-by-six-inch postcards. She encouraged pupils to look at the reproductions carefully and to keep a favorite. The students later studied the lives of the artists of their favorite paintings before *preparing biographical sketches* to read to their classmates.

Art Reproductions

In the midst of their unit on Japan, the fourth-grade class became interested in *writing haiku, senryu, and tanka.* After the initial drafts had been completed, large sheets of wrapping paper were spread around the room and the nine-year-olds copied their poems with large vigorous strokes of their paintbrushes or thick-tipped felt pens.

Social Studies Unit

When two second graders reported during the same week that their pet cats had had litters, they and their classmates decided to *write a classified ad* of twelve words or less in which they would try to find good homes for the new kittens. The ad was later posted—in excellent manuscript—on the news board at the local market.

Free Kittens

The third graders enjoyed watching "The Electric Company" program. After several weeks of such viewing, the pupils were able to *write short reviews* of the program, advising their family members as to whether or not some of them would enjoy watching the show at home.

Telecasts

The sixth-grade class was responsible for writing, duplicating, and distributing the *Commonwealth Register* each month. Some of the boys and girls especially enjoyed *writing editorials* on such diverse topics as dress codes, longer lunch hours, and spanking.

School Newspaper

Fourth graders took a short trip to collect (with permission) such items from a nearby field as leaves, twigs, rocks, worms, feathers, insects, and bits of wood. They brought their collections back to the classroom where they chose the most interesting specimens for further examination. Each child was then asked to *write a description* of a favorite (unnamed) specimen. Later, papers were exchanged,

Nature Specimens

and sketches were drawn in accordance with the written description. Finally, comparisons were made among the items, the written descriptions, and the sketches.

School Camp

The sixth graders at Lakewood Elementary spent five days camping in the mountains with their teachers. Since five pupils in the grade had been unable to attend the activities, the teachers asked the campers to *write a summary* of the week's experiences to share with their parents as well as the absentees.

Interclass Debate

The fifth graders in Room 15 were getting ready for a debate on the United Nations with their peers in Room 16. In order to be able to verify statements made by their team during the debate, the pupils in Room 15 *prepared a bibliography* listing all books (and the significant page numbers).

School Campaign

After a teller from the First National Bank had explained to the middle and intermediate grades how each pupil was welcome to participate in the school savings plan, he distributed deposit cards and enrollment slips. Children interested in the plan were asked to *complete the printed forms* carefully after discussing the matter at home.

Puppet Theater

The third graders first constructed hand puppets based on the tale of *The Three Billy Goats Gruff*. Then they built a puppet theatre out of a bicycle carton. When they began to *write scripts,* they decided to record them. Thus the puppet operators could concentrate on manipulating the puppets while the tape recording supplied the voices.

Geometric Shapes

During their review of geometric shapes which the class had studied, each fourth grader chose two different shapes and then wrote sentences or very short stories to go around each shape appropriately.

Example:

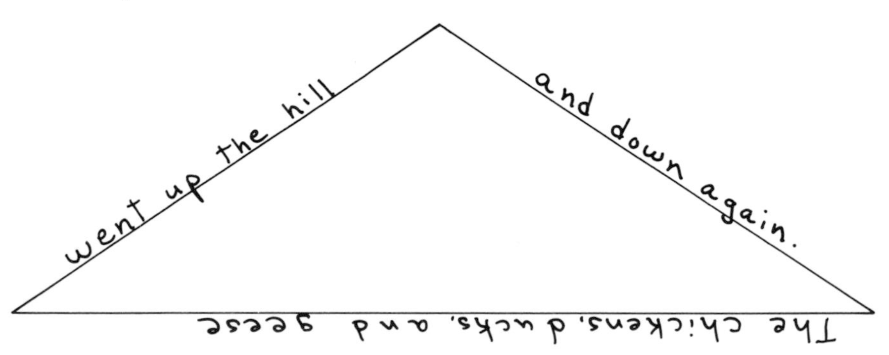

Filmstrip

After the second graders had seen the non-verbal filmstrip *Pancakes for Breakfast* (Weston Woods), they wanted to make a filmstrip of their own from sheets of wrapping paper. Later, although they kept their filmstrip silent, they chose to write appropriate captions for each picture frame.

The gifted sixth graders had read and discussed several novels. Then they learned that the school board had found it necessary to reduce the budget for the book collection at the media center. They decided to *write individual full-length books.* The writing process ran from November to April. The rest of the spring was devoted to copying the texts on unlined, margined paper with blue or black ink and to binding the books with the help of the art teacher. Most of the children wrote fiction. All of the books were placed in the library media center and permitted to circulate.

Library Media Center Budget

The fifth graders were provided with cameras and film. They took photographs of flowers, friends, trees, the kindergarten swing set, and the school building. Later each *wrote a lengthy poetic composition made up of several couplets* describing the subject of the picture or an impression/reaction to that subject.

Cameras

The sixth graders had glued to small individual cardboard sheets various objects such as steel wool, velvet, cotton balls, nylon, sandpaper, bits of fur, redwood bark fragments, long nails, and a sponge. The sheets were then placed into a large covered box which had a slot on top. After the children had carefully handled each object without seeing it they proceeded to *write jingles* consisting of a succession of sounds or a repeated phrase.

Buried Treasure

As the night for group parent conferences approached, the kindergarten children painted pictures about springtime. They then *dictated labels* for their paintings which were put on display both in the corridor and in the classroom.

Parents' Night

The third graders had been invited to perform some of the classroom experiments they had done with magnets at the school science fair. To assure a successful learning experience, their teacher urged that any pupil or group of pupils that had volunteered to do an experiment at the fair should *write down the steps of the selected experiment.*

Science Fair

Fourth graders became concerned with consumer education. Each child brought in one colorful label from a grocery item and *wrote a short television commercial* describing the product honestly. Some of the thirty-second commercials proved humorous.

Grocery Labels

After several weeks of construction work, the first graders were ready to participate in dramatic play concerning transportation. Still they needed such captions as Hangar and Garage to place on their sets. With the help of their teacher, they were able to *dictate and copy signs* that aided their activity.

Dramatic Play

The fifth- and sixth-grade pupils were eligible to join the Safety Patrol, whose members served as crossing guards for the children coming to and leaving school. The patrol meetings were held once a week, and their adviser selected a different secretary each month to *write up the club minutes.*

School Club

Clay Figures — Fifth graders created three-dimensional figures of fabulous beasts and monsters. They provided these nightmarish figures with original names. Then they began to *write character sketches* or stories about the creatures.

Wrapped Secrets — Pupils in the third grade each brought from home an inexpensive, inanimate, but carefully wrapped personal possession. The packages (with the owners' initials carefully hidden) were prominently displayed on the library table for most of the morning. Just before the noon recess, every child was allowed to *write a detailed guess* of the contents of a package other than his or her own.

Weather Conditions — The winter that their state was experiencing record snowstorms the sixth graders became interested in meteorology. They studied about the weather and *kept weather logs* for two weeks. Each daily log consisted of two sections: one for observations and one for actual weather measurements (temperature, humidity, barometric pressure, wind, and precipitation).

Color Posters — The second-grade teacher read aloud Rosetti's "Color" and Orlean's "Paints" and then created a picture-color poster with the help of the children. There were three word columns: color words, movement or action words, and describing words. The group then *wrote five-line cinquains* about a chosen color, first cooperatively and then individually. The cinquains were later mounted on sheets of construction paper that matched the color titles of the cinquains.

High School Sports — Some of the boys and girls in the third-and-fourth-grade combination class had brothers on the high school football team. The class was invited to see the game one Friday evening. The following Monday the children decided to *write new cheers* for the team.

Christmas/Hanukkah Gifts — During December when the newspapers were filled with advertisements of gift items for boys and girls, the fifth-grade teacher collected many pages of such advertisements. Each child chose one or two pages and *wrote a math story problem* involving some of the games, clothes, books, or other gift items. The following day the problems were exchanged and solved.

Party Invitation — Veronica, whose family had just recently arrived in Newton, invited all the girls in her first-grade class to a Halloween party. However, none of them was familiar with the new area where Veronica lived. So the teacher worked with the girls to help them *write down the directions* to Veronica's house.

Science Unit — As a result of their unit on sound, the fifth-grade class became interested in sound effects developed by radio stations. After each pupil who wanted to *write a radio commercial* about his or her favorite food had completed the assignment, the convincing—and sometimes comical—commercials were taped and appropriate sound effects added.

Nonsense Titles

The teacher posted on the chalk tray a variety of nonsense titles, including "How to Catch a Snapperdinck" and "The Day I Met a Rhinoraffoose." Each second grader selected one such caption to illustrate. Later the children were able to *write original fanciful stories* about their drawings and captions. Children who preferred to develop their own titles rather than use the teacher's stock were encouraged to do so.

Flannelboard Figures

Each reading group in the second grade chose its favorite basal story. The children then made felt figures of all the characters in that story. Finally they decided to *write new story endings* and present them on the flannelboard to the other groups.

Books for Beginning Readers

Fifth graders were permitted to *write original realistic stories for younger readers.* Working individually or in pairs, they had to be careful to choose subjects that would interest six-year-olds and had to develop a beginning-level vocabulary list. After the best stories—as rated by the class—had been copied in manuscript, the pages were carefully stapled and the books delivered to the first-grade pupils.

Study Trip

The second graders had visited the zoo on Monday. On Tuesday some children expressed a desire to learn more about the little-known animals they had seen, such as the llama. Other pupils wondered how the big bears, lions, and elephants were captured and brought to the zoo. The teacher encouraged each child or group of children to use the library media center in order to *make a report, gathering data from nonverbal sources,* about the animals in which there was special interest.

Homemade Objects

The sixth graders brought to class various items they had made at home, ranging from vases and pot holders to kites and model airplanes. As these objects began to collect on the display table, the class nicknamed them their Make-It Collection. Each pupil was able to *write an explanation* giving the steps for making or assembling his or her item.

New Wall Map

For securing the largest number of PTA members, the fifth-grade class earned a new wall map of the United States. Each child chose one state for an in-depth study and began to *write business letters for information* to the major chambers of commerce in that state. The replies, accompanied by some free materials, arrived within two months.

Mysterious Footprints

After school one day the teacher pasted large paper footprints on the floor and the walls of the classroom. The next morning the first graders were delighted to *dictate an experience chart story* about their strange visitors.

Snapshots from Home

When school opened in the fall, the third graders each brought some snapshots from home showing summer outdoor activities in which they had participated. After some discussion, the class voted to *write limericks.*

Pictures of Unusual Animals

Sixth graders were shown pictures of the star-nosed mole, the flamingo, some jellyfish, a pelican, a gar fish, and one gnu. Then each pupil was encouraged to *write appropriate similies and metaphors* involving these animals.

Numbers

Second graders discussed the significance of numbers in everyday life. They noted that four, for example, is the number of walls in a room, the number of seasons, the number of petals on the dogwood flower, and the number of directions on the compass. Then each boy and girl chose one number and prepared to *write a quatrain* about the number.

Story-Box Slips

In the fifth grade there were three story boxes. In the first were some slips with the names of the seasons; in the second, slips with the names of places; and in the third, slips with the names of actions. Each pupil drew one slip from each box (e.g., *summer, Pacific Ocean, sailing*) and then proceeded to *write a personal expository paragraph* incorporating the words on the three slips. The children stapled or pinned the story-box slips to their completed paragraphs.

Open House

The kindergarten class planned to bake cookies to serve to visitors for open house festivities. After each child had participated in purchasing, measuring, or mixing/shaping the ingredients, the group *dictated the recipe* for the teacher to post on a chart near the serving table. The cafeteria was happy to cooperate in the venture by handling the oven chores.

Samples of Children's Written Composition

Composition written by pupils aged five to twelve encompass a multitude of forms, ranging from the long-established prosaic paragraph to the relatively new, seven-lined diamond-shaped poem known as diamanté. Such written products may be quite brief, consisting of merely seventeen syllables of imagery in nature (in the form of haiku or senryu poetry). On the other hand, they may become fairly lengthy, expanding to several pages of expository prose relating to a plant-growth experiment. Some written communications may follow a predesigned structure; others may be arranged freely and extemporaneously.

In all instances, however, what truly matters is that the composition represents a boy's or girl's approach to life—straightforward, honest, inquisitive, observant. It is a reflection of the discoveries that a child makes in his or her day-to-day progress. Essentially, it displays the child's awareness. Each composition included in this section meets these standards.[29]

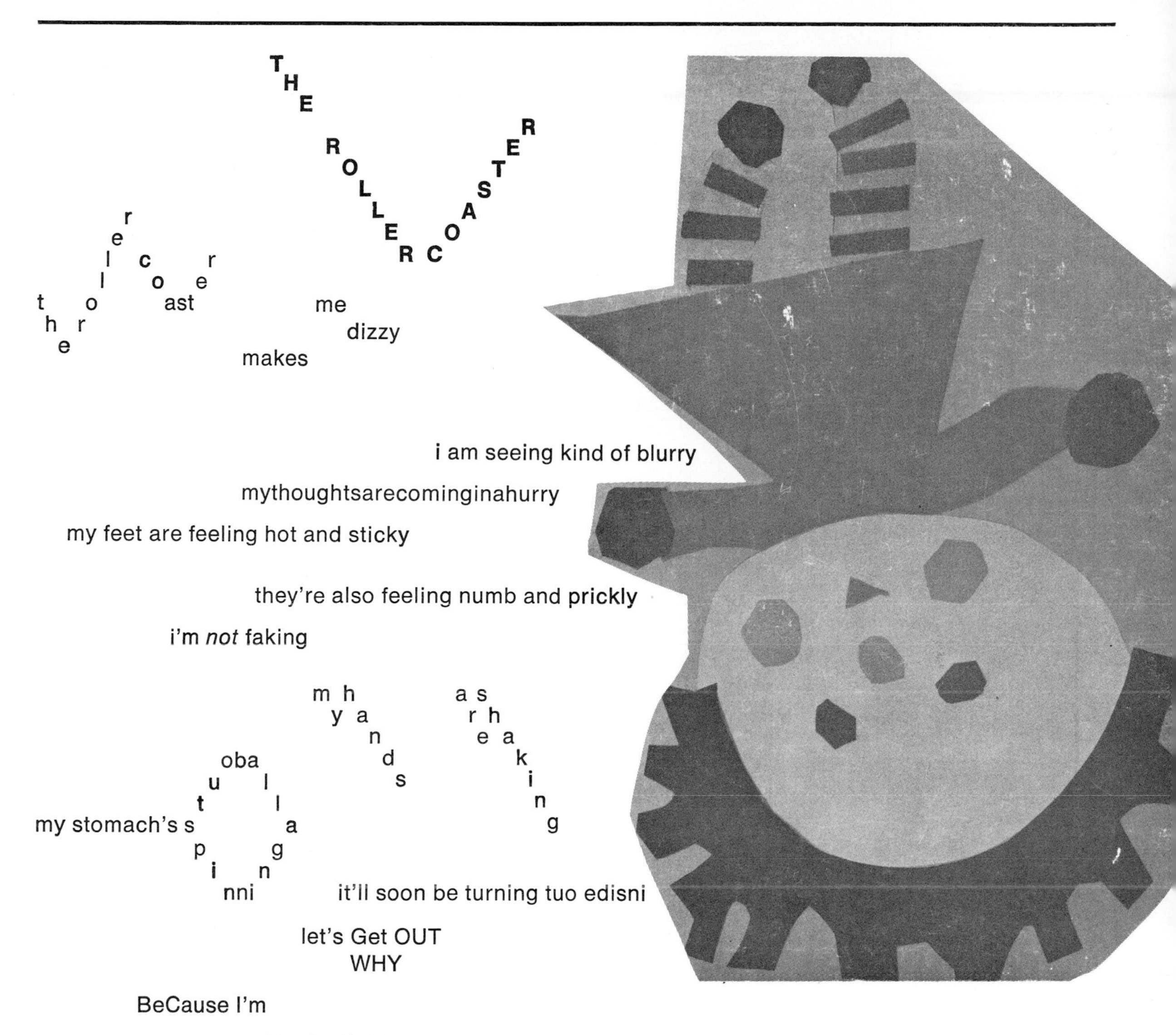

THE ROLLERCOASTER

the rollercoaster makes me dizzy

i am seeing kind of blurry

mythoughtsarecominginahurry

my feet are feeling hot and sticky

they're also feeling numb and prickly

i'm *not* faking

my hands are shaking

my stomach's spinning all about

it'll soon be turning tuo edisni

let's Get OUT

WHY

BeCause I'm

S c A r E d !

Janine
Written in Grade 6

Leland
Written in Grade 1

Kites

Zooming and swirling,
Kites go.
Dipping and twirling,
Kites flow.
Diving and whirling,
Kites blow
On a windy day.

Karen
Written in Grade 1

The Bear

The bear
Is
Just
A
Big
Bunch
Of
Hair.

Ellie
Written in Grade 4

Round is the center of a flower
so the petals will stay on.

Carol
Written in Grade 1

Turtle

Below the shell and
Above the plastron,
A little creature lurks.

Ben
Written in Grade 4

My Tree

My tree is an old tree. Its arms are tired from holding many leaves. Its feet are resting under the cool ground. See my tree go back and forth with the rocking-chair wind.

Tami
Written in Grade 3

Haiku

Please, little cricket,
Turn off your loud volumed
sound.
The trees are sleeping.

Wayne
Written in Grade 5

The Boston Massacre

No one person knows the boy's name, except he worked for a barber on King Street. King Street was the site of a mad massacre in 1770. The boy yelled at a guard and got quite personal, too. The guard smashed the butt of his rifle on the boy's head.

News spread fast through taverns and shops and warehouses. Soon men were prowling corridors and streets, both British and colonial. The mobs met at King Street and threw things at the guard. There were about one hundred men yelling at one guard. The colonists rushed into the porch of the customs house. The guard held them back with his bayonet. The frightened soldier yelled for help and got it from the 29th Regiment.

They warned the colonists to stay back or they would fire. The colonists dared them and threw things at them. They hit a soldier with a heavy stick. Montgomery accidentally pulled the trigger and shot Crispus Atucks.

In the excitement the other soldiers fired and people ran everywhere, leaving three dead and eleven injured. Jake was in the crowd and so were Paul and the twenty-two other men.

Written in Grade 5: Excerpt from James's 62-page Historical Fiction Book

The Rise and Fall of a Tree

From seed to seedling,
From seedling to tree,
The majestic fir
Rises high above me.

The tree falls to the ground,
Felled by thougtless men,
While the little seed starts
The cycle again.

David
Written in Grade 6

City

Fast, busy

Rushing, moving, hurrying

Streets, buildings, trees, fields

Yielding, rolling, harvesting

Quiet, free

Country

Martin
Written in Grade 6

Glen Canyon

Dramatic shapes
Emerge from mysterious canyons.
Eerie calls
Blow through the glens
Beauty glimmers
On cathedral ceilings.
Light seeps
Through the vast number of openings.
Mysterious forms
Dance along the sun-covered rocks.
Ancient writings
Cover the red sandstone walls.
All of the fascination
We once felt
Is gone forever.

Rita
Grade 6, age 12

The Cat and the Mouse

It was a stormy day. It was lightning outside. It was raining outside. The cat and the mouse were outside. The cat saw the mouse. The mouse was drowning. The mouse said, "Help! Help!" The cat picked the mouse up. He took him onto some dry land. The cat was getting ready to eat the mouse. The mouse got away. He looked at the cat and said, "Thank you but I don't like you chasing me or eating me."

Daren
Written in Grade 1

Dear Elders,

Please try to listen to what I have to say. Let me, please, tell you of my opinion. You may speak out when I am done; and if you listen and you think my opinions are valid, you may think differently than you do now.

The clothes I wear are different from yours. But is my outward appearance that important? Won't you look further? My hair is long, hanging loose; sometimes it's messy after I've played too hard and my cheeks are flushed, but need that close up our relationship? Sometimes I think differently than you—is that why I'm the foolish younger generation?

Sincerely,

Melinda
Written in Grade 6

My name is Don M. I live on a small dairy farm. It's a lot of work.

We milk the cows twice a day and have to make sure they have hay and water all the time. A cow drinks about 35 gallons of water a day. That's a lot. It's my responsibility to make sure their water tub stays filled. They drink out of an old bathtub. I fill it twice a day or three times when it's hot.

There should always be hay in the feeder, so the cows can eat it whenever they want. A cow has to spend a lot of time eating and chewing. First, she eats very fast, getting as much hay down her as she can. That hay goes into her first stomach or rumen. Then she lays down and just like a burp, a wad of food comes back up to her mouth so she can chew it. This is called chewing the cud or ruminating. A cow spends about eight hours a day just chewing her cud. A cow has four stomachs in all. She needs her complex stomach system in order to digest grass and hay and get food value out of them. Her fourth stomach is like ours, the other three are extra, just for digesting this roughage.

Don
Age 11

Skidder

This is a John Deere 540-A skidder. It weighs about thirty tons and is about ten or eleven feet tall. It lifts with a hydraulic blade. This skidder has a winch line on it. It winches about four-foot logs. There are 440, 540, 640, and 740 John Deere skidders. Sometimes they fill the tires of a skidder with water for extra weight.

Jim
Written in Grade 4

Who Am I?

I have many things I want to say
But
No one will listen.

I have many things I want to do
But
No one will let me.

I have many places I want to go
But
No one will take me.

And the things I write are corrected
But
No one reads them.

Jody
Age 8

If I were a pair of shoes,
I'd walk to the sundown.

Angela
Written in Grade 1

A poet's time
Flies by in rhyme.

Debbie
Written in Grade 3

At the Beach

We like the beach.
We make sand castles
And find starfish
While the sea talks to us.

Brian
Written in Grade 1

Ocean waves—here they come
And back they go,
Fighting a battle that
Will never end.
They go crashing on the rocks,
Crashing on the shore,
Crashing on me.

Steven
Written in Grade 3

Fog

Fog is like a blanket
Someone dropped from the sky.
It covers the earth with a
Cold and damp stillness
When you walk by.

Tammy
Written in Grade 6

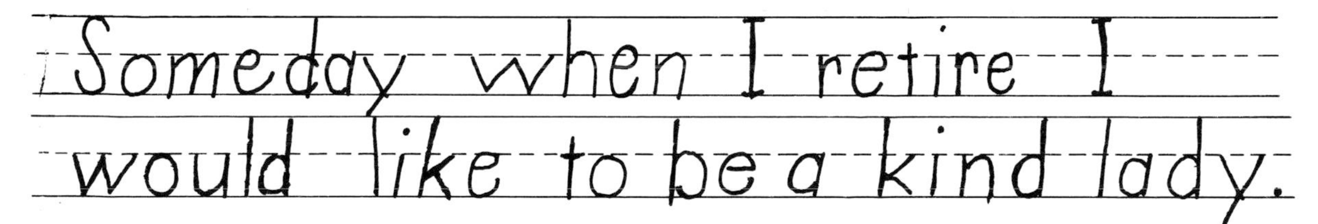

Brenda
Written in Grade 1

FISH

Fish swim and
bob and eat
food and swim
so gracefully and
have a stroke
like a butterfly
when I
watch them in my
fish tank.

Greg
Written in Grade 4

Diamante

Predator
Strategic, unpredictable
Hunting, stalking, attacking
Lions, Sarengeti dogs, gazelles, zebra
Fleeing, warning, eating
Careful, alert
Prey

Paul
Written in Grade 4

The Sad Worm

The sad worm is trying to climb up the tree to get the apple, but he couldn't climb up the tree.

It is a sunny day and the sad worm is trying to get in his hole, but he can't find it.

The sad worm climbs up the tree and finds his hole in the tree, then he changes into being happy.

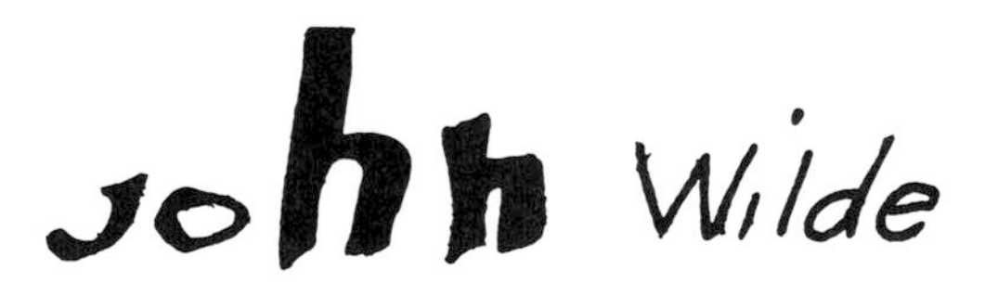

There was a young Frenchman
  of Cault
Who had but one little fault;
    He liked to rob banks
    To steal all their francs,
Until one day he got locked in
  a vault.

Paul
Written in Grade 6

Cat

Quiet, gentle

Rolling, playing, climbing

Yarn, mice, shoes, bones

Running, digging, jumping

Noisy, rough

Dog

Lori
Written in Grade 6

There was a young man from
  Orum
Who bought some new pants
  and he wore 'em.
He stooped and he sneezed;
He wiggled his knees;
And he knew right where he
  had tore 'em.

Jeff
Written in Grade 6

Just Before I Sneeze

There's a tingle
And a twitch,
A switch
And a tickle—
Until I just can't resist,
And then
And then
And then
I sneeze.

Simone
Written in Grade 6

The Two Ghosts

There once were two ghosts
sitting on a wall.
One of them was short and the
other was tall.

Then they heard someone
coming up the stairs.
They got all sorts of scares.

Then the one near the steeple
Said, "Do you believe in
people?"

Cheryl
Written in Grade 4

Fall Is Here

As I ran across a branch, I saw a winding road. There was a barn and a tall tree with colorful leaves. There must be houses nearby, for I could see mailboxes. I was right; the trees with colorful leaves did have acorns, but would the owner chase me away?

Dusk was falling, and I must collect my acorns before night falls. So back to my nest—a trunk of a tree! Perhaps I'll be braver tomorrow.

Tim
Written in Grade 5

Bam, Bam, Bam

Bam, bam, bam
Goes the steel wrecking ball;
Slam, slam, slam
Against a concrete wall.

It's raining bricks and wood
In my neighborhood;
Zam goes a chimney,
Zowie goes a door.

Bam, bam, bam
Goes the steel wrecking ball,
Changing it all,
Changing it all.

Eugene
Written in Grade 4

Why the Platypus Is So Mixed Up

When God was done creating the world, he had some leftover parts. He had a giant chimney, the skin of a beaver, the bill of a duck, and two pairs of geese feet.

Well, he thought and planned and pondered and finally thought of something to do with the giant chimney. He would stick it down in the United States and call it Chimney Rock!

Now he had gotten rid of the chimney, but what about the other things? Well, God thought and thought and at last came up with something. He would make it into an animal! It would be a little bit strange but so what?

So he mixed them together and came up with the duck-billed platypus. Poor creature!

Carol
Written in Grade 5

Sally

Sally was picking flowers. It started to rain. She started going into the tent. Then it started getting sunny again so she took a nap. Then she ran and skipped and walked.

Renee
Written in Kindergarten

Creativity: The Foundation of Composition

English educators during the past decade have directed significant attention to the development of creativity in students. They are aware that there now exists scientific evidence that creativity is not a free-wheeling, amorphous quality which operates as part of an unorthodox personality, but that it is an identifiable part of the intellect which (with its attendant skills) can be measured and taught. A survey of 142 experiments designed to provide information about the teachability of creativity revealed that the most successful approaches seem to be those that involve both emotional and cognitive functioning, supply adequate structure and motivation, and give opportunities for practice, involvement, and interaction with teachers and other students.[30]

Creativity as a subject presents a problem in definition. Behaviorists in creativity research describe as creative that which produces something unique either to the individual or to society or to both. Some data support the theory that divergent thinkers are more creative than other types of thinkers and that indeed the terms *divergent thinking* and *creativity* are largely synonymous.

Children (or adults) who exhibit creative behavior possess the ability to:

1. Maximize options. Creative individuals are generalists capable in many areas, possessing a variety of skills and interests. To them nothing is irrelevant.
2. Delay judgment. Creative persons accept all ideas as possible. Their lack of prejudice permits them to fully experience all situations.
3. Be inconsistent. Individuals who are creative act because a behavior is growth producing rather than being consistent with earlier actions or values.
4. Seek freedom. Creative behavior is free from habits and conventions and goes beyond ordinary limits.
5. Be active. Since creativity is an active process, its possessors act on good ideas rather than merely thinking about them.
6. Be aware of inner and outer worlds. Creative persons are always aware of their inner feelings even as they expand their sensitivity to the outer world. Change and experimentation is an integral part of the creative process.
7. Be responsible and responsive. Since growth depends upon decisions that individuals make for themselves, people who take responsibility for their actions accomplish more. Creative individuals are responsive to their own needs as well as to the environment.
8. Orient themselves positively. This increases their self-concept and allows them to take on greater self-responsibility.
9. Take risks. When persons go beyond behavioral boundaries, they take risks which can be potentially dangerous. However, by not taking risks, there can be a lack of growth, a routine existence, and limited horizons.[31]

A school climate that is most favorable to the development of creative attitudes and abilities is one that, according to Torrance, provides not only for periods of non-evaluated practice or learning but also provides opportunities—and even credit—for self-initiated learning.[32] Children are supplied with a model of self-determined exploration when learning is to some extent based on individual projects involving personal research in the media center. They need a responsive environment—rather than merely a stimulating one—that will lead to the controlled kind of freedom so necessary for productive, creative behavior.

The characteristics of their teacher are important too. Although not all the teacher's traits for producing creative endeavor in children have yet been determined, it is known that he or she must be resourceful in adapting to student leads and be pupil-centered. The teacher should be respectful of unusual questions or unusual ideas that the children propose and always indicate to the pupils that their thoughts have value. Ideally, the teacher should be knowledgeable and democratic by design, rather than merely cheerful and friendly. Moreover, he or she should perform as a facilitator of an atmosphere conducive to the individual thought of learners.

In addition, it is likely that creative efforts are stimulated by the teacher's confidence in the children's abilities to think adventurously and in new directions, which in turn will determine the children's estimation of themselves and their talents. A necessary condition of creativeness appears to be a certain self-confidence and particularly an absence of anxiety of nonconformist responses. Constant availability of varied media is also beneficial.

Factors identified as the most inhibitive to creative expression include: (1) discouragement of fantasy and imagination; (2) tests based on detailed memorization; (3) stereotyped sex roles; and (4) social expectation, including peer censure. The last named is especially important since international studies of children and their written imaginative compositions have revealed that American children show the greatest concern for peer censure.

What all this means to the teacher of writing is reasonably clear. The ideas of students must be valued first for their quality. Correctness of expression has to take second place. Children rated on standardized tests as less intelligent must be regarded as having creative potential just as those rated as most intelligent are. Finally, the teacher must tolerate occasionally unorthodox reactions among the pupils and keep an open mind.

Evaluation of Pupils' Progress

Positive correlations have been found between creativity and the teacher's use of the technique of rewarding children by personal interest in their ideas rather than by close grading of pupil compositions. Torrance concluded that unevaluated practice compared with evaluated practice is followed by a more creative performance in similar tasks requiring creative thinking.[33]

Ungraded Appraisal

In the noncritical environment so important for creative thought, teachers throughout the modern school cease to function as chief evaluators. Instead, the primary writing program is structured so that children gradually begin to function as their own editors (in the area of mechanical skills) and their own revisionists (in the area of content). By the intermediate grades most of the pupils can handle these responsibilities independently. By and large the teacher in each classroom serves as a supportive resource person who helps the students acquire the specific language skills as well as the technical skills they will need to serve as their own editors. The teacher also introduces the children to a self-check list, similar to the one shown in Figure 8.3, or helps them develop such a list cooperatively.

Checking My Writing

1) Is it clear?
   Does my writing make sense to me?
   Will others understand it?
   Do all sentences and words make sense?

2) Is it suitable?
   Who will my audience be?
   Did I write in a way that they will understand?
   Did I choose the best words?

3) Is it complete?
   Does my topic sentence say everything it needs to?
   Does it say too much?
   Have I said all I need to say about my subject in order for the audience to understand and enjoy it?

4) Is it well-designed?
   Do all of my sentences deal with the main idea?
   Are there any unnecssary sentences or words?
   Are my sentences in proper order?

Figure 8.3. Self-Check Writing List for Children.

Source: COMPOSITION IN THE LANGUAGE ARTS, GRADES 1-8: AN INSTRUCTIONAL FRAMEWORK, Wisconsin Department of Public Instruction, 1976, p. 38.

The foundation of any program in which students learn to revise their own work is the teacher-pupil conference. It is regularly scheduled about once each week. Each child keeps a writing folder of all work in progress (and may even choose to designate some papers as first drafts and others as final drafts) and brings this folder to the conference. The teacher works on the child's own level by attempting to identify the child's composition weaknesses in much the same fashion as he or she tries to diagnose the child's reading difficulties. With one child it may be difficulty in sequencing. With another, it may be paragraph unity. The teacher also helps every pupil develop an individualized editing guide which is posted on the inside of the writing folder to aid in proofreading.

While reviewing a pupil's composition during a conference, the teacher should take special note of the basic idea the child is trying to express with written symbols. The teacher should also consider these questions: Does this child communicate his or her thoughts? Does the child have a purpose for writing? Does the child have sufficient background from either real or vicarious experiences to deal properly with this topic? Does the choice of words contribute to the intended message? Is there a variety of sentence patterns? What conventions of spelling, capitalization, and punctuation are used successfully? Does the child apparently enjoy writing even though it demands close attention, effort, and thought?

Not all written work needs review or revision, however. Thus the conference can sometimes develop into a guided discussion period during which the student begins to see and feel elements and events previously unrecognized in his or her environment. The student needs the time to hear himself or herself express ideas and offer opinions. The listening teacher benefits as well. The teacher learns more about what interests the child and how he or she thinks.

It has been suggested that when boys and girls are involved in individual conferences beginning in the primary grades and are led to discover strengths and weaknesses in their own communication, *they* soon begin to tell the teacher what is needed to make their writing a stronger communication.

Probably the strongest advocate of the teacher-pupil writing conference is Donald H. Graves of the University of New Hampshire, who began his work on the composing process of elementary school children during the early 1970s.[34] Following are some of the more common questions asked about the conduct of such conferences together with abbreviated versions of the Graves' replies:

1. How do I find time to do conferences?
   — As writers learn to accept more responsibility, two or three ten-minute conferences every two weeks will suffice. At first, however, the teacher may confer with boys and girls according to this sample timetable:
   a. First ten minutes: children who need immediate help. Teacher in a "roving" type conference moves among six or seven children whose writing folders were reviewed the night before.
   b. Next 15 minutes: children who are regularly scheduled and meet the same day each week. They bring their folders to discuss their writing progress.
   c. Last 12 minutes: individual conferences with four or five children at critical stages of their writing pieces *or* one clinic group of five children needing to learn a common convention of writing.
2. What are the other children doing during conference time?
   — In some classrooms the other children are writing. In other classrooms the boys and girls are working at learning centers or are occupied with their workblocks of reading/math/science/writing. Routine classroom procedures must be established quickly in order to limit conference interruptions.
3. What is the easiest way to keep conference records?
   — Records must be kept simple or else they will not be used. A notebook can be maintained with each child's name on a tab for easy reference. Each lined page covers an entry showing the following: the date; the title of the writing; the skill shown; a brief rating; and a short note. At first, no more than 15 seconds are required per entry; later, more elaborate records may be kept.
4. How can I tell if I am improving in my conference conduct?
   — Keep your perspective on the entire writing program, and keep tape-recorded samples of your conferences with children who do well and those who are struggling. Videotape recordings may also help self-assessment.
5. What is the best way to start conferences?
   — Concentrate on one thing—the child's information.

6. How do I shorten conferences?
   __ Teach only one thing since overteaching leaves the child more confused at the end of the conference than he/she was at the start. When children speak first, much time is saved.
7. How do I do less talking and allow the children to do more?
   __ Do not feel the pressure of time; just wait. Expect the boys and girls to talk first.
8. What do I do when the piece has major problems and the boy or girl believes that it is good just the way it is?
   __ Ask the child why he/she thinks that it is worthwhile because children should be asked to tell the teacher why a piece is good far more frequently than is the actual practice. Should there be problems of meaning with the piece, choose a section for teaching which demonstrates a skill the child can handle or an area the child knows well.
9. How can skills or conventions of writing be taught in conference? Why not teach them in group settings instead?
   __ Skills last longest when presented within the context of the child's own paper. However, some skills can be taught in a group setting after the teacher has reviewed writing folders and discovered that several children needed to discuss quotation marks, for example.

Recently, Williams visited elementary school writing classes in three countries and found that the most important difference among them lay in the methods the teachers used to give pupils feedback about writing efforts.[35] While teachers in the United States seemed prone to think that evaluating children's work and having the children make corrections somehow inhibits their creativity, teachers in England and Canada had no compunctions about making evaluations. In both these countries, in open settings, there was individual conferencing during which the children read their compositions aloud so that they could discover for themselves areas for improvement. The teacher would ask each pupil, "How can you make me understand better what you mean?" Subsequently, when the child would offer solutions, the teacher would either accept them or respond with more guiding questions.

Graded Appraisal

The teacher-pupil conference is still a rarity in the area of evaluation of written products. One survey of teachers from urban and suburban systems in Pennsylvania, New Jersey, and Florida showed that none of the 200 teachers questioned held such conferences.[36] Instead, 78 percent of these intermediate teachers used letter grades, or letter grades and comments, to evaluate children's compositions.

Since evaluation is a specific step in the writing process, a part of the stage of postwriting, many educators believe that, no matter how stimulating and creative the writing assignment may be and no matter how much prewriting may be involved, teachers have the responsibility for *scoring* compositions. Two principal methods currently used are holistic scoring and analytical scoring.

However, before attempting to score student compositions, the teacher must bear in mind some specific criteria by which to evaluate such writing. The following standards for good writing have been developed recently by some teachers in Massachusetts who recommend that the criteria be modified according to learning levels and increased mastery of writing skills:

CONTENT

Does the paper focus on a specific subject?
Does the writer demonstrate knowledge of the subject?
Is the purpose of the paper made evident to the reader?
Are generalizations supported by specific details?
Are ideas original and clear
or are borrowed ideas credited to their sources?

ORGANIZATION

Does the introduction prepare the reader for the content?
Is the organization easy to follow?
Is there a clear connection from one point to another?
Are all details related to the purpose of the paper?
Does the conclusion re-emphasize the purpose or summarize the content?

DICTION

Are words used accurately?
Where appropriate, do words appeal to the reader's senses?
Is the language appropriate to the purpose of the paper and to the intended reader?

SENTENCE STRUCTURE

Are sentences complete?
Are sentences separated by end-punctuation, rather than run-together?
Are sentences free of choppy, unnecessarily repetitive constructions?
Is sentence structure varied?

FORM

Is penmanship legible?
Is the writing free from errors in word-usage?
Are words spelled correctly?
Are punctuation marks and capital letters correctly used?

Holistic scoring is based on the idea that the whole composition is greater than its components, that all components should be judged simultaneously, and that the overall effectiveness of a piece of writing is ranked as a communication. It involves reading and scoring a paper on the total effect of the first impression. Instead of evaluating student writing with a red pencil in hand, the teacher responds to the entire piece with one score, and that is the only mark he or she puts on the paper. Usually the scale goes from one to four, from one to six, or from one to nine. A sample four-point scale could run as follows:

1. Needs intensive help.
2. Shows below grade-level competency.

3. Shows grade level competency.
4. Shows high competency.

This type of holistic judgment grading is probably the one most used in schools today and has been described as general impression marking and rated as the simplest of the procedures in holistic evaluation.[38] It demands neither a detailed discussion of features nor a summing of scores given to separate features.

It usually involves a team approach, with a minimum of two teachers scoring each paper and the student's final score being the average. A fairly accurate assessment of a student's overall writing ability can therefore be attained. Too, many papers can be read and scored in a relatively short time, with at least one estimate being that two minutes per paper is all the time that is needed.

Unlike analytical scoring (discussed below), holistic scoring does not provide for the correction of errors and the writing of comments to boys and girls about their compositions. Still, it is a valid means of assessing student writing if the teacher establishes and follows a reasonable set of criteria for evaluating such writing and if his/her evaluation is periodically compared to another rater's evaluations based on the same criteria.[39] It is a way to score large sets of compositions.

Analytical scoring requires raters to isolate one or more characteristics of a written piece and to score them individually. This method has been deemed precise and useful when a focus on specific elements of writing is desired. However, the overall quality of any piece of writing becomes difficult to estimate when using this method. Furthermore, emphasis is often placed on flaws rather than on the strengths of any paper, so unless the evaluator's comments are constructive, students may become convinced that writing is a punitive activity leading to failure.

While analytical scoring is time-consuming because it calls for careful examination of every paper, it simultaneously offers opportunities for teacher and student to focus on individual problem areas and possible remedies.

At least one analytic scale has been developed which lists a set of qualities that may be applied to any one piece of writing, with points assigned for each quality. It is the Sager Writing Scale intended for use with intermediate and junior high school students. It has four scales (vocabulary, elaboration, organization, and structure) with four ratings possible on each scale (ranging from zero to three or from poor to excellent). Developed by Carol Sager, the CWRS may be ordered on microfilm from ERIC under number ED 091 723.

Standardized Tests

Teachers may be asked to examine (or administer) nationally standardized instruments for written language.

Certain achievement batteries such as the *Comprehensive Tests of Basic Skills* (published by CTV/McGraw-Hill, Monterey, CA) include a section for language, with one subtest for expression and one for mechanics. In the CTBS (which is available for grades 2.5–4, 4–6, and 6–8) the expression subtest requires the student to add correct words and phrases to incomplete sentences, to replace underlined parts of sentences in a poem or story, and to recognize errors and usage. This battery has received good reviews critically.[40]

A diagnostic instrument for appraising normal and abnormal development of written language is the *Picture Story Language Test* (published by Grune and Stratton, New York). The children are presented with a picture about which they are asked to write a story. From these written stories, scales are developed to measure length (productivity) and correctness of expression (syntax), and to attempt to measure content or meaning of the sentence (abstract-concrete). The test, which is intended for children ages seven to seventeen, runs 20–30 minutes.

Discussion Questions

1. Describe the kind of teacher who is most likely to produce creative effort in children.
2. Which four of the factors affecting the writing performance of children do you perceive as being the most important?
3. How could it prove helpful to the composition program to have the pupils guided by a teacher who is also a writer?
4. How should teachers evaluate children's written expression?

Suggested Projects

1. Encourage a five-year-old to dictate a report of a personal experience to you; then share that report with your peers.
2. Collect several compositions written by children in a particular grade or age bracket. Note the variations in content. Determine the creativity of each.
3. Plan a middle-grade bulletin board which will encourage self-editing of written work.
4. Examine three national children's magazines which publish original prose or poetry by elementary school boys and girls.
5. If poetry is talking to one's self, share a collection of unrhymed poetry with intermediate children in order to show them that their own writing need not rhyme to be poetry.
6. Begin a picture file which will aid your composition program. On the back of each picture, place a typed label describing how you would introduce or use that picture with young writers.
7. Set up the learning center on written composition shown in Figure 8.4.

Related Readings

Bent, J., and Plaskon, S. 1983. "Children Writing for Other Children," *Childhood Education, 60,* pp. 22–27.

Charney, D. 1984. "The Validity of Using Holistic Scoring to Evaluate Writing: A Critical Overview," *Research in the Teaching of English, 18,* pp. 65–81.

Coop, R. H. et al. 1983. "A Program to Develop Basic Writing Skills in Grades 4–9," *Elementary School Journal, 84,* pp. 76–87.

Edelsky, C., and Smith, K. 1984. "Is That Writing—or Are Those Marks Just a Figment of Your Curriculum?" *Language Arts, 61,* pp. 24–32.

Jacobs, S. 1984. "Investigative Writing: Practice and Principles," *Language Arts, 61,* pp. 356–363.

Kreeft, J. 1984. "Dialogue Writing—Bridge from Talk to Essay Writing," *Language Arts, 61,* pp. 141–150.

Simms, R. 1984. "Techniques for Improving Student Writing," *Academic Therapy, 19,* pp. 579–584.

Tway, E. 1984. *What Happens When Children Write in School?* Urbana, IL.: National Council of Teachers of English.

Figure 8.4. Language Arts Learning Center: Written Composition.

TYPE OF CENTER:	**Creative Writing**	TIME: 20-30 minutes
GRADE LEVEL:	2-3	NUMBER OF STUDENTS: 2

INSTRUCTIONAL OBJECTIVE: Children will use their imaginations and write down what they think the animals might be thinking or saying.

MATERIALS: Supply of pictures of animals so they can be changed, paper and pencil, a folder for finished papers.

DIRECTIONS:

1. Think about each of these animals and what they might say about the world today and how human beings treat them.
2. Using your imagination, write your ideas on the paper.
3. Proofread what you have written.
4. When you have finished your paper, place it in the folder on the back of the learning center.

EVALUATION: The teacher will read the papers looking for originality; later the students will read their own papers aloud to the class, or mount them on a bulletin board.

Source: From PATHWAYS TO IMAGINATION by Angela S. Reeke and James L. Laffey, © 1979 by Scott, Foresman and Company. Reprinted by permission.

Vukelich, C., and Golden, J. 1984. "Early Writing: Development and Teaching Strategies," *Young Children, 39*(2), pp. 3–10.

Willer, A. 1984. "Creative Writing with Computers: What Do Elementary Students Have to Say?," *Computers, Reading and Language Arts,* II (1), pp. 39–42.

Chapter Notes

1. E. Amiran and J. Mann, eds., *Written Composition, Grades K–12* (Portland, Oregon: Northwest Regional Educational Laboratory, 1982), p. 3.
2. A. Humes, "Putting Writing Research into Practice," *Elementary School Journal,* 1983, *84,* pp. 3–17; National Assessment of Educational Progress, *Expressive Writing* (Denver; NAEP, 1976); J. Chall and V. Jacobs, "Writing and Reading in the Elementary Grades: Developmental Trends among Low SES Children," *Language Arts,* 1983, *60,* pp. 617–626; E. Jane Porter, "Research Report," *Language Arts,* 1975, *52,* pp. 1019–1026; D. Graves, "An Examination of the Writing Process of Seven Year Old Children," *Research in the Teaching of English,* 1975, *9,* pp. 227–241; P. Groff,

"Does Negative Criticism Discourage Children's Compositions?" *Language Arts,* 1975, *52,* pp. 1032–1034; J. S. Krzeski, "Effect of Different Writing Tools and Paper on Performance of the Third Grader," *Elementary English,* 1971, *48,* pp. 821–824; E. McDaniel and T. Pietras, "Conventional Test Scores and Creative Writing among Disadvantaged Pupils," *Research in the Teaching of English,* 1972, *6,* pp. 181–186; L. Golub and W. Frederick, "An Analysis of Children's Writing under Different Stimulus Conditions," *Research in the Teaching of English,* 1970, *4,* pp. 168–180; R. C. O'Donnell et al., *Syntax of Kindergarten and Elementary School Children: A Transformational Analysis* (Urbana, Illinois: National Council of Teachers of English, 1967); B. Miller and J. Ney, "The Effect of Systematic Oral Exercises on the Writing of Fourth-Grade Students," *Research in the Teaching of English,* 1968, *2,* pp. 44–61; H. Blake and D. Hammill, "Structural Linguistics and Children's Writing," *Elementary English,* 1967, *44,* pp. 275–278; W. Taylor and K. Hoedt, "The Effect of Praise upon the Quality and Quantity of Creative Writing," *Journal of Educational Research,* 1966, *40,* pp. 80–83; M. Woodfin, "The Quality of Written Expression of Third Grade Children under Different Time Limits," *Journal of Experimental Education,* 1969, *37,* pp. 89–91; P. Shapiro and B. Shapiro, "Two Methods of Teaching Poetry Writing in the Fourth Grade," *Elementary English,* 1971, *48,* pp. 225–228; and S. Zeman, "Reading Comprehension and Writing of Second and Third Graders," *Reading Teacher,* 1969, *23,* pp. 144–150.

3. W. Harpin, *The Second 'R'* (London: George Allen and Unwin, Ltd., 1976), pp. 83–84.
4. S. Stotsky, "Research on Reading/Writing Relationships: A Synthesis and Suggested Directions," *Language Arts,* 1983, *60,* pp. 627–643.
5. B. Eckhoff, "How Reading Affects Children's Writing," *Language Arts,* 1983, *60,* pp. 607–616.
6. M. Wilson, "A Review of Recent Research on the Integration of Reading and Writing," *Reading Teacher,* 1981, *34,* pp. 896–901.
7. S. Haley-James, "Twentieth Century Perspectives on Writing in Grades One through Eight," in *Perspectives on Writing in Grades 1–8,* S. Haley-James, ed. (Urbana, Illinois: National Council of Teachers of English, 1981) pp. 3–17; and C. Temple, R. Nathan, and N. Burris, *The Beginnings of Writing* (Boston: Allyn & Bacon, 1982), pp. 131–145.
8. J. Britton, *Language and Learning* (Harmondsworth, England: Penguin Books, 1970).
9. M. Klein, "Teaching Writing in the Elementary Grades," *Elementary School Journal,* 1981, *81,* p. 320.
10. S. Florio and C. Clark, "The Functions of Writing in an Elementary Classroom," *Research in the Teaching of English,* 1982, *16,* pp. 115–130.
11. Wisconsin Department of Public Instruction, *Composition in the Language Arts, Grades 1–8: An Instructional Framework* (Madison: The Department, 1976), p. 4.
12. C. Gay, "Reading Aloud and Learning to Write," *Elementary School Journal,* 1976, *77,* pp. 87–93.
13. Haley-James, "Twentieth Century Perspectives," p. 8.
14. F. Smith, "Myths about Writing," *Language Arts,* 1981, *58,* p. 797.
15. D. G. Hennings and B. Grant, *Written Expression in the Language Arts* (New York: Teachers College Press, 1981), pp. 13–15.
16. California Department of Education, *Handbook for Planning an Effective Writing Program* (Sacramento: The Department, 1982), p. 9.
17. N. Andreasen et al., "The Child and the Composing Process," *Elementary School Journal,* 1980, *80,* p. 251.
18. J. Hailey, *Teaching Writing K–8* (Berkeley: University of California, Instructional Laboratory, 1978), p. 66.

19. California Department of Education, *Handbook*, pp. 11–14.
20. Andreasen et al., "The Child and the Composing Process," p. 252.
21. California Department of Education, *Handbook*, pp. 14–22.
22. D. Greenberg, *Teaching Poetry to Children* (Portland, Oregon: Continuing Education Publications, 1978), pp. 13–15.
23. L. Markham, "Writing Cinquains: Start with a Word or Two," *Language Arts*, 1983, *60*, pp. 350–354.
24. W. Petty and P. Finn, "Classroom Teachers' Reports on Teaching Written Composition," in *Perspectives on Writing in Grades 1–8*, S. Haley-James, ed., p. 23.
25. L. Golub, "Syntactic and Lexical Deviations in Children's Written Sentences," *Elementary English*, 1974, *51*, pp. 144–145.
26. P. Cordeiro, M. Giacobbe, and C. Cazden, "Apostrophes, Quotation Marks and Periods: Learning Punctuation in the First Grade," *Language Arts*, 1983, *60*, pp. 323–332.
27. R. Smith and L. Hansen, "Integrating Reading and Writing: Effects on Children's Attitudes," *Elementary School Journal*, 1976, *76*, pp. 243–244.
28. T. Hogan, "Students' Interests in Writing Activities," *Research in the Teaching of English*, 1980, *14*, pp. 119–126.
29. Examples are taken from L. Jenkins, *Reading, Writing and Arithmetic* (Corvalis, Oregon: State University, 1980), pp. 35, 40; *How the Poet Got the Word*, R. Atkinson and K. Hearn, eds. (Dover, Delaware: Delaware State Arts Council, 1978), pp. 7, 8; *Let the Children Speak*, N. Welbourn et al., eds. (Washington, D.C.: Teacher Corps, U.S. Office of Education, 1976); and *Impressions*, Vols. 26–28 (San Diego, California: City Schools, 1970–1972).
30. E. P. Torrance and J. P. Torrance, *Is Creativity Teachable?* (Bloomington, Indiana: Phi Delta Kappa Educational Foundation, 1973), p. 46.
31. R. Klein, "An Inquiry into the Factors Related to Creativity," *Elementary School Journal*, 1982, *82*, pp. 259–260.
32. E. P. Torrance, "Give the Devil His Due," in *Creativity: Its Educational Implications*, J. C. Gowan, G. D. Demos, and E. P. Torrance, complrs. (New York: John Wiley, 1967).
33. E. P. Torrance and R. Myers, *Creative Learning and Teaching* (New York: Dodd, Mead, 1970), pp. 105–106.
34. D. H. Graves, *Writing: Teachers & Children at Work* (Exeter, New Hampshire: Heinemann Educational Books, 1983), pp. 141–148.
35. L. E. Williams, "Methods of Teaching Composition in Open Classes—England, Canada, and the United States," *Innovator;* 1978, *9*, pp. 1–3.
36. P. Alpren, "The Grading of Original Stories—A Survey," *Elementary English*, 1973, *51*, pp. 1237–1238.
37. Reprinted from Najimy's *Measure for Measure*, National Council of Teachers of English, 1981, p. 3. Used with permission.
38. C. Cooper, "Holistic Evaluation of Writing," in *Evaluating Writing*, C. Cooper and L. Odell, eds. (Urbana, Illinois: National Council of Teachers of English, 1977), pp. 11–12.
39. S. Straw, "Assessment and Evaluation in Written Composition: A Commonsense Perspective," in *Research in the Language Arts*, V. Froese and S. Straw, eds. (Baltimore: University Park Press, 1981), p. 195.
40. O. K. Buros, ed., *The Seventh Mental Measurements Yearbook*, Volume I (Highland Park, New Jersey: Gryphon Press, 1972), pp. 18–19.

Part C Reading, Literature, Drama, and Related Skills

Chapters

9 Reading
10 Vocabulary Development
11 Children's Literature
12 Library Media Center Skills
13 Children's Drama

Reading 9

Objectives

Beginning reading readiness
Widespread popularity of the basal reader approach
Major word recognition skills
Questioning and its relevance to reading comprehension

Discover As You Read This Chapter If*

1. There is a strong relationship between reading and the other language arts.
2. No matter how well a child reads orally, reading does not take place unless there is comprehension of the written material.
3. Today it is finally recognized that there is one best way to teach reading to children.
4. Readiness for reading is a factor restricted to the beginning stages of the program.
5. Teachers' evaluative judgments of reading readiness among beginning students have been discredited.
6. Today most boys and girls are ready to read at an earlier level than their counterparts were a few decades ago.
7. The kindergarten reading program must be highly structured if it is to be successful.
8. The basal reader is used daily in about half of all elementary classrooms.
9. The language experience approach is especially beneficial to children who are learning English as a second language.
10. The individualized reading approach is really a recreational reading program.

*Answers to these true-or-false statements may be found in Appendix 6.

An effective reading program in today's elementary school is based on understanding what reading is, why it should be taught, and what the levels of reading competence are. One popular definition of reading is that it represents an active process of extracting meaning from written symbols of language.[1] During the process there is an interaction between the reader's experiential background language ability and the printed message. Should a match occur between the two, then meaning or comprehension will result. Learning to read depends on many factors, including cognition, motivation, visual perception, the reader's self-image, the teacher's effectiveness, and the caliber of the reading selection.

Reading is taught because it is a direct link between individuals and ideas. It remains one of the best means of retrieving data and thoughts for it can transmit ideas across cultures and across generations. Those who read are said to have access to all of the accumulated knowledge of civilization. They are better able to think critically about a subject, they can fulfill personal interests and needs, and they can in the long run contribute to the well-being of society.

The essential skill in reading is getting meaning from a printed or written message, states Carroll, who then delineates the components of that skill as follows:[2]

1. The child must know the language that he or she is going to learn to read.
2. The child must learn to dissect spoken words into component sounds.
3. The child must learn to recognize and discriminate the letters of the alphabet in their various forms (uppercase letters, lowercase letters, printed, and cursive).
4. The child must learn the left-to-right principle by which words are spelled and put in order in continuous text.
5. The child must learn that there are patterns of highly probable correspondence between letters and sounds. He or she must learn those patterns that will help him/her recognize words familiar from the spoken language or that will help him/her determine the pronunciation of unfamiliar words.
6. The child must learn to recognize printed words from whatever cues he or she can use—total configuration, letters composing the words, sounds represented by those letters, and/or meanings suggested by context.
7. The child must learn that printed words are signals for spoken ones and that they have meanings analogous to those of spoken words. As he or she decodes a printed message into its spoken equivalent, the child must be able to apprehend the meaning of the total message in the same way that the meaning of the corresponding spoken message is apprehended.
8. The child must learn to reason and reflect upon whatever he or she reads, within the limits of personal talent and experience.

The reading program involves three levels of competence, which are both interrelated and continuous:

1. Learning to read. Students acquire decoding abilities and comprehension skills. They learn to read maps, directions, story problems in mathematics, and other specialized printed matter.

Even a young child can attain satisfaction from recreational reading, especially when the activity is shared with a parent. (Photo courtesy of National Education Association Publishing, Joe Di Dio.)

2. Reading to learn. Students want to gain information; however, they should also learn to recognize (and even question) the author's purpose and decide whether or not the printed material fulfills their current needs.
3. Reading for life. Students wish to pursue hobbies and to attain satisfaction from recreational reading. As they mature, they will wish to read to achieve career goals and to function capably in a democratic society.[3]

Principles of Teaching Reading

Generalizations about the teaching of reading drawn both from research and from classroom observation of actual practices have recently been compiled in an effort to guide all individuals in planning an effective reading program.[4] The first stresses that *reading and the other language arts are closely interrelated.* A review of the results of 89 correlational studies shows a particularly strong relationship between written expressive language and reading, which may offer support to those who advocate teaching reading through a combined reading and writing approach.[5]

The second and third principles state that *reading is a complex act with many factors that require consideration* and that *reading is the interpretation of the meaning of printed symbols.* All the varied aspects of the reading process should be understood by the teacher, who must also realize that reading does not occur without comprehension of the written passage no matter how well the child reads orally.

Principles four, five, and six emphasize that *learning to read is a continuing process* and that, while *there is no one correct way to teach reading,* still *reading should be taught in a way that allows each pupil to experience success.* Not only do children learn to read over a period of several years as more sophisticated skills are introduced to them gradually, but adolescents and adults also continue to improve their reading ability even after their formal education may have ceased. Such continuity serves to illustrate the need for teachers to be acquainted with a variety of reading methods so that they may be able to help each classroom learner succeed at assigned reading tasks. The pupil must be given instruction at his/her own level of accomplishment.

The seventh generalization stresses that *students should be taught word-recognition/language processing skills which will permit them to unlock the pronunciations and meanings of unfamiliar words independently.* No one can memorize all the words that appear in print. Pupils therefore must be instructed in such techniques as phonetic and structural analyses, for example, so that they may figure out new words for themselves when helpful peers/adults are not around.

The eighth and ninth principles state that *readiness for reading should be considered at all levels of instruction* and that *the teacher should diagnose each child's reading ability and then use the diagnosis for lesson planning.* The readiness of the student for instruction in any phase of reading must always be considered, regardless of grade level. Mastery of prerequisite skills is important and can be easily determined through the use of standardized and teacher-developed tests. Whole-class instruction is not possible in the area of reading.

The final group of principles emphasize that *the student needs to see why reading is important,* that *enjoyment of reading should be considered of prime importance,* and that *reading must be an integral part of all content area instruction within the educational program.* Since learning to read takes effort, each boy and girl must see the value of reading not only for assignments made in other curriculuar areas during the school day but for personal activities as well. Reading is both entertaining and informative. Teachers can convince young readers of the many benefits of reading by introducing a variety of appropriate materials which meet numerous interest and ability levels.

Beginning Reading Readiness

There are two basic methods for determining reading readiness among beginning students.[6] The first is observation of individual children, using a checklist of characteristics known to have significance in reading success. Teacher's judgments have long been recognized as potent evaluative instruments. A sample comprehensive checklist is found in Figure 9.1.

Not all of the 90 items will of course apply to any one child. However, the kindergarten/primary teacher will be better able to help boys and girls make a good start in reading if he or she observes the behavior of children related to the overlapping areas of their physical, social/emotional, and psychological readiness. When the teacher rates any pupil on a majority of the checklist items in the "Usually" or "Sometimes" column, then that boy or girl is more apt to encounter success as a beginning reader than a peer with lower ratings.

Figure 9.1. Teacher Checklist for Assessing Beginning Reading Readiness Among Young Children.

Child's Name ______________
Birthdate ______________

CHECKLIST FOR BEGINNING READING READINESS

Category	Item	No.	Usually	Some-times	Seldom	Never
A. Physical Readiness	I. General Health					
	1. Does the child appear well rested?	1.				
	2. Does the child seem well nourished?	2.				
	3. Does the child have sufficient energy to participate in class activity?	3.				
	4. Do his/her teeth and gums appear healthy?	4.				
	II. Eyes					
	5. Can the child see without squinting?	5.				
	6. Can the child see without rubbing his/her eyes?	6.				
	7. Does the child hold materials within normal range?	7.				
	8. Does his/her color recognition appear to be within normal range?	8.				
	III. Ears					
	9. Is it apparent through his/her responses that the child is able to hear what is said in class?	9.				
	10. Does the child respond to a low-voice test at 20 feet?	10.				
	11. Does the child respond to a whisper test at 15 inches?	11.				
	12. Can the child respond without visual contact?	12.				
	IV. Speech					
	13. Can the child talk without stuttering?	13.				
	14. Can the child talk without lisping?	14.				
	15. Does the child speak without gross errors in pronunciation?	15.				
	16. Is his/her voice pleasant, clear, and readily audible?	16.				

Category	Item	No.	Usually	Some-times	Seldom	Never
A. Physical Readiness (contd.)	V. Coordination					
	17. Can the child button/unbutton his or her clothes?	17.				
	18. Can the child bounce and catch a ball?	18.				
	19. Can the child control a writing instrument?	19.				
	20. Does the child consistently use one hand without vacillating from the left hand to the right hand?	20.				
	21. Can the child copy three different geometric shapes?	21.				
	22. Can the child distinguish between objects of different sizes?	22.				
	23. Can the child pick one specific shape out of a mixed group of shapes?	23.				
	24. Can the child trace a line going from left to right?	24.				
	25. Can the child draw a recognizable human?	25.				
	26. Can the child walk up and down the stairs?	26.				
	27. Can the child walk on a straight line?	27.				
	28. Can the child walk well on a balance beam?	28.				
	29. Can the child hop on the right foot and on the left?	29.				
	30. Can the child jump rope five times in succession?	30.				
	Subtotal A.					
B. Social/Emotional Readiness	VI. Social Readiness					
	31. Does the child assert himself/herself?	31.				
	32. Does the child meet new peers comfortably?	32.				
	33. Does the child meet new adults comfortably?	33.				
	34. Does the child seem comfortable in the environment?	34.				
	35. Does the child appear to deal confidently with others and with the environment?	35.				
	36. Does the child seek involvement with peers?	36.				
	37. Does the child assume a share of group responsibility?	37.				
	38. Does the child actively participate in group play?	38.				

Category	Item	No.	Usually	Some-times	Seldom	Never
B. Social/ Emotional Readiness (contd.)	VI. Social Readiness—contd.					
	39. Can the child be a follower as well as a leader?	39.				
	40. Does the child listen while others speak?	40.				
	41. Does the child comply with the teacher's requests?	41.				
	42. Does the child share materials?	42.				
	43. Does the child respect the rights and materials of other children?	43.				
	44. Does the child offer help to other children?	44.				
	45. Does the child await his/her turn in playing?	45.				
	46. Does the child await his/her turn for help from the teacher?	46.				
	47. Does the child share the teacher's attention with peers?	47.				
	48. Does the child take care of his/her own clothes and materials?	48.				
	49. Can the child take care of personal physical needs?	49.				
	50. Is the child self-directed?	50.				
	51. Can the child work independently?	51.				
	52. Does the child see a task through to completion?	52.				
	VII. Emotional Readiness					
	53. Does the child express feelings verbally?	53.				
	54. Does the child seem happy?	54.				
	55. Is the child able to cope with success?	55.				
	56. Is the child able to cope with failure?	56.				
	57. Does the child accept routines?	57.				
	58. Can the child accept changes in routines?	58.				
	59. Can the child resolve personal problems?	59.				
	60. Does the child seek help when it is needed?	60.				
	61. Does the child attempt new tasks?	61.				
	62. Does the child show curiosity about the environment?	62.				
	63. Does the child show pride in his/her work?	63.				
	64. Can the child comfortably leave the person who brings him/her to school?	64.				
	Subtotal B.					

Category	Item	No.	Usually	Some-times	Seldom	Never
C. Psychological Readiness	VIII. Awareness of Reading					
	65. Does the child appear interested in books and reading?	65.				
	66. Does the child ask the meanings of words or signs?	66.				
	67. Is the child interested in the shapes/sizes of unusual words?	67.				
	68. Does the child recognize common words in the environment; e.g., "stop" signs?	68.				
	IX. Mental Maturity					
	69. Can the child give reasons for his/her opinions about personal work or that of others?	69.				
	70. Can the child make or draw something to illustrate an idea as well as most of his/her peers?	70.				
	71. Is the memory span sufficient to allow memorization of a short poem, song, or commercial slogan?	71.				
	72. Can the child tell a story or relate an experience without confusing the sequence of events?	72.				
	73. Can the child listen or work for five minutes without becoming restless?	73.				
	X. Mental Habits					
	74. Does the child look at a succession of items from left to right?	74.				
	75. Does the child exhibit creative imagination when describing a given picture?	75.				
	76. Does the child understand that conversation may be presented in written form?	76.				
	77. Can the child predict possible outcomes for a story?	77.				
	78. Can the child add a logical conclusion to an open-ended sentence; i.e., "I am happy when . . . ?"	78.				
	79. Is the child aware of the consequences of his/her actions?	79.				
	80. Will the child alter his/her behavior in view of the consequences?	80.				
	81. Can the child recall the central thought of a story?	81.				
	82. Can the child recall the important parts of a story?	82.				

Category	Item	No.	Usually	Some-times	Seldom	Never
C. Psychological Readiness (contd.)	XI. Language Patterns					
	83. Does the child constructively contribute to class discussions and conversations?	83.				
	84. Is the child effective in expressing personal needs in large and/or small groups?	84.				
	85. Is the child effective in expressing personal needs on a one-to-one basis?	85.				
	86. Is his/her speaking and listening vocabulary part of the vocabulary used in pre-primers?	86.				
	87. Does the child understand words dealing with the concepts of spatial relationships, directionality, and size?	87.				
	88. Does the child listen to a story with evidence of enjoyment?	88.				
	89. Is the child able to express an experience through dramatic play?	89.				
	90. Is his/her dominant language English?	90.				
	Subtotal C.					
	TOTAL					

The second method of assessing reading readiness is administration of standardized readiness tests. Two group tools which have earned favorable reviews are:

. . . *Metropolitan Readiness Test, Revised Edition* Psychological Corporation, New York). Available in two forms, Level 1 for first-half kindergarten entrants covers auditory memory, rhyming, visual skills, and language skills; it is administered in seven sessions for a total of 105 minutes. Level 2 for second-half kindergarten entrants and first grade entrants covers auditory skills, visual skills, and language skills; it is administered in five sessions for a total of 110 minutes. A specimen set is available.

. . . *Murphy-Durrell Reading Readiness Analysis* (Harcourt Brace Jovanovich, New York). Administered in two sessions for a total of 60 minutes, it covers sound recognition, letter names, and learning rate. A specimen set is available.[7]

Since readiness test predictions are more likely to be valid for good students than for poor ones, the best determiner of any child's readiness for reading consists of a combination of teacher observation (as noted on a checklist) and the pupil score on a standardized readiness test.

The child who enjoys listening to a story is showing signs of psychological readiness for reading. (Photo courtesy of the Ocean View School District, Huntington Beach, California.)

The Kindergarten Reading Program

Due to the interrelated factors affecting reading readiness, it is no longer possible to name a specific mental or chronological age as a guarantee of success in reading. Children today have greater exposure to mass media than their counterparts a few decades ago, and, therefore, they have a higher readiness level at an earlier age. Results of evaluations of "Sesame Street," for example, show that young regular viewers (ages three to five) have a greater mastery of a wide range of visual and auditory perceptual skills of readiness than children who are not regular viewers.[8] These patterns hold true for all groups of children, regardless of socio-economic status, mental ability, geographic location, sex, or age.

Furthermore, many more young boys and girls are attending day care centers, Headstart programs, and nursery schools than ever before as the number of single-parent families remains high and even continues to rise in some communities. It is not uncommon for such parents to demand at least a semblance of structured academics in which children develop and are taught the skills that once had been exclusively emphasized in kindergarten.

Consequently, reading instruction in the kindergarten should be sufficiently flexible so that it may be adapted for use at each child's level of development. A responsible teacher will attempt to help the kindergartener progress toward the next level of ability while simultaneously respecting the pupil's need to function confidently at his/her present level. The teacher will limit the size of any instructional group in order to provide for every child's maximum progress, and he/she will delay beginning reading activities until the child is mature enough to learn to read without difficulty or unnecessary pressure. A flexible reading program in kindergarten will include three stages, with individual pupils working in various levels of the stages during any part of the reading process because the stages have not been designed as a step-by-step formula:[9]

Stage I: Reading development, during which readiness for reading can be determined. Activities suggested may be used in a total group situation, in small groups, or with individual boys or girls; they are not in sequential order nor do they demand any specific period of time. Should a child show little understanding or interest, the following skill activities should be postponed (and more informal activities continued): motor development; identification of self and surroundings; hand-eye coordination; logical sequence of events; visual discrimination; visual memory; language usage; auditory discrimination; and listening skills.

Stage II: Initial stage in learning to read. Skill activities include: using spoken context; listening for initial sounds; distinguishing letter forms; associating letter sounds and forms; and developing a recognition vocabulary.

Stage III: Stage of progress in fundamental reading attitudes, habits, and skills. Skill activities include: word recognition (both sight vocabulary and word attack); recognition of punctuation marks; ability to read for deeper meaning; adaptation of reading method to purpose and content (silent reading and oral reading); and ability to study independently.

Some children may complete Stage III during the kindergarten year while others will only progress as far as Stage I or Stage II. There should be some interaction among the stages since reading readiness activities are continued throughout all levels of learning to read. Nevertheless, it is strongly recommended that the child experience success in the elements of Stage II before attempting Stage III.

Instructional Strategies

This section will discuss at some length the three major systematic procedures that elementary school teachers presently employ to teach and develop the skills and abilities needed to guide each learner to mature reading. Some teachers prefer an eclectic approach whereby they borrow a few of the features from each of the major strategies and combine them confidently to meet the needs of one classroom of girls and boys.

The Basal Reader Approach

The basal reader is not just one book but represents a entire package of books and supplementary materials used to teach reading. This package (and every major publisher has one) is composed of a series of 15–16 pupil books, which range in size and difficulty from preprimers to sixth or seventh/eighth grade readers. It also includes teacher manuals which correspond to the pupil books, text-related workbooks, a management component or testing program, and supplementary materials such as tapes, flash cards, paperback enrichment books, and kits of readiness or audiovisual resources. No wonder that most researchers affirm that the basal reader approach is used in one form or another in 80–95 percent of elementary classrooms on any given day.

Features of contemporary basal series of the 1980s, in comparison to those of earlier decades, reveal better ethnic balance, better male/female balance, inclusion of the handicapped, inclusion of senior citizens, deletion of violence, better balance of urban/suburban/rural settings, better balance of geographic areas, vigorous graphic arts components, improved literary quality, a more balanced selection of literary genres, sections devoted to glossary study, and (in the teachers' manuals) developmental lesson plans.[10] Since on the surface so many of the basal series appear to be nearly identical, it is suggested that teachers who have been asked to examine several programs and then recommend one for their grade level or school use the checklist in Appendix 3 in order to determine significant differences among series and thereby locate the one that best fits their needs.

The typical procedure for teaching a lesson in the basal reader is the Directed Reading Activity (or DRA). It generally consists of four to five specific subsections:

1. Motivation, introduction of new vocabulary and/or concepts.
2. Guided silent reading and sometimes oral reading for definite purposes.
3. Skill-building activities usually focused on decoding or comprehension skills.
4. Follow-up practice, often through workbook exercises, *and/or*
5. Supplementary/enrichment activities, sometimes in materials furnished by the publisher and often relating the story to art, music or creative writing.

A current basal, such as these boys are sharing, shows a better balance of ethnic groups, sexes, geographic areas, and literary genres than earlier basal readers did. (Photo courtesy of the Fountain Valley School District, Fountain Valley, California.)

A viable alternative to the DRA is the DRTA or Directed Reading-Thinking Activity. It demands that pupils become actively involved in the reading process by asking questions about the story, by processing the information as they read the story, and by receiving feedback about their original questions. Its primary goal is to develop critical readers. Major differences between the DRA and the DRTA run as follows:

1. The DRA is "materials oriented" and "teacher-manual oriented" with specific guidelines, questions, and instructional materials. The DRTA has fewer explicit guidelines, giving the teacher considerable flexibility as well as sole responsibility for the development of the lesson. It can be used in teaching any of the other elementary school curricular areas which demand reading, unlike the DRA which is primarily concerned with basal reader programs.
2. The teacher's role in the DRA is to ask the boys and girls to supply answers to questions found in the manual, and most of such questions are at the literal level of comprehension which requires convergent thinking. In the DRTA, however, the teacher asks questions which require a higher-level of thinking known as divergent thinking. By so doing, he or she promotes comprehension skills that make reading a dynamic activity which goes beyond responding to factual questions.
3. In the DRA, new vocabulary is introduced before the children open their books. In the DRTA there is no preteaching of vocabulary. Instead, the girl or boy must make use of decoding skills to unlock new words as these appear in the story selection just as she or he would during similar situations outside of reading class.
4. In the DRA, the manual details which comprehension skills will be taught and when they will be presented. In the DRTA, however, there is no such prescription and, therefore, the teacher must develop the art of good questioning as well as the ability to accept alternative answers to certain questions.[11]

Briefly, for the beginning teacher concerned with attempting to meet the needs of all the children in his/her classroom every day, the basal reader approach offers several advantages. There is a gradual introduction of word analysis skills and of vocabulary. Skills are presented in sequential order and continued through all the levels. There are ready-made tests and seatwork. Finally, the organization is both horizontal (coordination of materials) and vertical (social organization, comprehension, word analysis skills, and vocabulary).

After inexperienced teachers have worked with the basals and learned the skills sequences, they are better able to organize their own resources and thereby grow in their confidence to handle a reading program competently.

The Language Experience Approach

Sometimes used in conjunction with the basal reader approach, the language experience approach is founded on the theory that reading and comprehending written language is an extension of listening to and understanding spoken language. The experiences of the children form the basis for reading materials. Boys and girls first dictate to the teacher, and later themselves write, stories about field

trips, school activities, and personal experiences outside of school, for example. These stories and other student-produced materials become the texts for learning to read. Many are in the form of charts.
The rationale for this approach has been stated as:

- I can think about what I have experienced and imagined.
- I can talk about what I think about.
- What I can talk about, I can express in some other form.
- Anything I can record, I can recall through speaking or reading.
- I can read what I can write by myself and what other people write for me to read.[12]

The main advantages of the language experience approach are as follows: It uses the language of the boys and girls as the avenue for teaching reading; skills are presented to the child as they are needed and applied in contextual reading; and the child comes to recognize reading as one part of the communication/language arts process.[13]

On the other hand, the approach has certain limitations. There is no printed scope and sequence of skills to develop, which may create a haphazard method of reading instruction. There is a lack of both vocabulary control in general and the systematic repetition of new words in particular. There is an unusually high expenditure of teacher time on preparing charts and worksheets concerned with past experiences as well as on planning activities to stimulate future experience stories. Students are apt to become bored with rereading the same stories and other passages again and again, and they may even memorize some of the sentences rather than actually read them.

Briefly, the language experience approach can be used at any elementary grade level by seasoned teachers interested in integrating their writing and reading programs. It has been well received as an appropriate way to present reading to those kindergarteners who display many signs of readiness. It has also proved successful with beginning readers in the primary grades and with remedial readers in the intermediate grades, principally due to the vocabulary and interest levels of the materials. Finally, the language experience approach has been especially beneficial to students who speak English as a second language or who speak a non-standard English dialect. Sample charts developed by children and teachers using this approach in beginning ESL classes are shown in Figure 9.2.

The Individualized Reading Approach

In this approach the teacher introduces skills as these are needed in reading. The core of the individualized reading approach is the child-teacher conference (held at least once a week) which is generally based on the books that pupils have selected for their own reading. A suggested format for such conferences is detailed below (although at times some steps are skipped) and covers the approximate 15 minutes usually planned:

1. Greet the child and converse with him or her briefly about a matter of personal interest; e.g., soccer. (½–1 minute)
2. Ask the child what he or she has read since the last conference and what is being presently read, inviting a brief account of the reading matter. (1–2 minutes)

Figure 9.2. Sample Language Experience Charts Developed in Beginning ESL Classes by Teachers and Children.

In Our Room

There are 18 boys in our room.

There are 14 girls in our room.

There are 10 goldfish in our room.

There are 2 teachers in our room.

On Mondays

We stand outdoors by the flagpole on Mondays.

We salute the flag.

We sing songs.

We hear speakers.

Every Morning

Teacher:	Good morning, class.
Class:	Good morning, Miss Johnson.
Teacher:	How are you today?
Class:	Fine, thank you. How are you?
Teacher:	I'm fine too. Thank you.

3. Have the child read a passage aloud from the book he or she is presently reading, noting vocal fluency as well as the level of difficulty of the material. Offer positive feedback. (2 minutes)
4. Check upon a skill you reviewed or introduced at the last conference and correct the assignment made (see step 6). Offer praise for any gains made. (2 minutes)
5. Review or introduce a new skill. (3 minutes)
6. Give a follow-up assignment to be checked at the next conference session. (1 minute)
7. Help the child set goals for completion by the next conference, as you tell him or her when that conference will be and which skills will be practiced. (1 minute)

8. If a new book must be chosen shortly, offer several suggestions and describe each book briefly. (1 minute)
9. Compliment the child on progress already made and then dismiss her or him. (½ minute)
10. Complete your records of matters completed during the conference before motioning to the next child to come to your desk. (1 minute)[14]

The individualized reading approach is not a recreational reading program, although both foster independent reading. Recreational reading programs are intended only to help pupils understand that reading can indeed be an enjoyable experience. They lack child-teacher conferences, plans for keeping records of pupil progress, book-sharing sessions, and skills-instruction components.

The need for the individualized approach clearly exists for three reasons. First, individualized reading does not depend upon basals but involves a variety of materials and can even occur in the absence of the teacher. It therefore simulates closely the type of reading method that literate adults use and helps students transfer school learning outside of the classroom. Furthermore, it places a heavy emphasis upon the personal enjoyment and satisfaction to be gained through reading, thereby establishing lifelong reading habits. Finally, the approach helps the classroom teacher meet the problem of differing reading abilities which exists at every grade level. Since the differences actually increase as children grow older, the range of ability in the sixth grade has been predicted to be a little more than seven years!

Other advantages of this approach include the development of a healthy rapport between child and teacher as instruction is adjusted to the specific needs of each learner and the equally important reduction of comparison/competition among readers. Small groups can be formed as needed for specific purposes when several children encounter similar and temporary difficulties in one area, such as contextual analysis. The key words to this approach are self-motivation, self-selection, and self-pacing.

Those same words, however, also relate to a major limitation of the individualized reading approach: a well-stocked school library with a minimum of 100 selected books in the classroom at any one time which are changed monthly and cover a wide range of reading abilities. Such a collection is both difficult to house in a convenient spot and expensive to gather. Furthermore, it leads to a second important disadvantage of this approach: the time-consuming effort by the teacher to be knowledgeable about the broad array of reading materials which can then be promoted to allow for the most beneficial conferences. Children can only be encouraged to read on a variety of subject matter if materials are available locally on those same subjects written on reading levels suitable for elementary school boys and girls.

Other weaknesses of the individualized reading approach include the heavy record-keeping burden on the teacher, the stressful requirement that he or she provide a mini-reading program for each pupil, the difficulty of interpreting the reading program to the parents who are generally much more familiar with and accustomed to the basal readers, and the danger of insufficient skill development due to poor management of time.

Briefly, the teacher introducing the individualized approach to the grade level (or to the school) might consider doing so under a compromise arrangement which also involves basal reader lessons, workbook exercises, and the development of library media center research skills. Such a program could include most of the advantages of individualized reading without all of the difficulties. Consequently, a sample weekly schedule for a first-grade, second-semester reading program, as based on the use of three flexible reading achievement groups, is shown in Figure 9.3.

Figure 9.3. Sample Weekly Reading Schedule: First Grade, Second Semester.

Sample Weekly Schedule—First Grade Reading Period 9:00–10:30 A.M.					
	Monday	Tuesday	Wednesday	Thursday	Friday
Above-average Group	Individualized Reading Four Individual Reading Conferences Informal Sharing of Reading Material with One or Two Classmates	Basal Reader Lesson with Most of Its Traditional Steps	Basal Reader Lesson with Most of Its Traditional Steps	Individualized Reading Four Individual Reading Conferences Research Group from Science on Topic "Baby Animals"	Individualized Reading Three Individual Reading Conferences Research Group from Science on Topic "Baby Animals"
Average Group	Basal Reader Lesson with Most of Its Traditional Steps	Individualized Reading Five Individual Reading Conferences Informal Sharing of Reading Material with One or Two Classmates	Basal Reader Lesson Presentation of New Vocabulary Guided Silent Reading	Basal Reader Lesson Purposeful Oral Reading Skill Development Enriching Experiences Workbook	Individualized Reading Five Individual Reading Conferences Research Group from Science on Topic "Baby Animals"
Below-average Group	Basal Reader Lesson Development of Experiential Background Presentation of New Vocabulary Guided Silent Reading	Basal Reader Lesson Oral Reading Skill Development Workbook	Basal Reader Lesson Development of Experiential Background Presentation of New Vocabulary Oral Reading	Basal Reader Lesson Skill Development Enriching Experiences Workbook	Individualized Reading Four Individual Reading Conferences Research Group from Science on Topic "Baby Animals"

Word Recognition Skills

Fluent, capable readers do not pause to identify every single word as they read. Instead, according to Goodman, mature readers merely sample enough of the printed cues to permit them to make and to confirm guesses about words and meanings.[15] Nevertheless, all readers—children and adults alike—do at times encounter words which they do not promptly recognize. When this occurs, the readers can resort to employing one or more of the following word attack skills to help them decode the unknown word(s):

1. Using the dictionary
2. Using context clues
3. Using structural analysis
4. Using phonic analysis

Throughout the elementary school instruction in these skills, however, it must be emphasized that the ultimate goal is to have the boy or girl eventually learn to identify words instantly as wholes. Once the words have become his or her *sight words,* the child no longer must analyze them by using one or more of the skills listed above. Therefore, the underlying need for *developing sight vocabulary* is crucial and basic.

Developing Sight Vocabulary

A large sight vocabulary is important for several reasons. First, it allows the reader to attend to the meaning of the written passage, and comprehension is a critical area. Second, it permits the use of the valuable word attack skill involving context clues because many unfamiliar words can be identified by close consideration of the context around them (provided of course that the words in that context can all be smoothly read). Thirdly, it encourages the development of another important word identification skill—phonic analysis—since children who know several sight words which begin with the same letter, for example, can then use those words as a basis for learning a generalization about sound-letter correspondences. Fourth, many of the most frequently used words in the English language are phonically irregular although they appear in many beginning reading programs and must therefore be recognized on sight as whole configurations. Finally, acquiring at least a beginning sight vocabulary at the very start of reading instruction gives boys and girls greater success in reading and consequently a more positive attitude toward the entire reading program.

Words should be introduced gradually, reviewed often, and always presented in a meaningful context. While some authorities espouse the idea of having the children themselves choose the words they would like to learn, a more sensible solution is to incorporate that idea with teacher selection of words from the varied lists described in Chapter Ten.

While many good commercial materials are available for developing sight vocabulary, the following is a sampling of teacher-developed activities which offer individualized practice:

A. *Build-a-Train* Engines and railway cards are cut from oaktag sheets. Each piece has one word printed on it. Boys and girls who pronounce the words correctly build a train which becomes longer and longer. The goal can be to see who is the best train builder.

B. *Classification* On individual cards are printed in color two (or more) words which constitute categories, such as *farm* or *house*. These cards are placed in an envelope along with many other cards on which are printed in black such words as *roof, barn, cows,* and *kitchen*. The latter group must be categorized under the two words printed in color. If the teacher numbers the backs of the word cards, the exercise can be self-correcting.

C. *Color Match* On pieces of oaktag are printed words pertaining to various colors. Clothespins of different colors are placed in an accompanying envelope. The participant must attach the properly colored clothespins to the word cards. If the teacher colors the backs of the word cards with the color printed on the front, the exercise can be self-correcting.

D. *Flashcard Group* Every member of the reading group is given a small pile of cards, each approximately 1½ × 2½ inches. As a reader encounters an unfamiliar word, he or she must write it on a card. Then, several times a week the children are permitted to meet in groups of three to quiz each other on their cards. Generally at least one of the three children will know the new word. However, there may be times when the teacher or a paraprofessional may be called on to supply help.

E. *Nouns in Color* On a sheet of oaktag are printed nouns associated with specific colors (e.g., *snow, grass*). Then in an attached envelope are placed small cards of different colors. The participant matches the colored cards with the nouns. If the teacher uses an identification scheme on the backs of the colored cards, the exercise can be self-correcting.

F. *Picture Checkerboard* The teacher writes 16 nouns on the chalkboard in numbered order. The children first fold a sheet of drawing paper into 16 squares and number them correspondingly. Then they draw pictures of the nouns on the numbered squares. Finally the boys and girls exchange and correct their papers.

G. *Picture Dictionary Match* The teacher obtains a small, inexpensive picture dictionary (available in most supermarkets). From it pictures are cut and pasted in a row on a card measuring 9 × 12 inches. Under each picture is drawn a space box measuring ½ × 1½ inches. Small word cards are prepared and placed in an envelope which remains attached to the large picture card. If the teacher numbers the pictures and the backs of the word cards, the exercise can be self-correcting.

H. *Picture Riddle Matcho* Children cut pictures out of old magazines and place them in envelopes, five per envelope. Then the teacher writes a riddle about one of the pictures in each envelope, and places the riddle in that same envelope. The child is allowed to choose one envelope, examine the pictures, read the riddle, and select the picture which answers the riddle. If the teacher can devise a marking scheme appropriate to the age level of the children, the exercise can be self-correcting.

I. *Word Authors* Words are printed on the corners of cards with four cards to a set. For example, a set consists of four animal words, four color words, etc. A deck of cards generally consists of 10 to 12 sets. Each participant is dealt four cards. One child begins the activity by calling for a word, and, if he or she gets that word, the child may continue to call for more words until a set is complete. When the opponent states that he or she does not have the word card called for, the first child draws from the deck which is face down on the table. The winner of the exercise is the child who acquires the most sets. Two to four children may participate at a time.

J. *Word File Pictures* At the top of each card is printed the name of an object while below is placed a picture or drawing which illustrates that noun. On the back of the card is printed only the noun. The child reads the words from the backs of the cards and then checks himself/herself by examining the pictures on the front sides.[16]

In a school which provides *tachistoscopes* (devices which allow the presentation of visual material for brief intervals of time), teachers can use them to expose words rapidly for sight-word recognition practice. Children thus become accustomed to the idea of identifying the word instantly and not sounding it out. Tachistoscopes range in complexity from simple handmade cardboard devices to elaborate laboratory instruments.

A recent review of research on methods of teaching sight words concluded that no one method alone was best for every child.[17] Still, it was recommended that words be presented in context rather than in isolation since reading is a language, meaning-getting process.

Using the Dictionary

Dictionaries can help readers determine pronunciations, derivations, and meanings of unfamiliar words. Should the children have some idea of how a word is spelled, dictionaries can also help with correct spelling. Incidentally, in matters of pronunciation, it should be pointed out that children must be urged to use the other three word-attack skills before turning to the dictionary because (a) readers do not always have a dictionary readily available, and (b) using a dictionary may disrupt interest in the reading passage and thereby hinder comprehension.

Further discussion of dictionary use and skills can be found in Chapter Twelve together with 25 activities promoting increased understanding and familiarity with this important tool for greater word identification ability.

Using Context Clues

Context clues are meaning cues contained in the passage that surrounds the unknown word. They may appear in the same sentence or in preceding or following sentences. Common types of context clues found in the same sentence are:

1. Definition; e.g., *Lava, which is melted rock, flowed down the mountainside.*
2. Restatement; e.g., *The hardware store sold me some rope made from jute—a tropical plant.*
3. Example; e.g., *The stage manager rented properties such as tables, chairs, and dishes for the play.*

Although context clues are heavily dependent upon each reader's own background, experience, and interpretation, it nevertheless has been suggested that children ought to be taught that (1) the first cue to word identification which they should attempt to use is context and (2) context should always be employed to confirm a guess made through structural analysis or phonetic analysis.[18]

While there are many good commercial materials available for developing the use of context clues, the following is a sample of teacher-developed activities which offer individualized practice:

A. Present sentences in which a phonics clue is provided to aid the child in eliciting missing words. Readers are told to think of words which fit the blanks appropriately, such as in the following examples:
   1. Sean said that he would th ________ the softball to me.
   2. The kitten dr ________ all the milk in the saucer.
   3. Mother was going to pl ________ vegetables in the garden.
B. Present sentences in which words are completely missing. Readers are told to examine the sentences and determine which words fit the blanks most appropriately, such as in the following examples:
   1. The day was bright, warm, and ________________ .
      (*sunny, dark, cloudy*)
   2. The general had to ________________ if the army should ____ the fort against attack. (*defend, decide*)
   3. The robbers took all the ________________ in the bank.
      (*money, letters, papers*)
C. Present sentences which contain unusual words whose meanings can be determined by using contextual clues. Readers are told to examine the sentences carefully before deciding on the answers, such as in the following examples:
   1. Father will *deflate* the tire by opening the valve.
      Deflate means (a) let air out; (b) put air in; (c) turn over; or (d) damage.
   2. The old steamer trunk was *capacious* enough to hold all of Tim's clothes.
      Capacious means (a) colorful; (b) small; (c) large; or (d) plentiful.
   3. My brother works in a brick *edifice* which covers an entire city block.
      Edifice means (a) building; (b) hut; (c) ship; or (d) service station.
D. Employ cloze exercises to encourage readers to look for clues in surrounding sentences (or even the entire paragraph) as well as the sentence in which the unfamiliar word first appears. A good way to work on promoting context-clue use is for the teacher to develop a cloze passage in which words have been systematically omitted and replaced with blanks of uniform size. Sometimes the teacher may delete only certain types of words (such as nouns or adjectives) rather than have random deletion. The passage is reproduced on a worksheet, chalkboard, or transparency so that the class can discuss reasons for the words selected to be inserted in the blanks. All synonyms should be accepted as well as any nonsynonyms for which students can offer reasonable bases.[19]

   Further discussion about using context clues can be found in Chapter Ten.

Using Structural Analysis

A word recognition skill which uses word parts to determine the meaning and pronunciation of unfamiliar words is termed structural analysis. Its subskills include the use of (a) roots or base words, (b) prefixes and suffixes (known together as affixes (c) compound words, (d) contractions, and (e) syllabication and accent. It becomes a worthwhile technique in the upper primary and intermediate grades because the meanings of affixes, in particular, can help readers add many new words to their vocabulary. As early as the second grade level, for instance, boys and girls can be introduced to several structural generalizations for changing base words before adding a suffix. Often such generalizations are derived inductively by the pupils through carefully planned lessons. Structural analysis rather than phonic analysis should be used by readers when attacking unknown words because it deals with units larger than single graphemes.

Further discussion of the mastery of roots and of affixes can be found in Chapter Ten.

Compound words are made up of two (or sometimes three) words that have been joined together to form a new word; e.g., *snowman.* That word may be one whose (a) meaning is the sum of its parts, such as *houseboat;* (b) meaning is related to but not totally represented by the meaning of its parts, such as *shipyard;* or (c) meaning is not literally related to the sum of its parts, such as *moonstruck,* or the compound has multiple meanings, such as *doghouse.*[20]

As early as first grade, children can be introduced to compound words and learn to divide such words between the smaller words that comprise them. They can even discuss the reasons for combining certain small words, such as *cow* and *boy, fire* and *man, play* and *house,* and *police* and *woman.*

Also introduced in the first grade, or at least by the second grade, are contractions. They should be presented by sight at first because beginning readers are generally unable to determine what part of the omitted word has been left out as the contraction was formed. Later students can be taught that a contraction is a word composed of two (or more) words in which one or more letters have been left out and replaced by an apostrophe. Common contractions and their meanings which should be presented to children include:

can't=cannot
couldn't=could not
didn't=did not
don't=do not
hadn't=had not
hasn't=has not
he'll=he will
he's=he is
I'll=I will
I'm=I am
I've=I have
isn't=is not
let's=let us
she'll=she will
she's=she is
shouldn't=should not
they'll=they will
they're=they are
they've=they have
wasn't=was not
we're=we are
weren't=were not
we've=we have
won't=will not
wouldn't=would not
you'll=you will
you're=you are
you've=you have

Syllabication and accent are often introduced also in the primary grades, with syllabication being presented in second grade and stress or accenting in the third grade. The teaching of accent is actually built upon the skills of syllabication, since accent has much to do with the vowel sound heard in a syllable.

A letter or group of letters that forms a pronunciation unit is termed a syllable, and every syllable contains a vowel sound. It is important not to confuse sounds and letters because some words (such as *weave*) have several vowel letters but only one vowel sound. Consequently, *weave,* for instance, contains only one syllable.

There are both open syllables (which end in vowel sounds) and closed syllables (which end in consonant sounds). There are also accented syllables (which are given greater stress) and unaccented ones (which are given little stress).

Some useful generalizations about syllabication and accent are as follows:

1. Prefixes and suffixes generally form separate syllables.
2. Usually the first syllable of a two-syllable word is accented.
3. Affixes usually are not accented.
4. When two consonants are located between two vowels, the word is divided between the two consonants; e.g., *mon/key.*
5. A compound word is divided between the two words that form the compound as well as between syllables within the component parts; e.g., *thun/der/storm.*
6. When there are two of the same consonant letters within a word, the syllable before the double consonants is generally accented; e.g., *but/ter.*
7. When one consonant is located between two vowels, the first syllable usually ends with the vowel and the second syllable usually begins with the second consonant. Therefore, the vowel in the first syllable is long and the syllable is said to be open; e.g., *ti/ger.*

Incidentally, readiness for learning syllabication involves the ability to hear syllables as pronunciation units. Consequently, even first graders can listen to words and clap for every syllable they hear.

Some supplementary instructional activities for correcting deficiencies in structural analysis include the following, which can be used with individual pupils or even small groups of children:

A. Roots and Affixes

1. A list of words containing common prefixes is distributed to the readers. They must identify the root or base in each word by underlining it.
2. A list of words containing common suffixes is distributed to the readers. They must identify the suffixes.
3. A list of words containing common prefixes is distributed to the readers. They must identify the prefixes.
4. A list of words containing common suffixes is distributed to the readers. They must identify the root or base in each word by underlining it.
5. Readers are given lists of words and must write a given prefix before each word and tell the meanings of the new words.
6. Readers are given lists of words with prefixes and must write each word without the prefix and tell how the meaning has changed.

7. Readers are given lists of words containing suffixes and must use each root word in a sentence.
8. Readers are given lists of unfamiliar words. They must separate the suffix from each word that contains a suffix and correctly pronounce both the suffix and the root word.
9. Readers are given lists of unfamiliar words with a known prefix. They must find the meanings of the new words.
10. Readers are each given a list of words with definitions after each word. They are also given a list of suffixes and must add one of the suffixes to each word so that the newly formed word complies with its definition.

B. *Compound Words*

1. Two columns of words are distributed to the readers. They then develop compound words by matching the words in the first column with the words in the second column.
2. Readers are given lists of compound words. They must write the two short words that make up the compound, next to the longer word itself.
3. Lists of compound words are distributed to the readers. They must draw a line between the two short words which comprise each compound.
4. Readers look for compound words which can be illustrated humorously. When they have compiled at least ten such illustrations, they place them in a booklet.

C. *Contractions*

1. Readers are given a one-paragraph story calling for many contractions. They must fill in the blanks with the missing contractions. Some students may prefer developing their own stories and exchanging these with partners.
2. Student voices are tape recorded during committee work, whole class discussion, or a learning game, without the knowledge of the participants. Later, as the tape is played, the readers must listen for contractions and note them on their workpapers. Finally they must write what words were combined for each contraction.
3. Students are asked to search through a browsing book (which they have checked out of the library media center) and write down numerous different contractions. They may also copy the sentences in which the contractions appear. (The teacher may wish to limit the list to common contractions, excluding colloquial expressions such as *ya'all,* for greater clarity.)

D. *Syllabication and Accent*

1. Students are assigned (or choose) a page from their science or social studies text and are then handed a worksheet with four columns. They must record all one-syllable words in the first column, all two-syllable words in the second column, and so on. Each word, however, can only be recorded once.

2. Readers are each given a sheet of paper ruled into large squares, totaling either nine or 16. They draw an object in each square and write its name by syllables under the picture.
3. Readers are given a list of multisyllabic words taken from a current unit in math/health/science. The words appear in a column on the left side of the paper. Next to each word is a blank line on which the readers must write the number of syllables appearing in that word.
4. Readers are given a worksheet on which appear sentences using pairs of *homographs* (words with the same spelling but different meanings and sometimes different pronunciations, such as *léad/leád, próduce/prodúce, contént/cóntent.* By examining the context, each reader must determine the correct pronunciation and place the accent mark in the proper place. Dictionaries may be used.
5. Intermediate grade readers are each asked to write a silly paragraph using two-syllable homographs. As each student reads his/her paragraph aloud to the group, he or she must use the wrong pronunciation for each homograph. The chuckling listeners, however, must place the accent mark correctly on the homographs as they write them down on a worksheet.

Using Phonic Analysis

This word recognition technique, which has been used in elementary reading instruction for more than 175 years, involves the association of phonemes (or speech sounds) and graphemes (or written symbols) in unlocking the pronunciation of unknown words while reading. Its basic assumption is that the children are already familiar with the spoken forms and meanings of those same words, although it is admittedly possible for readers proficient in phonic analysis to determine pronunciations of words whose meanings they do not understand. For this reason mastering this word recognition skill should not be considered the end product of the reading program. The objective of all reading instruction is comprehension whereby the child will derive meaning from the printed page.

Phonic analysis depends upon sound auditory and visual perception and discrimination. Children must be able to perceive and distinguish among the more than 40 sounds of spoken English and the varied sequences of those sounds. This ability often may be affected by speech impediments, dialect variations, and differences in native language backgrounds. Children must also be capable of visually perceiving and discriminating among the 26 letters of the English alphabet and the sequences of those letters. Readers who are visually deficient may encounter difficulty in distinguishing between letters with similar features (such as *m* and *n*), between uppercase and lowercase forms of the same letter, and in various versions of script and print.

The two major kinds of phonic analyses or major approaches to phonics instruction are *analytic* and *synthetic.* The analytic involves teaching some sight words, as discussed earlier in this section, and then teaching the sounds of the letters within those words. It is used during the basal reader approach because it avoids the distortion which can occur when consonants are pronounced (whether blended or in isolation). Children can visually examine a polysyllabic word which has been divided into syllables, sound the portion of the word within each syllable, and then blend the syllables together to unite the complete word.

The synthetic method or synthetic phonic analysis is concerned with instructing boys and girls in the phonemes that are associated with individual letters, and it is generally accomplished by repeated drills on sound-grapheme relationships. Children blend the sounds of individual letters in a word to form the complete word, such as *cuh-a-tuh* to enunciate the word *cat*. The problem that promptly occurs is that speakers add a vowel (because a consonant sound can rarely be pronounced in isolation), and therefore the word becomes distorted as such blending takes place.

While controversy has enveloped the importance of phonic analysis for many years, most authorities agree with the following guidelines:

1. Basic to a phonics program is auditory perception.
2. Phonic analysis should not be used as an isolated word attack skill in order to be most effective.
3. Children should discover phonics generalizations (or learn them inductively) rather than be presented with them deductively as rules.
4. Phonics instruction should proceed from the simple to the complex with more time spent on generalizations with wide applicability.
5. Short frequent sessions devoted to phonics are more worthwhile and more enjoyable than long infrequent ones because there is nothing exciting about the subject of phonics.
6. The phonics program for each child should be individualized since girls and boys vary in their readiness and in their degree of mastery at any grade level.[21]

Most authorities also agree that consonant sounds should be presented before introducing vowel sounds because more words start with consonants than with vowels, because consonant letters are more consistent in the sounds which they represent in comparison to vowel letters, and because the more identifiable features of a word are usually made up of the consonants.

Before introducing any of the numerous important phonics generalizations to children, teachers should be completely familiar with the terminology listed in Table 9.1. Phonics principles or generalizations should be presented to boys and girls one at a time and inductively. They must be carefully chosen so that each is learned well. Although there is no agreement as to which or how many such principles should be introduced, Burns, Roe, and Ross consider the following generalizations to be useful in the majority of circumstances:

A. When two like consonants are adjacent to each other, only one is sounded; e.g., *lass*.
B. When the letters *c* and *g* are followed by *o, a,* or *u,* they generally have hard sounds: *c* has the sound of *k* and *g* has its own special sound; e.g., *cat, go, out, gut*. When the letters *c* and *g* are followed by *e, i,* or *y,* they generally have soft sounds: *c* has the sound of *s* and *g* has the sound of *j;* e.g., *city, gem, cyst, gym*.
C. The digraph *ch* usually has the sound heard in *church,* but it also sometimes sounds like *k* or *sh* as in *chord* or *chef*.

Table 9.1.
Definitions of Terms Commonly Used in Phonic Analysis.

Term	Definition and or Examples
Vowels	Letters *a, e, i, o,* and *u*. Letters *y* (when in the middle or final position in a word or syllable) and *w* (when in the final position of a word or syllable).
Consonants	Letters other than *a, e, i, o,* and *u*. Letter *w* and *y* when in the initial position in a word or syllable.
Consonant Blend or Consonant Cluster	Two or three adjacent consonant sounds which are combined although each retains its separate identity; e.g., *pl*ay, *str*ike, a*sk*, *br*ake, *dr*ove, *sm*ell, *sw*ing, *tw*ig.
Consonant Digraph	Two adjacent consonant letters which are combined into a single speech sound; e.g., *sh*ip, *ph*one, *th*is, *wh*at, ne*ck*, ri*ng*.
Vowel Digraph	Two adjacent vowel letters which are combined into a single speech sound; e.g., d*ay*, *ea*ch, f*oo*t, r*oa*d, f*ai*r, m*ee*t.
Diphthong	Two vowel sounds combined, beginning with the first and gliding smoothly into the second; e.g., *oi*l, t*oy*, *ou*t, pl*ow*.
Phonogram	Combination of letters within a word that functions as a pronounceable unit; e.g., r*ake*, m*ine*, f*ight*, b*all*, p*ick*, t*ack*.

D. When the letters *ght* are adjacent in a word, the *gh* is not sounded; e.g., *bought*.
E. When *kn* are the first two letters in a word, the *k* is not sounded; e.g., *know*.
F. When *wr* are the first two letters in a word, the *w* is not sounded; e.g., *wrong*.
G. When *ck* are the last two letters in a word, the sound of *k* is heard; e.g., *brick*.
H. The sound of a vowel preceding *r* is neither long nor short; e.g., *car, her*.
I. In the vowel combinations *oa, ee,* and *ay,* the first vowel is usually long, and the second is not sounded; e.g., *coat, beet, ray*. This rule may also apply to other double vowel combinations.
J. *Oi, oy,* and *ou* usually form diphthongs. While the *ow* combination often represents the long *o* sound, it may also form a diphthong; e.g., *now*.
K. When a word only has one vowel and that is at the end of the word, the vowel generally represents its long sound; e.g., *me*.
L. When a word only has one vowel and that is not at the end of the word, the vowel generally represents its short sound; e.g., *man*.
M. When there are two vowels in a word and one is a final *e,* the first vowel is usually long, and the final *e* is not sounded; e.g., *kite*.
N. The letter combination *qu* often represents the sound of *kw,* although it sometimes stands for the sound of *k;* e.g., *queen, quay,* respectively.
O. The letter *x* most frequently represents the sound of *ks* although it sometimes stands for the sound of *gz* or *z;* e.g., *box, exact, xylophone,* respectively.[22]

Teachers concerned about the utility of presenting phonics generalizations to children should be reassured by recent research that found that there were statistically significant relationships between knowledge of and ability to use such generalizations and reading achievement.[23] The fourth graders in the Ohio school were not always able to state a particular phonics rule, but this inability did not seem to hinder the children's effort to analyze unfamiliar words. Boys and girls in the elementary school apparently need not consciously know or verbalize generalizations in order to apply them.

While there are vast quantities of commercial materials available for developing phonic skills, the following is a sampling of teacher-developed activities which offer group or individualized practice:

A. *I Spy* Each child in a small group has a turn locating an object in the classroom which begins with a particular sound; e.g., "I spy something that begins like *cheese*." The player who names the correct object (*chair*) then has a turn to I Spy. The teacher may direct the choice of a beginning or final sound which the class has been learning.
B. *Mail Order Catalog* Boys and girls find in discarded mail order catalogs pictures of objects which begin with certain consonant blends or consonant digraphs. They mount the pictures on separate sheets of paper and label each one correctly.
C. *Planning a Meal* Children pretend to be meal-planners as each in turn names something to eat which begins with the letter *a*. When a child cannot add to the list of *a* foods, he or she begins naming foods starting with the letter *b*. This activity can be an ongoing one, taking place as children wait to be dismissed each day or as a culmination to a group reading session every day for one week.
D. *Snoopy Says* Every player is given a small card with *Yes* written on one side and *No* on the other. The teacher makes a statement which helps review the players' knowledge of phonics generalizations. Should the statement be true, the players hold up the *Yes* side of their card, but should the statement be false, they hold up the *No* side. If a player displays an incorrect response, he or she is out of the activity until the next time it is played. The winner is the last player remaining in the game.
E. *Newspapers* Copies of several newspapers are brought to class and distributed among the group members. Each child chooses an article and circles all the words in it which contain letters that are not sounded. She or he then exchanges articles with a partner. Partners mark through all the unsounded letters in the marked words. Finally articles are traded back and checked.
F. *Pictures* A series of pictures of objects is given to each child. She or he must name each object shown and also tell whether the vowel in the noun is long (glided) or short (unglided). This activity can be done orally or with a worksheet.
G. *Lists of Words* Each child is given a list of words. He or she is asked to do either of the following: (a) underline all the words which have the same vowel sound as that appearing in the first word; or (b) check all the words in the list that have the same vowel sound.

H. Table Display The teacher places on the table where the group is seated numerous small objects whose names call attention to certain sound elements that have been previously introduced. The teacher pronounces a sound, such as the diphthong *oy*. One child selects an object which contains that sound, names the item (*toy*), holds it up for the group to see, and then replaces it on the table. Once the word has been pronounced, the teacher should either write the word on the chalkboard or hold up a flashcard which contains the word.

Comprehension

Although no one really knows what comprehension is, it usually defines the skill of receiving information from the printed page. Factors influencing comprehension have generally been divided into two categories, according to Wilson and his associates: (1) characteristics of the reader; and (2) characteristics of the reading material.[24] Under the first category have come such factors as intelligence, experiential background, orientation skills (or the basic mechanics of reading), ability to use word attack skills, involvement or interest in the material, knowledge of word meaning, ability to read in thought units, ability to use punctuation marks, and ability to make predictions. Under the second category have appeared such factors as length of the material, readability factors (including sentence length and sentence complexity), difficulty level of the words, author's style of writing (including organization of ideas), the use of figurative language, and format (including type size and illustrations).

The major change in current views of comprehension is the focus on reader knowledge, as shown in the model in Figure 9.4.[25]

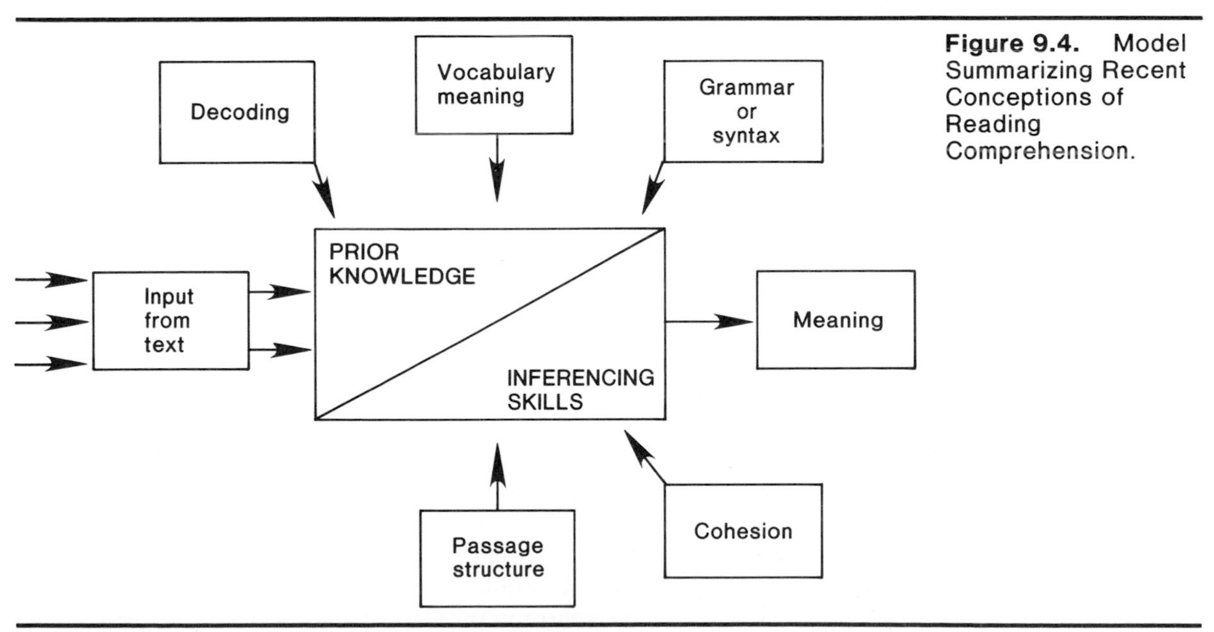

Figure 9.4. Model Summarizing Recent Conceptions of Reading Comprehension.

Source: Reprinted from Cathy R. Wilson "Teaching Reading Comprehension by Connecting the Known to the New," READING TEACHER, January 1983. Reprinted with permission of the author and the International Reading Association.

At the core of the model are the reader's inferencing skills and prior knowledge, reflecting the belief that comprehension occurs when information is connected from the text to information already stored in the reader's mind.

At the left of the model, information reaches the reader from the printed page. Then he or she uses information about decoding, vocabulary meaning, grammar, cohesion, and passage structure in an effort to help connect the new input to what is already familiar/known. The output is meaning, but the conception is interactive; each type of information may be used as necessary, and there is no set sequence in use of information sources. As readers are attempting to gain meaning from the text, each may use different information in order to comprehend. What must be stressed is that lack of information in any part of the model can create difficulties in comprehension.

Levels or Types of Comprehension

Survey of the literature reveals numerous labeling systems for the levels of comprehension, although there is a trend away from the use of the term *levels*. This is due to the fact that levels imply sequence, and, while the first type (or *literal* understanding) is necessary for other types of comprehension, the learner should develop skill in all three types simultaneously. The system that seems to be most widely accepted categorizes the comprehension process as follows:

1. *Literal* comprehension. Often described as "reading on the lines," this type requires the reader to process information which was explicitly stated in the text. It covers understanding what the author specifically stated. For example, the reader may be called upon to recall or locate specifically stated main ideas, details or sequences of events.
2. *Interpretive* comprehension. Frequently described as "reading between the lines," this type demands that the reader process ideas based upon what was read but not explicitly stated in the text. It covers understanding what the author meant, and the reader must call upon his/her intuition, personal experiences, and imagination as the foundation for making inferences. Children may be asked to predict outcomes or infer cause-and-effect relationships.
3. *Critical/Applicative/Problem-solving* comprehension. Often stated as "reading beyond the lines," this type requires the reader to evaluate, integrate, and apply information and ideas from the printed page to his/her own experiences and judgment. It calls for the student to think creatively or to develop original ideas based upon the pages read.

Questioning and Its Relevance to Comprehension

Question-and-answer sessions which accompany reading lessons (as well as lessons for reading content area texts) are an integral part of classroom life. Furthermore, the kinds of questions that the teacher asks are important since they directly influence the sorts of thinking that students do as they read. If they are consistently asked only literal or recall kinds of questions, children will focus their attention when reading on remembering details and not on analyzing or evaluating the information and storing it for future use. Instead, the information will probably only be remembered until the questions have been asked (and answered) and then often will be promptly forgotten. If, however, students are asked to read between or beyond the lines on the page, they will be forced to integrate new input with what they already know about the topic, and therefore much of it will more likely be retained.

Four general goals about the role of questions concern the likelihood that students will: (1) focus attention on significant aspects of the text; (2) relate information from the text to the most appropriate set of background experiences; (3) develop a coherent framework for remembering/understanding the text material; or (4) practice cognitive skills which they will ultimately be able to use alone.[26] A consensus which represents an effort to balance these goals where they conflict and also to integrate them where they agree with one another is as follows:

A. The teacher begins the lesson with questions which focus student attention on appropriate background experiences/knowledge; e.g., *Have you ever been on a farm? What do you know about farms?* Should knowledge or experiential background not be available or developed, then the teacher might attempt a longer question such as the following: *In our story today about South America, there is a family of jaguars. A jaguar is somewhat like a house cat, somewhat like a wolf, and somewhat like a sports car. Let's see if we can figure out how a jaguar is like all of those.*
B. The teacher then allows students to use background knowledge, whenever possible, to predict what might happen in the story; e.g., *If you were lost in the forest as the jaguar family is and needed food, how would you get it?*
C. The teacher sets up a purpose which lasts as long as possible throughout the story; e.g., *What did the jaguar family try to do to solve their problem?*
D. During the guided reading (which occurs *during* the reading in the primary classroom and immediately *after* the reading in the intermediate grades), the teacher asks questions which tie together the significant elements in the story "map" (or outline on the chalkboard that is a causal chain of events); e.g., *What was the first thing that Jenny tried to do to get rid of her tooth? What lesson did Jenny learn?*
E. Immediately following the reading, the teacher returns to the purpose-setting question(s), as suggested in item C above. Rewording or paraphrasing can occur; e.g., *Can you tell me in order the three things the jaguar family did to find food?*
F. In discussing the story, the teacher uses this sequence for generating questions: (1) retells the story map at a fairly high level of generality; (2) takes students beyond the literal stage by asking them to compare this story to their own experiences or to another selection or by asking them to speculate about the reactions of the characters when placed in a different situation; and finally, (3) returns to the selection in an effort to appreciate the talent of the author. Activities useful for item (1) include dramatization, discussion, production of a time line of events, or the development of a flow chart of events. (The last-named can be done with children as early as third grade.) Questions appropriate for item (2) would include: *Do you think that the jaguar family acted prudently? Why or why not?* and *What would you have done if faced with a similar situation?* Questions illustrative of item (3) would

include: *What is your favorite part of the selection? What made you choose that part?* and *How does the author tell you that the father jaguar feels proud?*[27]

There are three important elements of questioning: the teacher's question; the student's answer; and the teacher's response to the student's answer.[28] Student answers to teacher questions fall into three general categories: correct, partially correct, and incorrect. A correct response is one that is in line with the teacher question although it may differ substantially from the particular answer the teacher had hoped to elicit. What matters, however, is that the teacher be open to many different and possible correct answers to a particular question and not have a preconceived statement of one "correct" response. He or she should give the student immediate feedback concerning a correct answer to a reading comprehension question in order to reinforce learning. Should the student response only be partially correct, the teacher should recognize all of the correct aspects of the answer while simultaneously directing the student's thinking toward the correct response. Even when the child gives an incorrect answer which is irrelevant or incongruent to the teacher question, it is important that the teacher respond in an accepting manner and at the same time redirect the child's thinking by using clarification measures, such as *Let's go back to the story to check that fact* or *Let me ask the question in a different way.* Briefly, then, teacher responses to student answers fall into three broad categories: acceptance, clarification, and rejection, with rejection being defined as a teacher response which could damage the child's self-image and his or her subsequent learning.

Incidentally, an important factor which is often overlooked in developing reading comprehension is *wait-time.* This has been defined as the amount of time between a teacher's asking a question about the passage read and calling upon a child to respond to that question. It is particularly significant in the area of higher levels/types of comprehension because boys and girls must have adequate time in which to organize complete, original, and thoughtful answers. Research has shown that, while both the quantity of the student response (i.e., the actual number of words used in the answer) and the quality of that response (i.e., level of thinking demonstrated) are affected by the amount of wait-time, teachers give students an average wait-time of only one second![29] Furthermore, if the teachers respond too quickly following student answers, those answers are more often apt to be incomplete. Consequently, by increasing wait-time after a child's response, the teacher discovers that that response will probably be clearer and more elaborate while at the same time his or her own reply to the student will be more appropriate.

Strategies for Instruction

Directed comprehension instruction includes explaining the skills involved, providing practice in using those skills, assessing and (if necessary) reteaching the skills, and finally demonstrating how the skills can be applied. Teachers need to pose questions and then to show the students how those questions may be answered, by modeling aloud the thinking process used to come up with the responses. This includes sharing with students what kinds of clues are found within the selection itself, as well as how previously known information can be integrated.

By beginning lessons with questions which focus attention on what students already know about the topic and by encouraging them to use that knowledge to make predictions, teachers are helping the children deal with the questions in a more familiar framework. It is not enough to assign students to read a story and then answer questions about it. Instead, each teacher should have students share their thinking processes by going back to the assigned story and inquiring, "How did you know? Which words gave you clues that led you to this answer?" While children who give incorrect responses are often redirected through clarification measures, teachers generally overlook the value of questioning students who give correct responses. Such boys and girls can not only reinforce the thinking process of the individual but can model that process for their classmates. By sharing his or her own knowledge as a teacher and by drawing on the background and knowledge of students, the teacher can make the task of presenting comprehension skills more manageable.

Suggestions for comprehension instruction can be divided among those which occur before reading, during reading, and after reading.[30] *Before* the children begin their reading lesson, the teacher can first promote comprehension by (1) making certain the boys and girls are reading materials of an appropriate level of difficulty, with slower readers often needing to spend more time at a particular plateau than one basal series can accommodate and with advanced pupils doing most of their reading in content texts and other materials because they can read through their basals so quickly. Then the teacher can enhance comprehension by (2) making certain the children have appropriate background concepts by using the introductory activities outlined in the reading series in an effort to activate or build-upon prior knowledge, whether on the topic of laundromats, for instance, or life in the Amazon jungle. Finally, the teacher can promote comprehension by (3) making certain that the girls and boys understand that the purpose of reading is to get meaning and that what they already know can help them attain that purpose. Children must be made aware of what the teacher is doing and understand why she/he is doing it because they can indeed be taught to accept responsibility for comprehending, according to late research.[31] That study showed children how to answer questions based on whether the answer was textually explicit, textually implicit, or scriptally implicit. In the last-named category, the pupils were deemed to be on their own.

During the reading lesson the teacher can identify trouble spots (such as vocabulary or figurative language) and instruct boys and girls on how to solve those problem areas. (The questions that accompany each guided reading lesson in most basals may be helpful in this area.) However, the teacher's responsibility is not complete until each child assumes an equal share of the responsibility for comprehension. Pupils must be taught to monitor their reading, taught to identify problems (such as cohesion), and taught problem-solving strategies. Skilled readers can use the following general strategies: ignore and read on; suspend judgment; form a tentative hypothesis; reread the current sentence; reread the previous context; or go to an expert source.[32]

After the reading lesson the teacher should focus the instruction on summarizing the entire text and relating it to other information or to other books or stories. All groups, and particularly the slower readers, need this kind of comprehension activity. Other activities include having children write their own stories and participate in oral discussions concerning the comparison of the most recently completed story to other stories or the contrast of characters found in various assigned selections. One activity which does *not* belong in this segment of the reading lesson is asking a series of detailed literal-level questions because boys and girls must not get the impression that reading is only a factual recall exercise.

Sorting Out Comprehension Problems

Many so-called comprehension problems are not really failures to understand the author's message, state some educators.[33] Instead, the child who fails to respond properly to a comprehension assignment may actually be encountering other difficulties that masquerade as comprehension problems. Teachers should therefore consider the following questions before sending the child back for more directed practice in comprehension skills:

A. Was the reader able to decode most of the words in the selection?

If the pupil seems generally confused about an entire selection, the teacher should ask him/her to choose a particularly difficult passage and read it aloud. Then, if the problem seems to involve decoding, the teacher should try to ensure that the pupil's next assignment involves material at a more accpetable level of decoding difficulty.

B. Did the reader understand the specialized vocabulary of the selection?

When the code is too complex, decoding cannot occur. So the teacher must give careful attention to technical vocabulary and introduce such words prior to their appearing in a reading assignment. Students will then be able to recognize those words in print quickly and be alert to important points in the assignment before reading begins.

C. Did the reader follow directions?

Teachers must be certain that children understand directions before starting a task and can do so by (1) having the directions rephrased by a student or aide or by (2) having the pupils do one sample question together as a written guide for children to follow.

D. Did the reader's experiential background interfere with comprehension?

When the reader's background is substantially different from that of the author's or the teacher's, a "wrong" interpretation of a paragraph or passage is possible even though that interpretation is completely understandable in terms of the reader's own experience. The teacher consequently should evaluate readers' backgrounds through informal discussion before making reading assignments and then either (1) change the assignment or (2) introduce the necessary background or concepts.

E. Was the reader interested in the selection?

Comprehension is likely to be enhanced when students have questions which they are seeking to answer or when the teacher has introduced the assignment in such a way that their curiosity is piqued or their enthusiasm aroused.

F. Was the reader able to express the answer correctly?

Teachers must be able to distinguish between a child's composition, spelling, or handwriting problems and his/her comprehension problems. One way to handle this situation is to ask for oral answers if written responses are not decipherable. Student dictation may help, too.

G. Did the reader understand the question?

Sometimes misunderstandings arise due to the form in which a question is asked and not to the student's lack of knowledge. When a student can repeat a question accurately and still does not understand it, the teacher should either (1) rephrase the question or (2) have another student explain what was asked.

H. Could both the teacher's and the child's answers be right?

Or could the child's answer be right and the teacher's wrong? As mentioned earlier in this chapter, teachers must be open to the possibility of several correct answers and not restrict themselves to answers suggested in the manuals or those based on personal interpretations of the author's message. While a teacher can hardly accept every answer a child offers, he or she should examine each answer on its own merits.

Evaluation of Pupils' Progress

There are numerous standardized reading achievement tests which are normed (or norm-referenced) and therefore let the teacher know how the students are doing in relation to a given sample population that has taken the test earlier. Some which have been favorably reviewed include:

a. *American School Achievement Tests, Part 1, Reading, Revised Edition* (Bobbs-Merrill, Indianapolis, IN).
   1. Primary Battery, grades 2–3: 25–35 minutes.
   2. Intermediate Battery, grades 4–6: 25–35 minutes.

b. *Comprehensive Tests of Basic Skills: Reading, Expanded Edition* (CTB/McGraw Hill, Monterey, CA).
   1. Reading, two levels: kindergarten 6–1.9 and grades 1.6–2.9. Each runs 90–101 minutes in two sessions.
   2. Reading and Reference Skills, two elementary levels: grades 2.5–4.9 and grades 4.5–6.9. Each runs 99–105 minutes in two sessions.

c. *Cooperative Primary Tests: Reading* (Addison-Wesley, Reading, MA).
   1. Form 12A, 12B, grades 1.5–2.5: 35 minutes.
   2. Form 23A, 23B, grades 2.5–3: 35 minutes.

d. *Gates-MacGinitie Reading Tests* (Houghton Mifflin, Boston).
   1. Primary A, grade 1: 40 (50) minutes in two sessions.
   2. Primary B, grade 2: 40 (50) minutes in two sessions.
   3. Primary C, grade 3: 50 (60) minutes in two sessions.
   4. Survey D, grades 4–6: 45 (60) minutes in two sessions.

e. *Metropolitan Achievement Tests: Reading* (Psychological Corporation, New York).
   1. Primary, grades 2.5–3.4: 48–60 minutes.
   2. Elementary, grades 3.5–4.9: 40–50 minutes.
   3. Intermediate, grades 5.0–6.9: 40–50 minutes.

f. *Sequential Tests of Educational Progress: Reading,* Series II (Addison-Wesley, Reading, MA).
   1. Form 4A, 4B, grades 4–6: 45–55 minutes.

g. *Stanford Achievement Tests, Reading Tests* (Harcourt Brace Jovanovich, New York).
   1. Primary Level 1, grades 1.5–2.4: 120 minutes in two sessions.
   2. Primary Level 2, grades 2.5–3.4: 120 minutes in two sessions.
   3. Primary Level 3, grades 3.5–4.4, 110 minutes in two sessions.
   4. Intermediate Level 1, grades 4.5–5.4: 115 minutes in two sessions.
   5. Intermediate Level 2, grades 5.5–6.9: 110 minutes in two sessions.[34]

Another type of reading test is criterion-referenced and can compare students against a pre-determined objective. In contrast to a norm-referenced test, a criterion-referenced test offers the teacher more specific data about any one student's strengths and weaknesses in the field of reading. Most basal series include skill tests which are criterion tests.

The teacher may also choose to develop his/her own criterion tests, following a format of objective multiple-choice testing recently developed by the California State Department of Education.[35] Since the Department believes that comprehension is the central goal of reading, the majority of reading questions are comprehension items with percentages ranging from 60 percent in the third grade to 80 percent in the sixth grade. Sample items from the instrument administered to third graders follow Reading Passages A and B:[36]

Passage A

The time is midnight. The full *moon* is *high* in the sky. Here and there a bonfire lights the beach. People are gathered around the fires, waiting. Suddenly, the beach is alive with thousands of *wiggling* fish as wave after wave carries them to shore. At once the people are splashing through the waves, snatching up the fish.

Does it sound like a wild story? It is not just a story. It is a grunion run, and it happens several times every year in southern California.

The grunion is a small, silvery fish that is between five and six inches long. The season for laying eggs is from the middle of February to early September. During those months, on the nights of the highest tide, the grunion swim to shore to lay their eggs in the sand. The next high tide uncovers the eggs. The baby grunion burst out like *popcorn* and ride the waves to sea.

Passage B

George *woke* up one bright Saturday morning feeling wonderful. He and Gloria were at last going to Disneyland.

After an hour's drive on the freeway, they were there!

The first thing they *saw* was Mickey Mouse leading his band to the railway station. Uncle John took a picture of the twins with Mickey Mouse.

"Let's go on the Matterhorn," *shouted* Gloria. "*I'll* sit here and watch," said Uncle John.

They climbed into a *car,* and soon they were at the top of the mountain. Then down they rushed, *faster* and faster, in and out of tunnels, flying like the wind.

All of a sudden they came to a stop. They were glad to be safely on the ground again!

They had many more exciting rides and saw lots of wonderful things.

As they rode home, tired but happy, they thanked Uncle John for a thrilling treat.

Skill Area	Description of Skill Area	Illustrative Test Question
I. Word Identification		
A. Phonics		
1. Vowels	The student will identify a word which rhymes with a word used and underlined in a passage or will identify a word which contains the same tested vowel sound as a word used and underlined in a test passage.	Mark the word the rhymes with *moon.* ○ tin ○ tune ○ tan (See Passage A.) ○ tone
2. Consonants	The student will identify a word which rhymes with a word used and underlined in a passage or will identify a word which contains the same tested consonant sound(s) as a word used and underlined in a passage.	Mark the word that has the same sound as the *c* in *car.* ○ chose ○ circle (See Passage B.) ○ color ○ chick
B. Structural analysis		
1. Prefixes, suffixes, and roots	The student will identify (1) the way in which a suffix or prefix alters the meaning of a base word; (2) the root or base form of a tested regular verb (for example, *hurried* → *hurry*); and (3) the semantic association between an irregular past tense of a verb and its infinitive (for example, *taught* → *teach*).	In the word *faster,* the *er* makes the word mean ○ not as fast. ○ more fast. (See Passage B.) ○ just as fast. ○ less fast.

Skill Area	Description of Skill Area	Illustrative Test Question
2. Contractions and compound words	The student will identify the words which make up a contraction or compound word, both of which are used and underlined in a passage.	The two words in *popcorn* are ○ po + pcorn. ○ pop + corn. (See Passage A.) ○ popc + orn. ○ popco + rn. The word *I'll* means the same as ○ is all. ○ I will. (See Passage B.) ○ it will. ○ I fill.
II. Vocabulary		
1. Recognizing word meanings	The student will identify the definitions, synonyms, and antonyms of words which are used and underlined in a passage.	In this story, *shouted* means ○ watched. ○ climbed. (See Passage B.) ○ yelled. ○ pictured. The opposite of *high* is ○ small. ○ alive. (See Passage A.) ○ low. ○ tall.
2. Using context	The student will use the context of a passage to identify the meaning of a multiple-meaning word which is used and underlined in a passage.	In this story, *saw* means ○ a tool. ○ to cut wood. (See Passage B.) ○ a fun ride. ○ looked at.
III. Comprehension		
Literal		
1. Details		
a. From a single sentence	The student will identify the verbatim answer to a question which is derived entirely from a single sentence within a passage.	Who took a picture? ○ Uncle John ○ George (See Passage B.) ○ Mickey Mouse ○ Gloria
b. From two or three sentences	The student will identify the verbatim answer to a question which is derived from putting together two or three sentences within a passage.	Where were the people waiting? ○ in a boat ○ near a house (See Passage A.) ○ under a tent ○ on the beach
2. Pronoun references	The student will answer a question which involves identifying the antecedent of a pronoun.	Who saw Mickey Mouse? ○ the band ○ George and Gloria (See Passage B.) ○ the mountain men ○ Aunt Mary

Skill Area	Description of Skill Area	Illustrative Test Question
3. Sequence	The student will answer a question which involves identifying the sequence of events, facts, or other elements in a passage.	Which of these does the story tell about last? ○ the bonfire ○ the baby grunion (See Passage A.) ○ laying eggs ○ the waiting people
B. Inferential/Interpretive		
1. Main ideas	The student will identify the primary topic of a passage.	This story is mostly about ○ a ride in the car. ○ Uncle John. (See Passage B.) ○ a day at Disneyland. ○ the Matterhorn.
2. Cause and effect	The student will associate a cause with an effect.	Why were people waiting on the beach? ○ to ride on the waves ○ to cook the popcorn (See Passage A.) ○ to see the moon ○ to snatch up the fish
3. Drawing conclusions a. About characters	The student will draw a conclusion about the feelings or attitudes of a character(s).	At the beginning of the story, Gloria probably felt ○ sad. ○ angry. (See Passage B.) ○ excited. ○ disappointed.
b. From details	The student will draw a conclusion from a detail in a story.	You can tell from the story that baby grunion probably ○ will die in very deep water. ○ need to be taught to swim. ○ will lay five or six eggs. (See Passage A.) ○ can stay alive in deep water.
c. From overall meaning	The student will draw a conclusion from the overall meaning of a story.	This story tells about ○ a day of fun and excitement. ○ a day of hard work. (See Passage B.) ○ a night of worry and fear. ○ a night of quiet rest.

Discussion Questions

1. Why does the basal reader approach continue to be the most popular way to teach reading in the United States?
2. How could or does the computer contribute to reading instruction?
3. What should be the role of the parent in the elementary school reading program?
4. Describe the type of reading/language program that a professionally staffed preschool can offer in an effort to meet parental demands.

Suggested Projects

1. Administer the checklist for beginning reading readiness to a five- or six-year-old child. Record your findings.
2. Visit a kindergarten and observe which kinds of reading readiness skills are presented in that kindergarten. Take note of the amount of time spent on those skills.
3. Try using the language experience approach with an older nonreader or with an immigrant child who has only recently arrived in the United States and is either LEP (limited-English proficient) or NEP (non-English proficient).
4. Choose a basal reader story at a grade level that interests you. Then for that story develop four literal comprehension questions, four interpretive comprehension questions, and four critical/applicative/problem-solving questions.
5. Conduct an individual reading conference with a child in the primary or intermediate grades shortly after the girl or boy has read independently a self-selected book.
6. Examine six series of contemporary basal readers (together with their teachers' manuals) and evaluate each in terms of its balance of ethnic groups, sexes, geographic settings, and literary genres. Which of the manuals would you feel most comfortable using?
7. Set up the learning center on reading shown in Figure 9.5.

Related Readings

Aukerman, R. C. 1984. *Approaches to Beginning Reading.* Second edition. New York: John Wiley.

Criscuolo, N. P. 1984. "Parent Involvement in Reading: Surface or Meaningful?" *Childhood Education, 60,* pp. 181–184.

Durkin, D. 1984. "Is There a Match between What Elementary Teachers Do and What Basal Reader Manuals Recommend?" *Reading Teacher, 37,* pp. 734–744.

Fredericks, A. 1984. *The Reading Comprehension Idea Book.* Glenview, Il.: Scott, Foresman.

Kusik, P. 1984. "Winning at Reading Games," *Academic Therapy, 19,* pp. 341–349.

Reutzel, D. 1985. "Story Maps Improve Comprehension," *Reading Teacher, 38,* pp. 400–404.

Schickedanz, J., and Sullivan, M. 1984. "Mom, What Does U-F-F Spell?" *Language Arts, 61,* pp. 7–17.

Searloss, L., and Readence, J. 1985. *Helping Children Learn to Read,* Englewood Cliffs, NJ: Prentice-Hall.

Vukelich, C. 1984. "Parents' Role in the Reading Process: A Review of Practical Suggestions and Ways to Communicate with Parents," *Reading Teacher,* 37, pp. 472–477.

Warncke, E. W., and Shipman, D. A. 1984. *Group Assessment in Reading.* Englewood Cliffs, NJ: Prentice-Hall.

Figure 9.5. Language Arts Learning Center: Reading.

TYPE OF CENTER:	**Literature—Sequence Reinforcement**	TIME: Unlimited
GRADE LEVEL:	2-4	NUMBER OF STUDENTS: 3

INSTRUCTIONAL OBJECTIVE: The child will be able to analyze and read the comic strips and put them in sequential order, using the pictures and/or words as a guide.

MATERIALS: Ten 4-frame comic strips (each frame must be separated and pasted on a plain 4″ × 5″ index card), duplicates of the entire comic strip in correct order for the answer strips (these should be pasted on 3″ × 9″ construction paper). Each comic strip and its duplicate should have the same number. This number should be written on the back of each index card that contains a frame from that strip, and also on the corresponding duplicate answer strip. The center should have an answer pocket and a covered box for the playing cards.

DIRECTIONS:

1. One student plays "dealer."
2. The dealer removes the playing cards from the box. He deals four cards to every player.
3. Use the rest of the cards for playing cards. Take the top card from the pile of playing cards and place it next to the pile. This is the discard pile—all cards are face up.
4. The first player chooses a card from either pile. After the card has been chosen, the player may keep it but must put one down in the discard pile.
5. The game continues until one player has four cards with the same number on the back. The player must then try to put the comic strip in the correct order. The player must do both to win the game.
6. Answers can be found on the answer sheets.

EVALUATION: The children can check their own answers to see if they have accomplished the task. The teacher will observe whether the children become more proficient at placing pictures in sequential order. This activity may also indicate the students' ability to visualize a sequence of ideas.

Chapter Notes

1. California State Department of Education, *Reading Framework for California Public Schools* (Sacramento: The Department, 1980), p. 3.
2. J. B. Carroll, "The Nature of the Reading Process," in *Readings on Reading Instruction,* 3rd ed., A. J. Harris and E. R. Sipay, eds. (New York: Longman, 1984), pp. 31–32.
3. California State Department of Education, *Reading Framework,* pp. 2, 4.
4. P. Burns, B. Roe, and E. Ross, *Teaching Reading in Today's Elementary Schools,* 3rd ed. (Boston: Houghton Mifflin, 1984), pp. 20–24.
5. D. Hammill and G. McNutt, "Language Abilities and Reading: A Review of the Literature on Their Relationship," *Elementary School Journal,* 1980, *80,* p. 273.
6. D. Lapp and J. Flood, *Teaching Reading to Every Child,* 2nd ed. (New York: Macmillan, 1983), p. 79.
7. O. K. Buros, *The Eighth Mental Measurements Yearbook,* Volume II (Highland Park, New Jersey: Gryphon Press, 1978), pp. 1336–1338, 1341.
8. P. Weaver, *Research within Reach* (Washington, D.C.: National Institute of Education, 1978), p. 44.
9. Clark County (Nev.) School District, *Reading and the Kindergarten Child* (Las Vegas: The District, n.d.), pp. 1–12.
10. R. C. Aukerman, *The Basal Reader Approach to Reading* (New York: John Wiley, 1981), pp. 8–11.
11. W. Otto, R. Rude, and D. Spiegel, *How to Teach Reading* (Reading, Massachusetts: Addison-Wesley, 1979), pp. 243–247.
12. R. V. Allen, *Language Experiences in Communication* (Boston: Houghton Mifflin, 1976), pp. 51–53.
13. J. D. Cooper and T. W. Worden, *The Classroom Reading Program in the Elementary School* (New York: Macmillan, 1983), pp. 205–206.
14. L. Harris and C. Smith, *Reading Instruction: Diagnostic Teaching in the Classroom,* 3rd ed. (New York: Holt, 1980), pp. 363–364.
15. K. Goodman, "Reading: A Psycholinguistic Guessing Game," in *Readings,* A. J. Harris and E. R. Sipay, eds., pp. 45–52.
16. D. Schubert and T. Torgerson, *Improving the Reading Program,* 5th ed. (Dubuque, Iowa: Wm. C. Brown Company Publishers, 1981), pp. 249–252.
17. M. Ceprano, "A Review of Selected Research on Methods of Teaching Sight Words," *Reading Teacher,* 1981, *35,* pp. 314–322.
18. Otto, Rude, and Spiegel, *How to Teach Reading,* pp. 112–113.
19. Schubert and Torgerson, *Improving the Reading Program,* pp. 255–256.
20. A. J. Harris and E. R. Sipay, *How to Increase Reading Ability,* 7th ed. (New York: Longman, Inc., 1980), pp. 390–391.
21. Schubert and Torgerson, *Improving the Reading Program,* pp. 258–259.
22. Burns, Roe, and Ross, *Teaching Reading,* pp. 113–114.
23. B. R. Rosso and R. Emans, "Children's Use of Phonic Generalizations," *Reading Teacher,* 1981, *34,* pp. 653–657.
24. R. M. Wilson et al., *Programmed Reading for Teachers* (Columbus, Ohio: Charles E. Merrill, 1980), pp. 126–130.
25. C. R. Wilson, "Teaching Reading Comprehension by Connecting the Known to the New," *Reading Teacher,* 1983, *36,* pp. 382–385.
26. P. D. Pearson, "Asking Questions about Stories," in *Readings,* A. J. Harris and E. R. Sipay, eds., p. 274.
27. *Ibid.,* pp. 281–282.
28. Wilson et al., *Programmed Reading,* pp. 138–141.

29. M. Rowe, *Teaching Science as Continuous Inquiry* (New York: McGraw Hill, 1973), pp. 243–293.
30. C. R. Wilson, "Teaching Reading Comprehension," *Reading Teacher*, pp. 385–389.
31. T. Raphael, *The Effect of Metacognitive Strategy Awareness Training on Students' Question-Answering Behavior* (Urbana: University of Illinois, Center for the Study of Reading, 1983).
32. A. Collins and E. Smith, *Teaching the Process of Reading Comprehension*, Technical Report No. 182 (Urbana: University of Illinois, Center for the Study of Reading, 1980).
33. D. Spiegel, "Ten Ways to Sort Out Reading Comprehension Problems," in *Readings*, A. J. Harris and E. R. Sipay, eds., pp. 298–302.
34. O. K. Buros, *The Eighth Mental Measurements Yearbook*, Volume II (Highland Park, New Jersey: Gryphon Press, 1978), pp. 1163–1226.
35. California Assessment Program, *Survey of Basic Skills, Grade 3: Rationale and Content* (Sacramento: California State Department of Education, 1980); and California Assessment Program, *Survey of Basic Skills, Grade 6: Rationale and Content* (Sacramento: California State Department of Education, 1982).
36. California Assessment Program, *Survey of Basic Skills, Grade 3*, pp. 7–12.

Vocabulary Development 10

Objectives

General vocabularies that each child possesses
Factors that influence vocabulary growth
Guidelines for a curriculum in vocabulary development
The three major approaches for learning English vocabulary

Discover As You Read This Chapter If*

1. Reading comprehension improves only when children have opportunities to practice their new words.
2. Girls and boys in the intermediate grades know more words than children in the primary grades.
3. Elementary school children have three general vocabularies.
4. The first vocabulary to develop is the speaking vocabulary.
5. The vocabulary to grow most rapidly during the elementary school years is the reading vocabulary.
6. Environment is a major factor influencing vocabulary growth.
7. Direct instruction in vocabulary is relatively unimportant in the teaching of content areas.
8. Internal context clues concern mastery of affixes and mastery of roots.
9. Learning to use a thesaurus is a skill for students beyond the elementary school.
10. Students' names provide an interesting springboard for an etymology project in the elementary grades.

*Answers to these true-or-false statements may be found in Appendix 6.

The modern teacher plans many firsthand experiences for young children in order that they may become more able to attach meanings to words and to supply a variety of expressions. (Photo courtesy of the *Daily News Tribune,* Fullerton, California.)

School success depends heavily upon the size and utility of the child's stock of words. Due to the verbal nature of most classroom activities, a knowledge of words and the ability to use those words competently are essential to academic success.

In reality, a vocabulary building program is a service program. It is valuable both in its own right as well as for its contribution to reading and other curricular areas and to the personal development of boys and girls.

Classroom teachers then should be vitally interested in establishing a systematic approach to vocabulary development. They should seize every opportunity to awaken the children to the joy of hearing, repeating, and understanding new words. The boys and girls in turn are faced with a twofold task. First, they must learn as many as possible of the thousands of words or symbols that their culture has assigned to various objects, sensations, and processes. Then they must be able to recall the object, sensation, or process when the naming word is mentioned.

As children begin to acquire a vocabulary, the words they learn will have meaning if each word is linked with something the children have actually experenced through their senses. Vocabulary development is generally understood to be the result of the combined study of concepts and of symbols. Only experience can provide the mind with the concepts for which the spoken or visual symbols must be located as needs arise. Children cannot and do not acquire a large vocabulary by accumulating a stock of words as symbols for definitions apart from concepts.

Nor do boys and girls increase their vocabulary banks without repeated opportunities to *practice* each new word with which they are presented. A recent review of eight vocabulary studies completed between 1963 and 1982, mostly with pupils in grades four through six, has shown that, while all of the programs did increase children's word knowledge, very few of them reported any corresponding improvement in reading comprehension.[1] Those that did had demanded large amounts of practice of the instructed words. Length and breadth of training in the use of the words helped promote automacity of lexical access and, thereby, comprehension. Active attempts by the children to use the new words and even to make decisions about their use also had positive effects on performance of reading comprehension tasks.

Growth in Word Meaning

As boys and girls acquire experiences and learn to regard the environment in various ways, their ability to attach meaning to words changes and grows. Four ways in which this growth develops have been identified.

First, *children are able to see and label an increasing number of critical properties of events, objects, persons, and actions.* Young boys or girls are solely concerned with the physical attributes of size, color, and texture. More experienced children, however, can describe an object or condition in terms of other physical attributes as well. Similarly there is growth in the connotative meanings that boys or girls attach to a person or an object. Initially they may have only been able to experience anger or happiness but later they experience many other reactions as well to events or people. As their experience broadens they are able to identify more functional attributes and more aesthetic qualities of objects and actions.

Second, *children acquire a more precise label for any critical property as they begin to differentiate shades of meaning.* Young girls or boys experience everything so simply that they only need words for either end of the meaning spectrum: *rough/smooth, happy/sad, round/square.* More experienced children differentiate the extremes of meaning and try to qualify their words. Still later, pupils acquire standard labels or create their own metaphors for clear meaning.

Third, *children's words become more generalized words;* a single word may be applied to more objects, in more contexts, from more physical points of view, and in more time frames. Pencils for example, are no longer just yellow or wooden. Instead, they can be purple or green, dull or sharp, thin or oversized. They may be used in school or at home, in the car or at the library media center. They may be mechanical pencils, drawing pencils, grease pencils.

Fourth, while they are differentiating and generalizing their experiences, *children are building a supply of expressions relating to any one element of meaning.* Young boys or girls have only one way to describe a certain color. More experienced pupils retain their original expressions but simultaneously collect new expressions. They thereby become better able to communicate personally and to understand the speech and writing of others.

In an effort to examine these aspects of growth in word meaning, children at four different maturity levels were asked to define or describe the word *horse*. The responses revealed that *boys and girls at every level tend to observe and label a common property of size*. The children's answers were categorized by properties, connotations, synonyms, class names and contexts, and these are enumerated in Figure 10.1.

Figure 10.1. Children's Meanings for *Horse,* by Developmental Levels.

Properties

Level 1
a black one
hair
legs -ride it -walk

Level 2
big, high
brown, white
long tails, 4 feet, whiskery things on their necks
walk, run, gallop
ride 'em
(*demonstrates noise*)

Level 3
kinda big, some are little
brown, white, spotted, kinda blonde
some have short tails, usually long though, manes
trot, gallop, some do fancy steps
work, pull things, ride 'em
makes a sort of snorting noise (*demonstrates*)

Level 4
big compared to ponies, small compared to elephants;
tall—measure height in hands—about 4 hands high
many color combinations; color often indicates what *kind* of horse it is
manes (sometimes braided); hooves-shod;
walk, gallop, trot, canter, fight with teeth and hooves
used for work, entertainment, transportation

Connotations

Level 1
nice

Level 2
scary
neat
yech
stinks
nice

Level 3
sometimes scary
nice if they just stand still!
the ones I've seen are friendly

Figure 10.1 (cont.)

Level 4
can be mean if mistreated
brave (like Black Beauty)
depends on what kind of horse it is

Synonyms

Level 1	horsie	
Level 2	horse	colt pony
Level 3	horse	pony colt Shetland
Level 4	horse, "cheval," nag plough horse, beast of burden stallion	 pony mare

Class Names

Level 1
horse

Level 2
animal
horse lion cat elephant

young = colt, pony

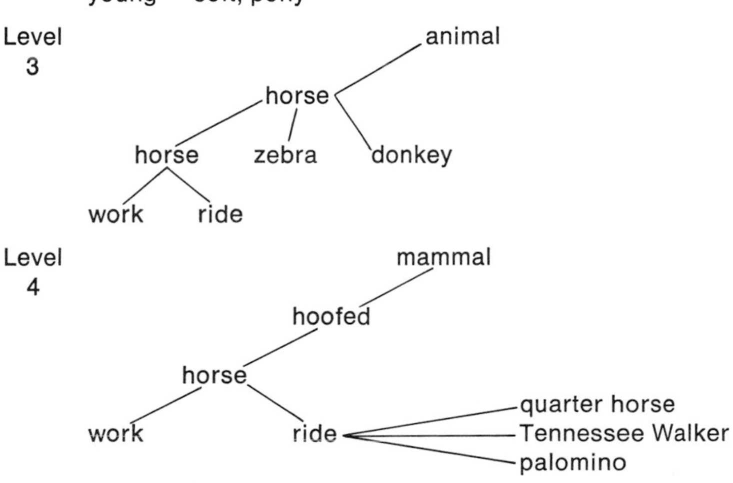

Figure 10.1 (cont.)

Contexts

Level 1	at Storyland Zoo
Level 2	on my grandpa's farm a horse at Storyland stampede my brother in grade 6 knows a girl who has one
Level 3	on farms — pasture, barn here, Texas circus riding stable TV — cowboy stories, parades
Level 4	farms show ring use in past — warriors, Robin Hood historical development all over the world, not on the moon

Source: ELEMENTARY LANGUAGE ARTS HANDBOOK (Edmonton: Alberta Department of Education, 1973), pp. 19–21.

Factors Influencing Vocabulary Growth

There are many specific factors which significantly affect the development of vocabulary in children. While some of them are beyond the domain of the teacher, others can be influenced by his or her planning.

The first factor is the controversial matter concerning the *socioeconomic status of the child's family.* Johnson and Barrett's survey of word recognition among 210 primary children revealed that boys and girls from schools that served families of upper socioeconomic status did better than children from schools that served families of lower socioeconomic status.[2] While the age at which significant differences first appear in vocabulary performance among boys and girls of varying socioeconomic groups has not been firmly set, some studies do indicate that these differences have been established by age three.

Nevertheless, a language-model, home environment alone cannot assure a wide vocabulary for children who are not alert and able to learn. Since there is a high correlation between vocabulary and *intelligence,* what children gain from their environment is conditioned by their native capacities to learn. Retarded readers have a limited writing vocabulary and possess a listening vocabulary that is larger than their reading vocabulary. Bright children, on the other hand, remember their experiences with greater clarity. They can abstract and generalize words and terms that are beyond those of pupils of limited mental ability.

The *age or grade level* of the child is an important factor too. The older the child, the more words he or she knows. Eighth graders commonly recognize four to six times as many words as first graders. Even second graders outperform first graders, according to two separate vocabulary surveys.[3] Children in grade two recognized 90 percent of the 306 words presented; children in grade one, 64 percent.

The factor of *motivation* is always crucial. Dale and O'Rourke believe that motivated individuals can increase their working vocabularies by 10 percent.[4] Such an increase will result, in part, from bringing into sharper focus those words, those parts of words, and those expressions whose meanings are presently fuzzy. The teacher can help motivate students into moving some of their words/word phrases out of a so-called twilight zone into their working vocabularies.

Such *instruction and guidance in the use of words* is vital. Besides teachers, children's parents, grandparents, and other interested adults—at home and in the community—can and should take the time to explain unfamiliar vocabulary to boys and girls. Conversing with someone like the mail carrier, for instance, can help children enrich and refine their use of words.

The *continued and regular listening to storybooks* is a critical factor. Vocabulary appears to be learned best by young children in a context of emotional and intellectual meaning. Pupils, especially those who are slow academically, find it difficult to deal with words in isolation. Reading aloud to boys and girls, however, has resulted in increasing their knowledge of words as well as the quality of their vocabularies.

Another contributing factor covers the *personal interests* that the child has developed. Boys and girls engrossed in sports or science readily acquire the specialized vocabulary that their avocation demands. Interest centers in the classroom which are properly planned and frequently changed can stimulate word study too.

Sex differences have also been noted in all types of vocabularies. Girls develop larger speaking vocabularies prior to school entrance and they soon exceed elementary school boys in reading vocabularies. These differences, however, level off as the pupils enter adolescence.

Television viewing is yet another factor. It offers simultaneous visual-auditory presentation of vocabulary. It promotes concept building and offers experience with standard English, allowing many pupils to increase both their speaking and reading vocabularies. However, the teacher must stress *selective television viewing* if he or she wishes to insure that the medium will make a useful contribution to the vocabulary growth of the children.

The *social organizations* to which boys and girls belong make a difference in their vocabularies. If they regularly attend a synagogue or church, for example, they are more likely to be acquainted with Biblical terms than if they did not attend.

The final factor is *locale* and this is growing less significant under the influence of the mass media. Still, there are words dealing with coal mining or condominiums that are not commonplace to everyone in the nation.

Types of Vocabularies

Each child has four general and related vocabularies with which the elementary teacher must work. Two of them—the listening and reading vocabularies—are receptive and emphasize understanding and decoding. Speaking and writing vocabularies, on the other hand, are expressive and can be viewed as encoding in its broadest definition. All four vocabularies overlap and develop continuously, although at different rates, into adulthood. Of course, initially it is the listening and speaking vocabularies which contribute to reading and writing skills.

The *listening or hearing vocabulary* refers to all the words that children recognize and understand when they hear them in an oral context. It is the first vocabulary to develop during the language acquisition stage and is also the one that continues to grow most rapidly during the elementary school years. It remains substantially larger than a pupil's visual vocabulary until the age of ten, at which time the size difference diminishes.

The teacher must realize that the listening child may comprehend one meaning of a word or one shade of meaning and yet be wholly ignorant of the other denotations. In addition, the teacher must recognize that the size of a primary child's listening vocabulary ordinarily will not affect the reading progress experienced by the pupil until the third grade.

The *speaking vocabulary* includes all the words that children use in everyday speech. It forms the basis for the development of the reading and writing vocabularies, and it is at the oral/aural level that vocabulary development generally takes place in the classroom. The recommendation has been made that pupils should possess sizable speaking vocabularies in a language before they begin reading lessons in that language whether it be their first or second tongue.

The *reading vocabulary* consists of all the words that children recognize and understand in print or in writing. When boys and girls enter school, their reading vocabularies are generally limited to their names and the few words they have learned to recognize from billboards, television, and food container labels. It is during reading instruction that children build their word banks. By the time they reach reading maturity in the upper grades their reading vocabularies overtake and surpass their oral/aural vocabularies. The more pupils read, the more their reading vocabularies grow.

Reported to lag perpetually behind the other three vocabularies is the *writing vocabulary*. It is the last to develop and includes only the words that children can use in written compositions. It is closely tied to spelling instruction. Pupils' writing vocabularies reportedly overlap more than 90 percent with their speaking vocabularies. Moreover, writing vocabularies are generally nonexistent when children begin school.

Planned instruction in any one area of vocabulary tends to result in improvement in all four areas. They are interrelated and uniformly based on conceptual development.

A planned and systematic approach to vocabulary instruction yields greater gains than incidental instruction, and a variety of instructional methods seems to be more beneficial than any single method. (Photo courtesy of the Fountain Valley School District, Fountain Valley, California.)

Guidelines for a Curriculum in Vocabulary Development

Based upon research studies and classroom experience, the following dozen principles are suggested for promoting vocabulary growth among elementary school pupils.

Developing a vocabulary requires understanding of the meanings and concepts which underlie words. Concepts may be expanded both by differentiation and by generalization. Children learn to group lemons and limes under *fruit.* They also learn to separate *cats* into Angora, Manx, and Persian. Boys and girls with learning difficulties or bilingual backgrounds find it hard to recognize different meanings of a single word such as *big.*

Vocabulary development is closely related to general maturation and varied interaction with a stimulating environment. Teachers generally cannot expect adequate vocabularies in immature, impoverished, or retarded children. Although heredity sets the limits of possible development, the child with an IQ slightly below normal who is growing up in an environment favorable to language development is likely to have a better vocabulary than the child with an IQ slightly above normal who is being reared in relatively sterile surroundings.

The vocabulary of the home and home community greatly affects the school program in vocabulary development. Not only have children learned to listen and speak long before they enter kindergarten, but even after they have been enrolled in school, they continue to spend many hours listening and talking at home and in their neighborhoods. Little wonder that if the type of vocabulary that the boys and girls hear and use outside of school is inadequate, it will partly offset the teacher's efforts to help them improve their stock of words. In this delicate area of home-school relations it is critical that care be taken so that children do not develop feelings of inadequacy about their families or communities due to matters of vocabulary.

Children need direct instruction in vocabulary, and teachers of beginning readers especially must be certain that the labels and terms they use are fully comprehended by the pupils.[5] Since word boundaries are almost impossible to identify during oral language, it is better to have the children's own words shown in print; e.g., during language-experience activities, both group and individual. Such direct instruction of vocabulary is also important in the teaching of social studies, science, mathematics, and other content areas.

Not only does planned vocabulary instruction yield greater gains than incidental or unorganized instruction but a variety of instructional methods appears to be more effective than any single method. Wide reading or listening alone will not guarantee vocabulary growth. Yet either or both skills bring children in contact with new words once they have become sensitive to contextual and structural analyses. Word games may be useful in heightening motivation, but their use is probably as an accessory rather than as a primary instructional device. The three major groups of useful strategies for fostering vocabulary development are labelled *learner's independent approach, learner's dependent approach,* and *teacher's direct instructional approach.* Each is described later in this chapter.

For beginning readers word shape alone does not seem to be a useful word recognition technique. Too many first-grade words have the same configuration. Fluent readers, however, as well as other students who are beyond the developmental level of beginning readers, do find and use helpful information in word configurations.[6]

In the lower grades growth in the pupil's meaning vocabulary is obtained chiefly through oral methods. The words that boys and girls encounter in primary reading books are chosen partly from concepts that have meaning for those children. Therefore, it is in these grades that much emphasis must be placed on vocabulary improvement through oral communication. The issue is critical in view of the fact that the absolute scale of vocabulary development and the longitudinal studies of educational achievement indicate that approximately 50 percent of general achievement at grade twelve has been reached by the end of grade three.

Vocabulary development must grow out of experiences that are real to the learner. A teacher cannot overlook the need for carefully structured experiences. For primary children especially, firsthand experiences are the best and often the only source of conceptual development. The teacher must recognize that pupils at any level who lag behind their peers in vocabulary growth do not need additional written work. Instead they will profit from nonprint media and direct experiences.

Comprehension, an integral part of word knowledge, was once defined as relating new experiences to those already known. Little wonder then that students with enriched backgrounds of experience bring more to the vocabulary which they hear or read than do children with limited experiential backgrounds.

Children's work with words should be as active as the teacher can arrange. They can participate in physically active word games, they can discuss literal/figurative word meanings, and they can record words in their personal notebooks. Other instructional activities are outlined later in this chapter.

Context has a facilitative effect on the learning of new words, although the role which it plays in the recognition of any one single word will depend upon the level of sophistication of the reader, the strength of the context, and the word itself.[7] Teaching words in isolation creates a transfer problem for children who have "learned" words separately one at a time or else in random order but have difficulty later recognizing in context. One recent study of fourth graders in a rural elementary school showed that, while both good readers and poor readers were significantly more accurate when reading connected text compared to reading the identical words in random order, it was the poor readers who particularly benefitted from the additional information contained in the contextual clues.[8]

Furthermore, contexts presented for the purpose of vocabulary development should be *pedagogical* contexts or those particularly designed for teaching designated unfamiliar words.[9] The second kind of contexts are *natural* contexts, covering four categories (mis-directive, non-directive, general, and directive) of which only the directive type is apt to lead the reader to the specific meaning for a word.

The dictionary is a valuable tool for extending vocabularies. Although the proper use of the picture dictionary is introduced in grade one, some pupils never seem to grasp the importance of any dictionary or develop the habit of using one. The teacher should therefore informally evaluate the dictionary competencies of the class and periodically schedule group lessons in the use of the dictionary. Also the teacher should insist that each child have access to a dictionary appropriate to his or her reading and maturity levels.

Vocabulary improvement requires periodic use of the new words by the teacher and by the pupils in conversation and discussion as well as in printed material. There must be adequate opportunities to use the new vocabulary in order to classify and reinforce word meanings. Only when a child has made a word his or her own has that word been mastered. The process does take time and rapid gains in vocabulary occur less frequently than in comprehension or rate of reading.

Sometimes children who have acquired words in their reading vocabularies fail to use them in their speech. It may be that they do not know how to pronounce those words properly and they need to be reminded of still another use of the dictionary.

Teaching English Vocabulary: Methodology

The foundations of vocabulary development are laid in the home during the preschool years. The school builds upon those foundations. It introduces new words to children during each curricular activity. It also teaches them how to develop their word power independently both in and out of school.

The process of vocabulary building involves sensory perception of an object (or the attributes of an object) or perception of the relationships of objects with one another. As each new perception is added to the earlier ones, the composite is then associated with familiar words or with new words spoken or written by other people.

Teachers must recognize that the more pupils learn about a given vocabulary concept, the broader and deeper their understanding of that concept becomes. O'Rourke terms this the BVD strategy for enlarging children's word stock; i.e., the broader (B) the knowledge of synonyms for the vocabulary (V) concept of *old,* for example, the deeper (D) the knowledge of the basic concept.[10] Conversely, the deeper the children's understanding of the concept of *old,* the broader their knowledge of suitable synonyms.

There are many ways to help children acquire word knowledge and proficiency, including audio and visual experiences. Which method of vocabulary instruction works best at a particular grade level or with a particular type of student, however, has not yet been firmly established. Nevertheless, there are three broad headings of approaches for developing vocabulary growth in the classroom: the *teacher's direct instructional approach;* the *learner's independent approach;* and the *learner's dependent approach.* Whether any specific method falls into one category or another depends primarily upon the amount of teacher/adult follow-up that is required once the child has acquired the technique.

Teacher's Direct Instructional Approach

One-five step strategy for teaching new words, especially sight words which have unusual or infrequent letter combinations, is as follows:

1. *Seeing the word.* The new word is first written on a flashcard, a wall chart, the chalkboard, or worksheet. It is then uttered in an oral context. Finally, with some nouns (e.g., *clock, squash*), three-dimensional objects or realia can be displayed and labelled, in much the same way that this occurs in ESL (English as a Second Language) classrooms. With many other words (e.g., *astronomer, cloud*), flat pictures can be used to promote understanding of the new terms.
2. *Discussing the word.* After step one, the new word (e.g., *cavity*) is reviewed orally and tied to earlier or on-going experiences/interests of the boys and girls.
3. *Using the word.* Following steps one and two, the children relate orally or write a sentence which uses the new word. Sometimes they may offer synonyms or synonymous phrases. In either case, the teacher writes the sentence on the chalkboard in an effort to clear up promptly any misunderstandings (as in homographs like *lead/lead, conduct/conduct*).
4. *Defining the word.* After steps one, two, and three, the boys and girls tell in their own words what the new term means. They should not need to use a dictionary to define a common word like *manufacture.*

5. *Writing the word.* Following steps one-four, boys and girls can practice writing the new word in their personal dictionaries. They can also write the word during some of the instructional activities outlined later in this chapter. It takes considerable repetition of practice and review in a variety of contexts to provide the necessary overlearning of an unfamiliar word to make it part of the children's vocabulary.[11]

All of the steps described above are involved in the Vocabulary Self-Collection Strategy (VSS) which can be implemented in the classroom, especially with intermediate students, with no additional costs or lengthy curriculum revisions.[12] While teachers will wish to make adaptations to meet individual classroom needs, the Strategy essentially works like this:

> On Monday the teacher and every pupil each bring in two words which the owner feels the entire class should know. The words are *written* on the board (with the teacher offering assistance with spelling if necessary) so that everyone can *see* them. Each owner *defines* his/her words and *tells* why they are important to learn.
>
> The class now prunes the list to a pre-determined size by eliminating duplicates and familiar words and by keeping high-frequency/important words. Then the owner of each word still on the list *defines* it again, and the teacher and class *discuss* the words while the students *write* the words in their vocabulary journals together with the definitions.
>
> During the next few days the students *use* the words from the class list in *writing* stories, dialogues, or plays, in making or solving crossword puzzles, or in other activities.
>
> At the end of the week the students may be tested on the class list. The following Monday the cycle begins again.

Since VSS emphasizes context because students must describe where they found their words and why those words are important, it is also a worthwhile approach for use in classes enrolling children learning English as a second languge. Too, it is a technique which stresses daily encounters with the words under study, preferably on a five-day cycle.

One recent two-year study with fourth graders also called for daily (30-minute) lessons, with each set of words taught during a five-day cycle.[13] The researchers concluded that it was the frequency and richness of the pupil encounters with the new vocabulary that contributed to how well those words were learned. Each word was given between 10 and 15 exposures during the weekly cycle, and strategies included oral production, defining, sentence generation, learning games involving speed of response, and competition for points on a Word Wizard Chart awarded to children who had heard/seen/used the new words outside of class. Results showed that the instructed children made significantly greater gains, after the first year of implementation, on a standardized measure of reading comprehension and vocabulary than did the boys and girls who had not received the instruction.

Learner's Independent Approach

As soon as the teacher has introduced a child to any one of the three major techniques or subheadings of this approach, the boy or girl may unlock the meaning of many unknown words by using knowledge of familiar words. The three techniques are using *external context-clue methods* of word attack, *mastery of affixes,* and *mastery of roots.* The last two may also be grouped together as morphological or internal context-clue methods.

Using External Context Clues

By using such clues a child can frequently figure out the meaning of a strange word without using the dictionary. Therefore, the teacher must demonstrate the various kinds of external context clues so that the child will be aware of their availability. The teacher can (a) construct several sentences to illustrate each kind of clue; (b) point out random context clues in paragraphs the pupil may be reading; or (c) present sentences which typify three or four kinds of clues and let the pupil explain which kind each sentence represents. Dale and O'Rourke have delineated the following kinds of external clues (together with illustrative sentences) which students can learn to recognize:

1. *Formal definition* or expressing the meaning of a word in a direct statement. *Example:* A phoneme is one of a group of distinct sounds that comprise the words of the English language.
2. *Definition by example* or defining a word by example alone or further clarifying a formal definition. *Example:* An example of a phoneme is the *f* in *fan* or the *n* in *fan.*
3. *Definition by description* or listing the physical characteristics of the object representing the word. *Example:* An orange is a reddish-yellow, round, juicy fruit. (A definition by description often does not distinguish one word from others in its class. It does, however, distinguish among classes.)
4. *Definition by comparison* or stretching the meanings of words creatively even to the extent of sometimes using similes or metaphors. *Example:* The map of Italy is shaped like a boot.
5. *Definition by contrast* or telling the reader what the word is not. *Example:* A tomato is not a vegetable. (The effectiveness of this context clue depends heavily on the reader's experience.)
6. *Defining by synonym* or providing a short similar word that is closer to common usage than the original word. *Example:* Bondage is slavery.
7. *Defining by antonym* or providing a short, opposite word often used to show the extreme of an object or idea. *Example:* She was willing but he was loath to walk to the stadium.
8. *Definition by apposition* or placing a clarifying word or phrase next to another noun or pronoun. *Example:* Jute, the plant, grows in India.
9. *Definition by origin* or providing a setting in which the word was first used. *Example:* Samuel Maverick was a Texan whose cattle were unbranded wanderers.[14]

Most context clues demand some degree of inferential thinking. The reader should gradually learn to use the sense of the sentence or the surrounding sentences as an aid in identifying the probable meaning of a difficult word.

Teachers should be aware of the results of a recent study in the use of context clues for vocabulary growth.[15] It involved third and fifth graders in a midwestern semi-rural community school who worked for eight weeks with four different methods of learning 12 new and difficult words each week. The context method proved significantly more effective than (a) using the dictionary, (b) categorizing the new word with other familiar words, or (c) associating known synonyms with the new word. It worked equally well for girls and for boys. Although good readers not unexpectedly did significantly better with the method than did poor readers, nevertheless the context technique was the most effective for both groups and for both third and fifth graders.

In this instance the context method introduced new words in several sentences, one of which was defining. Then after these sentences had been studied with the assistance of the teacher, the student was asked to apply the meaning of the new word in a written response concerning his/her personal experiences.

Incidentally, current language arts texts for the elementary school sometimes contain exercises to help pupils learn about context clues. Those that do may begin as early as the primary levels. Teachers' manuals and/or pupil workbooks for major basal reading series always include such exercises.

Using Internal Context Clues: Mastery of Affixes

While most boys and girls accept the importance of context, some of them do not understand morphology and how words also derive meaning from their component parts. To introduce this valuable generalization, the teacher must start with a familiar word, break it into meaningful parts, and then transfer the meaning of these parts to new words. The teacher should move stepwise from known words (*triangle* or *good*) to unknown words (*tricolor* or *goodness*). Children will then be able to infer the meaning of a difficult word if (a) they know the meaning of the prefix/suffix used to form the word, and (b) they realize that meanings of mastered prefixes and suffixes can be transferred from one word to another.

The value of such mastery can be quickly shown by an examination of Edward Thorndike's list of the 20,000 most common words in the English language. Five thousand words or 25 percent of those listed have prefixes. Of this group 82 percent use one of these fourteen prefixes: *ab* (away from), *ad* (toward or to), *be* (overly or on all sides), *com, con, co* (together or with), *de* (downward, reversal, or from), *dis* (apart from, not, opposite), *en* (in, into, or to cover), *ex* (former or out of), *in* (not or into), *pre* (before), *pro* (for, before, or in favor of), *re* (again or restore), *sub* (beneath or under), and *un* (not or the opposite of).

Common derivational suffixes that children should learn in an effort to develop their vocabularies independently include: *able, ble, ible* (can be done or inclined to), *al, ial* (relating to), *fy* (make or form into), *ic* or *ical* (in the nature of), *ism* (system or state of), *ist* (person who), *less* (without), *let* (small), *ment* (concrete result, process, or state of), *ness* (quality or condition of), *ory* (place where), and *ward* or *wards* (course or direction).

Inflections or inflectional suffixes which pupils can readily learn include: verb tenses (*helps, helped, helping*); plurals (*dogs, plates, watches, babies*); possessives (*Wendy's, boys'*); and comparisons (*smaller, smallest*). Inflectional suffixes differ from derivational suffixes because they do not change the part of speech (or form class) to which a word belongs; derivational suffixes generally do.

The exact value of an understanding of inflections (or inflected endings) has not been finally established. On the one hand, a study of 54 average fourth graders and 56 poor readers (from grades six through nine) in Illinois, Texas, and Ohio—all reading at the fourth grade level—showed that many students recognize one form of a word and not another.[16] Errors among the 87 words tested could not be explained in terms of frequency of use of a particular word form, and the unpredictability of word recognition was not confined to poor readers. The researcher concluded that recognition vocabularies exist on a continuum, with some words being recognized immediately wherever and whenever they appear and others never being recognized no matter how many times students are tested. In the broad area between these extremes are words which are sometimes recognized and sometimes not.

On the other hand, a closer relationship exists between children's reading abilities in grades one and two and children's abilities to apply inflections than exists between reading ability and either auditory or visual perception.[17] Young children surveyed were able to change pseudowords (like *wog*) to plurals, past and progressive verb tenses, possessives, and comparatives/superlatives with ease.

Incidentally, current language arts texts for the elementary school do contain exercises to help pupils learn about affixes. They generally introduce suffixes by level three and prefixes by level four, although some begin even earlier. Sample textbook exercises in prefixes are shown in Figure 10.2.

Using Internal Context Clues: Mastery of Roots

Unlike affixes, which are bound morphemes, most roots are free morphemes. Still, mastery of roots or base words will also help children attack new words which may come up outside the classroom. With a knowledge of base words, children will be able to unlock dozens of words by transferring the meaning of a single root to other words.

During a beginning lesson, for instance, the students could be asked to underline the common element in the following words: *telephone, microphone, saxophone, earphone, phonics*. They could discuss the meaning of *phon* (sound) and then write other words they know that contain the same root. They might even make up new words.

Common roots which the children can learn include: *cap* (head), *cav* (hollow), *circ* (ring), *dent* (tooth), *form* (shape), *geo* (earth), *gram* (letter), *mari* (sea), *min* (small), *mov* (move), *scrib* or *script* (write), and *vis* (see). Some current language arts texts for the elementary school contain exercises to help boys and girls learn about the roots of words. Samples of such exercises are found in Figure 10.3.

Five Useful Prefixes

Figure 10.2.
Exercises Using Prefixes.

Here are five prefixes that are often used in English. Each prefix has one or two meanings. Learn the meanings of these five prefixes. You will then be better able to understand hundreds of English words.

mis- This prefix means "wrong" or "wrongly." A *misstep* is a step in the wrong place. To *mistreat* is to treat wrongly.

non- This prefix always means "not." *Nonliving* means "not alive." *Nonstop* means "having no stops, continuous."

pre- This prefix always means "before." *Preschool* is the school before elementary school. *Presoak* means "to soak clothes before they are washed."

un- This prefix may mean "not." *Unnamed* means not named. The prefix may also mean "the reverse of." *Unzip* means the reverse of *zip*. Therefore, it means "to open or unfasten."

re- This prefix also has two meanings. It may mean "back." *Repay* means "to pay back." The prefix may also mean "again." *Reappear* means "to appear again."

Sometimes you may come across a word that looks as if it has a prefix but really doesn't. For example, the letters *un-* are not a prefix in *unit*. The letters *re-* are not a prefix in *real*.

How can you tell when a group of letters is a prefix and when it is not? Decide whether the word makes sense when you take off the prefix. Is *mis-* a prefix in *miser*? Take off *mis-* and test what is left. There is no such word as *er*. Then *mis-* is not a prefix in *miser*.

Figure 10.2
(cont.)

Exercises Prefixes

A. One word in each of the following pairs has a prefix discussed in this chapter. The other does not. Write only the words with prefixes. Draw a circle around each prefix.

1. nonviolent, none
2. pressure, prewar
3. reckless, replace
4. unkind, unite
5. misty, misprint

B. Here are a list of prefixes and a list of base words. Build as many new words as you can. Use any of the prefixes with any of the base words. For example, from the base word *pay* you could make *repay* and *prepay*. Not all of the base words and prefixes will go together. Use your dictionary to check your new words.

Prefixes	Base Words
mis-	named
non-	called
pre-	smoking
un-	made
re-	heated

mismatch

C. Answer these questions.

1. If a *conception* is an idea, what is a *misconception?*
2. If *compliance* is giving in to the wishes of others, what is *noncompliance?*
3. If *dawn* is the beginning of daylight, what is *predawn?*
4. If a *grateful* person is thankful, what is an *ungrateful* person?
5. What do these mean?
   a. to *redo* a project
   b. to *replay* a tape

Source: Reprinted from BUILDING ENGLISH SKILLS, Silver Level, Copyright 1984. McDougal, Littell & Company, Evanston, Illinois. Used with permission.

Figure 10.3. Exercises Using Base Words.

Part 1 Base Words

Some new words are built. That is, a beginning or an ending is added to a word you already know. For example, the beginning *un-* is added to the word *tie* to make a new word. The new word is *untie*. Also, the ending *-ment* is added to the word *move* to make *movement*. The words *tie* and *move* are examples of base words. A **base word** is the word to which a beginning or ending is added.

Beginning		Base Word		Ending		New Word
un	+	tie			=	untie
		move	+	ment	=	movement

What base word is in these three words?

reader
misread
readable

The base word is *read*. The ending *-er* was added to make *reader*. The beginning *mis-* was added to make *misread*. The ending *-able* was added to make *readable*. These three new words were built. They all have the same base word.

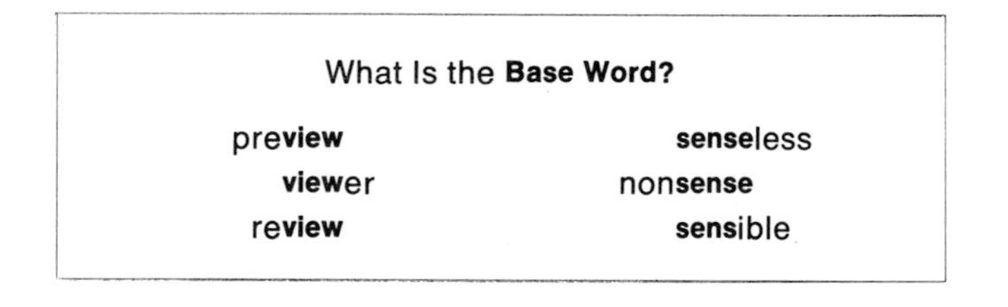

Figure 10.3 (cont.)

Exercises **Base Words**

A. Copy each of the following words on a sheet of paper. Find the base word in each. Write the base word after each word.

1. rebuild
2. unthinkable
3. nonspeaker
4. laborer
5. precooked
6. joyous
7. misspell
8. hopeless
9. thoughtful
10. unfit

B. Follow the directions for Exercise A.

1. careless
2. misbehave
3. untouchable
4. caller
5. unhelpful
6. hazardous
7. unwanted
8. preview
9. remake
10. harmless

Source: Reprinted from BUILDING ENGLISH SKILLS, Silver Level, Copyright 1984. McDougal, Littell & Company, Evanston, Illinois. Used with permission.

Learner's Dependent Approach

A dependent approach does not teach for transfer. Instead, the child studies one word at a time and learns it only under the close supervision of the teacher (or paraprofessional aide). Still the approach is organized, and any systematic strategy to vocabulary growth is preferable to incidental or unorganized learning. The two major techniques or subheadings of the dependent approach are *mastery of a word list* and *dictionary/thesaurus study.*

Mastery of a Word List

The teacher assigns, weekly or monthly, a specific number of whole words from lists suggested in children's texts or from word counts developed by educators or psychologists. Such lists vary in length as is readily apparent from an examination of some basic word lists in use today, including those by Edgar Dale and Joseph O'Rourke (1981, Living Word Vocabulary of more than 44,000 entries), Edward Fry (1980, 300 New Instant Words), William Durr (1973, 188 words most often used in primary library books), Robert Hillerich (1973, 240 Starter Words), Albert Harris and Milton Jacobson (1982, a Core List of 5167 words), John Carroll, Peter Davies, and Barry Richmond (1971, 86,740 different words for grades 3–9), Dale Johnson (1971, 306 Basic Vocabulary Words for Beginning Reading), and Henry Kučera and W. Nelson Francis (1967, 50,406 different words).

Older lists which still appear in the literature and are often used include those by Edgar Dale and Jeanne Chall (1948, 2946 words used in the Dale-Chall Readability Formula), Henry Rinsland (1945, 25,632 different words), Edward Thorndike and Irving Lorge (1944, 30,000 words), and Edward Dolch (1936, 220 Basic Sight Words).

Generally, the longer lists are for those teachers or students interested in writing vocabulary. The shorter lists are for those concerned with reading vocabulary.

Mastery of such a basic word list readily meets demands for behavioral objectives and classroom accountability. The children may be quickly assessed by means of a short test on the number of words they have learned from all those assigned. Teachers may also choose to use lists of words introduced during science or social studies units.

Dictionary/Thesaurus Study

Such study is sometimes linked with mastery of a word list. The teacher may ask the children to look up one or more words from their list in the dictionary so that they become familiar with the meaning of the assigned word or words.

At other times a new word may appear in the current events lesson, math assignment, or basal reader. The children locate this word in their dictionaries, or sometimes in their thesauruses, at the teacher's suggestion. Later they may find that the new word reappears in a follow-up activity planned by the teacher.

Of course the dictionary is more than a book of word meanings, and proper use of the dictionary is an important skill. Locating one or two unrelated words in the dictionary, however, does not lead to substantial vocabulary growth. The children learn only those exact words which their teacher has assigned and which they must use in a written exercise or test. Further discussion about dictionary skills can be found in Chapter Twelve.

Unlike the dictionary, which arranges entries alphabetically and provides considerable information, including pronunciations and word meanings, a *thesaurus* arranges entries by topics and contains lists of synonyms and antonyms only. It begins with a meaning and presents in context words which represent some part of that meaning.

Children can consult a thesaurus to find replacements for tired words like *interesting, nice, happy, big,* and *little.* They can also use it to find synonyms for such multisyllabic words as *parsimonious, euphemistic, caricature,* and *serendipity.* Most important, however, is the use of the thesaurus during the preparation of written compositions.

A current and recommended thesaurus is *In Other Words: A Junior Thesaurus* (Scott, Foresman, 1982) by W. Greet et al.

Teaching English Vocabulary: Etymology

When in 1983 it was announced that there were 11,000 new words—words added in one decade alone—in *Webster's Ninth Collegiate Dictionary* (G. & C. Merriam Company), interest was expressed in the increasing number of sources for new words. Primary sources such as science and technology had remained productive, but new words had also arrived from almost every aspect of life, including health, food, government, politics, music, the economy, and varing lifestyles.

The study concerned with the origins of words, their relations to similar words in other languages (also known as *cognates*), and the way word meanings have changed over the years is called *etymology.* Its significance is not restricted to college students and other adults, however. Young children too need to know that language is living and changing and that their own use of words contributes to the evolution of vocabulary. Dixon recommends that a good etymological dictionary be required in even the primary classroom and that any girl or boy who wishes to use it should be shown how to do so.[18] Possible adoptions include:

E. Pinkerton's *Word for Word: A Dictionary of English Cognates* (Gale, 1982)
R. Smith's *Dictionary of English Word Origins* (Littlefield, 1980)
E. Partridge's *Origins: A Short Etymological Dictionary of Modern English* (Macmillan, 1977)
E. Klein's *A Comprehensive Etymological Dictionary of the English Language* (Elsevier, 1971)

Students' names provide a good springboard for an etymological project in the elementary grades. Each child can discover what his or her first name means and also in which country it originated. Pupils can consult:

G. Stewart's *American Given Names: Their Origin and History in the Context of the English Language* (Oxford, 1979)
L. Dunkling's *First Names First* (Universe Books, 1977)
F. Loughead's *Dictionary of Given Names with Origins and Meanings* (Arthur Clark Co., 1974)

Then additional vocabulary growth can be promoted by listing words from the dictionary that involve that student's first name. For instance, after *Ann* has been introduced with the meaning for *year* and its Latin root, words such as *annual, annuity,* and *anniversary* can be discussed. Crist describes an activity in which a different child's name was honored each week and a class notebook developed with a separate page for each member of the class.[19] In some instances the matter of colloquialisms also arose so that *Bill* was linked to *fill the bill, foot the bill* and *bill and coo.*

Family names also have interesting origins. Children may wish to examine Hazen's *Last, First, Middle and Nick: All About Names* (Prentice-Hall, 1978) or Smith's *New Dictionary of American Family Names* (Harper, 1973).

Other topics which provoke the interest of boys and girls include words about people (e.g., *barber*), words about the animal world (e.g., *hippopotamus*), words about plants (e.g., *tangerine*), words about food and beverages (e.g., *ketchup* and *chocolate*), words about clothes (e.g., *pajamas*), and words about transportation (e.g., *bicycle*).

More advanced students may wish to determine how some places got their names (by reading Fletcher's *100 Keys: Names Across the Land,* Abingdon, 1973), how the days and months were named (by checking Asimov's *Words from the Myths,* Houghton, 1961), how slang expressions developed (by examining Carothers' and Lacey's *Slanguage,* Sterling, 1979), how brand names evolved (by consulting Arnold's *What's in a Name: Famous Brand Names,* Messner, 1979), and how some common everyday expressions or folk idioms originated (by using Nevins' *From the Horse's Mouth,* Prentice-Hall, 1977).

Teaching English Vocabulary: Instructional Activities

Vocabulary building requires attention. Every day at least a few minutes should be taken for discussion of words used or needed for the communication of ideas. This is the only way that precise meanings can be learned. Teachers must understand that when a word is introduced too quickly or too casually, pupils often receive only a vague impression of its definition.

Some of the following instructional activities appeal especially to children with learning disabilities or to younger pupils. Others will interest gifted pupils at all levels or intermediate students. Finally, there are activities that are suggested for all elementary classes, primary and intermediate alike.

1. Listing things needed to (a) bake cookies; (b) build a tree house; (c) go camping; (d) set the table; or (e) go to school on a rainy day.
2. Giving more than one meaning for such words as *run, pipe, can, shell, ice, bark, sheet, park, slip, call, date, yarn, strike, spring, roll, light, fall, cut, check,* and *charge.*
3. Making interesting beginnings for these endings:

   ". . . slipped down the icy slope"
   ". . . struggled wildly"
   ". . . called for help"
   ". . . huddled in the cave"

4. Constructing definitions from handling such objects as a *locket, darning needle, abacus,* or *avocado.*
5. Illustrating such mathematical and geographical terms as *plateau, diagonal, perpendicular,* and *plain.*
6. Constructing a simple crossword puzzle that uses a series of related words, for example, *airplane, pilot, fly, sky, hangar.*
7. Drawing a pear (pair) tree and adding pears. On each pear should be written a word and its homophone.
8. Describing scenes on picture postcards.
9. Making a sound-train by painting and lettering shoe boxes, and filling them with realia whose names begin or end with the letters shown.
10. Keeping a list of unfamiliar words which appear in newspaper headlines during one week.
11. Discovering colorful words in travel brochures or in newspaper travel advertisements.
12. Examining the *Reader's Digest* section entitled "It Pays to Increase Your Word Power."
13. Listing "moody" words that make readers/listeners feel angry or keep them in suspense.
14. Collecting job words about computer technicians or anthropologists.
15. Reading juvenile magazines such as *Cricket, Children's Digest, Highlights for Children, Jack and Jill, The Electric Company Magazine,* and *Ebony, Jr.*
16. Describing one food item (*pickles*) according to the five senses (*green, crunchy, sour, slippery, brined*).
17. Discovering how three acronyms (e.g., *radar*) have developed.
18. Collecting "loaded" words gleaned from speeches made by political candidates at election times.
19. Preparing menus based on a single food specialty such as desserts or sandwiches.
20. Writing or listing reduplications (*helter-skelter, dilly-dally, wishy-washy*).
21. Discussing environmental sounds.
22. Keeping word folders after study trips, such as "Visiting a Greenhouse" or "Going to the Planetarium."
23. Consulting Greet, Jenkins, and Schiller's *In Other Words: A Beginning Thesaurus* (Scott, Foresman, 1969) to locate five synonyms each for *break, go, jump, push, say,* and *send.*
24. Charting specialized words for such pastimes as tennis, bowling, fishing, or stamp collecting.
25. Promoting alliterative phrases (*ferocious flea, courteous crocodile*) that are humorous.
26. Making an illustrated dictionary relating to a special project which incorporates magazine pictures or personal drawings.
27. Using an opaque projector to display pictures of people or animals that plainly describe adjectives such as *grim, impatient, excited,* or *amazed.*

28. Creating names of imaginary animals by combining names of zoo or farm animals (*kangarooster, elephanteater*).
29. Drawing a favorite baked food such as chocolate cake and then writing all of the recipe ingredients of that food underneath the picture.
30. Adding up words instead of numbers (e.g., *high speed* plus *careless driving* equals *a highway accident*).
31. Creating a mysterious art gallery on a large bulletin board by posting several exciting and colored pictures (clipped from magazines) which have each been covered by sheets of numbered construction paper. A small rectangle is cut out of each numbered sheet so that one segment of each picture becomes visible. The caption above the gallery reads: "Can you solve the mystery of the hidden pictures?" Children can relate their guesses orally or on paper.
32. Writing words to reveal their meanings (e.g., *fat* would be drawn or written with plump thick letters, *f, a,* and *t* while *flag* could have a flag drawn in place of the *f*).
33. Rewriting familiar proverbs or creating new ones.
34. Writing some homophone riddles (e.g., Why is Sunday the strongest day of the *week*? Because the others are all *weak* days).
35. Illustrating humorously some compound words, as in Basil's *Breakfast in the Afternoon* (Morrow, 1979).
36. Collecting definitions of common television terms much like Carolyn Miller does in *Illustrated TV Dictionary* (Harvey House, 1980).
37. Examining some of the specialized vocabulary found in Scout manuals.
38. Miming *outrage, delight, terror* and other emotional reactions.
39. Listing items (*nylon, vinyl*) composed wholly or partly of synthetics.
40. Playing commercial word games such as Junior Scrabble, Concentration, Spill and Spell, or Password.
41. Charting words which first surfaced during the past decade (e.g., *microchip*).
42. Developing fresh similes (*fragile as a new pencil point*) or collecting familiar ones (*nose like a cherry*).
43. Listening to newscasters to elicit five current terms.
44. Expressing one action word (*lag* or *leap*) graphically through one of the art media.
45. Listing some of the specialized vocabulary used by sportscasters or found on the sports pages.
46. Identifying some of the photographs found in Loss's *What Is It*? (Doubleday, 1974) which employ macrophotography effectively.
47. Writing word puns after perusing Basil's *Nailheads and Potato Eyes* (Morrow, 1976).
48. Charting antonyms for five common words much like Richard Hefter does in *Yes and No: A Book of Opposites* (Larousse, 1975).
49. Drawing some amusing and confusing figures of speech such as *fork in the road* and *foot in his mouth.*
50. Listing some one-word palindromes (*nun, rotor, Otto*) or words that can be read backwards and forwards with the same result.

51. Writing some intonation riddles (e.g., Why did the pilot take his pony on the airplane? Becaues he wanted to see a horse fly [*horsefly*]).
52. Drawing five UGH(!) pages of terms such as *fish guts, a dead mouse,* and *a moldy cucumber.*
53. Collecting oxymorons (such as *jumbo shrimp* and *cruel kindness*) or contradictory words or groups of words that are opposite in meaning although they are often used in our language.
54. Developing an alphabet of words originating from famous names (e.g., *pasteurization* from Louis Pasteur). The list might begin with *America* (Amerigo Vespucci), *Braille* printing (Louis Braille), *Celsius* thermometer (Anders Celsius), and *diesel* engine (Rudolph Diesel).
55. Perusing from the library table one of the following:

    C. Basil, *How Ships Play Cards: A Beginning Book of Homonyms* (Morrow, 1980)

    N. Bossom, *A Scale Full of Fish and Other Turnabouts* (Greenwillow, 1979)

    J. Hanson, *More Similes: Roar Like a Lion, as Loud as Thunder. . . .* (Lerner, 1979)

    J. Hanson, *Plurals* (Lerner, 1979)

    B. Kohn, *What a Funny Thing to Say* (Dial, 1974)

    C. I. Kudrna, *Two-Way Words* (Abingdon, 1980)

    J. Rosenbloom, *Daffy Dictionary: Fun Abridged Definitions from Aardvark to Zuider Zee* (Sterling, 1977)

    A. Steckler, *101 Words and How They Began* (Doubleday, 1979)

    J. Thayer *Try Your Hand* (Morrow, 1980)

    A. Weiss, *What's That You Said? How Words Change* (Harcourt, 1980)

Learning Games

As more and more commercial word games are being produced, teachers in increasing numbers are using vocabulary games in the classroom. They should therefore be aware of the results of a study recently conducted in a large urban school system concerning the use of games to increase sight vocabulary among black first-grade remedial readers.[20] Teachers introduced two new words each morning, Monday through Thursday, for six weeks. After 10 minutes of introductory activity (using the chalkboard and flashcards), the children spent the next 20 minutes in one of three treatment groups: playing active games (such as Word Toss); playing passive games (such as Word Rummy); or completing vocabulary worksheets. Posttest results showed that games led to increased learning in children who had earlier mastered few words, with physically active games being the most effective treatment of the three. Boys and girls apparently enjoy competition and are more interested in playing a game in order to learn words than in using pencil and paper exercises.

Regardless of their grade level or their academic achievement, children do enjoy playing instructional games. Most of the non-commercial group games described below require little, if any, special preparation.

Break-Down

1. The teacher writes a long word on the chalkboard (e.g., *hippopotamus*).
2. At their desks, the players write as many smaller words as they can from any arrangement of the letters contained in the board word.
3. The winner, the player with the most words correctly written, is allowed to put a new word on the board for the class to use.
4. Suggestions: Seasonal words such as *pumpkin* or *valentine* are appropriate and interesting to break-down. Gifted classes enjoy sesquipedalian words (or long words) to break down such as *pneumonoultramicroscopicsilicovolcanoconiosis* with 45 letters.

Classified Information

1. The teacher writes the name of a category (e.g., *sports*) on the board.
2. The players write at their seats as many words as they can recall that fit that category (e.g., *boxing, tennis, baseball, soccer*).
3. One point is awarded for each word correctly listed. (The teacher may also award an extra point for each item correctly spelled.)
4. The winner is the player with the highest number of points. The winner may choose the next category (e.g., *trees*) of Classified Information.

College Words

1. The pupils are divided equally into teams. The teacher uses a timer.
2. The teacher calls out a simple word (e.g., *wash*), which is generally of one syllable. The first player on Team One must match the teacher's word with an advanced synonym or College Word (e.g., *launder*), which need not be longer than one syllable (e.g., *rinse*) but must definitely be more erudite.
3. If the first player on Team One fails to match the teacher's word before the timer buzzes, the first player on Team Two gets a chance to score.
4. The team with the most synonyms wins College Words and can label itself after its favorite (or local) college.
5. Examples include: *eat/dine, sweat/perspiration, pants/trousers, job/occupation.*

Dash-Dillers

1. The teacher writes on the board a short sentence, using only the first letter of each word and a dash for the rest of the word, (e.g., *M— b— c— f— t— p—*).
2. At their seats, the players try to complete the sentence by writing in their versions of the letters needed to complete each word, (e.g., *Mother baked cookies for ten people.*)
3. The winners of Dash-Dillers are the pupils whose sentences are not only reasonable, but comply with the board arrangement (even though the final sentences may not be ones the teacher had in mind).

Definition

1. Each player receives a portion of a newspaper and then circles five published words which he or she can define but believes will be difficult or impossible for others to define.
2. The teacher chooses a player to read one of his or her words. Should one of the other players be able to give an acceptable definition, then that player in turn reads a word for the class to define.
3. The winners are all pupils who announced words for which only they could furnish a satisfactory definition.

Descripto

1. The teacher writes on the chalkboard a sentence containing two or three nouns but no adjectives (e.g., *Children are eating apples and oranges.*)
2. The players rewrite the sentences, using one or more uncommon adjectives before each noun.
3. The winners of Descripto are the players who chose unique but appropriate adjectives not selected by the rest of the class.

Fill-In

1. The teacher writes an incomplete sentence on the chalkboard (e.g., *Sam lives in a* ______).
2. Each player copies the sentence and completes it with the most original word he or she knows.
3. The winners are the players with suitable words that no one else has chosen. They may help to write the next incomplete sentence that requires a fill-in word.

Name-O

1. The teacher writes a pupil's name on the chalkboard vertically like this:

    J
    A
    M
    E
    S

2. The players copy the name on their papers exactly as it appears on the board.
3. They use each letter of the name as the first letter of a word to be completed on the paper.
4. The winner is the first player who has used all the letters correctly. This player's name heads the next round of Name-O.
5. Variation: The winner is the first player who has used all the letters correctly and formed a sentence out of the words.

Printers' Words

1. The teacher distributes a portion of a newspaper (advertisements and articles) to each player, who is then asked to circle with a crayon or colored pencil any three affixes.
2. At a signal from their teacher, all children who have completed the task stand at their seats. Every pupil who can give the meaning of the printers' words that he or she has circled is a winner.
3. Variation: The game may be repeated for root words, depending upon the interest and maturity of the group.

Riddle Word

1. The teacher, or a child chosen as "It," draws one card from the word box or one entry from a word notebook.
2. "It" then describes the word drawn; for example, "The word has two syllables; it begins with *Q* and means to shake or tremble. What's the riddle word?
3. The other players try to write the riddle word at their seats.
4. "It" now says the riddle word (*quiver*) and also writes it correctly on the board.

5. Players award themselves one point if they guessed the word correctly. They get one additional point if they spelled the riddle word correctly.
6. The winners are the players with the highest number of points after a designated number of rounds.

Sentence Relay

1. The pupils are divided equally into teams.
2. The first player on each team writes any word he or she chooses on the chalkboard. The second player on the same team adds another word toward building a sentence placing it either before or after the first player's word. Each pupil receives a turn. But if a player cannot add a suitable word, the player forfeits his or her turn and the next team begins to build a sentence.
3. The team with the longest sentence after every player has had at least one turn wins Sentence Relay.

Stretcher

1. The teacher writes a short word on the chalkboard (e.g., *pin*).
2. The players, at their seats or at the board, then write as many words as they can by adding one or more letters before or after the chosen word (e.g., *spin, pint, spinning, pints*).
3. The winner of Stretcher is the player with the longest list of words correctly written when the round has been completed.
4. Suggestion: The teacher may wish to use a simple kitchen timer to stop a round after only 30 to 40 seconds if the group of players is mature.

String of Words

1. The teacher writes a key word on the chalkboard (e.g., *chair*).
2. The players, at their seats or at the board, then each write a word starting with the first two letters of the chosen word (e.g., *charm*).
3. Within a time limit of one to three minutes each player must compile a string of words, starting each word with the first two letters of the key word.
4. The winner is the player with the longest string of words correctly written when the round has been completed.

Substitute

1. The teacher writes a one-syllable word on the chalkboard (e.g., *bid*).
2. The players, at their seats or at the board, then write as many words as they can by substituting one or more vowels for the orignal vowel (e.g., *bad, booed, bead, bud*).
3. The winner of Substitute is the player with the longest list of words correctly written when the round has been completed.
4. Variation: Teams may be chosen and then provided with individual dictionaries.

Tic-Tac-Toe

1. Two pupils compete, each in turn, either at the chalkboard or using a sheet of writing paper.
2. The object is to write correctly three words, in a line or diagonally, which contain a common element such as an affix, phonogram (graphemic base), or root word. For example, if the first player wrote words all in capital letters

and the second player wrote words in small letters, the Tic-Tac-Toe board might look like this after three turns:

SEND		erased
	erase	
LEND	eraser	TEND

The first player could write in *MEND* (or any word containing the phonogram *end*) in the first column and so win Tic-Tac-Toe with a completed vertical line.

3. Variation: Teams of three to four members each may be chosen with the game played only at the chalkboard.

Evaluation of Pupils' Progress

To assist in the planning of a program of vocabulary building, the teacher needs measured insight into the progress made by individual pupils in their acquisition of broad listening, speaking, reading, and writing vocabularies.

Numerous standardized reading and reading-readiness tests contain sections on vocabulary as do various standardized achievement batteries, including the *Comprehensive Tests of Basic Skills* (published by CTB/McGraw-Hill of Monterey, CA), the *Metropolitan Achievement Tests* (published by the Psychological Corporation of New York City), and the *SRA Achievement Series* (published by Science Research Associates of Chicago).

There are also two recently-developed standardized instruments specifically intended to assess vocabulary growth among young children:

1. *Johnson Basic Vocabulary Test.* A group test for children in grades one and two, which requires 30–45 minutes. The examiner pronounces the words one at a time, and the pupils are told to draw a circle around each printed word they have just heard. Publisher is Personnel Press of Columbus, OH.
2. *Vocabulary Comprehension Scale.* An individually-administered test for children ages two through six, which requires 20 minutes. Each word is included in a separate sentence which is read by the examiner to the child and which asks him/her to perform an activity involving one or more objects arranged in a pre-staged scene. Publisher is Learning Concepts of Austin, TX.

A teacher may also choose to devise his or her own tests. There are four major ways of testing vocabulary, according to Dale and O'Rourke: (1) *identification,* whereby pupils respond orally or in writing by identifying a word according to its use or definition; (2) *multiple-choice,* whereby the students choose the correct definition of the tested word from three or possibly four meanings; (3) *matching* (which is really another form of multiple-choice), whereby the tested words are presented in one column and the matching definitions are listed out of order in another column; and (4) *checking,* whereby pupils check the words they know or do not know although they may also be required to define the words they have checked.[21]

Within these four groups the teacher can employ a variety of techniques to test vocabulary. Hopefully, with middle-grade or intermediate children the teacher will often choose self-tests which allow individual students to make an inventory of their stock of words to determine its strengths and weaknesses. Words contained in an easy-to-hard sequence in a sample self-inventory checklist (relevant to a fourth-grade unit on nutrition) might each be marked with a simple ✓ (to indicate knowledge of the word) or ○ (to indicate lack of such knowledge):

____ nutrition	____ strength
____ diet	____ calories
____ muscle	____ calcium
____ vitamin	____ cholesterol
____ protein	____ carbohydrate
____ energy	____ thiamine

The most important evaluation of vocabulary growth, however, is that which looks to the performance of the pupil in all the other areas of instruction. Proper measurement of word recognition and understanding is best seen in the light of evaluation of the pupil's progress in the total process of education.

Discussion Questions

1. Why is it necessary to see vocabulary development as conceptual development?
2. Which of the factors affecting vocabulary growth may be influenced by teacher planning?
3. When should the teacher ask a student to look up the meaning of a word in the dictionary?
4. With what kinds of exceptional children would some of the independent methods for teaching vocabulary be especially successful?
5. How could a unit on word origins be made appealing to a heterogeneous group of intermediate pupils of varying abilities and backgrounds?

Suggested Projects

1. Design a learning game that could be used to teach vocabulary to kindergarten pupils. Then try it out with a small group of school beginners.
2. Examine and evaluate two of the following commercial word games listed by the International Reading Association: *Picture Dominoes* (Childcraft), *Phonetic Quizmo* (Milton Bradley Company), *Scrabble* (Selchow and Righter), *Match* (Garrard Publishing Company), and *Judy's Match-Ettes* (Judy Company).
3. Discover how antonyms are presented in two current language art series.

4. Compare the presentations on suffixes in various language texts for children at the intermediate levels. Are any of them appropriate for pupils with learning disabilities or for gifted pupils?
5. Develop an animal crossword puzzle appropriate for either upper primary or intermediate boys and girls. Possible clues could include: the official bird of the United States, a baby cow, the king of beasts, etc.
6. Set up the learning center on vocabulary shown in Figure 10.4.

Related Readings

Duffelmeyer, F. A. 1982. "Expanding Children's Vocabulary," *Reading Horizons, 23*(1), pp. 64–66.

Fry, E. et al. 1984. *The Reading Teachers' Book of Lists*. Englewood Cliffs, NJ: Prentice-Hall, Inc.

Greenman, R. 1983. *Words in Action*. New York: Times Books.

Figure 10.4. Language Arts Learning Center: Vocabulary.

TYPE OF CENTER: **Etymology** TIME: 30-40 minutes

GRADE LEVEL: 4-6 NUMBER OF STUDENTS: 1-2

INSTRUCTIONAL OBJECTIVE: The pupil will recognize how rich our vocabulary is with words that we have borrowed from other languages.

MATERIALS: A dictionary, sheets of paper with the following sentence at the top: Worldly Sentence—The *gypsy girl* wearing a *scarlet belt*, an *indigo veil*, a *cotton blouse*, a *gingham skirt*, a *sprig* of *heather*, and a *fez*, and carrying a *tangerine*, a *boomerang*, a *ukulele*, and an *umbrella*, walked down the street with a *negro tycoon*, who lived in an *igloo* and traveled only by *canoe*, *sled*, or *dinghy* to a *bungalow* with a *dirty tile floor*, to make *telephone calls* and to *purchase* some *wine*, *vodka*, *brandy*, *cocoa*, *tomatoes*, *balsam ointment*, *tobacco*, *chop suey*, *yams*, and *goulash* for her *clan*.

McNutt, G. 1984. "Up, Down, Over, Under: Spatial Relationship Words," *Academic Therapy, 19,* pp. 553–560.
Mayher, J., and Brause, R. 1983. "Learning through Teaching: Teaching and Learning Vocabulary," *Language Arts, 60,* pp. 1008–1016.
Nagy, W., and Anderson, R. 1984. "How Many Words are There in Printed School English?" *Reading Research Quarterly, 19,* pp. 304–330.
Sauro, N. 1985. *Wordplay.* Great Neck, NY: Todd and Honeywell.
Swisher, K. 1984. "Increasing Word Power Through Spelling Activities," *Reading Teacher, 37,* pp. 706–710.
Wood, K. D., and Robinson, N. 1983. "Vocabulary, Language and Prediction: A Prereading Strategy," *Reading Teacher, 36,* pp. 392–395.
Word Mastery the Easy Way. 1985. Woodbury, NY: Barron's Educational Series.

Additional Materials

Folders for finished papers and key sheet, picture of girl (try to use some of the colors and items mentioned as well as the action).

DIRECTIONS:

1. Read the sentence below the picture.
2. Look up the origin of the underlined words, using the dictionary. Use the guide in the front of the dictionary for the meaning of abbreviations.
3. Write your answers on the paper provided in the *worksheets* folder.
4. Make sure to write your name on your paper.
5. Compare your origins to those on the key sheet. Are yours right? Can you identify anything in the picture with the words you have just looked up?
6. Place your paper in the *finished papers* folder.
7. Return the key sheet to its folder.

KEY

gypsy—Egyptian
girl—Anglo-Saxon
scarlet—Persian
belt—Latin
indigo—India
veil—Latin
cotton—Arabic
blouse—French
gingham—Malayan
skirt—Scandinavian
heather—Scottish
fez—Turkish
tangerine—French
boomerang—Australian

ukelele—Hawaiian
umbrella—Italian
street—Latin
negro—Spanish
tycoon—Japanese
igloo—Eskimo
canoe—Arawak
sled—Flemish
dinghy—Bengali
bungalow—Hindi
dirty—Scandinavian
tile—Latin
floor—Anglo-Saxon
telephone—Greek

call—Anglo-Saxon
purchase—French
wine—Latin
vodka—Russian
brandy—Dutch
cocoa—Nahuatl
tomatoes—Nahuatl
balsam—Greek
ointment—Latin
tobacco—Arawak
chop-suey—Chinese
yams—Portuguese
goulash—Hungarian
clan—Irish

EVALUATION: Self-checking: The students will compare their findings to correct derivations provided on the key sheet.

Source: From PATHWAYS TO IMAGINATION by Angela S. Reeke and James L. Laffey, © 1979 by Scott, Foresman & Company. Reprinted by permission.

Chapter Notes

1. K. Mezynski, "Issues Concerning the Acquisition of Knowledge: Effects of Vocabulary Training on Reading Comprehension," *Review of Educational Research,* 1983, *53,* pp. 253–279.
2. D. D. Johnson and T. C. Barrett, "Johnson's Basic Vocabulary for Beginning Reading and Current Basal Readers: Are They Compatible?" *Journal of Reading Behavior,* 1972, *4,* pp. 1–11. Also see W. Loban, *Language Development: Kindergarten through Grade Twelve* (Urbana, Illinois: National Council of Teachers of English, 1976), p. 85.
3. Johnson and Barrett, "Johnson's Basic Vocabulary;" and D. D. Johnson and E. Majer, "Johnson's Basic Vocabulary: Words for Grades 1 and 2," *Elementary School Journal,* 1976, *77,* pp. 74–82.
4. E. Dale and J. O'Rourke, *Techniques of Teaching Vocabulary* (Addison, Illinois: Field Educational Enterprises, Inc., 1971), p. 8.
5. T. C. Standal, "How Children Recognize Words in Print," in *Research in the Language Arts,* V. Froese and S. Straw, eds. (Baltimore: University Park Press, 1981), p. 251.
6. K. Rayner and E. Hagelberg, "Word Recognition Cues for Beginning and Skilled Readers," *Journal of Experimental Psychology,* 1975, *20,* pp. 444–455.
7. Standal, "How Children Recognize Words," p. 252.
8. R. Allington and A. McGill-Franzen, "Word Identification Errors in Isolation and in Context: Apples vs. Oranges," *Reading Teacher,* 1980, *33,* pp. 795–800.
9. I. Beck, M. McKeown, and E. McCaslin, "Vocabulary Development: All Contexts Are Not Created Equal," *Elementary School Journal,* 1983, *83,* p. 181.
10. J. O'Rourke, *Toward a Science of Vocabulary Development* (The Hague: Mouton, 1974), pp. 83–86.
11. D. D. Johnson and P. D. Pearson, *Teaching Reading Vocabulary,* 2d ed. (New York: Holt, 1984), pp. 101–102.
12. M. R. Haggard, "The Vocabulary Self-Collection Strategy: An Active Approach to Word Learning," *Journal of Reading,* 1982, *26,* pp. 203–207.
13. I. Beck and M. McKeown, "Learning Words Well: A Program to Enhance Vocabulary and Comprehension," *Reading Teacher,* 1983, *36,* pp. 622–625.
14. Dale and O'Rourke, *Techniques,* pp. 28–34.
15. J. P. Gipe, "Use of a Relevant Context Helps Kids Learn New Word Meanings," *Reading Teacher,* 1980, *33,* pp. 398–402; and J. P. Gipe, "Investigating Techniques for Teaching Word Meanings," *Reading Research Quarterly,* 1978–79, *14,* pp. 624–644.
16. R. Hillerich, "Recognition Vocabularies: A Research-Based Caution," *Elementary School Journal,* 1981, *81,* pp. 313–317.
17. M. Brittain, "Inflectional Performance and Early Reading Achievement," *Reading Research Quarterly,* 1970, *6,* pp. 34–50.
18. G. Dixon, "Investigating Words in the Primary Grades," *Language Arts,* 1977, *54,* p. 419.
19. B. Crist, "Tim's Time: Vocabulary Activities from Names," *Reading Teacher,* 1980, *34,* pp. 309–312.
20. D. P. Dickerson, "A Study of Use of Games to Reinforce Sight Vocabulary," *Reading Teacher,* 1982, *36,* pp. 46–49.
21. Dale and O'Rourke, *Techniques,* pp. 20–26.

Children's Literature 11

Objectives

The emergence of children's literature

Distinctions in reading preferences among primary and intermediate children

Titles useful for bibliotherapy

Instructional activities incorporating literature

Discover As You Read This Chapter If*

1. A good literature program for children provides a balance among the various genres of literature.
2. Picture books are now published for readers beyond the preschool and primary grades.
3. Elementary school children are too immature to exhibit strong sex differences in reading choices.
4. Boys and girls prefer fiction to nonfiction.
5. Most teachers are well-informed about current juvenile books.
6. An important criterion for all children's books is the format.
7. The majority of wordless picture books are fantasy.
8. Surprisingly, most children enjoy poetry.
9. Choral speaking is inappropriate for girls and boys with speech defects.
10. Teachers inexperienced in choral speaking sessions wisely begin with unison arrangements.

*Answers to these true-or-false statements may be found in Appendix 6.

The best opportunity in the school curriculum for boys and girls to examine the codes of conduct by which people live is through literature. It helps children compare value systems and relate them to their own standards. It also helps children discern what has perplexed people in the past and what these people have done about it. By understanding and evaluating the experiences of life as described in literature, the boys and girls become better able to integrate vicarious experiences with their own daily lives. In the process they also become more sensitive to the needs of others and to their own needs.

Books written especially for children are a relatively recent kind of literature, first emerging as a significant category in the eighteenth century. From Anglo-Saxon times until the early 1700s, children's books were inseparably linked with educational or moral purposes with hornbooks first appearing in the 1440s. Children who read fiction at all read easy adult works—fables, romances, fairy tales, and adventure stories. The change from uncensored adult literature for children to a literature written specifically for a child audience developed from the change which had occurred in the social pattern of Western life. As the life of adults became separated from the life of children and increased in technological complexity, children began to read a literature radically different from that of adults.

The first book especially designed for children's entertainment and quite apart from a schoolbook was published in England in 1744 by John Newbery. Entitled *A Little Pretty Pocketbook,* it was sold with a ball for boys and a pincushion for girls, and consisted mostly of games. A major shift in literature slowly followed, and by the mid-nineteenth century Hans Christian Andersen, Louisa May Alcott, Charles Kingsley, and dozens of other talented authors were producing many kinds of juvenile entertainment, surprisingly similar to that being generated for children today.

Modern authors of children's literature are aware that their writing cannot involve the same criteria of literary excellence as adult literature does. Most children have a more limited range of language experience and understandable experience (in both kinds and amounts) than many adults. Most children are also limited in their ability to attend to experiences over lengths of time, as compared to adults, and cannot normally manipulate as many elements at once, as most older persons can. Finally, they are less inclined than their elders to concern themselves with what may happen in the future.

Teachers and media specialists must also be aware of differences between good books for children and books in childlike format intended for adult buyers.[1] What is *not* a children's book is:

> A book which does not deal forthrightly with boys and/or girls, portraying them accurately as children, and/or
> A book which expects children to bring associations or have knowledge which they seldom possess.

While the children's first exposure to literature is Mother Goose and other rhymes and stories, children should gradually experience every type and form of literature in a school program that is comprehensive and sequentially plotted throughout the elementary grades. Such a program not only strengthens the developmental reading curriculum but contributes in a significant way to the attainment of several other objectives of elementary education:

- The school aims to meet the needs of individual pupils—and literature is widely diversified.
- The school aims to provide a learning program which will utilize the natural interests of its pupils—and literature appeals to all age groups.
- The school aims to provide socially satisfying experiences for its children and to develop in its pupils a wider social understanding—and good stories and pleasing verse are enjoyed more when they are shared with others.
- The school aims to give each child self-insight—and books introduced in childhood can sometimes bring about a profound change in one's outlook on life.
- The school aims to give each pupil a knowledge and appreciation of his or her cultural heritage—and literature is the means whereby much of that heritage is preserved and perpetuated.
- The school aims to stimulate and foster creative expression—and book experiences are an exciting springboard to art, drama, and other expressionistic activities.

Yet, teaching literature should not be considered synonymous with teaching reading. Neither should it be thought to be the same as the library media skills program, though both reading and the library media center support a literature program. It is not even the same as free reading, whereby pupils have a chance to choose their own books, read them during school time, and perhaps share them with their peers or the teacher. Should free reading turn into guided reading and parents/teachers/media specialists help pupils choose books, it still does not replace a literature class.

Literature as a subject in the elementary school deserves a special period to itself and should appear as such on the class schedule. Children can then regularly hear/read and understand writings of quality both from the past and the present.

A properly-structured literature program provides a balance among the various genres relevant to this segment of the language arts. Children thereby have at least minimal encounters with each genre of literature at every age level while teachers simultaneously are reminded of the need to explore the many and diverse offerings included within each genre. A balance is readily attained between traditional literature and contemporary fiction, between poetry and prose, between modern informational books and wordless books, and between realism and fantasy. Such a balanced offering actively strengthens and expands the pupils' skill in language and composition as well as in literature. It could be charted, as shown in Table 11.1.

Table 11.1
Planning Guide for a Literature Program in the Elementary School: By Genre (Recommended Sample Selections from *Adventuring with Books* [NCTE, 1981])

Age Level	Wordless Books	Poetry	Traditional Literature	Modern Fantasy
4–7	(1) *Alligator's Toothache* (Crown, 1977) (2) *A Birthday Wish* (Little, 1977)	(1) *Finger Rhymes* (Dutton, 1980) (2) *A Bunch of Poems and Verses* (Seabury, 1977)	(1) *Nursery Rhymes* (Crowell, 1978) (2) *Three Little Pigs* (Lothrop, 1979)	(1) *No More Baths* (Doubleday, 1980) (2) *Teddy Bear's Scrapbook* (Atheneum, 1980)
6–9	(1) *The Mystery of the Giant Footsteps* (Dutton, 1977) (2) *Max* (Atheneum, 1977)	(1) *Go to Bed!* (Knopf, 1979) (2) *Elves, Fairies, & Gnomes* (Knopf, 1980)	(1) *The Bremen-Town Musicians* (Doubleday, 1981). (2) *Snow Maiden* (Prentice, 1979)	(1) *The Talking Turnip* (Parents, 1979) (2) *Walking Shoes* (Doubleday, 1980)
7–10	(1) *The Wonder-Ring* (Doubleday, 1978) (2) *Up and Up* (Prentice, 1979)	(1) *Think of Shadows* (Atheneum, 1980) (2) *An Arkful of Animals* (Houghton, 1978)	(1) *The Diviner* (Lippincott, 1980) (2) *Jason and the Golden Fleece* (Troll, 1981)	(1) *The Water of Life* (Four Winds, 1980) (2) *Humphrey, the Dancing Pig* (Dial, 1980)
8–12	(1) *The Silver Pony* (Houghton, 1973) (2) *Lily at the Table* (Macmillan, 1979)	(1) *Cornucopia* (Atheneum, 1978) (2) *Moments* (Harcourt, 1980)	(1) *Two Pairs of Shoes* (Viking, 1980) (2) *The Seventh Day: The Story of the Jewish Sabbath* (Doubleday, 1980)	(1) *Algonquin Cat* (Delacorte, 1980) (2) *A Troll in Passing* (Atheneum, 1980)

Objectives/ Functions, Satisfactions, and Trends

Literature teaching means that elementary classes receive a planned program of activities designed to achieve certain general objectives:

1. To help pupils realize that literature is for entertainment and can be enjoyed throughout their entire lives
2. To acquaint children with their literary heritage
3. To help pupils understand what constitutes literature and—hopefully—to persuade them to prefer the best
4. To help children evaluate their own reading and extend beyond what is to what can be
5. To help pupils in their growing up and in their understanding of humanity in general[2]

For schools that prefer to follow behavioral objectives for the teaching of literature, Peterson has listed ten major headings.[3] Under the *cognitive domain,* the children will know literary forms; they will know, analyze, and evaluate the theme and supporting details, the plot, the characterization, the setting, the literary and artistic style; and they will know and evaluate the physical format. Under the *affective domain,* the children will enjoy hearing selections read, will enjoy reading independently, and will enjoy sharing literature experiences.

The school literature program should be structured to attain certain objectives because literature itself performs particular functions. It provides both pleasure and understanding. It shows human motives for what they are, inviting

Historical Fiction	Contemporary Fiction	Informational Books	Biography
(1) *Cornstalks and Cannonballs* (Carolrhoda, 1980) (2) *The Adventures of Obadiah* (Viking, 1972)	(1) *Moving Molly* (Prentice, 1979) (2) *Daddy* (Harper, 1977)	(1) *Picking & Weaving* (Four Winds, 1980) (2) *Wheels* (Crowell, 1979)	(1) *Self-Portrait: Erik Blegvad* (Addison, 1979) (2) *Self-Portrait: Margot Zemach* (Addison, 1978)
(1) *The Courage of Sarah Noble* (Scribner, 1954) (2) *How Far, Felipe?* (Harper, 1978)	(1) *Two Homes for Lynn* (Holt, 1979) (2) *The Best Burglar Alarm* (Morrow, 1978)	(1) *The Popcorn Book* (Holiday, 1978) (2) *Locks and Keys* (Crowell, 1980)	(1) *The Columbus Story* (Scribner, 1955) (2) *What's the Big Idea, Ben Franklin?* (Coward, 1976)
(1) *Fanny's Sister* (Dutton, 1980) (2) *The War Party* (Harcourt, 1978)	(1) *My Island Grandma* (Warne, 1979) (2) *Who's Afraid of the Dark?* (Whitman, 1980)	(1) *Careers at a Zoo* (Lerner, 1980) (2) *Heavy Equipment* (Scribner, 1980)	(1) *White House Children* (Random, 1979) (2) *Charles Lindbergh: Hero Pilot* (Garrard, 1978)
(1) *Wilkin's Ghost* (Viking, 1978) (2) *Hunt the Thimble* (Oxford, 1978)	(1) *Blind Outlaw* (Holiday, 1980) (2) *Branded Runaway* (Westminster, 1980)	(1) *Know about Alcohol* (McGraw, 1978) (2) *Ice Skating* (Rand, 1980)	(1) *Presidents at Home* (Messner, 1980) (2) *She Never Looked Back: Margaret Mead in Samoa* (Coward, 1980)

Source: *Adventuring with Books* (Urbana, Illinois: National Council of Teachers of English, 1981) Each book listed in the guide has met two criteria: "high potential interest for children" and "a significant degree of literary merit." The selection committee was also concerned with "equitable treatment of minorities and the recognition of quality books of the past."

the readers/hearers to identify with or react to fictional characters. Literature provides a form for experience, placing relevant episodes into coherent sequence and thereby showing life's unity or meaning. Literature reveals life's fragmentation as well, sorting the world out into segments that can be identified and examined. It helps focus on essentials, permitting readers/hearers to experience with different intensity but with new understanding the parts of life they have known. Literature reveals how both the institutions of society and nature itself affect human life. Finally, literature leads or entices the readers/hearers into meeting a writer-creator whose medium (words) they know, whose subject (human nature) they live with, and whose vision (life's meaning) they hope to understand.[4]

Children are eager to know about innumerable subjects and literature can satisfy their curiosities. Boys and girls exhibit and share:

An inward-looking *curiosity about themselves,* and a book like Berger's *I Have Feelings Too* (Human Sciences, 1979) responds to this concern.

A *curiosity about the natural world,* and Gans' *When Birds Change Their Feathers* (Crowell, 1980) helps them appreciate their environment.

A *curiosity about people and places,* and writers like Margaret Ronan, Jean Fritz, and Ronald Syme help young readers discover facts about various American states, historical Americans, and famed explorers, respectively.

A *curiosity about machines and how they work,* which is satisfied by writers like Jan Adkins and Gail Gibbons.

A *curiosity about facts and proofs of facts,* and so a popular book is the *Guinness Book of World Records,* revised annually by the Sterling Publishing Company of New York City.

A *curiosity about the ideals by which men live,* which leads children to ponder Black's *The First Book of Ethics* (Watts, 1975).

A *curiosity about the social world and how to get along in society,* which is satisfied by books like Hoke's *Etiquette, Your Ticket to Good Times* (Watts, 1970) and Naylor's *Getting Along with Your Friends* (Abingdon, 1980).

A practical and energetic *curiosity about creative experiences,* and writers like Ed Emberley and James Seidelman help children have fun with arts and crafts.

A *curiosity about the world of make-believe,* and books about science fiction written by John Christopher or Daniel Pinkwater are welcomed.

A *curiosity about the unknown world,* which is satisfied by books about unexplained phenomena by an author like Daniel Cohen.[5]

Contemporary Trends

Books published since 1970 offer a splendidly diversified reading fare for boys and girls, according to Cianciolo, who has identified some of the modern trends.[6] Most of the current writers for young readers have restated rather than abandoned the cultural traditions and so traditional literary forms are still very much present. Still there are three forms of iconoclastic novels that have been created for the juvenile reader: existentialist or activist novels like Tate's *Ben and Annie* (Doubleday, 1974); impressionist novels like Blume's *Are You There God? It's Me, Margaret* (Bradbury, 1970); and antirealistic or surrealistic novels like Wersba's *Amanda, Dreaming* (Atheneum, 1973). The contemporary authors of literature for children do not sentimentalize childhood but presume that boys and girls have basically the same emotions as adults although children's emotions are less complex. Children are reading this new literature with enthusiasm and pleasure.

Other trends in literature have been recognized too. There are many more picture books and those books that are profusely illustrated but not truly "picture books" per se have been offered to readers of all ages, not just to preschool and primary children. Then there are books displaying various art styles, with some artists creating sophisticated drawings or paintings as carefully as if the illustrations were intended for exhibition in an art gallery.

Another noticeable trend since 1970 has been the increasing number of children's novels about World War II and the Great Depression as well as many antiwar books. Also, an antiestablishment theme of disillusionment is now being reflected in some of the literature written for children. In addition, books are currently available about physical, mental and emotional disorders and handicaps, as well as books concerned with the plight of the elderly and the addiction of the young to drugs or alcohol. Finally, the advancement of technology has made available for young readers some excellent foreign literary selections in translation.

One contemporary trend, which actually first surfaced about 100 years ago, is the movable or pop-up book. The art work in many of these books is so outstanding that there are those who predict that the 1980s may well have been the start of the second Golden Age of movable books for children. Notable current pop-ups include Pienkowski's *Dinnertime* (Price/Stern/Sloan, 1981), Carle's *The Honeybee and the Robber* (Philomel, 1981), and Crowther's *The Most Amazing Hide-and-Seek Counting Book* (Viking, 1981). Reissues of productions of movables published in the 1800s are also available, such as Nister's *Magic Windows* (Collins, 1981) and *Revolving Pictures* (Collins, 1979). Modern young readers often react to such movable books by creating simple greeting card pop-ups.

Children's Literary Interests/ Preferences

Since the beginning of the century, several hundred studies of children's literary *interests* (actual reading behaviors) or reading *preferences* (expressed attitudes) have been completed. Although interest studies pinpoint what the population actually has read or does read, while preference studies concern hypothetical situations, the terms are often used interchangeably by researchers[7] and therefore by this writer.

Although reading preference is highly variable and children can be expected to display different preferences by grade (maturation) or by community, boys and girls exhibit the most stable difference in terms of specific likes and dislikes for males and females.[8] Results from a most recent study of 1127 intermediate-grade children are consistent with previous findings in identifying strong sex differences in reading choices. Generally, boys have stronger preferences for the themes of history/geography, sports, science, fantasy, and travel. Girls have stronger preferences for animals, child/family, poetry, biography, romance, and mystery. Both, however, have similar preferences for adventure, humor, and nature study.

Other earlier research regarding children's literary preferences revealed that:

1. Children prefer books with happy endings.
2. Primary children like animal stories best.
3. White and Hispanic subjects like to read poetry more than their Black agemates.
4. Children prefer to watch television rather than read.
5. Fiction rates high, especially humorous fiction.
6. The overwhelming majority of both primary- and intermediate-level children are initially attracted to a book by its subject matter.
7. Children's reading tastes have largely crystallized by the fifth grade.[9]

An examination of books listed recently as "Children's Choices" in a joint and annual project by the International Reading Association and the Children's Book Council showed that these books usually teach a lesson, have detailed descriptions of settings, are not sad, and possess plots which are faster paced than those found in less-liked books.[10] Their most outstanding quality, however, is warmth. Young readers like books in which characters express their feelings.

Thousands of boys and girls across the United States were surveyed in the early 1980s for their reading interests.[11] Out of 1060 book nominations, the top 50 titles included 31 books of realistic (contemporary) fiction, 11 modern fantasy (of which two—*Charlotte's Web* and *Charlie and the Chocolate Factory*—were in the top ten), three picture story books, two books of historical fiction, two poetry books, and one book of traditional literature. The author clearly dominating the selections was Judy Blume, whose name appears ten times in the Top 50 Titles Chosen by Children, as shown in Table 11.2.

Unfortunately, when the aforementioned list of many respected books was compared to the juvenile best-seller list issued by Dalton bookstores for the same year, only three titles out of the fifty appeared on both lists. Since the Dalton list included many spin-offs from television shows and films, popularity once again did not necessarily equal high-quality literature. Or, in the words of 1978 Nobel Laureate Isaac Bashevis Singer, children read books, not reviews.[12] Singer, whose picture books and short story collections for children have won many awards, has insisted that a child will accept or reject a book only because of his real taste and that telling him that Freud or Moses praised the story will leave the child unimpressed. The need, then, for a balanced literature program in the elementary grades appears paramount to the development of *good* literary taste in each and every child.

Sources and Criteria for Selecting Well-Written Books

Until approximately 1960, the volume of literature for children was relatively small, averaging less than 1000 juvenile titles published annually. Then came federal funding for the support of library materials. As a result, 2895 titles were published in 1965, 2640 in 1970, and 2235 in 1975. By 1980 the average annual output was 2500 new titles, with 10,000 new children's trade books published from 1977 through 1980.[13]

Since 1919, when Macmillan established the first children's department in a publishing house in the United States (and probably the world), the children's book market has become a twentieth-century phenomenon. More than 200 publishing houses are presently engaged in printing juvenile books, and in a recent year (1978) this country alone had an output of 105,700,000 copies of children's books.[14]

Despite this deluge, discriminating selection of a fine book for a specific class or pupil cannot yet be computerized. It still requires a knowledge of the interests, reading ability, and maturity level of that class or child, coupled with a knowledge of the best books to meet those interests and abilities.

The classroom teacher who has personally enjoyed some of the finest children's books can speak convincingly when introducing those books to the boys and girls. Children need to know a little of what each book is about, and a brief preview—or sales pitch—concerning a particular volume helps them gain this information. These days children can receive satisfaction from a variety of readily accessible media, including television and motion pictures, and so the satisfaction a well-written book can bring must be explored in every classroom. This demands

Table 11.2
Books chosen by children: top 50 titles (in order of popularity)*

Blume, Judy. Superfudge. Dutton.
Blume, Judy. Tales of a fourth grade nothing. Dutton.
Blume, Judy. Are you there God? It's me, Margaret. Bradbury.
White, E. B. Charlotte's web. Harper.
Blume, Judy. Blubber. Bradbury.
Silverstein, Shel. Where the sidewalk ends. Harper.
Farley, Walter. The black stallion. Random.
Dahl, Roald. Charlie and the chocolate factory. Knopf.
Rawls, Wilson. Where the red fern grows. Doubleday.
Blume, Judy. Deenie. Bradbury.
Tolkien, J. R. R. The hobbit. Houghton.
Cleary, Beverly. Ramona the pest. Morrow.
Blume, Judy. Forever. Bradbury.
L'Engle, Madeleine. A wrinkle in time. Farrar.
Hinton, S. E. The outsiders. Viking.
Wilder, Laura Ingalls. Little house on the prairie. Harper.
Blume, Judy. Tiger eyes. Bradbury.
Warner, Gertrude. The boxcar children. Albert Whitman.
Cleary, Beverly. The mouse and the motorcycle. Morrow.
Rey, H. A. Curious George. Houghton.
Lewis, C. S. The lion, the witch, and the wardrobe. Macmillan.
Rockwell, Thomas. How to eat fried worms. Watts.
Dahl, Roald. James and the giant peach. Knopf.
Silverstein, Shel. A light in the attic. Harper.
Cleary, Beverly. Ramona Quimby, age 8. Morrow.
O'Brien, Robert. Mrs. Frisby and the rats of NIMH. Atheneum.
Blume, Judy. Freckle juice. Scholastic/Four Winds.
DeClements, Barthe. Nothing's fair in fifth grade. Viking.
Sobol, Donald J. Encyclopedia Brown series. Various publishers.
Seuss, Dr. The cat in the hat. Random.
Seuss, Dr. Green eggs and ham. Random.
Danziger, Paula. The cat ate my gymsuit. Delacorte.
Blume, Judy. Otherwise known as Sheila the great. Dutton.
Dixon, Franklin W. Hardy boys books. Grosset.
Keene, Carolyn. Nancy Drew books. Grosset.
Tolkien, J. R. R. Lord of the rings trilogy. Houghton.
Wilder, Laura Ingalls. Little House books (as a group). Harper.
Andrews, V. C. Flowers in the attic. Pocket.
Blume, Judy. It's not the end of the world. Bradbury.
Cinderella. Various publishers.
Schulz, Charles M. Charlie Brown and Peanuts books (as a group). Various publishers.
Lewis, C. S. Narnia chronicles (as a group). Macmillan.
Choose your own adventure series. Bantam.
Cleary, Beverly. Ramona and her mother. Morrow.
O'Dell, Scott. Island of the blue dolphins. Houghton.
Paterson, Katherine. Bridge to Terabithia. Crowell.
Sewell, Anna. Black Beauty. Various editions.
Byars, Betsy. The pinballs. Harper.
Howe, Deborah and **Howe, James.** Bunnicula. Atheneum.
Parish, Peggy. Amelia Bedelia. Harper.

*Reprinted by permission of the American Library Association from Barbara Elleman, "Chosen by Children," in BOOKLIST 79(7):508-9 (Dec. 1, 1982); copyright © 1982 by the American Library Association.

a personal knowledge by the teacher of many books in order that he or she may convey some of the excitement, wonder, and beauty of the printed page to young listeners and readers.

Yet many teachers, according to a five-state investigation conducted recently, need to update their information in the field of children's literature.[15] A total of 773 preservice and inservice teachers in California, Georgia, Maine, Nebraska, and Texas were asked to name their three favorite books *as a child,* the three best children's books *now,* and the three most popular children's books *now.* On the best books list, out of 440 titles, the teachers chose only seven titles published since 1970 and also selected 39 percent of the titles from their list of childhood favorites. On the popular books list, out of 308 titles, the teacher selected only four titles (plus "Star Wars") published since 1970 and also picked 45 percent of the titles from their compilation of childhood favorites. Even more distressing was the 65 percent overlap of titles on both the best and the most popular lists! The researchers concluded that, while teachers' opinions regarding best and most popular books influence the selection of what teachers will read to and recommend to their classes, it is important that teachers expand their own experiences with literature so that they may in turn introduce some of those current high-quality books to children.

To learn more about new books and recent editions of older books, elementary school teachers can consult such periodicals as *Booklist* (published twice monthly and once in August), *Horn Book Magazine* (issued bimonthly), *Childhood Education* (published five times a year), and *Language Arts* or *School Library Journal* (each issued eight times a year), or examine book-review sections in such national newspapers as *The New York Times* or *The Christian Science Monitor,* which regularly compile material about new children's books. There are also published bibliographies (available in many public libraries) including:

Adventuring with Books (NCTE, 1981)
Best Books for Children (Bowker, 1981)
The Best in Children's Books (University of Chicago Press, 1980)
The Black Experience in Children's Books (New York Public Library, 1979)
The Bookfinder (American Guidance Service, 1981)
Books for the Gifted Child (Bowker, 1980)
Books for Today's Young Readers (Feminist Press, 1982)
Children's Books Too Good to Miss (University Press Books, 1980)
Children's Catalog (Wilson, 1981) and its annual supplements
A Comprehensive Guide to Children's Literature with a Jewish Theme (Schocken, 1981)
The Elementary School Library Collection (Bro-Dart, 1982)
A Hispanic Heritage (Scarecrow Press, 1980)
Let's Read Together (American Library Association, 1981)
Literature By and About the American Indian (NCTE, 1979)
Reading for Young People: The Northwest (American Library Association, 1981)
———Other titles in the series include: *The Rocky Mountains* (1980), *The Southeast* (1980), *The Middle Atlantic* (1980), *The Great Plains* (1979), and *The Midwest* (1979).
The Single-Parent Family in Children's Books (Scarecrow, 1978)

Use of such book-selection aids will help keep classroom teachers informed of titles worthy of being termed children's literature. They can also keep in mind the many award-winning books, especially the Caldecott Medal and Newbery Medal winners (together with their Honor Books) listed in Appendix 4. Finally, they can request catalogs from publishers specializing in children's books, such as Scholastic, Viking, Dell, and Atheneum.

With the ever increasing number of juvenile books from which to choose, the classroom teachers must be aware of certain criteria to help them identify a quality book for children.

The first criterion concerning all children's books is format or the physical appearance of a volume. Technological improvements in printing and picture reproduction are making possible attractive books for young readers. Although no book should ever be selected on the basis of format alone, matters of illustration, typography, binding, spacing, and paper quality cannot be ignored when books are chosen for classroom use. Such books must represent the combined efforts of the best editors, illustrators, book designers, printers, and authors.

The importance of format was recently confirmed in a study of 145 third and sixth graders in New York State, representing all reading ability groups, who were each interviewed individually.[16] Third graders and children in the low and middle reading groups considered format very important to book selection. Preferred by the total sample were books of larger page size, larger type size, and the sans serif (without small finishing strokes at the top and bottom of letters) type style. In the area of illustrations children are not as concerned with eye-appeal as they are with a desire to avoid confusion when reading. Consequently they prefer illustrations placed at the bottom or top of the page.

Other criteria besides format for fiction, biography, informational books, and wordless books are discussed below.

Fiction

Although the pupils' reading will not be limited to stories, they will remain the first and enduring favorite of the boys and girls. Good stories possess seven strong elements.

Plot

Children are most interested in the action or plot of the story. In a well-written book the action is plausible and credible, developing naturally from the behavior and decisions of the characters, and is not dependent upon coincidence or contrivance. A story must have a beginning, a middle, and an ending. Children prefer an orderly sequence of events and generally lack the maturity to understand flashbacks. A well-plotted book for the intermediate grades is Garner's *The Owl Service* (Walck, 1968).

Setting

The setting is the time and place of the action. It may be in the past, the present, or the future. The story may take place in a specific locale, or the setting may be deliberately vague to convey the feeling of all large cities or rural communities. It should, however, be clear, believable, and, in the case of historical fiction, authentic.

Both the time and the place should affect the action, the characters, and the theme. Younger readers can quickly grasp the setting of Monjo's *The Secret of the Sachem's Tree* (Coward, 1972) and Skorpen's *Old Arthur* (Harper, 1972). Older readers understand the setting of Sutcliff's *The Witch's Brat* (Walck, 1970).

Theme

A good book needs a worthy theme which provides a dimension of the story beyond the action of the plot. It may be the acceptance of self or others, the overcoming of fear or prejudice, or simply growing up. The theme of a book reveals the author's purpose in writing the story.

In a well-written book the theme avoids moralizing and yet effectively evolves from the events in the story and unifies them. Such a book is Cunningham's *Dorp Dead* (Pantheon, 1965), which older children especially enjoy.

Style

The style of writing in a book is the manner in which the author has selected and arranged words in presenting the story. A quality book possesses a style which respects children as intelligent individuals with rights and interests of their own. Children resent books whose style is patronizing or overly sentimental, or contains too much description or material for contemplation. Some pupils prefer books not written in the first person.

Primary grade children like to listen to Goble's *The Girl Who Loved Wild Horses* (Bradbury, 1978). Intermediate-grade pupils appreciate the contemporary dialogue in many of the books by E. L. Konigsburg.

Characterization

The personalities (animal or human) portrayed in children's books must be convincing and lifelike, displaying realistic strengths and weaknesses, and must be consistent in their portrayal. While not every character in a well-constructed story will change, there is frequent personality development as happenings occur and problems are solved. Too, characters should speak and behave in accordance with their culture, age, and educational experience.

Books with sound characterizations for primary children include Lindgren's *Pippi Longstocking* (Viking, 1950) and Caudill's *Did You Carry the Flag Today, Charley?* (Holt, 1966). Two for intermediate-grade pupils are the Cleavers' *Me Too* (Lippincott, 1973) and Greene's *A Girl Called Al* (Viking, 1969).

Point of View

A single incident may often be described differently by each individual witnessing or experiencing it. Consequently, point of view refers to the teller of the story and his/her values, feelings, or background. Contemporary fiction for middle-grade children is often told from a first person point of view (i.e., the viewpoint of a child) whether he or she is the main character or only a bystander. Sometimes an author may choose to offer a variety of viewpoints by letting the actions of the characters speak for each of them. Other times an author may restrict the viewpoint, with the only change coming from the evolving attitude of one narrator. Points of view must be consistent to encourage readers to believe the character(s) or narrator and the ensuing action.

The popular Ramona stories by Beverly Cleary are a good example of stories told from the viewpoint of a bright seven- or eight-year-old.

Nonstereotyping

Good literature does not contain bias and stereotyping in its portrayal of men, women, blacks, whites, the old, the young or any group that can be singled out and distinguished from any other. Such bias can be expressed by language, by illustrations, and by messages in the form of omissions and/or distortions.

Although awareness of such stereotypes has escalated since the civil-rights movement of the 1960s, surprisingly little progress has been made in some areas. In that of sex-role development in children's picture books, for example, a survey of the acclaimed Caldecott Medal and Honor Books for 1976–1980 revealed that there are still far more male (72%) than female (28%) characters and far more male (74%) than female (26%) images.[17] Yet both characters and images influence a child's developing concept of sex roles. The researcher believes that the causes contributing to sexual inequality and stereotyping in children's picture books are: male bias in career preparation and reading materials; the peculiarities of the English language; a sexist literary heritage; a preponderance of male artists; and the conditions of the 1950s which strengthened the idea that a woman's place was only in the home.

Informational Books

Since trade books today are being used more and more to supplement texts and other curricular resources, teachers must be familiar with the varied criteria used to evaluate informational books. The first of these is *author qualification,* covering competence in the chosen field, ability to communicate knowledge to children, and responsibility to distinguish between opinions/theories and facts. The second criterion is *accuracy and currency* because children cannot be supplied with facts that are out of date, superficial or rely on anthropomorphism; in many informational books the copyright date is critical. A third criterion is *imaginative and accurate illustrations* which help children comprehend technical principles and terms. A fourth criterion is the *scope and organization* of the text with logical sequencing and both a simplification and limitation of material. A fifth criterion is *elimination of stereotyping and the presentation of differing views on controversial subjects. Self-containment* is the sixth criterion so that children need not consult other books in an effort to understand the material therein presented. The enthusiasm or interest that boys and girls have for a particular subject may be quite brief. The seventh and final criterion is *style,* which should be lively and employ vocabulary geared to the reading ability of the children.

Older boys and girls like to read Wolf's *Firehouse* (Morrow, 1983) and Gilbert's *How to Take Tests* (Morrow, 1983). All ages enjoy Sattler's *The Illustrated Dinosaur Dictionary* (Lothrop, 1983).

Biography

The essentials of good biography are history (with authentic and verifiable facts), the person (considered as an individual rather than a type or paragon), and literary artistry with pleasing style.[18] There are three kinds of biography presented in children's literature. The first is authentic biography that is a well-documented and researched account of a person's life. It corresponds to adult biography and often includes photographs. Any conversations that are described include only those statements that are actually known to have been made by the subject. Outstanding examples are Meigs' *Invincible Louisa* (Little, 1961) and McKown's *The World of Mary Cassatt* (Crowell, 1972).

The second kind is fictionalized biography. Though grounded in thorough research, it allows the author more freedom to dramatize certain events and personalize the subject. The author may invent dialog, but the conversations are usually based upon actual facts taken from journals and diaries of the period. Fictionalized biography makes use of the narrative approach and is the generally accepted form for juvenile books. Recommended examples are Felton's *Mumbet, The Story of Elizabeth Freeman* (Dodd, 1970) and Judson's *Abraham Lincoln, Friend of the People* (Follett, 1950).

Biographical fiction is the third kind of children's biography. It consists entirely of imagined conversation and reconstructed action. Outstanding examples include Robert Lawson's amusing *Mr. Revere and I* (Little, 1953), and Fritz's *Where Do You Think You're Going, Christopher Columbus?* (Putnam, 1980).

Children may also become interested in biographical series, such as the *Troll Adventurers* (Troll Associates), *Focus on Women Series* (Greenhaven Press), *Sports Hero Series* (Putnam), and *Breakthrough Books* (Harper). In all well-written biographies the young readers enjoy a style that is vigorous and a narrative that is fast moving. The research material never detracts from the absorbing account of the life of the subject.

Wordless Picture Books

Almost unknown as recently as 1970, books without words now constitute a new genre in literature in the United States and appear regularly from reputable publishers. They are useful for reading-readiness activities and stimulate both language development and creative writing. Since their interpretation depends solely on the illustrations, it is crucial that the immediate action of each picture as well as the cumulative sequence of action in all the pictures be distinctly portrayed and readily understood by children of the age group for whom the books are intended. In other words, only two criteria apply when evaluating wordless pictures: the quality of the illustrations and the quality of the story.

Larrick conducted an informal survey concerning wordless picture books among elementary classroom teachers and children in three Pennsylvania towns.[19] Kindergarten teachers used wordless books with small groups of pupils who later role played or produced their own "surprise books" (using personal drawings or magazine photos). Primary children also responded more creatively to such follow-up activities as the taping of stories when a wordless book was introduced to a very small group or even on a one-to-one basis. Finally, those sixth graders who were poor readers thought that a wordless book would be "a good starter" for young readers because it challenges the imagination, resembles a silent movie, gives the readers more to ponder, and allows them to experience feelings which they must then put into words. For themselves, however, the sixth graders agreed that they preferred books with words since "you've got to learn to read sometime and we need words at our age." Rated as the top favorite author of wordless books in the survey was Mercer Mayer.

Although the majority of wordless picture books are fantasy and most of their main characters are animals, there are also informational books, realistic stories, and subtle books with pictures that do not tell stories. Animal fantasy is shown in Goodall's *Paddy's New Hat* (Atheneum, 1980). Child fantasy is the core of Heller's *Lily at the Table* (Macmillan, 1979). Informational wordless books include Crews' *Truck* (Greenwillow, 1980) and Koren's *Behind the Wheel* (Holt, 1972) while realistic stories without words include Krahn's *Catch That Cat!* (Dutton, 1978) and Ormerod's *Sunshine* (Lothrop, 1981). Finally, there are wordless books that do not tell stories, such as Ungerer's *Snail, Where Are You?* (Harper, 1962) and Anno's *Upside-Downers: More Pictures to Stretch the Imagination* (Weatherhill, 1971).

One of the longest wordless books is Ward's *The Silver Pony* (Houghton, 1973) which has some 80 pictures and appeals particularly to children in grades two to four.

Poetry: Literary Work in Metrical Form

Since children are entitled to hear satisfying poetry as well as fine prose, their teacher should be cognizant of three important elements in good poetry:

1. *Distinguished diction.* The words and phrases must be carefully chosen and rich in sensory and associated meanings. Both connotative and descriptive words are interwoven in Updike's *A Child's Calendar* (Knopf, 1965) and Milne's *When We Were Very Young* (Dutton, 1961).
2. *Significant content.* Poems should appeal to the intellect as well as to the emotions. Long or short, poems need a well-defined theme, such as those found in Ciardi's *Fast and Slow* (Houghton, 1975) and Frost's *You Come Too* (Holt, 1959). Poetry should provide new meaning to the students' everyday experiences.
3. *Singing quality.* Some poems have as much melody as does music, for the rhythm and the arrangement of the lines are suggestive of the mood of the poem. There is movement as well. De La Mare's *Peacock Pie* (Knopf, 1961) and Behn's *The Golden Hive* (Harcourt, 1966) are filled with poems with pronounced melody and movement. Children are helped to understand the rhythm in poetry as they complete exercises in some of the current language arts series, as shown in Figure 11.1.

In selecting a poem for children, the teacher must consider their background and age level, their needs, their previous experience with poetry, and the modern setting in which they live. The teacher should begin where the children are. For preschool and kindergarten pupils, the rhymes in *The Mother Goose Book* (Random, 1976) represent a strong and pleasant beginning. If primary children have not heard much poetry, the teacher can start with some of the traditional rhymes for games and tongue-twisters found in Lee's *Alligator Pie* (Houghton, 1975) as well as more modern poems such as those in Cole's *I'm Mad at You* (Collins, 1978). Older boys and girls who have not yet been introduced to poetry may be reached through books of narrative or humorous poems, such as Noyes' *The Highwayman* (Viking, 1983) and Bodecker's *Let's Marry Said the Cherry and Other Nonsense Poems* (Atheneum, 1974), respectively. The teacher can use country or folk music as a prelude to poetry with pupils in all grades. With older students the teacher may wish to develop an introductory unit centered about a poet to whom pupils can relate, such as Myra Cohn Livingston.

Figure 11.1.
Exercises in Hearing the Rhythm in Poetry.

Exercises Hearing the Rhythm in Poetry

A. Copy this poem on your paper. Read it aloud. Mark the strong beats in each line.

B. Discuss the rhythm of the poem. Answer these questions.

1. Is the rhythm strong?
2. Do the beats form a pattern?
3. Does the rhythm seem right for the meaning of the poem?

C. Think of a lively subject. Write a short poem that has strong rhythm. Mark the strong beats in each line. Change words to make the beats into an even pattern.

The poetry presented should have relevance for today's child. It should be appropriate in theme and mood to the maturity of the group. It should not be didactic or filled with archaic vocabulary. Neither should it be coy, nostalgic, or sarcastic. Finally, it should generally be true poetry and not always merely verse.

The teaching of poetry can follow no set pattern. Unless the teacher enjoys poetry, the students will not respond enthusiastically. The teacher's personal choice of poetry guides pupils in building their own individual yardsticks. Therefore, the teacher's personal definition of poetry will determine how far he or she will carry the children into the realm of poetry.

Forms of Poetry for Children

One of the literary understandings to develop in elementary school literature is knowledge of types of poetry. These understandings grow gradually, so the wise teacher will provide balance in the selection of poetic forms as children exhibit readiness for them. There are several major forms.

Most of the poetry written for children is *lyric poetry.* It is usually descriptive or personal, with no prescribed length or structure except that it be melodic and music-making. Many of the poems of Robert Louis Stevenson, Christina Rossetti, Eleanor Farjeon, Elizabeth Coatsworth, Sara Teasdale, Eve Merriam, and Henry Behn have this singing quality and can therefore be termed lyrical.

One of the best ways to capture pupil interest in poems is to present a variety of *narrative poetry.* Each of these so-called story poems relates a particular episode/event or tells a long tale. Seven- and eight-year-olds enjoy the long narrative verses of the many books by Dr. Seuss. Older children respond to Longfellow's *Paul Revere's Ride* (Windmill, 1973) and Thayer's *Casey at the Bat* (Coward, 1978). An outstanding classical narrative poem is Browning's *The Pied Piper of Hamelin* (Scroll Press, 1970) which has wide appeal. Narrative poems may appear as lyrics, sonnets, or free verse.

A special type of narrative poem that has been adapted for singing and that contains repetition, rhythm, and a refrain is a *ballad.* With the current popularity of folk singing there has been renewed interest in the ballad form. There are both literary ballads with recognized authors and popular ballads with no known authors. Children in the middle grades will enjoy popular ballads like "The Raggle, Taggle Gypsies," "Get Up and Bar the Door," and "Lord Randal." Literary ballads appropriate for use with children are included in Plotz' *As I Walked Out One Evening* (Greenwillow, 1976).

Children enjoy *limericks,* a nonsense form of five-lined verse. The first and second lines rhyme, as do the third and fourth lines, but the fifth line generally ends in a surprising or humorous statement. Contrary to popular belief, Edward Lear did not originate the limerick. He did, however, do much to popularize it, and pupils listen eagerly to many of the limericks in his *Whizz* (Macmillan, 1973). Middle-grade children also find Smith's *Typewriter Town* (Dutton, 1960) challenging because it combines limericks with pictures made by using the typewriter.

Pupils who have the opportunity to hear *free verse* are relieved to discover that all poetry does not rhyme. Free verse sounds much like other poetry when read aloud, but often looks different on the printed page. Sandburg's "Fog" and Hughes' "April Rain Song" are popular examples of the effective use of free verse which depends upon cadence or rhythm for its poetic form.

Some children enjoy hearing—and others enjoy writing—a Japanese verse form of three lines called *haiku.* Containing a total of only seventeen syllables, the first and third lines of the haiku have five syllables each, and the middle line has seven. Nearly every haiku may be divided into two parts: first a simple description that refers to a season; and second, a statement of feeling or mood. The teacher may wish to share with the class two volumes of haiku translated by Harry Behn and entitled *Cricket Songs: Japanese Haiku* (Harcourt, 1964) and *More Cricket Songs* (Harcourt, 1971).

Other old Japanese poetic forms are *senryu* and *tanka.* The first is identical to haiku, with seventeen syllables in three lines, except that it may deal with any topic; it is named after the poet who originated the form. Tanka is identical to haiku for its initial three lines, but adds two more lines of seven syllables each, for a total of thirty-one syllables; it usually completes a thought or tells a story. Elementary children may wish to hear or read some Japanese poetry compiled by Virginia Baron, in her *The Seasons of Time: Tanka Poetry of Ancient Japan* (Dial, 1968), and by Richard Lewis, in his *There Are Two Lives: Poems by Children of Japan* (Simon, 1970).

Children's Preferences

Since adults are unable to accurately predict which poems children will like, it is important to examine children's preferences directly.

Two national samplings, using the same schools but in different years, found that elementary children as a whole prefer limericks and narrative poems and dislike free verse and haiku.[20] Children in both the primary and intermediate grades enjoy poems that are funny as well as poems about animals and familiar experiences. They all dislike poems relying upon metaphor, simile or personification but like rhymed poems and those with sound effects (alliteration and onomatopoeia). Boys and girls in grades one to three enjoy poems about fantastic and strange events, but those in grades four to six prefer more realistic content. A second area of distinction is that younger children prefer traditional poetry, but the older pupils like modern poems. There were no overall sex differences.

What may be even more significant is the conclusion reached in a national survey of 1,401 elementary students in urban, suburban, and rural schools with varied socioeconomic backgrounds: *two out of three pupils like poetry.*[21] Urban students like poetry more than either the suburban or rural pupils.

Boys and girls in most of the elementary grades find nothing peculiar, boring, or silly about poetry because so many of the experiences of the children and their language are related to poetic experiences and language. Elements that are shared by both young pupils and poets, such as love of concrete imagery, use of accentuated rhythm, and indulgence in playfulness, work positively for the interest that children have for poetry—at least through grade four. And fifth and sixth graders, whose teacher possesses a realistic concept of poetry and couples pupils and poems as subtly as pupils and prose, will also continue their initial enthusiasm for poetry. However, interest in poetry begins to wane as students mature.

Boys and girls in the primary grades enjoy a wide variety of verse and poetry. They respond readily to nonsense and humor, ballads and narrative poetry, poems about animals, automobiles, and trains, and poetry that deals with daily activities. A sampling of the kinds of poetry and verse that they enjoy includes:

Austin's "Texas Trains and Trails"
Baruch's "Automobile Mechanics"
Bennett's "A Modern Dragon"
Brown's "Jonathan Bing"
Ciardi's "Mummy Slept Late and Daddy Fixed Breakfast"
Farjeon's "Cat"
Field's "The Duel"
Hoberman's "A Bookworm of Curious Breed"
Lear's "The Owl and the Pussy-Cat"
Lenski's "Bad Boy"
Lindsay's "The Little Turtle"
Merriam's "The Motor-Boat Song"
Nash's "The Tale of Custard the Dragon"
Prelutsky's "The Lurpp is on the Loose"
Richards' "Eletelephony"
Starbird's "Eat-It-All Elaine"
Wells' "The Tutor"

Children in the intermediate grades like poems which are related to their interests and experiences, poems that are humorous, and poems with strength of rhythm and rhyme. They will accept narrative verse that has action and excitement, such as Carmer's *The Boy from Vincennes* (Harvey, 1972) and may be exposed to some serious poems such as the Benets' "Nancy Hanks." They enjoy popular ballads that are not too difficult to read, including the traditional ones like Abisch and Kapian's *Sweet Betsy from Pike* (Dutton, 1970). They like the element of mystery in Stevenson's "Windy Nights."

Teachers concerned with helping children express their feelings will be interested in sharing one or more of the following books with their classes:

Adoff's *I Am the Running Girl* (Harper, 1979)
Grimes' *Something on My Mind* (Dial, 1978)
Hopkins' *By Myself* (Crowell, 1980)
Larrick's *Bring Me All of Your Dreams* (Evans, 1980)
Maher's *Alice Yazzie's Year: Poems* (Coward, 1977)
Marzollo's *Close Your Eyes* (Dial, 1978)
Tudor's *The Springs of Joy* (Rand, 1979)

Lastly, the teacher should be aware of the results of national polls of approximately 10,000 children in classrooms across the country for top selections among recently published poetry books.[22] The finalists which appeared in the "Children's Choices" for 1981 or 1982 were: Cole's *Poem Stew* (Lippincott, 1981); Moore's *The Night Before Christmas* (Holiday, 1980); Prelutsky's *Rainy Rainy Saturday* (Greenwillow, 1980); Silverstein's *The Missing Piece Meets the Big O* (Harper, 1981); and Viorst's *If I Were in Charge of the World and Other Worries* (Atheneum, 1981).

Modern Poetry for Children

Children should hear poems—and poems were written to be read aloud—published earlier in this century as well as those printed for them in the eighteenth and nineteenth centuries. And teachers can readily locate such poems in the fine anthologies compiled by May Hill Arbuthnot (1967), Edward Blishen (1963), Helen Ferris (1957), Elizabeth Sechrist (1946), Burton Stevenson (1956), and Louis Untermeyer (1935, 1959).

However, elementary pupils are also entitled to listen to poetry/verse compiled or written more recently. The recommended publications listed here are divided among those appealing to all ages, to younger children, and to intermediate students.

For all ages:

- Abercrombie's *The Other Side of a Poem* (Harper, 1977)
- Adoff's *Friend Dog* (Lippincott, 1980)
- Hopkins' *To Look at Any Thing* (Harcourt, 1978)
- Prelutsky's *Nightmares: Poems to Trouble Your Sleep* (Greenwillow, 1976)
- Watson's *Blueberries Lavender* (Addison, 1977)
- Wilner's *The Poetry Troupe* (Scribner, 1977)
- Wood's *War Cry on a Prayer Feather* (Doubleday, 1979)

For ages 4–9:

- Cole's *Oh, Such Foolishness!* (Lippincott, 1978)
- Farber's *Never Say Ugh to a Bug* (Greenwillow, 1979)
- Hopkins' *Go to Bed!* (Knopf, 1979)
- Lewin's *Animal Snackers* (Dodd, 1980)
- Lewis' *Up and Down the River: Boat Poems* (Harper, 1979)
- Wallace's *Ghost Poems* (Holiday, 1979)
- Yolen's *How Beastly! A Menagerie of Nonsense Poems* (Collins, 1980)

For ages 8–12:

- Baylor's *The Other Way to Listen* (Scribner, 1978)
- Larrick's *Bring Me All of Your Dreams* (Evans, 1980)
- Livingston's *A Lollygag of Limericks* (Atheneum, 1978)
- McCord's *Speak Up* (Little, 1980)
- Morrison's *The Sidewalk Racer and Other Poems of Sports and Motion* (Lothrop, 1977)
- Oliver's *Cornucopia* (Atheneum, 1978)
- Worth's *More Small Poems* (Farrar, 1976)

Bibliotherapy—or Books That Help Children to Cope

As children grow and develop, they encounter a multitude of problems stemming from sibling relationships, family mobility, hospital confinement, parental separation, physical handicaps, or other sources. Some of their concerns arise chiefly within themselves, while others evolve from outside events/conditions that affect the boys and girls: Jim and his divorced mother live alone; Jennifer is fat and friendless; Kim Chu is the first Asian in the school; and seven-year-old Chris has already lived in nine different states.

To help these children attain some degree of understanding of their personal difficulties, there are books that can be used to enable the reader or listener to accept problems in a wholesome manner. Books for precisely such mental hygiene comprise *bibliotherapy* and provide a source of insight and relief from the varied pressures that young readers face during the ups and downs of normal development. Bibliotherapy may help boys and girls relieve conscious problems in a controlled manner and gain information about the psychology and physiology of human behavior. What it cannot do, however, is to provide therapy through literature for those who have emotional or mental illnesses and are in need of clinical treatment.

Once defined as a process of dynamic interaction between literature and the personality of the reader (which may be utilized for personality assessment, adjustment and growth), bibliotherapy may generally be used by the teacher in two ways. With *therapeutic* bibliotherapy the teacher may attempt to solve children's actual problems by presenting similar experiences vicariously through books. By recognizing their problems and possible solutions in literature, the children presumably gain new insight and are then able to take a step toward resolving their personal difficulties. On the other hand, the teacher who employs *preventive* bibliotherapy believes that pupils will be better able to make satisfactory adjustments to some trying situations in the future provided that they have met similar problems in stories which they presently read or hear. In a sense, preventive bibliotherapy is analogous to an inoculation to prevent a contagious disease. It contributes to understanding and compassion as it offers children attitudes and standards of behavior that will help them to adjust to some or most of the personal difficulties they will encounter.

Choosing and Using Books to Help Pupils Cope

Books designed to help change social and emotional behavior among nonclinical cases should still exemplify good literature. Their content must be worthwhile and their style respectful to children. Racial, religious, or nationality groups must each be pictured with accuracy and dignity. In short, any book selected for bibliotherapy should be a book that boys and girls today want to read.

The teacher may choose to use a particular book either with a large-group guidance session, a small-group session, or in an individual conference. The large session is especially suited for preventive bibliotherapy where each member can benefit from exposure to the book. The small-group session, much like a group reading lesson, is appropriate for therapeutic bibliotherapy where several children all have a common problem. Individual conferences may incorporate preventive bibliotherapy when the teacher has been made aware of a forthcoming

Some of the problems associated with starting school may be resolved for this child through therapeutic bibliotherapy. (Photo courtesy of Charles Campbell.)

change in a child's life, e.g., that seven-year-old Rhonda will be leaving California for upstate New York before the end of the term. An unforeseen occasion may also demand therapeutic bibliotherapy, e.g., when Mike's grandfather suddenly dies. In preparation for either the personal conference or the group session the teacher is advised to maintain a supply of index cards, each containing the title and subject matter of a recommended book available in the school library media center.

After either the individual conference or the group guidance sessions, the teacher must assign follow-up activities. Younger children can be challenged through such projective devices as drawing, painting, puppetry, or dramatic play. Older pupils, however, often wish to retell what happened in the story itself and explore the results of certain behaviors or feelings before reaching a generalization about the consequences of particular conditions or traumas. With both age groups follow-up activities are important, for without them no significant amount of behavioral change can occur.

Selected Books Useful in Bibliotherapy

Of the books included in the following list, those marked with an *E* are picture books or easy books planned especially for the primary grades, while juvenile books marked with a *J* are intended for intermediate-grade children. In either case the teacher will wish to personally examine each book to determine its appropriateness and utility for the individual child's or group's needs.[23]

A. Exceptionality: Adjustments to Handicaps
   Autism
      (E) Gold's *Please Don't Say Hello* (Human Sciences, 1976)
      (J) Spence's *The Devil Hole* (Lothrop, 1977)
   Cerebral Palsy
      (E) Mack's *Tracy* (Raintree, 1976)
      (E) Robinet's *Jay and the Marigold* (Childrens, 1976)
   Epilepsy
      (J) Hermes' *What If They Knew?* (Harper, 1980)
      (J) Young's *What Difference Does It Make, Danny?* (Deutsch, 1980)
   General Handicaps
      (J) Kamien's *What If You Couldn't . . . ? A Book about Special Needs* (Scribner, 1979)
      (J) Jones' *The Acorn People* (Bantam, 1977)
   Hearing Impairment
      (E) Arthur's *My Sister's Silent World* (Childrens, 1979)
      (J) Wolf's *Anna's Silent World* (Lippincott, 1977)
   Intellectual Impairment
      (J) Clifton's *My Friend Jacob* (Dutton, 1980)
      (E) Hasler's *Martin Is Our Friend* (Abingdon, 1981)
   Orthopedic Impairment
      (J) Cook's *To Walk on Two Feet* (Westminster, 1978)
      (J) Wolf's *Don't Feel Sorry for Paul* (Lippincott, 1974)
   Stuttering
      (E) Christopher's *Glue Fingers* (Little, 1975)
      (J) Kelley's *The Trouble with Explosives* (Bradbury, 1976)
   Visual Impairment
      (E) Montgomery's *"Seeing" in the Dark* (Garrard, 1979)
      (E) Wosmek's *A Bowl of Sun* (Childrens, 1976)
B. Adjustment to New Environment/Condition
   Camp
      (J) Angell's *In Summertime, It's Tuffy* (Bradbury, 1977)
      (J) Shaw's *Shape Up, Burke* (Nelson, 1976)
   Death of a Grandparent
      (E) Bartoli's *Nonna* (Harvey House, 1975)
      (E/J) Grollman's *Talking About Death: A Dialogue Between Parent and Child* (Beacon, 1976)
   Death of a Parent
      (J) Mann's *There Are Two Kinds of Terrible* (Doubleday, 1977)
      (J) Wallace-Brodeur's *The Kenton Year* (Atheneum, 1980)
   Home with Working Mother
      (E) Cleary's *Ramona and Her Mother* (Morrow, 1979)
      (E) Power's *I Wish Laura's Mommy Was My Mommy* (Lippincott, 1979)

Hospital

(J) Singer's *It Can't Hurt Forever* (Harper, 1978)

(E) Sobol's *Jeff's Hospital Book* (Walck, 1975)

New Country

(E) Moore's *Tomas and the Talking Birds* (Herald, 1979)

(J) Madison's *Call Me Danica* (Four Winds, 1977)

New Home

(E) Isadora's *The Potters' Kitchen* (Greenwillow, 1977)

(E) Jacobson's *City, Sing for Me: A Country Child Moves to the City* (Human Sciences, 1978)

School

(E) Bram's *I Don't Want to Go to School* (Greenwillow, 1977)

(E) Wolf's *Adam Smith Goes to School* (Lippincott, 1978)

C. Family Relationships

Adopted Child

(E) Caines' *Abby* (Harper, 1973)

(E) Lapsley's *I Am Adopted* (Bradbury, 1975)

New Baby

(E) Berger's *A New Baby* (Raintree, 1975)

(E) Burningham's *The Baby* (Crowell, 1975)

Siblings

(E) Berger's *Big Sister, Little Brother* (Raintree, 1975)

(E) Kraus's *Big Brother* (Parents, 1973)

Foster Child

(J) Dunlop's *Fox Farm* (Holt, 1979)

(J) Gordon's *The Boy Who Wanted a Family* (Harper, 1980)

Stepmothers

(E) Bunting's *The Big Red Barn* (Harcourt, 1979)

(J) Martin's *Bummer Summer* (Holiday, 1983)

Stepfathers

(E) Clifton's *Everett Anderson's 1–2–3* (Holt, 1977)

(E) Keats' *Louie's Search* (Four Winds, 1980)

Grandparents

(J) Byars' *The House of Wings* (Dell, 1973)

(E) Lasky's *My Island Grandma* (Warner, 1979)

Single Parent Homes

(E) Rogers' *Morris and His Brave Lion* (McGraw, 1975)

(J) Wolitzer's *Out of Love* (Farrar, 1976)

D. Personal Traits

Courage

(E) Tester's *That Big Bruno* (Child's World, 1976)

(J) Cohen's *Bee* (Atheneum, 1975)

Greed

(E) Ginsburg's *Two Greedy Bears* (Macmillan, 1976)

(E) Jones' *I Didn't Want to Be Nice* (Bradbury, 1977)

Honesty/Dishonesty

(J) Levy's *Lizzie Lies a Lot* (Delacorte, 1976)

(E) Sharmat's *A Big Fat Enormous Lie* (Dutton, 1978)

Loneliness

(J) Holmes' *Amy's Goose* (Crowell, 1977)

(J) O'Hanlon's *The Other Michael* (Dial, 1977)

Obesity

(J) Holland's *Dinah and the Green Fat Kingdom* (Lippincott, 1978)

(J) Lipsyte's *One Fat Summer* (Harper, 1977)

Resourcefulness

(E) Lattimore's *Adam's Key* (Morrow, 1976)

(E) Pape's *Snowman for Sale* (Garrard, 1977)

Shyness

(J) Corcoran's *The Faraway Island* (Atheneum, 1977)

(E) Wold's *Tell Them My Name Is Amanda* (Whitman, 1977)

Sportsmanship

(J) Neigoff's *Runner-Up* (Whitman, 1975)

(J) Slote's *The Hotshot* (Watts, 1977)

Minority-Americans in Modern Children's Literature

Learning to accept and respect the diverse cultures in our pluralistic society—another phase of bibliotherapy—involves more than recognition of differences in family custom, diet, and language pattern, according to the Committee on Reading Ladders for Human Relations of the National Council of Teachers of English. Literature which goes beyond a mere acknowledgment of difference to an appreciation of the richness of cultural distinctions leads to sensitivity and feelings of empathy. It also allows the reader or listener to span the barriers of race, color, and religion which keep people apart.

Carefully planned literary experiences that expose children to books other than those of the dominant culture can help them realize that:

1. No one cultural group has a corner on imagination, creativity, poetic quality, or philosophic outlook. Each has made important contributions to the total culture of the country and the world.
2. People belonging to ethnic groups other than the pupils' are real people with feelings, emotions, and needs similar to theirs.
3. Other cultures have ways of looking at life and expressing ideas which can expand the pupils' own understandings. Therefore, pupils who judge other cultures in terms of their own lose the opportunity to broaden their bases of choice in developing values and modifying their life-styles.
4. While in other cultures people may have different value systems, individuals in all cultures can and must live together in harmony.[24]

Sample selections in each category listed on the next page appear either in the new edition of *Adventuring with Books* (National Council of Teachers of English, 1981) or in the sixth edition of the *Reading Ladders for Human Relations* (American Council on Education, 1981). Books preceded by (*E*) are easy books particularly appropriate for younger children, while those preceded by (*J*) are more truly books for intermediate pupils.

A. Black Americans
- (E) Clifton's *Everett Anderson's Friend* (Holt, 1976)
- (J) Greene's *Philip Hall Likes Me, I Reckon Maybe* (Dial, 1974)
- (J) Grimes' *Something on My Mind* (Dial, 1978)
- (J) Hamilton's *M. C. Higgins, the Great* (Macmillan, 1974)
- (J) Yarbrough's *Cornrows* (Coward, 1979)

B. Asian-Americans
- (J) Estes' *The Lost Umbrella of Kim Chu* (Atheneum, 1978)
- (E) Politi's *Mr. Fong's Toy Shop* (Scribner, 1978)
- (J) Uchida's *Journey Home* (Atheneum, 1978)
- (J) Yep's *Child of the Owl* (Harper, 1977)
- (J) Yep's *Dragonwings* (Harper, 1977)

C. Native Americans
- (E/J) Brown's *Tepee Tales of the American Indian* (Holt, 1979)
- (J) Lampman's *The Potlatch Family* (Atheneum, 1976)
- (E) Mills' *Annie and the Old One* (Little, 1971)
- (J) Rockwood's *To Spoil the Sun* (Holt, 1976)
- (E/J) Thayer and Emanuel's *Climbing Sun: The Story of a Hopi Indian Boy* (Dodd, 1980)

D. Puerto-Rican Americans
- (E) Bouchard's *The Boy Who Wouldn't Talk* (Doubleday, 1969)
- (J) Gonzalez' *Gaucho* (Knopf, 1977)
- (J) Lexau's *Jose's Christmas Secret* (Dial, 1963)
- (J) Mohr's *In Nueva York* (Dial, 1977)
- (J) Mohr's *Nilda* (Harper, 1973)

E. American Jews
- (J) Brooks' *Make Me a Hero* (Dutton, 1980)
- (J) Chaikin's *Finders Weepers* (Harper, 1980)
- (E) Eisenberg's *A Mitzvah Is Something Special* (Harper, 1978)
- (J) Konigsburg's *About the B'Nai Bagels* (Atheneum, 1969)
- (J) Taylor's *Ella of All-of-a-Kind Family* (Dutton, 1978)

F. Mexican-Americans
- (J) Bonham's *Viva Chicano* (Dell, 1971)
- (J) Lampman's *Go Up the Road* (Atheneum, 1972)
- (J) Molnar's *Graciela: A Mexican-American Tells Her Story* (Watts, 1972)
- (J) Newton's *Famous Mexican Americans* (Dodd, 1972)
- (J) Smith's *Josie's Handful of Quietness* (Abingdon, 1975)

Instructional Activities

Literature can be shared in a variety of meaningful ways in which children enjoy taking part and which grow naturally from the love of books. Such learning experiences furnish an avenue through which children can relate their personal feelings and develop their creative potential. These experiences also provide exposure to new media and new ways of thinking about books while they simultaneously build appreciations and develop standards in literature.

The activities that teachers can plan with or for their pupils should meet varying ability levels. Some are primarily *motivational* activities and others are especially *interpretive* experiences and the division between the two groups is not always clear-cut. Often an interpretive or culminating activity for one pupil will serve as a motivating literary experience for another child. While the teacher serves as the primary force bringing literature into the classroom to motivate children's reading, he or she also guides and assists the readers when they wish to share their books with one another. Aware that each book which is read need not be followed by some kind of report or interpretive exercise, the teacher is not disturbed when some children (notably the higher achievers) prefer to continue reading rather than to participate in creative expression.

Nearly 60 selected motivational and interpretive activities that have been used successfully in elementary classrooms are described as follows:

Motivational Experiences

Storytelling

The most appropriate way developmentally for children first to be exposed to narrative literature is through the medium of the storyteller—and not through movies, television, records, or even books. Once introduced to storytelling, boys and girls can begin to understand the oral tradition of literature and may even be stimulated to tell their own stories, especially after completing exercises from some language arts series, as shown in Figure 11.2.

The heart of any storytelling experience is the tale itself. Consequently, the teacher-storyteller should develop a familiarity with different kinds of story collections by spending some time reading in the children's room of the public library. When the teacher has located a promising tale he or she should consider: Is the story one that personally excites me? Is it a story that I wish to share with others? Is it a story that *I* can tell? Is it a tale that lends itself to telling (or should it be read aloud instead)? Is it a tale that will appeal to the age group of the listeners? Is the length of the tale correct for the attention span of the audience for which it is intended?

Storytelling is not difficult and child audiences generally are highly appreciative. Busy teachers must therefore discount the notably tough requirements from the traditional writers on storytelling which call for exceptional efforts at memorization, overlearning of stories, and considerable speech work.

Instead, once the teacher-storyteller has chosen a tale and prepared adequately, he or she needs only to establish an effective setting for the narration before proceeding with the performance. Successful storytelling does demand an informal and relaxed atmosphere in which every child can see and hear the teller without strain. It also demands that the modern teacher-storyteller perform with as much dramatization as possible—including gestures, body movements, facial expressions, and voice changes—for the child audience is truly television-minded.

When the story is over, there is often no follow-up planned by the teacher, for the simple responses of the children are adequate. Trite remarks such as "Wasn't that a nice story?" add nothing to the story hour, although questions prompting insight into cultural similarities or into social values may seem in order after certain kinds of tales.

Figure 11.2.
Exercises in Choosing a Story to Tell.

Part 1 Choosing a Story

It is important to choose a story that will capture the interest of your listeners. You may need to read several tales before you find one that is just right for you.

Where To Find a Story

Take plenty of time when you look for a story to tell. Ask your teacher or librarian to suggest tales that you might like. Read through them carefully. Look for stories among your books at home, too.

You might like to tell a story about yourself or someone close to you. Ask your parents and relatives if they remember any good family tales. Sometimes they have been handed down for generations.

How You Should Feel About Your Story

Your feelings about your story should be very strong. You should be eager to share it with others. If a story does not hold your interest, you should not tell it.

The more you practice telling your story, the closer you will feel to it. Try to make it part of you. It should feel as comfortable as an old shoe.

What To Look For in a Story

The story you choose should have important features:

1. **It should be short and simple.** Find a story that comes to the point quickly. A short tale is easy to remember. You can spend your time learning to tell it well. It's best to make your listeners wish you would tell more.

2. **It should have a lot of action.** An action story grips you. It makes you feel its excitement. A good action story will have a strong plot. The **plot** is the series of events that the author weaves together. A strong plot makes you follow the events eagerly. You want to know what happens next. Your listeners will share your feeling of suspense.

Guides for Choosing a Story

1. Ask your teacher, librarian, and parents to help you find stories to tell.
2. Read or listen to several of those stories.
3. Choose two stories that you especially like.
4. Check your stories. Are they short, simple, and strong in action? If not, look for others.

Exercises Choosing a Story

The exercises below will give you practice in choosing a story to tell. Be sure to follow the guides. When your teacher returns your paper, save it.

A. Find five stories you might wish to tell. Read them or listen to them carefully. Write their titles and authors on your paper.

B. From the stories you have found, choose two that would be good stories to tell. On your paper, answer the following questions about each one of them:

1. What is the most exciting event in the story?
2. Why do you think this story would be a good one to tell?

A two-year study involving 298 intermediate pupils concluded that children exposed to storytelling make significant gains in library usage and interest in literature as well as in reading ability, positive self-concept, creativity, and empathy. During the investigation the children participated for a 28-week period each year at public library branches representing a cross section of a metropolitan area. Librarians served as storytellers and generally told two folktales and four or five poems during the half-hour story time. A discussion followed each session only if the children responded with comments on the ending(s), the character(s), or events.[25]

By setting an example as a storyteller, the librarian or teacher can inspire children to try storytelling themselves. Some may wish to tell stories to their classmates while others will desire to entertain younger pupils. Children and teacher alike will find many good tales for the storyteller in such collections from the *Best Books for Children* (1981) as:

Bang's *The Buried Moon and Other Stories* (Scribner, 1977)
Carpenter's *Tales of a Chinese Grandmother* (Tuttle, 1973)
D'Aulaires' *Norse Gods and Giants* (Doubleday, 1967)
Gittins' *Tales from the South Pacific Islands* (Stemmer, 1977)
Grimm Brothers' *Grimm's Tales for Young and Old* (Doubleday, 1977)
Haviland's *The Fairy Tale Treasury* (Coward, 1972)
Holme's *Tales from Times Past* (Viking, 1977)
Leach's *The Lion Sneezed: Folktales and Myths of the Cat* (Crowell, 1977)
MacManus' *Hibernian Nights* (Macmillan, 1963)
Tashjian's *Three Apples Fell from Heaven* (Little, 1971)

Story Reading

While many stories may either be told or read aloud to the children, there are two broad categories of stories which can never be told but must always be read. The first covers picture books because their illustrations are an integral part of the story, as shown in Keats' *The Trip* (Greenwillow, 1978) and Graham's *Benjy's Dog* (Harper, 1973). The second includes stories whose charm lies in their language, due to either (a) the marked use of dialect as exemplified in NicLeodhas' *Heather and Broom* (Holt, 1960) and Lenski's *Strawberry Girl* (Lippincott, 1945) or (b) the strong individualistic style of the author as in Kipling's *Just So Stories* (Doubleday, 1952), and Seuss' *Horton Hears a Who* (Random House, 1954).

For reading aloud to boys and girls, teachers should look for materials which they know and genuinely like and which they believe the pupils are not apt to read themselves. Some of the older Newbery Medal Books, for example, are considered dull by the standards of today's children until the teacher reads them aloud to the group.

Story reading is an important and pleasurable experience for the children from all socioeconomic levels. For younger pupils, it is also a precursor to success in learning to read, for such children often score significant increases in vocabulary, word knowledge and reading comprehension in contrast to children denied the opportunity to hear good stories. With intermediate boys and girls, listening to stories helps them significantly to understand or draw inferences from selections of good literature. Yet only 60 percent of the teachers in the middle grades read aloud to their pupils, according to a national survey of nearly 600 teachers.[26]

Nevertheless, older pupils like to hear their teacher read to them from Supraner's *Think About It, You Might Learn Something* (Houghton, 1973) or Sobol's *Encyclopedia Brown Carries On* (Four Winds, 1980). Primary children enjoy hearing Parish's *Teach Us, Amelia Bedelia* (Greenwillow, 1977) or Travers' *Mary Poppins in the Park* (Harcourt, 1952). Some elementary pupils enjoy reading stories to their classmates or to younger children in the neighborhood or school.

Incidentally, teacher readers should be interested in the results of a study of behaviors which contribute most substantially to the quality of oral reading, especially in primary children.[27] In the order of influences, these behaviors are: child involvement in the story reading; the amount of eye contact between reader and audience; the amount of expression injected into the reading; the voice quality of the reader; the pointing to words or pictures by the reader; the reader's familiarity with the story; the selection of an appropriate book; the proper seating of boys and girls so that all can see; and finally, the highlighting of words and language by the reader.

Listening to Records and Cassette Tapes

The teacher may plan a listening period for playing some of the fine commercial cassettes or records of dramatizations or readings of such children's stories as Andersen's *The Emperor's New Clothes* (Four Winds, 1977) or Carroll's *Alice's Adventures in Wonderland and Through the Looking Glass* (Macmillan, 1963). Poets like Robert Frost and John Ciardi have also read from their own works for children, and such presentations have been carefully recorded for classroom use. Some school districts carry a collection of such materials. Others prefer that their teachers borrow the records or audio cassettes from the public library.

Attending Children's Theatre Productions

The teacher may occasionally see an announcement in the daily paper concerning the production of a children's theatre group that will be presented locally. Classroom discussions of the book on which the production will be based may then be planned. Paul Galdone's *Puss In Boots* (Seabury, 1976) is one of the tales often dramatized by professional or college groups for child audiences.

Often the admission prices for such productions are substantially reduced for young pupils. In some districts, school buses are used to transport the children to the theatre, particularly on Saturdays.

Watching Telecasts

The teacher should check the listings in the weekly television guides in order to suggest or assign the pupils to watch a suitable production of a story like Byars' *The Winged Colt of Casa Mia* (Viking, 1973) that is done with taste and fidelity.

Opening a Private Children's Library

Some pupils may be interested in following the example of two boys in Wellesley, Massachusetts, who each organized a library in one room of his home. The Great Library and the Kid's Library stocked tapes, records, and magazines in addition to books which had been donated or purchased at rummage sales. Dues-paying members of either library received an official monthly publication entitled *The Bookworm* in one case and *Book Life* in the other. The children's librarian of the Wellesley Hills Public Library had supported the boys' efforts, as would other public librarians or school media specialists.

Attending Book Fairs

During the annual Public Schools Week or National Children's Book Week, some schools schedule book fairs where all the grades are invited to display their creative reactions to certain children's books. The fairs are generally held in the school library media center and may involve commercial exhibits and films.

In other schools the teachers prefer to plan book fairs within their own classrooms, holding these on a bimonthly basis and encouraging children to participate in the planning. Parents are often invited to the fairs so they may have the opportunity to discover more about the school reading and literature program and to learn how they may assist the classroom library.

Watching Filmstrips

The class may sometimes enjoy listening to the teacher (or one of the members) read aloud from Turkle's *Obadiah the Bold* (Viking, 1965) as the filmstrip is run silently. On other occasions the boys and girls may wish to watch and hear one of the many acclaimed sound strips of children's stories issued by such studios as Weston Woods. Many filmstrip-cassette and filmstrip-record combinations are listed in Appendix 1.

Reading in a Basal Series

Some basal reading series for the middle and intermediate grades include excerpts from such books as Owens' *Jesse: The Man Who Outran Hitler* (Fawcett, 1978) and Clark's *All This Wild Land* (Viking, 1976). Children are more eager to read the complete story after they have enjoyed discussing an introductory selection.

Writing Goodbye Book Briefs

Children can copy their favorite literary passages on slips of paper and place the signed slips into a large envelope which hangs by the classroom door. Then, as the boys and girls are lined up for dismissal near that door—and a few minutes remain before the bell—a child can be chosen to reach into the envelope and draw out one of the selections. The pupil who copied the passage is pleased to hear his or her choice read aloud. In the meantime, classmates become acquainted with still another good book, like Naylor's *Eddie Incorporated* (Atheneum, 1980).

Examining Free or Inexpensive Materials from Publishers

Publishers of children's books often supply free or inexpensive bookmarks, maps, illustrations suitable for framing, buttons, brochures, photographs, and other display materials, sometimes in quantity lots. Such offers are described in *The Calendar,* issued quarterly by the Children's Book Council, Inc., 67 Irving Place, New York 10003, and are directed to all its members. The Council invites teachers to join its ranks at a onetime charge of ten dollars.

Planning an Author's Afternoon

An Author's Afternoon is an exciting event during which children hear an author discuss his or her life and books. The Children's Book Council, Inc., offers speakers' lists of authors and illustrators who are willing to speak to various groups—sometimes for fees and sometimes for the payment of transportation costs alone. The lists are compiled by states and available for the price of a large self-addressed stamped envelope. Publishing houses, local libraries, and educational organizations can also help the children in arranging an Author's Afternoon.

Making Bulletin Board Displays

Bulletin boards can announce new books or book events, display unusual book illustrations, and encourage imaginative writing in the classroom. Some boards point up authors like Katherine Paterson or Roald Dahl. Others stress categories like sports stories or tall tales. An interesting addition is a pegboard which holds books and other three-dimensional objects.

Studying Assigned Units

Background for in-depth understanding of many units in social studies and a few units in science can be furnished through broader use of literature. A primary unit on transportation, for example, helps develop familiarity with Marston's *Big Rigs* (Dodd, 1979) and Pierce's *The Freight Train Book* (Carolrhoda, 1980). An intermediate unit on the expansion of the American West encourages reading of Levenson's *Homesteaders and Indians* (Watts, 1971) and Seidman's *The Fools of '49: The California Gold Rush, 1848–1856* (Knopf, 1976).

Attending Storytelling Workshops

In schools with media centers and professional media specialists, a series of storytelling workshops may be held under the supervision of the specialist. Interested pupils from the middle and intermediate grades are invited to attend in order to learn how to tell folktales and other stories to kindergarten and primary children.

In schools without library media centers, the children's librarian from the nearest public library may schedule the workshops, which help introduce good stories and good storytelling techniques to older boys and girls.

While some schools prefer to hold the workshops during National Children's Book Week, nearly any time during the academic year that is convenient for the librarian is appropriate for the children.

Using Community Resources

Primary classes that visit the harbor during a study trip return to school with a special desire to read Plowden's *Tugboat* (Macmillan, 1976). Classes in districts whose budgets do not allow for many trips away from the school building may be privileged to hear resource speakers from the community, who visit schools to make presentations to the students and thereby elicit interest in books like Branley's *Feast or Famine? The Energy Future* (Crowell, 1980).

Reviewing Books for Publication

School newspapers and magazines often have a column for book reviews, and children throughout the building can be encouraged to write reviews of new and old favorites in order to inform their friends of books they have personally enjoyed.

Older pupils may even review books for readers outside the immediate school-community. In one elementary school in Austin, Texas, for example, the book editor of the local newspaper came to discuss book reviewing with the more advanced members of the sixth grade. She provided a number of new books for them to review, and subsequently all their reviews were published in the book section of the Sunday edition. Later, reviewing new books for the paper became a regular activity at the school.

Meeting Book Characters in Person

Children can dress up as their favorite book characters and tell about themselves and their experiences. Sometimes they may even be invited to parade through a neighboring classroom and introduce briefly the characters they are representing.

Pupils who like to read realistic stories of the here and now, like Conford's *Felicia the Critic* (Little, 1973), find it easy to borrow appropriate costumes for the characters they want to be in the parade.

Joining a Book Club

Some boys and girls become interested in literature through membership in a book club which caters to their age bracket. Sponsors of book clubs for elementary school children include:

Grolier Enterprises, Inc., Sherman Turnpike, Danbury, CT: Beginning Readers' Program and Disney Book Club.

Junior Literary Guild, 245 Park Avenue, New York (ages three to fourteen). Hardcover selections. Six age groups.

Parents Magazine's Read Aloud and Easy Reading Programs, division of Gruner & Jahr USA, Inc., 685 Third Avenue, New York (ages two to seven). Original hardcover picture books from Parents Magazine Press.

Scholastic Book Services, 730 Broadway, New York
Paperback reprints and originals.
- (1) See-Saw Book Program (kindergarten and grade one)
- (2) Lucky Book Club (grades two and three)
- (3) Arrow Book Club (grades four to six)

Xerox Education Publications, 245 Long Hill Road, Middletown, CT
- (1) I Can Read Book Club (ages three to eight). Hardcover selections from Harper & Row's *I Can Read* Series.
- (2) Paperback Book Clubs. Quality paperbacks from major publishers.
  - (a) Buddy Books Paperback Book Club (kindergarten and grade one)
  - (b) Goodtime Books Paperback Book Club (grades two and three)
  - (c) Discovering Books Paperback Book Club (grades four to six)
- (3) Weekly Reader Children's Book Clubs (ages five to eleven). Hardcover selections from all children's book publishers. Three age groups: primary (5–7), intermediate (8–9), and senior (10–11).

Reading and Writing Newspaper Headlines

A provocative headline such as "U.N. Ambassador Receives Penguin Support" might be tacked on the bulletin board and children encouraged to guess which book is represented. The answer, of course, is Freeman's *Penguins, Of All People!* (Viking, 1971). Older pupils can develop their own headlines to intrigue their classmates.

Keeping an Author's Birthday Calendar

The primary teacher can post a large monthly birthday calendar and mark it with pictures of authors whose prose or poetry the class has enjoyed hearing and reading. In the intermediate grades the calendar can include a list of the author's books as well. Such calendars are more stimulating to young readers if pupils' names are also listed, especially when a class member was born on the same day of the year as a favorite writer-illustrator like Maurice Sendak (June 10).

Playing Charades and Other Games

Some children, singly or in small groups, can act out the names of books while their friends try to identify the correct titles. Others will enjoy matching book-jacket pictures with their corresponding titles. Still other pupils can take turns unscrambling the names of authors or story characters out of jumbled letters fastened to a magnetic board.

Working in the School Media Center or Classroom Library

Boys and girls can help with the charging out and returning of books. They can prepare magazines and books for circulation. They can repair torn pages, make catalog cards, and shelve books. They can set up attractive displays and exhibits. All of these activities which involve the handling of books and magazines stimuluate interest in the contents of the materials.

Watching Films

A class that can observe on the screen the famed doughnuts episode from McCloskey's *Homer Price* (Viking, 1943) is generally anxious to read the entire story. Watching a full-length film of a book like O'Brien's *Mrs. Frisby and the Rats of Nimh* (Atheneum, 1971) will also entice children to examine the published story.

Interpretive Activities

Using Story Dramatization

Children who have heard or read Galdone's *The Three Billy Goats Gruff* (Seabury, 1973) or Carrick's *Happy Jack* (Harper, 1979) are quickly prompted into participating in story dramatization. Any properties that are needed can be readily improvised by the players.

Singing

The class may be interested in singing some of the poems written by Robert Louis Stevenson that have been set to music. Several series of elementary music books carry songs based on his poems from *A Child's Garden of Verses* (Shambhala, 1979). Another favorite poem that has been set to music is the lengthy *The Night Before Christmas* (Holiday, 1980) written by Clement Moore.

Making Puppets and Holding Puppet Shows

Children of every grade level can construct puppets of their favorite book characters, using a variety of materials ranging from paper bags to soda straws. Some groups may even prefer to hold puppet shows based on such stories as de Regniers' *Beauty and the Beast* (Bradbury, 1978) or Galdone's *The Little Red Hen* (Seabury, 1973).

Filing Instant Replays

In an attempt to avoid overstructured book reporting, children can be encouraged to dictate or write on index cards their brief accounts of the most exciting or critical incident in a book they have read, such as Moyes' *Helter-Skelter* (Holt,

1968). The cards are placed in a small box on the library table and shared by both teacher and class.

Making Collages

Boys and girls, individually or in groups, can prepare a collage depicting a favorite scene from a book like Monjo's *The Secret of the Sachem's Tree* (Coward, 1972) which they have heard or read. On a background of a large piece of brown wrapping paper or burlap is attached an assortment of materials to represent the characters and objects. The finished collage may later be displayed if its producers approve.

Using Flannel or Felt Characters

Children can cut out of remnant pieces of flannel or felt the animals, persons, or objects described in a book such as Rose's *How Does A Czar Eat Potatoes*?(Lothrop, 1973) which the group has enjoyed. Sometimes the pupils will wish to decorate the pieces or to back tiny lightweight realia with flannel. Finally, they are ready to share their book adventure by means of a cloth board.

Constructing Mobiles

Although the framework of the three-dimensional design is made of wire or wood, the pendants or suspended objects on the mobile are made from a wide collection of materials which the pupils can bring from home. The class may prefer to restrict the pendants to represent the characters or events from a single story (like Seuss' *If I Ran the Zoo,* Random House, 1950) or to confine them to the stories of a single author (as Virginia Hamilton).

Sometimes it is the teacher that supplies the materials for the mobile-making project. First the students make a list of important quotations, incidents, words, or characters from a book recently heard or read. Then they are given some index cards, glue, thread, and scissors. The cards are cut into different shapes, e.g., squares for quotations. The students copy each item on their list on a different card. Finally, they hang the card shapes one below the other in proper vertical sequence.

Modeling Clay

Children can use clay to model their favorite characters or scenes. Later, after the clay has been fired, painted, and glazed, the models are displayed before a backing made of a folded piece of cardboard on which the pupils can write the words best describing their representations. The text may be copied from a book such as Cleary's *Ramona and Her Father* (Morrow, 1977) or created by the children.

Creating Finger Plays

Both nursery rhymes (as in Fujikawa's *Mother Goose,* Golden Press, 1980) and counting poems (as Rosenburg's *One, Two, Buckle My Shoe,* Simon, 1981) lend themselves to adaptation to finger plays. Kindergarten and first-grade children enjoy creating rhymes for such activities.

Making Films

When they use a Super 8-mm camera with a built-in viewfinder, children can be taught quickly how to take movies. The teacher can borrow a camera from a staff member or from one of the room parents. If the school lacks indoor lighting equipment, the pupils can paint scenery on large sheets of heavy cardboard and film all scenes outdoors. The major expenses incurred in this activity, therefore, lie in the cost of film and film development.

Many of the folktales that the teacher reads aloud or tells to the class—such as Galdone's *The Gingerbread Boy* (Seabury, 1975)—are suitable for an elementary class project in filmmaking.

Making Mosaics

When children have read a satisfying book such as Maruki's *Hiroshima No Pika* (Lothrop, 1982) or McHugh's *Karen's Sister* (Greenwillow, 1983), they can prepare a mosaic report. They sketch on a sheet of white paper a character or scene from the story. Next they paste small pieces of colored tissue paper on the sketch, using a brush dipped in liquid starch. Then they fold black construction paper and cut it to make a frame for the mosaic. Finally, they tape the mosaic to a window. When the light shines through the mosaic, the sketch assumes the appearance of stained glass.

Designing Book Jackets

Boys and girls can design their own book jackets and display them next to the original ones issued by the publishers. Inside the jacket may be written or dictated a synopsis of a book, like Kishida's *The Lion and the Bird's Nest* (Crowell, 1973). A biographical sketch of the author can be substituted for the synopsis if adequate reference books are available and the boy or girl is skilled in using them.

Making Transparencies

In schools where overhead projectors are readily available, pupils can make transparencies of drawings of selected characters or scenes from books that they have enjoyed reading. Once the drawings are completed, the book (like Peck's *Soup's Drum,* Knopf, 1980) can be read aloud, wholly or in part, as the transparencies are projected on the screen.

Producing Shadow Boxes

Large shallow boxes can be quickly converted into shadow boxes when the box fronts have been removed; the remaining frames are then painted and hung on the wall. In them the children can display three-dimensional objects that are essential to the plot of a favorite story like Hicks' *Alvin's Swap Shop* (Holt, 1976). The boxes can also be prepared to represent the settings for a story like Hodges' *Plain Lane Christmas* (Coward, 1978).

Making Dioramas

Children can build dioramas of several scenes from a book like Estes' *The Coat-Hanger Christmas Tree* (Atheneum, 1973). Similar to shadow boxes in construction, dioramas can be made simply from cartons, or made more elaborately from wood and heavy cardboard. When the teacher helps the boys and girls to see the relationships between the available materials and the mood or scene they are trying to depict, children find more creative ways of making dioramas realistic and attractive.

Constructing Box Theaters

Dioramas with some sort of movement added are box theaters. They can be adapted to finger puppets and used for a children's favorite like Colver and Graff's *The Wayfarer's Tree* (Dutton, 1973) when the pupils or teacher wish to depict a scene or story without too much preparation. Larger box theaters can be used with hand puppets.

Drawing Maps

Maps can be made of individual states, countries, continents, or of the entire world. On them are sketched or marked the birthplaces of authors like Donald Crews; the settings of favorite books like Taylor's *All-of-a-Kind Family* (Dutton, 1978), *Downtown* (Follett, 1972); or the travels of a character like Chakoh in Baker's *Walk the World's Rim* (Harper, 1965). Where fictitious places are key points in books, the class members may create original maps, as for Baum's *Wizard of Oz* (Macmillan, 1970).

While some children may prefer to make small individual desk maps, others will wish to work together on a huge wall map.

Attending a Mad Hatter's Party

With the aid of room mothers, the teacher can arrange an unusual Halloween or end-of-the-semester party. Each pupil, at home or during an earlier school art period, makes a hat to help depict a well-known story character and then wears the hat to the Mad Hatter's Party.

Creating Rhythms and Dances

When a group or the entire class has completed a book like Emberley's *Drummer Hoff* (Prentice, 1968), the boys and girls may like to create a rhythmical interpretation of the story. Their teacher may either compose music for the dance or use a recorded accompaniment. More than one series of basic movements may be possible, and the audience can then select the dance interpretation that it prefers.

Making Roll Movies

Scenes from a well-liked story such as Goodall's *Jacko* (Harcourt, 1972) can be painted or crayoned on a long sheet of shelf paper. Then the sheet is rolled up on two dowels inserted through the holes in the back of a puppet stage. As the movie rolls slowly along, a pupil reads the matching excerpt from the book.

Painting Murals

Brightly colored murals involving tempera paint, construction paper, and colored chalk may develop from the reading of a single book like George's *Julie of the Wolves* (Harper, 1972). They may also represent the composite of many books on a single unit like "The Zoo."

Making Posters

Posters of every size and sort can be created by readers who wish to inform others of an exciting book such as McDermott's *Arrow to the Sun* (Viking, 1974). When they are three-dimensional, posters add special interest to book exhibits.

Participating in Panel Discussions

Children enjoy panel discussions during which they informally explore a popular or current topic. One group of intermediate-grade students that had read biographies of Maria Mitchell, Margaret Mead, Jane Goodall, Susan La Flesche, Marie Curie, and Elizabeth Blackwell centered its panel discussion on the theme of Women in Science.

Presenting Pantomime Skits

Some young readers, particularly those with speech handicaps, enjoy sharing with their peers scenes from a book like Haywood's *Eddie's Valuable Property* (Morrow, 1975). The pantomimes they present are short, lasting five minutes or less.

With the help of their teacher, the boys are planning a poster for the library media center which will describe their favorite book. (Photo courtesy of the Fullerton Elementary School District, Fullerton, California.)

Dressing Character Dolls

A child who has read a story such as Estes' *The Hundred Dresses* (Harcourt, 1944) may want to show classmates how some of the characters in the story looked. Should the teacher have a stock of small inexpensive dolls available from a variety store as well as a supply of colorful remnants donated by room mothers, the child may easily sew the clothes to dress the book characters. At other times, a group of children enjoys making paper clothes for a sturdy paper doll character.

Writing Classified Ads

A student can write a "Lost and Found" ad for a person, object, or pet from a story, such as Schneider's *Uncle Harry* (Macmillan, 1972). He or she may also wish to write an ad for the "Jobs Wanted" or "Help Wanted" column after reading a book like Varga's *Circus Cannonball* (Morrow, 1975).

Preparing Rebus Reviews

Primary pupils especially enjoy preparing a rebus review of a book like Viorst's *Alexander and the Terrible, Horrible, No Good, Very Bad Day* (Atheneum, 1976). In place of certain portions of a sentence or paragraph, old magazine pictures are substituted. Such clippings can cover significant persons, places, objects, or actions. Some exceptional children in the upper grades enjoy writing rebus reviews too.

Cooking and Eating

Pupils from six to ten can make pancakes after the group has read or heard Lobel's *The Pancake* (Green willow, 1978). The younger children especially will each like to make a "happy day pancake" by first forming the eyes and smile with batter, then letting it bake a while before adding the rest of the batter, and finally flipping the pancake over to see its "happy face."

Drawing Cartoons

Intermediate boys and girls familiar with newspaper and magazine cartoons can draw their own cartoons to depict important situations, problems, and events from a favorite book such as Kerr's *Dinky Hocker Shoots Smack* (Harper, 1972).

Creating Ballads

Several children who have heard or read the same story such as Daudet's *The Mule of Avignon* (Crowell, 1973) may wish to turn it into a ballad which may later be presented either with or without a musical accompaniment. One pupil in the group begins and then points to another child to continue the ballad until all have had an opportunity to participate.

Performing in Shadow Plays

Almost any story or poem lends itself to a shadow play, which may be done in pantomime or with voices and movement. Scenes for such a play can be made by cutting simple shapes from wrapping paper or newspaper and pinning them to a sheet. Then a bright light is placed behind that sheet and the pupils stand between the sheet and the light. Even shy children enjoy performing in a shadow play by acting out roles from a favorite such as Lenski's *Policeman Small* (Walck, 1962).

Preparing Picture Reports

Beginning readers can cut pictures from magazines to prepare a report of a story such as Cazet's *The Duck with Squeaky Feet* (Bradbury, 1980). Each picture is properly mounted and accompanied by an appropriate caption.

Preparing Written Reports for a Reason

Pupils may occasionally prepare book reports to communicate their feelings about books in purposeful, written fashion. While some children are ready to begin such reports in the middle primary years, others are not ready until the intermediate grades. There are, however, five levels of book-report writing adaptable to children's written language maturity.

- Level One—The pupils record on a four-by-six-inch card the title and author, the number of pages read, and a one-sentence opinion of the book. They later arrange their cards in chronological order of books completed.
- Level Two—The pupils use a five-by-eight-inch index card to record the title and author, and to write one sentence on each of the following: the general idea of the book, the part liked best, the reasons for recommending or not recommending the book, and the place where a copy of the volume was located.
- Level Three—The pupils use the same form as at Level Two, but expand to a short paragraph each of the following points: the general idea of the book, the part liked best, and the reasons for recommending or not recommending the book. Pupils may substitute in place of one of the aforementioned points a discussion of the plot or an analysis of the

characterization. In this case, however, the pupils abandon the index card for writing paper.

- Level Four—The pupils respond at length about the title and author, the type of story, its main idea or subject, its outstanding qualities or features, and their general comments or opinion. They write or use a typewriter.
- Level Five—The pupils follow the assignment for Level Four, but they also complete one or more of the following activities: a biography of the author, a discussion of the effect of the book on the reader, a different ending for the story, a commentary on the characterizations, or a comparison of books by the same author or on the same subject. They write on notebook paper or type the report.

Choral Speaking: A Unique Interpretive Activity

Choral speaking is sometimes called "choral reading," "verse choirs," or "choric speaking." All of these terms refer to a similar technique of group recitation or reading of poetry (or poetic prose) without music but under the direction of a leader.

Suitable for any group of elementary school children (even those with speech handicaps), choral speaking is also appropriate for any class size. It produces positive personal, social, psychological, cognitive, affective, and language values.[28] It is a beneficial experience because it synchronizes three linguistic skills: listening, reading, and speaking. It improves the everyday speech of children. It builds positive group attitudes and offers an acceptable outlet for emotional expression. It promotes desirable personality traits and offers a socializing activity for both the shy and the forward. It develops imagination and heightens the appreciation of poetry.

To make effective use of choral speaking, however, teachers must first understand the rhythm and the tempo of the poetry as well as the color and quality of the children's voices. Then, with that background in mind, they must be able to choose wisely among the five different types of arrangements that are possible.

The Refrain Arrangement

Easiest for beginners are poems with a refrain or chorus. The teacher or pupil leader recites most of the narrative, with the class responding with the words that constitute the refrain or the repeated line(s). Typical examples of poems with refrains include:

Hoberman's "Whale"
Lindsay's "The Mysterious Cat"
Stevenson's "The Wind"
Guthrie's "This Land Is Your Land"

and (by Unknown)

Little Brown Rabbit

Leader: Little brown rabbit went hoppity-hop,
Group: Hoppity-hop, hoppity-hop!
Leader: Into a garden without any stop,

Group:	Hoppity-hop, hoppity-hop!
Leader:	He ate for his supper a fresh carrot top,
Group:	Hoppity-hop, hoppity-hop!
Leader:	Then home went the rabbit without any stop,
Group:	Hoppity-hop, hoppity-hop!

The Antiphonal or Dialog Arrangement

Poems demanding alternate speaking between two groups require an antiphonal or dialogue arrangement. High voices may be balanced against low voices or boys' voices may be contrasted with girls' voices. This arrangement may simply be a question and answer session. Poems that provide dialogue between two people can also be used for this form of choral speaking. Typical examples include:

Meigs' "The Pirate Don Durk of Dowdee"
Rossetti's "Who Has Seen the Wind?"
Fyleman's "Witch, Witch"
Coatsworth's "Who Are You?"

and (by Unknown):

To London Town

Group A:	Which is the way to London Town To see the king in his golden crown?
Group B:	One foot up and one foot down, That's the way to London Town.
Group A:	Which is the way to London Town To see the queen in her silken gown?
Group B:	Left! Right! Left! Right! Up and down, Soon you'll be in London Town!

The Line-a-Speaker or Line-a-Choir Arrangement

This arrangement differs from the antiphonal variety only in that it engages not two, but three or more individual children or choirs. The line-a-speaker or line-a-choir arrangement is always popular with pupils because it possesses variety and offers the challenge of picking up lines quickly in exact tempo. Children must come in on cue, of course, so early effort with this kind of choral speaking should find the students standing in the order in which they present their lines. Teachers who wish to use it with younger children, however, will find it helpful to choose poems that have lines or couplets that end with semicolons, periods, or even commas, so that the poet's thoughts are not broken up after the assignment of parts. Typical examples include:

Coleridge's "The Months of the Year"
Field's "The Duel"
Turner's "Dark-Eyed Lad Columbus
Eastwick's "Where's Mary?"

and (by Unknown), for five children or five groups of children that begin and end their reading together:

Five Little Squirrels

All:	Five little squirrels sat in a tree.
Group A:	The first one said, "What do I see?"

Group B:	The second one said, "A man with a gun."
Group C:	The third one said, "We'd better run."
Group D:	The fourth one said, "Let's hide in the shade."
Group E:	The fifth one said, "I'm not afraid."
All:	Then bang went the gun, and how they did run.

The Cumulative Arrangement

The cumulative arrangement differs from the line-a-choir arrangement in that the addition of each group to the presentation is permanent, not temporary, in order to attain a crescendo effect. It is one of the more difficult forms of choral speaking because it involves the use of voice quality to achieve interpretation. The addition of voices is not simply to gain greater volume but to build, too, toward a more significant climax. An entire class can readily take part. Typical examples of poems for cumulative arrangement include:

Lear's "The Owl and the Pussycat"
Lindsay's "The Potatoes' Dance"
Ciardi's "Mummy Slept Late and Daddy Fixed Breakfast"
Silverstein's "Smart"

and (by Mother Goose):

The House That Jack Built

Group A: This is the house that Jack built.

Groups A-B: This is the malt
That lay in the house that Jack built.

Groups A-C: This is the rat,
That ate the malt
That lay in the house that Jack built.

Groups A-D: This is the cat,
That killed the rat,
That ate the malt
That lay in the house that Jack built.

Groups A-E: This is the dog,
That worried the cat,
That killed the rat,
That ate the malt
That lay in the house that Jack built.

Groups A-F: This is the cow with the crumpled horn,
That tossed the dog,
That worried the cat,
That killed the rat,
That ate the malt
That lay in the house that Jack built.

Groups A-G: This is the maiden all forlorn,
That milked the cow with the crumpled horn,
That tossed the dog,
That worried the cat,
That killed the rat,
That ate the malt
That lay in the house that Jack built.

Groups A-H: This is the man all tattered and torn,
That kissed the maiden all forlorn,
That milked the cow with the crumpled horn,
That tossed the dog,
That worried the cat,
That killed the rat,
That ate the malt
That lay in the house that Jack built.

Groups A-I: This is the priest all shaven and shorn,
That married the man all tattered and torn,
That kissed the maiden all forlorn,
That milked the cow with the crumpled horn,
That tossed the dog,
That worried the cat,
That killed the rat,
That ate the malt
That lay in the house that Jack built.

Groups A-J: This is the cock that crowed in the morn,
That waked the priest all shaven and shorn,
That married the man all tattered and torn,
That kissed the maiden all forlorn,
That milked the cow with the crumpled horn,
That tossed the dog,
That worried the cat,
That killed the rat,
That ate the malt
That lay in the house that Jack built.

Groups A-K: This is the farmer sowing his corn,
That kept the cock that crowed in the morn,
That waked the priest all shaven and shorn,
That married the man all tattered and torn,
That kissed the maiden all forlorn,
That milked the cow with the crumpled horn,
That tossed the dog,
That worried the cat,
That killed the rat,
That ate the malt
That lay in the house that Jack built.

The Unison Arrangement

Even more difficult than the cumulative variety is the unison type of choral speaking. An entire class or group reads or recites every line together. Only an experienced teacher-leader can skillfully direct a large number of voices speaking simultaneously.

Unison reading is unfortunately where most teachers begin choric speech, although it is the hardest of all the popular arrangements and often elicits the singsong monotony that results when inexperienced children read together. However, when the class—and the teacher—have developed considerable background in choral speaking, unison arrangements become dramatically effective. Obviously they are better suited to intermediate-grade children. Young children will enjoy saying nursery rhymes and other simple verse together, but they should not be given a heavy dose of unison experience because of the problems of coordinating timing and inflection. Typical examples of poems for unison recital include:

Morrison's "On the Skateboard"
Livingston's "Whispers"
Thurman's "Campfire"
Falls' "September"

and (by Unknown):

Weather

Whether the weather be fine,
Or whether the weather be not,
Whether the weather be cold,
Or whether the weather be hot,
We'll weather the weather,
Whatever the weather,
Whether we like it or not.

Guided Sessions

The teachers who experience little difficulty in commencing choral speaking are the ones who enjoy poetry themselves and share it often with their classes. These are the same men and women who write poems on charts and display them about the room, and who encourage pupils to create their own poetry. Such class saturation of all kinds of possible selections for verse choirs is a natural beginning because the children acquire an ear for rhythm, a sense of mood, and a desire to say enjoyable poems with their teacher. It can also be a successful beginning if the sessions are short, simple, and well directed. The director or teacher must set the example for the choral reading periods insofar as phrasing, tempo, diction, and emphasis are concerned. He or she must help the pupils understand that with choral speaking, every word must be readily understood by the listeners. To make direction easier, the teacher groups the children in a standing position where all can see.

The first poems presented should be those that the class had memorized earlier. Later the group's repertoire can be increased by duplicating and distributing copies of other longer poems that the pupils have enjoyed.

After everyone is familiar with the content of the material and has had several pleasing experiences with choral speaking, the children should be encouraged to suggest a variety of interpretations and executions. Sound effects may be introduced upon occasion.

Two techniques for helping groups improve their choral efforts include: (1) the use of tape recordings so that all may share in the evaluation, and (2) the appointment of a small group within the class to divorce itself from the chorus and act as a critical audience of listeners.

Finally, the teacher must learn the progressive phases through which a choral speaking moves so that he or she can place the whole experience in proper perspective. The first phase is an understanding of rhythm and tempo, and its purpose is to encourage each child to sense that rhythm and tempo. The second phase is an understanding of the color and quality of the voices which demands that the teacher also comprehend the meaning of such specialized terms as *inflection* (the rise and fall within a phrase), *pitch level* (the change between one phrase and another), *emphasis* (pointing up of the most important word) and *intensity* (loudness and softness of the voices). And the third phase that the teacher must understand is the arrangement or orchestration of choral speaking to help convey the meaning of a poem.

Appropriate Selections

Literature for choral speaking should have a story or theme that is both dramatic and simple so as to be understood promptly by an audience that hears it for the first time. It should possess a marked rhythm and express a universal sentiment. Prose suitable for group reading includes—for older children—portions of Rachel Carson's *The Sea Around Us* (Golden Press, 1958) and selections from Scott O'Dell's *Island of the Blue Dolphins* (Houghton, 1960). For younger readers there is the text from Beatrix Potter's *The Tale of Peter Rabbit* (Grossett, 1968) as well as some portions of Robert McCloskey's *Time of Wonder* (Viking, 1957).

Whether the selection is prose or poetry, it must not only meet the teacher's criteria for literature and fulfill a specific objective in the day's planning but also win the pupils' interest and involvement as well. Children prefer selections that contain humor, repetition, surprise, action—and brevity.

Anthologies and literature textbooks are crowded with poems and pieces of poetic prose which can readily be done by a choral group. In selecting material for choric interpretation, the classroom teacher should consider: (1) the appropriateness of the subject matter as well as its treatment; (2) the richness of the rhythmic elements and tone color or sound values; and (3) the author's overall method of organization in order that a vocal group can be utilized impressively.

Pitfalls

Besides the danger of mediocre material, choral speaking has several other possible pitfalls of which the teacher must be aware. One of these that occurs when children speak together is the mounting volume of their voices. Therefore, the teacher must listen continually to the tone quality of the individuals in the choir, marking the time firmly, and keeping the voices warm and light. Another pitfall is the children's tendency to singsong their lines. Consequently, the teacher must focus the attention of the class on the meaning, the story, or the idea of the selection, and not upon the delivery. Still another pitfall is the lapse into cuteness or overdramatics, which makes the children believe that it is they and not their accomplishments that are being put on exhibition.

The teacher must also be certain that the class develops and maintains unity in the following areas of choral speaking: articulation, pitch, inflection, and thought/feeling. Good diction and articulation must be accomplished first, and individuals who speak at various rates of speed must learn to enunciate each word clearly at the exact time in group work. Pitch will become more uniform as children develop better understanding of poetry and as they become accustomed to the voices of those around them. Due to a tendency to end sentences on an upward inflection, unity in the modulation of the voice is difficult to accomplish. Speakers must first hear themselves to correct any bad habits. Finally, all participants must have the same understanding of any poems and possess a depth of feeling and a sensitivity to words.

Evaluation

Classroom teachers can briefly rate the results of their choral speaking sessions if they will ask themselves:

- Has there been an improvement in the speech and voice quality of the children?
- Do the pupils have a greater enjoyment of poetry because they have spoken it together, and are they genuinely eager for more and better poetry?
- Are the pupils developing growing powers of interpretation so that they speak their selections with understanding and vitality?
- Has the anonymity of choir work helped individual children?
- Are some of the pupils able to take over the leadership of the choir, showing a real feeling for the possibilities of the work?
- Are the children completely simple, natural, and sincere in their work?

A majority of positive answers would indicate that the teacher is doing sound and careful work.

Evaluation of Pupils' Progress

More attention needs to be given to the evaluation of literature learning than has been done in recent decades.

For the present, the teacher must continue to rely heavily on day-to-day observations of pupils to get an accurate idea of how the class and individuals in that class are reacting to experiences in literature. These questions can provide the teacher with a quick appraisal of the group's interests and enjoyments:

- Does the class look forward to the literature period?
- Does the class enter into the motivational or interpretive activities with enthusiasm?
- Is its attention span prolonged during those activities?
- Is there a high degree of group interaction?
- Does the class wish to share its literary findings with other classes or with parents?

Information regarding each pupil's growth toward the objectives of the literature program can be secured by inquiring:

- Does the student read widely in different genres?
- Does the student like to share his or her pleasure in reading?
- Does the student express in composition form some of the ideas he or she has gained from books read or discussed?

- Does the student's speaking vocabulary include new words from the books he or she has read or discussed?
- Does the student's writing vocabulary include new words from the books he or she has read or discussed?
- Has the student read books related to personal interests?
- Has the student's reading helped with personal problems?
- Does the student use a variety of art media to illustrate situations from the book he or she has read or discussed?
- Do the student's comments indicate the building of a personal philosophy that appears to be influenced by the books he or she has read or discussed?
- Does the student visit the public library regularly?

In evaluating student growth in interaction with literature, the teacher must always bear in mind that the primary goal is enjoyment, and enjoyment is difficult to assess.[29]

There is presently available for grades four to six only one published test: *A Look at Literature—The NCTE Cooperative Test of Critical Reading and Appreciation* (published by Educational Testing Service, Princeton, NJ). It takes 60 to 70 minutes to administer and may be purchased in either of two forms. Each form contains 14 short literary selections and 54 option-multiple-choice questions. The first half of the test is read aloud by the administrator (partially to decrease the effect of students' reading ability on the test results) while the second half is read silently by the examinee. The selections were chosen to represent as many as possible of the modes of literary expression found in imaginative prose and poetry deemed suitable for children. Since there are no norms or validity data, the use of the test is fairly well limited to criterion-referenced testing or to districts that wish to develop local norms. It can also be used informally as an aid in instruction. Bearing in mind the disadvantages of the test, which lie in interpretation, reviewers generally approve the instrument.[30]

Discussion Questions

1. How can literature contribute to the achievement of some of the objectives of elementary education? Document your answer with specific book titles if possible.
2. What are some of the means by which busy classroom teachers can readily keep up on at least a small percentage of the hundreds of new children's books published each year? Could this responsibility be handled more efficiently by grade levels or on a district-wide basis?
3. When and how should a teacher employ bibliotherapy in the classroom?
4. Which motivational experiences in literature would you use comfortably with a class of slow achievers?
5. Why is it difficult to secure the participation of high achievers in exercises and activities involving the books they read? How can a teacher promote at least minimal creative expression among such readers?

Suggested Projects

1. Begin a collection of pictures of illustrators and/or authors of children's books.
2. Design and construct a hanging book mobile to interest children in reading biographies and informational books.

3. Make an annotated file of at least 20 book titles (arranged by genre) which you would include in a balanced literature program for the elementary grade of your choice.
4. Select ten poems suitable for choral speaking. Then plan how you would use at least two of them, utilizing appropriate arrangements.
5. Compile a list of classroom activities for National Children's Book Week celebrated in November.
6. Read, and later tell, a story suitable for a kindergarten class, using the flannelboard if you like. Finally, record that story on a cassette tape.
7. Set up the learning center on literature shown in Figure 11.3.

Figure 11.3. Language Arts Learning Center: Literature.

TYPE OF CENTER: **POETRY APPRECIATION**
GRADE LEVEL: K–3
TIME: Varies
NUMBER OF STUDENTS: 1 (or a small group)

INSTRUCTIONAL OBJECTIVE: The children will listen to several poems on tape. They will draw a picture of one that has meaning for them.

MATERIALS: Manila paper, crayons or paints, a tape recorder, and a cassette of recorded poems.

DIRECTIONS:

1. Press down the green button (the "on" button is colored green).
2. Listen to the poems.
3. Press the red button (the "off" button is colored red).
4. Pick the one you liked best.
5. Draw a picture of what you heard, saw, or felt.
6. Put your picture on the left side of the table.

SUGGESTED IDEAS: The poems could be read into three different tapes and children could select one.

EVALUATION: The teacher will be able to determine how interested the students are in poetry by observing the number that use the center and whether the students understand the poems by the pictures drawn. The teacher may also discuss the pictures and the meaning of the poetry with the children individually or as a group. The pictures could be displayed on a bulletin board near the center.

Related Readings

Barron, P., and Burley, J. 1984. *Jump Over The Moon: A Reader for Children's Literature*. New York: Holt.

Benton, M. 1984. "The Methodology Vacuum in Teaching Literature," *Language Arts, 61,* pp. 265–275.

Collins, L. J., Ingoldsby, B., and Dellmann, M. 1984. "Sex-Role Stereotyping in Children's Literature: A Change from the Past," *Childhood Education, 60,* pp. 278–285.

Jalongo, M. R. 1984. "Imaginary Companions in Children's Lives and Literature," *Childhood Education, 60,* pp. 166–171.

Moss, E. 1983. *Picture Books for Young People 9–13*. New York: Greenwillow Books.

Rudman, M. K. 1984. *Children Literature: An Issues Approach*. Second edition. New York: Longman.

Saltman, J. 1985. *The Riverside Anthology of Children's Literature*. Sixth edition. Boston: Houghton Mifflin.

Smando, F. 1984. "Using Children's Literature as a Prelude or Finale to Music Experiences With Young Children," *Reading Teacher, 37,* pp. 700–705.

Sutherland, Z., and Livingston, M. C. 1984. *The Scott, Foresman Anthology of Children's Literature*. Glenview, IL: Scott, Foresman.

Wagoner, S. A. 1984. "The Portrayal of the Cognitively Disabled in Children's Literature," *Reading Teacher, 37,* pp. 502–508.

Chapter Notes

1. J. W. Stewig, *Children and Literature* (Chicago: Rand McNally, 1980), pp. 9–10.
2. H. Huus, "Teaching Literature at the Elementary School Level," *Reading Teacher,* 1973, *26,* pp. 797–798.
3. G. Peterson, "Behavioral Objectives for Teaching Literature," *Language Arts,* 1975, *52,* pp. 969–971.
4. R. J. Lukens, *A Critical Handbook of Children's Literature* (Glenview, Illinois: Scott, Foresman, 1981), pp. 1–6.
5. R. E. Toothaker, "Curiosities of Children That Literature Can Satisfy," *Childhood Education,* 1976, *52,* pp. 262–267.
6. P. J. Cianciolo, in *Adventuring with Books* (Urbana, Illinois: National Council of Teachers of English, 1977), pp. 1–10.
7. K. Spangler, "Reading Interests Vs. Reading Preferences: Using the Research," *Reading Teacher,* 1983, *36,* pp. 876–878.
8. E. G. Summers and A. Lukasevich, "Reading Preferences of Intermediate Grade Children in Relation to Sex, Community, and Maturation (Grade Level): A Canadian Perspective, *Reading Research Quarterly,* 1983, *18,* pp. 347–360.
9. A. Mendoza, "Elementary School Children's Preferences in Literature," *Childhood Education,* 1983, *59,* pp. 193–197; J. T. Feeley, "Interest Patterns and Media Preferences of Middle Grade Children," *Elementary English,* 1974, *51,* pp. 1006–1008; Beta Upsilon Chapter, Pi Lambda Theta, "Children's Reading Interests Classified by Age Level," *Reading Teacher,* 1974, *27,* pp. 694–700; S. Tibbetts, "Sex Differences in Children's Reading Preferences," *Reading Teacher,* 1974, *28,* pp. 270–281; L. Oliver, "Reading Interests of Children in the Primary Grades," *Elementary School Journal,* 1977, *77,* pp. 401–406; E. J. Porter, "Research Report: Children's Reading Interests," *Elementary English,* 1974, *51,* pp. 1003–1013; H. Robinson and S. Weintraub, "Research Related to Children's Interests and to Developmental Values in Reading," *Library Trends,* 1973, *22,* pp. 81–108; and Lian-Hwang Chiu, "Reading Preferences of Fourth Grade Children Related to Sex and Reading Ability, *Journal of Educational Research,* 1973, *66,* pp. 269–273.

10. S. Sebesta, "What Do Young People Think about the Literature They Read?" *Reading Newsletter #8* (Boston: Allyn & Bacon, 1979).
11. B. Elleman, "Chosen by Children," *Booklist* 79(7), December 1, 1982, pp. 508–9.
12. M. Berkley, "Isaac Bashevis Singer," *Publishers' Weekly,* February 18, 1983, pp. 65–66.
13. *The Bowker Annual of Library and Book Trade Information* (New York: R. R. Bowker, 1982).
14. *UNESCO Statistical Yearbook: 1980* (New York: United Nations Publications, 1981), Table 8.9.
15. K. H. Wendelin, R. A. Zinck, and S. M. Carter, "Teachers' Memories and Opinions of Children's Books: A Research Update," *Language Arts,* 1981, *58,* pp. 416–424.
16. M. J. Weiss, "Children's Preferences for Format Factors in Books," *Reading Teacher,* 1982, *35,* pp. 400–406.
17. R. Engel, "Is Unequal Treatment of Females Diminishing in Children's Picture Books?" *Reading Teacher,* 1981, *34,* pp. 647–652.
18. Z. Sutherland, D. Monson, and M. Arbuthnot, *Children and Books,* 6th ed. (Glenview, Illinois: Scott, Foresman, 1981), p. 402.
19. N. Larrick, "Wordless Picture Books and the Teaching of Reading," *Reading Teacher,* 1976, *30,* pp. 743–746.
20. C. A. Fisher and M. Natarella, "Young Children's Preferences in Poetry: A National Survey of First, Second, and Third Graders," *Research in the Teaching of English,* 1982, *16,* pp. 339–354; and A. C. Terry, *Children's Poetry Preferences: A National Survey of Upper Elementary Grades* (Urbana, Illinois: National Council of Teachers of English, 1974).
21. M. Roush, "Is the Role of Literature Different in Urban, Suburban, and Rural Classrooms throughout the Nation?" *Elementary English,* 1973, 50, pp. 745–747.
22. *Children's Choices for 1982* and *Children's Choices for 1981* (Newark, Delaware: International Reading Association).
23. Most of the titles listed appear in Volume 2 of S. Dreyer's *The Bookfinder: A Guide to Children's Literature About the Needs and Problems of Youth Aged 2–15* (Circle Pines, Minnesota: American Guidance Service, 1981).
24. E. Jenkins, "Multi-Ethnic Literature: Promise and Problems," *Elementary English,* 1973, *50,* p. 695.
25. E. M. Ziegler, "A Study of the Effects of Creative Dramatics on the Progress in the Use of the Library, Reading Interests, Reading Achievement, Self-Concept, Creativity, and Empathy of Fourth and Fifth Grade Children," *Dissertation Abstracts International,* 1971, *31,* p. 6482A.
26. Chow Loy Tom, *A National Survey of What Teachers Read to Children in the Middle Grades.* Unpublished doctoral dissertation, Ohio State University, 1969.
27. L. Lamme, *Reading Aloud to Children: A Comparative Study of Teachers and Aides.* Unpublished research report, 1977.
28. J. W. Stewig, "Choral Speaking: Who Has the Time? Why Take the Time?" *Childhood Education,* 1981, *57,* p. 25.
29. California State Department of Education, *English Language Framework for California Public Schools* (Sacramento: The Department, 1976), p. 57.
30. O. K. Buros, ed., *The Eighth Mental Measurements Yearbook,* Volume I (Highland Park, New Jersey: Gryphon Press, 1978), pp. 157–159.

Library Media Center Skills 12

Objectives

The role of the media specialist
Major library media center skills
The various types of catalog cards
How media centers serve exceptional children

Discover As You Read This Chapter If:*

1. The school library media center program must function as an inseparable part of the educational program.
2. Children usually request library materials by title.
3. Teachers/media specialists should introduce boys and girls to the Dewey Decimal Classification System rather than the Library of Congress Classification System.
4. Presenting the skill of understanding the parts of a book should be delayed until the intermediate grades.
5. Publishers of most of the good general encyclopedias follow the continuous-revision policy.
6. Unlike other catalog cards, the cross-reference card is generally not introduced until the third grade.
7. ESL students in the intermediate grades can and do make good use of picture dictionaries.
8. Many school library media centers allow primary children to check out audiovisual equipment.
9. Kindergarteners are too immature to profit from regular visits to the media center.
10. Simple research assignments on the materials located in the school library media center can be given to and completed by pupils as early as the fourth grade.

*Answers to these true-or-false statements may be found in Appendix 6.

The school library media program and the educational program are interdependent and inseparable, according to Davies.[1] To attempt to understand one in isolation from the other would be comparable to an attempt to build a school without specifications or a blueprint. Only when it functions as an integral support component of the total teaching-learning enterprise does the school library media program truly become an instructional source and force for excellence. The media center's program is designed to assist boys and girls to grow in their ability to find, generate, evaluate, and apply information that helps them to function effectively as individuals and to participate fully in society.[2] Nothing that children learn in school today is likely to continue to serve them so well throughout life as an interest in books and a skill in using both nonbook and book materials.

The development of such an interest and skill is primarily the responsibility of the elementary school librarian or *media specialist* (as this person is described in a joint statement of the American Association of School Librarians and the Association for Educational Communications and Technology). Since an educational program of excellence demands the multimedia approach to teaching and learning, the media specialist must help each student acquire and strengthen skills in reading, viewing, listening, and in communicating ideas. The specialist must also assist pupils in the development of independent study habits and must teach library research skills and the use/care of media resources.

As important as these duties may be, however, there remains an insufficient number of media professionals to handle them in elementary schools at the present time due both to budgeting problems and the relative lack of properly qualified personnel.

It is notable, therefore, that there is a direct relationship between the elementary classroom teacher's library background and reading habits and the amount and kind of library media skills and reading interests maintained by his or her students. When the teacher's library skills and reading habits are significantly high, the reading and library media skills of his or her pupils are high also.

However, at least one survey of elementary teachers' mastery of basic study skills has revealed surprisingly low results.[3] Sixty-five teachers in six schools in Wisconsin, Illinois, and Virginia took tests of study skills' attainment intended for use with students completing elementary or junior high school. The median percent of skills mastered was found to be in the 51–60 percent bracket, with a low of 23 percent of the teachers showing mastery of card catalog skills and a high of 90 percent displaying mastery of the use of the (abridged) *Reader's Guide to Periodical Literature*.

The only apparent solution, then, to the problem of who is to teach every child the library media skills deemed necessary in today's society involves two steps. First, the classroom teacher must acquire and maintain mastery of elementary study skills. And second, in schools without media specialists, boys and girls must attain library media skills from their classroom teacher while children attending schools that maintain strong library media facilities and staff can acquire the needed skills from a teacher-specialist team. Only in this way can students eventually become independent and expert public library patrons. A comprehensive school program should encourage the love of literature and the habit of individualized reading, should build attitudes of good citizenship, must develop reference and study skills, and should promote the use of nonbook materials.

Such a program may be presented to elementary school children in a variety of ways. In Concordia, California, seventh graders learn library media skills through tape recordings prepared in the school from scripts written and narrated by other students. In Islip, New York, fifth- and sixth-grade boys and girls are able to use the card catalog after two instructional sessions presented by closed-circuit television. In Phoenix, Arizona, transparencies prepared for use with an overhead projector are employed to teach library citizenship to primary children and to provide intermediate grade children with the opportunity to learn about author, title, and subject catalog cards, and to review correct ways of filling out date-due slips and circulation cards. In Charleston, Illinois, the transparencies supplement an audiovisual program consisting of two-by-two-inch color slides accompanied by taped narration. Finally, in Wayne County, Michigan, certain shelves in the library media center are specially marked with large Dewey decimal numbers and children are taught to shelve their own books. As they return the books that they have checked out, the clerk removes the transaction cards and hands the books back to the children for shelving. Since it is believed that boys and girls who cannot shelve a book also cannot locate a book on the shelf, self-shelving has become an activity that not only gives the children needed practice in handling books but also increases their opportunities to become familiar with all the areas of the library media center.

Such familiarity is important due to the many objectives of the library media center in K–8 schools, according to the New York City Board of Education:

1. To impart a lasting and genuine love of reading and an appreciation of fine literature.
2. To develop an understanding and aesthetic appreciation of aural and visual art forms.
3. To assist with programs for the development of competency in reading, listening, and viewing skills in the content areas.
4. To encourage reading, listening, and viewing as aids toward the achievement of the basic developmental tasks of children.
5. To support curriculum programs at all grade levels by providing a variety of book and nonbook materials.
6. To develop a continuity of instruction in the skillful use of school library media resources.
7. To reinforce, extend, and enrich classroom learning through planned library experiences.
8. To promote an understanding and appreciation of American institutions and ideals as well as a responsibility for supporting them.
9. To develop an understanding and appreciation of different ethnic groups and their contributions to the world.

10. To be an active participant in curriculum development, schoolwide projects and experiments, and school-related community programs.
11. To provide incentive for lifelong productive and satisfying use of libraries, museums, and other multimedia information centers.[4]

Another set of objectives for school library media center programs can be found in the Library Bill of Rights of the American Library Association, as shown in Figure 12.1.

Figure 12.1.
Library Bill of Rights.

Library Bill of Rights

The American Library Association affirms that all libraries are forums for information and ideas, and that the following basic policies should guide their services.

1. Books and other library resources should be provided for the interest, information, and enlightenment of all people of the community the library serves. Materials should not be excluded because of the origin, background, or views of those contributing to their creation.

2. Libraries should provide materials and information presenting all points of view on current and historical issues. Materials should not be proscribed or removed because of partisan or doctrinal disapproval.

3. Libraries should challenge censorship in the fulfillment of their responsibility to provide information and enlightenment.

4. Libraries should cooperate with all persons and groups concerned with resisting abridgment of free expression and free access to ideas.

5. A person's right to use a library should not be denied or abridged because of origin, age, background, or views.

6. Libraries which make exhibit spaces and meeting rooms available to the public they serve should make such facilities available on an equitable basis, regardless of the beliefs or affiliations of individuals or groups requesting their use.

Adopted June 18, 1948.
Amended February 2, 1961, June 27, 1967, and January 23, 1980, by the ALA Council.

Source: Reprinted by permission of the American Library Association.

Many of the above-named objectives have been met at the Point Road School Media Center, which recently served as a demonstration media center for the state of New Jersey.[5] Although it started as a "hallway library," it has been able to skillfully overcome the limited physical facilities available, and it is presently housed in one large room (approximately the size of three classrooms).

Many of its furnishings are mobile, including its checkout desk, its card catalog, its large puppet stage, its storage cabinet, and its atlas stand. Even the center's bookcases are large book carts on wheels. Furthermore, some of the mobile furnishings are also multipurpose items, such as the wardrobe which has a movie screen on the back and the supply closet which has a chalkboard back. All this mobility allows any adult to quickly turn areas of the center into a theatre, a puppet factory, an inviting storytelling corner, a large meeting room, a research center for reports, or several quiet reading corners.

Another feature of the Point Road School Media Center is integrated shelving. This arrangement of its collections shelves print and nonprint materials together, thereby offering additional accessibility to faculty and students. Integrated shelving increases learning experiences for both fast and slow learners, promotes social adjustment and sharing, and makes it possible for both students and staff to find related resources more quickly.

Since this media center is interested in enlisting boys and girls in lifelong education, it offers many opportunities for personal growth such as the Great Art and Music Appreciation Program, the Poetry Read-In and Eat-In Program, the Great Books Discussion Groups, the Theatre-in-the-Round, the Paperback Exchange, and the Magazine Give-A-Way. The center also awards an Assistant Librarian Certificate to each student who completes a course covering various library chores, responsibilities, and skills.

Major Library Media Center Skills and Instructional Activities

Instruction in the use of the media center must be functional and preferably related directly to classroom work experiences in social studies, science, and other curricular areas. It can, however, also occur indirectly through separate units that parallel curricular units. A fourth-grade class, for example, is pursuing a unit on weather, so the media specialist may plan a unit on folklore, myths, and legends which have evolved as people have attempted to explain climatic and seasonal changes. In this way the specialist or teacher-specialist can use classroom science to motivate pupils to learn more about the realm of imaginative literature.

The instructional program should incorporate the interests, needs, and developmental tasks of the children, including activities within the pupils' understanding and ability. It should contain a sequence of growth and emphasize ten major skills.

First Skill: Understanding the Classification of Books

Since the minimal book collection in schools with 500 or fewer pupils (according to standards established by the American Association for School Librarians and AECT) contains 8,000 to 12,000 volumes, any child looking for a book needs a knowledge of the basic arrangement of books and of the Dewey Decimal System for the classification of books. Lessons that relate to call numbers and the proper placement of books on the shelf should begin by stressing the importance of careful arrangement of volumes and reviewing the division of books into fiction and nonfiction groupings. Then the lessons could proceed as follows:

Fiction and Call Numbers

While showing flash cards with enlarged call numbers (covering both fiction and nonfiction), the teacher-specialist establishes the difference between the two categories of numbers. He or she emphasizes that a fiction call number is the intial letter or letters of an author's surname and then sends several children to get fiction books from the shelves. The children discuss the selections and justify the call numbers appearing on the book spines.

Next, the teacher tells how fiction is arranged, explaining why shelf labels are a quick way of locating the right call number, and how the library media center "landmarks" (corners, windows, pictures, and doors) will save the readers' time in finding the proper shelf label. Finally, the teacher drills on locating fiction via call numbers by showing certain flash cards and calling on the pupils to walk to the shelves to point out the books bearing the desired call numbers.

Nonfiction and Call Numbers

The teacher-specialist randomly arranges on the chalk tray some flash cards with enlarged nonfiction call numbers, and asks the class to suggest a way to place the cards in numerical order. The children will usually respond correctly, although the teacher must be careful not to omit a card with a 000 number in the tray. Another more time-consuming way of introducing the arrangement of nonfiction is by working from the numbers on the shelf labels: pupils are carefully dispatched to each of the nonfiction shelves—except individual biography—and, one by one, they read the numbers off the shelf labels.

To establish "landmarks" in the nonfiction section of the library media center, the teacher hands out flash cards representing the major classifications to each of ten children and asks the pupils to place their cards on the top shelf of the proper section. In this way the class can easily see, for example, that the 500s are under the clock or the 800s are by the door.

Next, the teacher distributes copies of the abridged Dewey Decimal Classification System appropriate for elementary school library media centers, as exemplified in Table 12.1. The teacher explains that most libraries in the United States use the Dewey System to determine which number to use on each book. Then he or she selects a few examples from the handout sheet and has various pupils verify these numbers on the shelves. Finally, the teacher refers back to the flash cards and reminds the children that nonfiction numbers are composed of a first line, which indicates the subject of a book according to the Dewey System, and a second line, which—like the fiction call numbers—indicates the initial letter or letters of an author's surname. (In those few elementary schools which use the Library of Congress Classification System, as shown in Table 12.2, the teacher-specialist should use the same teaching strategies to introduce that system as have been described for the Dewey System).

Table 12.1
Dewey Decimal Classification Numbers in Use in Elementary Schools

020	Library Science	540	Chemistry	914.4	France
028	Reading	550	Geology, Rocks, etc.	914.5	Italy
030	Encyclopedias	551	Weather	914.6	Spain
070	Journalism	560	Prehistoric Life	914.7	Russia
150	Psychology, Ethics	570	Anthropology	914.8	Sweden, Norway
220	Bible	574	Wildlife	9.14.9	Other European
					Countries
260	Christian Church	580	Plants, Trees		
290	Myths	594	Seashore Life, Shells	915	Asia
300	Social Science	595	Insects, Worms	915.1	China
310	Almanacs	598	Birds	915.2	Japan
320	Political Science	599	Animals	915.3	Arabian Countries
323	Community Life	600	Useful Arts, Industries	915.4	India
330	Banking, Trade, Money	608	Inventions	915.5	Iran
333	Conservation	614	Health, Fire Protection,	915.6	Syria
			Safety		
338	Commercial Establishments	620	Aviation	915.9	Other Asiatic Countries
340	Law	621	Radio, Television	916	Africa
341	United Nations	625	Highways, Roads, Bridges	917	North America
352	Police	629	Automobiles, Trucks,	917.1	Canada
			Machines		
353	Citizenship	630	Farming, Gardening, Lumber	917.2	Mexico
355	Armed Forces	636	Domestic Animals	917.3	United States
371	Vocations	640	Food, Clothing	917.94	California
380	Transportation,	655	Printing	917.98	Alaska
	Communication, Commerce				
680	Handicrafts	918	South America	918	South America
383	Postal Service, Stamps	700	Fine Arts	919	Oceania
385	Railroads, Trains	740	Drawing	919.8	Polar Regions
387	Waterways, Ships	770	Photography	920	Collective Biography
					(Real People)
390	Costume	778	Motion Pictures		
392	Families, Homes	780	Music	921	Biography (Individual)
394	Holidays	790	Games, Sports	929	Flags
395	Etiquette	800	Literature	930	Ancient History
398	Fairy Tales, Folklore	811	Poetry	940	European History
400	Language	812	Plays	940.5	World War II
423	Dictionaries	900	History	942	Great Britain, History
425	Grammar	910	Geography	970.1	Indians of North America
500	Science, Nature Study	912	Atlases	973	United States, History
510	Mathematics	914	Europe	978	The West
520	Astronomy	914.1	Scotland, Ireland	979.4	California, History
530	Physics, Electricity, Atomic	914.2	England	E	Easy Book
	Energy	914.3	Germany	F	Fiction

Table 12.2
Library of Congress Classification System

Classes A to Z			
A	General Works	L	Education
B	Philosophy, Psychology, and Religion	M	Music
		N	Fine Arts
C-D	History: General, European, African, Asiatic	P	Language and Literature
		Q	Science and Mathematics
E-F	History: United States and American	R	Medicine
		S	Agriculture
G	Geography, Anthropology, etc.	T	Engineering, Technology, etc.
H	Social Sciences (General), Economics, Sociology, etc.	U	Military Science
		V	Naval Science
J	Political Science	Z	Bibliography and Library Science
K	Law		

Other Activities

The children may play a relay game in locating and returning books to the shelves or may straighten shelves of books that have been scrambled. They may arrange themselves in alphabetical order as if they were fiction books on the shelf or may rearrange oversized sample book spines made of felt board. They will enjoy completing a floor plan of the library media center on which they designate the locations of different classifications of books. Some pupils may wish to read and report on pertinent topics such as the Library of Congress or the life of Melvil Dewey. Others will be interested in visiting their local public library to compare its book locations and arrangements with those used in the school center. Still other pupils will enjoy completing the exercises (found in some language arts series) which concern arranging/locating fiction and nonfiction books, as shown in Figure 12.2.

Second Skill: Using the Card Catalog

Since the card catalog is a distinctive and important tool, children must attain an understanding of it as a complete index to all the materials in the library media center. Sample catalog cards are shown in Figures 12.3 through 12.10 (see pages 439–442).

Figure 12.2. Exercises in Arranging/Locating Fiction and Nonfiction Books.

Exercises **Arranging Fiction Books**

A. Copy this list of authors. Underline the first letter of each author's last name. Then write the names in alphabetical order.

Taro Yashima	Elizabeth Coatsworth
Rodney Peppé	Kristin Hunter
Symeon Shimin	Ellen Raskin
Ezra Jack Keats	A. A. Milne
Ludwig Bemelmans	Alice Dalgliesh

B. Here are two groups of authors' names. The last names within each group begin with the same letter. Write the names in alphabetical order.

1.	2.
Leo Lionni	Roger Duvoisin
Arnold Lobel	Tomie de Paola
Hugh Lofting	James Daugherty
Joan M. Lexau	Bruce Degen
Astrid Lindgren	Glen Dines

C. Here is another list of authors. Write the last names in alphabetical order.

Albert Lamorisse	Mercer Mayer
Eros Keith	Kenneth Grahame
Maurice Sendak	Charlotte Zolotow
George Mendoza	Yoshiko Uchida

Nonfiction Books

Nonfiction books are about real persons, places, and things. They are arranged according to what they are about. They are arranged by their **subjects.** All books about the same subject are grouped together. For example, all books about history are together. All books about science are together.

Figure 12.2 (cont.)

Exercises Arranging Nonfiction Books

A. Here is a list of books. Each book falls into one category of the Dewey Decimal System. Name the category. Tell what numbers are given to books in the category.

1. *How Did We Find Out About Outer Space?* Isaac Asimov
2. *Stories from the Bible* Walter de la Mare
3. *World Book Encyclopedia*
4. *Monster Poems* Daisy Wallace
5. *How We Choose a President* Lee Learner Gray
6. *Kids Camping* Aileen Paul
7. *Sequoya, The Cherokee Who Captured Words* Lilli Patterson
8. *Ice Hockey Rules* Robert Scharf
9. *You Can Write Chinese* Kurt Wiese
10. *Slapdash Cooking* Carol Barkin and Elizabeth James

B. Go to your school, neighborhood, or city library. Draw a floor plan of the young people's section. Show where these books are shelved:

1. Fiction books
2. Nonfiction books
3. Encyclopedias

The media specialist can help students to locate those catalog subject cards that relate to their social studies assignments or special hobbies. (Photo courtesy of National Education Publishing, Joe Di Dio.)

HORSES—FICTION

HEN Henry, Marguerite.
One Man's Horse. Illustrated by
Wesley Dennis. Rand, McNally, c1977
103 p. illus.

1. Horses—Fiction 1. Title

Figure 12.3. Sample Catalog Subject Card: Fiction.

Figure 12.4.
Sample Catalog
Author Card: Fiction.

HEN Henry, Marguerite.
One Man's Horse. Illustrated by
Wesley Dennis. Rand, McNally, c1977
103 p. illus.

1. Horses—Fiction 1. Title

Figure 12.5.
Sample Catalog Title
Card: Fiction.

One Man's Horse

HEN Henry, Marguerite.
One Man's Horse. Illustrated by
Wesley Dennis. Rand McNally, c1977
103 p. illus.

Figure 12.6.
Sample Catalog
Subject Card:
Nonfiction.

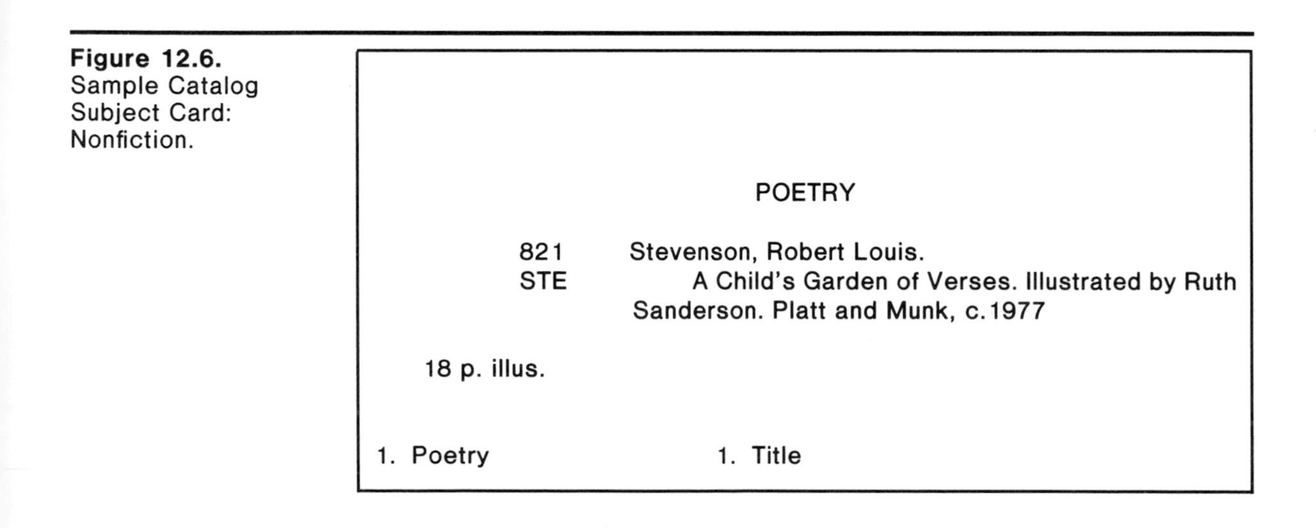

POETRY

821 Stevenson, Robert Louis.
STE A Child's Garden of Verses. Illustrated by Ruth
Sanderson. Platt and Munk, c.1977

18 p. illus.

1. Poetry 1. Title

Figure 12.7. Sample Catalog Author Card: Nonfiction.

821 STE Stevenson, Robert Louis.
A Child's Garden of Verses. Illustrated by Ruth Sanderson. Platt and Munk, c.1977

18 p. illus.

1. Poetry 1. Title

Figure 12.8. Sample Catalog Title Card: Nonfiction.

A Child's Garden of Verses

821 STE Stevenson, Robert Louis.
A Child's Garden of Verses. Illustrated by Ruth Sanderson. Platt and Munk, c.1977.

18 p. illus.

Figure 12.9. Sample Catalog Audiovisual Card: Author.

821 STE Stevenson, Robert Louis
A Child's Garden of Verses; read by Judith Anderson. (AA).

Phonotape Cassette
CAEDMON CDL 51077.

1. Poetry 1. Title

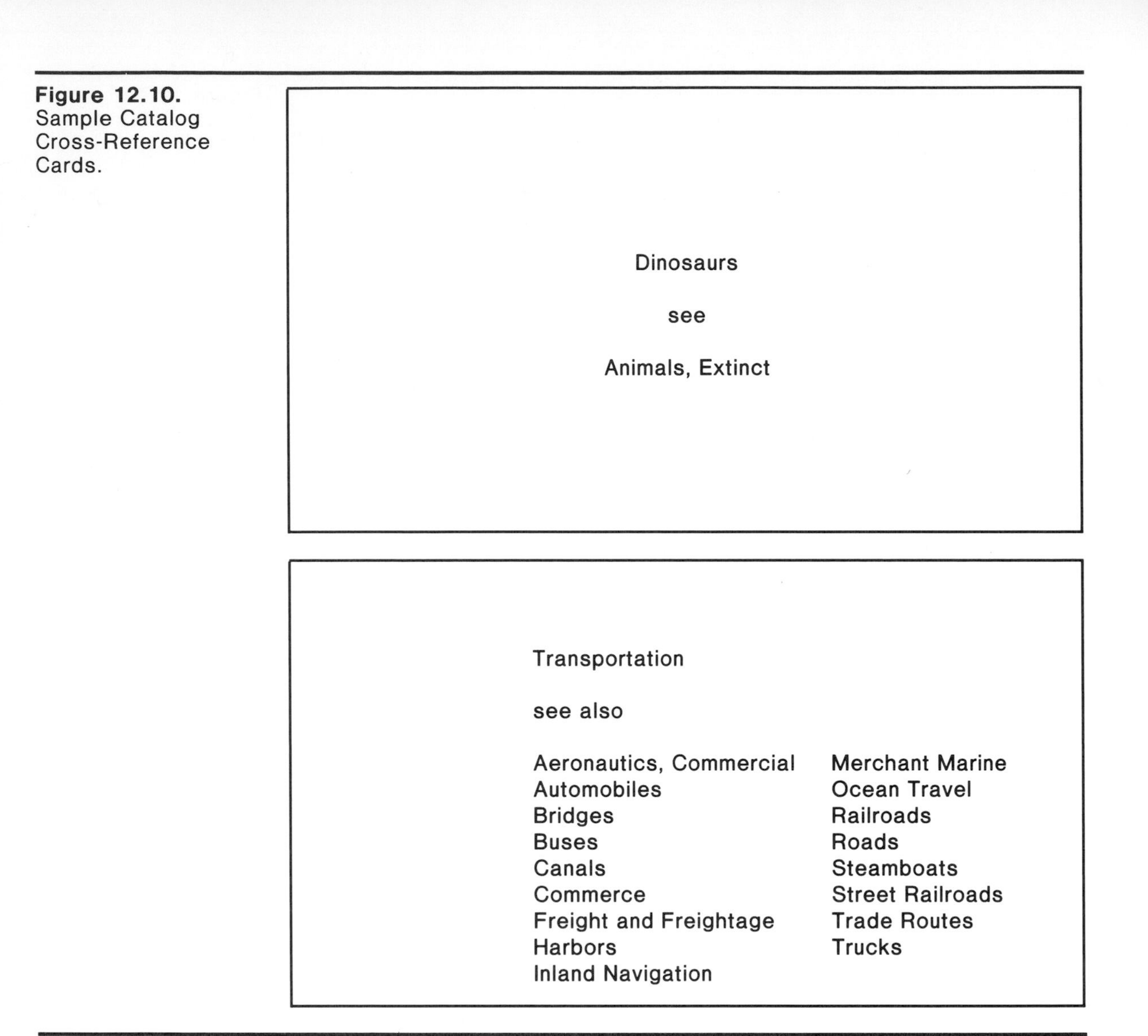

Figure 12.10. Sample Catalog Cross-Reference Cards.

More than one lesson may be needed to acquaint pupils with this skill. The first could relate to the cabinet itself and the use of labels on the drawers (and include a poster-sized chart of the front of the card catalog showing the labels on each drawer, if the group of children is too large to sit directly in front of the cabinet). The teacher explains that it is through the card catalog that the pupils can learn to find independently the materials they want and that while catalogs are sometimes in book form, they are more generally in card form in order to be kept up-to-date easily. Then the teacher calls the group's attention to the guide letters on the catalog drawers, which are a means of finding the right drawer, and demonstrates how guide cards save the reader's time. Since elementary school children almost invariably begin to inquire for materials by subject rather than author or title, the teacher now shows them a poster-sized catalog subject card and discusses what questions the card is intended to answer. Finally, as the class studies the labels on the catalog drawers, the teacher lists some subjects or topics that will require a choice between two drawers containing the same letter or that will require finding a letter not shown on the labels.

A second lesson would begin with a review of the poster-sized catalog subject card, proceed to a display of poster-sized cards showing the author and title cards for the same book as the subject card, and culminate in a discussion with the pupils of the information contained on the three cards. The teacher then shows through the opaque projector sample author cards, title cards, and subject cards taken from the catalog in the school library and points out the publisher's name and the copyright date. He or she explains how to find titles of other books written by a favorite author and how to compare dates of books on one subject when recency of publication is an important factor. Finally, each pupil is provided with a set of questions based on the cards in one catalog drawer in the library. Since there are not enough drawers to provide one for each pupil in an average-sized class, plans are made for some of the children to read while the others work on the catalog lesson. As pupils complete the catalog assignment, they become readers, viewers, or listeners, and the drawers that they have been using are given to other members of the class.

A third lesson, especially appropriate for sixth graders, would begin with a brief review of author, title, and subject cards, and then proceed to an introduction of cross-reference cards. These "see" and "see also" cards refer the reader from one subject to another.

During other activities that lead to skill acquisition, the pupils may alphabetize sets of discarded catalog cards, demonstrate various ways that a single book may be located in the catalog, or practice locating books on the shelves by referring to the card catalog. They may make simplified author, title, and subject cards by using the title pages of ten nonfiction books, or use prepared slips with which to practice locating book titles in the catalog. They may arrange a notebook on the use of the card catalog or find answers to specific questions by using the catalog. The children may make guide cards for some of the drawers, or may interpret the bibliographic data on a few catalog cards. Some may wish to explain how to use the catalog to classmates who had been unable to attend school on the days when the teacher-specialist initiated the study of the card catalog. Others may enjoy demontrating the use of the catalog to the group through an improvised skit or dialog. Older boys and girls will be interested in keeping a record of their recreational reading in the form of catalog cards, complete with guide cards, or in using the catalog to compile lists of books on unusual subjects or by favorite authors. Some may wish to complete exercises concerned with the use of the card catalog, which are found in current language arts series, as shown in Figure 12.11.

Figure 12.11. Exercises Using the Card Catalog.

Exercises Using the Card Catalog

A. For each group below, number the entries in the order in which you would find them in the card catalog.

1. a. LAW
   b. The last frontier
   c. Last race
   d. The law of life
   e. The last out

2. a. The new math
   b. Newman, James R.
   c. NEWSPAPERS
   d. NEW YEAR
   e. New tall tales of Pecos Bill

B. What subject cards would give you information about each of the following topics? Discuss your answers in class.

1. Painting a van
2. How to make slides
3. How to sail a boat
4. Cures for diseases
5. How to enter a rodeo
6. Houdini's best magic tricks
7. Olympic medal winners
8. Wilderness camping
9. Television commercials
10. Grooming your dog

C. Use the card catalog to find the title, author, call number, and publication date of a book on one of the following subjects.

1. A book on metrics
2. A book about the Boston Marathon
3. A collection of stories by Arthur Conan Doyle
4. A book on World War I uniforms
5. A book about mountain climbing
6. A book on holidays
7. A book of short stories by Alfred Hitchcock
8. A book about country and western music
9. A book of science fiction stories
10. A book about Beverly Sills

Source: Reprinted from BUILDING ENGLISH SKILLS, Red Level, Copyright 1984, McDougal, Littell & Company, Evanston, Illinois. Used with permission.

Incidentally, catalog cards for audiovisual materials are filed like any other cards—up to the parentheses that enclose the type of medium. The elements, arrangement, and style of the catalog cards for nonprinted materials are essentially the same as for printed matter. The library media center which uses Dewey numbers for books would use these for audiovisual materials as well. Color-coding of catalog cards for such materials or the use of symbols or abbreviations in place of fully spelled-out media designations is no longer recommended because such techniques emphasize form over content and confuse the catalog users. The AECT uses certain generic media designators (such as AA for audiorecordings, FA for filmstrips, and MA for motion pictures) in an effort to achieve standardized terminology.

Third Skill: Understanding the Parts of a Book

Children must gradually gain an understanding of the parts of a book, the publication of books, and the technical vocabulary that relates to books. Early in the second grade the pupils learn about the parts of a book beginning with the spine ("you have a spine, too, that runs down your back") and discover that books are always kept on the shelf with the spines facing out. A few weeks later the children become acquainted with the title page when the librarian brings in several stacks of books with appealing titles, shows them the title pages of several books, and then asks each child to select one book and attempt to locate the title page. By the end of the third grade the pupils have been introduced to three items in the physical makeup of books (front and back covers, spine, and text or body of book) and two printed parts of the book (title page and table of contents).

Older children become familiar with the parts of a book which precede and follow the main text: frontispiece, title page, copyright page, dedication, table of contents, list of maps—plates—illustrations, foreword, preface, acknowledgements, inroduction, appendix, glossary, bibliography, index, and end papers. They may be introduced to the signature (or printed sheet containing a section of a book) and may also participate in a demonstration of the making of a signature by folding, numbering, and cutting large sheets of newsprint. Sixth graders may be taken through the steps involved in the physical production of a book from the original idea to the finished volume, may attend demonstrations on book mending, or may tour local printing plants.

All pupils may enjoy hearing a presentation by an author, printer, publisher, illustrator, or binder who can describe his or her contribution to the evolution of a book. They can make original title pages for book reports, draw book jackets of favorite books to be displayed in the library media center, or create a book individually or in cooperation with their peers. They can occasionally demonstrate the proper handling of books when new sets are distributed for classroom assignments. Sometimes they may be allowed to take apart a discarded volume in order to demonstrate the construction of a book.

Fourth Skill: Using an Index

Because of the nature of reference tools, children must necessarily acquire the ability to locate and use indexes. They will enjoy comparing the tables of contents to the indexes in several books, but it should be pointed out to them that while the table of contents gives the broad areas of a book's coverage, the index offers a more detailed listing of the contents of that book. A teacher-specialist in Clearlake Oaks, California, for example, has one of the fifth graders draw from a hat a slip of paper containing an easily located subject, such as "the moon," "Abraham Lincoln," or "bluebirds." The child then locates a book which has that subject listed in its table of contents. Presuming that the fifth grader has drawn a slip with the word "bluebirds" written on it, the discussion can soon revolve about an opaque projection of the following initial index entry:

> BLUEBIRDS, 32–48; description, 32–33;
> food, 35, 38–40; migration, 46–48;
> nests, 34, 36–37.

The teacher-specialist reminds the children that when they use the table of contents they are looking for a broad area of information such as a chapter on bluebirds generally. Then, he or she asks the girls and boys if they wish to learn more about bluebird nests in particular, how can they locate this specific information and locate it readily? A few pupils may suggest skimming through the entire chapter, but gradually the class begins to realize that using an index will make the locational task much easier.

In an attempt to help elementary teachers present the index skill, an analysis was once made of more than 100 actual index entries in several curriculum subjects at three grade levels of representative textbooks and elementary encyclopedias. Components of index entries included the following twenty: main topic, page numbers, comma, period, semicolon, hyphen, colon, synonymous subtopic, related by not synonymous subtopic, *see, see also, illus., map, diag., pict.,* underscore, bold face, definitions, pronunciation (both phonetic and with diacritical marks), and others (chart, figure, volume). The analysis concluded that the larger the number of components the more difficult was the entry. In other words, the criterion of complexity was the number of components. Consequently, boys and girls must be given experiences which will enable them to develop insight into the composite nature of the index skill.

Fifth Skill: Using Encyclopedias

Before children are abruptly plunged into certain kinds of supplementary assignments, they must attain the ability to use encyclopedias to discover information about broad topics. Since many pupils and a few teachers speak of the encyclopedia as though there were only one and it were entitled The Encyclopedia, it is better from the first to have both pupils and teachers refer to encyclopedias by their individual names.

A two-part demonstration is generally effective in teaching discrimination among sets. During the first portion, which emphasizes the number of different encyclopedias available, the children are given a week to look at various sets found in public libraries and homes and then return to class to draw up a composite list of titles. During the second portion, the children become aware of the differences among encyclopedias and the need to comprehend the arrangement and content of each set, for they must examine several identical topics in three or more different sets. An opaque projector can be used during the second part of the demonstration in order to save class time. Publishers of juvenile encyclopedias also sometimes supply printed aids for teaching the use of their particular sets.

Among the multivolume encyclopedias for children ages 9–18, the *World Book Encyclopedia* (22 vol.) is rated as best by independent surveys of both United States and Canadian public librarians.[6] Its chief challenger is the *Merit Students Encyclopedia* (20 vol.). Among the multivolume encyclopedias for children ages 7–14, the two leaders in almost every aspect are *Britannica Junior Encyclopedia* (15 vol.) and *The New Book of Knowledge* (20 vol.). All of these four sets use the continuous-revision policy (presently followed by most of the good general encyclopedias, according to the American Library Association) which means that, instead of publishing thoroughly revised editions at spaced intervals, the editorial staffs make changes with each annual printing to bring some articles up to date.

While children often learn at home about general encyclopedias, which are alphabetically arranged and discuss many subjects, they need to be introduced at school to special subject encyclopedias. These bring together related materials under broad topics in a nonalphabetical arrangement. Examples include *The Book of Popular Science* (10 vol.) and *The International Encyclopedia of Wildlife* (20 vol.).

Encyclopedias are not difficult to use, particularly for pupils already familiar with the card catalog. The principal teaching problems lie in the different methods of indexing (including the use of the cross-reference) and in the different spine markings. To help the children acquire facility in the use of encyclopedias, the teacher-specialist should discuss finding words alphabetically, understanding volume letter(s) or words, using an index or an index volume, and using guide words and cross-references. The teacher should be certain that pupils understand the definition of an encyclopedia and the difference between an encyclopedia and a dictionary. Moreover, the teacher should explain the importance of reading for facts, and then rewriting or retelling those facts honestly in the reader's own words. He or she should also alert older children to the significance of the date of publication and to the use of the encyclopedia for validating material in textbooks and newspapers.

A good exercise for use in beginning research work is to have the class locate pictures in an encyclopedia by using the index to look for illustrations, which are listed in italics. Pencils and paper are not needed as each pupil is asked to locate a picture of a particular person, place, animal, or item. (For example, a child who picks up the last-designated volume in most general sets must find a picture of a zebra.) While the completed task can be evaluated at a glance, the teacher must be sure to assign an interesting list of illustrations that are readily located under the proper headings.

Competence in using the encyclopedia is cumulative and involves alphabetizing, searching, reading, and acquiring-organizing information. These skills are also necessary for using the *yearbooks* which are annual supplements to most encyclopedias. They give new, factual information on the highlights of the year and update some of the material already in the encyclopedia set. Kister warns, however, that with the exception of the *World Book Year Book* and, for adults, the *Britannica Book of the Year,* most yearbooks are usually not a good buy because they are not only overly expensive but often are related to the encyclopedia in name only.[7]

Incidentally, at least one recent national survey of public libraries of varying sizes has documented an interesting phenomenon: widespread teacher bias against student use of encyclopedias.[8]

Sixth Skill: Using Dictionaries

Primary and intermediate pupils alike must possess the ability to use dictionaries to discover information about words. They will enjoy examining different dictionaries which have been set up on the library table and which range from a picture dictionary to an unabridged volume. They may compile a list of the kinds of information that can be found about most words in the dictionary or define terms that relate to dictionary usage. They may engage in contests to see how long it takes to locate a particular word in order to prove the usefulness of guide words.

In the primary grades the children should have an opportunity to become familiar with the picture dictionary. This is a suitable readiness device which generally presents words in most of the following ways: picture and caption, simple explanation of the word, the word used in a sentence, the word used in a quotation, and the word and its antonym used in a phrase.

Although the picture dictionary is less a reference book than an enrichment source (since no dictionary which most primary children can read themselves will be comprehensive enough to function as a real dictionary), picture dictionaries can be used in the classroom, library media center, and home in a variety of ways. They can teach the order of the alphabet, encourage independence in learning words, and teach the users to discover meanings and develop an interest in words through browsing. Through the picture dictionary, the children can recognize various forms of the same letter (uppercase and lowercase, cursive, and printed) and identify various words which begin with the same letter. They can also learn to spell. Should they come from a foreign language background, the picture dictionary will also help them learn English as a second language.

Among the current and better picture dictionaries are:

The Cat in the Hat Beginner Book Dictionary (Random House), 1350 entries, grades K–1
The Golden Picture Dictionary (Western Publishing Co.), 2500 entries, grades K–1
My First Picture Dictionary, Revised Edition (Lothrop/Scott, Foresman), 800 entries, grades K–1
My Pictionary (Lothrop/Scott, Foresman), 535 entries, grades K–1
My Second Picture Dictionary (Lothrop/Scott, Foresman), 4000 entries, grades K–3
The New Golden Dictionary (Western Publishing Co.), 2000 entries, grades K–1
Storybook Dictionary (Western Publishing Co.), 2500 entries, grades K–3
The Strawberry Picture Dictionary (Larousse), 375 entries, grades K–1

The pupils' readiness for instruction in dictionary skills should include recognizing each letter and learning its name, becoming familiar with the location of the letters in relation to each other, learning the consecutive arrangements of letters in the alphabet, and making alphabetical arrangements of words starting with a limited group of different letters.

Middle-grade children should be told about the aids contained in the dictionary for the location of words (the thumb index by letters and the guide words on each page) and the information provided by the dictionary on spelling, abbreviations and other arbitrary signs, pronunciations, definitions, proper geographical names, synonyms, antonyms, English usage, foreign words and phrases, parts of speech, quotations, and word derivation.

While each major area of the dictionary has specific skills that should be presented in the elementary grades, some of the skills are more important than others and should therefore be taught first. A majority of dictionary authorities

The elementary schoolchild enjoys examining various dictionaries that have been placed on the library media center table.

has graded 19 items as indispensable.[9] Should a pupil then master all of these items prior to leaving the sixth grade, the teacher can be confident that the child is well prepared in five areas of dictionary matter:

1. **Pronunciation**
   Knowing the pronunciation key being used
   Knowing that correct pronunciation is regional
   Knowing that pronunciations are usage reports
2. **Location**
   Knowing location of pronunciation keys
   Knowing alphabetical order
   Knowing how to locate idioms
3. **Meaning Selection**
   Selecting the meaning to fit the context
   Understanding status or usage labels
   Interpreting status or usage labels
   Knowing how the parts of speech are abbreviated
   Knowing each definition is numbered under different parts of speech

4. **Spelling**

Knowing there are alternate spellings to some words
Knowing that the basis of spelling is custom and usage
Knowing how to locate plural spellings
Knowing that the dictionary gives the principal point of view
Knowing that the dictionary shows capitalization
Knowing homographs
Knowing that the dictionary shows syllabication of words

5. **History and Structure of the Dictionary**

Knowing that the dictionary is a guide, not a rule book

Among the current and better dictionaries for the middle-school and upper-elementary grades are these:

The American Heritage School Dictionary (Houghton Mifflin), 55,000 entries, grades 6–10
Macmillan School Dictionary, Revised Edition (Macmillan), 65,000 entries, grades 6–10
Thorndike-Barnhart Intermediate Dictionary (Doubleday), 57,000 entries, grades 5–8
The Random House Dictionary, School Edition (Random House), 45,000 entries, grades 6–10
Webster's Intermediate Dictionary (G. & C. Merriam), 57,000 entries, grades 6–10

Described as strictly elementary-school dictionaries are these current and recommended titles:

The Charlie Brown Dictionary (Random House), 2400 entries, grades K–3
Scott, Foresman Beginning Dictionary (Doubleday/Scott, Foresman), 25,000 entries, grades 3–8
Troll Talking Picture Dictionary (Troll Associates), 1400 entries, grades K–3, cassette tapes and booklets
Macmillan Dictionary for Children, trade edition, or *Macmillan Beginning Dictionary,* text edition (Macmillan), 30,000 entries grades 3–8
Weekly Reader Beginning Dictionary, trade edition (Grosset & Dunlap) or *The Ginn Beginning Dictionary,* text edition (Ginn), 5000 entries, grades 2–4
Xerox Intermediate Dictionary, trade edition (Grosset & Dunlap) or *The Ginn Intermediate Dictionary,* text edition (Ginn), 34,000 entries, grades 3–8

Elementary school children should be allowed to peruse at least one unabridged dictionary so they may realize that that is one volume to which they can refer for quick answers to a variety of questions.

Incidentally, children and teachers alike should be aware that the name "Webster" in the dictionary field can now be used by any publisher. Although it once distinguished the dictionaries published by the reputable G. & C. Merriam Company, it no longer has any bearing on the worth of a dictionary. Publishing houses of every quality are now permitted to label their dictionaries as "Webster's". It therefore becomes even more important for educators to consider the following areas when evaluating a dictionary: purpose and scope; authority; vocabulary treatment; encyclopedic features; graphics; physical format; and price.[10]

Activities

Selected activities which teachers may wish to plan with and for their classes generally demand that each pupil have a copy of an appropriate dictionary. Less advantaged districts, however, sometimes distribute dictionaries on a one-to-three or one-to-four basis (meaning one dictionary per three or four pupils). Therefore, the sample activities briefly described here may be conducted either as whole-class or group assignments.

1. Drill: What letter comes right before *L?*
   What is the second guide word on page 172?
   On what page can you find a picture of a prehistoric animal?
   How many nouns can you find on page 212? (A small letter *n* will be printed after the word or at the end of the definitions.)
   How many pictures of birds can you find under the *K* section of the dictionary?
   See if you can find the pictures of three musical instruments. Then list the name of the instrument and the number of the page on which you found its picture.
2. Examine the quarters of the dictionary and list which letters are located in each quarter.
3. Look up the following words and write "yes" after the hyphenated words and "no" after those that are not hyphenated: *baseball, workman, takeoff, overcoat,* and *tonguetied.*
4. Find a homophone for each of the following: *way, ewe, be, our, cent,* and *seen.*
5. Decide which of the two spellings of the following pairs of words is the correct one: *acqueduct/aqueduct, business/busness, calendar/calander,* and *certainly/sertainly.*
6. Substitute synonyms for five words in the following sentence: *The lad with the pallid and morose countenance peered into the murky bayou.*
7. Paraphrase sentences to accommodate general meanings of specific words which are underlined (e.g., Jeff looked <u>puzzled</u>. Jeff looked as if he didn't understand.)
8. Practice opening the dictionary at a given letter, without thumbing through the pages, on a timed basis.
9. Answer yes-no questions involving words that are not in the present vocabulary of the members (e.g., Can Lisa and Sandy play a *duet* at the piano recital?)
10. Find many different meanings for such common words as *safe, husband,* or *signal.*
11. Determine the meaning of one prefix (e.g., *sub*) and then find "sub" words to fill the blanks in a list such as the following:
    A boat that travels under water sub ________
    An underground electric railway sub ________
12. Supply one root word and then list other members of the same family (e.g., *kind*).
13. Determine roots of words used in modern advertising (e.g., *Aqua Velva*).

14. Change phonetic spellings of certain words to the regular spellings (e.g., *fikst* to *fixed*).
15. Make up a list of words in which
    ph or *gh* sound like *f*
    ch or *ck* sound like hard *c*
    c, x, and *s* sound like *sh*
16. List the plurals of words like *alumnus, basis, index, stratus,* and *bacillus.*
17. Look up English words which have been adapted or borrowed from other languages, such as *ski, coffee, kimono, sonata,* and *waltz.* Then identify the language in which the word first appeared.
18. Tell whether each of the following is found in the air, on land, or in the water: *sturgeon, tripod, coracle,* and *obelisk.*
19. Write the words for which the following abbreviations stand: *PO, RFD, pp., dept., riv., a.m., ans.,* and *inc.*
20. Write the phrase or sentence from your dictionary that shows the correct use of the following words: *urge, noble, mellow, rummage,* and *commerce.*
21. Write the abbreviation for the word class of each of the following words: *whereas, hereby, gratis, forever, martial,* and *confident.*
22. Copy from your dictionary the following words, properly divided into syllables: *dirigible, final, nicety,* and *miraculous.*
23. List the guide words connected with each word of the current social studies lesson.
24. Extract root forms of ten words in the weekly spelling lesson (e.g., *unpaved/pave*).
25. Indicate the syllable with the primary stress in a list of ten familiar two-syllable words (e.g., *cár toon*).

Seventh Skill: Using Specialized Reference Books

The ability to use almanacs, atlases, gazetteers, handbooks, and other special reference sources to discover geographical, historical, biographical, and statistical information becomes an increasing preoccupation of school children from the time that they are first introduced to these editions until they gradually develop or improve their techniques for independent study. By using late issues of the *World Almanac and Book of Facts* or the *Information Please Almanac,* pupils may participate in a "scavenger hunt" by finding answers to such prepared questions as "Who was the first black American to play professional baseball?" and "Which motion picture won the Acadamy Award last year?." In some areas of the country there are state almanacs published which boys and girls can also peruse.

The pupils themselves may write questions whose answers are found in such references as an atlas ("Which states border Texas?"); a gazetteer ("Where is the Isle of Man?"); the *Fourth Book of Junior Authors and Illustrators* ("As an adolescent, which musical instrument did Myra Cohn Livingston play professionally?"); *Who's Who in America* ("From which service academy did former President Jimmy Carter graduate?"); or a handbook like Bartlett's *Familiar Quotations* ("Who said, 'The only thing we have to fear is fear itself'?").

The ability to use atlases, gazetteers, and other general reference works is a vital library media center skill for pupils in the middle and upper grades. (Photo courtesy of National Education Association Publishing, Joe Di Dio.)

The boys and girls can produce a chart or table comparing various atlasses or statistical reference books available in the library. They can define specialized words pertaining to gazetteers. They may even find it interesting to examine some dictionary indexes such as the *Illustrations Index,* and the *Index to Children's Poetry,* each of which is a separate volume. The class may also enjoy locating in an atlas the places which are mentioned on the front page of the daily newspaper.

Incidentally, for the sake of those teacher-specialists who fear that many of the children in the middle- and upper-elementary grades have not developed sufficient reading skills to be effective users of such tools as *Current Biography, Contemporary Authors,* the *Negro Almanac,* the *Guinness Book of World Records,* or the *Atlas of American History,* it must be mentioned that the introduction of these tools shold best be left to the discretion of the media specialist or teacher-specialist. Some classes can work successfully with these resources and should be properly encouraged to do so. In other classes the introduction of these materials must be postponed until junior high school.

Eighth Skill: Organized Printed Information and Compiling Bibliographies

As soon as children are mature enough to come to the library media center for reference work, they can begin to acquire the ability to select, organize, interpret, and evaluate information from printed material through skimming, note taking and outlining. Although any number of teaching strategies might be used to develop such research study skills, there is one four-stage scheme which appears to be particularly promising.[11] The first stage introduces the skill, clarifying its use or purpose; this could be accomplished through an expository, inquiry, or problem-solving approach. Second stage offers focused practice in a controlled situation demanding a particular skill with short drill exercises sometimes included at this level. The third stage reinforces or reteaches the first lesson on a specific skill. The final stage of independent application involves assignments requiring the use of the newly learned skill in a content area such as social studies.

Skimming occurs when pupils read at about twice their normal rate, selectively eliminating nearly one-half of the material because they are in a hurry and therefore willing to accept lowered comprehension. They may read only the topic sentence and then let their eyes drift down through the paragraph, picking up a date or a name. Their intention is to get the main thought from each paragraph, with a few specific facts. Drills useful for teaching skimming involve asking a group of pupils (all of whom are reading the same book) to see who will be the first to find a particular fact buried in a given chapter, or who will be the first to locate a subject-matter area in the index, and then report on which pages it can be found in the text. Similar activities can be done with dictionaries, encyclopedias, or even telephone books. Skimming is a useful skill that can be consciously developed, although children should not consider it a substitute for other kinds of reading or for study activities.

Since there are procedures and information which elementary pupils are expected to write down for future reference, the technique of *note taking* is a critical one. Its significance as a basis for an outline, for a valuable record, or for critical evaluation of an oral or written presentation must be explained to the class. Then the children can be helped to develop some group standards for note taking, including the following:

1. Read or listen first before writing down the information in your own words.
2. Write down only the important facts, rechecking for accuracy whenever possible.
3. Use underlining to indicate emphatic ideas.
4. Never record every word, except for laws, rules, and quotations.

In early grades, note taking is generally a group subject culminating in an experience chart. In the middle and upper grades, however, children can be encouraged to keep individual notes (sometimes written on file cards) during a field trip or as they listen to a resource speaker, watch a film, or help prepare a committee report. Older boys and girls should also understand how to use other media for note taking in the modern school, such as transferring pictures, graphs, or diagrams to transparencies for sharing with the class.

Organizing factual material that has been collected and assimilated demands *outlining* ability. While the purpose of an outline is the more significant point for pupils to learn, some attention should also be paid to promoting an understanding of the structure of an outline. Such a form generally reflects a hierarchy of ideas or a sequence of events much like the following example:

I. A main topic demands a roman numeral.

   A. A subtopic requires indentation and a capital letter.
      1. A detail needs indentation and an arabic numeral.
         a. A subdetail must have indentation and a lowercase letter.
      2. Another detail on the same subtopic needs an arabic numeral too.
   B. Another subtopic requires a capital letter too.

II. Another main topic demands another roman numeral.

   A. Subtopic
      1. Detail
         a. Subdetail
      2. Detail
      3. Detail

   B. Subtopic
      1. Detail

   C. Subtopic
      1. Detail
      2. Detail

To help beginners learn outlining, the teacher-specialist may read aloud several, short, selected paragraphs from different volumes, asking the pupils promptly after each reading to state the main topic in as few words as possible. The teacher may also deliver a well-organized but informal talk on a popular theme and then outline its major topics, using the board or overhead projector. Sometimes a common experience such as a walking trip or a carefully chosen movie may introduce the class to an outline form. Once an outline has been completed, however, the boys and girls should be reminded that it may serve as the basis for either a written or an oral report.

During their experiences with beginning research children gain a knowledge of the compilation and use of a bibliography. To help the pupils acquire this skill some schools present each sixth grader with a dittoed sheet containing bibliographical forms for books, encyclopedias, and magazines. Then different parts of each form are posted on a cloth board or magnetic chalk board, and the class compares the forms to see the differences in arrangement. In other schools each intermediate pupil brings to class either one book that contains a bibliography or one list of five different books that pertain to a single hobby or sport. The class may also choose to keep a random record of all books and periodicals consulted during the preparation of a report for social studies before deciding to arrange the entries in alphabetical order for the bibliography.

Since inquiry and independent study are both such critical areas in education today, the school library media center's resources and the teacher-specialist's program of teaching research and study skills are basic components of all levels of elementary curricula.

Ninth Skill: Using and Evaluating Nonbook Media

Learning how to view and how to listen, and developing the art of perception that evaluation and appreciation of the nonbook media demand, represent two abilities that students must acquire in much the same way that they master the word recognition skills and developmental aspects of reading. Such instruction includes guidance in aiding children to turn naturally to media other than print as forms of communication. It also involves teaching them to realize when nonbook media complement printed materials and when they have no relevance to the task at hand.

While instruction in using many of these resources is being handled on an individualized basis, in one or more classroom lessons the teacher-specialist can demonstrate how to find and read quickly the table of contents (of a magazine) or the index (of a newspaper) and how to evaluate readily the pictures, physical format, and contents of the magazine or paper. The teacher may discuss the kinds of readers to whom the magazine or newspaper would appeal and the types of services that it can render for those readers. The children can bring to class a copy of one of the local papers and summarize at least three of its front-page stories into one statement each. They can examine some of the more popular juvenile magazines as well as some general adult magazines that have been recommended as interesting and informative for pupils in the intermediate grades.

Advanced students may be introduced to the *Reader's Guide to Periodical Literature,* in which over 180 periodicals are indexed by author and subject. Once the pupils have noted the list of periodicals included and the abbreviations used for each, they should be encouraged to consult the *Readers' Guide* routinely before completing assigned reports.

The teacher-specialist should also acquaint children with vertical-file materials. These are miscellaneous items which are not individually catalogued because of poor physical durability, varied sizes, and short subject treatment. Examples include pamphlets, leaflets, clippings, and unmounted pictures printed on lightweight paper. Such materials often brighten displays in the classroom and hall, and meet the informational needs of both beginning and older readers.

Incidentally, the base collection of nonbook media for a school with 500 or fewer users (according to standards established by the AASL and the AECT) includes 50 to 175 titles of *periodicals and newspapers;* 1,500 to 2,000 *audio recordings* (tapes, cassettes, discs, and audio cards); 500 to 2,000 *filmstrips* (sound and silent); 2,000 to 6,000 *slides and transparencies;* 200 to 500 *models and sculpture reproductions;* 800 to 1,200 *graphics* (posters, art and study prints, maps and globes); 200 to 400 *specimens;* 500 to 1,000 *Super 8-mm films* (silent); and access to 3,000 titles of 16-mm and Super 8-mm *sound films, videotapes and television reception.*

Tenth Skill: Operating the Audiovisual Equipment

In many school library media centers primary and intermediate pupils alike are being permitted to check out the audiovisual equipment just as they do books. Anyone can learn to operate the basic equipment and children do so more rapidly than adults. Primary boys and girls in Montgomery County, Maryland, for example, learn to operate a record player, a cassette-tape recorder, a listening station, a filmstrip viewer (or previewer), an 8-mm filmloop projector, an opaque projector, a slide viewer (or previewer), an overhead projector, a filmstrip projector, and a microprojector.[12] Intermediate children in the same county become familiar with the operation of a reel-to-reel tape recorder, a slide projector, an 8-mm or 16-mm film projector, and a videotape recorder.

Step-by-step instructions for operating typical equipment found in media centers can be located in most standard audiovisual instruction texts. The teacher or media specialist can demonstrate the proper procedures on an individualized or small-group basis.

The base collection of equipment for a school with 500 or fewer users, according to standards established by the AASL and the AECT, should include:

Filmstrip equipment: ten projectors and thirty viewers
Slide and transparency equipment: six slide projectors, ten slide viewers, ten overhead projectors
16-mm and Super 8-mm sound projection and video playback and reception equipment: six units (with two assigned to the media center) plus one more unit per 100 users
Super 8-mm equipment: twenty cartridge-loaded projectors, enough open-reel projectors to accommodate available films plus one more projector per 75 users
Audio equipment: thirty tape recorders and record players, one set of earphones for each audio reproduction unit plus one portable listening unit per 25 users
Opaque projectors: one per media center and one per 500 users (or one per floor in multistory building)
Microform equipment: two readers plus one reader-printer
Microprojectors: one per media center and one or more per school

With the widespread advent of computer-assisted instruction, school media centers should also include one or more microcomputers. Even preschool children at ages three or four (at Stanford University's Bing Nursery School and at North Texas State University Nursery School, for example) can and do use microcomputers just as eagerly and profitably as do kindergarten, primary, and intermediate children in many public and private school systems.[13]

Learning Experiences through the Grades

The sequence of learning should be developed from kindergarten through the sixth grade, and library media center skills that have been introduced in any one grade must be reviewed and practiced in succeeding grades.

In order that each pupil may be at ease in the school library media center an orientation session should be held for every class at the beginning of the school year before any personal borrowing is done. At this time there are two main concepts which can be brought out in discussion or summarized on the chalkboard:

- *Everyone reads and uses public libraries or school media centers to some extent* because people read for fun, for information they need for school or work, and for information on hobbies or other subjects in which they are especially interested.

- *Everyone wants to know how to get along well in a public library or school media center* so that many people can all use the facility at once, and take out the special materials that each desires.

The principal objectives of the orientation session are: (1) to present the broad range of appealing and attractive books and audiovisual materials available for curricular and personal needs; (2) to facilitate finding these materials by demonstrating their location; and (3) to provide the pupils with an opportunity to browse, examine, and try out these materials before borrowing them for classroom or home use. The atmosphere during orientation is the same as that which prevails throughout all media center activities—informal, relaxed, and warm.

Beginning Grades

The *kindergarten* class should come to the library media center at least once a month. The children can be introduced to the world of books through storytelling, through attractive displays, and through many opportunities to browse. During these visits children learn how to carry a book, how to turn its pages properly, how to replace a book on the shelf, how to place books on a book cart, and how to use book markers. They also begin to develop the habit of relying on the library as a source of information. Its facilities are truly an extension of their classroom.

After listening to stories, the five-year-olds should have time to select books from the regular shelves or to sit at tables where the teacher-specialist has placed some new picture books. They can listen to story records, look at filmstrips, or handle flat pictures, models and specimens. Although the children do not check out either book or nonbook materials, they are able to observe the media aides and technicians and thus become acquainted with some of the functions of the center. It is important that kindergarteners enjoy their visits to the library media center and learn to become good library citizens. Whatever activity is presented in the center's instructional program for five-year-olds, its prevailing objective is to present an environment which will instill in the children a love of good reading materials and the recognition of the library media center as a friendly, helpful place to browse and to work.

Following an initial briefing in the classroom, the *first-grade* children should have a weekly opportunity to go to the center for at least 30 minutes and to check out one book at a time. The teacher-specialist will wish to informally stress the concept of library responsibility and to enumerate the qualifications for personal borrowing.

As six-year-olds listen to the teacher read or recite rhythmic prose and poetry, they continue to gain literary appreciation. As they examine more picture books, they may slowly begin to sense the relationship between illustrations and plot. They can be shown the gross differences between an encyclopedia and a dictionary, and they will begin to realize the importance of alphabetizing as they are introduced to the easy picture dictionaries. To acquaint them with simple informational books, the teacher-specialist can—

1. tell the children that both books and people have names, show them books with titles that are names of people, and conclude by displaying books with other kinds of titles;
2. develop the concept that some books tell stories and some books give information;
3. show the children several books that have titles which indicate their contents; and
4. introduce and guide pupils on a restricted basis in the individual use of suitable audiovisual resources according to their ability to handle such media.

As first graders continue to use the school library media center for simple research and to develop independence in the selection of resources, they are also learning to improve their library manners and to practice proper handling of materials. Hopefully they are also discovering public library facilities and beginning to think of books in terms of possible ownership.

The *second grade* should maintain its weekly half-hour visits to the center, listening to stories and sharing reading experiences. The children can refine alphabetizing skills and enjoy simple "location" games in the library media center. They can learn the purpose of the book card and date-due slip, and recall how to sign out and return books independently. They can locate title pages, use tables of contents, read chapter titles, and find page numbers of books. The pupils will also enjoy browsing in beginning dictionaries, and can learn to locate and use more nonbook materials such as primary globes.

The simple research work done in the kindergarten and first grade is maintained in the second grade with little change. Each teacher continues to help young children recognize the center as a source of information and an aid to their classroom and personal work. When second graders have completed their research, they may be asked to present their findings to their peers, thereby involving the use of multimedia resources with which they have become familiar.

Seven-year-olds can be encouraged to confer with their teacher regarding the books they are reading. They should be allowed to check out two books each week, one to read themselves and one to share with their parent(s) in order to further home-school ties and broaden the pleasure of reading. They may also be permitted to check out one audiovisual resource if the school media collection is sufficiently large to allow second graders the privilege of borrowing cassette tapes, story records, or other nonbook items.

In the *third grade* the weekly story period may be continued (if scheduling arrangements can accommodate these more knowledgeable media center visitors), for creative expression is stimulated with such reading-listening experiences. The children should be taught the difference between fiction and nonfiction, and where books in each of these broad classifications are found in the center. Their information-finding skills will grow as the teacher-specialist points out the table of contents in each book examined and encourages the pupils to identify the names of the title and author on both the cover and title page of every new book they read or share. Their maturing alphabetizing skills, which may even lead to the introduction of a simple card catalog, will involve alphabetizing by first, second, and third letters, and relate to shelving of fiction books. Their reporting skills and their use of the library as a research resource will continue to develop, even among boys and girls reading below grade level.

The children complete the transition from the picture dictionary to the standard beginning dictionary and start to read primary magazines. The teacher-specialist will also find them capable of grouping the books in the classroom by broad subject areas (such as sports, science, and animal stories). They are also capable of taking care of the shelves and tables in the school library media center and in the class library corner.

Each member of the class should be allowed to check out three books at once from any part of the library media center, and one nonbook reference because the most important aim of third-grade library media center instruction is to encourage independent selection of materials. Their use of public library facilities should be extended, and their observation of library rules reinforced.

By the end of the third grade pupils have learned to:

Locate all kinds of books which interest them.
Use various parts of books for desired information.
Consult picture and beginning dictionaries.
Use simple audiovisual materials and equipment for enjoyment and information.
Recognize the school media center and the public library as distinct and pleasant places as well as sources of information.

Intermediate Grades

Instruction in the care of print and nonprint materials is reviewed briefly with the older boys and girls. It receives special emphasis only in those classes that have enrolled many transfer students. Basic research techniques are frequently mentioned.

By the time the children have reached the *fourth grade* they are ready to concentrate on technical skills. They can begin work with the card catalog and learn how the call numbers on the catalog cards enables readers, viewers, and listeners to find the resources on the shelves. They can analyze their textbooks as they become familiar with additional parts of a book and the purpose that each serves.

Nine-year-olds recognize the need for orderly arrangement of materials on the shelves and can locate main library media center resources for guests. They show their awareness of the varied kinds of materials available in both school and public libraries by embarking on year-round use of such facilities.

At the beginning of the *fifth grade* a comparison of different standard encyclopedia sets will enable the pupils to realize how each set differs as to the number of volumes, method of indexing, location of maps, and signed articles. In this way they may learn to evaluate the various sets in such areas as arrangement, authority, recency of publication, and accuracy of illustrations.

They learn to understand the purpose of the Dewey Decimal System and memorize the 10 major divisions with key numbers. They make independent use of the card catalog to locate both book and nonbook materials needed for assignments, and enjoy filing catalog cards in classroom relay activities. They use the dictionary to find new and additional information about their spelling words or reading vocabulary.

Ten-year-olds can become familiar with award-winning books, particularly the Newbery Medal books, and may be persuaded to share some of these through oral book reports. They consult book lists and learn to distinguish among biographical fiction, authentic biography, and fictionalized biography. They should have access to many materials dealing with the American heritage to amplify the theme of their social studies units.

In the *sixth grade* children are becoming more efficient in note taking, outlining, and making short bibliographies. They can therefore be introduced to more advanced research tools such as the yearbook, the atlas and gazetteer, and the unabridged dictionary. Boys and girls are capable of using several reference sources independently, including nonbook materials. They can demonstrate their research findings during debates and while preparing committee reports.

The pupils begin to understand the provisions for cross-references made in different encyclopedia sets. They use the dictionary in order to trace the etymology of words and complete crossword puzzles. They are able to interpret the information contained on catalog cards for both book and nonbook materials, becoming acquainted with cross-reference cards which help them locate additional kinds of data. Finally, in their work with the Dewey Decimal System, the children begin to understand the breakdown of the 10 major classifications into subclasses, and they are able to locate subheadings on the shelves, as identified by guide tabs. Pupils also learn how individual biography is shelved.

The sixth graders in one Washington school keep individual reading records as an incentive to discover different types of books in the library media center. Upon completing a book, they list on a sheet of paper the title, the author's name, the publisher's name, the copyright date, the type of book it was, and the month that it was read; and then assign a number to the title. The number is then placed in one of two circles posted on the reading record: the first has divisions for various kinds of fiction (sports, folk and fairy tales, home and family, etc.) and the second has divisions for the major areas of nonfiction according to the Dewey System. In this way, the children can determine promptly which groups of books they have not yet explored and may, eventually, remedy the imbalance.

By the end of the sixth grade pupils have learned to:

Consult encyclopedias, atlases, gazetteers, and dictionaries.

Update informatoin on a topic by reading periodicals, pamphlets, and newspapers.

Select and use audiovisual materials with discrimination and independence.

Obtain inspiration and stimulation from fiction, poetry, and biography.

Integrate information taken from various media and from different information sources and organize it into a sequential entity.

Explore new fields of interest through print and nonprint materials.

Work independently in the library media center due to an understanding of the classification of resources provided by the Dewey Decimal System.

The Exceptional Child and the Library Media Center

The concept of the school library media center as the chief source of insructional materials should be extended to the service of the exceptional child.[14] Whether that pupil comes to the center alone or with regular classes, the experiences through which the media specialist guides him or her are similar to those offered to other children.

To compensate for the reading deficiencies of *the hearing impaired* the specialist chooses simple materials on a high interest level commensurate with the maturity development of the pupil. The visual is emphasized in an effort to provide experiences that cannot be obtained through audition—films, filmstrips with printed copies of the narrative, film loops, art and study prints, maps and globes, models and specimens. From the United States Office of Education have come captioned classroom films for the hard-of-hearing.

Since much of the school program is geared toward learning through vision, *the visually impaired* must be encouraged by the media specialist to utilize all their capabilities. The specialist must provide tapes and records of stories suitable for the interests and maturity of the visually limited children (including some stories of the achievements of persons with visual handicaps), records and cassettes of music of all kinds, and aids to the reading/sharing of experiences (including magnifying glasses, blank tapes and primary typewriters). Books that the media specialist purchases for the visually limited should be printed in large, clear type (preferably 24 point) on white paper so that print and pictures stand out distinctly; they should have lines that are widely spaced with ample margins. The specialist may receive sources of materials for visually handicapped pupils from the National Library Service for the Blind and Physically Handicapped, Washington, D.C. 20542; and from the American Foundation for the Blind, Inc. (Publications Division), New York 10011.

In providing for *the intellectually impaired* the media specialist recognizes that few retarded pupils have a reading ability above the fourth-grade level and that all have difficulty with abstract ideas. The specialist therefore selects magazines on arts/crafts/hobbies, simple fiction and well-illustrated information books, picture and "easy" books, combination kits of picture books/filmstrips/cassettes, collections of models and prints associated with science and social studies, and games and toys. The specialist may also prepare tapes of literature which the children would enjoy but cannot read.

To meet the interests and needs of *the emotionally handicapped* the teacher or media specialist chooses print and non-print materials which are stimulating (but relatively easy) and which may be used individually to provide a necessary break from group activities. Wide use of bibliotherapy whereby such pupils can identify with book characters is also recommended.

Due to the difficulty which *the orthopedically impaired* have in getting to the public library and to other resource places, they must often depend solely upon the school libarary media center. The materials collection for these children must be extensive and include many paperbacks (due to light weight), audiovisual resources (which can be easily handled), periodicals, high-interest/low-vocabulary books, materials about particular disabilities, and reference collections. To provide vicarious excitement there should be a larger number of books in the fiction category than in the nonfiction. And all materials should be accessibly located so that they can be readily removed from and returned to the shelves by the children without assistance.

To satisfy the wide range of interests of *the gifted* the media specialist must provide an expanded collection of reference sources, absorbing stories with contemporary themes, a rich selection of folklore/legend/poetry, all kinds of audiovisual materials, books on arts and hobbies, and advanced print and nonprint information sources. All of these resources, including the availability of numerous microcomputers with accompanying programs, are needed to challenge the potential of gifted children and to develop their powers of critical thinking.

Worksheets and Learning Games Involving Library Media Center Skills

Worksheets on library media center skills have been designed by some school districts for both the primary and intermediate grades. Teachers may use them for either enrichment, follow-up, or diagnostic experiences. A sample worksheet for upper primary children runs as follows:

Library Terms: author, title, title page, table of contents, illustrator, illustration

Directions: Read the sentences below and fill in the blank spaces with the correct library term.

Sentences:

1. We call the person who draws pictures for a book the ___________ .
2. The name of a book is called the ___________ .
3. The ___________ is a picture found in a book.
4. The ___________ is a person who writes a book.
5. We look in the ___________ if we want to find the chapters in a book in page number order.
6. The author's name is found on the ___________ .

Misspell (for either the classroom or the library media center)

1. The class or group is evenly divided into teams whose members are seated in rows.
2. On the first desk (or table) in each row are placed a copy of the class dictionary, a pencil, an empty red box, and a blue box filled with slips. Each slip contains three spellings of a single word, of which only one is correct and appears in the class dictionary.
3. At a signal from the teacher-specialist, the first player on each team draws one slip from the blue box, checks the spellings in the dictionary, circles the correct spelling, and drops the slip in the red box. The first player then moves to the end of the row, all the other team members move up one desk, and the game continues.
4. The winning team has proved that it cannot "misspell" when it has been able to empty its blue box of slips first, and when its red-box entries have been approved by a class committee or the teacher-specialist.

Order Please (for the classroom only)

1. The class is evenly divided into teams.
2. On the chalkboard in front of each team is written or placed a list of authors' names which are not in alphabetical order. Each team receives a different list, and that list always contains one more name than there are players on that team.
3. At a signal from the teacher-specialist, the first player on each team walks to the board and marks with the numeral 1 the author's name which should appear in the initial position on that list. The first player then returns to his or her seat and the second player goes to the board to indicate the second name in alphabetical order with the numeral 2.
4. The first team to mark all of its authors' names properly wins the Order Please game.

Shelf Fever (for the library media center only)

1. The class or group is divided into two teams.
2. The first player on each team chooses one card from a large box of cards with book titles on them. The player then uses the card catalog to find the call number of the title on the card. Last, he or she removes the book from the shelf and hands it to the second player on the team.
3. The second player promptly returns the book to the shelf. Then he or she touches the shoulder of the third player, who chooses a card and follows the actions of the first player.
4. The game continues until every odd-numbered player has removed his or her chosen book and every even-numbered player has reshelved a book.
5. The team which performs best within a designated period of time is the winner of Shelf Fever.

Evaluation of Pupils' Progress

There are both formal standardized and informal teacher-made written tests for evaluating library media center skills among elementary school children.

Sample items (with correct answers circled) from an achievement test on library media skills which the teacher-specialist could devise and administer to intermediate grade children are as follows:

1. There are three main types of catalog cards. Two of them are known as the author and subject cards, and the third is:
   a. the book card
   (b.) the title card
   c. the date-due card
   d. the circulation card
2. A list of subjects arranged in alphabetical order at the back of the book is called:
   a. a table of contents
   b. a title page
   c. a glossary
   (d.) an index
3. To find out how many informational resources your school library media center has about Texas, you would use:
   a. a magazine about new books
   b. the Dewey Decimal System of Classification
   (c.) the card catalog
   d. the encyclopedia
4. When you are looking for books on the shelves, the call number is found:
   (a.) on the spine of the book
   b. on the pocket
   c. on the title page
   d. on the table of contents
5. In looking up information about a person in the card catalog or encyclopedia, you would look up the person alphabetically by his or her:
   a. first name
   (b.) last name
   c. middle name
   d. initials
6. Cards in the card catalog which have "see" and "see also" on them are called:
   a. author cards
   b. guide cards
   (c.) cross-reference cards
   d. subject cards

There are also standardized study-skills tests designed to measure the ability of elementary pupils to use library catalog cards, atlases, almanacs, indexes, books, encyclopedias, maps, and graphs. Specimen sets of three well-reviewed tests may be purchased from—

1. Science Research Associates of Chicago, which publishes the *SRA Achievement Series: Work-Study Skills* (Blue Level for grades 4.5 to 6.5 and Green Level for grades 6.5 to 8.5), available in two forms for each level. Administration times run from 70 to 80 minutes.
2. CTV/McGraw-Hill of Monterey, CA, which publishes the *Comprehensive Tests of Basic Skills: Study Skills* (Level 1, grades 2.5 to 4.0; Level 2, grades 4.0 to 6.0, and Level 3, grades 6.0 to 8.0), available in two forms for each level. Administration times run from 21 to 50 minutes depending upon the form and level.
3. N.C.S. Interpretive Scoring Systems of Minneapolis, which publishes the *Wisconsin Tests of Reading Skills Development: Study Skills* (Level A, grades K–1; Level B, grades 1–2; Level C, grades 2–3; Level D, grades 3–4; Level E, grades 4–5; Level F, grades 5–6; and Level G, grades 6–7). Criterion-referenced tests with heavy emphasis on skills, their administration times run from 25 minutes (in one session) in Level A to 180 minutes (in four sessions) in Level G.

Discussion Questions

1. How can the school media center help remedial readers?
2. Is it as important to have a well-staffed library media center in each elementary school as it is to have one in every secondary school? How can teachers persuade taxpayers to fund more such centers for young children?
3. Should an elementary school media center be open during the summer months? Should it be open on Saturdays during the regular school year?
4. How can parents assist in the media center?

Suggested Projects

1. Plan a library corner for a third-grade classroom.
2. Make a card catalog, using discarded shoe boxes for file drawers. Be sure to label each "drawer" carefully.
3. Inquire of several elementary school media specialists which teaching strategies and materials each has found to be especially useful in presenting library media skills to boys and girls.
4. Prepare a bulletin board on the Dewey Decimal System which might be used in the fifth grade.
5. Visit the children's room of the main public library in your community and determine how you as a classroom teacher could best utilize its resources.
6. Set up the learning center on library media center skills shown in Figure 12.12.

Figure 12.12. Language Arts Learning Center: Library Media Skills.

TYPE OF CENTER:	**Library Skills—Biography**	TIME: Varies
GRADE LEVEL:	5-6	NUMBER OF STUDENTS: 3 or 4

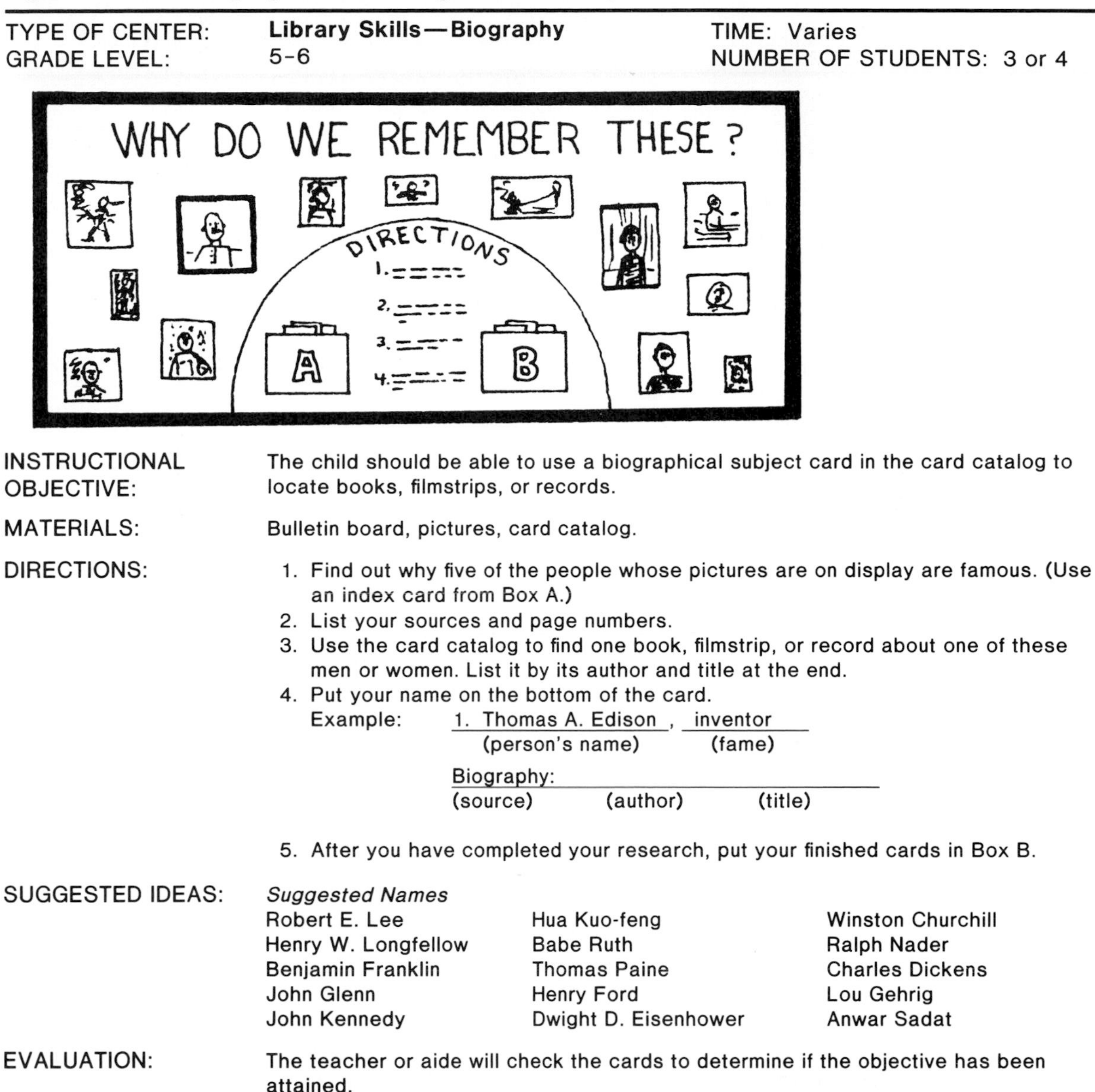

INSTRUCTIONAL OBJECTIVE: The child should be able to use a biographical subject card in the card catalog to locate books, filmstrips, or records.

MATERIALS: Bulletin board, pictures, card catalog.

DIRECTIONS:

1. Find out why five of the people whose pictures are on display are famous. (Use an index card from Box A.)
2. List your sources and page numbers.
3. Use the card catalog to find one book, filmstrip, or record about one of these men or women. List it by its author and title at the end.
4. Put your name on the bottom of the card.

   Example: 1. Thomas A. Edison , inventor
   (person's name) (fame)

   Biography: ______________________
   (source) (author) (title)

5. After you have completed your research, put your finished cards in Box B.

SUGGESTED IDEAS: *Suggested Names*

Robert E. Lee	Hua Kuo-feng	Winston Churchill
Henry W. Longfellow	Babe Ruth	Ralph Nader
Benjamin Franklin	Thomas Paine	Charles Dickens
John Glenn	Henry Ford	Lou Gehrig
John Kennedy	Dwight D. Eisenhower	Anwar Sadat

EVALUATION: The teacher or aide will check the cards to determine if the objective has been attained.

Source: From PATHWAYS TO IMAGINATION by Angela S. Reeke and James L. Laffey, © 1979 by Scott, Foresman and Company. Reprinted by permission.

Related Readings

Baker, D., 1984. *The Library Media Program and the Schools.* Littleton, CO: Libraries Unlimited, Inc.

Jalbrant, F., and Malley, I. 1984. *User Education in Libraries.* Second edition. Hamden, CT: Shoe String Press.

Karpisek, M. E. 1983. *Making Self-Teaching Kits for Library Skills.* Chicago: American Library Association.

Marshall, K. 1983. *Back to Books: 200 Library Activities to Encourage Reading.* Jefferson, NC: McFarland & Company.

Nickel, M. 1984. *Steps to Service: A Handbook of Procedures for the School Library Media Center.* Revised edition. Chicago: American Library Association.

Prostano, E. T., and Prostano, J. S. 1982. *The School Library Media Center.* Third edition. Littleton, CO: Libraries Unlimited, Inc.

Salinger, T. 1983. "Study Skills: A 'Basic' in Elementary Reading Instruction," *Reading Improvement, 20,* pp. 333–337.

Smallwood, C. 1984. *Exceptional Free Library Resource Materials.* Littleton, CO: Libraries Unlimited, Inc.

Tamor, L., and Walmsley, S. 1983. "Using a Thesaurus in the Elementary School," *Language Arts, 60,* pp. 554–557, 660.

Wilkins, L. 1984. *Supporting K–5 Reading Instruction in the School Library Media Center.* Chicago: American Library Association.

Chapter Notes

1. R. A. Davies, *The School Library Media Program,* 3rd ed. (New York: R. R. Bowker, 1979), p. 13.
2. American Association of School Librarians, American Library Association, and Association for Educational Communications and Technology, *Media Programs: District and School* (Chicago: ALA; and Washington, D.C.: AECT, 1975), p. 4.
3. E. Askov, K. Kamm, and R. Klumb, "Study Skill Mastery among Elementary School Teachers," *Reading Teacher,* 1977, *30,* pp. 485–488.
4. Board of Education of the City of New York, *The School Library Media Center: A Force for Learning* (New York: The Board, 1975), p. 101.
5. E. Silverman, *101 Media Center Ideas* (Metuchen, New Jersey: Scarecrow Press, 1980), pp. 1, 41.
6. K. Kister, *Encyclopedia Buying Guide,* 3rd ed. (New York: R. R. Bowker Co., 1981), pp. 339, 353–54, 398.
7. *Ibid.,* p. 501.
8. K. Kister, "U.S. Public Librarians Rate the Encyclopedias: A Survey," *Library Journal,* 1979, *104,* pp. 890–893.
9. M. L. Mower and L. Barney, "Which Are the Most Important Dictionary Skills?" *Elementary English,* 1968, *45,* pp. 468–471.
10. K. Kister, *Dictionary Buying Guide* (New York: R. R. Bowker, 1977), pp. 19–24.
11. J. H. Shores and J. F. Snoddy, "Organizing and Teaching the Research Study Skills in the Elementary School," *Elementary English,* 1971, *48,* pp. 648–651.
12. H. T. Walker and P. K. Montgomery, *Teaching Media Skills* (Littleton, Colorado: Libraries Unlimited, 1977), pp. 34–36.
13. G. E. Mason, J. S. Blanchard and D. B. Daniel, *Computer Applications in Reading,* 2nd ed. (Newark, Delaware: International Reading Association, 1983), pp. 58–75.
14. In this section the author has drawn upon: Board of Education of the City of New York, *The School Library Media Center,* pp. 145–148.

Children's Drama 13

Objectives

Distinctions between children's theatre and creative drama

The major groups of activities in creative drama

How sociodrama differs from dramatic play

Why children should first dramatically interpret some stories before attempting improvisation

Discover As You Read This Chapter If*

1. Children's theatre is concerned chiefly with the audience.
2. Creative drama is product-oriented.
3. Emotionally disturbed children should not participate in creative drama.
4. Most classroom teachers do not really favor creative drama, but they do teach it.
5. Dramatic play is an insignificant area of the preschool/kindergarten curriculum.
6. Pantomime is not portrayal-centered.
7. Role-playing always concerns a group situation.
8. Sociodrama increases skill in communication.
9. Interpretation involves going beyond a basic story in order to expand upon its theme.
10. The discussion and resolution of inferential questions about a particular story must precede any improvisation of that story.

*Answers to these true-or-false statements may be found in Appendix 6.

Children's drama in the United States is a twentieth-century educational endeavor. It encompasses two aspects: children's theatre and creative drama. Children's theatre is formal, product-oriented, and concerned primarily with the audience, while creative drama is informal, process-oriented, and concerned chiefly with the players. Although its performances are occasionally staged in a school auditorium, children's theatre is neither the curriculum responsibility nor the language art that creative drama is.

No conflict prevails between the two areas of children's drama, for both exist as an art form when given the proper guidance (creative drama) or direction (children's theatre). Experiences in creative drama build appreciation for formal plays because the pupils learn about play construction as they work out their own plays with the assistance of an adult familiar with formal drama. On the other hand, children's theatre provides standards for pupils' work in creative drama by helping the children to visualize and to be objective.

Ordinarily the two areas are distinct and separate. At least one attempt has been made recently, however, to combine children's theatre with creative drama. Financed by a grant from the Bronx Council on the Arts, the Theatre of Creative Involvement in New York was able to offer a short children's theatre production and then have the adult actors serve as leaders while the children created their own plays. A total of three creative encounters was involved in each session with the inner-city boys and girls. During the first, the actors presented a professional dramatization of a story or poem such as "Little Miss Muffet," "Little Red Riding Hood," or "The Gingerbread Man." In the second, each actor or pair of actors became leaders of a small group of the spectators and assisted them in the creation of an original play. The third encounter found each group of children presenting its own play to other young spectators/participants and to the adult actors.

Statement of Purposes

The objectives of drama/theatre for students are sevenfold, according to the California State Board of Education:

1. The students will develop the "self," learning to discover themselves, express themselves, and accept themselves. They will become increasingly aware of and learn to trust their sensations, feelings, fantasies, memories, attitudes, thoughts, and values as they seek to give these entities coherent expression in theatrical form.
2. The students will communicate effectively in seeking to express something which has value and meaning to others. Because theatre is a cooperative act in every phase, they will learn how to articulate their intentions with increasing clarity in many verbal and nonverbal ways and to receive with sensitivity what others have to express.
3. The students will solve problems inventively in both real and imagined situations, discovering or creating patterns of relationships among people and ideas in fantasy and fact. Whether they deal with imaginary people or real people, they will learn how to play many roles, to try on or simulate a broad range of life experiences, and to evaluate the results.

4. The students will learn from society, past and present, including the rich contributions of the multiethnic and multicultural groups which make up the American heritage.
5. The students will use critical and creative skills. The rigors of the discipline will help them to develop skills which they can apply to any area of chosen study.
6. The students will be awakened to theatre as an art form. They will become more discerning, perceptive, and responsive theatregoers and viewers of other theatrical media (film and television).
7. The students will approach other art forms with insight. Theatre has processes and concepts necessarily related to those of the other arts, and incorporates aspects of all of them.[1]

Children's Theatre

Children's theatre is the drama *for* children where the audience is the first consideration. Regardless of whether the play is being acted by adolescents or adults (or both), or whether the players are amateurs or professionals, the value of the experience to the actors must be secondary to what the experience means to the boys and girls who see the play, for the success of the project is judged by the cultural value and enjoyment that it gives to the child audience.

Children's theatre is based on the traditional theatre concept. Concerned with a polished production involving a stage, it does not in this respect differ from theatre for adults. Lines written by professional playwrights are memorized, action is directed, and scenery and costumes are used. The director attempts to offer a finished product for public entertainment and engages the best actors available, for the goal in this area of children's drama is perfection.

Beginning with the establishment of the first significant children's theatre in the United States, which was founded in a New York settlement house in 1903, the children's theatre movement has always been guided by worthy objectives. During the movement's first decades of existence the theatre projects, as conceived and administered primarily by social workers, boosted social welfare purposes like cultural integration and the teaching of English as a second language. Then, as the movement spread under the auspices of community-oriented organizations, universities, and professional companies, its direction changed to an emphasis on theatre as an aesthetic device. Currently, therefore, the American children's theatre promotes the development in boys and girls of a high standard of taste, provides them with the joy of seeing good stories come alive upon a stage, and helps them grow in the understanding and appreciation of life values from the human experiences seen on the stage.

The more than five million children who annually see the productions receive other benefits as well. Pedagogically, the theatre can capitalize on each pupil's heightened motivation to indirectly inculcate ideas and facts regarding cultural patterns of thought, theatrical conventions, and the Judeo-Christian ethical code that is at the base of most Western drama. Psychologically, the theatre teaches the child, through role awareness and character identification, socialization skills and personal maturation. Aesthetically, the theatre is the only art form that deals with human behavior in a totally recognizable way.[2]

The national organization for the children's theatre movement is presently the Children's Theatre Association of America (CTAA), formed in 1944 as a division of the American Educational Theatre Association in order to encourage experience in live theatre for all children everywhere, to promote in all communities children's theatre activities conducted by educational, community, and private groups, and to encourage high standards in all types of children's theatre activity throughout America.[3] Its current membership of some two thousand adults is drawn from all kinds of professional and amateur groups, since agencies producing theatricals for children may be either community, educational, or professional organizations.

Community groups, which often present their plays in municipal auditoriums, have such varied sponsors as city recreation departments, the Junior League, and civic theatres in cities like Seattle, Nashville, Palo Alto, and Midland, Texas. *Educational institutions* (public and private) include universities, colleges, and high schools that offer plays in their own auditoriums and theatres. University activity today is centered at Northwestern, Minnesota, Kansas, UCLA, Florida State, Denver, and Washington. There are also some *professional studios and touring companies* that produce several plays a year. The commercial companies include The Children's Theatre Company and School (Minneapolis), The Traveling Playhouse, The Paper Bag Players, The Mask, and the Honolulu Theatre for Youth. The noncommercial theatres for children are either attached to museums (as in Los Angeles and Chicago) or to adult regional companies (as in New Haven and Atlanta). Incidentally, ticket prices vary considerably from theatre to theatre, ranging recently in price from free (Los Angeles Children's Museum) to 50 cents for children and $1.00 for adults (Fort Lauderdale Children's Theatre) to $2.00 for all (Louisville Children's Theatre) to $4.00 for all (New York's First All-Children's Theatre) to $5.75 for all (The Paper Bag Players).

The most successful plays staged by these various groups for the child audience, stresses Goldberg, are those that maintain:

1. *Respect*—for the child's sense of wonder, naive emotionality, and physical/psychological weaknesses.
2. *Entertainment*—comprising nonverbal communication, repetition, direct address, slapstick, childish behavior in adults, romanticism, physical pleasures, suspense, and the antagonist's realization of defeat.
3. *Contemporaneity*—for children lack historical perspective and become most involved in a play when they sense its relevance to them.
4. *Action*—for theatre is what is done and what is seen and not what is said: "Show it, don't tell it."
5. *Unity of organization*—or a careful adherence to whatever dramatic element it is that serves to organize and unify a particular script, such as a basic story line.
6. *Variety and rhythm*—since with their short attention spans, children like a rhythm of short and long scenes, talk and action, humor and seriousness, calm and tension.[4]

There can be no doubt that the creative drama program in the elementary school has benefited considerably from the growth in children's theatre. While half of a century ago only a few pioneers bothered with play production for boys and girls, today several hundred producers devote their time and energy to the development in children of an artistic appreciation for drama.

Incidentally, there is a technique known as readers theatre which is sometimes mistakenly described as a form of children's drama. It is in reality a speech art and another form of oral reading. Scripts are used and literature ranging from short stories to poetry to plays is shared by the readers with their listeners. Unlike children's theatre, readers theatre is not a polished, organized production. And unlike creative drama, readers theatre is not spontaneous and its action or physical movement is merely suggested. This speech art was discussed in Chapter Five.

Creative Drama

Creative drama is drama *with* children. Originated by a group of youngsters who are guided (not directed) by a teacher, it is always played with spontaneous dialog and action and is often termed *playmaking*. Participation is all-important for creative drama is not for the talented few, and the experience of the child who lacks ability is often as meaningful and as enjoyable as that of the child with marked dramatic talent. It may be created from an everyday experience, a story, a poem, a special event or holiday, or from an object or an idea. While it frequently develops from literature or the social studies, creative drama is not confined to a certain subject or time schedule but may be employed in an area of the curriculum where it can be used effectively for the sake of the pupils' social and emotional development.

Studies have shown that problem-solving ability, personality, behavior, oral language growth, and reading achievement can all be altered positively through creative dramatic activities.[5] Primary pupils in an integrated school, for example, who engaged in an 11-week dramatic play program (developed to teach social studies) showed significant improvement in problem-solving skills and the acceptance of social responsibility; the children took part once or twice a week. Third graders who participated in a 15-week program of creative drama improved in both personal and social adjustment, with the boys making even greater gains than the girls; the class met forty minutes a week. Fourth and fifth graders who had 20 creative drama sessions increased significantly their total verbal output, total clause output, and total T-unit (one main clause with all subordinate clauses attached) output. When the study was replicated with seventh graders, their growth increased not only in the three areas where the younger students had improved but in a fourth area (type-token ratio, measuring vocabulary diversity) as well. And advantaged and disadvantaged pupils alike gained in reading achievement and in self-concept after a 15-week program of reading and dramatizing stories. Children from the primary and the intermediate grades dramatized self-selected stories from their basal and supplementary readers, their science and social studies texts, and from library browsing books as they met in small committees, three to five times weekly.

Teachers of the ever-increasing number of emotionally disturbed children can freely use creative drama too. Gillies has found that it (1) helps build the troubled children's sense of respect for their own ideas and consequently for themselves; (2) offers them a chance to become aware of and understand their feelings; (3) provides them with the social contacts often eliminated from their daily lives; (4) helps them experience firmness and inner control, so often lacking, in an enjoyable way; and (5) provides an opportunity for the children to be heard alone as well as in a group situation.[6]

That creative drama can bring teachers in contact with insightful clues as to the basis of pupils' emotional illness is readily understood. After all, this form of children's drama is a much more natural form of expression for all young students than is formal drama because it results from their own thoughts and feelings. All children in the group are encouraged to volunteer for all the parts, acting and, with the exception of pantomime, talking as they believe the characters they are portraying would act and talk. Pupils begin to realize that what they say and do is important to other people. They acquire the habit of thinking about what they are saying rather than memorizing a recitation, since the play is not rehearsed but develops with each presentation. The importance of creative drama, therefore, lies not in the product but in the process, and no school experience in the estimation of many teachers gives children a better opportunity to be creative than does playmaking. Still, most schools continue to view creative drama as strictly a peripheral activity, as exemplified in a recent Wisconsin study of 346 classroom teachers.[7] Although 75 percent favored creative drama, less than 25 percent of the teachers actually taught it to their students.

McCaslin, however, reiterates the many values that prevail in creative playing and contends that these exist in some measure for all participants, regardless of age, circumstances, or previous experience.[8] Consequently, the teacher need not assign different values to various age levels in the elementary school, but she or he should accept the following ten basic values which exist at all levels, although they may vary somewhat in degree: an opportunity for independent thinking; an opportunity to develop the imagination; an opportunity for cooperation; an opportunity to build social awareness; a healthy release of emotion; an experience with good literature; an introduction to the theatre arts; better habits of speech; recreation; and the freedom for the group to develop its own ideas.

Not all of the above values will of course appear at once because the total creative process is slow. Within its context, however, a number of different linguistic, mental, and physical activities or processes takes place, according to Youngers, who points out that creative drama fits a definition of problem solving in which discovery by doing receives the focus.[9] In a thorough exploration of a problem or topic, the processes generate one another and are tapped sequentially, as outlined in the multidimensional model shown in Figure 13.1.

At other times, however, the processes may overlap and lack distinctive boundaries. And, while younger children may only use the first two dramatic processes of *perceiving* and *responding,* older pupils may employ the additional

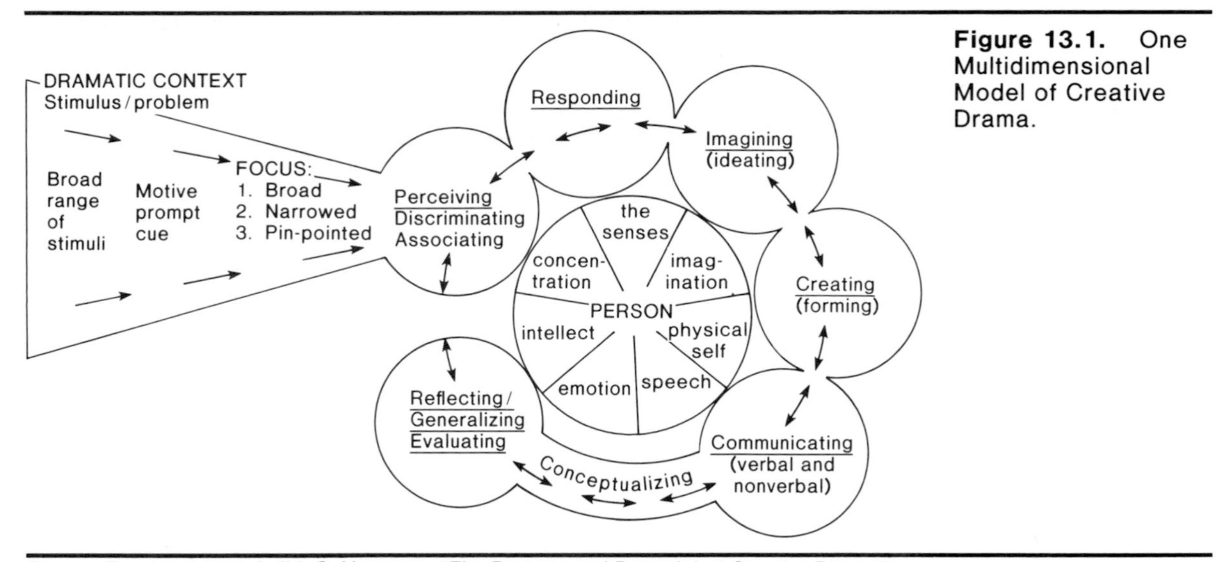

Figure 13.1. One Multidimensional Model of Creative Drama.

Source: Reprinted from Judith S. Youngers "The Process and Potential of Creative Dramatics for Enhancing Linguistic and Cognitive Development" in RESEARCH IN THE LANGUAGE ARTS edited by V. Froese and S. Straw. University Park Press, 1981, p. 96, Figure 1.

processes of *imagining* (or ideating), *creating* (forming or improvising), and *communicating*. The sixth and final process of *reflecting* is more typically part of the problem-solving sequence of children who have attained an advanced level of development in creative drama.

It must be stressed that, regardless of whether the boys and girls are beginners or advanced students, creative drama remains participant-centered. And the only audience, as a rule, is the part of the group not playing at the moment. Still, it is vital that there be onlookers (especially with older children) because they assist in evaluating the production while they themselves are developing an appreciation for drama. Should the creative thinking of the pupils result in a particularly good play, it may sometimes be shared with another group of children or with the parents. Such a sharing is not considered a performance, however, but rather an informal demonstration incidental to the creative experience. The players, nevertheless, are generally so fluent that should the audience be unaware that the dialog is being improvised, they might readily believe that the play has a written script.

Elementary teachers skilled in playmaking establish a physical setting and an emotional tone in the classroom that stimulate creative drama. Although they do not talk much themselves, they draw out the pupils' ideas through subtle questioning and courteous consideration of all responses. They quietly stress the importance of sense memory (or improvisations based on the five senses) and emotion memory (or improvisations based on feelings). They place emphasis on spontaneity, encouraging the children to create in their own way and to believe in themselves and their abilities. These teachers provide enrichment, as the need arises, with materials and properties, factual information, stories and verse, and audiovisual aids that help develop depth and understanding. At times when children appear unable to make suggestions necessary for the improvement of a play, thoughtful questions from teachers will elicit creative thinking among the group members.

Children up to the age of approximately eleven or twelve years should participate in creative drama exclusively, according to the CTAA Committee on Basic Concepts. Only when pupils are older and have had a background in creative drama and only after they have formed the habit of thinking through their speeches can they be counted on for a much greater degree of naturalness in children's theatre roles. Pupils who are enrolled in a school that offers them a program in creative drama, will, beginning in kindergarten, enjoy during their elementary school years these five major groups of activities:

1. Dramatic play: nonsocial and social
2. Pantomime
3. Role-playing
4. Story dramatization: interpretation
5. Story dramatization: improvisation

Dramatic Play

Much of the knowledge children absorb is best acquired by exploration in the real world where they may freely and actively construct their vision of reality, rather than be passively instructed about it. Happily, therefore, one of the most spontaneous interests of young children is dramatic play. It involves neither plot nor sequence, just conversation and action. In their dramatic play, children reenact their own experiences, imitate the activities of adults, animals, and inanimate objects, and live in an imaginary world. They are the father, teacher, truck driver, mother, doctor, nurse, fire fighter, and scores of other characters in the home, school, and community. During the play period, children move about freely, choosing their own activities, materials, equipment, and companions as long as their selections do not interfere with the welfare of the classroom.

What the children do in this initial kind of creative drama is wholly exploratory and experimental. Although they lack the background to bring full knowledge to the situation, they are capable of conceiving ideas, planning their own dramatizations, and performing with the "dress-up" materials, playhouse, boxes, planks, or other properties that will help them produce something that provides them at least with gratification. Sometimes they may shift swiftly from one character to another, playing each role for only a few minutes. In other cases, they may continue the same role for days or weeks, becoming the person, animal, or object with which they have an impulse to identify. Children may play the part of a barking dog, a galloping pony, or a soaring airplane. Dramatic play concerns being rather than playing and incorporates feeling with action. It is fragmentary and fun.

There is no definite beginning, middle, or end. Dramatic play may start anywhere and may conclude abruptly, especially in its early stages, when a child says, "I'm finished."

Sequence of Growth and Social Context

Teachers should keep in mind the sequence of growth through which children progress in their play and recognize that there is a gradual transition from simple movement and manipulation through the following phases:

Solitary play. The child plays alone, with little or no attention to other children. Although the child may show interest in others, he or she will not play with them.

Parallel play. The child still plays independently, but alongside of other children, and he or she enters into the same types of activities that they do. There is very little conversation.

Associate play. Children may share some ideas and materials. Though their activities may be similar, each child plays according to individual interests.

Sociodramatic play. Two or more children attempt to recreate real life situations through cooperative play. This type is more complex than nonsocial dramatic play and requires longer periods of time. In Piagetian terms it has been classified as the most highly developed form of symbolic play.

Sociodramatic Play

Both Smilansky and Christie list the following elements as essential to sociodramatic play: persistence (of at least ten minutes for a single play episode); make-believe in regard to objects; make-believe in regard to actions and situations; imitative role play; verbal communication covering both metacommunications (or exchanges about the play episode) and pretend communications (or exchanges within the episode); and interaction.[10]

For children who are already engaging in an advanced form of sociodramatic play, teacher intervention is not needed and may even disrupt the play. However, should it be noted that the play of the older kindergarten or first grade children lacks some of the six essential elements, teachers may wish to use either outside intervention (by remaining outside the play episode and only offering special comments to encourage particular behaviors) or inside intervention (by joining the play and demonstrating behaviors previously lacking in the episode). The teacher will most often be called upon to interfere in the play of children from low socioeconomic backgrounds or the play of children with emotional problems. Cultural differences, too, may create differences in play behavior.

The teacher should also be aware that as children mature, the character of their dramatic play changes. Older children demand a higher degree of organization than younger children before beginning to play, as they assume roles and divide responsibilities. Older children also have a desire for some properties that are real, while younger children are able to participate in dramatic play in which all the properties they use exist only in their imaginations. As children mature, a distinction between "work" and "play" develops: work involving the constructing, gathering, or arranging of materials for dramatic play; and play concerning the use of those materials for dramatizing an idea or a situation. Consequently, the intervals between play periods obviously lengthen as the children create the properties they need. Finally, the amount of time that is devoted to dramatic play and the place of dramatic play in the daily schedule will differ according to the maturity of the children.

Conditions and Developmental Steps

Play is the child's vehicle of growth. And teachers who have successfully guided dramatic play have discovered factors which contribute to stimulating play in the kindergarten and early grades. There must be adequate space to promote free expression, and numerous and different kinds of properties to encourage participation. Proper stimuli from both firsthand and vicarious experiences are needed before young children can play creatively. Development of the children's own ideas, not those imposed by the teacher, is always an encouraging factor. Sufficient time for children to employ previous learnings and explore additional ones is an especially significant matter in the early grades. Participation by the children in all phases of the play from problem solving to evaluation honestly furthers creative expression. Finally, there is no unnecessary interference or criticism on the part of the teacher.

After its beginning weeks in any classroom, dramatic play usually encompasses the following steps, according to the Shaftels:

1. There is an environment arranged by the teacher.
2. The boys and girls explore that environment and are permitted to manipulate and discuss all the materials and tools that it contains.
3. A story may be heard or read to further stimulate interest in the selected area and provide data.
4. The boys and girls elect to play a part of the story or improvise their own situation.
5. The first play is unguided, but carefully observed by the teacher.
6. A sharing period follows the play to clarify dissatisfactions and unexpressed needs.
7. There is a planning period for problem solving and work assignments.
8. A period of extension of experiences through research, excursions, and multimedia ensues before and beside further play.
9. Play proceeds on a higher level due to enriched experience.[11]

Pantomime

Stated in its simplest terms, pantomime is acting without words. It can help children become prepared for story dramatization by letting them become accustomed to transmitting ideas, emotions, and actions to the audience through the medium of body movement, facial expression, and posture. Confidence gained through success in pantomime quietly prepares the way for subsequent success in handling dialog. After all, psychologists claim that no less than 55 percent of the total communicated message is determined by *kinesics,* or bodily movements made by arms, hands, shoulders, and face.

Mime is an ancient and universal art form which is also a nonlinguistic means of communication common to all humanity. Perhaps this is why children enjoy it, even those who are shy and generally find oral activities distressing. It offers each child an opportunity to develop physical freedom and a feeling of self-worth without the additional problem of dialog.

Participants learn to use all parts of the body to express a single action. To indicate drowsiness, for example, they can rub their eyes, stretch their arms, droop their shoulders, cover a yawn, or sit down wearily.

Children must realize that during a pantomime performance every action takes place in total silence. They can be reminded that while it is permissable to move one's lips as if talking, the lips must not form actual words. This basic tenet of pantomime is a difficult one for most boys and girls to follow.

Although properties are generally not allowed, a chair or table may occasionally be permitted. Should the performers be holding an imaginary object, they should practice with actual objects first. In that way, during the actual pantomime they will remember to leave space between the fingers just as if the object were actually in the hand.

The mark of an effective pantomime is that it is clearly presented so that it becomes easy to identify. Sometimes children get the mistaken impression that a pantomime has been well performed if the class is unable to decipher the activity shown. The contrary is true.

Consequently, as the pupils become more adept at their presentations, it is a wise policy for the teacher to encourage them to prepare their pantomimes in advance. They must think through their movements and not rely upon impromptu actions. While it is hardly necessary that all the movements to be used in a prepared pantomime be written down, it is still helpful if the teachers know in advance just which pantomimes will be presented. They may sometimes have to caution children about using good taste in their performance.

Introductory Pantomime

All of the pantomime exercises during the introductory period involve gross actions only. What is being portrayed should be easily recognized by one and all.

If drama is new to both the primary teacher and the class, one starting point is a simple exercise executed in the form of a charade. The teacher asks, "If right at this moment you could do the one thing you enjoy doing most of all in the world, what would it be?"; and then as children raise their hands, the teacher adds, "Don't tell us what it is; show us!" Each child then pantomimes an activity that he or she especially enjoys, such as playing ball, helping to sail a boat, running with a dog, or riding a bicycle.

Should the group be timid or afraid of ridicule, the teacher should first set the mood verbally ("It is a snowy day") and then establish a feeling of confidence by doing the first large-movement pantomime. The teacher then asks the children to guess the situation, giving them the opportunity later to present their own interpretations of the same situation. Finally they are ready to enact some familiar actions for their classmates to decipher.

Besides charades and guessing games like "Secret" or "Who Am I?", riddles and Mother Goose rhymes are other ways to introduce pantomime to young children. One rhyme that works well is:

One, two, buckle my shoe;
Three, four, knock at the door;
Five, six, pick up sticks . . .

The teacher quickly recites the rhyme, demonstrating the actions that might accompany each part. Then he or she asks the children to present their interpretations individually as the rest of the class recites the rhyme. In a few instances the children merely imitate the teacher's actions, but in other cases the pupils create and express their own ideas.

In teaching pantomime to intermediate grade boys and girls who have never engaged in such dramatic activities before, the teacher must always assume the lead and give an informal demonstration. The teacher can pantomime, for example, the humorous efforts to retrieve a pencil that has rolled under a heavy piece of furniture in the corner of the room. This demonstration will generally elicit other amusing pantomimes by the more extroverted pupils. Their demonstrations will, in turn, probably provoke pantomimes by shyer students.

Suggested exercises which may be effective for freeing inexperienced or withdrawn pupils to perform in front of their peers include the following pantomimes:

- Pretend to eat—an ice cream cone—a sour pickle—a freshly toasted marshmallow.
- Pretend to—nail two boards together—put on a pullover sweater—brush your teeth.
- Pretend that you are walking—on hot sand—through fallen leaves—through very deep snow.
- Pretend to throw—a baseball—a basketball—a football.

Developmental Stages

True pantomiming concerns more than mere mute action. It expresses vividly the participant's feelings and thoughts as well. For example, is there anyone who cannot interpret fully the facial expression and wordless actions of (1) a rider caught between floors in a self-service elevator when the control panel buttons fail to respond, or of (2) a burglar on the second floor of an empty house when the residents unexpectedly return home?

Consequently, once children have learned to react to the typical large-movement pantomimes that make suitable class beginnings, it is time for pantomimes focusing on emotional attitudes, sensory awareness, and occasional conflicts or problems.

The first group of these should be *short individual pantomimes* that will allow each member of the class to perform at least once during the lesson. Either a boy or girl may pretend to be—

- Biting into a sour apple
- Drinking cocoa that is too hot
- Hiking up a rocky hill
- Walking on an icy sidewalk
- Picking up a crying baby

After children have had some experience performing and watching brief pantomimes, they will be encouraged to select topics for *lengthy individual pantomimes*. At this stage, they may either develop their own themes or choose to mime situations like these:

- Seeing a kindergartner who is mistreating a small cat that does not belong to her, becoming very angry, running between the girl and the cat, rescuing the frightened kitten, and finally scolding the unkind child.

- Walking down the street on the way home from school, noticing a three-year-old boy dart into the street after a ball just as a truck comes rapidly around the corner toward him, and reacting properly.
- Receiving a letter from your favorite aunt with an invitation to take a trip to Florida to visit Disney World, thinking about what fun it will be, and hurrying to tell a parent the good news.

A third stage in pantomime activities is reached when children choose partners and perform *double pantomimes* such as—

- a barber cutting the hair of a wiggling boy;
- a Boy Scout walking an elderly person across the street;
- an indifferent student showing a poor report card to a parent;
- a bank robber holding up a frightened teller; or
- a beginning driver backing out of the garage with a nervous friend.

A variation of the double pantomime is the *mirror pantomime* where two players must harmonize their movements so as to give the impression of one person looking at his/her reflection in a full-length mirror. All actions are done in unison as the players face each other (and appear sideways to the audience). They should be of approximately the same size, though they need not be dressed alike. They should use broad gestures which are clearly visible to the audience, and make all movements with moderate speed.

After some practice with double pantomimes, the children may wish to attempt *group pantomimes* with character analysis and finer movements. Demanding the cooperation of several children, group pantomimes are especially suited for those pupils who are hesitant about giving individual performances but who still enjoy pantomime. Groups in the primary or middle grades may decide to do individual themes or variations on the same theme. They may even wish to perform a narrative pantomime in sequence from a complete story such as:

Bright's *Gregory* (Doubleday, 1969)
Daughterty's *Andy and the Lion* (Viking, 1966)
Garelick's *Just Suppose* (Scholastic, 1969)
Mayer's *There's a Nightmare in My Closet* (Dial, 1968)
Miller's *Mousekin's Family* (Prentice-Hall, 1965)
Seuss's *The Lorax* (Random House, 1971)
Tolstoy's *The Great Big Enormous Turnip* (Watts, 1968)
Yolen's *No Bath Tonight* (Crowell, 1978)

Material suitable for group pantomime in the intermediate grades includes many of the fables, folktales, legends, and fantasy stories to which the pupils have been introduced during their literature periods. Readily found in several anthologies are such stories that can be pantomimed as "Pecos Bill and His Bouncing Bride," "The Emperor's New Clothes," "The Mad Hatter's Tea Party," "The Crow and the Pitcher," and "The Milkmaid and Her Pail." Narrative pantomimes may also be developed from such complete stories as:

Ambrus' *The Three Poor Tailors* (Harcourt, 1965)
Belpre's *Ote: A Puerto Rican Tale* (Pantheon, 1969)
Chaikin's *Ittki Pittki* (Parents, 1971)
Kanzawa's *The Selfish Old Woman* (Bobbs-Merrill, 1971)
Withers' *Painting the Moon* (Dutton, 1970)

One successful group pantomime consists of having one fluent student read aloud a lively story while a selected cast simultaneously pantomimes the action.

Role-Playing

Like pantomime and both kinds of dramatic play, role-playing is participant-centered and encourages spontaneous actions. Unlike them, however, role-playing *always* concerns a group situation in which a problem in human relations is enacted and reenacted until alternatve solutions have been elicited. Observers evaluate the variables involved as well as the possible solutions. The purpose of role-playing is educative and preventive rather than therapeutic, and its specific goal is the social growth of individuals.

Children often learn to resolve problems in real life by working them out successfully in role-playing situations. They find that by exchanging roles they gain a better understanding of the dilemmas that others face. They learn to develop awareness of their own feelings and to release those feelings safely. They acquire new ways of handling acceptance and rejection, criticism and praise, failure, and success, and such confusing predicaments as sibling rivalry, parent-child conflicts, social isolation, and integrity in friendship relations.

One specialized kind of role-playing is *sociodrama,* which has been defined as decision making in a social crisis involving a conflict of values. Should a controversial issue such as racial tensions, for example, exist in the school/community and should the children be mature enough to understand some of their own anxieties, elementary classroom teachers may wish to use sociodrama. They may also choose to schedule some sociodrama sessions during the presentation of certain social studies units if the children are intermediate students and have had earlier experiences with structured dramatic play.

Sociodrama and role-playing alike increase skill in communication. Role-playing, however, is the more useful method of helping pupils resolve the many routine problems that arise daily. A quarrel develops on the playground, for instance, because there is a shortage of equipment. The teacher arranges an enactment by getting the attention of all the children, discussing the setting of the "play" situation, and choosing the participants: Sean has the role of an aggressive child who will not share the equipment; Heather plays a polite child who wishes to use the equipment but will not fight to get it; and Brian plays a shy pupil who is disturbed by the quarrel.

It is helpful when the situations chosen are representative of the problems of the group, and the members want to explore them. Situations in which the pupils feel misunderstood, those in which they have difficulty in making up their minds about what is right to do or say, or those that make them unhappy are all suitable for role playing. There should never be a feeling that there is only one right way of behaving in a given situation. Instead, the same situation may be played several times in order that the children can reinterpret the factors and reach solutions that are personally satisfying. Through this method participants and their audience both can find ways of behaving that will expand the present skills they possess in dealing with problems of deep personal concern. Generalizations about human relations appropriate to the age and maturity of the group involved may also be discovered.

In organizing and directing role-playing, teachers should choose a problem that the children cannot meet adequately or toward which they have conflicting attitudes; that problem should involve three or more participants. Teachers should take sufficient time to clarify the various roles and explain the situation—not the solution—before they ask for volunteers for the different roles. (If there are no volunteers, they should select those pupils who are neither shy nor readily upset.) Next, they can arrange the details of the situation, discuss the physical setting, and prepare the nonparticipants for their role as observers. Promptly after the first unrehearsed enactment, teachers and children should discuss the presentation and summarize how the problem was met. Then the first actors may be replaced by new ones who have different ideas of how the roles should be played, and again the enactment should be evaluated and modifications suggested. Sometimes a third version may ensue.

One of the most effective stimulants for decision making through role-playing is the unfinished problem story which presents an unresolved conflict or dilemma which demands alternative solutions. Some teachers choose to use the more than 60 such stories written by the Shaftels concerning areas like moral development, citizenship, interpersonal and intergroup relations, and self acceptance.[12] Other teachers elect to produce their own stories, believing that they know best their own students' maturity level and interests as well as the attitudes and values to be explored with the individual group. Under the circumstances, these teacher-authors also understand more clearly the numbers and types of character parts to be included in the unfinished story.

In an effort to aid beginning teachers in the upper elementary grades who are interested in role-playing sessions, the Fairfield (Connecticut) schools have developed a checklist for guiding teachers during such sessions involving problem stories.[13]

Classroom Teachers' Checklist for Guiding Role-Playing

Part A

1. Define the problem (Recall).
   After reading the story, allow time for the children to reflect and to make voluntary comments. Then ask: What is happening here? Should the children still seem to be having difficulty in moving into the situation, ask further recall questions: Who is involved? How are they affected by this situation? How is Chief Character feeling? Why is he or she feeling this way? How are Other Characters feeling? Why?
2. Delineate alternatives (Projection).
   Ask: What do you think will (*not* should) happen now?

Invite ideas from the children.
Both antisocial and socially sanctioned solutions will generally be mentioned. If only one kind of solution is offered, however, ask: Is this the only way in which such a situation usually ends? Then if still no other solution is proposed, proceed into role-playing.

3. Explore alternatives.
   If the group has offered both negative and positive proposals for solving the story dilemma, begin with a consideration of the antisocial or impulsive solutions first.
   a. Negative solutions
      (1) Choose one negative solution and hold a brief discussion.
      (2) Choose a volunteer to role-play the proposal. Ask the volunteer: Whom will you need to help you? Then assist him or her in selecting other volunteer role-players.
      (3) Set the stage for the role-playing session by asking: Where is this happening? What time of year (or day) is it? What is each of you doing?
      (4) Prepare the audience. If beginners, ask the group to evaluate, as they watch, how realistic the role-playing is by pondering: Could this really occur? Are the persons behaving as they would in real life?
          If the class is experienced in role-playing, divide the members into observer groups and ask Group I to observe for true-to-life behaivor, Group II to observe how individual players feel, and Group III to consider next steps for solving the dilemma.
      (5) Start the role-playing and continue it only until the acting has clearly delineated the proposed solution.
      (6) Start the discussion by asking: What has been happening? How does Chief Character feel? Why does he or she behave in that way? What will happen next?
   b. Interim
      Decide whether it is worthwhile to continue further enactment exploring the negative solution or to go on to explore proposals offering alternative courses of behavior. Should time allow for elaborated role-playing, consult Part B.
   c. Positive solutions
      (1) Choose one positive solution and hold a brief discussion.
      (2) Proceed as outlined under 3a—sections (2) to (6).
4. Make a decision.
   a. If the group has reached some definite understanding of the alternatives explored and of the consequences that may ensue, ask: Which one of the solutions to this problem do you believe to be the best? Why? For whom is it best? Who will benefit from the solution and who will suffer? If you were (One Story Character), how would you decide? If you were (Another Story Character), how would you decide?

b. Ask: At which point in the story could a choice have been made that would have precipitated an acceptable solution?

Part B

1. Add extra steps to role-playing when time allows.
   For occasions when the group may be guided into role-playing with some depth, up to three additional steps may be added to the process.
   a. Extend exploration of the consequences of the proposed solution to the dilemma by suggesting another scene to be enacted. This second scene should logically be an aftermath of the proposed behavior.
   b. Reverse the roles of the chief characters in the problem story. (In order to convince an individual who is unaware of the effect of his or her behavior upon others, it is often impressive to put this individual into the position of the person most seriously affected by that behavior.)
   c. Seek out the implications of the proposed alternative by means of analogy. Apply the principle suggested by the alternative to other situations outside the story.

Story Dramatization: Interpretation

Constituting the most popular means that pupils and their teachers have to get behind the printed word, story dramatization helps develop a new dimension in understanding literature.

Children who are younger or less experienced in creative drama generally want to do stories already familiar to them and only gradually abandon stereotypes and conventions for more original creations. Briefly, this illustrates the sequence of *interpretation* and *improvisation.* In planning story dramatization with students, the teacher begins with an interpretation of the story or an accurate re-creation of the author's intent and statement. Then as the pupils mature and become more knowledgeable in dramatization, the teacher can proceed to improvisation, for that involves going beyond the basic story in an attempt to extend or expand upon the thematic material.

Developmental Steps

When the class has shown readiness for story dramatization *the teacher tells or reads a well-structured story* that possesses most or all of the following characteristics:

1. Brevity—as in one of Kipling's *Just So Stories* (Doubleday, 1972)
2. A simple, strong, dramatic conflict—as in Seuss' *The 500 Hats of Bartholomew Cubbins* (Vanguard, 1938)
3. One setting—as in Slobodkina's *Caps for Sale* (Scott, 1947)
4. Natural, interesting characters—as in Brown's *Stone Soup* (Scribner, 1947)
5. A simple plot that hinges on action—as in the Grimm Brothers' *The Shoemaker and the Elves* (Scribner, 1960)
6. Dialog that furthers that action—as in Galdone's *The Three Little Pigs* (Seabury Press, 1970)
7. A strong climax and a quick, definite ending—as in Galdone's *The Three Wishes* (McGraw, 1961)

Listening to the teacher tell or read a well-structured story promotes the interest of young children in creative drama. (Photo courtesy of the *Daily News Tribune,* Fullerton, California.)

Before reading or telling the intended story, the teacher becomes so familiar with it that he or she can reflect upon the thoughts, movements, appearances, and feelings of the characters in order to make these figures real. The teacher attempts to establish in their minds one version to which the pupils can repeatedly return in the dramatization. During the recitation the teacher watches for external clues from the children that may indicate their interest and involvement. It is vital that all or most of the children like the narrative which will be dramatized. The teacher may be certain that they will enjoy a story if it appeals to their emotions.

The teacher's own viewpoint about the story is also important. The teacher can hardly guide children to create successful dialog and action from literary selections concerned with values or characterizations that he or she personally finds unacceptable.

Once a story has been told, *the teacher poses questions to stimulate discussion of sequences, characters,* and *setting.* The children must be able to bring out in their dramatization the essential elements of the story just read. So the teacher asks the pupils carefully framed questions to point up the key actions and lines which will move the play along. In some instances more than one discussion period may be necessary to stimulate thoughts about the story plot and people, for it is wise not to pose more than five specific questions during a single discussion.

After they have carefully analyzed the story, *the children determine the characterization and the scenes.* Whether the story requires one scene or several, the pupils will find that the playing proceeds more smoothly if they decide in advance the number of scenes and the characters who appear in each scene, and plot all these details on the chalkboard.

Characterization being principally a matter of imagination, the teacher should always stress developing a character from within. Boys and girls should try first to understand how the other person thinks and feels before they attempt to act like the person. In one New York classroom, for example, there is a "Magic Stage," a special space reserved for creative drama activities. Once children step onto this stage, they are encouraged to be the characters they have chosen to portray by acting like them with both their bodies and their minds. To help the boys and girls keep clear about the characters and their goals and obstacles in the story, the teacher and the class play a game called Circle of Characters, in which they take turns asking the characters on the Magic Stage various questions to help them establish who they are: Where do you live? What is your favorite color? What hobby do you have? Which animals do you like? Which foods do you prefer to eat? What is your favorite sport? What do you like to do best? How old are you? Who is your best friend?

As they follow the general outline of the story, *the children create the dialog and the dramatization.* As a consequence of the discussion periods held earlier, the boys and girls generally can speak all or nearly all of the key lines, adding other phrases to make the play their own and to round out the characters they will be portraying. For the first performance, the teacher designates a space within the room as a stage or playing area and selects five or six confident volunteers (explaining to the others that each will be given an opportunity in turn to play a role). The group of players for the initial performance is then permitted a planning conference among themselves, away from the rest of the class, in order to prepare in greater detail exactly what each member will do and how he or she will do it. This conference, serving as a brief orientation period for the players, runs about five minutes and takes place just prior to the start of the dramatization.

Once the play has begun, it must move along without interruption because to the children this step is the most important of all. The teacher should attempt to limit the performances in the lower grades to five minutes, and those in the middle and intermediate grades to fifteen minutes.

As soon as the performance has been completed, *the class promptly evaluates the presentation.* Such appraisal under the positive guidance of the teacher is a training of vital importance, according to Gillies, for all age levels, beginning in the second grade.[14] It starts with an acknowledgment of strengths: What did you see that you liked? What was good (about Cinderella's step-sisters)? Once trained to look for what is good or what they liked, children can soon reach the second level of discussion: How can we make that scene more real (or more powerful, more exciting)? What shall we change or add the next time we play it? Throughout the discussion the boys and girls should examine the action and consider the voice and diction of the actors. They can study the characterizations, using the names of the characters rather than those of the players in order to be more objective in their criticism. They can ask one another these questions:

Was the play just like the story we heard?
Were the characters the way we had imagined them to be?
What did we like about the opening scene?
What did we like best about the performance?
How could we improve the play the next time we act it out?

Slowly the class can be led through creative group appraisal to realize that while first dramatic attempts may appear uneven and crude, story dramatizations gradually become more convincing. Therefore, every sincere effort of each child is acceptable and praiseworthy and every child retains the right to reject or modify proposed changes in the role that he or she has undertaken.

Finally, *the children reenact the dramatization,* incorporating the constructive criticisms just discussed. Properties are still kept at a simple minimum, with no costumes necessary. Eventually, several casts are drawn up, with every child playing at least one role. Variations in actions and dialog are anticipated and appreciated during each performance.

Suggested Stories

All of the traditional folk tales listed here have proved suitable for informal dramatization and can be adapted to different age groups. Readily located in most standard anthologies of children's literature, they include:

"Briar Rose"
"Cinderella"
"Hansel and Gretel"
"Jack and the Beanstalk"
"Little Red Riding Hood"
"Puss in Boots"
"The Gingerbread Boy"
"The Three Bears"

Those same anthologies are also apt to include some stories in verse form that children and teachers may enjoy dramatizing, such as:

Browning's "The Pied Piper of Hamelin"
Field's "The Duel"
Follen's "Three Little Kittens"
Moore's "A Visit from St. Nicholas"

Stories in prose form which invite dramatization by elementary school children, in addition to the folk tales listed earlier, include the following:

- Balet's *Fence, a Mexican Tale* (Delacorte, 1969)
- Freeman's *Corduroy* (Viking, 1968)
- Grahame's *The Reluctant Dragon* (Holiday, 1953)
- Hodges' *The Wave* (Houghton, 1964)
- LeGallienne's *The Nightingale* (Harper, 1965)
- Piper's *The Little Engine That Could* (Platt & Munk, 1961)
- Sawyer's *Journey Cake, Ho!* (Viking, 1953)
- Selden's *Sparrow Socks* (Harper, 1965)
- Seuss' *Bartholomew and the Oobleck* (Random House, 1949)

Story Dramatization: Improvisation

Improvisation involves going beyond the basic literary material. The children are compelled to extrapolate and enrich the material by drawing from within themselves. Their thoughts, emotions, and conclusions are based upon, but not truly found in, the poem or story in question.

This type of story dramatization encompasses many of the same developmental steps that were discussed earlier for the interpretation category. The major difference lies in the sort of questions that the teacher must write. Unlike the literal variety demanding strict recall, which are a significant part of interpretation, questions that are developed in preparation for an improvisation session are inferential. They require original, creative thinking.

A teacher, for example, who had told the familiar myth of King Midas to a class that had been interpreting stories for months, might pose such questions as the following as a prelude to improvisation:

1. Why do you believe the king was so greedy? What might have caused him to be that way?
2. Why was his daughter so sweet, despite the fact that she had been raised alone in the castle with her father as an example?
3. How did the king react to other people? (Remember that the story did not show him interacting with others). How did he treat his servants? The townspeople?
4. In what other ways might he have resolved his problem?[15]

Other, more general questions could be asked regarding the physical, social, and psychological facets of additional characters in the story.

What the teacher must emphasize to the class is that there is no one right answer to an inferential question and that all responses are valuable. Children will then be encouraged to offer a variety of opinions and insights before any improvisation session begins.

Only after the children have had sufficient time to carefully ponder both the questions and answers can they proceed to the final three developmental steps previously explored under Story Dramatization: Interpretation. They create the dramatization complete with dialog and that event in turn provokes an evaluation session and a subsequent reenactment of the improvisation.

Evaluation of Pupils' Progress

Appraisal of the growth of the child in this area of the English language arts can be made on an informal and individual basis through observing to what extent he or she fulfills the following:

- Does the child participate freely and wholeheartedly in imaginative play-making?
- Does the child find enjoyment and satisfaction as a member of the audience at informal creative drama activities and/or formal children's theatre productions?
- Does the child control situations by words rather than physical force?
- Is the child developing the nonverbal elements of communication such as body language?
- Is the child able to interact comfortably with others?
- Does the child recall a series of episodes in sequence and distinguish between central ideas and subordinating details?
- Is the child's vocabulary expanding properly?
- Is the child able to organize stories, verse, and other media for dramatic expression?
- Has the chid developed physical coordination and good posture habits?
- Has the child's voice quality and projection improved?
- Has the child increased in self-confidence and self-direction, whether working alone or before an audience?
- Has the child formed the habit of original flexible thinking?
- Has the child's problem-solving ability expanded?
- Has the child developed a respect for the creative forms that he or she has experienced and for the creative efforts that fellow classmates have demonstrated?

Discussion Questions

1. As a beginning teacher, how would you explain your creative drama program to a group of stolid parents?
2. How can a teacher interest fifth graders into doing pantomime or story dramatization if they have never attempted either one before?
3. Listening is said to improve after creative drama sessions. How can you explain this improvement?
4. Should a teacher assign a letter grade to the young performer in creative drama? How can the teacher best evaluate the child's participation in this critical area?

Suggested Projects

1. Write an unfinished problem story which could serve as the basis of a role-playing session in the fourth grade.
2. Observe a group of pupils in kindergarten or first grade who are engaged in dramatic play. What values are apparent in this type of creative drama?
3. List the organizations in your community that are currently sponsoring children's theatre productions. Visit one of their performances and assess its reception by the young audience.

4. Plan a beginning pantomime lesson for primary pupils.
5. Examine one of the standard anthologies of poetry for children, such as the Opies' *The Oxford Book of Children's Verse* (Oxford, 1973). List several ballads and story poems that pupils might enjoy dramatizing.
6. Set up the learning center on creative drama shown in Figure 13.2.

Figure 13.2. Language Arts Learning Center: Creative Drama.

TYPE OF CENTER:	**Creative Dramatics**	TIME:	10–15 minutes
GRADE LEVEL:	2–4	NUMBER OF STUDENTS:	3–5

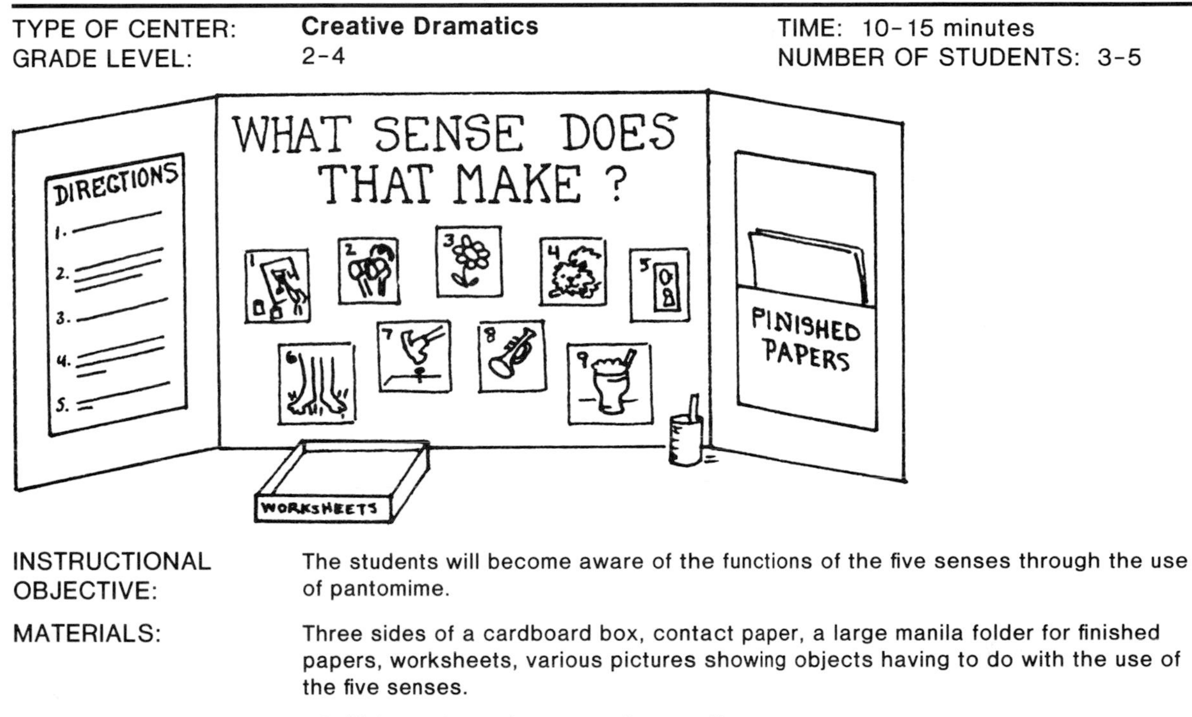

INSTRUCTIONAL OBJECTIVE: The students will become aware of the functions of the five senses through the use of pantomime.

MATERIALS: Three sides of a cardboard box, contact paper, a large manila folder for finished papers, worksheets, various pictures showing objects having to do with the use of the five senses.

DIRECTIONS:

1. Take a piece of paper and a pencil.
2. Look at the pictures on the center. Decide what you would do with the objects in the pictures if you had them, using the words *see, smell, taste, hear, touch.*
3. Write your answers on the worksheet.
4. Think how you could pantomime several of the items so the class could guess what you are doing. You may act them out when told to.
5. Put your finished paper in the *Finished Papers* folder.

SUGGESTED IDEAS: Pictures could include flowers, types of food, someone playing a musical instrument, someone hammering a nail, a keyhole, someone looking through a pair of binoculars, a furry animal, someone walking with bare feet on a green lawn or a thick rug, someone painting or drawing a picture, making a clay bowl, weaving a pattern, sewing. Every other day, change the pictures to add to the variety and interest the children.

EVALUATION: Look over the ideas given by the students on the worksheet. Set aside a period at a convenient time to permit students to dramatize a given item.

Source: From PATHWAYS TO IMAGINATION by Angela S. Reeke and James L. Laffey, © 1979 by Scott, Foresman and Company. Reprinted by permission.

Related Readings

Bolton, G. 1984. *Drama As Education.* New York: Longman.

Galda, J. 1983. "The Effect of Dramatic Play on the Story Retelling of Second Grade Children," *Journal of Instructional Psychology, 10,* pp. 200–206.

Griffing, P. 1983. "Encouraging Dramatic Play in Early Childhood," *Young Children, 38*(2), pp. 13–22.

Heathcote, D. 1983. "Learning, Knowing, and Languaging in Drama," *Language Arts, 60,* pp. 695–701.

Lehr, F. 1983. "Developing Language and Thought through Creative Drama," *Language Arts, 60,* pp. 385–389.

Manna, A. 1984. "Making Language Come Alive through Reading Plays," *Reading Teacher, 37,* pp. 712–717.

Miller, G., and Mason, G. 1983. "Dramatic Improvisation: Risk-Free Role Playing for Improving Reading Performance," *Reading Teacher, 37,* pp. 128–131.

Piggins, C. 1984. "Learning to Act, Acting to Learn," *Learning, 12*(7), pp. 54–56.

Siks, G. 1983. *Drama With Children.* Second edition. New York: Harper & Row.

Verriour, P. 1983. "Toward a Conscious Awareness of Language through Drama," *Language Arts, 60,* pp. 731–736.

Chapter Notes

1. California State Department of Education, *Drama/Theatre Framework for California Public Schools* (Sacramento: The Department, 1974), pp. 6–7.
2. E. C. Smith, "Drama and the Schools," *Elementary English,* 1972, *49,* p. 300.
3. *Children's Theatre Review,* 1981, *30*(2), p. 2.
4. M. Goldberg, *Children's Theatre: A Philosophy and a Method* (Englewood Cliffs, New Jersey: Prentice-Hall, Inc., 1974), pp. 127–135.
5. E. Hartshown and J. C. Brantley, "Effects of Dramatic Play on Classroom Problem-Solving Ability," *Journal of Educational Research,* 1973, *66,* pp. 243–46; E. C. Irwin, "The Effect of a Program of Creative Dramatics upon Personality as Measured by the California Test of Personality, Sociograms, Teacher Ratings, and Grades," *Dissertation Abstracts,* 1963, *24,* p. 2188; J. W. Stewig and L. Young, "An Exploration of the Relation Between Creative Drama and Language Growth," *Children's Theatre Review,* 1978, *27*(2), pp. 10–11; J. W. Stewig and J. A. McKee, "Drama and Language Growth: A Replication Study," *Children's Theatre Review,* 1980, *29*(3), pp. 10, 14; and L. Carlton and R. H. Moore, *Reading, Self-Directive Dramatization and Self-Concept* (Columbus, Ohio: Charles E. Merrill, 1968).
6. E. Gillies, *Creative Dramatics for All Children* (Washington, D.C.: Association for Childhood Education International, 1973), p. 48.
7. E. Littig, "Drama as an Important Classroom Tool," *Project Overview* (Northeast Wisconsin In-School Television Project, 1975).
8. N. McCaslin, *Creative Drama in the Classroom,* 3rd ed. (New York: Longman, Inc., 1980), pp. 11–17.
9. J. S. Youngers, "The Process and Potential of Creative Dramatics for Enhancing Linguistic and Cognitive Development," in *Research in the Language Arts,* V. Froese and S. B. Straw, eds. (Baltimore: University Park Press, 1981), pp. 97–100.
10. J. F. Christie, "Sociodramatic Play Training," *Young Children,* 1982, *37*(4), pp. 27–28; and S. Smilansky, *The Effects of Socio-Dramatic Play on Disadvantaged Preschool Children* (New York: John Wiley, 1968).

11. F. R. Shaftel and G. Shaftel, *Role Playing in the Curriculum,* 2nd ed. (Englewood Cliffs, New Jersey: Prentice-Hall, Inc., 1982), p. 89.
12. *Ibid.,* pp. 153–316.
13. Abridged from J. Strauss and R. DuFour, "Discovering Who I Am: A Humanities Course for Sixth Grade Students," *Elementary English,* 1970, *47,* pp. 100–103.
14. Gillies, *Creative Dramatics,* p. 19.
15. Adapted from J. W. Stewig, *Spontaneous Drama: A Language Art* (Columbus, Ohio: Charles E. Merrill, 1973), pp. 9–10.

Part D

Teaching English to Non-Native Speakers

Chapter
14 English as a Second Language

English as a Second Language 14

Objectives

General goals for learning English as a second language

Second language learning model patterned after Bloom's Taxonomy

Cognitive-developmental and social-affective strategies for ESL

Activities promoting ESL as a vehicle of real communication

Discover As You Read This Chapter If*

1. More than ten percent of all Americans come from non-English-speaking homes.
2. The basic concepts of non-English-speaking children are always and totally different from those of native speakers of English.
3. At any given time the limited-English-proficient students are at a higher level in external language skills than they are in the corresponding internal language skills.
4. Older ESL pupils need less instructional time in reading and writing than do younger ESL children.
5. The chief priority in teaching ESL reading should be comprehension.
6. Boys and girls acquire both their first and their second languages by learning how to carry on a conversation.
7. The most highly motivated ESL learners are those pupils who are most eager to identify with English speakers.
8. The English language skills of nonnatives do not develop in the same sequence and definite way as do those of native speakers.
9. Beginning ESL learners often go through a silent period which may last for several weeks or months.
10. Language learning is best promoted in a setting where language is used for genuine communication.

*Answers to these true-or-false statements may be found in Appendix 6.

Standard English is the language system that is habitually used, with some regional variations, by the majority of educated English-speaking persons in the United States. It is the level of language that facilitates communication in a highly complex and interdependent society. No wonder then that current language arts series not only emphasize standard English but even point out distinctions between the formal and informal varieties of standard English, as shown in Figure 14.1.

Figure 14.1. Exercises Using Standard English.

Part 1 Standard English

Standard English is language that most people understand easily. There are different kinds of standard English. Sometimes you need to choose your words very carefully. At other times, you can be more informal.

When To Choose Words Carefully

Suppose you have something special to say or to write. You must think about the language you use. Here is an example.

> You are asked to make an announcement about the school talent show at the PTA meeting. You say this:
>
> "On Wednesday evening, October 25, the boys and girls of Jefferson School will present their annual talent show. The program will be presented in the auditorium at 7:30 P.M. All parents, relatives, and friends are cordially invited to attend."

In this announcement, you are careful to make your thoughts clear. You use words in a way everyone will understand. You use complete sentences. This is formal standard English.

Here are some other special situations. In these situations, you will want to choose your words carefully.

1. You are giving a book report to your class.
2. You are writing a letter to your town newspaper.
3. You are applying for a job to mow lawns.

Can you think of other times when your words should be chosen carefully?

Yet according to the 1980 United States Census, 11 percent of all Americans come from non-English-speaking homes.[1] While they live in all 50 states, they comprise over 25 percent of the population in Hawaii and New Mexico and between 16 and 25 percent of the population of Arizona, California, Connecticut, Louisiana, Massachusetts, New Jersey, New York, North Dakota, Rhode Island, and Texas. Briefly, the non-English minority constitutes 10 percent or more of the total population in 23 states scattered all over the country, with the fastest

When To Speak Informally

Informal language is everyday talk. It is another kind of standard English.

Here is an example of informal language.

> You tell your cousin about the show. You say this:
>
> "Doing anything next Wednesday night? How about coming to my school talent show? It should be pretty good. Everyone's in it. It's in the auditorium at seven. Want to come?"

In the example above, your grammar is correct, but your language is informal. Although you leave out a few words, your friend understands you. You are speaking simply and naturally.

To speak or write in standard English, follow these guides:

Guides for Using Standard English

1. Use correct grammar.
2. Choose words that most people understand.
3. Fit your words to your situation.

Exercises Using Standard English

A. Suppose you meet the mayor of your town. You want to invite him or her to speak to your class. Write down three things you would say to the mayor. Write in standard English. Choose your words carefully.

B. Imagine that you are going to an amusement park. Invite a friend to go with you. Write down three things you might say to your friend. Write in standard English. Use informal language.

growing ethnic minority group being the Asians. Of these millions, an estimated 7.6 million are children enrolled in United States schools.[2]

The elementary school program must therefore provide a structured learning situation that will help all of its students become participating members of the classroom and the total community. An ESL or English as a Second Language program recognizes the following:

1. Children enter school with good control of the sound system and structure of their native language. While their language may not meet the accepted level of usage employed by the educated adults in their culture, it is practical and functional from the children's point of view in terms of communication needs in the home and community.
2. Non-English-speaking children bring to school a well-developed set of personal concepts that have grown out of their own experience. The teacher must not assume that the children lack an experiential base which can serve as a starting point for instruction. Nor should the teacher believe that their basic concepts are always and totally different from those of native speakers of English.
3. The range and distribution of intelligence in a group of non-English-speaking pupils are identical to those found in a similar group of English-speaking pupils. Although instruments that adequately measure potential do not seem to exist today, a creditable job of evaluating pupil performance can be done through individual interviews and through the judgment of trained personnel knowledgeable about both the children and their cultures.
4. Non-English-speaking children have the same human needs as their English-speaking classmates. Their psychological needs, for example, including a positive self-image, are as intense as those of children who speak English fluently.
5. While children are learning a second tongue, their thought processes will probably continue in their first language since that is the language in which they have learned to think and in which they feel comfortable. The first language may remain their preferred language for communication in many social situations even after the children have become fluent in standard English.

Such an ESL program incorporates four general goals for learning English as a second language. First, students must be able to carry on and understand a conversation with a native English speaker on topics of interest to persons of their peer group. Secondly, students must be able to read materials in English with comprehension, ease, and enjoyment, consistent with their level of oral proficiency. Thirdly, students must be able to write correctly, and in time creatively, in English consistent with their level of oral proficiency. And finally, students must recognize the differences between their own culture and that of their English-speaking peers, as expressed through the various arts.

Beginning ESL pupils should be encouraged by their teacher to speak English only after they have had numerous listening experiences. (Photo courtesy of the Fountain Valley School District, Fountain Valley, California.)

Guidelines for Instruction

Since teachers are ultimately accountable for all formal instruction that occurs in their classroom, their skill in working with the NEP (non-English-proficient) student or the LEP (limited-English-proficient) student will be related to their understanding of the types of conditions which help establish a strong language learning environment. Guidelines for assisting the NEPs or the LEPs in the elementary classroom are listed below:

1. Permit these children to speak only when they are ready. Otherwise, psychological blocks may develop which inhibit language learning. Some of these children may even experience a "silent period" for several weeks or even months during which they volunteer no language at all.
2. Be patient because it may take several months for some of these boys and girls to display any semblance of communication skill.
3. Accept the accents of the children in order to promote communication. Phonological changes will occur later during interaction with native English speakers.
4. Use resources already in the classroom/school. Manipulatives and readiness materials of many kinds usually found in K–1 rooms can be adapted for use in ESL in all grades.

5. Provide a model of the behavior you expect the children to attain by using gestures and other nonverbal means of communication.
6. Ask the boys and girls if they understand your directions. If they do not, try to reword the instructions or ask an English-speaking classmate to explain what is expected. Pupils often understand peers better than they do adults.
7. Smile genuinely to show the children that you are glad that they are enrolled in your classroom and that you want to help them learn.
8. Develop questions which require multiple-word answers and for which there is no one single correct response. This will prevent rote replies which are often meaningless during ordinary conversation or written communication.
9. Talk with the children in normal tones and on a variety of topics. They must be given many opportunities to converse in the classroom.
10. Explain the purpose of lessons to the children in their native language whenever you can. This aids comprehension and thereby facilitates achievement of the lesson goals.
11. Listen for meaning. Make every effort to interpret what these children are trying to communicate.
12. Separate production and competence. Provide considerable practice in using English with many different persons and in many different settings.
13. Encourage the children to take chances in trying out the English language. Do not correct their mistakes unless they themselves have reached the stage where they ask for such assistance.[3]

Second Language Learning Model

The model in Table 14.1 is patterned after the well-known Bloom's taxonomy and represents the cognitive aspects of second-language learning described at six levels. Each level builds on the skills and concepts acquired at previous levels, and the line of asterisks between levels three and four represents a threshold level of proficiency. Levels 1–3 cover survival language skills while levels 4–6 concern more academic language used for instructional purposes. Teachers must realize that, at any given time, the children are at a higher level in receptive skills (internal language skills) than they are in the corresponding productive or external language skills.

The language proficiency of levels 1–3 is the language of social communication or *context-embedded* communicative proficiency, which is crucial to a child's adjustment to a new culture and language.[4] It allows him or her to interact socially and affectively with others. Recent Canadian research has shown that most young children attain native-speaker ability in this type of language proficiency within two years of exposure to an English-speaking environment.[5] This may be due in part to the fact that the social context includes a variety of paralinguistic aids to comprehension (e.g., gestures, intonation, objects).

Levels 4–6 cover *context-reduced,* academic communicative proficiency, which is used in content subjects and on achievement tests. It is related to cognition and to the more formal language used to refer to concepts. Since it exists primarily in books (and oral lectures), children can attain understanding of the words and phrases only when they comprehend the concepts expressed. Most boys

Table 14.1.
Second Language Learning Model

Cognitive Domain Taxonomy	Linguistic Process	Internal Language Skills	External Language Skills
1 Knowledge	Recalling	Discrimination of and response to sounds, words, and unanalyzed chunks in listening. Identification of labels, letters, phrases in reading.	Production of single words and formulas; imitation of models. Handwriting, spelling, writing of known elements from dictation.
2 Comprehension	Recombining	Recognition of and response to new combinations of known words and phrases in listening and oral reading. Internal translation to and from L_1.	Emergence of interlanguage/telegraphic speech; code-switching and L_1 transfer. Writing from guidelines and recombination dictation.
3 Application	Communicating	———Social Interaction———	
		Understanding meaning of what is listened to in informal situations. Emergence of silent reading for basic comprehension.	Communication of meaning, feelings, and intentions in social and highly contextualized situations. Emergence of expository and creative writing.
• • •	• • •	• • •	• • •
4 Analysis	Informing	Acquisition of factual information from listening and reading in decontextualized situations.	Application of factual information acquired to formal, academic speaking and writing activities.
5 Synthesis	Generalizing	Use of information acquired through reading and listening to find relationships, make inferences, draw conclusions.	Explanation of relationships, inferences, and conclusions through formal speech and writing.
6 Evaluation	Judging	Evaluation of accuracy, value, and applicability of ideas acquired through reading and listening.	Expression of judgments through speech and writing. Use of rhetorical conventions.

Source: Reprinted from Anna Uhl Chamot, "Toward a Functional ESL Curriculum in the Elementary School," TESOL QUARTERLY, 1983, 17, p. 462, fig. 1. Used with permission of publisher and Anna Uhl Chamot.

and girls need five to seven years to reach a context-reduced level in English comparable to that of native-speaking peers. This gap may be shortened if more academic language skills are taught within the ESL curriculum.

Guidelines for a Functional ESL Curriculum

A functional ESL curriculum for elementary school children provides them with the language functions and notions needed in order for them to study school subjects in English.[6] Since it looks at language from a pragmatic rather than a descriptive viewpoint, such a curriculum represents a dramatic departure from the grammatical/structural approach to second language learning. *Functions* have been defined as objectives which can be attained through language (e.g., socializing, giving and receiving data). *Notions* have been divided into specific categories (e.g., relations with other people, personal identification) and general semantic categories (e.g., spatial, temporal). When notions are combined with functions, practical language goals are produced which focus on what language does rather than on how it works grammatically. Since a single language function can generally be expressed with more than one group of vocabulary items or more than one grammatical structure, it becomes possible to recycle each function throughout the second language curriculum with a widening group of vocabulary and structures.

Teachers planning a functional ESL curriculum must first become thoroughly familiar with the regular curriculum. Then they must compare the regular curriculum with the ESL one currently used. Third, non-English-proficient children must be assessed for their language and content achievement in their first language, while limited-English-proficient boys and girls must have both their first language and their English ability evaluated prior to entering the ESL program. Finally, teachers must allow for individualized instruction because the NEP and LEP students at all elementary levels will enter the program with substantially different background experiences and conceptual understandings.

In an effort to help teachers plan learning activities within a functional ESL curriculum, the following suggestions have proved useful:

1. Keep the realities of the regular classroom in mind when planning exercises which promote different language skills (e.g., older ESL pupils need more instructional time in reading and writing than do younger ESL children).
2. Initiate content area instruction in English in areas such as art, math, physical education, and music where little is demanded in reading and writing skills.
3. Remember that comprehension should be the chief priority in teaching ESL reading since a child's ability to pronounce a word is not nearly as important as his or her ability to recognize the meaning of that word in a written context.
4. Use concepts and vocabulary from content areas when developing ESL exercises at appropriate grade levels.
5. Encourage participation in small group discussions, in oral reports, and in responding to teacher questions because these types of speaking skills are necessary for completion of academic activities.
6. Assign simple expository writing rather than strictly creative writing because it is a more useful skill in the regular classroom.
7. Teach test wiseness because language-minority children often have great difficulty understanding directions for taking standardized tests and thereby suffer unnecessary penalties.[7]

Strategies and Second Language Learning

Recently 450 children's conversations which occurred in classroom or play activities across the United States were recorded from such diverse native-language groups as Italian, Spanish, Haitian, Chinese, Portuguese, and Japanese.[8] The conversations were then analyzed for strategies which were used often by children learning English as a second language, regardless of their first language.

Such strategies allow children to exploit available information to improve their own competence in the second language and also allow boys and girls to communicate in social situations. They can be divided into two major groups: cognitive-developmental and social-affective.

Cognitive-Developmental Strategies

The three described chronologically are *bridging, chunking,* and *creating.* In bridging, children tie English words to concepts which they already understand in their first language. Pictures, objects, and actions are important. The children go from perception to understanding to labeling, and they depend heavily upon the skills of the teacher to present words in meaningful contexts. The vocabulary must be organized into units and gradually expanded. All senses must be utilized in teaching vocabulary through such unit presentations as A Trip to the Zoo, Building a House, Buying New Shoes, or Going to the Restaurant. Learning games and activities, along with various word cards, are all helpful.

The second strategy, *chunking,* occurs when girls and boys imitate chunks of the second language. Such chunks consist of phrases or units of more than one word that are memorized as wholes rather than segments. They serve as a transition from labeling to sentence fluency and are best remembered when they have a special meaning for the child or can be directly related to experience. They are not learned in isolation but must be practiced in social interactions where they make sense. As girls and boys receive language input from their environment, they selectively imitate those chunks or phrases which have meaning for them and then proceed to use those chunks holistically again and again. Teachers are cautioned, however, not to plan drill/habit-formation lessons divorced from gamelike situations. Such sterile drills have little transfer value and cannot be ultimately integrated into sentence patterns promoting communicative fluency. Incidentally, among the first chunks of language mastered by second-language pupils are social greetings.

During *creating,* the final cognitive-developmental strategy, children are able to combine the words (acquired during bridging) and the phrases (learned during chunking) to express their ideas creatively. When girls and boys first begin to learn English as a second language, they do so without any comprehension of its underlying structure. Gradually, however, their syntactic development in English begins as they break down chunks and analyze them into component parts in order to build many new sentences.[9] Teachers must accept the fact that boys and girls acquire both their first and their second languages by learning how to carry on a conversation.[10] Classroom curricula must encourage children to become involved in as many highly specific language interactions as possible, with channeled conversations ranking as one of the best media for the development of the creative use of the second language. For that end, Ventriglia stresses that:

1. The perception of patterns should be emphasized and not the intensity of the practice.
2. The teacher should respond to what the children are saying rather than to the grammatical structures they use to say it.

3. The teacher should plan lessons involving language patterns in game-like settings and verbal play with partial repetitions of sentences and appropriate expansions of pupil sentences.
4. Above all, language should be integrated in all subject matter teaching and not be restricted to a 20-minute segment in the day. Only thus can the ESL pupils become creators.[11]

Social-Affective Strategies

There are nine strategies which children use naturally.[12] The first of these is a *receptive-expressive strategy,* which can be labeled *listening in and sounding out.* It involves listening comprehension and expressive fluency and is based on numerous research findings which indicate that the development of listening skills must precede, and not accompany, the development of speaking skills. Some of these studies have been done by James Asher utilizing the Total Physical Response approach, which requires that beginning students not respond verbally to commands in the second language but instead respond with appropriate physical actions.[13] It appears that delayed oral practice during the early stages of second-language learning can effectively develop both listening and speaking skills, provided there is a substantial period of active listening practice together with numerous physical responses.

Listening comprehension or "listening in" can be developed through the expressive arts, employing listening posts with headsets, and through the use of pictures and objects. The second or "sounding out" portion of this first strategy occurs when children engage in sound play as they chant in sing-song rhythms or make repetitive vocalizations. Both are important phases which allow children eventually to make associations from the sounds of words to the meanings of words, thereby promoting social interactions.

Follow the phrase or the *pattern-practice strategy* is the second social-affective strategy, and it is primarily concerned with the learning of the syntax of the second language. Word patterns are practiced and eventually varied by changing one or more words. Teachers, however, must provide many opportunities for the children to creatively experiment with the language already acquired, regardless of how limited it may be, so that pattern practice does not become mechanical and meaningless. When phrases are tied to a topic (e.g., Foods I Like) and practiced in game-like situations, teachers can utilize all four types of pattern drills (chain, question-answer, repetition, and substitution) effectively. Later, children are able to transfer meaningful patterns to new social contexts.

Socializing, the third and *formal-informal style social relations strategy* in this group, represents a process by which girls and boys acquire social expressions holistically as chunks. They hear the expressions during various communication contexts (e.g., structured sports activities, games, small group discussions), imitate them, and finally apply them to other appropriate social settings. Since language learned during interaction is always modified by the immediate situation, socializing must be considered an accomodating strategy. Essential to the development of a second language are the following social relations' components: social interaction; the establishment and maintenance of relationships/friendships by using social formulas; the acquisition of formal and information language styles; receiving feedback from teachers and peers; and possessing social skills which further language learning. Teachers must use both controlled exercises and decontrolled activities in order to help boys and girls acquire language naturally.

When children use gestural (involving sensory-motor actions), visual, or interpersonal cues for linguistic problem solving, they are pursuing an *inference-guessing strategy* labelled *cueing*. They are anxious to derive meaning from verbal input and rely on more proficient language speakers to give them cues. Since their desire to communicate is strong, they actively seek to interpret cues to better decode the meaning of language and eventually participate fully in the speech arena. Major functions of the teacher's cueing are to promote dialog and demonstrate meaning. Advantages of cueing the second-language learner in classroom situations include the following: students are prompted to infer meanings and respond correctly; they are encouraged to participate actively (not passively); student attention is carefully directed; and boys and girls are given corrective feedback and compelled to understand exactly structures and vocabulary that often may go unnoticed.

An *imitative-repetitive strategy* known as *peer prompting* enables children to acquire the second language through modeling and feedback. Boys and girls learn from each other and are able to acquire language from both patterned and spontaneous encounters that demand verbal exchanges. Peer pairs can consist of one dominant or proficient English-speaking child who serves as a model and one child with only limited expressive ability in the language. Often the last-described pupil acquires a friend along with increased English vocabulary and grammatical structures during play interactions or even during subject-matter activities. The peer model uses repetition in an effort to encourage the LEP child to imitate correct speech. This kind of buddy system is a flexible approach demanding only the interaction of two children who become involved in language on personal, emotional, and academic levels.

The sixth social-affective strategy encourages switching to the language which the listener knows best so that he/she can convey cultural meaning to others, and it is termed *wearing two hats*. It is a *bilingual-bicultural strategy* and is most successful with children who have internalized the following aspects of both languages: a sense of personal identity with each language; social situational meanings upon which effective communication is based and code-switching employed; cultural beliefs, attitudes, and values; emotional and psychological factors since language enforces and reinforces behavior; and linguistic flexibility which is an enriching dimension. Because language and culture cannot be separated, the strategy of *wearing two hats* is best developed in a multidimensional setting of bilingual-bicultural education.

When second-language learning occurs through a *role-playing strategy,* it can be termed *copycatting.* It involves dramatic dialogues in the classroom both as free imaginative role-play and structured role-play activities. Boys and girls imitate language and also learn to use their hands, faces, and bodies to portray emotions. They become able to integrate English expression into a complete system of communication and conversational competency. They develop empathy and problem-solving skills because role-playing concentrates language around student attitudes, interests, concerns, and feelings. Further opportunities for practicing the second language evolve creatively.

The eighth social-affective strategy bridges motivational, social, and cognitive predispositions into several styles of second-language learning and is termed *putting it together.* Children learn language by different routes/processes/styles, of which three have been labeled *beading, braiding,* and *orchestrating.* The first frames language in terms of semantics or word meanings and strings words one after another, focusing attention on content rather than form. The second frames language around syntax or language patterns and chunks words together into phrases so that attention is paid to form and the sequence of words. Orchestrating is occupied with phonology or the sounds of the language, placing initial emphasis on listening comprehension and concentrating on sounds first by syllables, then as words, and then as sentences.

As teachers begin to recognize the beaders, braiders, and orchestrators within any one classroom, they must plan group lessons accordingly. Beaders require highly structured lessons which do not contain too many concepts at once. Braiders prefer social interaction and function best in a fairly open-ended environment. And since orchestrators stress auditory input, they enjoy songs and other rhythmic poems/chants and are continually imitating the teacher's language behavior. Since the goal of the ESL program is to permit boys and girls to learn English in the style that is most suitable to them, the teacher must be familiar with the major learning styles in order to define the learners and gain new insight into instructional planning.

The final and ninth affective strategy, known as *choosing the way,* describes children's three motivational styles in acquiring a second language. When boys and girls lack the desire to identify with English speakers, they also lack the motivation to learn the English language. Conversely, those who have a strong desire to identify with English speakers also possess a strong motivation to acquire the language. Since the primary model of the second language and culture is the teacher, it is important that the teacher's relationship with the students be a strong, positive, and sensitive one.

In their effort to resolve a psychosocial identity crisis, minority children can adopt any one of three different *motivational styles* that reflect the owner's preferred way of participating in second-language acquisition. The first is called *crystalizing* and includes boys and girls who initially reject the second language because they want to maintain their identity with their first language culture.

They crystalize their native language identity and refuse to participate in any interaction which would lead to learning the new language/culture. They also refuse to speak English until they are able to do so perfectly. As passive second-language learners, they are highly dependent on structured classroom activities and communicate with the teacher in English only when prodded to do so. Basically they are shy children who are cautious learners, stressing the receptive, not expressive, understanding of the English language. Only as a final step do they express themselves socially in the second language.

On the other hand, children who use the *crossing over* motivational style choose to identify with the second culture rather than their first culture, even to the extent of giving up speaking in their first language in the classroom. They interact with English speakers and capitalize on every opportunity to practice the new language both in and out of school. They admire English speakers and are anxious to identify with them, believing that immersion in the second language is the quickest method for developing proficiency. They are active language learners, flexible, impulsive, and independent.

The third motivational style, *crisscrossing,* applies to children who identify equally with both cultures and readily adapt languages to the situations which occur. They switch back and forth between languages and cultures, adopting a bicultural identity. They are versatile, spontaneous, and adaptable, adjusting communication patterns comfortably. They are able to socialize between groups of English speakers and native language speakers.

Although no one motivational style is better than another, the teacher must comprehend how children differ in their approaches to learning English as a second language. Since he or she represents the role model of the second language/culture, the more the boys and girls can identify positively with their teacher and their English-speaking classmates, the more easily they will adjust to the English language and culture. The teacher must make every effort to match instructional strategies with children's motivational styles: indirect methods for Crystalizers; integration of English into the total school program for Crossovers; and additive bilingualism for Crisscrossers.

Through individualization in ESL instruction, teachers can employ learning centers or other classroom arrangements which allow students to learn English easily and confidently.

Stages in the Acquisition of English Language Skills

Teachers concerned with mainstreaming NEP and LEP children into the regular classroom may wish to use the Student Oral Language Observation Matrix, shown in Figure 14.2, which must of course be administered individually. Others whose ESL students are strictly native Spanish speakers may also employ the Oral Language Rating Scale shown in Figure 14.3 when planning English lessons for those children.

Figure 14.2. Student Oral Language Observation Matrix for English Proficiency.

Teacher Observation
Student Oral Language Observation Matrix
(SOLOM)

Student's Name ______________ Grade ________ Signature ______________
Language Observed ______________ Date ______________

	1	2	3	4	5
A. COMPREHENSION	Cannot be said to understand even simple conversation.	Has great difficulty following what is said. Can comprehend only "social conversation" spoken slowly and with frequent repetitions.	Understands most of what is said at slower-than-normal speed with repetitions.	Understands nearly everything at normal speech, although occasional repetition may be necessary.	Understands everyday conversation and normal classroom discussions without difficulty.
B. FLUENCY	Speech is so halting and fragmentary as to make conversation virtually impossible.	Usually hesitant; often forced into silence by language limitations.	Speech in everyday conversation and classroom discussion is frequently disrupted by the student's search for the correct manner of expression.	Speech in everyday conversation and classroom discussions is generally fluent, with occasional lapses while the student searches for the correct manner of expression.	Speech in everyday conversation and classroom discussions is fluent and effortless approximating that of a native speaker.
C. VOCABULARY	Vocabulary limitations so extreme as to make conversation virtually impossible.	Misuse of words and very limited vocabulary make comprehension quite difficult.	Frequently uses the wrong words; conversation somewhat limited because of inadequate vocabulary.	Occasionally uses inappropriate terms and/or must rephrase ideas because of lexical inadequacies.	Use of vocabulary and idioms approximates that of a native speaker.
D. PRONUNCIATION	Pronunciation problems so severe as to make speech virtually unintelligible.	Very hard to understand because of pronunciation problems. Must frequently repeat in order to make himself understood.	Pronunciation problems necessitate concentration on the part of the listener and occasionally lead to misunderstanding.	Always intelligible, though one is conscious of a definite accent and occasional inappropriate intonation patterns.	Pronunciation and intonation approximates that of a native speaker.
E. GRAMMAR	Errors in grammar and word-order so severe as to make speech virtually unintelligible.	Grammar and word-order errors make comprehension difficult. Must often rephrase and/or restrict himself to basic patterns.	Makes frequent errors of grammar and word-order which occasionally obscure meaning.	Occasionally makes grammatical and/or word-order errors which do not obscure meaning.	Grammatical usage and word-order approximates that of a native speaker.

The student oral language matrix has five categories on the left: A. Comprehension, B. Fluency, C. Vocabulary, D. Pronunciation, E. Grammar, and five numbers on the top—1 being the lowest mark to 5, being the highest.

According to your observation, indicate with an X across the square in each category which best describes the child's abilities. Those students whose (X) check marks are to the right of the darkened line will be considered for reclassification to FES, if test scores and achievement data also indicate English proficiency.

Source: Beverly Hills (CA.) Unified School District, ENGLISH AS A SECOND LANGUAGE (ESL) GUIDELINES, September 1, 1981

Figure 14.3. Oral Language Rating Scale Indicating Areas of Interference and Difficulty for Spanish-Speaking ESL Pupils.

Oral Language Rating **Spanish Interference**	**5**	**4**	**3**	**2**	**1**	**0**
School ______ **Date** ______ **Name** ______ **Grade** ______ **Teacher** ______	**Never**	**Almost Never**	**Some-times**	**Usually**	**Almost Always**	**Always**
Pronunciation (Sounds): Distinguishes between vowel sounds such as *sheep-ship, cut-cat, cut-cot, pool-pull,* and between consonant sounds as *sink-zinc, vote-boat, sink-think, yellow-jello, cheap-jeep.*	____	____	____	____	____	____
Pronunciation (Clusters): Pronounces initial consonant clusters as in *school, speak, study,* and final consonant clusters as in *land, fast, old, box, act, desk, pulled, touched.*	____	____	____	____	____	____
Pronunciation (Suprasegmentals): Pronounces sentences with appropriate rhythm, stress, pause, and pitch.	____	____	____	____	____	____
Pronouns: Uses appropriate pronoun forms in subject position (*I, he, she,* etc.), in object position (*me, him, her,* etc.) and possessives (*my, mine; her, hers;* etc.).	____	____	____	____	____	____
Negative: Uses *not* to express the negative after forms of *be* (*Bill is not here.*) and between auxiliary and verb in other sequences (*Bill was not talking. Bill did not talk.*). Uses singular rather than double negative.	____	____	____	____	____	____
Noun Modifier: Uses adjectives appropriately, as in *the big dog* as opposed to *the dog big* and *Is the dog big?* as opposed to *Is big the dog?*.	____	____	____	____	____	____
Comparison: Uses the correct form of comparison such as *bigger, biggest, more beautiful, most beautiful,* rather than *more bigger, beautifuller.*	____	____	____	____	____	____
Present Tense: Uses the appropriate present forms of regular verbs, with subject-verb agreement when *he* or *she* is used as subject, as in *He walks,* rather than *He walk.*	____	____	____	____	____	____
Plurals: Distinguishes between singular and plural in regular forms such as *dog-dogs, boot-boots, horse-horses,* and in irregular forms such as *foot-feet, knife-knives.*	____	____	____	____	____	____
Past and Perfect Tenses: Uses the past forms of regular verbs as in *walk-walked, glue-glued, land-landed,* and of irregular verbs as in *go-went-gone, dig-dug, cut-cut.*	____	____	____	____	____	____
Uses of Be: Uses appropriate forms of *be* as an auxiliary and as a verb.	____	____	____	____	____	____
Uses of Do: Uses appropriate forms of *do* in questions, answers, and in negative statements.	____	____	____	____	____	____
Future Tense: Uses the appropriate future forms of regular verbs as in *run-will run.*	____	____	____	____	____	____
Possessive: Uses appropriate possessive forms as in *John's wagon.*	____	____	____	____	____	____

Source: *Michigan Oral Language Series* (New York: ACTFL, 1970).

Furthermore, they should keep in mind the most frequent errors of Spanish speakers learning English, according to recent taped conversations of 150 students in grades K–6 in the Denver Public Schools.[14] The two most common errors were the omission of the final *d* and the substitution of *d* for *ŏ*. Other frequent mistakes involved the use of the present for the past tense, the omission of articles, the improper subject/verb number, the omission of prepositions, improper pronouns, improper formation of the present participle, the omission of a coordinate conjunction, and the omission of the final *t* or *l*.

It has been recognized for some time that English language skills of nonnatives develop in much the same sequential and definite way as do those of native speakers. These stages are shown in Figure 14.4, the Cardona Oral Language Index.

Figure 14.4. Cardoza Oral Language Index: States in the Acquisition of English.*

Acquisition of Syntax	Acquisition of Semantic Structures
Stage 1 1. Yes/no answers 2. Positive statements 3. Subject pronouns: *he, she,* etc. 4. Present habitual verb tense 5. Possessive pronouns; *my, your,* etc.	1. Sentences with 1 part: agent or object or locative (attribute + noun = 1 part) 2. Sentences with 2 parts agent + action or + object or + locative action + object or + locative
Stage 2 1. Simple plurals of nouns 2. Affirmative sentences 3. Subject and object pronouns (all) 4. Possessives: *'s* 5. Negation 6. Possessive pronouns: *mine,* etc.	1. Substitution of pronouns for nouns 2. Fragmentary grammar 3. Beginning regularization of sentence order 4. Sentence with 3+ parts: agent + *to* action/infinitive/ + object, or action + agent + object or locative, or agent + object + action or locative
Stage 3 1. Present progressive tense 2. Conjunctions: *and, but, or, because, so, as,* etc.	1. Regularized sentence order 2. Conjoining with *and,* using deletions 3. Addition of modifiers: agent + (modifier) action + object or locative
Stage 4 1. Questions: *who? what? which? where?* 2. Irregular plurals of nouns 3. Simple future tense: *going to.* 4. Prepositions	1. Sentence with 4 parts: agent + action + 2 other parts, selected from additional agent, agent modifier, action modifier, 1-2 objects, object modifier, locative

Figure 14.4 (cont.)

Acquisition of Syntax	Acquisition of Semantic Structures
Initial reading readiness	
Stage 5	
1. Future tense: *will* 2. Questions: *when? how?* 3. Conjunctions: *either, nor, neither, that, since,* etc.	1. Sentence with 5+ parts agent + action + 3 other parts, additional agent, agent in additional action, 1-2 objects, object modifier, locative
Stage 6	
1. Regular past tense verbs 2. Question: *why?* 3. Contractions: *isn't,* etc. 4. Modal verbs: *can, must,* etc., and *do*	1. Permutations in word order 2. Substitution of phrases and sentence parts
Stage 7	
1. Verb tense: irregular past 2. Past tense questions 3. Auxiliary verbs: *has, is* 4. Passive voice	
Stage 8	
1. Verbs: conditional 2. Summary of verb forms 3. Verb tense: the imperfect 4. Conjunctions: *though, if, therefore,* etc. 5. Verb mood: subjunctive	

*Adapted from Cardona, 1980

Source: Reprinted from Phillip C. Gonzales "Beginning English Reading for ESL Students," READING TEACHER, November 1981. Reprinted with permission of Phillip C. Gonzales and the International Reading Association.

This Index has been used well by teachers of English-Spanish bilingual children in the Pacific Northwest to assess the stage of productive English language skill of each nonnative student as well as to evaluate the language demands of first-grade basals used for beginning English reading.[15]

Prior to Stage 1 a child may well exhibit a "silent period" until he/she becomes comfortable with the English-speaking environment. During the first stage most commonly heard are one- and two-word utterances (usually consisting of nouns, verbs, or a combination of the two) which cover a multitude of situations and allow the speaker to appear to comprehend what is going on at any given time. Sample utterances would include "yes," "no," and "my turn." Egocentric speech also occurs as do overextensions and overgeneralizations of meanings.

During Stages 2 and 3 there is frequent mixing of English and native language. The concern appears to be communication by any means possible. Children use more readily recognized language and sentence structure.

During each of the subsequent stages boys and girls incorporate additional sentence parts (such as modifiers or objects) into the basic sentence utterances. Each such addition indicates an increase in the acquisition of complex language; e.g., the use of prepositional phrases during Stage 4 and the use of conjunctions during Stage 5.

By the conclusion of Stage 5, the children have a language which is related to initial reading readiness. They are then capable of making judgments concerned with correctness of form and may even ask for adult approval regarding such "correctness." They understand several hundred words and have refined both their lexical knowledge and use through actual language practice in numerous situations.

During the final stages—6, 7, and 8—boys and girls begin to experiment with changes in the order of parts of sentences and also start to substitute phrases and clauses for the main portions of sentences. They can use language well for purposes of problem solving or hypothesis testing.

Using the Oral Language Index

The teacher can determine the language proficiency of any nonnative child by tape-recording samples of spontaneous, informal speech which occur during nonthreatening situations between student and teacher evaluator. The language samples are first examined for grammatical forms and their location in the Index; e.g., "Why does it rain?" relates to Stage 6 and "why" questions.

Then the same samples are examined for types of grammatical structures by identifying and counting major sentence parts. Also at this point they are checked to see if the samples follow the common English order: subject, action, object or locative.

Such analysis of a child's conversational language easily reveals the boy's or girl's command and use of different syntax structures and form. It helps the teacher locate reading materials with syntax at (or not too far above) that of the student's listening and speaking abilities. Obviously this is significant during the beginning stages of English reading.

Consequently, a second use of the Oral Language Index occurs during an examination of the linguistic demands made by various first-grade basals. If too great a discrepancy exists between the language used in a particular text and the actual language proficiency of the young reader, the teacher must plan special lessons stressing language structures and grammatical forms found in that chosen text. If, however, a better match occurs between the language used by the beginning reader and that printed in the book, the teacher may then plan more lessons in comprehension and word attack skills.

A third and final use of the Oral Language Index takes place when the teacher initially examines the text for linguistic structures that have proven difficult for many ESL speakers and then proceeds to plan lessons around those structures and forms in an effort to aid comprehension and promote reading enjoyment. It has been suggested that, in this instance, direct and concrete hands-on experiences might be best, especially if they use language which is both appropriate to the situation and readily understood by the ESL students.[16] Role-playing and the employment of visuals are both effective. Another suggestion calls upon the teacher to simplify the language found in the basal to structures already familiar to the nonnative pupil, e.g., writing several simple sentences on the chalkboard based on one lengthy compound sentence.

Briefly, then, an efficient ESL teacher about to introduce reading to the class will first assess the language proficiency of the children, then evaluate the structures found in the assigned books, and finally plan lessons so that both the NEP and the LEP pupils will comprehend the language used in the reading books.

Instructional Activities

Activity-centered classrooms promote language learning in a setting where the language is not an object of study but a vehicle of real communication.[17] Repetition occurs often and naturally as the learners interact with the teacher and with their peers in real situations. The newly-discovered English language becomes a tool for cognitive growth, thereby promoting the learning of additional vocabulary and structures.

Other advantages of such classrooms include a nonthreatening atmosphere which allows physical movement during the lessons and support for self-concept development in areas such as problem solving and decision making. The interaction with their classmates gives children immediate feedback on their language performance or product at an impersonal level directed at the information presented. The motivation to communicate is strong, and students assume some degree of responsibility for their own progress.

Activities may be divided into in-school and out-of-school categories, with the former including (1) events which commonly take place during the school year such as science fairs, (2) academic themes including an art unit on colors and a science unit on birds, and (3) development of personal skills through sewing projects and cooking.[18] Out-of-school activities involve field trips and the celebrations of regional festivities.

Specific classroom activities planned for individualized instruction have been outlined by Rodrigues and White and are described in this section according to their levels of difficulty.[19] Each can of course be readily adapted to small-group or even large-group sessions.

Beginning-Level activities include:

Rhyming. The purpose is to give the child a chance to recall as many English words as possible which rhyme with words the teacher uses (e.g., *map, run, say, ant, wing*). The teacher says one of the words, and the pupil offers as many rhyming words as possible. Or the teacher says three words which are alike but of which only two rhyme, and the student must choose the word that does not rhyme. Sometimes the teacher begins a couplet with a line which ends with a word to be rhymed, and the pupil must respond accordingly with the next line. (This is strictly a listening/speaking exercise).

Acting Out Emotions. The teacher prepares flashcards containing English words stating emotions (e.g., *afraid, happy, sad, angry, excited*). The teacher displays one flashcard at a time to the student and acts out the emotion. Then the pupil holds each card and acts out the appropriate emotion. Later, three flashcards are shown simultaneously to the student, and he/she must point to and pronounce the word for the one emotion the teacher is acting out.

Vocabulary Around the House. The teacher collects pictures of rooms in various houses and shows them one at a time to the student. The pupil must name all the objects that he/she can identify in the pictures and also relate how each is used. The teacher then reviews the pictures and names any objects which the student has missed, asking the boy or girl to repeat the names of the objects originally omitted. Later, the student may draw a map of the objects in his or her own bedroom, living room, or kitchen.

Beginning- to Intermediate-Level activities include:

Using a Telephone. The teacher reviews with the student the following terms: *ring* or *ringing, telephone, dial tone, busy signal, information, area code, operator, receiver, telephone number.* If the boy or girl is unfamiliar with any of the terms, the teacher should draw a picture or demonstrate using sounds and gestures. Finally, the teacher and the pupil role-play the following situations:

—— The teacher calls the student to give a message.
—— The student calls and gets a busy signal.
—— The student dials the operator for assistance in reporting a fire.
—— The student places a local call at a pay telephone.
—— The student calls the teacher to give a message.

Asking Directions in a New Town. The teacher supplies a map of the local city (or any other city) and reviews with the student the following key terms: *left, right, street, avenue, sign, stop, straight, turn, traffic light.* Common expressions of courtesy are also reviewed. The teacher and the student take turns pretending to be a newcomer in town and the police official/other information provider. The map may be used to answer such model questions as: Where is the ____ ? How do I get to the ____ ? First responses must be brief, but later ones may become more complex.

Giving Dictation to the Teacher. The purpose is to give the child a chance to discuss in English a topic mutually agreed upon by teacher and student. The child dictates to the teacher-secretary who spells and punctuates all sentences properly but is careful to write down exactly what has been said. Later, the two go over the composition, and the student is encouraged to correct or improve the language. Possible topics for dictation include favorite television shows, hobbies, and ways that the child's native land differs from that of the teacher.

Taking Dictation from the Teacher. The teacher selects a book which is apt to interest the student and meet his or her ability level. As the teacher slowly reads aloud short selections from the book, the student must write down the passages. A second reading aloud by the teacher of the same selections is done at a normal rate of speed so that the boy or girl may check the dictation. A third reading is done by the student alone from the handwritten copy. The fourth and final reading is done by teacher and student working together from the student copy and noting any mistakes. Incidentally, during all the readings the punctuation marks are read aloud also (e.g., Hello comma how are you question mark).

Intermediate-Level activities include:

Visiting a Library. The purpose is to give the child a chance to visit the library media center and learn how to locate and check out a book. Upon arrival at the center, the teacher introduces the child to the following terms: *librarian, library, card catalog, check-out desk, stacks, media center, reference section, library card.* The teacher also introduces the following model questions: (a) How do I find a book about ____ ? (b) Where is the card catalog? (c) When is this book due? The visit culminates with the student locating and checking out a book selected earlier by the teacher because it would especially interest that child.

Table Manners. The teacher places in front of the boy or girl all of the following items: tablespoon, teaspoon, knife, dinner fork, salad fork, cup and saucer, dinner plate, bread plate, salt shaker. The teacher picks up one item at a time, names it, and asks the student to repeat the name. Then the teacher demonstrates how Americans eat at the table and discusses with the student such matters as the proper way to hold a fork, the polite way to ask for salt or butter or any other food on the table, and the correct way to cut a piece of meat and eat it. The teacher and student should practice their table manners as often as it seems necessary.

Learning Games

The games described in this section are a viable and enjoyable method of attaining a variety of educational objectives.[20] They can *reinforce* newly acquired information, *review* material presented days or even weeks ago, *relax students* after grueling oral or written exercises, *raise attentiveness, aid retention, reward* students, *reduce inhibition* among shy or linguistically weak pupils, and provide the teacher with a method of *rapidly rectifying students' errors.* Although they provide motivation for learning, these games do not entail excessive preparation. The pictures, flashcards, or objects/materials which some of the games require are the kinds of resources routinely found in elementary ESL classrooms.

Auction

1. Objects are placed on the "auction" table in front of the room, with one item secretly tagged by the teacher, who is the first "auctioneer." All the players come to the auction with an equal amount of play money.
2. The auctioneer describes each item on the table as it comes up for auction, and each interested player is allowed to shout a bid only when he or she has been recognized by the auctioneer.
3. A fixed number of bids should be agreed upon in advance, and the player winning the bid then walks up to the auctioneer to collect his or her purchase.
4. The player purchasing the secret item becomes the next auctioneer.

5. Suggestions: (a) The auctioneer should be garrulous. (b) Objects for sale may be brought from home or constructed in the classroom. (c) The player with the most purchases may be designated as the "big spender."

Baseball

1. The teacher selects one umpire, one scorekeeper, and two teams; and provides large picture cards or sentence cards.
2. After each team has chosen its own catcher and pitcher, the pitcher of Team A flashes a card to the catcher of Team A and to the first batter of Team B, both of whom are standing at home plate.
3. If the catcher answers first and correctly by identifying the picture or reading the card, there is a strike against the batter. If the catcher and batter answer simultaneously, the umpire calls it a foul ball. If the batter answers first and correctly, he or she advances to first base and the next player on Team B comes to bat. When the batter has three strikes, he or she is out and the next player on Team B is up.
4. Players advance one base at a time, runs are scored, three outs constitute a change of teams' position, and the team with the greater number of runs in the designated time wins Baseball.
5. Suggestion: For simpler scoring among younger children, one strike constitutes an out.

Book Bag Relay

1. Each row receives an empty book bag, school bag or bike bag that is placed on the desk or table of the first player.
2. Each player in turn takes the bag and puts into it one school article which he or she can identify properly (e.g., "This is my spelling book.")
3. Though each player in one row must insert a different item from his or her table or desk and must identify it properly (for duplication of items within one row is not permitted) a player may insert more than one of any specified item (e.g., three pencils, two pens) into the book bag.
4. The first row to have the greatest number of items correctly identified within a specified time wins Book Bag Relay.

Buried Treasure

1. "Buried treasure" (objects or pictures) is placed into a large box in front of the room, and teams are chosen.
2. One player at a time from each team walks to the box and draws out a buried treasure. If the player can identify or describe the treasure correctly, his or her team retains it. If the player fails, he or she must return the treasure to the box.
3. Each team continues to choose and identify items until one of its players misses. The team with the most treasures when time is called wins Buried Treasure.

Eraser Relay

1. Each row, consisting of the same number of players, receives an eraser that is placed on the desk or table of the first player.
2. The teacher asks the first player of the first row a question (e.g., "What day is this?"). If the player can answer it successfully, he or she passes the eraser

down the row to the next player. If any player in the row fails to answer, he or she retains the eraser. The teacher then proceeds with the second row of players, questioning each briefly until one player is unable to respond or responds incorrectly.

3. The row that first passes its eraser down to its last player wins Eraser Relay.
4. Variation: For less advanced classes, the teacher reads some questions aloud and each player in turn responds "Yes" or "No" followed by a short sentence to indicate reasonable comprehension.

Hot Potato

1. The teacher is "It" first. While the teacher turns his or her back to the class, the players pass a small rubber ball quickly around the circle or up and down the rows as if it were a "hot potato."
2. As each player receives the ball, he or she must say, "I have the ball" before passing it on.
3. Each time "It" turns around and calls, "Stop," the player holding the hot potato must come up and stand in front of the room. Then the game continues until each player has passed the ball at least once.
4. "It" must then issue simple penalties (e.g., "Count from 20 to 30," "Draw a cat on the board," or "Give the names of three vegetables") to all players who are standing in front of the room.
5. Suggestion: A baseball, tennis ball, or football may be used to stimulate interest during different seasons of the year.

Knock, Knock

1. The teacher must provide an assortment of paper masks or a collection of paper hats.
2. All the players close their eyes, and the teacher quietly taps one player to be "It." "It" dons one of the masks or hats to assume a different identity.
3. "It" now hides under the teacher's desk or behind a screen. When "It" begins to "knock, knock" on the floor, the other players open their eyes and demand, "Who is there?"
4. "It" answers, "Guess if you can," and begins to describe his or her new identity (e.g., fire fighter, cowboy).
5. The first player to identify "It" correctly becomes "It" for the next round.
6. Suggestions: (a) Players may construct simple masks or hats during an art period. (b) Whenever possible, with older children, masks of famous national heroes of the United States or the native lands of the ESL players may be used.

Look at Me

1. The teacher selects a timekeeper, and space is cleared for "It" to perform.
2. The player chosen as "It" mimes an action, and the other players, either individually or chorally, offer guesses as to what "It" is doing (e.g., "You are drinking water" or "You are washing your hands").
3. The first player to identify the action correctly becomes "It" for the next round. When there has been a choral response, "It" selects his or her own successor.

4. The player chosen as "It" who can puzzle the class the longest with a pantomime wins Look at Me.
5. Suggestions: This game is especially appropriate when the children have been overactive.

Red Ball

1. The teacher chooses a player to be "It" and allows "It" to hide the "red ball" somewhere in the room while the other players close their eyes.
2. Once the red ball has been hidden, all eyes are opened and each player is allowed one guess as to the location of the ball; for example, "The ball is by the door."
3. If a player's identifying statement is correct, he or she is permitted to look for the red ball in that place.
4. The first player to find the ball is "It" during the next round.
5. Suggestion: Instead of using the relatively large red playground ball, the teacher may prefer to paint a golf ball red or substitute a red tennis ball since a small ball is easier to hide.

Robber, Robber

1. The teacher places large pictures on the chalk tray, and chooses one player to be "It."
2. While the other players close their eyes, "It" removes one of the pictures and places it facedown on the teacher's desk.
3. All eyes are opened, and the class shouts, "Robber, Robber, what do you have?"
4. Then, each player is allowed one chance to identify correctly the missing picture, using a complete sentence, and the first player to do so successfully becomes "It" for the next round.
5. Variations: (a) "It" is permitted to rearrange the pictures each time; (b) Instead of using pictures, the teacher places objects on a table where everyone can see them, and "It" must remove one of the objects.

Show Me

1. Large pictures are placed on the chalk tray in front of the room or on the bulletin board. Two teams are chosen, and a scorekeeper is selected.
2. The first player on Team A asks the first player on Team B, "Show me a duck," and the first player on Team B must walk up and point to the correct picture and identify it (e.g., "This is a duck"). Then the second player on Team B asks the second player on Team A, "Show me. . . ."
3. The scorekeeper allows one point for each command that is properly issued, and one point for each correct identification. The team with the greater number of points wins the Show Me game.
4. Variation: The game may be called Draw Me if sufficient chalkboard space is available and the students are talented.

Super Chair

1. The players sit in a semicircle, with the teacher seated at one end on a "super chair" (high stool). A timekeeper stands nearby.
2. While holding up picture or sentence cards, one at a time, the teacher calls on a player in the semicircle to identify the item(s) shown, using a complete

sentence, or read the card. If the player succeeds, all the players remain in their own seats. If the player fails, he or she moves to the end of the line and the other players move up clockwise.

3. The teacher is soon replaced by the player who formerly sat at his or her right but who now has succeeded to the Super Chair and must continue the game.
4. The player who remains longest in the Super Chair is declared the winner.

Three Chances

1. After one player leaves the room, the teacher selects another player to be "It" and describes "It" softly to the class (e.g., "He has brown hair, blue eyes, and wears a red shirt").
2. The outsider now returns to the room and must guess which player is "It" by asking three questions (e.g., "Is it a boy?"; "Is he tall?"; "Is he wearing a sweater?"). The class answers chorally "Yes" or "No."
3. Then, the outsider has Three Chances to identify "It." If the outsider is successful, he or she may select the next player to leave the room. Should the outsider fail, the player who has been "It" becomes the next outsider.
4. Suggestion: In the primary grades, the outsider is told, before beginning his or her questioning, the row or part of the room in which "It" is seated.

Triple Play

1. Three teams are chosen, a scorekeeper is selected, and everyone stands.
2. The teacher holds a stack of large pictures or large sentence cards which can be readily seen about halfway across the room. The first players on all three teams try simultaneously to identify the picture (using a complete sentence) or read the card which the teacher flashes to them.
3. The first player to succeed scores one point for his or her team and the game continues with the next trio of players. In case of a tie identification or reading during the "triple play," the teacher puts the cards back into the pile, and the next trio steps up.
4. The team with the most points after a specified period of time wins Triple Play.
5. Suggestion: If the class is small or if the game is played for a long time, a Most Valuable Player can be chosen.

Evaluation of Pupils' and Teachers' Progress

Elementary teachers who are responsible for classroom ESL programs, and the paraprofessionals who in some districts assist the teachers, may use self-evaluation sheets. They may also periodically employ individual checklists to rate pupil progress in oral skills. Typical checklists are found in Figures 14.5, 14.6, and 14.7.

To help teachers and their aides evaluate literacy skills of the children, individual files may be kept of reading work papers, written exercises, independent compositions, or informal written group tests.

Figure 14.5. Teacher's Self-Evaluation Checklist in the ESL Program.

Self-Evaluation of Teacher	Yes	No
1. Do I demonstrate adequate planning and sequencing?	____	____
2. Do I use material that is relevant to the students' world and at an appropriate level for the students?	____	____
3. Is the aim of my lesson clear to the students, i.e., is the target structure or activity clearly delineated and reflected in my preparation?	____	____
4. Do I have a clear understanding of the structure so that I will not be "surprised" by irregular items?	____	____
5. Are my directions clear and to the point?	____	____
6. Do I keep rules, diagrams and explanations to a minimum?	____	____
7. Are my handouts well prepared and legible and NOT poor duplications characterized by light print or minute type which students, already struggling in a second language, must struggle to read?	____	____
8. Do I speak naturally, at normal speed?	____	____
9. Do I maintain an appropriate pace to keep the class alert and interested?	____	____
10. Do I have good rapport with my class, respecting the students' time as well as exhibiting sensitivity to the students as children and offering positive reinforcement?	____	____
11. Do I listen to my students and am I aware of student errors, limiting correction to what is necessary and relevant?	____	____
12. Do I promote student self-editing?	____	____
13. Do I utilize peer correction?	____	____
14. Do I respect students' abilities to use their own grey matter to come up with new items, and do I invite them to use their own powers of analogy or analysis to make "educated guesses"?	____	____
15. Do I promote student participation and activity?	____	____
16. Am I aware of the ratio of student and teacher talk, keeping teacher talk to a minimum rather than dominating the class?	____	____
17. Do my students have an opportunity to communicate with each other in real language activities so that the emphasis is not on pattern practice?	____	____
18. Is my class arranged for successful communication between students and easy accessibility to the teacher?	____	____
19. Can my students do something new linguistically after the class?	____	____
20. Would I, as a student, enjoy my own class?	____	____

Source: GUIDELINES OF THE NEW YORK STATE TEACHERS OF ENGLISH TO SPEAKERS OF OTHER LANGUAGES AND THE BILINGUAL EDUCATION ASSOCIATION (n.d.).

Figure 14.6. Paraprofessional's Self-Evaluation Checklist in the ESL Program.

Self-Evaluation of Paraprofessional Aide	Frequency		
Item	Occasionally	Often	Always
Do I:			
Prepare carefully?	_____	_____	_____
Demonstrate enthusiasm?	_____	_____	_____
Provide for individual differences?	_____	_____	_____
Use a variety of materials?	_____	_____	_____
Invent new activities?	_____	_____	_____
Read professional literature?	_____	_____	_____
Do boys and girls with whom I work:			
Attend class regularly?	_____	_____	_____
Show enthusiasm?	_____	_____	_____
Participate willingly?	_____	_____	_____
Continue to understand more English?	_____	_____	_____
Continue to use more English?	_____	_____	_____

Source: GUIDELINES FOR THE TUTOR IN TEACHING ENGLISH AS A SECOND LANGUAGE. (Los Angeles: Los Angeles City Schools, 1970), p. 126.

Figure 14.7. Teacher's Evaluation of Pupil Growth in the ESL Program.

Pupil's Name ______________ **Age** ______________ **Grade** ______________

Item	Progress in ESL			
	Little Improvement	Fair Improvement	Good Improvement	Excellent Improvement
Listens with interest	_____	_____	_____	_____
Listens with accuracy	_____	_____	_____	_____
Understands directions	_____	_____	_____	_____
Understands concepts	_____	_____	_____	_____
Repeats sentence structures accurately	_____	_____	_____	_____
Recalls sentence structures accurately	_____	_____	_____	_____
Repeats vocabulary words accurately	_____	_____	_____	_____
Uses language spontaneously	_____	_____	_____	_____

Source: GUIDELINES FOR THE TUTOR IN TEACHING ENGLISH AS A SECOND LANGUAGE. (Los Angeles: Los Angeles City Schools, 1970), p. 125.

Teachers should also be familiar with two nationally-distributed instruments often used in ESL programs, especially in English/Spanish bilingual programs.[21] The first is SOBER—Spanish (System for Objectives-Based Evaluation of Reading—Spanish), published by Science Research Associates of Chicago. Covering grades K–3, it is customized and can include 10–30 objectives (with three items per objective) locally chosen from a list of 203 objectives in four areas: encoding, decoding, vocabulary, and comprehension. Pictures are used and most test items require the student to fill in a circle. About four minutes is allowed per objective.

The second instrument is the Bilingual Syntax Measure, published by Harcourt Brace Jovanovich of New York, and concerned with second-language oral proficiency in English or Spanish syntax. It is available in two editions, English Student and Spanish Student, and it is suitable for grades K–12. It is individually administered and employs cartoon-type pictures with simple questions in an effort to identify the student's control over basic syntactic structures. Administration time is 10–15 minutes. The scorer can assign the child to one of five proficiency levels, ranging from no speaking proficiency to a top level of comprehension.

Incidentally, schools in Des Moines, Iowa, were able to use the BSM (English Student) to test students from southeast Asia, administering it both at the beginning and end of the school year to detect progress in ESL.[22] More instruction in English appeared to be beneficial during the first year of schooling with diminishing effects during the second and third years. The report covered 567 students in grades 2–10 and concluded that the first year was the most effective period of instruction for these southeast Asian students learning ESL.

Procedures designed to reveal students' overall language proficiency and ability to use language in real communication contexts include observations, oral interviews, cloze tests, and dictation.[23] Regular periodic *observations* provide the teacher with an informal ongoing evaluation process as well as with help in planning appropriate classroom activities. Another informal measure of student progress is *oral interviews,* which allow the teacher to become better acquainted with students and student needs and which also stimulate a sampling of the language ability of students. Interviews may be taped and can follow the format shown in Figure 14.8.

A typical example of a *cloze test* consists of a paragraph of some 250 words at a level appropriate to that of the student. While the first and last sentences are left untouched, all other sentences have every fifth word deleted from the passage. The student must use contextual and grammatical clues to fill in the blanks with possible words. Particularly useful for beginning ESL students is a cloze test which permits the use of several word choices for each blank. Incidentally, the results of the cloze test correlate highly with results of listening comprehension tests.

Dictation tests require several readings by the teacher. First, the students merely listen. Second, they try to write down what they hear. Third, they attempt to correct mistakes and fill in any blanks they still have. Finally, they reread what they have written, making further corrections and additions. These tests evaluate general language ability and can also be used to diagnose specific language problems.

Figure 14.8. Checklist for Interview Findings.

Student Name: ____________________ Age _____ Grade _____ Date _______

Speaking and Listening

Accent

Grammar
- One word
- Two words
- Complete sentence
- Word order in sentence
- Complex sentences
- Use of idioms or figurative language
- Knowledge of deep structure of questions

Vocabulary

Fluency

Comprehension
- Understood main idea of questions
- Understood details of questions
- Answered inference questions

Reading

Vocabulary

Rate of reading

Comprehension
- Understood main idea of note
- Understood details in note
- Understood inference in note

Writing

Vocabulary

Grammar
- One word
- Two words
- Complete sentence
- Word order in sentence
- Complex sentences
- Use of idioms or figurative language

Comments: (interests, desires, needs)

Source: R. Rodrigues and R. White, MAINSTREAMING THE NON-ENGLISH SPEAKING STUDENT (ERIC Clearinghouse on Reading and Communication Skills, 1981), p. 45.

Discussion Questions

1. What is your reaction to the possible introduction of a Constitutional Amendment which declares that the English language shall be the official language of the United States?
2. In school districts where funds are limited and ESL students numerous, what type of program should there be to promote English as a second language (e.g., how many levels of proficiency should it cover)?
3. Why do you feel that the activity-centered classroom constitutes a better approach to learning English as a second language?
4. How should a teacher evaluate the progress of ESL students? How can she/he adequately inform their parents about the program?

Suggested Projects

1. Determine the non-English minority in your state and in your local school district.
2. Tape the conversations of five children learning English as a second language. Then analyze the results to see which of the twelve strategies the boys and girls are using to attain fluency and understanding.
3. Prepare a unit about the culture of the country or territory—such as Vietnam or Puerto Rico—from which some of the local ESL students have emigrated.
4. Examine some of the reading books used in local ESL classes.
5. Set up the learning center for ESL shown in Figure 14.9.

Related Readings

Downing, J. 1984. "A Source of Cognitive Confusion for Beginning Readers: Learning in a Second Language," *Reading Teacher, 37,* pp. 366–371.

Ford, C. 1984. "The Influence of Speech Variety on Teachers' Evaluation of Students With Comparable Academic Ability," *TESOL Quarterly, 18,* pp. 25–40.

Higgs, T. V., ed., 1984. *Teaching for Proficiency: The Organizing Principle.* Lincolnwood, IL: National Textbook.

Jackson, P. et al. 1983. *BETA: Beginning English Through Actions.* Reading, MA: Addison-Wesley.

Krashen, S. D., and Terrell, T. D. 1983. *The Natural Approach: Language Acquisition in the Classroom.* Hayward, CA: Alemany Press.

Leibowicz, J. 1984. "Classrooms, Teachers, and Nonstandard Speakers," *Language Arts, 61,* pp. 88–91.

Long, M. 1983. "Does Second Language Instruction Make a Difference? A Review of Research," *TESOL Quarterly, 17,* pp. 359–382.

Nakamura, Y. 1984. "Purposeful Listening for ESL Students," *TESL Reporter, 17*(1), pp. 3–5.

Saracho, O. 1983. "Essential Requirements for Teachers in Early Childhood Bilingual/Bicultural Programs," *Childhood Education, 60,* pp. 96–101.

Smith, S. 1984. *The Theater Arts and the Teaching of Second Languages.* Reading, MA: Addison-Wesley.

Figure 14.9. Language Arts Learning Center: English as a Second Language.

TYPE OF CENTER:	**Oral Language**	TIME: 15 minutes
GRADE LEVEL:	1-3	NUMBER OF STUDENTS: 1

INSTRUCTIONAL OBJECTIVE: Given stimuli, the child should be able to carry on a conversation on the telephone.

MATERIALS: A display board, toy telephone, tape recorder, people pictures, "Talk About" cards, and a make-believe switchboard.

DIRECTIONS:

1. Take a picture from the pocket on the left. Put the other pictures back.
2. Pick something you would like to talk about from the pocket on the right.
3. Put the plug in the hole next to the person on the switchboard to whom you're going to talk.
4. Push the two flowered buttons on the recorder at the same time.
5. Pick up the phone receiver. Say "Hello!" and begin talking.
6. When you are through, push the "Stop" button on the recorder.
7. Pull the plug out carefully.
8. Hang up the phone and put your "Talk About" card and picture back.

SUGGESTED IDEAS:

People Pictures:

aunt	uncle
grandparents	sick friend
pen pal	cousin
friend	sister

"Talk About" cards will say:

What happened one time on your birthday?
What new place would you like to visit?
Where did you go on a vacation you took with your family?
What would you do with a million dollars?
What would you like to be when you grow up?
Tell about your favorite story.
Tell about a trick you played on someone.
Tell about a pet you have or would like to have.
What is your favorite television show?
Tell a story you made up.

EVALUATION: The teacher will listen to the tape and note the vocabulary used and the sequence of events as related by the child. If needed, the teacher should hold individual conferences with children, offering them constructive ideas.

Source: From PATHWAYS TO IMAGINATION by Angela S. Reeke and James L. Laffey. © 1979 by Scott, Foresman & Company. Reprinted by permission.

Chapter Notes

1. N. Conklin and M. Lourie, *A Host of Tongues* (New York: Macmillan/Free Press, 1983), p. 3.
2. D. Waggonner, "Non-English Language Background Persons: Three U.S. Surveys," *TESOL Quarterly,* 1978, *12,* pp. 247–263.
3. P. Gonzales, "How to Begin Language Instruction for Non-English Speaking Students," *Language Arts,* 1981, *58,* pp. 178–179.
4. J. Cummings, "The Construct of Language Proficiency in Bilingual Education," in *Current Issues in Bilingual Education,* J. Alatis, ed. (Washington, D.C.: Georgetown University Press, 1980), pp. 81–103.
5. J. Cummins, *Tests, Achievement, and Bilingual Students* (Rosslyn, Virginia: National Clearinghouse for Bilingual Education, 1982).
6. A. U. Chamot, "Toward a Functional ESL Curriculum in the Elementary School," *TESOL Quarterly,* 1983, *17,* pp. 459–460.
7. *Ibid.,* pp. 466–467.
8. L. Ventriglia, *Conversations of Miguel and Maria: How Children Learn a Second Language* (Reading, Massachusetts: Addison-Wesley, 1982), pp. 3–27.
9. L. A. Fillmore, *The Second Time Around: Cognitive and Social Strategies in Second Language Acquisition.* Unpublished doctoral dissertation, Stanford University, 1976.
10. E. Hatch, ed., *Second Language Acquisition: A Book of Readings* (Rowley, Massachusetts: Newbury House, 1978).
11. Ventriglia, *Conversations,* p. 26.
12. *Ibid.,* pp. 31–161.
13. J. J. Asher, *Learning Another Language Through Action: A Complete Teacher's Guide* (Los Gatos, California: Sky Oaks Productions, 1977).
14. F. Moore and R. Marzana, "Common Errors of Spanish Speakers Learning English," *Research in the Teaching of English,* 1979, *13,* pp. 161–167.
15. P. C. Gonzales, "Beginning English Reading for ESL Students," *Reading Teacher,* 1981, *35,* p. 155.
16. *Ibid.,* p. 160.
17. F. Stevens, "Activities to Promote Learning and Communication in the Second Language Classroom," *TESOL Quarterly,* 1983, *17,* p. 269.
18. *Ibid.,* pp. 262–267.
19. R. Rodrigues and R. White, *Mainstreaming the Non-English Speaking Student* (Urbana, Illinois: ERIC Clearinghouse on Reading and Communication Skills, and the National Council of Teachers of English, 1981), pp. 18–27.
20. J. Steinberg, "Laugh and Learn," *TESL Reporter,* 1983, *16,* p. 54.
21. O. K. Buros, ed., *The Eighth Mental Measurements Yearbook,* Volume I (Highland Park, New Jersey: Gryphon Press, 1978), pp. 232–236, 244–245.
22. D. Weslander and G. Stephany, "Evaluation of an English as a Second Language Program for Southeast Asian Students," *TESOL Quarterly,* 1983, *17,* 473–480.
23. Rodrigues and White, *Mainstreaming,* pp. 41–43.

Appendix 1
Award-Winning or Highly Recommended Media Resources for Elementary School Language Arts

NOTE: In this list, the proper names which appear in parentheses after the titles are those of narrators or authors. All films and filmstrips are in color unless otherwise noted. Under the *Medium* category, dots (. . . .) indicate that the title is available in several media from the same producer as exemplified under *Other Information*. A complete list of producers concludes this Appendix. Every production listed has either earned an award or been highly recommended by reviewers in various media journals/columns.

Level	Producer	Medium	Title	Other Information
P	Random	....	*A Is For Alphabet*	11 min., film or videocassette
PI	Random	filmstrips	*Adventures in Library Land*	set of 6 w/cassettes
P	SVE	filmstrips	*Aesop's Famous Fables*	set of 6 w/cassettes
I	Caedmon	cassettes	*African Heritage Core Collection*	set of 6
P	Random	filmstrips	*ALA Notable Children's Filmstrips*	Set 1: 4 w/cassettes Set 2: 11 w/cassettes
I	Xerox	....	*Alexander Hawkshaw's Skill Series:* *—Building Word Power* *—Reading for Comprehension* *—Using Context Analysis* *—Using Structural Analysis* *—Phonic Analysis* *—Critical Reading/Thinking*	8–10 min. each; film or videocassette
PI	Troll	filmstrips	*American Folk Heroes and Tall Tales*	set of 6 w/captions or cassettes
I	Random	filmstrips	*American Folklore Series*	Set I: 5 w/cassettes Set II: 5 w/cassettes
PI	Texture	film	*Anansi the Spider* (G. McDermott)	10 min.
P	Weston	film	*Andy and the Lion* (J. Daugherty)	10 min., iconographic
PI	Ency.B.	filmstrips	*Animals from the Prehistoric Ages*	set of 4 captioned w/cassettes
PI	Random	film	*Annie and the Old One* (M. Miles)	14½ min.
PI	Texture	film	*Arrow to the Sun* (G. McDermott)	12 min.
P	SVE	filmstrips	*Basic Reading Skills:* *—Base Words & Word Parts* *—Consonant Sounds:* Group 1 Group 2 *—Reading Readiness* —Vowel Sounds: Group 1 Group 2	set of 6 w/cassettes set of 6 w/cassettes set of 6 w/cassettes set of 6 w/cassettes set of 6 w/cassettes set of 6 w/cassettes set of 6 w/cassettes
I	Random	filmstrips	*Basic Study Skills: Learning How to Learn*	set of 6 w/cassettes

Level	Producer	Medium	Title	Other Information
PI	Churchill	film	*Beep Beep*	12 min., animation
P	SVE	filmstrips	*Beginning Writing Skills*	set of 4 w/cassettes
P	Troll	filmstrips	*Beloved Fairy Tales*	set of 6 w/captions or cassettes
PI	Ency.B.	film	*The Blue Dashiki*	14 min., no narration
PI	Barr	film	*Cabbages and Kings* (Grimm Brothers)	17 min.
I	Pathways	records	*Charlotte's Web* (E. B. White)	set of 4 LPs
PI	Ency.B.	filmstrips	*Christmas Classics*	set of 4 w/cassettes
PI	Caedmon	cassettes	*Classics of Amer. Poetry for the Elementary Curriculum*	set of 2
PI	Caedmon	cassette	*Classics of English Poetry for the Elementary Curriculum*	1 cassette
P	Weston	film	*The Clown of God* (T. DePaola)	10 min., animation
I	Aims	film	*Conrad, Josie & the Zoomerang*	15 min.
I	Xerox	....	*The Cricket in Times Square* (G. Selden)	26 min., film or videocassette
P	Ency.B.	film	*Crosstown Adventure*	14 min., 3 endings
P	Random	filmstrips	*Curious George Learns the Alphabet*	set of 2 w/cassettes
PI	Aims	film	*The Dead Bird* (M. Brown)	13 min.
PI	Xerox	....	*Desire to Read Series* —*Most Marvelous Cat* —*Peasant's Pea Patch* —*A Firefly Named Torchy* —*The Seventh Mandarin* —*World's Greatest Freak Show* —*Strange Story of the Frog Who Became a Prince*	8–12½ min. each; film or videocassette
P	Sterling	film	*Dick Whittington and His Cat*	16 min.
I	SVE	filmstrips	*The Dictionary*	set of 4 w/cassettes
PI	Barr	film	*Dictionary—The Adventure of Words*	16 min.
I	Troll	kit	*Dictionary Skill Box*	set of 6 cassettes w/spirit masters
PI	Random	film	*Dr. Seuss on the Loose*	25 min.
P	Random	filmstrips	*Easy-Read Stories*	Set I: 6 w/cassettes Set II: 6 w/cassettes
I	SVE	filmstrips	*Elementary School Library*	set of 4 w/cassettes
PI	Texture	film	*Exchange Place*	10 min., no narration
I	Xerox	film	*A Fable* (M. Marceau)	19 min., no narration
P	SVE	filmstrips	*Fables of Aesop*	set of 6 captioned w/cassettes
I	Ency.B.	filmstrips	*Fact or Fiction?*	set of 6 captioned w/cassettes
PI	Caedmon	cassettes	*Fairy Tales From Around the World*	set of 6
PI	Random	film	*Fast Is Not a Ladybug* (M. Schlein)	11 min.
PI	Troll	filmstrips	*Favorite Poems to Read, See, and Hear*	set of 6 w/captions or cassettes
PI	Random	film	*A First Film On Our Library*	12 min.
P	Ency.B.	film	*Follow Mr. Willoughby*	14 min., 3 endings

Level	Producer	Medium	Title	Other Information
I	Aims	film	*Francine, George & the Ferryboat*	15 min.
PI	Caedmon	cassettes	*A Gathering of Great Poetry for Children*	Kdgn. and Up: 1 cassette Second Grade and Up: 1 cassette Third Grade and Up: 1 cassette Fourth Grade and Up: 1 cassette
P	Sterling	film	*Georgie to the Rescue* (R. Bright)	10 min.
PI	Troll	filmstrips	*Getting Ready to Write Creatively*	set of 6 w/cassettes
P	Random	....	*The Gingerbread Man*	10 min., film or videocassette
I	Ency.B.	film	*The Golden Lizard*	19 min.
P	Random	....	*Goldilocks and the Three Bears*	10½ min., film or videocassette
I	SVE	filmstrips	*Grammar*	
			—Basic Word Functions	set of 5 w/cassettes
			—Sentences and Paragraphs	set of 4 w/cassettes
PI	Xerox	....	*Grammar Rock*	set of 7 films or 1 videocassette
P	Spoken	....	*Grimm's Fairy Tales*	set of 3 records or 5 cassettes
PI	Sterling	film	*Hailstones & Halibut Bones* (M. O'Neill)	Part I: 6 min. Part II: 7 min.
PI	Random	film	*Hansel and Gretel*	11 min.
PI	Pyramid	film	*The Happy Prince* (O. Wilde)	25 min.
PI	Ency.B.	film	*The Hare & the Tortoise*	10 min.
P	Weston	....	*The Hat* (T. Ungerer)	cassette, film, or filmstrip w/ cassette
P	Ency.B.	film	*The Haunted House*	14 min., 3 endings
PI	Aims	film	*How The Beaver Stole Fire*	12 min.
PI	Churchill	film	*How the Kiwi Lost His Wings*	12 min.
PI	SVE	filmstrips	*How to Use Library Media*	set of 4 w/cassettes
PI	Churchill	film	*The Hundred Penny Box* (S. Mathis)	18 min.
PI	Spoken	cassettes	*I Heard It With My Own Two Ears*	set of 12 w/guide
P	Pathways	record	*I Met A Man* (J. Ciardi)	1 LP
P	SVE	filmstrips	*Improving Listening Skills*	set of 4 w/cassettes
P	Random	film	*Ira Sleeps Over* (B. Waber)	17 min.
PI	FilmFair	film	*Isabella and the Magic Brush*	13½ min.
P	Weston	....	*Island of the Skog* (S. Kellogg)	13 min., film or videocassette
I	Random	filmstrips	*Kipling's Jungle Books*	set of 8 w/cassettes
PI	Churchill	film	*A Kite Story*	25 min., no narration
PI	Caedmon	cassette	*Lear's Nonsense Stories and Poems*	1 cassette
PI	Pyramid	film	*Legend of Paul Bunyan*	13 min.
I	Pyramid	film	*Legend of John Henry*	11 min.
I	Pyramid	film	*Legend of Sleepy Hollow* (W. Irving)	13 min., black/white
P	Troll	filmstrips	*Let's Learn the Alphabet*	set of 8 w/4 cassettes
P	Troll	filmstrips	*Let's Print the Alphabet*	set of 8 w/4 cassettes
P	Troll	filmstrips	*Let's Write the Alphabet*	set of 8 w/4 cassettes
PI	Churchill	film	*Let's Write a Story* (2d ed.)	11 min.
I	Troll	kit	*Library Skill Box*	set of 10 cassettes w/duplic. masters

Level	Producer	Medium	Title	Other Information
I	Barr	film	*Library World*	16 min.
I	Ency.B.	filmstrips	*A Likely Story*	set of 4 captioned w/cassettes
I	Churchill	film	*Listen, Cindy*	17 min.
P	Troll	filmstrips	*Listening Clearly*	set of 4 w/cassettes
PI	Pathways	records	*Little House in the Big Woods* (L. Wilder, J. Harris)	set of 4 LPs
PI	Ency.B.	film	*The Little Mariner*	21 min., no narration
PI	Pyramid	film	*The Little Mermaid* (H. Andersen)	25 min.
P	Random	....	*The Little Red Hen*	9½ min., film or videocassettes
PI	Texture	film	*Little Red Riding Hood*	17 min.
PI	Random	film	*The Littlest Angel*	14 min.
P	Weston	film	*Little Tim and the Brave Sea Captain* (E. Ardizzone)	11 min., iconographic
I	Troll	filmstrips	*Look It Up*	set of 4 w/cassettes
I	Ency.B.	film	*The Loon's Necklace*	11 min.
PI	Random	film	*The Lorax* (Dr. Seuss)	25 min.
PI	Sterling	film	*The Magic Pipes*	15 min.
PI	Pyramid	film	*The Magic Rolling Board*	15 min.
PI	Texture	film	*The Magic Tree* (G. McDermott)	10 min.
I	Ency.B.	film	*Making Haiku*	9 min.
PI	Pyramid	film	*The Marble*	10 min.
PI	Pyramid	film	*The Morning Spider*	22 min., no narration
I	Xerox	....	*Mowgli's Brothers* (R. Kipling)	26 min., film or videocassette
PI	Barr	film	*My Grandson Lew* (C. Zolotow)	13 min.
PI	Higgins	film	*My Parrot, Brewster*	17 min.
P	Ency.B.	filmstrips	*My Senses and Me*	set of 4 w/cassettes
I	SVE	filmstrips	*Nancy Drew's Guide to Book Reports*	set of 4 w/cassettes
I	Ency.B.	filmstrips	*The Near Future*	set of 4 captioned w/cassettes
PI	Troll	filmstrips	*New Adventures in Language*	set of 15 w/cassettes
P	Troll	cassettes	*New Goals in Listening*	set of 18 w/spirit masters
PI	Aims	film	*One Kitten for Kim* (A. Holl)	16 min.
P	Weston	film	*Panama*	11 min., animation
P	Weston	....	*Petunia* (R. Duvoisin)	10 min., film or videocassette
PI	FilmFair	film	*Petronella* (J. Williams)	13½ min.
PI	Pathways	record	*The Pickety Fence & Other Poems* (D. McCord)	1 LP
I	Random	filmstrips	*Poetry Classics*	Set I: 8 w/cassettes Set II: 8 w/cassettes
P	Caedmon	cassettes	*Poetry for the Primary Grades*	set of 6
P	Random	filmstrips	*Popular Picture Book Filmstrips*	Set 1: 4 w/cassettes or records Set 2: 4 w/cassettes or records Set 3: 4 w/cassettes or records
P	Random	....	*The Puppy Who Wanted a Boy*	23 min., film or videocassette
P	Troll	filmstrips	*Putting Words in Order*	set of 6 w/cassettes
P	SVE	filmstrips	*Reading for Meaning*	set of 4 w/cassettes
P	Random	filmstrips	*Reading the Signs in Your World*	set of 4 w/cassettes
I	Random	filmstrips	*Real-Life American Legends*	set of 6 w/cassettes

Level	Producer	Medium	Title	Other Information
P	Weston	....	*Really Rosie* (M. Sendak)	26 min., film or videocassette
I	Barr	film	*The Reference Section*	22 min.
I	Ency.B.	film	*Reflections*	19 min.
PI	Churchill	film	*The Reluctant Dragon* (K. Grahame)	12 min.
I	Xerox	....	*Rikki-Tikki-Tavi* (R. Kipling)	26 min., film or videocassette
P	Spoken	cassettes	*Road to Reading: Phonics Program*	set of 33 w/duplic. masters, guide
PI	Churchill	film	*Roundabout*	19 min.
PI	Random	film	*Sam, Bangs & Moonshine* (E. Ness)	15 min.
I	SVE	filmstrips	*Seasons of Poetry*	set of 4 w/cassettes
PI	Pyramid	film	*The Selfish Giant* (O. Wilde)	27 min., animation
PI	Churchill	film	*Seven With One Blow*	10 min.
PI	Ency.B.	filmstrips	*Show Me a Poem*	set of 6 w/cassettes or records
P	Random	filmstrips	*Sights and Sounds Filmstrips*	Sets 1-6: 6 each w/cassettes
PI	Caedmon	cassette	*Silver Pennies*	1 cassette
PI	Weston	film	*The Sorcerer's Apprentice* (L. Weil)	14 min., live action
I	Churchill	film	*Speak Up, Andrew*	17 min.
PI	Barr	film	*A Special Trade* (S. Wittman)	17 min.
P	Weston	film	*Stone Soup* (M. Brown)	11 min., iconographic
P	Churchill	film	*Stories*	14 min.
P	Caedmon	cassettes	*Stories to Develop Listening Skills*	set of 6
PI	Caedmon	cassettes	*Stories for Beginning Readers*	Set I: 6 Set II: 6
I	Ency.B.	filmstrips	*Stories Told by Native Americans*	set of 4 w/cassettes
P	Weston	film	*The Story of Ping* (M. Flack)	10 min., iconographic
PI	Pathways	records	*Stuart Little* (E. B. White, J. Harris)	set of 2 LPs
P	Weston	....	*The Swineherd* (H. Andersen)	13 min., film or videocassette
P	Troll	kit	*Talking Picture Dictionary*	set of 16 cassettes, 64 paperbacks
P	Troll	kit	*Talking Picture Dictionary of More New Words*	set of 16 cassettes, 64 paperbacks
P	Spoken	cassettes	*Talking with Mike*	set of 14 w/guide
PI	FilmFair	film	*A Tale of Till*	11 min.
P	Weston	....	*Teeny Tiny and the Witch Woman* (B. Walker)	14 min., film or videocassette
P	Ency.B.	filmstrips	*That's Delightful*	set of 4 w/cassettes
I	Ency.B.	filmstrips	*That's Fantastic*	set of 4 captioned w/cassettes
I	Pathways	records	*Thirteen Clocks* (J. Thurber)	set of 2 LPs
I	Weston	film	*This Is New York* (M. Sasek)	12 min., iconographic
P	Weston	....	*The Three Little Pigs* (E. Blegvad)	cassette or filmstrip w/cassette
P	Weston	....	*Tilly's House* (F. Jacques)	cassette or filmstrip w/cassette
I	Aims	film	*Tommy, Suzie & the Cardboard Box*	15 min.
P	SVE	filmstrips	*Treasury of Animal Stories* (B. Potter)	set of 4 w/cassettes
P	Spoken	....	*Treasury of Nursery Rhymes*	set of 3 cassettes or 2 records

Level	Producer	Medium	Title	Other Information
PI	Troll	cassettes	*Troll Listening Lab*	Grades 1-2: set of 10 w/duplic. masters Grades 3-4: set of 10 w/duplic. masters Grades 5-6: set of 10 w/duplic. masters
I	Pathways	records	*The Trumpet of the Swan* (E. B. White)	set of 5 LPs
PI	Ency.B.	film	*Tschou Tschou*	15 min., no narration
P	Weston	....	*The Ugly Duckling* (H. Andersen)	15 min., film or videocassette
I	SVE	filmstrips	*Understanding Poetry*	set of 4 w/cassettes
PI	SVE	filmstrips	*Using Good English*	set of 6 captioned
I	Troll	filmstrips	*Vocabulary Development*	set of 6 w/cassettes
I	Ency.B.	filmstrips	*What's New in Space?*	set of 4 captioned w/cassettes
I	Spoken	....	*The Wind in the Willows* (K. Grahame)	1 cassette or 1 record
P	Pathways	record	*Winnie-The-Pooh* (A. Milne)	1 LP
PI	Random	film	*Word Wise: Prefixes*	10½ min.
P	Churchill	film	*Words*	14 min.
P	Troll	filmstrips	*Working with Blends & Digraphs*	set of 6 w/cassettes
P	Troll	filmstrips	*Working with Consonants*	set of 6 w/cassettes
P	Troll	filmstrips	*Working with Vowels*	set of 6 w/cassettes
P	Troll	filmstrips	*Working with Words*	set of 6 w/cassettes
PI	Spoken	cassettes	*World of Just So Stories* (R. Kipling)	Set 1: 4 w/books Set 2: 3 w/books
P	Weston	....	*Zlateh the Goat* (I. Singer)	20 min., film or videocassette

Producers

Aims Media, 626 Justin Avenue, Glendale, CA 91201
Barr Films, P.O. Box 5667, Pasadena, CA 91107
Caedmon, 1995 Broadway, New York, NY 10023
Churchill Films, 662 N. Robertson Blvd., Los Angeles, CA 90069
Encyclopaedia Britannica Educational Corp., 425 N. Michigan Ave., Chicago, IL 60611
FilmFair Communications, 10900 Ventura Blvd., P.O. Box 1728, Studio City, CA 91604
Alfred Higgins Productions, Inc., 9100 Sunset Blvd., Los Angeles, CA 90069
Pathways of Sound, 6 Craigie Circle, Cambridge, MA 02138
Pyramid Films & Video, Box 1048, Santa Monica, CA 90406
Random House School Division, 400 Hahn Road, Westminster, MD 21157
Society for Visual Education, Inc., 1345 Diversey Parkway, Chicago, IL 60614
Spoken Arts, Dept. R., P.O. Box 289, New Rochelle, NY 10802
Sterling Educational Films, 241 East 34th St., New York, NY 10016
Texture Films, P.O. Box 1337, Skokie, IL 60076
Troll Associates, 320 rt. 17, Mahwah, NJ 07430
Xerox, The Center for Humanities, Communications Pk., Box 1000, Mt. Kisco, NY 10549
Weston Woods, Weston, CT 06883

Appendix 2
Language Arts Textbook Evaluation*

Evaluation Form

Directions for use:

1. In each section indicated by a roman numeral, place a 3 before each item on which you think the text is outstandingly satisfactory.
2. Place a 2 before each item on which you think the text is more satisfactory than unsatisfactory.
3. Place a 1 before each item on which you think the text is more unsatisfactory than satisfactory.
4. Place a 0 before each item on which you think the text is completely unsatisfactory.
5. Total your points within each section. Record these totals on the Summary Sheet and compare them with those from other textbooks being evaluated. The book having the highest total is the most effective for your purposes.

I. Attitudes toward Language

_____ A. How effectively does the text capitalize on students' native understanding of language?

_____ B. How effectively does the text recogize that students may speak various dialects of English?

_____ C. How effectively does the text emphasize that several styles of speech and writing are appropriate to various situations?

_____ D. How effectively does the text emphasize that language changes constantly?

_____ E. How much attention does the text give to teaching reading, writing, listening, and speaking as skills of communication?

_____ F. How much attention does the text give to language as used outside the classroom in television, newspapers, magazines, and advertising?

_____ G. How much attention does the text give to the regional and social dialects of the United States?

_____ H. How much attention does the text give to the history of the English language?

_____ I. How much attention does the text give to the making and using of dictionaries?

_____ J. How clearly does the text explain that dictionaries describe usage and do *not* prescribe it?

Explanatory Notes and Comments: ______________________________

____

____

*Reprinted from UNDERSTANDING LANGUAGE: A PRIMER FOR THE LANGUAGE ARTS TEACHER, by Jean Malmstrom. Copyright © 1977 by St. Martin's Press, Inc. Reprinted with permission of the publisher.

II. Motivation of Students

_____ A. How effectively will the text motivate the better students?
_____ B. How effectively will the text motivate the slower students?
_____ C. How effectively will the text encourage inductive thinking?
_____ D. How effectively will the text encourage deductive thinking?
_____ E. How successfully does the text describe options rather than present rules?
_____ F. How well does the text interrelate language study, composition, and literature?
_____ G. How originally does the text present material?
_____ H. How effectively does the text emphasize ideas and minimize linguistic terminology?

Explanatory Notes and Comments: ______________________________

____

____

III. Adaptability

_____ A. How adaptable is the text for slow students?
_____ B. How adaptable is the text for average students?
_____ C. How adaptable is the text for superior students?
_____ D. How adaptable is the text for speakers of nonstandard dialects?
_____ E. How useful is the text as a reference tool?
_____ F. How useful is the text as a supplement to the curriculum?
_____ G. How useful is the text as a curriculum guide?

Explanatory Notes and Comments: ______________________________

____

____

IV. Diction and Style

_____ A. How well will students like the writing style of the text?
_____ B. How accurately is word choice adjusted to the students for whom the text is intended? (Consider using a cloze test in reaching your conclusions.)
_____ C. How effectively does sentence variety increase the text's appeal?
_____ D. How much will the style of the text enhance your own effectiveness in the classroom?

Explanatory Notes and Comments: ______________________________

____

____

V. Authority and Reliability

_____ A. How clearly are the instructional goals of the text presented?
_____ B. How effectively do these goals mesh with your own instructional goals?
_____ C. How consistently is the viewpoint of the introductory comments and/ or the teacher's manual maintained throughout the text?

Explanatory Notes and Comments: ______________________________

____

____

VI. Miscellaneous Features

Rate the text on the quality of each of the following.

_____ A. Reference features
(table of contents, index, illustrations)
_____ B. Physical features
(size, binding, printing, margins, paper)

Explanatory Notes and Comments: ______________________________

____

____

Summary Sheet

_____ I. Attitudes toward language
_____ II. Motivation of students
_____ III. Adaptability
_____ IV. Diction and style
_____ V. Authority and reliability
_____ VI. Miscellaneous features

Overall Explanatory Notes and Comments: ______________________

____

____

Appendix 3
How to Judge a Basal Reader Series*

On the surface, all basal reader series appear to be very much alike. This is understandable, because one that is too unusual or maverick will stand little chance of success in the market place. On close inspection, however, there are some significant differences; some dictated by philosophy, some by financial restrictions, some by differences in the editorial teams, and some by expediency. As an aid for comparison and, perhaps, for selection of the basal series that best fits certain situations and particular learners, the following check sheet is presented.

In addition to checking "yes" or "no," you may wish to make some subjective, qualitative judgments as well. For example, it may not be enough to check "yes," that the series includes cassettes for individual learning. A value judgment may well be in order to answer such questions as: "How appropriate is the cassette material?" "Does the cassette material go slowly enough for my particular pupils?" "How easy to understand is the voice on the cassette?"

Other value judgments are certainly appropriate when judging artwork, the literary selections, the suitability of the selections for children in a particular economic and geographic region, and so forth.

The following check sheet is not meant to yield a definitive score, but to highlight the many facets of the basal reader series and to make comparisons possible on these many standard features.

COMPONENTS OF PUPIL TEXTS	**Yes**	**No**
Are the covers attractive?		
Are the book titles meaningful?		
Are the covers easy to clean?		
Is there a library binding that allows the book to lie open flat?		
Is the "level" coded on the spine? On the back?		
Are the books easy to stack?		
Which of the following literary genre are included?		
Short stories		
Plays		
Songs		
Poems		
Informational articles		
Vignettes from longer novels		
Legends and myths		

*Reprinted from Robert C. Aukerman THE BASAL READER APPROACH TO READING, John Wiley & Sons, Inc., 1981, pp. 13-17. Used with permission.

	Yes	No
Letters and speeches		
Newspaper reports and journal excerpts		
Science fiction		
Advertisements, flyers, etc.		
Directions, recipes, etc.		
Biography and autobiography		
Historical fiction		
Is there a balance of informational articles from the following?		
Social studies		
Science		
Health and sports		
Arts and artists		
Travel and adventure		
Home economics		
Recreation		
Business, commerce, etc.		
Invention, technology, etc.		
Careers and the world of work		
Is there an adequate balance of selections in the "real" and "make believe"?		
Is there a satisfactory balance of selections from the "children's classics" and from contemporary children's literature?		
Are many of contemporary award-winning authors' works represented?		
Are the stories "devised" by a group of relatively unknown writers?		
Are the literary selections "relevant" to today's young readers?		
Do the selections represent an adequate cross section of contemporary living?		
Does the artwork provide an environmental setting and mood for the story or article?		
Does the artwork illustrate the action in the story?		
Are realistic male/female roles in keeping with the conditions existing at the time and place of the story or selection?		
Are positive cultural images of today's socioethnic groups adequately presented?		
Where there is cultural bias and/or propaganda, is it made clear that this is the case and the purpose for including it?		
Are the following literary devices adequately developed in the pupil texts and in the teacher's edition plans?		
Plot		
Characterization		
Simile/metaphor		
Sounds (alliteration; onomatopoeia, etc.)		

	Yes	No
Rhythm and rhyme		
Imagery		
Implied, "deep" meanings		
Verbal description		
Loaded language, sales pitch, "snow" job		

MATERIALS FOR INDIVIDUAL DIFFERENCES	**Yes**	**No**
Are the following materials available?		
Boxed collection of books arranged and coded for various reading levels.		
Transition books		
Pupil workbooks for reinforcing skills		
Pupil workbooks or sheets for reteaching skills to slower learners		
Games for small-group activities		
Individual game-type activities		
Cassettes for individual listening		
Pupil-progress record charts or sheets		
Self-corrective materials		
Every-pupil response cards		

ANCILLARY MATERIALS TO ENHANCE SKILLS LEARNING	**Yes**	**No**
Are the following available?		
Games		
Filmstrips		
Flashcards		
Wall charts		
Picture-word cards		
Tachistoscopic programs		
Alphabet letters		
Puppets, and other gimmicks and gadgets		

AUTHORSHIP AND EDITORSHIP	**Yes**	**No**
Are the senior authors recognized as distinguished reading authorities? Does the team of authors include the following?		
A children's literature specialist		
A reading supervisor		
A classroom teacher at each level		
A child-development specialist		
An elementary education specialist		
A graphic arts specialist		
A language arts specialist		
A linguistics specialist		
A testing and evaluation specialist		
Was the series developed by the publisher's in-house group of editors?		

RELEVANCE AND VIABILITY OF THE SERIES	Yes	No
Are the selections in the books relevant to today's children?		
Are the selections appropriate for the interests and abilities of the particular children in your school?		
What is the level of the readability of the books?		
Too difficult		
Too easy		
Just right		
Are the selections "dated," so they will be out of date in five years?		
Is the artwork attractive and relevant to the environments of today's children?		
Are the selections old-fashioned?		
Are the books of the series in traditional sequence so children may transfer in and/or out easily?		
If you had to select a series that you would have to stay with for 10 years, would this one do?		

STORAGE OF COMPONENTS	Yes	No
Are books standard size for shelf storage?		
Do the workbooks have a place *on* the cover for the pupil's name?		
Are the books color-coded according to level?		
Are there self-contained boxes for any of the following?		
Filmstrips		
Cassettes		
Games		
Flashcards and flipcards		
Are the container boxes sturdy?		

THE INSTRUCTIONAL PROGRAM	Yes	No
Do the teacher's editions (or manuals) contain the following aids to teaching?		
Story synopsis		
Suggestions for introduction and motivation for each selection		
Comprehension questions		
Notations highlighting special details		
Objectives for each lesson		
List of materials to be assembled prior to teaching each lesson		
Oral reading suggestions		

	Yes	No
Review of previously learned skills		
Suggestions for follow-up activities		
List of related "enrichment" reading materials		
Specific information on location of those enrichment materials		
Reproduction of pages from the pupil's reading book		
Information on the authors of the stories, poems, and other selections		
Background information on the region and/or environment that is the setting of the selection		
Suggestions for diagnostic/prescriptive teaching		
Realistic continuous-progress planning		
Practical plans for ad hoc grouping		
Plan for vocabulary development and enrichment		
A total language-arts program or strand		
Thorough plans for a sequential phonics program		
A reading study-skills developmental program		
Suggestions for oral speaking and dramatics		
A composition and expository writing sequence		
A planned use of the library		
A plan for information search using library skills		
A thorough, sequential word-recognition program (phonics, word structure, contextual clues, etc.)		
Do all the lessons in the teacher's edition (manual) follow the same routine?		
Are the lessons in the teacher's edition (manual) varied for interest?		
Could a novice teacher work successfully with the plans in the teacher's edition?		
Is there a definite, identifiable phonics strand?		
Does the phonics strand, if any, follow a developmental sequence?		
Does the phonics strand, if any, appear to be "helter-skelter"?		
Is it possible to know which word-recognition skills are covered in the first grade and which are covered in the second grade (i.e., within reason)?		
Is there undue repetition from one level to the next and to the next?		

WOULD YOU BE HAPPY USING THE MATERIALS OF THIS SERIES?	**Yes**	**No**
Would this be your first choice?		
Would this be your middle choice?		
Would this be your last choice?		

Appendix 4
Caldecott Medal and Newbery Medal Books and Their Honor Books Since the Mid-Century

Caldecott Medal Books

The Caldecott Medal is named in honor of Randolph Caldecott (1846–1886), an English illustrator of children's books. The Medal is presented annually by a committee of the Children's Service Division of the American Library Association to "the artist of the most distinguished American picture book for children." The book must be an original work by a citizen or resident of the United States.

1985 Award: *St. George and the Dragon.* Illustrated by Trina Schart Hyman. Retold by Margaret Hodges. Little, Brown.

Honor books: *Hansel and Gretel.* Illustrated by Paul O. Zelinsky. Retold by Rika Lesser. Dodd.
Have You Seen My Duckling? Written and illustrated by Nancy Tafuri. Greenwillow.
The Story of Jumping Mouse. Written and illustrated by John Steptoe. Lothrop.

1984 Award: *Glorious Flight Across the Channel with Lewis Bleriot.* Written and illustrated by Alice Provensen and Martin Provensen. Viking.

Honor books: *Ten, Nine, Eight.* Written and illustrated by Molly Bang. Greenwillow.
Little Red Riding Hood. Illustrated and retold by Trina S. Hyman. Holiday House.

1983 Award: *Shadow.* Illustrated by Marcia Borwn. Written by Blaise Cendrars. Scribner.

Honor books: *A Chair for My Mother.* Written and illustrated by Vera Williams. Greenwillow.
When I Was Young in the Mountains. Illustrated by Diane Goode. Written by Cynthia Rylant. Dutton.

1982 Award: *Jumanji.* Written and illustrated by Chris Van Allsburg. Houghton.

Honor books: *On Market Street.* Illustrated by Anita Lobel. Written by Arnold and Anita Lobel. Greenwillow.
Outside Over There. Written and illustrated by Maurice Sendak. Harper.

A Visit to William Blake's Inn. Illustrated by Alice Provensen and Martin Provensen. Written by Nancy Willard. Harcourt.
Where the Buffaloes Begin. Illustrated by Stephen Gammell. Written by Olaf Baker. F. Warne.

1981 Award: *Fables.* Written and illustrated by Arnold Lobel. Harper.

Honor books: *The Bremen-Town Musicians.* Illustrated and retold by Ilse Plume. Doubleday.
The Grey Lady and the Strawberry Snatcher. Written and illustrated by Mollie Bang. Four Winds.
Mice Twice. Written and illustrated by Joseph Low. Atheneum.
Truck. Written and illustrated by Donald Crews. Greenwillow.

1980 Award: *Ox-Cart Man.* Illustrated by Barbara Cooney. Written by Donald Hall. Viking.

Honor books: *Ben's Trumpet.* Written and illustrated by Rachel Isadora. Greenwillow.
The Garden of Abdul Gasazi. Written and illustrated by Chris Van Allsburg. Houghton.
The Treasure. Written and illustrated by Uri Shulevitz. Farrar.

1979 Award: *The Girl Who Loved Wild Horses.* Written and illustrated by Paul Goble. Bradbury.

Honor books: *Freight Train.* Written and illustrated by Donald Crews. Greenwillow.
The Way to Start a Day. Illustrated by Paul Parnall. Written by Byrd Baylor. Scribner.

1978 Award: *Noah's Ark: Story of the Flood.* Written and illustrated by Peter Spier. Doubleday.

Honor books: *It Could Always Be Worse.* Illustrated and retold by Margot Zemach. Farrar.
Castle. Written and illustrated by David Macaulay. Houghton.

1977 Award: *Ashanti to Zulu: African Traditions.* Illustrated by Leo and Diane Dillon. Written by Margaret Musgrove. Dial.

Honor books: *The Golem: A Jewish Legend.* Illustrated and retold by Beverly McDermott. Lippincott.
The Contest: An Armenian Folktale. Adapted and illustrated by Nonny Hogrogian. Greenwillow.
Hawk, I'm Your Brother. Illustrated by Peter Parnall. Written by Byrd Baylor. Scribner.
The Amazing Bone. Written and illustrated by William Steig. Farrar.
Fish for Supper. Written and illustrated by M. B. Goffstein. Dial.

1976 Award: *Why Mosquitos Buzz in People's Ears.* Illustrated by Leo and Diane Dillon. Retold by Verna Aardema. Dial.

Honor books: *The Desert Is Theirs.* Illustrated by Peter Parnall. Written by Byrd Baylor. Scribner.

Strega Nona. Illustrated and retold by Tomie de Paola. Prentice.

1975 Award: *Arrow to the Sun.* Adapted and illustrated by Gerald McDermott. Viking.

Honor book: *Jambo Means Hello—Swahili Alphabet Book.* Illustrated by Tom Feelings. Written by Muriel Feelings. Dial.

1974 Award: *Duffy and the Devil.* Illustrated by Margot Zemach. Retold by Havre Zemach. Farrar.

Honor books: *Cathedral: The Story of Its Contruction.* Written and illustrated by David Macaulay. Houghton.

Three Jovial Huntsmen. Adapted and illustrated by Susan Jeffers. Bradbury.

1973 Award: *The Funny Little Woman.* Illustrated by Blair Lent. Written by Arlene Mosel. Dutton.

Honor books: *Anansi the Spider.* Adapted and illustrated by Gerald McDermott. Holt.

Hosie's Alphabet. Illustrated by Leonard Baskin. Written by Hosea Tobias, and Lisa Baskin. Viking.

Snow-White and the Seven Dwarfs. Illustrated by Nancy Ekholm Burkert. Translated from the Brothers Grimm by Randall Jarrell. Farrar.

When Clay Sings. Illustrated by Tom Bahti. Written by Byrd Baylor. Scribner.

1972 Award: *One Fine Day.* Illustrated and retold by Nonny Hogrogian. Macmillan.

Honor books: *If All the Seas Were One Sea.* Written and illustrated by Janina Domanska. Macmillan.

Moja Means One: Swahili Counting Book. Illustrated by Tom Feelings. Written by Muriel Feelings. Dial.

Hildilid's Night. Illustrated by Arnold Lobel. Written by Cheli Duran Ryan. Macmillan.

1971 Award: *A Story—A Story: An African Tale.* Retold and illustrated by Gail E. Haley. Atheneum.

Honor books: *The Angry Moon.* Illustrated by Blair Lent. Retold by William Sleator. Little, Brown.

Frog and Toad Are Friends. Written and illustrated by Arnold Lobel. Harper.

In the Night Kitchen. Written and illustrated by Maurice Sendak. Harper.

1970 Award: *Sylvester and the Magic Pebble.* Written and illustrated by William Steig. Windmill.

Honor books: *Goggles!* Written and illustrated by Ezra Jack Keats. Macmillan.

Alexander and the Wind-up Mouse. Written and illustrated by Leo Lionni. Pantheon.

Pop Corn and Ma Goodness. Illustrated by Robert Andrew Parke. Written by Edna Mitchell Preston. Viking.

Thy Friend, Obadiah. Written and illustrated by Brinton Burkle. Viking.

The Judge: An Untrue Tale. Illustrated by Margot Zemach. Written by Harve Zemach. Farrar.

1969 Award: *The Fool of the World and the Flying Ship: A Russian Tale.* Illustrated by Uri Shulevitz. Retold by Arthur Ransome. Farrar.

Honor book: *Why the Sun and the Moon Live in the Sky: An African Folk Tale.* Illustrated by Blair Lent. Retold by Elphinstone Dayrell. Houghton.

1968 Award: *Drummer Hoff.* Illustrated by Ed Emberley. Adapted by Barbara Emberley. Prentice.

Honor books: *Frederick.* Written and illustrated by Leo Lionni. Pantheon.

Seashore Story. Written and illustrated by Taro Yashima. Viking.

The Emperor and the Kite. Illustrated by Ed Young. Written by Jane Yolen. World.

1967 Award: *Sam, Bangs and Moonshine.* Written and illustrated by Evaline Ness. Holt.

Honor book: *One Wide River to Cross.* Illustrated by Ed Emberley. Adapted by Barbara Emberley. Prentice.

1966 Award: *Always Room for One More.* Illustrated by Nonny Hogrogian. Written by Sorche NicLeodhas, *pseud.* (Leclaire Alger). Holt.

Honor books: *Hide and Seek Fog.* Illustrated by Roger Duvoisin. Written by Alvin Tresselt. Lothrup.

Just Me. Written and illustrated by Marie Hall Ets. Viking.

Tom Tit Tot. Illustrated by Evaline Ness. Edited by Joseph Jacobs. Scribner.

1965 Award:	*May I Bring a Friend?* Illustrated by Beni Montresor. Written by Beatrice Schenk de Regniers. Atheneum.
Honor books:	*Rain Makes Applesauce.* Illustrated by Marvin Bileck. Written by Julian Scheer. Holiday House. *The Wave.* Illustrated by Blair Lent. Written by Margaret Hodges. Houghton. *A Pocketful of Cricket.* Illustrated by Evaline Ness. Text by Rebecca Caudill. Holt.
1964 Award:	*Where the Wild Things Are.* Written and illustrated by Maurice Sendak. Harper.
Honor books:	*Swimmy.* Story and pictures by Leo Lionni. Pantheon. *All in the Morning Early.* Illustrated by Evaline Ness. Text by Sorche Nic Leodhas, *pseud.* (Leclaire Alger). Holt. *Mother Goose and Nursery Rhymes.* Illustrated by Philip Reed. Atheneum.
1963 Award:	*The Snowy Day.* Story and pictures by Ezra Jack Keats. Viking.
Honor books:	*The Sun is a Golden Earring.* Illustrated by Bernarda Bryson. Text by Natalia M. Belting. Holt. *Mr. Rabbit and the Lovely Present.* Illustrated by Maurice Sendak. Written by Charlotte Zolotow. Harper.
1962 Award:	*Once a Mouse.* Retold and illustrated by Marcia Brown. Scribner.
Honor books:	*The Fox Went Out on a Chilly Night.* Illustrated by Peter Spier. Doubleday. *Little Bear's Visit.* Illustrated by Maurice Sendak. Written by Else H. Minarik. Harper. *The Day We Saw the Sun Come Up.* Illustrated by Adrienne Adams. Written by Alice E. Goudey. Scribner.
1961 Award:	*Baboushka and the Three Kings.* Illustrated by Nicolas Sidjakov. Written by Ruth Robbins. Parnassus Press.
Honor book:	*Inch by Inch.* Written and illustrated by Leo Lionni. Ivan Obolensky, Inc.
1960 Award:	*Nine Days to Christmas.* Illustrated by Marie Hall Ets. Written by Marie Hall Ets and Aurora Labastida. Viking.
Honor books:	*Houses from the Sea.* Illustrated by Adrienne Adams. Written by Alice E. Goudey. Scribner. *The Moon Jumpers.* Illustrated by Maurice Sendak. Written by Janice May Udry. Harper.

1959 Award: *Chanticleer and the Fox.* Adapted from Chaucer's *The Canterbury Tales* and illustrated by Barbara Cooney. Crowell.

Honor books: *The House that Jack Built: La Maison Que Jacques A Batie.* Text and illustrations by Antonio Frasconi. Harcourt.
What Do You Say, Dear? Illustrated by Maurice Sendak. Written by Sesyle Joslin. W. R. Scott.
Umbrella. Story and pictures by Taro Yashima. Viking.

1958 Award: *Time of Wonder.* Written and illustrated by Robert McCloskey. Viking.

Honor books: *Fly High, Fly Low.* Story and pictures by Don Freeman. Viking.
Anatole and the Cat. Illustrated by Paul Galdone. Written by Eve Titus. McGraw.

1957 Award: *A Tree is Nice.* Illustrated by Marc Simont. Written by Janice May Udry. Harper.

Honor books: *Mr. Penny's Race Horse.* Written and illustrated by Marie Hall Ets. Viking.
1 Is One. Story and pictures by Tasha Tudor. Walck.
Anatole. Illustrated by Paul Galdone. Written by Eve Titus. McGraw.
Gillespie and the Guards. Illustrated by James Daugherty. Written by Benjamin Elkin. Viking.
Lion. Written and illustrated by William Pène du Bois. Viking.

1956 Award: *Frog Went A-Courtin'.* Illustrated by Feodor Rojankovsky. Text retold by John Langstaff. Harcourt.

Honor books: *Play With Me.* Story and pictures by Marie Hall Ets. Viking.
Crow Boy. Written and illustrated by Taro Yashima. Viking.

1955 Award: *Cinderella, or the Little Glass Slipper.* Illustrated and translated from Charles Perrault by Marcia Brown. Scribner.

Honor books: *Book of Nursery and Mother Goose Rhymes.* Illustrated by Marguerite de Angeli. Doubleday.
Wheel on the Chimney. Illustrated by Tibor Gergely. Written by Margaret Wise Brown. Lippincott.
The Thanksgiving Story. Illustrated by Helen Sewell. Text by Alice Dalgliesh. Scribner.

1954 Award: *Madeline's Rescue.* Written and illustrated by Ludwig Bemelmans. Viking.

Honor books: *Journey Cake, Ho!* Illustrated by Robert McCloskey. Text by Ruth Sawyer. Viking.
When Will the World Be Mine? Illustrated by Jean Charlot. Written by Miriam Schlein. W. R. Scott.

The Steadfast Tin Soldier. Illustrated by Marcia Brown. Story by Hans Christian Andersen, trans. by M. R. James. Scribner.
A Very Special House. Illustrated by Maurice Sendak. Written by Ruth Krauss. Harper.
Green Eyes. Story and pictures by A. Birnbaum. Capitol.

1953 Award: *The Biggest Bear.* Written and illustrated by Lynd Ward. Houghton.

Honor books: *Puss in Boots.* Illustrated and translated from Charles Perrault by Marcia Brown. Scribner.
One Morning in Maine. Written and illustrated by Robert McCloskey. Viking.
Ape in a Cape: An Alphabet of Odd Animals. Text and pictures by Fritz Eichenberg. Harcourt.
The Storm Book. Illustrated by Margaret Bloy Graham. Written by Charlotte Zolotow. Harper.
Five Little Monkeys. Story and illustrations by Juliet Kepes. Houghton.

1952 Award: *Finders Keepers.* Illustrated by Nicolas, *pseud.* (Nicolas Mordvinoff). Written by Will, *pseud.* (William Lipkind). Harcourt.

Honor books: *Mr. T. W. Anthony Woo.* Story and pictures by Marie Hall Ets. Viking.
Skipper John's Cook. Written and illustrated by Marcia Brown. Scribner.
All Falling Down. Illustrated by Margaret Bloy Graham. Written by Gene Zion. Harper.
Bear Party. Written and illustrated by William Pène du Bois. Viking.
Feather Mountain. Written and ilustrated by Elizabeth Olds. Houghton.

1951 Award: *The Egg Tree.* Written and illustrated by Katherine Milhous. Scribner.

Honor books: *Dick Whittington and His Cat.* Told and illustrated by Marcia Brown. Scribner.
The Two Reds. Illustrated by Nicolas, *pseud.* (Nicolas Mordvinoff). Written by Will, *pseud.* (William Lipkind). Harcourt.
If I Ran the Zoo. Written and illustrated by Dr. Seuss, *pseud.* (Theodor Seuss Geisel). Random House.
The Most Wonderful Doll in the World. Illustrated by Helen Stone. Written by Phyllis McGinley. Lippincott.
T-Bone, the Baby Sitter. Story and pictures by Claire Turlay Newberry. Harper.

1950 Award: *Song of the Swallows.* Written and illustrated by Leo Politi. Scribner.

Honor books: *America's Ethan Allen.* Pictures by Lynd Ward. Story by Stewart Holbrook. Houghton.
The Wild Birthday Cake. Illustrated by Hildegard Woodward. Written by Lavinia R. Davis. Doubleday.
The Happy Day. Pictures by Marc Simont. Story by Ruth Krauss. Harper.
Bartholomew and the Oobleck. Written and illustrated by Dr. Seuss, *pseud.* (Theodor Seuss Geisel). Random House.
Henry Fisherman. Written and illustrated by Marcia Brown, Scribner.

Newbery Medal Books

The Newbery Medal is named in honor of John Newbery (1713–1767), an English bookseller and publisher. The Medal is presented annually by a committee of the Children's Service Division of the American Library Association to "the author of the most distinguished contribution to American literature for children." The book must be an original work by a citizen or resident of the United States.

1985 Award: *The Hero and the Crown.* Robin McKinley. Greenwillow.

Honor books: *Like Jake and Me.* Mavis Jukes. Knopf.
The Moves Make the Man. Bruce Brooks. Harper.
One-Eyed Cat. Paula Fox. Bradbury.

1984 Award: *Dear Mr. Henshaw.* Beverly Cleary. Morrow.

Honor books: *A Solitary Blue.* Cynthia Voigt. Atheneum.
Sugaring Time. Kathryn Lasky. Macmillan.
Wish Given: Three Tales of Coven Tree. Bill Brittain. Harper.
The Sign of the Beaver. Elizabeth G. Speare. Houghton.

1983 Award: *Dicey's Song.* Cynthia Voight. Atheneum.

Honor books: *The Blue Sword.* Robin McKinley. Greenwillow.
Doctor De Soto. William Steig. Farrar.
Graven Images. Paul Fleischman. Harper.
Homesick: My Own Story. Jean Fritz. Putnam.
Sweet Whispers, Brother Rush. Virginia Hamilton. Philomel.

1982 Award: *A Visit to William Blake's Inn.* Nancy Willard. Harcourt.

Honor books: *Ramona Quimby, Age 8.* Beverly Cleary. Morrow.
Upon the Head of a Goat: A Childhood in Hungary 1939–1944. Aranka Siegel. Farrar.

1981 Award: *Jacob Have I Loved.* Katherine Paterson. Crowell.

Honor books: *The Fledgling.* Jane Langton. Harper.
A Ring of Endless Light. Madeleine L'Engle. Farrar.

1980 Award:	*A Gathering of Days: A New England Girl's Journal 1830–32.* Joan W. Blos. Scribner.
Honor book:	*The Road from Home: The Story of an Armenian Girl.* David Kherdian. Greenwillow.
1979 Award:	*The Westing Game.* Ellen Raskin. Dutton.
Honor book:	*The Great Gilly Hopkins.* Katherine Paterson. Crowell.
1978 Award:	*Bridge to Terabithia.* Katherine Paterson. Crowell.
Honor books:	*Anpao: An American Indian Odyssey.* Jamake Highwater. Lippincott.
	Ramona and Her Father. Beverly Cleary. Morrow.
1977 Award:	*Roll of Thunder, Hear My Cry.* Mildred Taylor. Dial.
Honor books:	*A String in the Harp.* Nancy Bond. Atheneum/McElderry.
	Abel's Island. William Steig. Farrar.
1976 Award:	*The Grey King.* Susan Cooper. Atheneum/McElderry.
Honor books:	*The Hundred Penny Box.* Sharon Bell Mathis. Viking.
	Dragonwings. Lawrence Yep. Harper.
1975 Award:	*M. C. Higgins the Great.* Virginia Hamilton. Macmillan.
Honor books:	*My Brother Sam Is Dead.* James Lincoln Collier and Christopher Collier. Four Winds.
	Philip Hall Likes Me, I Reckon Maybe. Bette Greene. Dial.
	Figgs & Phantoms. Ellen Raskin. Dutton.
	The Perilous Gard. Elizabeth Marie Pope. Houghton.
1974 Award:	*The Slave Dancer.* Paula Fox. Bradbury.
Honor book:	*The Dark Is Rising.* Susan Cooper. Atheneum/McElderry.
1973 Award:	*Julie of the Wolves.* Jean George. Harper.
Honor books:	*Frog and Toad Together.* Arnold Lobel. Harper.
	The Upstairs Room. Johanna Reiss. Crowell.
	The Witches of Worm. Zilpha Keatley Snyder. Atheneum.
1972 Award:	*Mrs. Frisby and the Rats of NIMH.* Robert C. O'Brien. Atheneum.
Honor books:	*Incident at Hawk's Hill.* Allan W. Eckert. Little, Brown.
	The Planet of Junior Brown. Virginia Hamilton. Macmillan.
	The Tombs of Atuan. Ursula K. Le Guin. Atheneum.
	Annie and the Old One. Miska Miles. Little, Brown.
	The Headless Cupid. Zilpha Keatley Snyder. Atheneum.

1971 Award:	*The Summer of the Swans*. Betsy Byars. Viking.
Honor books:	*Kneeknock Rise*. Natalie Babbitt. Farrar.
	Enchantress from the Stars. Sylvia Louis Engdahl. Atheneum.
	Sing Down the Moon. Scott O'Dell. Houghton.
1970 Award:	*Sounder*. William Armstrong. Harper.
Honor books:	*Our Eddie*. Sulamith Ish-Kishor. Pantheon.
	The Many Ways of Seeing: An Introduction to the Pleasures of Art. Janet Gaylord Moore. World.
	Journey Outside. Mary Q. Steele. Viking.
1969 Award:	*The High King*. Lloyd Alexander. Holt.
Honor books:	*To Be a Slave*. Julius Lester. Dial.
	When Schlemiel Went to Warsaw and Other Stories. Isaac Bashevis Singer. Farrar.
1968 Award:	*From the Mixed-Up Files of Mrs. Basil E. Frankweiler*. E. L. Konigsburg. Atheneum.
Honor books:	*Jennifer, Hecate, Macbeth, William McKinley, and Me, Elizabeth*. E. L. Konigsburg. Atheneum.
	The Black Pearl. Scott O'Dell. Houghton.
	The Fearsome Inn. Isaac Bashevis Singer. Scribner.
	The Egypt Game. Zilpha Keatley Snyder. Atheneum.
1967 Award:	*Up a Road Slowly*. Irene Hunt. Follett.
Honor books:	*The King's Fifth*. Scott O'Dell. Houghton.
	Zlateh the Goat and Other Stories. Isaac Bashevis Singer. Harper.
	The Jazz Man. Mary Hays Weik. Atheneum.
1966 Award:	*I, Juan de Pareja*. Elizabeth Borton de Trevino. Farrar.
Honor books:	*The Black Cauldron*. Lloyd Alexander. Holt.
	The Animal Family. Randall Jarrell. Pantheon.
	The Noonday Friends. Mary Stolz. Harper.
1965 Award:	*Shadow of a Bull*. Maia Wojciechowska. Atheneum.
Honor book:	*Across Five Aprils*. Irene Hunt. Follett.
1964 Award:	*It's Like This, Cat*. Emily Neville. Harper.
Honor books:	*Rascal*. Sterling North. Dutton.
	*The Loner.*Ester Wier. McKay.
1963 Award:	*A Wrinkle in Time*. Madeleine L'Engle. Farrar, Straus.
Honor books:	*Thistle and Thyme: Tales and Legends from Scotland*. Sorche NicLeodhas, *pseud.* (Leclaire Alger). Holt.
	Men of Athens. Olivia Coolidge. Houghton.

1962 Award:	*The Bronze Bow.* Elizabeth George Speare. Houghton.
Honor books:	*Frontier Living.* Edwin Tunis. World.
	The Golden Goblet. Elois Jarvis McGraw. Coward-McCann.
	Belling the Tiger. Mary Stolz. Harper.
1961 Award:	*Island of the Blue Dolphins.* Scott O'Dell. Houghton.
Honor books:	*America Moves Forward.* Gerald W. Johnson. Morrow.
	Old Ramon, Jack Schaeffer. Houghton Mifflin.
	The Cricket in Times Square. George Seldon, *pseud.* (George Thompson). Farrar, Straus.
1960 Award:	*Onion John.* Joseph Krumgold. Crowell.
Honor books:	*My Side of the Mountain.* Jean George, Dutton.
	America Is Born. Gerald W. Johnson. Morrow.
	The Gammage Cup. Carol Kendall. Harcourt.
1959 Award:	*The Witch of Blackbird Pond.* Elizabeth George Speare. Houghton.
Honor books:	*The Family Under the Bridge.* Natalie S. Carlson. Harper.
	Along Came a Dog. Meindert DeJong. Harper.
	Chucaro: Wild Pony of the Pampa. Francis Kalnay. Harcourt.
	The Perilous Road. William O. Steele. Harcourt.
1958 Award:	*Rifles for Watie.* Harold Keith. Crowell.
Honor books:	*The Horsecatcher.* Mari Sandoz. Westminster.
	Gone-Away Lake. Elizabeth Enright. Harcourt.
	The Great Wheel. Robert Lawson. Viking.
	Tom Paine, Freedom's Apostle. Leo Gurko. Crowell.
1957 Award:	*Miracles on Maple Hill.* Virginia Sorensen. Harcourt.
Honor books:	*Old Yeller.* Fred Gipson. Harper.
	The House of Sixty Fathers. Meindert DeJong. Harper.
	Mr. Justice Holmes. Clara Ingram Judson. Follett.
	The Corn Grows Ripe. Dorothy Rhoads. Viking.
	Black Fox of Lorne. Marguerite de Angeli. Doubleday.
1956 Award:	*Carry On, Mr. Bowditch.* Jean Lee Latham. Houghton.
Honor books:	*The Secret River.* Marjorie Kinnan Rawlings. Scribner.
	The Golden Name Day. Jennie Lindquist. Harper.
	Men, Microscopes, and Living Things. Katherine Shippen. Viking.
1955 Award:	*The Wheel on the School.* Meindert DeJong. Harper.
Honor books:	*The Courage of Sarah Noble.* Alice Dalgliesh. Scribner.
	Banner in the Sky. James Ullman. Lippincott.

1954 Award:	. . . *and now Miguel.* Joseph Krumgold. Crowell.
Honor books:	*All Alone.* Claire Huchet Bishop. Viking.
	Shadrach. Meindert DeJong. Harper.
	Hurry Home, Candy. Meindert DeJong. Harper.
	Theodore Roosevelt, Fighting Patriot. Clara Ingram Judson. Follett.
	Magic Maize. Mary and Conrad Buff. Houghton.
1953 Award:	*Secret of the Andes.* Ann Nolan Clark. Viking.
Honor books:	*Charlotte's Web.* E. B. White. Harper.
	Moccasin Trail. Eloise McGraw. Coward-McCann.
	Red Sails to Capri. Ann Weil. Viking.
	The Bears on Hemlock Mountain. Alice Dalgliesh. Scribner.
	Birthdays of Freedom, Volume 1. Genevieve Foster. Scribner.
1952 Award:	*Ginger Pye.* Eleanor Estes. Harcourt.
Honor books:	*Americans Before Columbus.* Elizabeth Baity. Viking.
	Minn of the Mississippi. Holling C. Holling. Houghton.
	The Defender. Nicholas Kalashnikoff. Scribner.
	The Light at Tern Rock. Julia Sauer. Viking.
	The Apple and the Arrow. Mary and Conrad Buff. Houghton.
1951 Award:	*Amos Fortune, Free Man.* Elizabeth Yates. Aladdin.
Honor books:	*Better Known as Johnny Appleseed.* Mabel Leigh Hunt. Lippincott.
	Gandhi, Fighter Without a Sword. Jeanette Eaton. Morrow.
	Abraham Lincoln, Friend of the People. Clara Ingram Judson. Follett.
	The Story of Appleby Capple. Anne Parrish. Harper.
1950 Award:	*The Door in the Wall.* Marguerite de Angeli. Doubleday.
Honor books:	*Tree of Freedom.* Rebecca Caudill. Viking.
	The Blue Cat of Castle Town. Catherine Coblentz. Longmans.
	Kildee House. Rutherford Montgomery. Doubleday.
	George Washington. Genevieve Foster. Scribner.
	Song of the Pines. Walter and Marion Havighurst. Winston.

Appendix Guidelines for Review and Evaluation of English Language Arts Software*

In 1981 the National Council of Teachers of English established the Committee on Instructional Technology to investigate the potential of using technology, particularly computers, in the teaching of English language arts. A major priority of the Committee was to develop a set of criteria that could be used by educators at all levels to evaluate educational software. The Committee set about this task with the full recognition that it would be difficult to develop a single evaluation form that could be applied to all software. The approach to the task, therefore, was to try to develop criteria that embraced the most dynamic capabilities of the computer and, at the same time, to take into account the various instructional strategies which could be included in the design of a software program.

The Committee on Instructional Technology hopes that the Guidelines will help you with the difficult task of evaluating software. We welcome your comments about how you used them and about the kind of criteria that should be included in future revisions.

Using the Guidelines

STEP 1: FAMILIARIZE YOURSELF WITH THE GUIDELINES

Read through the Guidelines to acquaint yourself with the format, the criteria, and the general procedures for using them. You will notice that the Guidelines are divided into five (5) sections, or categories. The criteria in four (4) of these sections can be used to evaluate almost any type of instructional software. Section III, however, includes variable criteria which can be applied to a software package depending upon the instructional strategy used in the program. The criteria listed in Section III within the body of the Guidelines address programs that use a tutorial/drill and practice strategy. However, if the program you are reviewing uses an instructional game or a simulation, simply turn to the GUIDELINES ADDENDUM section and use the criteria listed there to evaluate the strategy being used. This section lists criteria for evaluating Simulations and Problem-Solving, Educational Games, Teacher Utilities (A program that allows teachers to alter the content or format of the program), and Word Processing. Not all of the sections included in the ADDENDUM are truly instructional strategies in the strictest sense. However, the ADDENDUM section does allow you to evaluate programs which might deviate from a typical drill and/or tutorial program.

*Reprinted from GUIDELINES FOR REVIEW AND EVALUATION OF ENGLISH LANGUAGE ARTS SOFTWARE, 1981. Prepared by the Committee on Instructional Technology (Robert Caldwell, Chair), National Council of Teachers of English, Urbana, Illinois. Used with permission.

STEP 2: USE THE SOFTWARE YOURSELF

Proceed through the software program and use it as if you were a student. Occasionally, make an error deliberately in the same way that one of your students might. By doing this you will be able to see how the program handles errors or prompts incorrect responses.

STEP 3: LET YOUR STUDENTS USE THE SOFTWARE

Allowing students to use the program is the ultimate evaluation. Observe their responses to the program. Try to determine whether they are learning anything from it. Does it motivate them and involve them in learning or do they look bored and uninvolved?

STEP 4: USE THE GUIDELINES TO EVALUATE THE SOFTWARE

When you have thoroughly familiarized yourself with the software program, go through each section of the Guidelines and respond to each item. You might want to write marginal notes by some items for reference later when you write your summary comments.

STEP 5: COMPLETE THE OVERALL EVALUATION AND WRITE SUMMARY COMMENTS

The Overall Evaluation section of the Guidelines provides for four (4) types of information:

1. *A summary evaluation of each of the five (5) sections.*
   In this section you have the opportunity to make a qualitative judgment about the program you are reviewing. Rate each section using the scale of 1–5 with 1 (poor) representing the lowest rating and 5 representing the highest (excellent). A rating of NA has also been provided in case the program lacks a management system, supplementary materials, or some other feature that does not detract from the programs effectiveness.
2. *Summary Comments*
   Here you can write anecdotal comments about the program's strengths and weaknesses. This is an important section because it provides an opportunity to include comments about qualities in the program which are not included in the criteria for each section. This section allows you to provide both a description and an evaluation of the software for yourself and your colleagues.
3. *Students' Responses to the Program*
   The true measure of any instructional program is whether it teaches what it was intended to teach. In this section you can summarize the observations you made when you allowed your students to use the program.

4. *Recommendations*
This section could be the most important of all, particularly if you review software for your district or school building. Try to summarize the reasons why you are not recommending the software or how you think it might fit into your language arts program. Try to recommend a specific use for the piece of software and how it might fit in with software programs you already have.

Compared with other educational media, instructional software is still in its very earliest stages of development. Developers and publishers of software are still learning how to best use the computer as a teaching medium. For this reason, the evaluation of software remains an imprecise process. Therefore, perhaps the best guidelines for evaluating software is to judge it against its producer's claims. That is, compare the product's performance against what the publisher claims it will do. Also, compare it against other products that attempt to teach the same concepts and skills. Finally, try to review a wide range of software and note how each uses the computer to present the instruction.

Guidelines for Software Review and Evaluation

Program: ______________________________

Producer ______________________________

Required Equipment: ______________________________

____

Grade Level: ____________________ Cost: ____________

Overall Program Objectives: ______________________________

____

Single Lesson Objectives (if you are reviewing one lesson only):

Answer *yes* or *no* for the following criteria in Section I through V.

I. MANAGEMENT FEATURES

____ 1. Program provides teacher with a management system. (If *no,* go to Section II.)

____ 2. Program has record-keeping system that is useful and efficient.

____ 3. Records are easily retrievable.

____ 4. Teacher can assign or change performance levels and otherwise modify or add to records.

II. CONTENT

____ 1. Content is accurate.

____ 2. Content is appropriate to grade levels for which it is intended.

____ 3. Content can be modified by student or teacher.

____ 4. Possible content modifications are appropriate to the subject matter.

____ 5. Program can contribute integrally to the total English language arts curriculum.

____ 6. Program achieves its purpose.

____ 7. Program is likely to be motivating to students.

III. INSTRUCTIONAL STRATEGY

Note: If the software you are reviewing uses an instructional strategy other than tutorial or drill and practice, go to the Guidelines Addendum (Alternate Section III) to complete this section. Then continue with Section IV.

____ 1. Program is attractive.

____ 2. Program provides opportunity for practice.

____ 3. Practice is sufficient to help ensure mastery.

____ 4. Examples are provided.

____ 5. Examples are clear.

____ 6. Presentation is logical and well organized.

____ 7. Student has control over rate of presentation.

____ 8. Feedback for incorrect responses is helpful for discovering correct answers.

____ 9. Program allows learner to review, repeat, or advance according to performance.

____10. Program reports student performance periodically.

____11. Program provides an appropriate balance between content presentation and student interactions or responses.

____12. Program offers a variety of interactions, varying keys pressed or responses required.

____13. Program stimulates cognitive growth (or promotes thinking skills beyond recall of information).

____14. Program complements (or enhances) other English language arts materials.

____15. Program calls for meaningful application of English language arts skills.

IV. EASE OF OPERATION

____ 1. Directions to student are clear.

____ 2. Directions are accessible when needed.

____ 3. Student can operate program independently.

____ 4. Student is prevented from getting lost in the program, with no way out.

____ 5. Student is provided with option to quit or continue at any time.

V. SUPPLEMENTARY MATERIALS

___ 1. Program provides teacher's guide.
___ 2. Program provides supplementary student materials.
___ 3. If *yes,* materials are appropriate and useful.
___ 4. Program provides pre- and post-tests.
___ 5. Replacement print materials are available from producer.

Overall Evaluation

Use the scale at the right to rate this program. (1 is lowest; *NA* means *Not Applicable.*)

I. MANAGEMENT FEATURES	**1 2 3 4 5 NA**
II. CONTENT	**1 2 3 4 5 NA**
III. INSTRUCTIONAL STRATEGY	**1 2 3 4 5 NA**
IV. EASE OF OPERATION	**1 2 3 4 5 NA**
V. SUPPLEMENTARY MATERIALS	**1 2 3 4 5 NA**

SUMMARY COMMENTS
(Continue on back of sheet, if necessary.)

Program's Strengths and Weaknesses ______________________________

____
____
____
____
____
____

STUDENTS' RESPONSES TO PROGRAM
(Briefly indicate number of students, grade levels, etc.): ______________________________

____
____
____

RECOMMENDATIONS: ______________________________

____
____
____

Guidelines Addendum (Alternate Section III)

Choose the description which best fits the software you are reviewing, and respond to each criterion under that heading with a *yes* or *no.*

A. SIMULATION/PROBLEM-SOLVING

(A program in which students learn through discovery and decision making)

____ 1. Problem-solving situation is realistic.
____ 2. Design is motivating.
____ 3. Procedural tasks are clearly sequenced.
____ 4. Feedback about user's decision is helpful.
____ 5. Suggestions are given for optimum performance.
____ 6. Outcomes or choices are explained.
____ 7. The program is relevant to the acquisition of English language arts skills.

(Go on to Section IV.)

B. EDUCATIONAL GAME

____ 1. Format is motivating.
____ 2. Graphics are appropriate to presentation.
____ 3. Content is relevant to English language arts skills.
____ 4. Learner has access to help or review.
____ 5. There is an appropriate reward for success and no "reward" for incorrect responses.
____ 6. Additional information or clues are provided by error feedback.

(Go on to Section IV.)

C. TEACHER UTILITY

(A program which allows teacher to "author" the content within a programmed format)

____ 1. Directions to teacher are clear.
____ 2. Items are easy to enter.
____ 3. Editing is possible.
____ 4. Format for presenting items to student is appropriate.
____ 5. Student directions are clear.
____ 6. The type of interaction is appropriate to the skills taught.
____ 7. Record keeping capability is provided.

(Go on to Section IV.)

D. WORD PROCESSING/TEXT EDITING

1. Management Features

____ a. Utility functions (e.g., cataloging, renaming, protecting, deleting, copying files) are adequate.

____ b. Supplemental materials (such as summary command cards, worksheets, spelling checkers) are provided.

____ c. Editing utilities (e.g., capacity for adding words to spelling checkers) are adequate.

____ d. Management options (such as printing files) are available to and easy to use by students.

2. Safeguards

____ a. Directions or warnings at critical decision points (e.g., "Are you sure you want to delete this paragraph?") are given.

____ b. Back-up disks are available.

____ c. User can undo a previous action (e.g., return paragraph to its original position).

3. Editing

____ a. Formating features (e.g., upper/lower case, centering, underlining, tabs, subscripts) are adequate for intended audience and use.

____ b. Editing features (such as deletion and insertion of characters, words, paragraphs) are adequate for intended audience and use.

____ c. Command keys are logical and relatively easy to use.

4. Visual Presentation

____ a. Displayed characters are sufficiently readable for intended audience (e.g., 25, 40, 80 characters per line).

____ b. There is adequate space between lines or print.

____ c. Lines terminate at word boundaries.

5. Printing

____ a. Print formats (e.g., page width, page length, spacing) are flexible and adequate for intended audience and use.

____ b. The selected print format can be displayed on the screen prior to printing.

(Go on to Section IV.)

E. OTHER TYPES OF SOFTWARE

If the software you are reviewing does not fall into any of the above categories, you may wish to give a brief description of it below, followed by your evaluative comments.

____

____

____

____

____

____

____

____

(Go on to Section IV.)

Committee on Instructional Technology National Council of Teachers of English

Robert M. Caldwell, Chair, PANDA Learning Systems, Inc., Dallas, Texas: Phyllis Caputo, Classroom Computer News; Ricky Carter, Lesley College; Phil Cousins, Harvard University; Richard P. Cummins, PANDA Learning Systems; Collette Daiute, Harvard University; Lester Golub, Baruch College; William Horst, Fairfax County Schools, Virginia; Shirley Keran, Minnesota Educational Consortium; George Mason, University of Georgia; Jayne Moliterno, Science Research Associates; Bill Oates, University of Miami; Karen Piper, Developmental Learning Materials; Sallie Sherman, Ohio State University; Robert Shostak, Florida International University; Sally Standiford, University of Illinois; Irene Thomas, IOTA, Inc.; Robert F. Yeager, InterCom, Inc.; Robert Wisher, Army Research Institute, PERI-IC; Anne Auten, ERIC/RCS, NCTE Staff Liaison; Skip Nicholson, Burbank High School, Burbank, California, NCTE Executive Committee.

Appendix

Answers to *Discover as You Read This Chapter If* Statements

Chapter 1	1. true	2. false	3. true	4. false	5. true
	6. false	7. false	8. false	9. true	10. false
Chapter 2	1. false	2. true	3. true	4. true	5. false
	6. true	7. true	8. false	9. false	10. false
Chapter 3	1. true	2. true	3. true	4. false	5. false
	6. false	7. true	8. false	9. true	10. true
Chapter 4	1. true	2. false	3. false	4. false	5. true
	6. false	7. false	8. true	9. false	10. true
Chapter 5	1. false	2. false	3. false	4. true	5. true
	6. true	7. false	8. false	9. true	10. true
Chapter 6	1. true	2. false	3. true	4. true	5. false
	6. false	7. true	8. false	9. true	10. true
Chapter 7	1. true	2. false	3. false	4. true	5. true
	6. false	7. true	8. false	9. false	10. true
Chapter 8	1. true	2. false	3. false	4. false	5. true
	6. false	7. true	8. false	9. false	10. false
Chapter 9	1. true	2. true	3. false	4. false	5. false
	6. true	7. false	8. false	9. true	10. false
Chapter 10	1. true	2. true	3. false	4. false	5. false
	6. true	7. false	8. true	9. false	10. true
Chapter 11	1. true	2. true	3. false	4. true	5. false
	6. true	7. true	8. true	9. false	10. false
Chapter 12	1. true	2. false	3. true	4. false	5. true
	6. false	7. true	8. true	9. false	10. false
Chapter 13	1. true	2. false	3. false	4. false	5. false
	6. false	7. true	8. true	9. false	10. true
Chapter 14	1. true	2. false	3. false	4. false	5. true
	6. true	7. true	8. false	9. true	10. true

Author Index

a

Addy, P., 202
Adorable, E., 112
Alatis, J., 530
Allen, R., 340
Allington, R., 376
Alpern, R., 158
Alpren, P., 295
Alvermann, D., 112
Amiran, E., 293
Andersen, D., 201
Anderson, R., 375
Andreasen, N., 294
Anisfeld, M., 49
Arburthnot, M., 427
Asher, J., 508, 530
Askov, E., 201, 470
Aukerman, R., 338, 340
Ayris, B., 201

b

Backlund, P., 114, 160
Baker, D., 470
Barbe, W., 201, 202
Barney, L., 470
Barrett, T., 348, 376
Barron, P., 426
Beck, I., 376
Beers, C., 236, 238
Beers, J., 236, 238
Bent, J., 292
Benton, M., 426
Berkeley, M., 427
Berns, M., 20
Berry, M., 114
Bingham-Newman, A., 44, 50
Bissex, G., 236
Blair, T., 238
Blake, H., 294
Blanchard, J., 14, 20, 470
Bloomfield, L., 58
Blume, J., 384, 385
Bolton, G., 494
Boodt, G., 112
Bornstein, D., 80
Brantley, J., 494
Brause, R., 375
Brittain, M., 376
Britton, J., 294
Brooks, K., 114
Brown, R., 50
Bullock, A., 201
Burley, J., 426
Burns, P., 340
Buros, O., 50, 81, 160, 239, 295, 340, 341, 427, 530
Burris, N., 294
Burton, G., 201
Busching, B., 20, 159
Byrne, M., 151, 160

c

Carlton, L., 494
Carpenter, D., 235
Carroll, J., 300, 340, 363
Carson, D., 158
Carter, S., 427
Cazden, C., 295
Ceprano, M., 340
Chall, J., 293, 363
Chamot, A., 530
Charney, D., 292
Chiang, B., 235
Childers, P., 239
Chiu, L. H., 426
Chomsky, C., 214, 236, 238
Chomsky, N., 60, 207
Christie, J., 80, 479, 494
Cianciolo, P., 382, 426
Clark, C., 294
Clausen, G., 160
Clements, D., 20
Coles, R., 201
Collins, A., 341
Collins, L., 426
Conklin, N., 530
Cook, J., 114
Cooney, J., 20
Coop, R., 292
Cooper, C., 295
Cooper, J., 202, 340
Cordeiro, P., 295
Cothran, A., 202
Cowe, E., 159
Cramer, R., 209, 237, 239
Criscuolo, N., 338
Crist, B., 365, 376
Cummins, J., 530
Cunningham, P., 112
Curtis, J., 160

d

Dahl, S., 50
Daiker, D., 80
Dale, E., 349, 356, 363, 372, 376
Damico, J., 160
D'Angelo, K., 201
Daniel, D., 14, 20, 470
Darley, F., 50
Davies, P., 363
Davies, R., 430, 470
Dellmann, M., 426
DeLoach, R., 202
Devine, T., 96, 114
Dickerson, D., 376
Dickson, S., 160
DiStefano, P., 20, 235, 238
Dixon, G., 364, 376
Dolch, E., 363
Downing, J., 528
Dreyer, S., 427
Duffelmeyer, F., 374
Du Four, R., 495
Durkin, D., 202, 338
Durr, W., 363

e

Eckhoff, B., 244, 294
Edelsky, C., 292
Edwards, C., 158
Eisenhardt, C., 50
Eisenson, J., 160
Elleman, B., 427
Emans, R., 340
Engel, R., 427
Erickson, R., 114

f

Feeley, J., 426
Fielding, L., 114
Fillmore, L., 530
Finn, P., 295
Fisher, C., 114, 201, 427
Fisher, K., 80
Fitzgerald, J., 217
Fitzgerald, S., 159
Fitzsimmons, R., 238
Flake-Hobson, C., 49
Fleming, C., 158
Flood, J., 20, 340
Florio, S., 294
Ford, C., 528
Forster, R., 201
Francis, W., 217, 363
Frederick, W., 294
Fredericks, A., 338
Freeman, E., 49
Frentz, T., 114
Friedlander, Z., 114
Frith, U., 239
Froese, V., 86, 113, 201
Fry, E., 363, 374

g

Galda, J., 494
Ganshow, L., 238
Gay, C., 294
Gentry, J., 49
Gentry, R., 237
Gerard, H., 114
Getman, G., 201
Giacobbe, M., 295
Gillet, J., 20, 49
Gillies, E., 476, 490, 494, 495
Gipe, J., 376
Goldberg, M., 474, 494
Golden, J., 293
Goldman, R., 202
Golladay, W., 238
Golub, L., 294, 295
Gonzales, P., 530
Goodman, K., 316, 340
Goodman, Y., 201
Gordon, H., 20
Gottfried, A., 49
Graham, S., 238
Gralley, R., 160
Grant, B., 294
Grant, K., 238
Graves, D., 288, 293, 295
Gray, R., 159
Green, E., 80
Greenberg, D., 295
Greenman, R., 374
Greff, K., 201
Griffin, W., 40, 50
Griffing, P., 494
Gumperz, J., 50

h

Hagelberg, E., 376
Hagerty, P., 235, 238
Haggard, M., 376
Hailey, J., 294
Haley-James, S., 53, 81, 159, 247, 294
Halle, M., 207
Halliday, M., 34, 50
Halpin, G., 201
Hammill, D., 238, 294, 340
Hansen, L., 260, 295
Hardyck, C., 202
Hare, V., 49
Harpin, W., 244, 294
Harries, R., 201
Harris, A., 340, 363
Harris, L., 340
Hartshown, E., 494
Hasselbring, T., 235
Hatch, E., 530
Haugh, E., 89, 114
Hayes, D., 201
Heath, S., 158
Heathcote, D., 494
Helwig, J., 202
Henderson, E., 235, 236
Hennings, D., 294
Higgs, T., 528
Hildyard, A., 89, 114
Hillerich, R., 363, 376
Hirsch, E., 201
Hobson, C., 159
Hodges, R., 238, 239
Hoedt, K., 294
Hoffman, S., 88, 114, 158
Hogan, T., 295
Holbrook, H., 80, 235
Homer, S., 159
Horton, L., 202
Huckleberry, A., 159
Hull, F., 160
Humes, A., 294
Hunt, K., 40, 50
Hurst, C., 235
Huus, H., 426
Hymes, D., 50

i

Ingoldsby, B., 426
Irwin, E., 494

j

Jackson, P., 528
Jacobs, S., 292
Jacobs, V., 293
Jacobson, M., 363
Jalbrant, F., 470
Jalongo, M., 426
Janiak, R., 114
Jann, G., 160
Jenkins, E., 427
Jenkins, L., 295
Johns, J., 202
Johnson, D., 348, 363, 376
Johnson, T., 238
Jones, J., 202
Jones, T., 159

k

Kaake, D., 202
Kaelber, P., 159
Kamm, K., 470
Karpisek, M., 470
Kean, J., 56, 81, 114
Kerek, A., 80
King, R., 160
Kirk, U., 201
Kister, K., 447, 470
Klein, M., 80, 81, 119, 122, 159, 294
Klein, R., 295
Klumb, R., 470
Kopatic, N., 160
Kowalski, S., 239
Krashen, S., 528
Kreeft, J., 292
Krzeski, J., 201, 294
Kučera, H., 217, 363
Kuchinskas, G., 20
Kusik, P., 338

l

Lamme, L., 201, 427
Langford, K., 238
Lapp, D., 340
Larrick, N., 390, 427
Larsen, S., 238
Larson, G., 114

Lawler, J., 80
Lazarus, P., 159
Lefevre, C., 81
Lehman, C., 202
Lehr, F., 494
Leibowicz, J., 528
Lemons, R., 88, 114
Levine, S., 80
Littig, E., 494
Livingston, M., 426
Loban, W., 40, 50, 376
Long, M., 528
Loomer, B., 238
Lorge, I., 363
Lourie, M., 530
Lukasevich, A., 426
Lukens, R., 426
Lundsteen, S., 86, 113

m

McCarthy, A., 80
McCaslin, E., 376
McCaslin, N., 376, 494
McCully, B., 158
McDaniel, E., 294
McGill-Franzen, A., 376
McKee, J., 494
McKeown, M., 376
McMahon, M., 114
McNutt, G., 238, 340, 375
Majer, E., 376
Malley, I., 470
Malmstrom, J., 50, 80
Mann, J., 293, 494
Manolakes, G., 238
Markham, L., 295
Marshall, K., 470
Martin, M., 114
Marzana, R., 530
Mason, G., 202, 470, 494
Mayher, J., 375
Mendoza, A., 426
Mezynski, K., 376
Middleton, T., 80
Miller, B., 80, 294
Miller, G., 494
Milone, M., 201, 202
Monson, D., 427
Montessori, M., 165
Montgomery, P., 470
Moore, F., 530
Moore, R., 494
Moore, S., 88, 114
Morenberg, M., 80
Morency, A., 160
Morris, D., 235
Moss, E., 426
Mower, M., 470
Mumford, S., 113
Myers, R., 295

n

Nagy, W., 375
Najimy, N., 295
Nakamura, Y., 528
Natarella, M., 427
Nathan, R., 294
Nelson, D., 159
Newman, A., 20
Ney, J., 80, 294
Nickel, M., 470
Nirgiotis, N., 159
Norman, J., 202
Norris, R., 40, 50
Noyce, R., 80
Nunberg, G., 80

o

O'Donnell, R., 40, 50, 294
Ogilvie, M., 160
O'Hare, F., 80
Oliver, L., 426
Oller, J., 160
Oratio, M., 160
O'Rourke, J., 349, 354, 356, 372, 376
Oskendahl, W., 202
Otto, W., 340
Owens, S., 235

p

Papert, S., 20
Partoll, S., 228, 239
Paul, R., 236
Pearson, P., 114, 340, 376
Perney, J., 235
Perron, J., 80
Petersen, B., 114
Peterson, G., 380, 426
Petitclerc, G., 185, 202
Petrinovich, L., 202
Petty, D., 20
Petty, W., 20, 295
Piaget, J., 42, 43
Pickering, M., 159
Pietras, T., 294
Piggins, C., 494
Plaskon, S., 292
Porter, E., 293, 426
Prostano, E., 470
Prostano, J., 470

q

Quorn, K., 238

r

Ramsey, I., 114
Raphael, T., 341
Rayner, K., 376
Read, C., 236, 237
Readence, J., 338
Reutzel, D., 338
Richmond, B., 363
Riedesel, C., 20
Rieke, R., 159
Rinsland, H., 217, 363
Rivers, R., 20
Robinson, H., 426
Robinson, N., 375
Rodrigues, R., 517, 530
Roe, B., 324, 340
Ross, E., 324, 340
Rosso, B., 340
Rothschild, I., 239
Roush, M., 427
Rowe, M., 341
Rubin, D., 114
Rude, R., 340
Rudman, M., 426
Rupley, W., 238
Russell, P., 236
Russell, S., 159
Rutherford, W., 114

s

Safran, J., 80
Sager, C., 291
Salinger, T., 470
Saltman, J., 426
Salus, P., 20
Saracho, O., 528
Saunders, R., 44, 50
Sauro, N., 375
Schickedanz, J., 338
Schilling, M., 235
Schubert, D., 340
Schwartz, J., 20

Searloss, L., 338
Sebesta, S., 427
Seidler, A., 160
Seiler, W., 159
Serio, M., 235
Shafer, R., 50
Shaftel, F., 480, 485, 494, 495
Shaftel, G., 480, 485, 494, 495
Shapiro, B., 294
Shapiro, P., 294
Shervanian, C., 151, 160
Shipman, D., 338
Shores, J., 470
Signoretti, L., 160
Siks, G., 494
Silverman, E., 470
Simms, R., 292
Sinatra, R., 20, 80
Sinclair, C., 201
Singer, I., 384
Sipay, E., 340
Skeen, E., 20
Smallwood, C., 470
Smando, F., 426
Smilansky, S., 479
Smith, C., 159, 340
Smith, E., 341, 494
Smith, F., 50, 248, 294
Smith, K., 292
Smith, R., 260, 295
Smith, S., 528
Snoddy, J., 470
Sovik, N., 201
Spangler, K., 426
Spiegel, D., 340, 341
Stahl-Gemake, J., 20
Stammer, J., 114
Standal, T., 376
Stein, M., 235
Steinberg, J., 530
Stephany, G., 530
Stevens, F., 530
Stewig, J., 20, 426, 427, 494, 495
Sticht, T., 89, 114
Stotsky, S., 80, 244, 294
Stoudt, R., 160
Strauss, J., 495
Straw, S., 80, 295
Strother, E., 159
Sullivan, M., 338
Summers, E., 426
Sutherland, Z., 426, 427
Swisher, K., 375

t

Tagatz, G., 202
Tamor, L., 470
Taylor, W., 294
Temple, C., 20, 294
Templeton, S., 238
Terrell, T., 528
Terry, A., 427
Thomas, V., 217
Thompson, G., 88, 114
Thorndike, E., 357, 363
Thurber, D., 178
Tibbetts, S., 426
Timmons, R., 160
Tinzmann, M., 89, 114
Tom, C., 427
Toothaker, R., 426
Torgerson, T., 340
Torrance, E., 285, 295
Torrance, J., 295
Trachtman, P., 50
Trap, J., 202
Trap-Porter, J., 201
Tway, E., 293

v

Van Riper, C., 151, 160
Venezky, R., 205
Ventriglia, L., 508, 530
Verriour, P., 494
Vockell, E., 20
Vukelich, C., 293, 338

w

Waggoner, D., 530
Wagoner, S., 426
Walker, H., 470
Walmsley, S., 470
Warncke, E., 338
Waslyck, T., 201
Wassermann, S., 113
Watts, A., 40, 50
Way, J., 159
Weaver, C., 81
Weaver, P., 340
Weaver, S., 114
Weintraub, S., 426
Weiss, M., 427
Wendelin, K., 427
Weslander, D., 530
Wetstone, H., 114
White, R., 517, 530
Wilcox, M., 123, 159
Wilkins, L., 470
Wilkinson, L., 159
Willbrand, M., 159
Willer, A., 293
Williams, F., 159
Williams, L., 289, 295
Wilson, C., 327, 340, 341
Wilson, M., 294
Wilson, R., 340
Winitz, H., 50
Wise, M., 168
Wood, K., 375
Woodfin, M., 294
Woods, C., 160
Worden, T., 340
Worell, J., 50
Wylie, P., 202

y

Yost, H., 20
Young, L., 494
Youngers, J., 476, 494

z

Zaharias, J., 20
Zelazo, P., 50
Zeman, S., 294
Ziegler, E., 427
Zinck, R., 427
Zonshin, J., 50
Zutell, J., 237

Subject Index

a

Activities, instructional, in
beginning language, 10–14
dictionary skills, 451–52
ESL, 517–19
grammar, 72–73
language history, 25–26
listening, 93–102
literature, children's, 402–23
phonic analysis, 326–27
speech arts, 118
spelling, 221–23
structural analysis, 321–23
vocabulary development, 365–68
word recognition skills, 316–18, 319, 321–23, 326–27
written composition, 262–63
Affixes
mastery of, 357–58
prefixes, 33, 207, 357, 359–60
suffixes, 33, 207, 357–58
derivational, 33, 357
inflectional, 33, 357
Alignment in handwriting, 170, 176, 197
Alphabet, handwriting
cursive, traditional, 175–76
D'Nealian, 179–80
italic, 181
manuscript, traditional, 170–71
Alphabetic orthography, English, 204–7
American Handwriting Scale, 199
Analytic phonic analysis, 323–24
Analytic scoring of written composition, 291
Announcing/explaining/directing, 127
Appreciative listening, 94–95
Articulation
disorders, 153–54
exercises, 147
Attentive listening, 95–98
Audiovisual equipment, operating, 456–57
Ayres Handwriting Scale, 199

b

Basal reader approach, 309–11
Basal reader series, evaluation checklist, Appendix 3
Base words, 33, 358, 361–62
Bay Area Writing Project, 242, 250
Behavioral objectives in
listening, 102–3
literature, 380
Behavioristic theory of language acquisition, 35
Bibliographies, compiling, 455
Bibliotherapy, 397–401
Biography for children, 381, 389–90
Biological theory of language acquisition, 35
Book clubs, juvenile, 410
Book reports/reviews, 416–17
Buzz groups, 126

c

Caldecott Medal books, list of, Appendix 4
Calendar, The, 408
Capitalization, 259
Card catalog, library
sample cards, 439, 440–41, 442
using, 436–44
Cardoza Oral Language Index, 514–15
Cassette tapes, recommended titles, Appendix 1
Checklist, pupils' self-evaluation (*See* Evaluation, pupils' self)
Checklist, teacher's for guiding role-playing, 485–87
Children's Book Council, 408
Children's drama (*See* Theatre, children's *and* Drama, creative)
Children's literature (*See* Literature, children's)
Children's theatre (*See* Theatre, children's)
Choral reading (*See* Choral speaking)
Choral speaking
arrangements for, 417–22
pitfalls of, 422–23
selections for, 422
Cinquains, writing, 256–57
Classroom environment (*See* Environment, classroom)
Cloze reading, 18, 319
Cloze test in ESL, 526
Club meetings, evaluating, 129
Cognitive theory of language acquisition, 36
Communicative development, 117, 141–51

Communicative remediation for handicapped children
  articulation disorders, 153–54
  delayed language development, 156–57
  stuttering, 155–56
  voice disturbances, 155
Competencies for English language programs, 6–9
Composition, written
  content of, 249
  conventions or mechanics of, 257–60
  creativity and, 285–86
  evaluation of pupils' progress in, 286–92
  factors affecting, 242–45
  functions of, 245–46
  guidelines for teaching, 245–48
  instructional activities in, 262–63
  poetry, 256–57
  process, 249–57
  reading and, 243
  samples of children's, 272–84
  stimuli for, 260–72
Compound words, 207, 322, 330
Comprehension, listening, 88–89, 90
Comprehension, reading
  conceptions of, 327
  factors influencing, 327
  levels or types, 328
  problems, 332–33
  role of questioning in, 328
  strategies for instruction, 330–32
Concrete operations period (Piaget), 42
Conferences, teacher-pupil, in
  handwriting, 192–93
  individualized approach to reading, 312–14
  written composition, 287–89
Consonant sounds, English
  symbols for, 206
Constituents, 60
Construction, English, 60
Content of written composition, 249
Context clues
  activities using, 319
  external, 356–57
  internal, 357–62
  types, 318
Contractions, 320, 322
Conventions of writing, 257–60
Conversation and dialogue, 121–23
Copying in handwriting, 164
Creative drama (*See* Drama, creative)
Creativity, 285–86
Criterion-referenced tests, 334
Critical listening, 99–101
Cursive handwriting, traditional, 173–78

d

Debating, 118, 127–28
Decoding, 218, 220, 327
Deep structure of language, 60
Delayed language development, 156–57
Delayed speech (*See* Delayed language development)
Derivational affixes (*See* Affixes, suffixes)
Determiners, noun, 61, 77
Development, child
  Piagetian principles, 43–44
Dewey Decimal Classification System, 435
Dialect
  nonstandard, 29, 30
  regional, 28–29
  regions of the United States, 28
  social, 29
  standard, 29, 500
Dialogue, 121–23
Dictionaries
  elementary, 450
  instructional activities for using, 451–52
  picture, 448
  skills for, 448–50
Directed Reading Activity (DRA), 310, 311
Directed Reading-Thinking Activity (DRTA), 311
Discrimination skills in listening, 89
Discussion, 123–27
  evaluation of, 127
  forms of, 126
Divergent thinking, 285
Double-base transformations, 62, 64–65
Drama, creative (*See also* Dramatic play; Dramatization, story; Pantomime; Role-playing; *and* Theatre, children's)
  evaluation of pupils' progress in, 492
  model of, 477
  objectives of, 472–73
  teacher's role in, 477–78
  values of, 476
Dramatic play, 478–80
  conditions for, 480
  developmental steps in, 480
  sequence of growth in, 479
Dramatization, story
  improvisation, 491
  interpretation, 487–91

e

Editing, 254
"Electric Company, The," 12
Encoding, 218, 220
Encyclopedias, using, 446–47
English as a second language (ESL)
  cognitive development strategies for, 506–8
  curriculum guidelines for, 505–6
  evaluation of progress in, 523–26
  guidelines for instruction in, 503–4
  instructional activities for, 517–19
  learning games for, 519–23
  program goals of, 502
  second language learning model, 504–5
  social affective strategies for, 508–11
  stages in skills' acquisition, 511, 514–16
English for speakers of other languages (ESOL) (*See* English as a second language)
English language (*See* Language, English; Grammar, English, *and* English as a second language)
Environment, classroom, 92, 117, 211, 243, 246
Environmental skills in listening, 90
Error pattern analysis, 212
Etymology, 364–65, 374
Evaluation, basal reader, Appendix 3
Evaluation, language arts textbook, Appendix 2
Evaluation of pupils' progress in
  choral speaking, 423
  conversation, 123
  debating, 128
  drama, 492
  ESL, 523, 525, 526–27
  grammar, 74–77
  handwriting, 192–99
  interviewing, 131
  language development, 48–49
  library media center skills, 467–68
  listening, 108–10, 111
  literature, children's, 423–24
  puppetry, 141
  readers theatre, participating in, 135
  reading, 333–37
  reading readiness, 303–7
  speech, 147–51
  speech arts, 157
  spelling, 230–34
  talks, giving, 121
  telephone usage, 134
  vocabulary development, 372–73
  written composition, 286–92
Evaluation, pupils' self, in
  handwriting, 193
  listening, 109–10
  speech, 149
  spelling, 233–34
  written composition, 287
Evaluation, teacher's self, in
  ESL, 524
  listening, 111
  speech education, 148
Exceptional children and
  communicative remediation, 151–57
  drama, 476
  library media center, 462–63
Experience charts, language, 12, 313
Experiences, 10–11, 246
External context clues, using, 356–57
Eye dominance, tests for, 191–92

f

Fantasy, modern, 380
Fiction in children's literature
  contemporary, 381
  elements of, 387–89
  historical, 381
Films/Filmstrips, recommended titles, Appendix 1
Formal operations period (Piaget), 42
Freeman Handwriting Scale, 199

g

Games, learning
  for ESL, 519–23
  for library media center skills, 464–66
  for listening, 102–7
  for spelling, 224–27
  for vocabulary development, 368–72
Generative transformational grammar (*See* Transformational grammar)
Genetic theory of language acquisition, 36
Goals (*See also* objectives)
  of ESL program, 502
  of handwriting program, 162
  of language arts program, 9–10
  of questioning during reading, 329
Grammar, English
  controversy over, 52–53, 56
  definitions of, 52
  evaluation of pupils progress in, 74–77
  generalizations about, 56
  instructional activities in, 72–73
  structural, 56, 58–60, 244

traditional, 56, 57–58
transformational, 56, 60–71, 244
values of teaching, 52
written composition and, 244
Graphemes, 205, 219, 323
Growth and development, child (*See* Development, child)

h

Hand dominance, 166
tests for, 190–91
Handwriting
alphabets, 170–71, 175–76, 179–80, 181
areas of difficulty in cursive, 177–78
chalkboard writing, 169
cursive, traditional, 173–78
D'Nealian, 178–79, 180
evaluation of pupils progress in, 192–99
guiding rules for cursive, 176–78
guiding rules for manuscript, 169–72
individualized instruction in, 186–87
italic, 179–81
learning-disabled children and, 187–89
left-handed children and, 190–92
legibility in, 162, 193
manuscript, traditional, 168–73
modality-based curriculum program, 172–73
prerequisite skills for, 165–68
problem areas in cursive writing, 195–97
readiness for, 165–68
sample lessons in, 187
scales, 198–99
speed in, 162, 193
written composition and, 258–59
Hard-of-hearing children, 92–93
Hearing sense, 90
History, language (*See* Language, English, history)
Holistic scoring of written composition, 290–91
"House that Jack Built, The," 419–20

i

Improvisation (*See* Dramatization, story)
Indexes, using, 445–46
Individual differences, providing for, 44–48
Individualized instruction in
handwriting, 186–87
spelling, 216–18
Individualized reading approach, 313–15
advantages of, 313
limitations of, 313
Inflectional affixes (*See* Affixes, suffixes, inflectional)
Informational books for children, 381, 389
Instructional activities (*See* Activities, instructional)
Intellectual development (Piaget), 42–44
Intelligence and
handwriting, 163
school readiness, 116
vocabulary, 348
written composition, 242
Interaction puppetry, 136
International Reading Association, 17, 383
Interpretation (*See* Dramatization, story)
Interpretive comprehension in reading, 328
Interviewing, 130
Intonation, 31–32, 58
Introductions, making, 132
Invented spelling, 209–11

j

Juncture phonemes, 32

k

Kernels, 60, 61–62
Kernel sentences (*See* Kernels)
Kindergarten, 40, 164, 458
reading program in, 308–9
Kinesics, 480
Kits, instructional, recommended, Appendix 1

l

Language arts programs, English
competencies for, 6–9
programs goals of, 9
Language arts textbooks, evaluation of, Appendix 2
Language development, delayed, 156–57
Language, English
acquisition/development of, 35–42, 208
beginning activities in, 10–14
history of, 23–25
nature of, 22–23
sound system of, 143, 206
structure of, 31–35
universal functions of, 34
usage and dialect, 26–29
Language experience approach in reading, 220–21, 311–12
advantages of, 312

charts using, 313
limitations of, 312
rationale for, 312
Language processing, 87
Language skills, 86 (*See also* specific skills such as Listening, Speaking, Reading, *and* Written Composition [writing])
Latin language, 24, 57
Learning centers, 78–79, 112–13, 158, 200, 236–37, 293, 339, 374–75, 425, 469, 493, 529
Learning disabilities in
handwriting, 187–90
spelling, 227–30
Learning games (*See* Games, learning)
Left-handed children, 190, 192, 244
Legibility in handwriting (*See* Handwriting, legibility in)
Letter formation in handwriting, 172, 177, 197
Library Bill of Rights, 432
Library media center
and exceptional children, 462–63
learning experiences in, 457–62
objectives of, 431–32
skills in using, 433–57
Library of Congress Classification System, 436
Line quality in handwriting, 172
Listening
appreciative, 94–95, 102
attentive, 95–98, 102, 103
critical, 99–101, 103
evaluation of progress in, 108–10, 111
factors influencing, 90–92
hierarchy of skills in, 89–90
importance of, 86–87
instructional activities in, 102–3
learning games for, 102–7
relationship to other language arts, 87–89
vocabulary, 350
Literal comprehension in reading, 328
Literary interests/preferences of children, 383–84
Literature, children's
as bibliotherapy, 397–401
contemporary trends in, 382–83
evaluation of pupil progress in, 423–24
functions of, 380–81
history of, 378
minority Americans in, 401–2
poetry as, 391–96
sources for selecting, 384, 386–87
Literature program, school
instructional activities in, 402–23
objectives of, 380
planning grid for, 380–81
written composition and, 243
Logographic writing, 204

m

Manuscript handwriting, traditional, 168–73
Mechanics of writing, 257–60
Media center (*See* Library media center)
Media resources for language arts, recommended, Appendix 1
Media specialist, 430
Microcomputers for language arts classrooms, 14–19
Minority Americans in children's literature, 402
Morphemes
affixes, 33
bases, 33, 358, 361–62
bound, 33
classes of, 33
free, 33, 358
roots, 33, 358, 361–62
Morphology, 32–33
Movable books, 383

n

National Council of Teachers of English (NCTE), 17, 19
Nativistic theory of language acquisition, 35–36
Newbery Medal books, list of, Appendix 4
Noble Handwriting Scale, 199
Nonbook media, using and evaluating, 456
Nonstandard dialect (*See* Dialect, nonstandard)
Nonstandard English (*See* Dialect, nonstandard)
Norm-referenced tests, 333
Note taking, 454
Noun determiners, 61, 77
Noun phrase, 61

o

Objectives (*See also* Goals) of,
children's literature, 380–81
creative drama, 472–73
drama/theatre, 472–73
elementary education, 379
library media center program, 430
library media centers, 431–32

Orthography
English alphabetic, 204–7
logographic, 204
syllabary, 204
Outlining, skill in, 454–55

p

Panel discussion, 126
Pantomime, 12, 480–84
Paragraphing, 259
Parliamentary procedure, following, 118, 128–29
Phonemes
juncture, 32
nonsegmental, 31
pitch, 32
segmental, 31
stress, 31
suprasegmental, 31
Phonic analysis
generalizations regarding, 324–25
instructional activities for, 326–27
major kinds of, 323–24
teaching guidelines about, 324
terms used in, 325
Phonology of English language, 31–32
Piagetian theory, 42
Picture books, wordless, 380, 390–91
Picture dictionaries, 448
Pitch phonemes, 32
Poetry for children
elements of, 391
forms of, 393–94
modern, 396
preferences by boys and girls for, 394–96
Poetry, writing, 256–57
Pop-up books, 383
Post writing stage in composition, 247
Prefixes (*See* Affixes, prefixes)
Preoperational period (Piaget), 42
Preschool child's language behavior, 37–38
Prewriting stage in composition, 247, 250, 251–52
Problem stories for sociodrama, 485
Proofreading
in spelling, 213
in written composition, 254, 255
marks, 255, 257–58
Punctuation, 259
Puppetry, classroom
interaction, 136
steps in, 136–37
stories for, 137
Puppets, 138–39
Puppet stages or theatres
permanent, 140–41
temporary, 139–40

q

Questioning
elements of, 330
goals of, 329
relevance to reading comprehension, 328–30

r

Readers theatre, 118, 134–35, 475
Readiness
beginning language, 10–14
for cursive writing, 174
for manuscript writing, 165–68
for reading, 302–7
Reading
components of, 300
comprehension, 327–33
definition of, 300
evaluation of pupils' progress in, 333–37
instructional strategies for, 309–16
principles of teaching, 301–2
readiness for, 302–7
recreational, 314
relationship to other language arts, 88–89, 218–21, 243
vocabulary, 350
Reading program 300, 301–2
Reading readiness checklist, 303–7
Records, recommended titles, Appendix 1
Reference books, using specialized, 452–53
Regional dialect, 28–29
Reporting, 118, 119–20
Revision of written composition, 254, 255
Robert's Rules of Order, Newly Revised, 128
Role-playing, 484–87
Roots, 33, 321, 358
Round table discussion, 126

s

Scales, handwriting, 198–99
Semantics, 34–35
Sensorimotor period (Piaget), 42
Sentence combination/manipulation, 52–53, 54–55, 69–71, 75
Sentence patterns, 56, 59

"Sesame Street", 12, 308
Sex differences and
literary interests/preferences, 383
stuttering, 155
vocabulary development, 349
written composition, 243
Show-and-tell, 119
Sight words, development of
activities for, 316–18
importance of, 316
Single-base transformation, 62, 63–64
Size and proportion in handwriting, 171, 176, 197
Skimming, 454
Slant in handwriting, 172, 176, 198
Social courtesies, developing, 131–34
Social dialect, 29
Sociodrama, 484
Sociodramatic play, 479
Software evaluation checklist, 15–16
Spacing in handwriting, 171–72, 176, 198
Speaking (*See* Communicative development; Communicative remediation for handicapped children; *and* Speech arts)
Speech arts, 117–41
choral speaking, 417–23
conversation and dialogue, 121–23
debating, 118, 127–28
discussion, 118, 123–27
drama, creative, 475–91
interviewing, 130–31
parliamentary procedure, following, 118
puppetry, 118, 136–41
readers theatre, participating in, 118, 134–35
social courtesies, developing, 131–34
storytelling, 403–6
talks, giving, 119–21
Speech community, 27, 29
Speech correction (*See* Communicative remediation for handicapped children)
Speech improvement (*See* Communicative development)
Speed in handwriting, 162, 193
Spelling
and reading, 218–21
and written composition, 258
early, 209, 210–11
evaluation of pupils' progress in, 230–34
for learning disabled children, 227–30
individualized, 216–18
instructional activities in, 221–23
invented, 209–11
learning games in, 224–27
psychology of, 207–9
problem areas in, 229
recommended teaching practices in, 215–16
sample lessons in, 219
teaching guidelines for, 211–15
Stages, puppet (*See* Puppet stages)
Stammering, 155
Standard English (*See* Dialect, standard)
Stereotyping in literature, 389
Story dramatization (*See* Dramatization, story)
Story reading, 406–7
Storytelling, 95, 403–6
Stress phonemes, 31
Structural analysis, using, 319–23
Structural grammar, 56, 58–60
Structure words, 58, 59
Stuttering, 152, 155–56
Suffixes (*See* Affixes, suffixes)
Surface structure of language, 60
Syllabary, 204
Syllabication and accent, 321, 322–23
Syntax, 33–34, 57, 59
Synthetic phonic analysis, 323, 324

t

Tachistoscopes, 318
Talks, giving, 119–21
Tape recordings (*See* Cassette tapes)
Telephone, using the, 133–34
Television, educational, 12, 308
Tests, commercial
American School Achievement Tests, 333
Arizona Articulation Proficiency Scale, 154
Bilingual Syntax Measure, 526
California Achievement Tests, 108
Carrow Elicited Language Inventory, 151
Circus—Listen to the Story, 108
Circus—Say and Tell, 151
Comprehensive Tests of Basic Skills, 108, 291, 333, 374, 468
Compton-Hutton Phonological Assessment, 154
Cooperative Primary Tests, 333
Durrell Listening-Reading Series, 108
Fisher-Logemann Test of Articulatory Competence, 154
Fundamental Achievement Series, 108
Gates-MacGinitie Reading Tests, 333
Goldman and Fristoe Test of Articulation, 154

Iowa Tests of Basic Skills, 254
Johnson Basic Vocabulary Test, 372
Language Facility Test, 151
McDonald's Screening Deep Test of Articulation, 154
McDonald's Screening Deep Test of Articulation: Picture and Sentence Form, 154
Metropolitan Achievement Tests, 108, 234, 333, 372
Metropolitan Readiness Tests, 307
Murphy-Durrell Reading Readiness Analysis, 307
NCTE Cooperative Test of Critical Reading and Appreciation, 424
Northwestern Syntax Screening Test, 48
Picture Story Language Test, 292
PRI Primary Reading Systems, 108
Sequential Tests of Educational Progress (STEP), 108, 334
SOBER, 526
SPAR Spelling Test, 234
SRA Achievement Series, 108, 468
Stanford Achievement Tests, 108, 334
Stanford Early School Achievement Tests, 108
Templin-Darley Test of Articulation, 154
Test of Listening Accuracy in Children, 108
Utah Test of Language Development, 48
Verbal Language Development Scale, 49
Vocabulary Comprehension Scale, 372
Wisconsin Tests of Reading Skills Development, 468
Textbooks, language arts, evaluation checklist, Appendix 2
Theatre, children's, 473–75
Theatre, readers (*See* Readers theatre)
Thesaurus, 364
Thinking, children's, 91
  Piagetian stages of, 42
Traditional grammar, 56
Transformational generative grammar (*See* Transformational grammar)
Transformational grammar, 56, 57–58
Transformations or transforms, 60, 62–71
  coordinating, 62, 64–65
  double-base, 62
  interrogative (yes/no), 62
  negative, 63
  relative clause, 62, 68–69
  single-base, 62
  subordinating, 62, 65–68
T-unit, 243, 475
Typewriting for children
  methodology for, 182–85
  rationale for, 182
  research summary of, 185–86
  sample lessons in, 183–84

u

Unit study, 13, 409
Usage, modern English, 26–27, 52, 259

v

Verb phrase, 61–62
Vertical files in library media center, 456
Vocabulary
  growth in, 345–48
  lists, 18, 217, 363
  types of, 350
Vocabulary development, English
  evaluation of pupils progress in, 372–73
  factors influencing, 348–49
  guidelines for curriculum in, 351–53
  instructional activities in, 365–68
  learning games for, 368–72
  methodology, 354–65
Voice disturbances, 155
Vowel sounds, English
  symbols for, 206

w

West Handwriting Scale, 199
Word attack skills (*See* Word recognition skills)
Wordless picture books, 380, 390–91
Word lists, 217, 363
Word processing, 18, Appendix 5
Word recognition skills
  context clues, using, 318–19
  dictionaries, using, 318
  phonic analysis, using, 323–27
  structural analysis, using, 319–23
Writing process, 249–57
Writing readiness (*See* Handwriting, readiness for)
Writing composition (*See* Composition, written)

y

Yearbooks, encyclopedia, 447